AN
ADEQUATE
RESPONSE

6/15

AN ADEQUATE RESPONSE

The War Poetry of Wilfred Owen & Siegfried Sassoon

by ARTHUR E. LANE
California State University,
Northridge

WAYNE STATE UNIVERSITY PRESS
DETROIT 1972

Library of Congress Cataloging in Publication Data

Lane, Arthur E., 1937–
An adequate response.

Includes bibliographical references.
1. Owen, Wilfred, 1893–1918. 2. Sassoon, Siegfried
Lorraine, 1886–1967. 3. European War, 1914–1918—
Poetry—History and criticism. I. Title. II. Title:
The war poetry of Wilfred Owen & Siegfried Sassoon.
PR6029.W4Z7   821'.9'1209   74-39905
ISBN 0-8143-1472-4

PERMISSIONS

G. T. Sassoon; Faber & Faber Ltd. Collected Poems of Siegfried Sassoon by Siegfried
Sassoon (London, 1961).
Executors of the Estate of the late Harold Owen, and Chatto Windus, Ltd. Wilfred
Owen, Collected Poems, Copyright Chatto & Windus, Ltd., © 1946, 1963. Re-
printed in U.S.A. by permission of New Directions Publishing Corporation.
Cambridge University Press. The Letters of Charles Sorley (Cambridge, 1919) and
Marlborough and Other Poems (Cambridge, 1916) by Charles Sorley.
Charles Scribner's Sons. A Farewell to Arms by Ernest Hemingway (New York, 1957).
Charles Scribner's Sons. Poems by Alan Seeger (New York, 1917).
Robert Graves. Goodbye to All That by Robert Graves (London: Cassell & Co., Ltd.,
1957).
Houghton Mifflin Company. The Void of War: Letters from Three Fronts by Reginald
Farrar (New York, 1918).
Little, Brown and Company. The Real War by Captain Basil Henry Hart Liddell
(Boston, 1930).
The Macmillan Company; the trustees of the Hardy Estate; Macmillan London and
Basingstoke; and The Macmillan Company of Canada Ltd. "In Tenebris II"; "And
There Was a Great Calm"; "The Pity of It"; and "The Dynasts" from Collected
Poems by Thomas Hardy (London, 1960).
Oxford University Press. Journey from Obscurity by Harold Owen (London, 1963–65).
Faber & Faber Ltd. Collected Poems of Rupert Brooke by Rupert Brooke (London:
Sidgwick & Jackson, Ltd., 1920); In Parenthesis by David Jones (New York: Chil-
mark Press, 1962).
Originally published by the University of California Press; reprinted by permission of
The Regents of the University of California. Blasting and Bombardiering by Wynd-
ham Lewis (London: Eyre & Spottiswoode, 1937).
From Rupert Brooke: A Biography by Christopher Hassall, © 1964 by Evelyn Helena
Hassall and Nicholas Edward Hassall and the Rupert Brooke Trustees. Reprinted
by permission of Harcourt Brace Jovanovich, Inc.
Harcourt Brace Jovanovich, Inc. Surprised by Joy by C. S. Lewis.

Contents

Introductory

Literary criticism of war poetry has usually assumed that the epic is the most satisfactory mode for dealing with war. Such an assumption, based on a division of poetry into epic and lyric, fails to account for the validity—both as art and as statement—of shorter war poetry like Wilfred Owen's and Siegfried Sassoon's. It was the First World War, not the artists, which lacked Homeric grandeur: they attempted to render its reality through fidelity to fact rather than fidelity to traditionally sanctioned abstractions.

As poets, Owen and Sassoon had to create a mode of expression adequate to their subject. Though Owen had learned from Keats, and Sassoon from Hardy and Masefield, these influences had to be reworked in the face of an experience which was both the milieu and the subject of their poetry. For the millions of men who lived and died at the front, the war was not an abstraction distanced by time or geography but a phenomenon which defied the traditional categories of military planners and poets alike. A comparison of the war's reality and the various abstractions traditionally available for characterizing it is made throughout this study.

A wide variety of poetic responses to the war is considered, including David Jones's *In Parenthesis*, contemporary newspaper verse, the Georgian reactions exemplified by Rupert Brooke and Charles Hamilton Sorley, and finally the work of Owen and Sassoon. Where poets have treated the war as an abstract issue, I have tried to define the criteria for abstraction and the relevance of those criteria to the event. Sorley is a particularly interesting example. Though his attitude toward the war is tougher and less sentimental than Brooke's, it too fails to encompass the reality of his experience. His poems become, in fact, a record of his attempt to transcend the unavoidable aspects of military conflict.

Siegfried Sassoon's prewar poems show nothing of the corrosive vitality so typical in his poetry of the years 1916 to 1918; as late as 1915 he was criticizing Robert Graves for writing in a "realistic" way about the war. Yet Sassoon's Georgian pastoralism, dependent more on metaphor than on experience, quickly faded when he encountered the actual conditions of modern warfare. His use of satire and parody and the complex contrasts evident in poems like "The Hero" show a significant departure from the poetic styles of his civilian contemporaries. His pictorial and dramatic nonmetaphorical imagery is closely analyzed in Chapter 4 as an indication of a deliberate shift toward a poetry of experience.

The most striking examples of this kind of poetry occur in the work of Wilfred Owen. Whereas Brooke works almost exclusively with metaphor, Owen concentrates relentlessly on the actual conditions—the experience—to be rendered as verse. By replacing figurative images with factual images, he relocates poetic value in human action; the poems seek to elicit a response to experience itself rather than to an imaginary world of graceful (and possibly irrelevant) fancy. Such use of images is not necessarily prosaic; Owen's rendering of visual and auditory images and his skilled verse-techniques modulate their subject into art in the act of revealing it. The radical redefinition of imagery and style in poems like "Greater Love" and "Apologia Pro Poemate Meo" shows a startling reversal of the conventional poetic process: here, instead of language bestowing significance on experience, the pressure of experience has begun to compel a new significance in the use of language.

The unique nature of the First World War, and the kinds of heroism it evoked, are more adequately rendered in such poetry than they could be in the epic. There were no "epic" heroes in the European theater of this war: the plains of Flanders were not the plains of Troy. To have imported alien abstractions to categorize the war would have been to betray the facts and the men who died in making the facts. Owen and Sassoon remained true to their experience and to the facts: they wrote what was, not what might have been.

I

FORM AND CONTENT

The greatness of literature cannot be determined
solely on literary grounds; though we must remember that whether it is literature or not can be determined only by literary standards.

T. S. Eliot

But if we understand morality in the singular, as a
generic decision on the part of consciousness, then it
appears that our response to art is "moral" insofar as
it is, precisely, the enlivening of our sensibility and
consciousness. For it is sensibility that nourishes our
capacity for moral choice, and prompts our readiness
to act, assuming that we do choose, which is a pre-
requisite for calling an act moral, and are not just
blindly and unreflectively obeying. Art performs this
"moral" task because the qualities which are intrinsic
to the aesthetic experience (disinterestedness, con-
templativeness, attentiveness, the awakening of the
feelings) and to the aesthetic object (grace, intelligence, expressiveness, energy, sensuousness) are also
fundamental constituents of a moral response to life.

Susan Sontag

The purpose of this study is to assess the several values of one type of poetic response to the experience of the First World War. The standards I intend to use are for the most part literary, since it is as poets and not as propagandists or moralists that both Wilfred Owen and Siegfried Sassoon should be considered. However, no examination of this particular poetry—poetry produced under a unique environmental stress—can afford to ignore its moral and propagandistic implications without doing less than justice to the stated intentions of both poets. Their poetry is as much a manifestation of conscience as of artistry; they spoke not simply because the Muse bade them, but also because an intolerable situation demanded it.

Although the poet's intention cannot be the sole criterion for estimating the value of his work, both of these poets may best be judged in the light of Owen's statement of purpose. He was concerned with the *subject* of his verse, he said, not with the process of verse-making as a self-justifying act. If for a moment we ignore the semantic intricacies currently associated with the words, we may say that for Owen poetry was a medium (simply because he was a poet—others tried to render the reality of the war in painting, which was *their* medium) and his primary aim was the most meaningful expression possible for his message. Thus, in a rare combination of simplicity and sensitivity, he stated his credo:

> Above all I am not concerned with Poetry.
> My subject is War, and the pity of War.
> The Poetry is in the pity.[1]

11

His concern was with his subject, a subject rendered in poetry. What Owen meant when he capitalized *poetry* was that poetry is a way of looking at things, as well as a way of rendering them. Pity, in Owen's sense, is not a maudlin weakness, but a compassionate understanding, the pity that the child understands in his prayerful request to Jesus, "Pity my simplicity."[2] In this sense, pity is a way of looking at things, a way available to poets, painters, and musicians alike. Owen was a poet, and when he said "The Poetry is in the pity" he postulated a far higher role for poetry than that of a skilled art to which moral standards are irrelevant. He was not Yeats's "golden bird"—a golden bird singing dispassionately about the war would have been ludicrous at the time, and would be as ludicrous today.

If a man must choose between utter dedication to his art for its own sake and the use of that art to express his sense of humanity, and if embracing the former aesthetic alone defines the true artist, then both Owen and Sassoon must be barred from Parnassus. But if a man is skilled in the art of poetry and dedicated to it as a *means* of expressing his humanity, and if he then uses it to inform the moral awareness of his fellow-men, the talent has been well used. W. H. Auden, speaking of poets involved in a later war, made a significant discrimination between this kind of poetry and simple propaganda:

> . . . poetry is not concerned with telling people what to do, but with extending our knowledge of good and evil, perhaps making the necessity of action more urgent and its nature more clear, but only leading us to make a rational and moral choice.[3]

This argument is not entered as an attempt to justify Owen and Sassoon as poets solely on the basis of their noble sentiments. Poetry may have a variety of effects, edification among them; but to argue backward from the effect to a definition of the poem is seriously to misjudge the principles of art. On the other hand, the confident assertion that a poem is a self-referential act seems an equally unsatisfactory assessment. Neither of these extremes is in itself sufficient to justify the existence of poetry, though the latter has the advantage of forestalling argument on all but the technical level. Poetry is a *means* of expression—a highly definitive means, to be sure—but no more than a means. Archibald MacLeish's "Ars Poetica," despite its brave last line, is not simply a self-referential poem; it has a point to make, an aesthetic statement to both make and illustrate. The poem is contextual illumination of informational concepts. There must be quality in both concept and mode of illumination, but for poets to aspire to the nonconceptual model of music is to ignore the intrinsically literary nature of poetry. Whether it will or no, the poem uses the materials of conceptual communication; and, despite MacLeish and the more thoroughgoing theoreticians of the French Symbolist school, it cannot but mean, and mean on several levels. Some of its total effect may be determined by the ideas, some by the contextual modification of those ideas; but the ideas, and some awareness of their quality, can never be excised. Only as a process for the modification of ideas can the poem "be"; but without what used to be called "content," it cannot exist as a poem. It is the function of the content to provide a material to mean, and it is not frivolous to assume a hierarchy of content, even in the art of poetry.

The content burdening Owen's poetry, and that of several other war poets, was the most important of all possible contents: the untold truth. The need to speak out about the war had its basis in a strong moral conviction—in Owen's case especially, a conviction so strong as to define his calling: "All a poet can do today is warn. That is why the true Poets must be truthful."[4] How Owen and Sassoon were true in their poetry, both morally and aesthetically, is one of the problems to be examined in succeeding chapters. It may suffice here to note the observation, made some twenty-five years later, of a contemporary writer who had his own exacting standards of honesty: "the only true writing that came through in 1914–18 was in the poetry." He added, "[the First World War] was the most colossal, murderous mismanaged butchery that has ever taken place on earth. Any writer who said otherwise lied."[5]

A frequent criticism leveled at the War Poets is that they were too close to their subject to attain the aesthetic distance necessary for great poetry.[6] But their subjective immediacy vivifies their poetry to the point where a broader critical basis than that traditionally reserved for "meditative" poetry seems called for. Both Sassoon and Owen trace their poetic ancestry to English Romanticism, Sassoon through Hardy and Owen through Keats, and it is this, the dominant strain of English poetry, which frequently baffles those critics who are committed to rehearsing the categories of classical poetics. It is only in the last decade or so that criticism has evolved an adequate series of approaches to English Romanticism, the central idea of which has been defined by one modern critic as follows:

> That central idea is, I would suggest, the doctrine of experience—the doctrine that the imaginative apprehension gained through immediate experience is primary and certain, whereas the analytic reflection that follows is secondary and problematical. The poetry of the nineteenth and twentieth centuries can thus be seen in connection as a poetry of experience—a poetry constructed upon the deliberate disequilibrium between experience and idea, a poetry which makes its statement not as an idea but as an experience from which one or more ideas can be abstracted as problematical rationalizations.[7]

Owen's capitalization of *poetry* takes on added significance if considered from this critical viewpoint. The "pity" evoked by the poem in the reader will do the meditative work—"the Poetry is *in* the pity"—the poet's task is to provide the experiential material rather than

14

himself to reflect on it or to console. Thus Owen's statement becomes clearer; if by "Poetry" we may understand the meditative working-out of the significance of the subject, then the poet's overriding concern with the subject can be seen as a responsibility to deal with it truthfully, so that the poetic material will honestly reflect it.

Critics of war poetry, the most recent being John H. Johnston and Bernard Bergonzi,[8] have to date been content with a simple twofold division based on form: the poetry is either epical in nature, or lyrical. The usual example of the former is David Jones's in Parenthesis; the usual examples of the latter are the works of Owen and Sassoon. However, these categories seem ultimately unsatisfactory because of their Procrustean nature. A more useful typology would be one based on the manner in which the poet's response to his subject makes itself evident as a poem. The response is shaped not only by the subject, but also by the environment—both physical and, more broadly, cultural—in which the poet exists at the time the poem is created. The two main divisions which result are the poetry of meditation and the poetry of immediate experience. The one is relatively impersonal and treats of general truths; the other is personal, frequently dramatic, and usually stops short of general statement.

The epic may be included without strain in the former category: although technically a narrative poem, it employs action as a deliberately selected vehicle for the illustration of themes considered culturally significant by the poet. The "idea" of the epic—be it of religious or racial significance—exists as a subject for thematic development prior to the act of poetic creation, prior to the moment when the poet with his tools and his talent applies himself to the task of objectifying it in verse.

The lyric, on the other hand, though elusive of definition, may be considered as poetry of experience, since it has the appearance of being a direct reaction to exter-

15

nal phenomena rather than a reflection on a reaction. Such are the love poems constituting the largest part of our lyrical poetry: poems which seem spontaneous, which—though many of them were no doubt the product of hours in a study—seem to be the efflux of a single sustained moment of passion.

If the lyric, in its apparent simplicity, is to have broad significance as utterance, it must operate within an area where the poet's response is itself recognizable and universal—hence the preponderance of love lyrics, lyrics which strike responsive chords in almost any listener. The fact of love, and the poet's reaction to its object, are part of our common experiential stock. Death, on the other hand, though as much a human preoccupation as love, is seldom the subject of lyrical poetry because it characteristically inspires the meditative mode; it is the significance of death, not the fact of death, which operates as the "content" of poems on mortality. Here, under the pressure of history, the simple categories break down. Poems like "Mental Cases," "The Sentry," "Does It Matter?" and "The Dug-Out," which deal with death and war and mutilation, are not epic in nature or intent, nor do they have the distancing, abstracting effect of the meditative mode. Yet even though Owen and Sassoon write with the immediacy and concreteness generally associated with the lyric mode, the brutality and seriousness of their subject make it impossible to classify their work as "lyrical." The broader and less perplexed category indicated by the phrase "poetry of experience" is more useful, because more accurate, especially since both poets did at times purposely develop lyric contrasts in some poems. Owen's "Spring Offensive" is a complex example; a simpler and more available instance is Sassoon's "Everyone Sang," in which he celebrates the resilience of men pushed to the limits of endurance, yet still able somehow to maintain their capacity for hope. No less than the grimmer poems, the occasional lyric demonstrates these poets' commitment to the evocation of meaning through experienced fact:

> For while [the poet] works only with extant facts, his meaning is not quite there for imitation; he must find his meaning by restoring to the facts a concreteness they have lost in the process of becoming facts, of being abstracted from their original human and historical situations. Thus the poet as "resuscitator" is the superlatively effective psychologist and historian, the arch-empiricist who works toward greater concreteness and not, as in traditional poetic theory, toward general truths. His talent lies in the "surplusage of soul" which enables him to project himself into the facts, apprehend them sympathetically in other words, and thus apprehend their life. His poem establishes a pole for sympathy, so that the reader, too, can project himself into the facts and apprehend their life. For both poet and reader, to "see into the life of things" is to see their meaning. Meaning comes not from theoretical interpretation but from the intensest concreteness.[9]

Owen's poetry, in particular, is notable for its radical concretization of the elegiac mode—a mode which, since the sixteenth century, has always been "meditative" in the sense indicated above. Owen calls his poems elegies—but makes an interesting qualification: "Yet these elegies are to this generation in no sense consolatory. They may be to the next. All a poet can do today is warn. That is why the true Poets must be truthful."[10]

In Milton, Gray, Shelley, and Arnold, the elegy *is*, in a sense, consolatory. But Owen's use of the word is relevant to his conception of "truth." The poems are not elegies in the sense that they make the occasion of mourning an occasion for philosophical abstractions about the meaning of life. They are, with very few exceptions, elegies of fact rather than elegies of reflection. Hence the denial of consolation: elegies, particularly Christian ones, generally aim at some form of reconciliation; Owen's elegies, however, are written at a time when reconciliation would be a betrayal of the truth: here "warning" is intended. Both Owen and Sassoon held by Hardy's dictum, "If way to the Better there be, it exacts a full look at the Worst"[11]: the fact of civilized life which was the war had been concealed from the people whose efforts made it continue; the poets, in horror and in despair, accepted the challenge, and distilled into their poetry the warning which had to be given. It was only appropriate, given the milieu in which the poems were composed, that many of them should evolve as elegies.

The Georgian reaction against the Victorian amplitude of poetic statement was toward concreteness of observation. While it is true that, as a poetic movement, the Georgian aesthetic was short-lived and its notes few, this brief reemphasis of the Romantics' preoccupation with immediate sensory data served to clarify Owen's technique. The leaning toward the concrete is a long-standing tradition in English poetry, one only temporarily in abeyance during the Neoclassical period; its rebirth at the end of the eighteenth century was vigorous enough to carry it into the twentieth century as a viable aesthetic, a continuing faith in the value of perceived reality. Those endowed with this perception are, as Wordsworth said,

> Willing to work and to be wrought upon,
> They need not extraordinary calls
> To rouse them; in a world of life they live,
> By sensible impressions not enthralled,
> But by their quickening impulse made more prompt
> To hold fit converse with the spiritual world,
> And with the generations of mankind. . . .[12]

The poetic perception of fact is also a perception of value; the mind is no "mere pensioner / On outward forms."[13] Only a cultural tendency to discriminate between "objective" and "subjective"—our inheritance, as Langbaum suggests, from Newton, Locke, and the Enlightenment[14]—has created the "twofold frame of body and of mind,"[15] the dualist's gulf of caution between **fact** and value. Dualism, however, rests uneasy in poetry, which uses language to communicate both fact and value; for the Romantics in particular, the act of poetry was an act of communicating fact and value simultaneously.

What Wordsworth called "spots of time," and a later age moments of "epiphany," are an unmistakable characteristic of the Romantic perception, precisely because of their experiential immediacy:

> The epiphany grounds the statement of value in perception; it gives the idea with its genesis, establishing its validity not as conforming to a public order of values but as the genuine experience of an identifiable person. It gives us the idea, in other words, before we have to pass judgment on its truth or falsity, before it has been abstracted from perception—while it is still in union with emotion and the perceived object.[16]

In epiphany fact is not separated from value; the two exist simultaneously in the poet's perception. The categories "objective" (strictly factual) and "subjective" (interpretive and evaluative) are irrelevant. By "dramatizing" the poem, the operative sensibility unites into a coherent and identifiable viewpoint the experienced fact and the resulting value, both of which are apprehended at the moment the poem's concrete detail is perceived. Both Owen and Sassoon developed this "dramatic" mode of rendering experience into art; Sassoon's "The Dug-out" and Owen's "The Chances" are typical examples:

The Dug-Out

Why do you lie with your legs ungainly huddled,
And one arm bent across your sullen, cold,
Exhausted face? It hurts my heart to watch you,
Deep shadow'd from the candle's guttering gold;
And you wonder why I shake you by the shoulder;
Drowsy, you mumble and sigh and turn your head . . .

19

You are too young to fall asleep for ever;
And when you sleep you remind me of the dead.

The Chances

I mind as 'ow the night afore that show
Us five got talkin',—we was in the know.
"Over the top to-morrer; boys, we're for it.
First wave we are, first ruddy wave; that's tore it!"
"Ah well," says Jimmy,—an' 'e's seen some scrappin'—
"There ain't no more nor five things as can 'appen:
Ye get knocked out; else wounded—bad or cushy;
Scuppered; or nowt except yer feelin' mushy."

One of us got the knock-out, blown to chops.
T'other was 'urt, like, losin' both 'is props.
An' one, to use the word of 'ypocrites,
'Ad the misfortoon to be took be Fritz.
Now me, I wasn't scratched, praise God Amighty,
(Though next time please I'll thank 'im for a blighty).
But poor young Jim, 'e's livin' an' 'e's not;
'E reckoned 'e'd five chances, an' 'e 'ad;
'E's wounded, killed and pris'ner, all the lot,
The bloody lot all rolled in one. Jim's mad.

Eliot's "dissociation of sensibility"—the incompatibility of thought and emotion—the reconciliation of which was begun by the Romantics, is here, in the poetry of experience, further reconciled.

One fact about the subject of Owen's and Sassoon's poetry is of particular significance in estimating their achievement: it was material which never before had been the subject for the poet's art to render. The experience of this war was factually unique; millions of men were exposed to manifestations of a technology new to human experience, and an alarmingly high proportion of them collapsed under the onset of neurasthenia. No war before or since has matched the First World War for the brutality of this confrontation. Soldiers in the trenches were at times so stunned by the bombardment laid down by their own artillery to clear the way for their advance that, when the time came for them to climb out and attack, they were unable to move—and were either shot where they dumbly stood by officers also strained beyond endurance, or were herded out into the relentless machine-gun fire which blanketed the zone between the trenches. One of the countless examples of such assaults was conducted by the British First Army at Neuve-Chapelle in March 1915. It was a limited assault, took three hours, and gained one thousand yards. It cost, as Hanson Baldwin has pointed out, 3,266 British soldiers per hour.[17] The western front, where both Owen and Sassoon served, was convulsed by such carnage for almost four years.

No arrangement of metaphors, be it ever so well drawn, could have done justice to such experience—hence Owen's statement, "Above all I am not concerned with Poetry." Only the facts themselves—those that the poets could personally vouch for—would suffice; and perhaps the very enormity of their subject removed the temptation to reduce it to metaphor, to dilute its dramatic and experiential actuality.

If we compare works written before actual contact with the war with those written after, the poetry itself demonstrates the effect of the confrontation. At the outbreak of hostilities both poets recorded their reactions in poems which were conventional, poems which reduced the pending conflict to a background for the playing-out of abstract ideas, a practice characteristic of Rupert Brooke, who died before combat, and of the hundreds of lesser poets who practiced their trade safely behind the lines. Owen's "1914" and Sassoon's "Absolution"—the latter written in 1915, before Sassoon's trench experience —will be examined later, not only in their own right as poems, but also as indications of how the actual experience of the war altered the poets' approach to their art. It is sufficient to note here that, in each case, the subject of the poem is a diffuse awareness of historical forces, forces impersonal and elevated, manifested through the

21

kind of metaphor available to any writer of literary sensibility. Though certainly not major examples of the mode, "1914" and "Absolution" are in the tradition of what I have called meditative poetry, as opposed to poetry of experience. Their concern is with Truth, not truth; the latter is simply a point of departure, located in the historical fact of a fallen world, for an exercise in a higher, more enduring Truth which is finally the "subject" of the poem. The fact is in each case subordinated to the idea.

When Sassoon and Owen came to experience the actuality which had provided them with their abstractions, both realized that their poetry was faced with a morally charged responsibility. A comment Owen made in 1918 shows not only his own awareness of his developing powers but also something of the ability of poetry *per se* to render the essence of experience without betraying it into metaphor. In a letter to Sassoon, written on 10 October 1918, less than a month before his death, Owen said,

> It is a strange truth: that your *Counter-Attack* frightened me much more than the real one: though the boy by my side, shot through the head, lay on top of me, soaking my shoulder, for half an hour.
>
> Catalogue? Photograph? Can you photograph the crimson-hot iron as it cools from the smelting? That is what Jones's blood looked like, and felt like. My senses are charred.
>
> I shall feel again as soon as I dare, but now I must not. I don't take the cigarette out of my mouth when I write Deceased over their letters.
>
> But one day I will write Deceased over many books.[18]

Owen's observation is based, in part, on the relationship obtaining between poem and reader. The act of reading a poem is, to some degree, an aesthetic experience in which, through the exercise of his conceptual imagination, the reader assimilates the content of the poem. This content is not experienced directly through the primary senses, but through the associative powers of the imagination:

> For to perceive [the experience in a work of art], a beholder must *create* his own experience. And his creation must include relations comparable to those which the original producer underwent. They are not the same in any literal sense. But with the perceiver, as with the artist, there must be an ordering of the elements of the whole that is in form, although not in details, the same as the process of organization the creator of the work consciously experienced.[19]

In certain kinds of experience there is an intensity which cauterizes the basic sensory apparatus so that it ceases to work as an experience-assimilator. Once this overload point has been passed, something essentially human has been lost: the capacity to feel, to know compassion—and, later, to communicate the nature of the experience. This brutalization of the senses, called "neurasthenia" at the time, was an experience with which Owen was familiar, and he perceived in it something of importance to the role of poetics. To expose his audience to the direct fact of intolerable suffering would be fruitless because their senses would swiftly dull to the level where survival under these conditions would be possible. Yet by somehow rendering the suffering into poetry, by invoking the sympathetic imagination rather than the basic senses, he could bring to their undulled sensibilities the horror of an experience which, as every combat soldier knows, provides its own anaesthetic. When experience exceeds the powers of primary comprehension, it can only be communicated by art. Ironically enough, the experience is itself too horrific to permit of its own assimilation: it can only be seen as Medusa was seen, in the mirror of art. Hence the strange truth: "your *Counter-Attack* frightened me much more than the real one: though the boy by my side, shot through the head, lay on top of me, soaking my shoulder, for half an hour."

In what must have been one of the most appalling struggles any artist has ever undergone, both Owen and Sassoon kept alive their sensibilities and took on the burden of their entire experience. There is no self-pity to undercut the compassion Owen feels for his men, men who are "troops who fade, not flowers / For poets' tearful fooling":

> Happy are these who lose imagination:
> They have enough to carry with ammunition.
> Their spirit drags no pack,
> Their old wounds, save with cold, can not more ache.
> Having seen all things red,
> Their eyes are rid
> Of the hurt of the colour of blood for ever.
> And terror's first constriction over,
> Their hearts remain small-drawn.[20]

These men have every right to insensibility; it is their only way of retaining sanity. But if the poet is to deal artistically with such experience, he must keep his sensibility alive, must force his sanity to risk what Owen speaks of: "In all my dreams, before my helpless sight, / He plunges at me, guttering, choking, drowning."[21]

The poet runs this risk because his art requires it, because he must communicate a felt reality to those who, by accident or by choice, are cut off from this reality and, in their ignorance or iniquity, permit it to continue. The latter, those who are safe from the terror of experience and remain insensitive through choice or ambition are, for both Owen and Sassoon, the real enemy:

> But cursed are dullards whom no cannon stuns,
> That they should be as stones;
> Wretched are they, and mean
> With paucity that never was simplicity.
> By choice they made themselves immune
> To pity and whatever mourns in man
> Before the last sea and the hapless stars;

Whatever moans when many leave these shores;
Whatever shares
The eternal reciprocity of tears.[22]

The war-profiteers and those whom Sassoon called "Yellow-Pressmen" and "Junkers [in] Parliament"[23] are the targets of the only hatred Owen ever shows. More readily aroused to satire, Sassoon deals with them most effectively, but they occur in Owen's poetry and prose in ways that, significantly enough, the German troops—the supposed "enemy"—never do. Convalescing in Scarborough in July 1918, before going out to the front again, Owen bitterly observed:

> There are only mock alarms of course. But this morning at 8.20 we heard a boat torpedoed in the bay, about a mile out, they say who saw it. I think only 10 lives were saved. I wish the Boche would have the pluck to come right in and make a clean sweep of the pleasure boats, and the promenaders on the Spa, and all the stinking Leeds and Bradford war-profiteers now reading *John Bull* on Scarborough Sands.[24]

Sassoon's own "Home Front" outbursts have a similar origin in a sense of despair over the wilful incomprehension of those profiting from the waste and horror of "a young man's war."[25]

One of the most frequent criticisms of war poetry like Owen's and Sassoon's is that it lacks scope, that it is too limited in its view. This criticism has already been mentioned and will be examined at length later. Here we must, however, dispose of one controversialist whom subsequent critics have taken too much at his own estimation. In 1930 Douglas Jerrold published a pamphlet titled *The Lie about the War: A Note on some Contemporary War Books*. Poetry was beyond Jerrold's purview; he chose sixteen novels to denounce for their "fundamentally false" picture of the war.[26] As a propagandist for the right wing—Wyndham Lewis called him "the brains of the Right"[27]—Jerrold's intention was to discredit the propaganda value of the liberal or socialist, or simply humanitarian, works which he saw corroding the spirit of the nation. It is, however, difficult to take seriously a propagandist writing almost eighty years after the publication of *Uncle Tom's Cabin* and setting forth his thesis in this way:

> That there are a lot of people going about today saying that they never knew until they read *All Quiet on the Western Front* what war was really like I can well believe. But as to the value of the moral indignation, the emotional force and the effective will of people who were unmoved by the deaths of nine million men in four years but waited till a novelist wrote a book about it before they sat up and took notice—well, that is a different thing. Of the tens of millions of people now living who saw service during the war most must have seen as much as Mr. Remarque, and very many saw a great deal more. These tens of millions, at any rate, and the hundreds of millions of their fathers, mothers, wives and children, do not need to be told, and if their own experience or the experience of their nearest relatives did not "turn them" effectively against the "idea of war," Mr. Remarque's book is unlikely to have done so.[28]

The point that Jerrold missed was precisely the reason for the popularity of such a book as *All Quiet on the Western Front*. The aspect of the war which aroused "moral indignation" in the book's readers—the brutality and violence Jerrold calls the "lie" about the war—was the side of the war which had never been presented to the civilian population. The newspapers, under War Department censorship, carefully edited it out of their reports, and the men who came back from the front usually chose not to talk about it, being more than thankful to be safely home again. Even were they to talk, their testimony would have been discounted in advance by Jerrold, for his thesis was that no individual soldier's experience is germane to the significance of the war, which was in actuality a clash of nations, of—at the very least—armies. Indeed, the "lie" perpetrated by Remarque and other writers consisted in their use of personal experience as representative of the fact of war.[29] Jerrold's views on the uses of art need not concern us here, but his insistence that the war must be viewed as a grand collision of nations makes him useful to some modern critics, who also insist that the "meaning" of war is more properly the subject of art than is the experience of war.

Hence the continuing demand for an epic. Hence the attacks on Owen and Sassoon for lacking Homeric grandeur—when it is the lack of Homeric grandeur in this war that they were trying to demonstrate.[30] They were not social historians, skillfully encapsulating their culture in a recognizable myth. Nor were they apologists for the fictions of geography. They were poets aware of the reality of their experience and of the experience of the men they led into battle. They chose to speak for themselves and for those men who were either dead or had not the talent to make themselves heard. That they were poets in an age when poetry was no longer a social force is part of their tragedy, and of the tragedy of their times.

They wrote as best they could. And the poetry they wrote is, finally, a poetry of protest. But it would be unwise to use such a label as a limiting device. Owen showed every sign of being a great poet; what little of his mature work we have is assured a permanent place in the body of English poetry. Sassoon, though perhaps not as accomplished a poet, was a good poet—at times very good—and deserves more recognition than he has yet received. They were poets, and they were men of conscience, and they made their protest on behalf of basic human values, on behalf of a world where poetry and the other arts would still be possible and still have relevance. Their warning is still a warning—not yet a consolation.

2

THE MILIEU

Owing to the summary rejection by the German Government of the request made by His Majesty's Government for assurances that the neutrality of Belgium would be respected, His Majesty's Ambassador in Berlin has received his passports, and His Majesty's Government has declared to the German Government that a state of war exists between Great Britain and Germany as from 11 P.M. on August 4.

> *Announcement issued at the Foreign Office, London, 12:15 A.M., 5 August 1914*

If Owen and Sassoon wanted to render, rather than reflect upon, their experience, could they have written about this war in the form which critics have attacked them for neglecting—the epic? The distinction made in Chapter 1 between the poetry of experience and the poetry of meditation suggests that the epic was a form neither possible nor desirable for Owen and Sassoon— but this negative must be qualified. The most useful qualification possible is the fact that, some twenty years after the war, a man who was both a combatant and a poet did write a poem about it which is undoubtedly epic in both aspiration and achievement. David Jones's *In Parenthesis,* is—with the exception of Hardy's *The Dynasts*—the only work of epic proportions to have dealt with war from the viewpoint of a twentieth-century sensibility, and to have used the war as its major theme. It is, significantly enough, an epic of passive suffering. Its magnificence is adequate reply to Yeats's *ex cathedra* statement that such experience is no valid theme for poetry, yet its novel use of its materials is an indication that the possibilities for heroic action in the traditional epic manner may no longer exist. 25201 Ball, Private Ball—his very name a synonym for small arms ammunition—is unlike the hero of any epic ever written to crystallize the aspirations of a self-conscious race. Not in him will we find the rallying power of an Achilles or the flair for control of a Ulysses. He is the unknown soldier, the hero of a new kind of war, the unwitting and pathetic center of events beyond his control and comprehension.

While Private Ball is not the Hero, he is not unheroic. His characteristics are those of the common man who must submerge his humanity in order to wage war —and his humanity will not be submerged. His story becomes an epic of rare and terrible beauty, the beauty of evoked immediacy, of wry acceptance, of resignation which knows it is resignation:

> Maiden of the digged places
> let our cry come unto thee.
> *Mam, moder,* mother of me
> Mother of Christ under the tree
> reduce our dimensional vulnerability to the minimum—
> cover the spines of us
> let us creep back dark-bellied where he can't see
> don't let it.[1]

There are many passages that remind one of Owen; and there are passages such as the following that owe something to Sassoon:

> you mustn't spill the precious fragments, for perhaps these raw bones live.
>> They can cover him again with skin—in their candid coats, in their clinical shrines and parade the miraculi.
>> The blinded one with the artificial guts—his morbid neurosis retards the treatment, otherwise he's bonza—and will learn a handicraft.
>
> Nothing is impossible nowadays my dear if only we can get the poor bleeder through the barrage and they take just as much trouble with the ordinary soldiers you know and essential-service academicians can match the natural hue and everything extraordinarily well.
>> Give them glass eyes to see
> and synthetic spare parts to walk in the Triumphs, without anyone feeling awkward and O, O, O, its a lovely war with poppies on the up-platform for a perpetual memorial of his body.[2]

But such satire is only one aspect of Jones's complex poem;

for it is a story of courage, of bravery dogged if undistinguished, and of unrelenting intelligent observation:

> The immediate, the nowness, the pressure of sudden, modifying circumstance—and retribution following swift on disregard; some certain, malignant opposing, brought intelligibility and effectiveness to the used formulae of command; the liturgy of their going-up assumed a primitive creativeness, an apostolic actuality, a correspondence with the object, a flexibility.[3]

There is an important difference of vantage point between Jones and the other poets we are considering: Jones was not an officer. His was the detached observation possible in those who were led; the officers had the burden—and both Owen and Sassoon demonstrate the anguish of that burden—of deploying men they respected and loved in accordance with impersonal orders which were frequently mass death-warrants. Neither took lightly his responsibilities as an officer. Both were appalled by their enforced complicity in Haig's grand schemes of slaughter, and the bitter awareness of their dilemma recurs constantly:

> For 14 hours yesterday I was at work—teaching Christ to lift his cross by numbers, and how to adjust his crown; and not to imagine he thirst till after the last halt. I attended his Supper to see that there were not complaints; and inspected his feet that they should be worthy of the nails. I see to it that he is dumb, and stands at attention before his accusers. With a piece of silver I buy him every day, and with maps I make him familiar with the topography of Golgotha.[4]

That is Owen; Sassoon is no less conscious of his role:

I'm looking at their blistered feet; young Jones
Stares up at me, mud-splashed and white and jaded;
Out of his eyes the morning light has faded.
Old soldiers with three winters in their bones

31

> Puff their damp Woodbines, whistle, stretch their toes:
> *They* can still grin at me, for each of 'em knows
> That I'm as tired as they are . . .
>   Can they guess
> The secret burden that is always mine?—
> Pride in their courage; pity for their distress;
> And burning bitterness
> That I must take them to the accursed Line.[5]

Two other factors make it unwise to use *In Paren-thesis* as a standard of comparison. The first is the historical fact of its composition: Jones was able to work in peacetime, sifting his memories of the war and blending them into a framework of Anglo-Welsh mythology; beautiful, evocative—and more available in the British Museum than in the trenches. Even so, he felt uneasy about the relationship between his subject and his chosen form. Speaking of the difficulty of "ennobling" the experience of this war, he said:

> Some of us ask ourselves if Mr. X adjusting his box-respirator can be equated with what the poet envisaged, in
>
> "I saw young Harry with his beaver on."
>
> . . . For the old authors there appears to have been no such dilemma—for them the embrace of battle seemed one with the embrace of lovers. For us it is different. There is no need to labour the point, nor enquire into the causes here. I only wish to record that for me such a dilemma exists, and that I have been particularly conscious of it during the making of this writing.[6]

Jones is not here speaking of any "dissociation of sensibility"; he is speaking of the artist's difficulty in rendering impersonal warfare conducted by "loosing poisons from the sky" in terms germane to "that creaturely world inherited from our remote beginnings."[7] This, coming from a man whose sensibilities were attuned to the possibilities of the epic form, should provide critical pause

for those whose literary categories have not taken technology into account.

The second factor which makes Jones's work unique
in its treatment of the First World War is acknowledged
by him in terms which, more than any simply literary
judgment, justify the mode used by Owen and Sassoon.
He makes it clear that, chronologically, he is not dealing
with the same war:

> This writing has to do with some things I saw, felt, &
> was part of. The period covered begins early in De-
> cember 1915 and ends early in July 1916. The first
> date corresponds to my going to France. The latter
> roughly marks a change in the character of our lives
> in the Infantry on the West Front. From then onward
> things hardened into a more relentless, mechanical
> affair, took on a more sinister aspect. The wholesale
> slaughter of the later years, the conscripted levies fill-
> ing the gaps in every file of four, knocked the bottom
> out of the intimate, continuing, domestic life of small
> contingents of men, within whose structure Roland
> could find, and, for a reasonable while, enjoy, his Oli-
> ver. In the earlier months there was a certain attrac-
> tive amateurishness, and elbow-room for idiosyncrasy
> that connected one with a less exacting past. The pe-
> riod of the individual rifle-man, of the "old sweat" of
> the Boer campaign, the "Bairnsfather" war, seemed to
> terminate with the Somme battle.[8]

The war covered by *In Parenthesis* ends, in effect, in
July 1916. Owen was commissioned in June 1916, and
went to France on active service in December 1916. Sassoon was on active duty by late 1915, but his experience
of the war is similar to Owen's, whose war poetry was
written between August 1917 and September 1918, the
period Jones calls "relentless," "mechanical," and "sinister," a period in which even so gifted a writer as he
could find no basis for an epic narrative.

The unspoken assumption of the "epic" writer is that
man is a history-making creature; but there is a feedback
in history-making—and it is that man is himself influ-

enced by the history which is his environment. The poet may succeed in assimilating new phenomena to traditional aesthetic precepts; Kipling's "And all unseen / Romance brought up the nine-fifteen" and Spender's "More beautiful and soft than any moth" airliner are examples which historically bracket the First World War, and show that technology is not necessarily alien to poetry. But if technology is used in a dehumanizing and literally life-destroying way, the poet is surely justified in regarding it as something more than mere furniture for poetical descriptions. Rightly or wrongly, Owen felt that the war was destroying a world in which poetry would retain meaning as an activity for both maker and reader alike. When he asked "What passing-bells for these who die as cattle?" ("Anthem for Doomed Youth"), he was questioning the validity of the old rituals, the old aesthetic norms, in a world which had chosen to disregard the sacredness of flesh formed in the likeness of the Deity. Owen had no ready answer; and though "Anthem" develops its response through instances of fact and human sincerity, one can understand Geoffrey Hill's comment that the remainder of the poem is a retreat from the impossibility of the dilemma posed by the first line.[9]

For millions of men the war was real, not an abstraction distanced by time or geography. Consider, for example, the implications of words like "abstract" and "real" for an incident which occurred after the 6 November assault on Passchendale:

> The following day Lieutenant General Sir Launcelot Kiggell paid his first visit to the fighting zone. As his staff car lurched through the swampland and neared the battleground he became more and more agitated. Finally he burst into tears and muttered, "Good God, did we really send men to fight in that?"
>
> The man beside him, who had been through the campaign, replied tonelessly, "It's worse further on up."[10]

Lieutenant General Sir Launcelot Kiggell was Haig's Chief of Staff, the officer responsible for the planning and ordering of the offensive on Passchendale in November 1917. He had never visited the battlefield area. The final attack took place on 6 November, and in the lull on the following day the incident cited above occurred. Passchendale concluded what is now called the Third Battle of Ypres, a six-month bloodbath which cost the British alone 448,614 casualties, 22,316 of whom were junior officers.[11]

The milieu of any art is of incalculable significance in determining not only the subject of the art, but the manner in which the art treats of its subject. The war was not only *what* Owen and Sassoon were writing about; it was *where they were* most of the time. And the First World War was a bewildering phenomenon, new in man's experience; neither poets nor generals foresaw the course it would take. The military caste, with more technological power at their command than ever before, were almost completely unprepared for its use. Not one army engaged in the conflict was under the direction of competent military planners. Although the Germans had a more rational and effective staff organization, even they misjudged the potential effectiveness and drawbacks of the new engines of war that technology supplied.

The military posture of the British Army seems to have been one of normal confidence. Major F. P. Crozier, for example, a professional soldier later to attain the rank of brigadier-general, was assigned to instruct the new officers of his battalion (the 9th Royal Irish Rifles) in basic tactical principles. He opened his first lecture to these young volunteers quite cheerfully:

> "Gentlemen, the Commanding Officer has asked me to undertake your training for war, by nightly lectures. I shall try to make you interested. I shall run through Field Service Regulations, Parts 1 and 2, Infantry training, combined training, a little topography,

> organisation and equipment, military law and certain campaigns of history. *I shall not stress the present war. All wars are much the same, the details merely vary,* owing to climate, geography, numbers engaged and equality or inequality of forces. We can teach you to form fours, drill, put out outposts, advance, flank and rear guards and the whole bag of tricks, in a short time."[12]

Crozier was, in many ways, an admirable man. An officer of the old school, he was a living example of all the clichés about the professional soldier able to trace his ancestry to Hotspur and determined to uphold the honor of his country in battle. Like most staff officers, he survived the war; unlike most, he changed his views about the morality of war. His conclusions must wait for a later chapter; it is sufficient here to note that the spirit he demonstrated at the outset was typical of the traditional warrior in every nation which sent its youth to the field.

The history of the war is not my main concern; what I wish to show is the peculiar combination of efficiency and blindness that resulted in the environment which gave rise to the poetry of Owen and Sassoon. The diplomatic and military preparations for the war have a fascinating inevitability about them; in a way that Hardy could best have appreciated, a machine was constructed which would eventually control its builders. The English preparations were typical, though not as thoroughgoing as the German; Haldane, the Liberal Party's Secretary for War, and Sir Henry Wilson, the General Staff's Director of Military Operations, were both brilliant and dedicated men who between them had by 1911 organized in minute detail the schedule for mobilization. More aware than many of his colleagues of the need for close cooperation with the French, Wilson is a particularly interesting figure. A conversation he had in 1910 with the then General Foch gave rise to a classic indication of the true nature of the alliance. Wilson asked, "What is the smallest British military force that would be of any practical assistance to you?" Foch's reply had all of European history behind it: "A single British soldier—and we will see to it that he is killed."[13]

The mobilization and commitment of the British Expeditionary Force was completely set forth in Plan W, a marvel of organizational expertise. Yet it suffered, like all the plans of all the nations involved in the war, from a failure to understand the new machines of war—and the consequent involvement of such industries as the heavy munitions factories—and also from the cultivated ignorance of the ruling political party, which was officially committed to peace and therefore chose not to know what its military staff was doing to prepare for war. The split between the military and the political establishments is the gulf in which Sassoon's official protest against the war ultimately foundered.

The General Staff of every nation was committed to the principle of the offensive—none more so than the French, whose casualties, as a result, approximated 5,651,000—in a war dominated from the first by the most effective of *defensive* field weapons, the machine gun. The only way of ensuring tactical mobility was with intensive heavy artillery bombardment, yet neither the Germans nor the Allies had made adequate provision for its use. As a matter of fact, it was only the Germans' underestimation of the role their heavy artillery was to play which caused their advance to stall after August 1914: they literally ran out of ammunition. Ironically enough, the French also ran out of artillery ammunition at the same time; they were therefore unable to throw back the Germans—who had swiftly entrenched—and they dug themselves in, to start the war of attrition which became the dominant feature of the next four years. The statistics of this deadlock are available in the histories:

[The French General Staff] anticipated a daily supply of 13,600 rounds for 75 mm. guns, 465 for 155 mm.

37

guns, and 2,470,000 cartridges for the infantry; a daily production of 24 tons of B powder; 50,000 workers to be employed in 30 factories. The estimated production was to be attained on the eighty-first day after general mobilization. [French General Mobilization was 1 August 1914.] On September 19, instead of 13,600 rounds the general staff asked the Ministry of Armament for 50,000. It obtained that quantity in March 1915, but meanwhile, in January, it had demanded 80,000. This last figure was reached in September 1915, but by then the general staff was demanding 150,000.[14]

On 15 September 1914 the French arsenals contained approximately 120,000 rounds of ammunition for their 75 mm artillery. At the then current rate of use, this stock represented less than three days' supply.[15]

From its inception, this was a war dominated by machines rather than by men, but both sides clung to patterns of operation which were technically irrelevant by the time war broke out. The insistence of the French on Plan 17, developed by Foch and finally codified in 1913, took no account of known German tactics, and may be summed up by its slogan: *attaque brusquée*. The Germans, somewhat more methodical, were committed to the Schlieffen Plan, formulated in 1899 by Count Alfred von Schlieffen, a Prussian staff officer, and modified in succeeding years until his death in 1913. His last words, surely the most individual deathbed utterance in modern history, were, "It must come to a fight. Only make the right wing strong."[16] There is some irony in the fact that his successor, General Helmuth von Moltke, failed at the critical moment to concentrate firepower in the pivoting right wing, thereby stalling the German advance on the entire front. Schlieffen's plan was flexible enough to have utilized the improvements in technology; but Moltke, with a peculiar combination of reverence for the work of his predecessor and timidity in its prosecution, crippled the advance at the crucial point by withdrawing troops from the right wing just at the time when they were most thinly spread, and when artillery ammunition—on both sides—was running low.

The character of the war was determined by the fact that neither General Joseph Joffre, the French commander-in-chief, nor Moltke exploited the technology at their command. Not until 1917 was curtain-bombardment by artillery deployed consistently and effectively; and, until the introduction at Cambrai in 1917 of workable tank tactics, infantry mobility in the face of entrenched machine guns was bought only at the expense of thousands of lives per foot of advance. As a matter of fact, Lieutenant General Julian Byng, who authorized the Cambrai attack of 20 November, did so at the risk of his command, since Haig, his commander-in-chief, distrusted tanks and wanted nothing to do with them. Cambrai was "one of the most startling and one-sided successes of the war";[17] but since Haig did not have the intelligence to exploit it and since Byng had almost no reserves, it petered out. Haig distrusted not only tanks. One of the least competent military leaders ever to lead a nation in war, he chose to ignore the machine gun, the "concentrated essence of infantry":

> Even when the machine-gun had obviously gained a dominance of the battlefield, General Headquarters in France resisted its growth from the puny pre-war scale of two in each battalion. One army commander, Haig, declared that it was "a much overrated weapon" and that this scale was "more than sufficient." Even Kitchener laid down that four were a maximum and any in excess a luxury — until the Ministry of Munitions [headed by Lloyd George] came to the rescue of the machine-gun advocates and boldly multiplied the scale by sixteen.[18]

While the various general staffs learned their lessons and kept their horses well groomed, the war continued, with men pitted against machines in a line of battle stretching from the Swiss border to the North Sea. The Germans, however, at the insistence of Lieutenant Colonel Max Hoffman—a staff theorist responsible for German successes on both eastern and western fronts—had equipped their infantry with machine guns to an extent matched by neither the British nor the French. Consequently, the cavalry-oriented leaders of the Allied armies, committed more through sentimental attachment than tactical commonsense to the principles of *arme blanche* and *offensive à outrance,* incurred casualties on the order of 60,000 a day.[19]

When infantrymen are thrown against machine guns in this way, a commander's most pressing problem, if he is to remain in the field, is replacements. In May 1916, Great Britain adopted conscription for the first time in her history. There was no other way to deal with the enemy's machine guns.

Conscription is an aspect of a nation in arms, a nation for which war is no longer an extension of its political existence, but an integral part of it. At the outbreak of modern war the civilian population must be convinced that the prosecution of the war is important to them personally—hence the rise of national propaganda and news management. In the first months of the Great War, with the issues sufficiently abstract to seem simple—Germany the aggressor, Belgium and France the innocent victims —there was no shortage of volunteers. The most idealistic young men of an entire generation rushed to serve the cause of Freedom and Justice. Their idealism, coupled with their immense respect for Field Marshal Lord Herbert Kitchener, ensured the army a large initial supply of young men: voluntary enlistment up to October 1915 resulted in more than 3,000,000 entering the service. But as these men disappeared into France and failed to return, the rush to serve dropped off. Enrollment by late 1915 was so low that the Derby Scheme was implemented; and even this, using a degree of social coercion which caused some qualms to its canvassers, resulted in only 350,000 more recruits.[20]

Some of the stratagems employed to bring in volunteers, particularly the newspaper advertisements, indicate the tone of an environment that would make men like Sassoon eventually turn away in disgust. These two newspaper advertisements, appearing in 1915, are typical:

FOUR QUESTIONS TO THE WOMEN OF ENGLAND.

1. You have read what the Germans have done in Belgium. Have you thought what they would do if they invaded England?

2. Do you realise that the safety of your Home and Children depends on our getting more men *now?*

3. Do you realise that the one word "Go" from *you* may send another man to fight for our King and Country?

4. When the War is over and your husband or your son is asked "What did you do in the great War?" —is he to hang his head because *you* would not let him go?

Women of England do your duty! Send your men *to-day* to join our glorious Army.

God Save the King.

FIVE QUESTIONS TO THOSE WHO EMPLOY MALE SERVANTS.

1. Have you a butler, groom, chauffeur, gardener, or gamekeeper serving *you* who, at this moment should be serving our King and Country?

2. Have you a man serving at your table who should be serving a gun?

3. Have you a man digging your garden who should be digging trenches?

4. Have you a man driving your car who should be driving a transport wagon?

5. Have you a man preserving your game who should be helping to preserve your Country?

A great responsibility rests on you. Will you sacrifice your personal convenience for your Country's need?

> Ask your men to enlist *to-day*.
> The address of the nearest Recruiting Office can be obtained at any Post Office.
>
> GOD SAVE THE KING.[21]

These advertisements, and others like them, seem no more than grotesque now, but in 1915 they were a fact of life—and death. Sassoon's "Memorial Tablet" is sufficient comment on what they said—and on what they omitted ever to say. This is the last stanza:

> At sermon-time, while Squire is in his pew,
> He gives my gilded name a thoughtful stare;
> For, though low down upon the list, I'm there;
> "*In proud and glorious memory*" . . . that's my due.
> Two bleeding years I fought in France, for Squire:
> I suffered anguish that he's never guessed.
> Once I came home on leave: and then went west . . .
> What greater glory could a man desire?

Perhaps the low point in recruiting posters was reached in a series of advertisements for Eno's Fruit Salts (*Eno's* was a gentle cure for "irregularity" or stomach upset):

> THE BRITISH EMPIRE! THE LAND OF
> BEAUTY, VIRTUE, VALOUR, TRUTH. OH!
> WHO WOULD NOT FIGHT FOR SUCH A LAND!
> IN SAD OR GLAD TIMES, OR ALL TIMES,
> TAKE ENO'S![22]

—an advertisement which certainly combined in appropriate amounts the qualities of spirit which had created the Empire.

But all the exhortations fell short, and compulsory military service became necessary to bring sufficient men to the flag. The summer of 1916 found men conscripted from all walks of life into unfamiliar uniforms, to drill with wooden rifles against the day when they would encounter real guns which fired real bullets which killed real men. Simple social history, to be sure, but relevant in several ways to art. The confrontation between men and machines had been prefigured by some of the artistic movements earlier in the century—particularly the Futurists, who extolled the virtues of the machine in terms which show a peculiar fascination with violence and destruction. Emilio Marinetti's 1909 essay in *Le Figaro* is an aesthetic, rather than a social statement, yet it lauds war as "the only hygiene of the world" and commends the beauty of a racing car that "goes like a machine gun."

Wyndham Lewis, though he called himself a Vorticist rather than a Futurist, subscribed to an aesthetic similar to Marinetti's. Philosophically he agreed with the antihumanist ethic of his friend T. E. Hulme; when the war broke out, he volunteered partly out of a sportsman's interest in a contest and partly out of an artist's fascination with violence. But the juxtaposition of the soft, organic human beings he fought beside and the powerful, nonhuman machines he tended caused him to reconsider the relationship between life and art. He speaks as a painter, faced with an experience "too vast for its meaning";[23] the visual effect of the Flanders front left him at an artistic loss:

> To make a reconstruction of the landscape for a millionaire-sightseer, say, would be impossible. The sightseer would be the difficulty—for the reasons I have given already in my dissection of romance. This is a museum of sensations, not a collection of objects. For your reconstruction you would have to admit Death there as well, and he would never put in an appearance, upon those terms. You would have to line the trenches with bodies guaranteed freshly killed that morning. No hospital could provide it. And unless people were mad they would not want—apart from the cost—to assemble the necessary ordnance, the engines required for this stunt landscape-gardening.—Except that they were mad, they would not have wanted ever to assemble it.[24]

This is the "subject" which so concerned Owen—how, for the millions of people who would never experience the Flanders front, could its totality be rendered so as to retain something of its character in the communication?

There is a troubled note underlying Lewis's customary sangfroid after he has experienced a real-life manifestation of antihumanism:

> The pathos got worse as one watched them month after month at the Front—telling themselves that this was a war-to-end-war, and that was why the free Britisher was in it: otherwise it would have been unthinkable. Just *this once* all the heirs of Magna Carta and the Bill of Rights were behaving like the conscript herds of less favoured nations, and dying too in unheard-of numbers.[25]

This is something more than the classicist's scorn for democracy's empty phrases; and when he refers to the war as the "Rape of the Crowd"[26] one may admire him for political awareness as well as for the careful ambiguity of the expression.

Lewis's inability to deal adequately with the war as an artist stems at least in part from the contradiction between his personal aesthetic and the experience he had to face as both artist and man. Owen's direction as an artist was consistent with his attitude as a man; the attention he wanted was not simply from people who would judge his poetry as well-executed art, but from people who would listen to what he had to say about the facts of his experience. This is why he abjures "Poetry" in his Preface, and insists on his and (by implication) the reader's concentration on his "subject." He was perhaps mistaken in thinking that his poetry would ever reach beyond the aesthetic coteries of Georgian London; but there is no doubt that it was aimed at an entire generation which had to be warned—a generation which read its verse in the newspapers where it also read what the War Office saw fit to tell it about the war. His concern was more than that of the professional poet. In his last conversation with his brother, he indicated something of what his poetry meant to him. To Harold Owen's question, "You have made up your mind to get back to the front line as soon as possible, haven't you?" Wilfred replied, "Yes I have, Harold, and I know I shall be killed. But it's the only place that I can make my protest from. What about you?"[27] There is all of Owen's unsentimental integrity in the bluntness of the reply, the integrity of a poet who, being more than a poet, wrote—in "The Calls"—

> I heard the sighs of men, that have no skill
> To speak of their distress, no, nor the will!
> A voice I know. And this time I must go.

Owen did not reach his intended audience in his own lifetime. Only three times before his death in 1918 did examples of his poetry appear in print: on 1 September 1917 the Craiglockhart magazine, *The Hydra*, published "Song of Songs," a slight piece exemplifying his youthful admiration for Keatsian imagery and diction; on 16 January 1918, *The Nation* published "Miners," and on 15 June 1918, "Futility" and "Hospital Barge at Cérisy." Of the four poems, only "Futility" has the unmistakable certainty and power of his major work. Not until 1919, in the Sitwells' *Wheels,* would a representative group (7 poems) of his war poetry see print.

The poets who both represented and influenced the home front attitudes toward the war were not only inferior to Owen as artists but—and the point is acutely important if we are to comprehend Owen's sense of purpose—they were unable to grasp the moral significance of the conflict. The reasons for this are several—some have already been mentioned—but the main fault was the categories, sanctified by time and tradition, to which they turned. It was Rupert Brooke, rather than Owen or Sassoon, who would be quoted from the pulpit, and although Brooke deserves better than he has received from later critics, he was being equally abused, though in a different way, by the patriotic preachers. It was a public who would never read his poetry that Owen was writing for, hoping that somehow he could bridge the gap of silence which had existed between poet and public for almost a generation. His despair of reaching this audience breaks out occasionally, as did Sassoon's; but he knew, with the older poet, that this was the audience to be reached—and that it was being reached only by patriotic versifiers such as Jessie Pope, the "you" of Owen's "Dulce et Decorum Est":

> If in some smothering dreams you too could pace
> Behind the wagon that we flung him in,
>
> . . . .
>
> My friend, you would not tell with such high zest
> To children ardent for some desperate glory,
> The old Lie: Dulce et decorum est
> Pro patria mori.

Jessie Pope's verse appeared in newspaper after newspaper. Collected, as *Jessie Pope's War Poems* (then, inevitably, as *More War Poems*), it went through several impressions—and this was its message:

> Who's for the trench—
>   Are you, my laddie?
> Who'll follow the French—
>   Will you, my laddie?
> Who's fretting to begin,
> Who's going out to win?
> And who wants to save his skin—
>   Do you, my laddie?
>
> Who's for the khaki suit—
>   Are you, my laddie?
> Who longs to charge and shoot—
>   Do you, my laddie?

Who's keen on getting fit,
Who means to show his grit,
And who'd rather wait a bit—
    Would you, my laddie?

Who'll earn the Empire's thanks—
    Will you, my laddie?
Who'll swell the victor's ranks—
    Will you, my laddie?
When that procession comes,
Banners and rolling drums—
Who'll stand and bite his thumbs—
    Will you, my laddie?[28]

More threatening than encouraging. But she had her romantic moments, as this stanza from "A Cossack Charge" demonstrates:

The torrent opens wider;
As one, move horse and rider,
One heart, one soul, one body, and one breath.
The narrow eyes are laughing,
The wine of war they're quaffing,
The glorious draught of swift, resistless death.[29]

If the subject were not so serious, one could afford to laugh off Miss Pope as the faintly ridiculous lady she was. But it was she, not Owen, who had the public ear, and her jingling verse was a lie no less terrible for the inanity it displayed.

Unlike the writers who sought to describe the war from the perspective of a war-intoxicated capital, Owen was in a position to see the human resources of his nation (and of the "enemy" nation) being destroyed daily. He was a soldier, and he was acutely aware of a clash of responsibilities: in the trenches he fought against Germans, while in his poetry he fought against war. He described himself as "a conscientious objector with a very seared conscience."[30] All but helpless, he watched the toll that war was taking from his people, his men, and himself; and he found the strength to hope that "The Next War" would be a "greater war,"

> when each proud fighter brags
> He wars on Death—for lives; not men—for flags.[31]

The war of men and machines was not only the subject of his poetry, it was the enemy of his poetry; and the dilemma of the artist who is also a compassionate man is evident in his treatment of the materials of the soldier's life—which were too often also the materials of the soldier's death. There is an artistic satisfaction to be derived from adequately rendering the observation of any phenomenon; but, as Wyndham Lewis discovered, the artist's necessary inhumanity may break down in the face of situations which demand from him the agonized response of the whole man. The two levels of the dilemma may be seen in Owen's "Sonnet: On Seeing a Piece of Our Artillery Brought into Action." The existence of this engine of war is morally indefensible but practically necessary; to the artist who is also a soldier falls the additional problem of dealing with an aesthetically beautiful but humanly reprehensible object. The artillery piece, the "subject" of Owen's poem, must be used. Whether its burden may ever be removed from the conscience of its users is a question which he has difficulty facing, and it underlies his untypical use of religious rhetoric:

> But when thy spell be cast complete and whole,
> May God curse thee, and cut thee from our soul!

Owen's resort to such language may well be an index of his deep perplexity. The violent efficiency of the cannon is admirable and deserves the rhetoric of grandeur which is sustained throughout the poem—but it is a rhetoric pregnant with irony and sadness:

> Sway steep against them, and for years rehearse
> Huge imprecations like a blasting charm!
> Reach at that Arrogance which needs thy harm. . . .

"Rehearse / Huge imprecations" bitterly undercuts the anthropomorphic grandeur of the big gun, while at the same time acknowledging it. The poet who also wrote "At a Calvary near the Ancre," "Le Christianisme," and "Soldier's Dream" could not but be aware of the terrible irony of

> thou long black arm,
> Great gun towering towards Heaven, about to curse. . . .

The poem is more than an exercise in the grand style; it is a poet's expression of the soldier's agony when he realizes the paradox of his function. It deserves close comparison with the following poem from the *Toronto Globe*, 23 July 1917. The style of the two poems is similar; the subject is the same; yet the attitude of the latter poem is symptomatic of the condition Owen's work sought to correct:

To the First Gun

Speak, silent, patient gun!
  And let thy mighty voice
Proclaim the deed is done—
  Made is the noble choice;
To every waiting people run
  And bid the world rejoice.

Tell them our heaving heart
  Has found its smiting hand,
That craves to be a part
  Of the divine command.
Speak, prove us more than ease or mart,
  And vindicate the land.

Thine shall the glory be
  To mark the sacred hour
That testifies the free
  Will neither cringe nor cower.
God give thy voice divinity,
  That Right be armed with Power.

Thou are not lifeless steel
  With but a number given,
But messenger of weal
  Hot with the wrath of heaven.
Go earn the right to Honor's seal—
  To have for Honor striven.

Lead us in holy ire
  The path our fathers trod;
The music of thy fire
  Shall thrill them through the sod.
The smoke of all thy righteous choir
  Is incense unto God.

And when long Peace is found
  And thou hast earned thy rest,
And in thy cave of sound
  The sparrow builds her nest,
By Liberty shalt thou be crowned
  Of all thy comrades, best.[32]

Leaving aside considerations of artistic value, the comparison demonstrates the immensity of the task Owen had set himself: the point at issue is not only how "artistic" the poet may be, but also how, in moral terms, he evaluates the fact—and the facts—of war. "To the First Gun" accurately reflects public sentiment; a thousand such poems could be culled from the pages of newspapers then as now, and it was the holding of such easy and uninformed attitudes that made the prosecution of the war possible. The pious tone of the last stanza of "To the First Gun," eminently suited to an age of diminished Christianity, is that of culpable ignorance; the strength of Owen's sestet is that of mature experience:

Yet, for men's sakes whom thy vast malison
Must wither innocent of enmity,
Be not withdrawn, dark arm, thy spoilure done,
Safe to the bosom of our prosperity.
But when thy spell be cast complete and whole,
May God curse thee, and cut thee from our soul!

The explicit contradiction of attitudes needs no gloss; but it demonstrates how insulated from the experience of the war the civilian world still was. Owen and Sassoon sought to penetrate, by means of art, the density of that insulation; their moral involvement precluded their taking Yeats's "professional-poet" disclaimer of responsibility:

> I think it better that in times like these
> A poet's mouth be silent, for in truth
> We have no gift to set a statesman right. . . .[33]

Owen and Sassoon may have been "meddling," as Yeats put it, but if one considers the quantity and quality of hortatory verse which urged uncritical and violent patriotism from the pages of every day's newspapers, theirs becomes an urgently needed note of sanity in a bewildered world.

It was an age when Christianity had become more convenience than conviction; yet the home front antidote to the stress of war sometimes took the form of strange and pathetic manifestations of religiosity. It was as if the finer instincts of all the belligerents had migrated to the front, there to be destroyed, while at home those who were to inherit the pillaged earth contented themselves with such wilful myths as the "Angels of Mons"—who made their first and only verifiable appearance in a short story by Arthur Machen printed in the *Evening News,* 29 September 1914. And in Machen's story the "angels" had been the ghosts of bowmen from England's finer days—but to those who waited and worried on the home front, nothing less than angels would do; and so a legend was born, sired on an unwitting storyteller by an impetuous public.

The mutual incomprehension between the home front and the war front was far out of proportion to the few hundred miles that lay between them. What could the Guardsman, fighting in the waist-deep mire of Flanders, say to his sister's commiserating letter, "You must be terribly tired when you get back to your barracks after the fighting"?[34] A German cavalry officer, writing home from West Flanders, demonstrates the sense of isolation and despair which lay over the war front:

> When I look deeply into it, it seems somehow another world from which there is no return—not only for those whose bodies are buried, but perhaps for no one. To do justice to this other world a new speech would have to be born. We would have to learn it, you would never understand it. This is what makes it so difficult to write. More and more we are to be counted among the dead, among the estranged—because the greatness of the occurrence estranges and separates us—rather than among the banished whose return is possible.[35]

But exhortations for the troops from the German home front were likely to take the form of the "Hymn of Hate" by Ernst Lissauer, published in thousands of copies and distributed by the Crown Prince of Bavaria to his entire army at the beginning of the war:

> French and Russian they matter not,
> A blow for a blow and a shot for a shot,
> We love them not,
> We hate them not,
> We hold the Weichsel and Vosges gate,
> We have but one and only hate,
> We love as one, we hate as one,
> We have one foe and one alone:—
>
> He is known to you all, he is known to you all,
> He crouches behind the dark gray flood,
> Full of envy, of craft, of gall,
> Cut off by waves that are thicker than blood.
> Come let us stand at the Judgment place
> An oath to swear to, face to face,
> An oath of bronze no wind can shake
> An oath for our sons and their sons to take,
> Come hear the word, repeat the word,

Throughout the Fatherland make it heard:
We will never forego our hate,
We have all but a single hate,
We love as one, we hate as one,
We have one foe and one alone,
                    England!

At the Captain's mess, in the Banquet-hall,
Sat feasting the officers, one and all,—
Like a sabre-blow, like the swing of a sail,
One raised his glass, held high to hail;
Sharp-snapped like the stroke of a rudder's play,
Spoke three words only: "To the day!"

Whose glass this fate?
They had all but a single hate.
Who was thus known?
They had one foe and one alone,
                    England!

Take you the folk of the earth in pay,
With bars of gold your ramparts lay,
Bedeck the ocean with bow on bow,
Ye reckon well, but not well enough now.
French and Russian they matter not,
A blow for a blow, a shot for a shot,
We fight the battle with bronze and steel,
And the time that is coming, Peace will seal.
You will we hate with a lasting hate,
We will never forego our hate,
Hate by water and hate by land,
Hate of the head and hate of the hand,
Hate of the hammer and hate of the Crown,
Hate of the seventy millions choking down.
We love as one, we hate as one,
We have one foe and one alone:
                    England![36]

France, an abstraction as convenient as England, if
one has sufficient perspective, receives its due elsewhere.

Herr Pastor Joh. Rump, lic. Dr. of Berlin, encouraged his Christian flock in these terms:

> For what should the sons of France be enthusiastic in this war? They really do not know. But we know. We fight for Kultur and cult, for right and morals, for life and welfare. Rejoice, my brethren! A holy mission has been entrusted to you, so holy that he who is unable to go forth with you and join in the precious work, seems to himself as an outcast from decent society! Verily, it has long been an honour and a joy, a source of renown and happiness, to be a German—the year 1914 has made it a title of nobility. What Geibel once prophesied, in the distich so often quoted, now can and shall and must at last become a reality in the life of the nations, that by the German nature, that nature blessed by the grace and hallowed by the spirit of God, shall the whole world be healed. Help in this, comrades! Rejoice in the call to make room, by means of German courage and German thoroughness, for this new world on earth.[37]

Some critics of the literature of the period, such as J. H. Johnston, make much of the limitations of viewpoint imposed upon those who fought—as contrasted with those who were able to see the struggle in perspective:

> Since the individual soldier can know little of the war outside his limited and generally passive experience of it, this fact . . . contributes even further to the reduction of perspective and the consequent loss of temporal, moral, and physical proportion.[38]

Johnston's point grows out of his conviction that the "epic"—as opposed to what he calls the "lyric"—response to war is the only literary mode which can adequately render its significance. Empirically, however, his point appears specious; the categories appropriate to the plains of Troy are not necessarily those most appropriate to the plains of Flanders, and the men who fulfilled their specialized functions along the lines of trenches had little opportunity for the kind of individual combat which makes a man a Hero as well as a hero. Moreover, the perspective of the epic narrator is that of the fully informed cultural historian; yet in the First World War the general tone of available documentary evidence shows undeniably that the only perspective maintaining a semblance of "temporal, moral, and physical proportion" was that of the men at the front. Second Lieutenant Arthur Conway Young of the Royal Irish Fusiliers shows how experience at the front acted as a solvent for moral prejudgments. His response would puzzle, and perhaps infuriate, those observers whose perspective enables them to view war as an epic contest between opposed cultures:

> However much you may hate the Huns when you are fighting them, you can only feel pity for them when you see them lying helpless and wounded on the ground. . . . Our men were very good to the German wounded. . . . In fact, kindness and compassion for the wounded, our own and the enemy's, is about the only decent thing I have seen in war. It is not at all uncommon to see a British and German soldier side by side in the same shell-hole nursing each other as best they can and placidly smoking cigarettes. . . . It is with a sense of pride that I can write this of our soldiers.[39]

Rudolph Binding, the German cavalry officer quoted previously, observed the same human reluctance toward the kind of categories that, based in abstraction, would subordinate real men to the grand movements of history or race:

> For truly . . . there is no longer any sense in this business. The fraternization that has been going on between our trenches and those of the enemy, when friend and foe alike go to fetch straw from the same rick to protect them from cold and rain and to have some sort of bedding to lie on—and never a shot is fired; this is a symptom of reason that only goes to prove the converse: that there is no longer any sense in this business.[40]

Binding viewed the war within the context of history, but his conclusions are profoundly unsympathetic to any possibility of creating a heroic myth out of the material of this actual warfare:

> When one sees the wasting, burning villages and towns, plundered cellars and attics in which the troops have pulled everything to pieces in the blind instinct of self-preservation, dead or half-starved animals, cattle bellowing in the sugar-beet fields, and then corpses, corpses, and corpses, streams of wounded one after another—then everything becomes senseless, a lunacy, a horrible bad joke of peoples and their history, an endless reproach to mankind, a negation of all civilization, killing all belief in the capacity of mankind and men for progress, a desecration of what is holy, so that one feels that all human beings are doomed in this war.[41]

Superficially, and out of the context of the war, this account may appear to support Johnston's point about the soldier's loss of perspective and proportion. But Binding is adding to history a record of experience; death and destruction will always seem radically different when present as physical phenomena than when they appear as distant—or literary—abstraction. While Rudolph Binding was recording the disintegration of his world in terrible and expressive sorrow, Walter Lehmann, Pastor of Hamberge in Holstein, had a different perspective; he saw the war in confident traditional terms:

> It might come to pass that we succumbed in this, the worst and perhaps the last fight of Germanism against the whole world, of righteousness and purity against falsehood and deceit. That could only happen, I am sure, over the dead body of the last German—but should it happen, I assert that we should all die happy in the consciousness of having defended God against the world. It is no longer a question of the life or death of the individual, but of the eternal ideas, of God's victory over all demons and idolaters, of all that will live even in death, ay, by means of death, as did Christ of old.[42]

Abstractions like "the eternal ideas" are empty vessels, forever ready to be filled with whatever prejudices are easiest to handle and accept. The physical fact of suffering, on the other hand, is subjective and difficult to communicate; but if the poet is to deal with a world of experience, he must come to terms—even if they be subjective terms—with that experience which is both significant and available to him.

It is quite evident that attitudes adopted toward the fact of war undergo a radical conceptual change in direct proportion to the distance—the experiential distance—from which it is viewed. To insist that the long view is the "true" one simply because it thereby achieves a qualitatively different perspective is to beg the question of the nature of the experience to be considered. There is a bitterness born of intolerable knowledge in Binding's statement, "The history of this War will never be written. Those who could write it will remain silent. Those who write it have not experienced it."[43] And elsewhere he notes, "if I could summon all the poets of past times to sing the War they might all remain silent—unless one should answer who has been through hell."[44]

There was, to humanity's shame, a hell available, its median defined by the few hundred yards of poisoned earth separating Binding and his German companions from their French and British fellow-sufferers. From there the poet of whose arrival Binding despaired would address an indictment to an uncomprehending world:

Nevertheless, except you share
  With them in hell the sorrowful dark of hell,
Whose world is but the trembling of a flare,
  And heaven but as the highway for a shell,

You shall not hear their mirth:
  You shall not come to think them well content
By any jest of mine. These men are worth
  Your tears. You are not worth their merriment.[45]

3

EARLY RESPONSES
The Men Who
Marched Away

Do not listen to my quotations with a sneer in your souls because they are "minor poetry." People who speak disparagingly of minor poetry are either stockbrokers and lawyers and rich practical people who don't understand, or reviewers in the Press, who are always young men fresh from a university with souls so stuffed full of intellectual pride that they might as lightly speak of minor roses or minor sunsets.

Rupert Brooke,
addressing the Eranos
Society, Rugby, 1906

Inscribed on the Memorial Arch which marks the entrance to the Royal Military College of Canada are the following lines: "Blow out, you bugles, over the rich dead; there's none of these so lonely and poor of old, but dying has made us rarer gifts than gold." There is no indication of the verse's origin. Though recruits are required to memorize the lines within twenty-four hours of their arrival at the college, there is little curiosity as to who might have written them; they are merely another aspect of the military establishment, requiring only dutiful acknowledgment and assimilation. The anonymous contributive voice is that of Rupert Brooke; "There he remains"—as Christopher Hassall observed of the five war sonnets—"fixed in the public mind, caught in the act of making a superb but not very characteristic gesture."[1]

Brooke was, it hardly needs saying, a Georgian. Indeed, to most critics who survey the field of Georgian poetry, he is a convenient focal point; his are the attitudes, the beliefs, the postures, which most indicate the Georgian tone. And though, for reasons that are more a matter of literary fashion than of impartial criticism, such an assessment of Brooke is made to his disadvantage, his poetry is an especially valuable point of departure for those critics who concentrate on the war poets. Both historically and ideologically, Brooke is the typical Georgian—well educated, socially conscious, and more bound by the conventions of his predecessors than he would have been willing to admit.

"There were," Robert Ross reminds us, "no Georgian manifestoes."[2] But there was a feeling of renewal,

59

even of renascence, in the air at the end of the first decade of the twentieth century. In his preface to the first (1911–1912) volume of *Georgian Poetry*, Edward Marsh voiced a widely held sentiment: "This volume," he wrote, "is issued in the belief that English poetry is now once again putting on a new strength and beauty."[3] The "new strength and beauty" came, in part, from the Georgians' commitment to realism and drama in their poetry. "There is no 'carpe diem' touch," one of them insisted,

> The joy is sure and fast. It is not the falling rose, but the rose for ever rising to bud and falling to fruit that gives us joy. We have faith in the vastness of life's wealth. We are always rich. . . . There is no winter that we fear.[4]

Hindsight adds a tinge of irony to D. H. Lawrence's 1913 pronouncement, but hindsight also imposes its own limitations on the viewer. Lawrence was sincere, and he spoke for his time. As Ross points out:

> [The first two volumes of *Georgian Poetry*] shared, for example, that sense of spiritual buoyancy common to most of the poets of Left and Center. The Georgians had abandoned, they thought, the effete skepticism of the poets of the nineties. They were possessed of positive, definite beliefs about life and art; they tried to see once again with their own eyes, feel with their own passions.[5]

The revolutionary aspect of Georgian poetry was its extension of the subject matter of poetry. Lascelles Abercrombie's "The Sale of Saint Thomas," which opens *Georgian Poetry, 1911–1912*, deliberately violates the canons of "good taste," particularly in the notorious "flies" section. In his own "Channel Passage," published in *Poems* (1911), Brooke had similarly offended those critics for whom poetry was a genteel diversion. Yet, though the Georgians sought to take all experience for their province, there is a sense of strain in their vulgarity; it is self-conscious, too evidently a deliberate departure from the manners of the class to which, with few exceptions, they belonged. Nowhere is this strain more evident than in the tension between the elevated "poetic" language they used so uncritically and the almost obscene subject matter they were determined to incorporate. A few lines from" The Sale of Saint Thomas" will illustrate this point:

> I abhor flies,—to see them stare upon me
> Out of their little faces of gibbous eyes;
> To feel the dry cool skin of their bodies alight
> Perching upon my lips!—O yes, a dream,
> A dream of impious obscene Satan, this
> Monstrous frenzy of life. . . .[6]

There is vitality here, just as there is careful observation of experience and sensation; but there is also the sadly reduced poetic manner of a much earlier period of English letters. Few among the Georgians (Masefield was the notable exception) had learned the lesson that the displacement of poetry by fiction had demonstrated: a gracefully adjectival style of speech was no fit medium in which to render the cruder realities which awaited communication.

But the critic should be wary of asking for too much too soon. We easily forget the storm of critical protest which greeted Brooke's first volume, *Poems* (1911); almost to a man the reviewers attacked what they considered the "disgusting," "harsh," "appalling," "ignoble," "nasty" elements in the book.[7] It is true that this reaction was to only a small proportion of the poems, but Brooke's determination to have these very poems included is worthy of notice. When Frank Sidgwick, his publisher, objected before publication to the offensive realism of some of the pieces—in particular one entitled "Lust"— Brooke replied:

> My own feeling is that to remove it [the poem "Lust"] would be to overbalance the book still more

in the direction of unimportant prettiness. There's plenty of that sort of wash in the other pages for the readers who like it. They needn't read the parts which are new and serious. About a lot of the book I occasionally feel like Ophelia, that I've turned "Thought and affliction, passion, hell itself . . . to favour and to prettiness." So I'm extra keen about the places where I think that thought and passion are, however clumsily, *not* so transmuted. This was one of them. It seemed to have qualities of reality and novelty that made up for the clumsiness. The expression is only good in places. But the idea seemed to me important and moving. . . .

I should like it to stand, as a representative in the book of abortive poetry against literary verse; and because I can't see any aesthetic ground against it which would not damn ¾ of the rest of the book too, on any moral ground at all.[8]

It is a good statement. And it is a useful corrective to that attitude which would have the "new poetry" of Eliot and Pound born in a literary vacuum.

Rupert Brooke came of a good family; his father, William Parker Brooke, was a housemaster at Rugby, whence Brooke graduated and went up to Cambridge in 1906. While at King's, Brooke—after conscientious self-examination—joined the Fabian Society, then in its early stages at Cambridge. In 1909 he was elected president of the Cambridge Fabian Society; he was its third president, following Hugh Dalton, an acquaintance who was to distinguish himself later as Labour Chancellor of the Exchequer. When the Webbs were trying to rally public sympathy for their Minority Report (which supplemented the 1909 Report of the Royal Commission on the Poor Law), Brooke embarked on a twelve-day caravan tour with Dudley Ward, distributing pamphlets and speaking on street corners and village greens in its support.

All the while, Brooke was entering poetry contests and supplementing his income with the prizes. But his viewpoint on social ethics, like his viewpoint on sexual ethics, bore the stamp of his time and class; it was a question of ideals rather than actual practice. The men of Brooke's circle regarded themselves as modern and sophisticated, and studiously addressed their feminine counterparts as equals—even going so far as to remain seated when one of the opposite sex entered the room—but in matters far wider-ranging than the sexual, their virginity sat heavy on them. Their hunger for experience, for tangible fact to bolster their endlessly argued ideals, runs as an undercurrent through their writings, and eventually surfaces in examples like the octave of Brooke's sonnet I in the "1914" sequence, pointedly entitled "Peace":

Now, God be thanked Who has matched us with His hour,
   And caught our youth, and wakened us from sleeping,
With hand made sure, clear eye, and sharpened power,
   To turn, as swimmers into cleanness leaping,
Glad from a world grown old and cold and weary,
   Leave the sick hearts that honour could not move,
And half-men, and their dirty songs and dreary,
   And all the little emptiness of love![9]

   It would be wrong to attack the unthinking youthfulness of such a poem, if only because of the existence of a poem like the following:

     Give me your hand, my brother, search my face;
     Look in these eyes lest I should think of shame;
     For we have made an end of all things base.
     We are returning by the road we came.

     Your lot is with the ghosts of soldiers dead,
     And I am in the field where men must fight.
     But in the gloom I see your laurell'd head
     And through your victory I shall win the light.[10]

   The young man who wrote the latter poem was soon to have more than his fill of experience to temper his idealism and toughen his metaphors. Brooke was not to be so fortunate. His complicated relationship with Katherine Cox, outlined with sympathy and insight in Christopher Hassall's biography, slowed his poetic development considerably. Noting the effect of the affair on Brooke's state of mind, Hassall comments,

> By now, mid-August [1912], it was growing clear. Within the compass of this one topic which brought about the break with Strachey—an emotional complex of love, hate, jealousy, recrimination, disillusion, self-reproach, and austere moral judgment—Brooke never lived to regain that wholesome objectivity and balance which restores the sense of proportion after a phase of breakdown. The injury had gone too deep. His condition remained—in this one sphere of memory and association alone—what scientists who chart the mind would have us call paranoiac. On the broader and more conscious plane the shock was such as to transform his anti-Victorian zeal into a respect for much that he had formerly despised and brushed aside as needless.[11]

Brooke was still piecing himself together from the ruins of this harrowing affair when the war came. And though, in the larger context of social responsibility, Brooke's apparently eager turning to the war "as swimmers into cleanness leaping" may be deplored, the responsible critic should take into account the factors which helped to determine the attitude. Brooke's response was not a simply emotional one, but it is not too fanciful to assume that, in at least some respects, the war provided him with the kind of welcome respite from personal problems that an earlier poet had so well described:

And as months ran on and rumour of battle grew,
"It is time, it is time, O passionate heart," said I,—
For I cleaved to a cause that I felt to be pure and true,—
"It is time, O passionate heart and morbid eye,
That old hysterical mock-disease should die."[12]

In order to qualify the image of Brooke we have from the five war sonnets—and, by implication, to begin to qualify our image of the Georgians as a whole—it is only necessary to take note of the man behind the poems. On 1 August 1914 he writes to Stanley Spencer:

> If fighting starts I shall have to enlist, or go as a Correspondent. I don't know. It will be Hell to be in it, and Hell to be out of it. At present I'm so depressed about the war, that I can't talk, think, or write coherently.[13]

After the declaration of war, he is in London, trying to assess where his responsibilities lie. He writes to Eileen Wellesley:

> It's not so easy as you think—for a person who has no military training or knowledge, save the faint, almost prenatal, remembrance of some khaki drilling at Rugby—to get to the "front." I'm one of a band who've been offering themselves, with vague persistence, to their country, in various quarters of London for some days, and being continually refused. In time, one of the various doors we tap at will be opened. Meanwhile, I wander.
>
> One grows introspective. I find myself in two natures—not necessarily conflicting, but—different. There's half my heart which is normal and English—what's the word, not quite "good" or "Honourable"—"*straight*," I think. But the other half is a wanderer and a solitary, selfish, unbound, and doubtful. Half of my heart is of England, the rest is looking for some home I haven't yet found. So, when this war broke, there was part of my nature and desires that said "Let me alone. What's all this bother? I want to work. I've got ends I desire to reach. If I'd wanted to be a soldier I should have been one. But I've found myself other dreams."[14]

What those "other dreams" might have consisted of is suggested in Brooke's last speech as president to the Cambridge Fabian Society, delivered on 10 December

1910. He has been considering the role of the artist within society, and has neatly dismissed the possibility of becoming an artist-propagandist; the artist, he concludes, cannot be merely a public voice "expressing the soul of the Community." "The Community hasn't got a soul; you can't voice the soul of the Community any more than you can blow its nose." Unlike later poets such as Auden and Day-Lewis, who would attempt to embody a social program in their poetry, Brooke held to his own modification of the nineties aestheticism which he had taken, with reservations, from St. John Welles Lucas-Lucas. Addressing his audience directly, he defines his separation from them—at least insofar as he is an artist:

> You are in the midst of insoluble problems of temperance reform and education and organization. The artist, as artist, is not concerned. He leads you away by the hand and, Mamillius like, begins his tale: "There was a man—dwelt by a churchyard"—it is purely irrelevant.[15]

Brooke obviously had no intention of becoming a poet of public sentiment like Tennyson—for whom he nurtured a well-developed dislike. Yet neither was he committed to the kind of "irrelevance" flouted by the Decadents. The skepticism evident in "Menelaus and Helen" (1909) is not what Robert Ross has called "the effete skepticism of the poets of the nineties";[16] it is the genial skepticism of a new age, an age which was more than willing to apply hardheaded standards of realism to even the most cherished myths. And the artistic control of the poem's material—in both its sections—is that of a poet becoming confident in his craft; the poems he sent to his friend, Edward Marsh, from Tahiti—among them "The Great Lover"—similarly demonstrate that a poet was beginning to emerge from his influences, and to find his own voice.

The war broke shortly after Brooke's return to England. He did not have to seek long to find a way of being

useful. Edward Marsh was secretary to Winston Churchill, then First Lord of the Admiralty, and on 27 September 1914 Brooke, together with Denis Browne, was in
uniform and traveling to join the Anson Battalion of the
Second Naval Brigade, R.N.D. Across the Channel, the
professional armies of Germany, France, and England
were undergoing swift and systematic destruction.

On 4 October the brigade sailed from Dover en
route for Antwerp. Churchill, taking an initiative which
neither Joffre nor Kitchener saw fit to exploit, was sending 3,000 marines in an attempt to save the Belgian capital. The troops were too few and too late; and, as they
fell back, Brooke found himself surrounded, if briefly,
by the chaos and horror of modern warfare. He was
amazed at the powers of endurance which he saw in his
troops, in himself, and in the thousands of fleeing civilian refugees, a toughness which had apparently lain dor-
mant because never before called on. A new awareness,
a new sense of purpose awoke in him as he led his men
through the flame-lit night (the petroleum tanks at
Hoboken had been ruptured, and flooded the country-
side with rivers of burning gasoline); *this* challenge, at
least, was unambiguous. On 9 October the brigade was
back in England, and Brooke was about to embark on
the personal statement that would catch so vividly the
imagination of a nation seeking to articulate unfamiliar
sentiments. On 10 October, Antwerp was occupied by
the Germans.

Recovering from an attack of conjunctivitis, Brooke
was absent from his unit in mid-October. It was during
this time that he read aloud Donne's *The Anniversarie*
to Cathleen Nesbitt. The fifth and sixth lines of Donne's
final stanza, "Who is so safe as we? where none can do /
Treason to us, except one of us two," are echoed in the
opening of Brooke's second "1914" sonnet, "Safety":

> Dear! of all happy in the hour, most blest
> He who has found our hid security,

> Assured in the dark tides of the world that rest,
> And heard our word, "Who is so safe as we?"[17]

It is important, in this case, to emphasize the obvious. The sonnet is not a public statement in the sense that its rhetorical structure is intended to capture a public mood; it is a personal, private poem—in fact, a love poem. And the Donnesque paradox of the concluding couplet seems much less culpable when one considers that Brooke was speaking only for himself, and not for a generation of young men under arms when he said: "Safe though all safety's lost; safe where men fall; / And if these poor limbs die, safest of all." Christopher Hassall makes a convincing case for the equally personal nature of the third sonnet, "The Dead"[18]—clarifying particularly the difficult seventh and eighth lines, ". . . and those who would have been, / Their sons, they gave, their immortality," which Frances Cornford, knowing Brooke's fear that he would die without issue, considered to be "a very *expensive* line."[19]

The personal nature of these poems gives some indication of the flaw for which we must criticize Brooke. He saw the war in personal, not social, terms—saw it as a means of escape from involvements he was unable to control. Of the five war sonnets the first expresses, through paradox, the nature of his relief at being confronted with an evident question of right and wrong; the second is a graceful farewell to Cathleen Nesbitt; the third, while it has personal touches, makes some claim as public statement and is oratorical in a way that shows his unfamiliarity with the "occasional" mode; the fourth is sufficiently complex to merit comparison in a later chapter; and the fifth is again an expression of personal sentiment, finding outlet as patriotism—but a private kind of patriotism which avoids completely the jingoistic clamoring soon to fill the popular press.

The fashionable practice of pillorying Brooke has led such critics as D. J. Enright to take exception to the lines from sonnet V, "There shall be / In that rich earth a richer dust concealed," when only obtuseness or perversity could fail to note that Brooke is using the same kind of ironic realism for which Donne and Shakespeare are admired. Enright also objects to the frequency with which references to England occur within the poem (six times), when it is evident that Brooke is making a fairly successful attempt to transcend the personal nature of his death by emphasizing the beauty and continuity of the things that he has loved. Certainly Brooke's five war sonnets are inadequate to the task of rendering the war which was to follow his death, but to say, with Enright, that "later writers showed how wrong Brooke was"[20] is to judge the poet by standards which were not part of his milieu—an unprofitable, if tempting, exercise. Sir Herbert Read made a more charitable observation:

> It must be remembered that in 1914 our conception of war was completely unreal. We had vague childish memories of the Boer War, and from these and from a general diffusion of Kiplingesque sentiments, we managed to infuse into war a decided element of adventurous romance. War still appealed to the imagination.[21]

Read was speaking for an entire generation of young Georgians who were still caught in the backwash of the nineties' reaction against the poetic amplitude of the High Victorian period. Yet it is of more than minor interest that there was available a poetic voice both steady and mature enough to judge the war as Owen and Sassoon would soon do. Living at Max Gate, Dorset, was a man to whom all the young poets made pilgrimages, to whom later generations would turn with increasing respect—a poet who, as the conflict accelerated into carnage, anticipated the essential sanity of Owen and Sassoon:

I walked in loamy Wessex lanes, afar
From rail-track and from highway, and I heard

In field and farmstead many an ancient word
Of local lineage like "Thu bist," "Er war,"
"Ich well," "Er sholl," and by-talk similar,
Nigh as they speak who in the month's moon gird
At England's very loins, thereunto spurred
By gangs whose glory threats and slaughters are.

Then seemed a Heart crying: "Whosoever they be
At root and bottom of this, who flung this flame
Between kin folk tongued even as are we,

"Sinister, ugly, lurid, be their fame;
May their familiars grow to shun their name,
And their brood perish everlastingly."[22]

Hardy was seventy-four when he sketched this indictment of those responsible for the war; Sassoon was
twenty-eight and, though already an admirer of the
older poet, had yet to learn from experience that the war
was no subject for the easy metaphorizing in which he
indulged that year:

The anguish of the earth absolves our eyes
Till beauty shines in all that we can see.
War is our scourge; yet war has made us wise,
And, fighting for our freedom, we are free.

Horror of wounds and anger at the foe,
And loss of things desired; all these must pass.
We are the happy legion, for we know
Time's but a golden wind that shakes the grass.

There was an hour when we were loth to part
From life we longed to share no less than others.
Now, having claimed this heritage of heart,
What need we more, my comrades and my brothers?[23]

There is little to distinguish Sassoon's poem from
Brooke's equally confident, equally innocent war verse.
It even reflects the same world as Brooke's: a young

man's world where experience is largely the subject matter for graceful metaphor, where suffering is thought to
ennoble, rather than degrade, those who must undergo
it. The echoes of Wordsworth, filtered by the intervention of Victoria's reign—an unmistakable Georgian characteristic—are apparent in both poets:

> There are waters blown by changing winds to laughter
> And lit by the rich skies, all day. And after,
> Frost, with a gesture, stays the waves that dance. . . .[24]

> Time's but a golden wind that shakes the grass.[25]

> She triumphs, in the vivid green
> Where sun and quivering foliage meet;
> And in each soldier's heart serene;
> When death stood near them they have seen
> The radiant forests where her feet
> Move on a breeze of silver sheen.[26]

But it is a misunderstood Wordsworth, a Wordsworth
seen on the pages of a schoolboy's book, an irrelevant
Wordsworth. What he could have taught them about the
shifting relationships between language and sense-data
never reached them; each had to discover for himself the
literary equivalents of experience—and Brooke died on
the threshold of this artistic awareness.

Perhaps for the sake of categorical neatness, critics
usually ignore Brooke's last poem, "I Strayed about the
Deck."[27] It is often classed as a "fragment," like Owen's
"Strange Meeting," though in each case the poem is
complete enough to warrant serious critical attention. In
"I Strayed about the Deck" one can sense Brooke testing
the boundaries of his Georgian vision and moving not
only toward a radical awareness of himself as poet, but
also toward an unmistakable criticism, perhaps even a
rejection, of his earlier mode of expression:

> I strayed about the deck, an hour, tonight
> Under a cloudy moonless sky; and peeped

71

In at the windows, watched my friends at table,
Or playing cards, or standing in the doorway,
Or coming out into the darkness. Still
No one could see me.

                         I would have thought of them
—Heedless, within a week of battle—in pity,
Pride in their strength and in the weight and firmness
And link'd beauty of bodies, and pity that
This gay machine of splendour 'ld soon be broken,
Thought little of, pashed, scattered. . . .

                             Only, always,
I could but see them—against the lamplight—pass
Like coloured shadows, thinner than filmy glass,
Slight bubbles, fainter than the wave's faint light,
That broke to phosphorus out in the night,
Perishing things and strange ghosts—soon to die
To other ghosts—this one, or that, or I.

If one considers the framework of the second and third stanzas, Brooke's advance toward a new kind of poetic integrity is startling in its overtness: "I would have thought of them / . . . in pity. / . . . Only, always, / I could but see them . . . pass / Like coloured shadows. . . ."

It is unlikely, given Brooke's critical intelligence, that after such a poem as this, he could have returned to seeing the world in a way that led T. Sturge Moore to comment, somewhat waspishly, "Smiling over his own fancies, Brooke seems to have sat half abstracted at a pleasure party till the outbreak of war."[28] The briefest survey of Brooke's life will belie this judgment, which, in its hostile reaction to the success of the "1914" sonnets, seems as unjustified as the uncritical approval with which they were received by the public. Sybil Pye, a less prejudiced observer, had noted in August 1910 the paradox of Brooke's vision of the world: ". . . all the while one was aware of that strange anachronism—the lighted eyes and serious face of a child's complete absorption, and again

the detached watchful intelligence. . . ."[29] By 1915 the
"detached watchful intelligence" had begun to see itself
in the world and to be troubled by what it saw. E. J. Dent,
a Cambridge contemporary still able to distinguish between the Brooke he knew and the Brooke who was being
made into a legend on the basis of the war sonnets, made
a vain plea for critical intelligence in *The Cambridge
Magazine:*

> It is grotesquely tragic—what a characteristic satire
> he would have written on it himself—that he should
> have died (at Lemnos too!) just after a sudden and
> rather factitious celebrity had been obtained by a few
> poems which, beautiful as they are in technique and
> expression, represented him in a phase that could only
> have been temporary. No Englishman can ever quite
> eradicate the national tendency to romanticism, just as
> there is, according to Romain Rolland, an essential
> Massenet that slumbers in the heart of every true
> Frenchman. In the first shock of the moment that
> romanticism he so hated came uppermost.[30]

Dent would, I believe, have us today read "sentimental-
ism" for "romanticism"; certainly the characteristic he is
referring to is the excessive play of emotion in an area
where the fact giving rise to the emotion deserves a
cooler, more hardheaded appraisal.

If Brooke represents the "classical" Georgian, skilled
in traditional metrics, given to satire as a defense against
openly expressed feeling—yet thereby all the more vulnerable to sentimental lapses—Charles Hamilton Sorley
may be taken as a representative of the other English
poetic tradition, the "native" assimilative tradition which
was already old when "Western wind, when wilt thou
blow" found its fortuitous way into literary history. Born
in 1895 and raised in an academic environment similar
to Brooke's, Sorley never fell prey to the urban aestheticism occasionally to be found in Brooke. Though the
comparison needs qualification, there is some validity in
linking Sorley with Hardy, and Brooke with Housman.

Though both older poets clearly influenced Sorley, it is Hardy's dogged affirmation which provides the positive note in such a poem as "Return."[31] These are the first two stanzas:

> Still stand the downs so wise and wide?
>   Still shake the trees their tresses grey?
> I thought their beauty might have died
>   Since I had been away.
>
> I might have known the things I love,
>   The winds, the flocking birds' full cry,
> The trees that toss, the downs that move,
>   Were longer things than I.

In its strongly personal attitude toward the objects which have aroused the poet's sensibility, "Return" bears a generic similarity to Brooke's "The Great Lover" (1914); but the Hardyan recognition of nature's endurance as a source of affirmation sets Sorley apart not only from Brooke, but from most of his other contemporaries. Hardy's resignation to his sense of mortality—often labeled "pessimism"—also appears in Sorley; indeed, as the war worsens, it moves dangerously close to that kind of stoic nonresponsibility which makes moral judgment impossible.

But that is to anticipate. Sorley was undoubtedly a Georgian; his careful poetic observation of nature, somewhat limited by the age's lack of a vital terminology, is evident in many of his poems,[32] as is a somewhat truculent impatience with the "everlasting afternoon" air of peace which had settled over England since the turn of the century. Like Brooke, he yearned for action as a cathartic. Brooke felt that God and the war had

> . . . caught our youth, and wakened us from sleeping,
> With hand made sure, clear eye, and sharpened power,
>   To turn, as swimmers into cleanness leaping,

Glad from a world grown old and cold and weary,
   Leave the sick hearts that honour could not move....[33]

Sorley, in an earlier (October 1912) poem, "A Call to
Action," voiced his frustration at the lack of challenge
offered by prewar England:

> It needs no thought to understand,
>   No speech to tell, nor sight to see
> That there has come upon our land
>   The curse of Inactivity.
>
> . . . .
>
> We question, answer, make defence,
>   We sneer, we scoff, we criticize,
> We wail and moan our decadence,
>   Enquire, investigate, surmise;
>
> We preach and prattle, peer and pry
>   And fit together two and two:
> We ponder, argue, shout, swear, lie—
>   We will not, for we cannot, DO.
>
> Pale puny soldiers of the pen,
>   Absorbed in this your inky strife,
> Act as of old, when men were men
>   England herself and life yet life.[34]

Before going up to Oxford, where he had won a schol-
arship to University College, Sorley went abroad to travel
and study. From January to July 1914 he was in Germany.
While his letters mingle admiration (for German efficiency) with condescension (for German dullness), always
there is evident a curious and lively intelligence, at times
detached, at times participative. He writes of German
soldiers singing on the march:

> And when I got home, I felt I was a German, and
> proud to be a German: when the tempest of the sing-
> ing was at its loudest, I felt that perhaps I could die
> for Deutschland—and I have never had an inkling of

75

> that feeling about England, and never shall. And if
> the feeling died with the cessation of the singing—well
> I had it, and it's the first time I have had the vaguest
> idea what patriotism meant—and that in a strange
> land. Nice, isn't it?[35]

Expelled from Germany at the outbreak of hostilities, Sorley immediately applied for a commission in the Army, though he had strong reservations about the patriotic fervor which held the country in a state of mindless excitement. He saw the war as a quarrel between sisters, "between Martha and Mary, the efficient and intolerant against the casual and sympathetic."[36] But he felt he had no choice:

> What a worm one is under the cart-wheels—big
> clumsy careless lumbering cart-wheels—of public opin-
> ion. I might have been giving my mind to fight against
> Sloth and Stupidity: instead, I am giving my body (by
> a refinement of cowardice) to fight against the most
> enterprising nation in the world.[37]

The last two quotations are as significant for their imagery as for their commonsense attitude to the war. Fatalism and a sense of the continuing Christian framework of existence served to insulate Sorley from the moral shock so evident in Owen and Sassoon; the unquestioning resignation of the sonnet "To Germany" is a characteristic which will determine the tenor of all of Sorley's war poems:

> You are blind like us. Your hurt no man designed,
> And no man claimed the conquest of your land.
> But gropers both through fields of thought confined
> We stumble and we do not understand.
> You only saw your future bigly planned,
> And we, the tapering paths of our own mind,
> And in each other's dearest ways we stand,
> And hiss and hate. And the blind fight the blind.

When it is peace, then we may view again
With new-won eyes each other's truer form
And wonder. Grown more loving-kind and warm
We'll grasp firm hands and laugh at the old pain,
When it is peace. But until peace, the storm,
The darkness and the thunder and the rain.[38]

"To Germany" certainly demonstrates Sorley's increasing poetic control of his material; but it is a control more akin to that of Brooke than that of Owen, a control of metaphor rather than of fact.

Yet Sorley was, at least theoretically, in favor of a more concrete rendering of experience in poetry. In an essay he wrote in November 1912, he stated the basis of what he hoped would be a newer, truer poetic:

> We stand by the watershed of English poetry; for the vastness and wonder of modern life has demanded that men should know what they write about. Behind us are the poets of imagination; before us are the poets of fact. . . . [Masefield] is the first of a multitude of coming poets (so I trust and pray) who are men of action before they are men of speech and men of speech because they are men of action.[39]

In "Marlborough," dated 1 March 1914, he shows signs of moving toward this more "realistic" (as opposed to "metaphoric") poetry. These are the last two stanzas:

I, who have lived, and trod her lovely earth,
  Raced with her winds and listened to her birds,
Have cared but little for their worldly worth
  Nor sought to put my passions into words.

But now it's different; and I have no rest
  Because my hand must search, dissect and spell
The beauty that is better not expressed,
  The thing that all can feel, but none can tell.

Here, at least, there is no retreat to metaphor; in the conventionally "poetic" sense, the poem is imageless—yet it

77

is strong, expressive, and pure, a statement poignant in its summation of the short-lived Georgian promise. Sorley's poetic dedication to "fact" rather than "imagination," admirably embodied in "Marlborough," is also implied in a passage from his essay on Masefield already quoted—a passage, ironically enough, as brilliant in its rhetoric as in its rejection of rhetoric:

> The voice of our poets and men of letters is finely trained and sweet to hear; it teems with sharp saws and rich sentiment: it is a marvel of delicate technique: it pleases, it flatters, it charms, it soothes: it is a living lie.[40]

Sorley, it must be said, failed to use his promising "realistic" aesthetic in his war poetry. Whether the reason was his increasing resignation or—a fact not to be ignored—his early death on 13 October 1915, before the war had degenerated into the "relentless, mechanical affair" of "wholesale slaughter"[41] with which Owen and Sassoon were faced, is not a matter for the literary critic to decide. In early 1915—even before David Jones went to the front—it was still possible for Sorley to incorporate the detached ironies of Housman into one of the war's truly lyric poems, numbered XXII in *Marlborough and Other Poems*. The following excerpts indicate one aspect of this tonally ambivalent poem:

> All the hills and vales along
> Earth is bursting into song,
> And the singers are the chaps
> Who are going to die perhaps.[42]
> . . . .
> Wherefore, men marching,
> On the road to death, sing!
> Pour your gladness on earth's head,
> So be merry, so be dead.[43]

But these ironies are embedded in a poem which is heavily freighted with Christian resignation, a poem which calls to mind the deep charity of Hardy's "The Blinded Bird" and its opening question, "So zestfully canst thou sing?" Here is an example of the more reflective strain in the poem:

> Earth that never doubts nor fears,
> Earth that knows of death, not tears,
> Earth that bore with joyful ease
> Hemlock for Socrates,
> Earth that blossomed and was glad
> 'Neath the cross that Christ had,
> Shall rejoice and blossom too
> When the bullet reaches you.[44]

Although Sorley criticized Hardy's "Men Who March Away" (a poem about which Hardy too had reservations) there was much in the older poet that he found congenial. There is a recognizable stylistic roughness in the last stanza of Sorley's "To Poets," a poem which also has affinities—of intention, if not style—with Owen's "Greater Love":

> We are the homeless, even as you,
> Who hope and never can begin.
> Our hearts are wounded through and through,
> Like yours, but our hearts bleed within.
> We too make music, but our tones
> 'Scape not the barrier of our bones.
>
> We have no comeliness like you,
> We toil, unlovely, and we spin.
> We start, return: we wind, undo:
> We hope, we err, we strive, we sin,
> We love: your love's not greater, but
> The lips of our love's might stay shut.
>
> We have the evil spirits too
> That shake our soul with battle-din.
> But we have an eviller spirit than you,
> We have a dumb spirit within:

> The exceeding bitter agony
> But not the exceeding bitter cry.[45]

This is experience reprimanding ease; but it also indicates Sorley's reticence to deal with concrete facts, to speak in other than the general terms used by the poets he is criticizing. The quickening imagery which makes almost physically comprehensible Owen's lines "Heart, you were never hot / Nor large, nor full like hearts made great with shot" is absent from Sorley's "Our hearts are wounded through and through, / Like yours, but our hearts bleed within," which fail to render, in any immediate way, the literal and all too physical fact which underlies both selections. The poetic quality of Owen's response, his deliberately nonmetaphorical use of the tropes of conventional love poetry, succeeds perfectly in communicating without brutality a thoroughly brutal fact. This is the manner of response I wish to term *adequate*.

Sorley had, in April 1915, attacked Brooke in a way which reveals as much about the critic as his subject. It is Brooke's attitude, rather than his manner of expressing it, which irritates Sorley: "He has clothed his attitude in fine words: but he has taken the sentimental attitude."[46] The expression "fine words" seems not to be ironical; Sorley approves of sonnet IV ("These hearts were woven of human joys and cares"), though not on any stylistic basis; simply because it is "not about himself." Yet sonnet IV[47] is a striking example of experience betrayed into metaphor; even if we disagree with D. J. Enright's comment ("The sestet describes water which has frosted over, and seems to have nothing to do with the octave")[48] it is a peculiarly unsatisfactory war poem—because it is inadequate in its relation to the experience it claims to render.

Sorley's prose statements imply an aesthetic not realized in his war poetry, which does not come to "factual" terms with his experience. As I mentioned earlier, the poems are more a record of his attempt to transcend the unavoidable aspects of the war. The sonnet "Such, Such Is Death," for example, begins by denying death the abstract values earlier poets had ascribed to it—but ends on a note of hope which, though admirable, is neither convincing nor very different from that of the "poets of imagination" he had condemned:

Such, such is Death: no triumph, no defeat:
Only an empty pail, a slate rubbed clean,
A merciful putting away of what has been.

And this we know: Death is not Life effete,
Life crushed, the broken pail. We who have seen
So marvellous things know well the end not yet.

Victor and vanquished are a-one in death:
Coward and brave: friend, foe. Ghosts do not say
"Come, what was your record when you drew breath?"
But a big blot has hid each yesterday
So poor, so manifestly incomplete.
And your bright Promise, withered long and sped,
Is touched, stirs, rises, opens and grows sweet
And blossoms and is you, when you are dead.[49]

The conclusion of this well-worked poem denies the validity of observed experience; in no way does it repudiate the "living lies" of his contemporaries. Sorley makes the same retreat to metaphor Brooke makes in sonnet IV; both poets exhibit a figurative response to the fact of death; both end with a reassurance drawn from the world of abstraction; both make the same escape from fact to imagination. The stoicism of Sorley's first three lines, qualified in a radical way by the possibly Christian metaphor of the last three lines, is always present in his war poetry; it underlies his reticence to protest the fact of war, and enables him to impose on his experience a frame of reference within which he can say—not without irony—"It is easy to be dead."[50]

Stoicism and irony are traditional means of defense

against those aspects of experience which the individual cannot influence. Sorley's view of himself as a soldier makes evident the type of compromise he had made:

> I wonder how long it takes the King's Pawn, who so proudly initiates the game of chess, to realize that he is a pawn. Same with us. We are finding out that we play the unimportant if necessary part. At present a dam, untested, whose presence not whose action stops the stream from approaching: and then—a mere handle to steel: dealers of death which we are not allowed to plan. But I have complained enough before of the minion state of the "damned foot." *It is something to have no responsibility—an inglorious ease of mind.*[51]

It is precisely this "inglorious ease of mind" that is so notably absent in Owen and Sassoon, both of whom, like Sorley, were infantry officers responsible for the lives of their men. Sorley's war experience appears devoid of moral content; his attitude toward death, his own as well as others', is blandly stoical. There is little ironic coloration in poem XXVII (undated), in which he addresses the living on behalf of the dead; he recommends acceptance, and criticizes only the unseemliness of grief, for where is the sense in grieving over those who can no longer hear? But it is not the dead who are the intended audience of Owen's elegies or Sassoon's bitter lyrics; they address themselves to the living who, through ignorance or ambition, permit such deaths to continue. Sorley shows no awareness that the soldiers' deaths could be averted:

When you see millions of the mouthless dead
Across your dreams in pale battalions go,
Say not soft things as other men have said,
That you'll remember. For you need not so.
Give them not praise. For, deaf, how should they know
It is not curses heaped on each gashed head?
Nor tears. Their blind eyes see not your tears flow.
Nor honour. It is easy to be dead.

Say only this, "They are dead." Then add thereto,
"Yet many a better one has died before."
Then, scanning all the o'ercrowded mass, should you
Perceive one face that you loved heretofore,
It is a spook. None wears the face you knew.
Great death has made all his for evermore.

There is bitterness here, but it seems peculiarly misdi-
rected ("Say not soft things as other men have said, / That
you'll remember"). Sorley's main concern is with the
inappropriate attitude of elegists; yet there is a disturbing lack of sensitivity in his own bluff paraphase of
Achilles' rebuke to Lycaon ("many a better one has
died before"), the use of which does not seem ironic. If
the poem is taken seriously as an attempt to diminish the
significance of individual death—a reading which the
last four lines appear to support—one can only deplore
the terms in which it does so. Neither quantity ("millions
of the mouthless dead") nor quality ("many a better one
has died before") are criteria relevant to the fact of death;
they operate as rationalizations to protect both poet and
reader from a truth too unpleasant to assimilate. One need
only read Owen's "Anthem for Doomed Youth," which
confronts the same problem ("What passing-bells for
these who die as cattle?"), to see how Sorley has manoeu-
vred away from truth into abstraction—an area wherein,
like Brooke, he is poetically more at ease. In so doing,
Sorley demonstrates an unfortunate reticence—perhaps
"decency" is a better word—at a time when nothing
short of the vulgar truth would convey the reality of war
to those who were unable to experience it and to whom
such personifications as "Great death" could have little
meaning. Sassoon, in such poems as "Remorse" and "The
Hero" was soon to show the extent of the moral dilemma
which is only implicit in the work of Sorley.[52]

For Sorley had quite evidently made his choice.
Whether his failure to deal adequately with the war as
material for the "poetry of fact" arose from personal

inability or from his too early death at a time when, in Herbert Read's words, the war "still appealed to the imagination"[53] is a question best left open. Eight days before his death, in a letter to the Master of Marlborough, Sorley revealed the pessimistic resignation which—even though he seems to have been aware of it—made it impossible for him to view the war in any other than the most sterile of categories—those which deny human responsibility:

> The chess players are no longer waiting so infernal long between their moves. And the patient pawns are all in movement, hourly expecting further advances—whether to be taken or reach the back lines and be queened. 'Tis sweet, this pawn-being: there are no cares, no doubts: wherefore no regrets. The burden which I am sure is the parent of ill-temper drunkenness and premature old age—to wit, the making up of one's own mind—is lifted from one's shoulders. I can now understand the value of dogma, which is the General Commander-in-chief of the mind. I am now beginning to think that free thinkers should give their minds into subjection, for we who have given our actions and volitions into subjection gain such marvellous rest thereby. Only of course it is the subjecting of their powers of will and deed to a wrong master on the part of a great nation that has led Europe into war. Perhaps afterwards, I and my likes will again become indiscriminate rebels. For the present we find high relief in making ourselves soldiers.[54]

4

COMING OF AGE
IN THE TRENCHES
Siegfried Sassoon

*I write . . . on "Innocents' Day," and who can help
thinking of those young and blameless lives laid
down so uncomplainingly in this war on the altar of
sacrifice? May this book comfort the many who
mourn and lead them to see, as one mother wrote so
nobly after losing her greatest treasure, "It does not
seem lonely to think of this noble band of young
knights going forth into the other world together."*

The Bishop of London, 1915

*What is this crazy croon of nobleness,
Of ancient human wisdom and honor?
What majesty itches on the grinning tongues
Of these who have died
That men might not live?*

Kenneth Patchen

Siegfried Lorraine Sassoon entered the war in much the same spirit as Rupert Brooke, though without Brooke's sense of escape from oppressive emotional problems. He enlisted two days before Great Britain declared war and, at first, while he was undergoing training near Canterbury, it seemed no more than "a mounted infantry picnic in perfect weather."[1] In the guise of his autobiographical analogue, George Sherston, he later wrote that his main concern at the time was for the welfare of his horse Cockbird, his "only tangible link with the peaceful past,"[2] which he had had to sell to the Army. He was, however, sensitive to the fragile nature of that briefly idyllic English summer of 1914:

> The flavour and significance of life were around me in the homely smells of the thriving farm where we were quartered; my own abounding health responded zestfully to the outdoor world, to the apple-scented orchards, and all those fertilities which the harassed farmer was gathering in while stupendous events were developing across the Channel. Never before had I known how much I had to lose. Never before had I looked at the living world with any degree of intensity. It seemed almost as if I had been waiting for this thing to happen, although my own part in it was so obscure and submissive.[3]

Sassoon, already a poet, had left Cambridge without taking a degree, and had—on one peculiarly Georgian occasion—even tried on Tennyson's hat and cloak. In other ways, too, he was a man of his time; a passage from *Memoirs of a Fox-Hunting Man* records an experience emblematic of the Georgian moment. It was the evening of "that ominous July 31st," and he was leaving home:

> I was alone in the twilight room, with the glowering red of sunset peering through the chinks and casting the shadows of leaves on a fiery patch of light which rested on the wall by the photograph of "Love and Death." So I looked my last and rode away to the War on my bicycle.[4]

His prewar poetry, like the war poetry he wrote before his experience in the trenches, gives no indication of the corrosive vitality which was to characterize his poetry of the years 1916 to 1918—a vitality as much of the man as of the poet, and which occasioned a remarkable letter from a younger poet whom Sassoon met in Craiglockhart War Hospital in 1917:

> Know that since mid-September, when you still re-garded me as a tiresome little knocker on your door, I held you as Keats + Christ + Elijah + my Colonel + my father-confessor + Amenophis IV in profile. What's that mathematically? . . . If you consider what the above names have severally done for me, you will know what you are doing. And you have *fixed* my Life—however short. You did not light me: I was always a mad comet; but you have fixed me. I spun round you a satellite for a month, but I shall swing out soon, a dark star in the orbit where you will blaze.[5]

So wrote Wilfred Owen. Yet Sassoon's first major volume of verse, *The Old Huntsman and Other Poems,* published in May 1917, though it was dedicated to Thomas Hardy, was a strangely uneven collection, containing seventy-two poems which ranged from his earliest weekend-in-the-country Georgianisms to such accomplished pieces as "The Redeemer," "A Working Party," and "They." "Nim-rod in September" may serve as an example of the poetry Sassoon was to leave behind:

> When half the drowsy world's a-bed
> And misty morning rises red,

> With jollity of horn and lusty cheer,
> Young Nimrod urges on his dwindling rout;
> Along the yellowing coverts we can hear
> His horse's hoofs thud hither and about:
> In mulberry coat he rides and makes
> Huge clamour in the sultry brakes.

It is far from being "bad" poetry; as a matter of fact, it is superior to the early (pre-trench) war poetry also included in the volume. I have already quoted "Absolution" and "To My Brother." Other examples are "France" and "The Dragon and the Undying," which, in their adjectival use of nature and their abstract use of human experience, bear a strong similarity to Brooke's war poems. Sentiment and style are academically correct; there is nothing to distinguish these productions from those of the many other Georgian poets who went willingly to their desks at the outbreak of this distant war. The terminal stanza of "The Dragon and the Undying" is typical:

> Yet, though the slain are homeless as the breeze,
> Vocal are they, like storm-bewilder'd seas.
> Their faces are the fair, unshrouded night,
> And planets are their eyes, their ageless dreams.
> Tenderly stooping earthward from their height,
> They wander in the dusk with chanting streams,
> And they are dawn-lit trees, with arms up-flung,
> To hail the burning heavens they left unsung.

It is necessary to keep in mind that, for the duration of the war, the prevalent home front images of "the slain" were on the order of "fair, unshrouded night" and "dawn-lit trees," even when Sassoon, having seen the slain for himself, offered conflicting testimony:

> The place was rotten with dead; green clumsy legs
> High-booted, sprawled and grovelled along the saps
> And trunks, face downward, in the sucking mud,
> Wallowed like trodden sand-bags loosely filled;

> And naked sodden buttocks, mats of hair,
> Bulged, clotted heads slept in the plastering slime.[6]

To quote from "Counter-Attack" is to anticipate some-what, but the title indicates a poetic challenge as well as a poetic subject. The anthologies of war poetry which flooded the market during and after the war years were, with some exceptions, stocked with pious and patriotic verse of the most fanciful kind. To ignore the existence of such verse was one possibility; both Sassoon and Owen were angrily democratic enough to challenge it for the public ear.

In 1915, however, Sassoon was a talent going to waste; had there been no war, he might never have been wrenched from his easygoing bucolics. But there was a war, and it became the milieu within which Sassoon the poet found his voice. The man who, in 1915, had said "fighting for our freedom, we are free"[7] had seen through his own glib phrases as well as those of his leaders when he risked his life in 1917 with the following statement:

> I am making this statement as an act of wilful defiance of military authority, because I believe that the War is being deliberately prolonged by those who have the power to end it. I am a soldier, convinced that I am acting on behalf of soldiers. I believe that this War, upon which I entered as a war of defence and libera-tion, has now become a war of aggression and con-quest. I believe that the purposes for which I and my fellow soldiers entered upon this War should have been so clearly stated as to have made it impossible to change them, and that, had this been done, the objects which actuated us would now be attainable by negotiation. I have seen and endured the sufferings of the troops, and I can no longer be a party to prolong these sufferings for ends which I believe to be evil and unjust. I am not protesting against the conduct of the War, but against the political errors and insincerities for which the fighting men are being sacrificed. On behalf of those who are suffering now I make this pro-test against the deception which is being practised

on them; also I believe that I may help to destroy the callous complacency with which the majority of those at home regard the continuance of agonies which they do not share, and which they have not sufficient imagination to realize.[8]

What lay between Sassoon the fox-hunting Georgian and Sassoon the polemicist and satirist was one inescapable fact: the experience of war. He maintained his innocence up to the last moment. In November 1915, Robert Graves, visiting the 'C' Company mess of the First Battalion, Royal Welch Fusiliers, found *The Essays of Lionel Johnson* on the table: "It was the first book I had seen in France (except my own Keats and Blake) that was neither a military text-book nor a rubbishy novel." Curious, he checked the flyleaf and found the name Siegfried Sassoon.

> Then I looked around to see who could possibly be called Siegfried Sassoon and bring *Lionel Johnson* with him to the First Battalion. The answer being obvious, I got into conversation with him, and a few minutes later we set out for Béthune, being off duty until dusk, and talked about poetry.
>
> Siegfried Sassoon had, at the time, published only a few privately-printed pastoral pieces of eighteen-ninetyish flavour, and a satire on Masefield which, half-way through, had forgotten to be a satire and turned into rather good Masefield. We went to the cake shop and ate cream buns. At this time I was getting my first book of poems, *Over the Brazier,* ready for the press; I had one or two drafts in my pocket-book and showed them to Siegfried. *He frowned and said that war should not be written about in such a realistic way.* In return, he showed me some of his own poems. One of them began:
> Return to greet me, colours that were my joy,
> Not in the woeful crimson of men slain . . .
> *Siegfried had not yet been in the trenches.* I told him, in my old-soldier manner, that he would soon change his style.[9]

Sassoon was to change more than his literary style; the experience forced upon him by the war changed his social and political allegiances. The easygoing young man of letters who had gone to Marlborough and ridden with the Cheshire Hunt would, after the war, be found campaigning in the industrial north of England for Philip Snowden, candidate of the Independent Labour Party, the man who was to become the first socialist viscount in British history.

Sassoon's transformation has been thoroughly described in two engaging autobiographical trilogies: *The Memoirs of George Sherston*, which includes *Memoirs of a Fox-Hunting Man, Memoirs of an Infantry Officer*, and *Sherston's Progress;* and a companion set comprising *The Weald of Youth, The Old Century and Seven More Years*, and *Siegfried's Journey*. In the former, Sassoon is George Sherston, a diffident recorder who continually subordinates himself and his opinions to the larger events and personalities which helped shape his saga. *The Memoirs of George Sherston* is in no way fictional, unless one balks at the use of pseudonyms such as Thornton Tyrrell (for Bertrand Russell) and David Cromlech (for Robert Graves). Sassoon's continual self-effacement perhaps makes for some distortion—but a self-effacing autobiography is no slight achievement, and a satisfactory proof of its factual accuracy may be found in the other trilogy where, to avoid unnecessary duplication, Sassoon will on occasion refer the reader back to the *Memoirs*.[10]

One cannot overemphasize the value of Sassoon's dual memoirs. Along with Graves's *Goodbye to All That* and Blunden's *Undertones of War*, they are our best prose record of a poet's personal involvement in the Great War —all the more valuable for their having been written after the event, when the creation of an adequate narrative was possible. In a limited way, such accounts fulfill the role once played by the epic: they take in a wide social view which provides perspective and background for the action, and the action is developed along historical, sequential patterns.[11] Furthermore, they supply a unique kind of validation for the kind of poetry which Sassoon and Owen had written from within the war. Sassoon has provided copious autobiographical material as a context for his poems—and even for some of Owen's. Whereas from Owen we have only his surviving letters, from Sassoon we have information of this nature:

> While learning to be a second-lieutenant I was unable to write anything at all, with the exception of a short poem called "Absolution," manifestly influenced by Rupert Brooke's famous sonnet-sequence. The significance of my too nobly worded lines was that they expressed the typical self-glorifying feelings of a young man about to go to the Front for the first time. The poem subsequently found favour with middle-aged reviewers, but the more I saw of the war the less noble-minded I felt about it. This gradual process began, in the first months of 1916, with a few genuine trench poems, dictated by my resolve to record my surroundings, and usually based on the notes I was making whenever I could do so with detachment. These poems aimed at impersonal description of front-line conditions, and could at least claim to be the first things of their kind. The only one which anticipated my later successes in condensed satire was "Good Friday Morning," a jaunty scrap of doggerel versified from a rough note in my diary. Here I broke into realism by introducing my Muse to the word "frowst." Six years later, the reprinting of these lines in a New Zealand Socialist paper caused the editor to be prosecuted for blasphemous libel. After several days of lawcourt proceedings the editor was discharged—the jury adding a rider "that similar publications of such literature be discouraged." Nevertheless it summarized the feelings of thousands of other platoon commanders, and I consider it one of the most effective of my war productions.[12]

Sassoon's wartime change to what he calls "realism" in poetry is the subject of the poem "Conscripts." His pastoral romanticism, dependent on an idea of what poetry ought to be, rather than on observed reality, fails him when he is confronted with a world which has not evolved in the modes of pastoral prettiness. "Conscripts" allegorizes his stock of poetic responses in terms of military reality; these are stanzas 1 and 4:

> "Fall in, that awkward squad, and strike no more
> Attractive attitudes! Dress by the right!
> The luminous rich colours that you wore
> Have changed to hueless khaki in the night.
> Magic? What's magic got to do with you?
> There's no such thing! Blood's red, and skies are blue."
> . . . .
>
> Their training done, I shipped them all to France,
> Where most of those I'd loved too well got killed.
> Rapture and pale Enchantment and Romance,
> And many a sickly, slender lord who'd filled
> My soul long since with lutanies of sin,
> Went home, because they couldn't stand the din.

Incidentally, the poem may itself provide an example of the dangers of poetic abstraction—or at least the dangers of not knowing when a poem is using figurative imagery. Perhaps remembering the embarrassments of the nineties, Sir Edmund Gosse objected strenuously to the fourth stanza of "Conscripts," particularly to its last three lines. Robert Graves, maintaining a straight face, records that Gosse considered that the lines "might be read as a libel on the British House of Lords. The peerage, he said, was proving itself splendidly heroic in the war."[13]

By November 1915, Sassoon had completed his training as an infantry officer at Litherland, near Liverpool, and was sent to the western front. As "Conscripts" and Robert Graves indicate, he took his myths with him; but he lost them swiftly, and set about to disabuse an audience which was eventually to include Winston Churchill. Whether Churchill was disabused—or could have been disabused—is a moot point; when he talked to Sassoon in 1918, his intention seems to have been that of enlightening the younger man:

> Pacing the room, with a big cigar in the corner of his mouth, he gave me an emphatic vindication of militarism as an instrument of policy and stimulator of glorious individual achievements, not only in the mechanism of warfare but in spheres of social progress. The present war, he asserted, had brought about inventive discoveries which would ameliorate the condition of mankind. For example, there had been immense improvements in sanitation. Transfixed and submissive in my chair, I realized that what had begun as a persuasive confutation of my anti-war convictions was now addressed, in pauseful and perorating prose, to no one in particular.[14]

Sassoon, understandably enough, avoided debate. Like Owen, he had come to realize that there were no easy solutions to the vexing problem of a war in progress. "Had I been capable of disputing with him," he concludes, "I might have well quoted four lines from *The Dynasts:*

> I have beheld the agonies of war
> Through many a weary season; seen enough
> To make me hold that scarcely any goal
> Is worth the reaching by so red a road."[15]

"Conscripts" is a convenient poetic marker. From this point on, Sassoon's own initiation into "the agonies of war," his poems will fall into two main categories: war poems of dramatic realism like "The Hero" and the more purely satirical war poems like "Base Details." There is a third category, the distortion of which results in the sharpness of the satirical poems; this is the lyric response, more basic to Sassoon than would seem evident from a first examination of his work during 1916–1918. But it is without doubt Sassoon who wrote the one pure lyric to result from the experience of war; a war lyric justified because it was born not in ignorance of pain, but in release from pain. "Everyone Sang" is a poem whose joyful transcendence has been won at the cost of blood and anguish. It breaks loose from the viciousness and filth of an exhausted war as a symbol of what Sassoon, more than twenty-five years later, felt to be his final attitude towards man's self-degradation: "The only effective answer that a poet can make to barbarism is poetry, for the only answer to death is the life of the spirit."[16]

Despite his moral reservations about the war, Sassoon performed well as an infantry officer. He earned the nickname "Mad Jack" for his soldierly exploits, at one point single-handedly attacking an entire German trench.[17] He was awarded the Military Cross and recommended for the Distinguished Service Order—but in 1917, in disgust and despair, he threw away his decoration:

> Wandering along the sand dunes I felt outlawed, bitter, and baited. I wanted something to smash and trample on, and in a paroxysm of exasperation I performed the time-honoured gesture of shaking my clenched fists at the sky. Feeling no better for that, I ripped the M.C. ribbon off my tunic and threw it into the mouth of the Mersey. Weighted with significance though this action was, it would have felt more conclusive had the ribbon been heavier. As it was, the poor little thing fell weakly onto the water and floated away as though aware of its own futility. . . .
> Watching a big boat which was steaming along the horizon, I realized that protesting against the prolongation of the War was about as much use as shouting at the people on board that ship.[18]

But Sassoon's poetry, while it frequently makes just such a doomed appeal, is manifestly more than that. The eight lines of "The Dug-Out," for example, succeed in conveying, despite their moderate tone, the unutterable horror of a world where nerves and imagination have been so swamped by death that the speaker can no longer bear the sight of a fellow soldier asleep:

> Why do you lie with your legs ungainly huddled,
> And one arm bent across your sullen, cold,
> Exhausted face? It hurts my heart to watch you,
> Deep-shadow'd from the candle's guttering gold;
> And you wonder why I shake you by the shoulder;
> Drowsy, you mumble and sigh and turn your head . . .
> *You are too young to fall asleep for ever;*
> *And when you sleep you remind me of the dead.*

By asking a question which, in any other context, would seem superfluous, Sassoon draws attention to the uniquely alien nature of this particular context—a world where death is more common than sleep.

"The Dug-Out" is an example of those poems which achieve their effect through pictorial nonmetaphoric imagery. All of the images are nonfigurative (with the possible exception of "candle's guttering gold"); the poem itself becomes the vehicle which uses connotation to indicate what is only made explicit in the tonally separated concluding two lines. In a sense, these last two lines are a gloss on what precedes them—the poem providing an exegesis of its own metaphoric process—but the poem remains simple, direct, and immensely suggestive, communicating immediately the agonized disorientation of life in the trenches.

It is this quality of immediacy, sometimes deceptively simple immediacy, which is Sassoon's chief poetic virtue. One need only compare "The Dug-Out" with Owen's "Exposure" to see that, though Owen exhibits a more sophisticated grasp of figurative language, Sassoon is more successful in conveying the mood, common to both poems, of sanity only barely maintained. Although Sassoon's war poems often lack what is conventionally understood as metaphor, they retain a high degree of symbolic value; "The Dug-Out" is a perfect example of the Coleridgean use of symbol "not as a sign that stands for something other than itself but as a living part or instance in the larger reality it manifests."[19] The speaker in the poem demonstrates in the final two lines his own awareness of the symbolic significance of what at first seems to be little more than an everyday scene: a man asleep. This stated awareness is necessary in disclosing to the reader the effect of environment on perception; without the two italicized lines the reader would not have the shock of reinterpreting the preceding six, of learning to assimilate the pictorial image in terms of war experience. By turning in on itself, by explicitly indicating the interpretation of its own dominant image, the poem creates the requisite contrast with the "normal" world—a world where the dead are usually described as sleeping.

The problem of communicating the abnormality of life and death at the front to those who, if not directly responsible, at least concurred in the prosecution of the war became a potent stimulus. Sassoon's poetry achieved a hardness and vigor untypical of his earlier or later work. Bernard Bergonzi observes that after 1916 Sassoon "was increasingly dominated by the desire to use poetry as a means of forcibly impressing on the civilian world some notion of the realities of front-line life."[20]

The "civilian world" was not a world which inspired admiration, especially in soldiers home as invalids or on leave. "Shameless madness" was how Robert Graves described the atmosphere of England in 1917;[21] Reginald Farrar, a correspondent who saw the war on three fronts, wrote home from Flanders:

> To find the real England you have to come to France: and there is something almost frightening and painful about the sudden intensity of the blaze in which it bursts upon you out here. England, at home, has had a difficult, unhappy atmosphere to judge in this past year. . . . It all seemed restless and feverish, passing greedily from the gush of war correspondents to Ephesia banners posturing perpetually for some new "Charity" or other, in some new form of frill.[22]

The "two Englands" concept was a commonplace among soldiers; most of them seem to have felt out of place when on leave in the homeland they had so recently left. Wilfred Owen, writing of wounded soldiers hospitalized in England, parenthetically observed:

> (This is the thing they know and never speak,
> That England one by one had fled to France,
> Not many elsewhere now, save under France.)[23]

And even the usually sanguine Grenfell had written home in 1915:

> I am glad not to be in England now. What a sad disgraceful, unennobled, burglarious huckster among nations we are; and we are not doing much out here to right it, whether because we cannot or because they won't let us, the Lord knows, but one suspects the latter; but at least we are cheerful and willing. . . .[24]

Recuperating from wounds in England in early 1917, Sassoon was infuriated by the complacent patriotism only a few hundred miles from the daily slaughter of the front line. Just before he returned to the front, he went to a music-hall revue at the Hippodrome in Liverpool; the blatant jingoism and tastelessness of the performance, and his typical soldier's reaction to it, are memorialized in "Blighters":

> The House is crammed: tier beyond tier they grin
> And cackle at the Show, while prancing ranks
> Of harlots shrill the chorus, drunk with din;
> "We're sure the Kaiser loves our dear old Tanks!"
>
> I'd like to see a Tank come down the stalls,
> Lurching to rag-time tunes, or "Home, sweet Home,"
> And there'd be no more jokes in Music-halls
> To mock the riddled corpses round Bapaume.

"Perhaps I was intolerant," he comments in *Siegfried's Journey*, "but I found a good many people—Thomas

99

Hardy among them—who agreed with me. Anyhow it was my farewell to England, and as such it was the sort of thing I particularly wanted to say."[25] While "Blighters" is hardly a profound poetic comment on the gap between home front ignorance and the horrors of war, it does show Sassoon's typical contrastive technique: the manifest function of the tank juxtaposed with the bawdy, gay atmosphere of the music hall. The poet who had written so confidently and so recently about such abstract concepts as "sacrifice," "death," and "the slain" was by now aware that visceral reality was ill-served by either abstract metaphor or patriotic obscurantism.

But angry satire is not, in itself, sufficient. The more complex poems, though they do not deny the satirical truth of "Blighters," indicate the moral difficulties involved in bridging the gap between the two fronts. "Remorse," for example, is bluntly realistic, but with significant reservations:

> Lost in the swamp and welter of the pit,
> He flounders off the duck-boards; only he knows
> Each flash and spouting crash,—each instant lit
> When gloom reveals the streaming rain. He goes
> Heavily, blindly on. And, while he blunders,
> "Could anything be worse than this?"—he wonders,
> Remembering how he saw those Germans run,
> Screaming for mercy among the stumps of trees:
> Green-faced, they dodged and darted: there was one
> Livid with terror, clutching at his knees . . .
> Our chaps were sticking 'em like pigs . . . "O hell!"
> He thought—"there's things in war one dare not tell
> Poor father sitting safe at home, who reads
> Of dying heroes and their deathless deeds."

Given these reservations, the satirical tone of "The Fathers" takes on additional overtones of pathos:

> Snug at the club two fathers sat,
> Gross, goggle-eyed, and full of chat.

100

One of them said: "My eldest lad
Writes cheery letters from Bagdad.
But Arthur's getting all the fun
At Arras with his nine-inch gun."

"Yes," wheezed the other, "that's the luck!
My boy's quite broken-hearted, stuck
In England training all this year.
Still, if there's truth in what we hear,
The Huns intend to ask for more
    Before they bolt across the Rhine."
I watched them toddle through the door—
These impotent old friends of mine.

It would be wrong to excuse the senile pugnacity of such
unattractive prototypes. But even reasonable people had
little concrete information with which to form an intelligent estimate of what was going on in the war. Sassoon
was acutely aware of the problem. On sick leave in England, he spent a day with his uncle Hamo Thornycroft,
the sculptor, and Mr. Horniman, a retired member of
Parliament. The incongruity of his two roles that day—
the conscience-troubled infantry officer and the politely
patriotic visitor to a world of Chinese lacquer screens and
water-clocks made in 1635—left him in perplexity:

> How had Uncle Hamo and Mr. Horniman managed,
> I wondered, to make the war seem so different from
> what it really was? It wasn't possible to imagine one-
> self even hinting to them, that the Somme Battle was
> —to put it mildly—an inhuman and beastly business.
> One had to behave nicely about it to them, keeping up
> a polite pretence that to have taken part in it was a
> glorious and acceptable adventure. They must know
> what it was costing in lives of course; the casualty lists
> had told them that. But when Uncle Hamo's well-
> meant remark had reminded me of our battalion raid
> in the Fricourt sector I had felt that no explanation of
> mine could ever reach my elders—that they weren't
> capable of wanting to know the truth. Their attitude
> was to insist that it was splendid to be in the front-

line. So it was—if one came out of it safely. But I resented their patriotic suppression of those aspects of war which never got into the newspapers.[26]

The directness which, for personal reasons, Sassoon could not achieve in talking to people he loved and respected is accomplished in the war poetry by a variety of means. He avoids the polite abstractions of his earlier poetry, uses colloquial language, and frequently resorts to a *persona* who presents, as direct experience, the soldier's point of view. In some cases, it is useful to regard the poem as a self-contained dramatic piece, with its chief effect—pathos or irony, as the case may be—brought about as much by the dramatic situation as by the imagery. This technique, characteristic of Hardy's *Satires of Circumstance*,[27] can be seen in "The Hero," where a difficult moral confrontation is sketched with great economy:

"Jack fell as he'd have wished," the Mother said,
And folded up the letter that she'd read.
"The Colonel writes so nicely." Something broke
In the tired voice that quavered to a choke.
She half looked up. "We mothers are so proud
Of our dead soldiers." Then her face was bowed.

Quietly the Brother Officer went out.
He'd told the poor old dear some gallant lies
That she would nourish all her days, no doubt.
For while he coughed and mumbled, her weak eyes
Had shone with gentle triumph, brimmed with joy,
Because he'd been so brave, her glorious boy.

He thought how "Jack," cold-footed, useless swine,
Had panicked down the trench that night the mine
Went up at Wicked Corner; how he'd tried
To get sent home, and how, at last, he died,
Blown to small bits. And no one seemed to care
Except that lonely woman with white hair.

As in the best of Hardy's satires, the "point" lies below the dramatic surface, or plot, of the poem. The Brother

Officer's disgust is evident in his thought, "how 'Jack,' cold-footed, useless swine, / Had panicked down the trench that night . . . "; but his overriding impression (and ours) is of the pathos of the scene being played out: "And no one seemed to care / Except that lonely woman with white hair." Yet behind the poem, and implied by it, is the knowledge that, in contributing to the fiction of the "hero's" death, the officer is helping to distort the realities of war and of what the war has done to Jack. The deception seems called for in this particular case— but every soldier's death is a particular case; and though there is no suggestion that the sordid facts of Jack's igno- bility be presented to his mother, the conundrum is plain: it is common decency itself which, on the personal level, helps to maintain a state of ignorance on the home front.

Both "The Hero" and "The Dug-Out" demonstrate Sassoon's mature use of nonmetaphoric imagery. Though one is dramatic and the other pictorial, neither is simply anecdotal; each develops the metaphoric possibilities of a factually presented situation which comes to mean "beyond the facts" because of the insight with which it is presented. The technique, learned at least partly from Masefield and Hardy, is well suited to the difficult task of rendering what Edmund Blunden called the "under- tones of war,"[28] a subject which has been poorly served by those poets given to metaphoric abstraction.

For such versifiers, the war seems to have presented no unusual challenge. Poetry for them was "Poetry," sentiment both decorous and decorative. When, therefore, at the call of history, they turned from expressing private passion to articulating the concern of a nation at war, they wrote on with easy confidence. The newspaper "Poetry Corner" became hortatory in tone, an editorial page with rhyme and metrical rhythm. Unfortunately, none of the ubiquitous "public voice" poets, so sincerely attempting to express the "soul of the community," had the talent or vision of a Tennyson; and in any case, the Victorian Age had passed.

The reader has already been exposed (see Chapter 2)

to the strenuous exhortations of Jessie Pope; a more touching example of home front war verse is Katherine Hale's
"Grey Knitting." The poem was popular, appeared in
anthologies, and is quite irrelevant to the war that was
being fought; this—coupled with its symptomatic use of
abstraction—is its importance. The seriousness of the reality Miss Hale so pathetically abuses is, I think, evident in
Sassoon's "Attack." A useful start at discriminating between the two modes of dealing with experience is to
consider the radically different roles the respective poets
assign to Jesus Christ:

Grey Knitting

Something sings gently through the din of battle,
Something spreads very softly rim on rim.
And every soldier hears, at times, a murmur
Tender, incessant,—dim.

A tiny click of little wooden needles,
Elfin amid the gianthood of war;
Whispers of women, tireless and patient,
Who weave the web afar.

Whispers of women, tireless and patient,
"This is our heart's love," it would seem to say,
"Wrought with the ancient tools of our vocation,
Weave we the web of love from day to day."

And so each soldier, laughing, fighting,—dying
Under the alien skies, in his great hour,
May listen, in death's prescience all-enfolding,
And hear a fairy sound bloom like a flower—

I like to think that soldiers, gaily dying
For the white Christ on fields with shame sown deep,
May hear the tender song of women's needles,
As they fall fast asleep.[29]

Attack

At dawn the ridge emerges massed and dun
In the wild purple of the glow'ring sun,
Smouldering through spouts of drifting smoke that
    shroud
The menacing scarred slope; and, one by one,
Tanks creep and topple forward to the wire.
The barrage roars and lifts. Then, clumsily bowed
With bombs and guns and shovels and battle-gear,
Men jostle and climb to meet the bristling fire.
Lines of grey, muttering faces, masked with fear,
They leave their trenches, going over the top,
While time ticks blank and busy on their wrists,
And hope, with furtive eyes and grappling fists,
Flounders in mud. O Jesus, make it stop!

"Grey Knitting," unfortunately, was typical of home front sentimentality—the wishful and false view of war that Sassoon and Owen strove to counteract with their own poetry.

Their art becomes thereby didactic writing, a fact they both acknowledged, but it remains art. Their insistence on public acceptance of the facts of war—an acceptance made difficult in England by heavy military censorship and the compliance of a jingoist press, to say nothing of the popular poets whose art favored metaphor at the expense of reality—was not new in English poetry. Thomas Hardy, whose observations of the darker side of things had caused him to be dismissed as a pessimist, was their precursor in both honesty and—in Sassoon's case—artistic technique. Hardy's credo, from "In Tenebris, II," that "if way to the Better there be, it exacts a full look at the Worst" could be taken as the foreword to the war poems of both poets. And D. H. Lawrence, another writer who had learned much of his art from Hardy, observed in 1916:

> The essence of poetry with us in this age of stark
> and unlovely actualities is a stark directness, without a

shadow of a lie, or a shadow of deflection anywhere. Everything can go, but this stark, bare, rocky direct- ness of statement, this alone makes poetry, to-day.[30]

"Directness of statement" in poetry implies a largely nonmetaphorical use of imagery. Of some aesthetic sig- nificance is the power that such a nonfigurative context can impart to a single well-placed metonymic image. Here, for example, is the last half of "A Working Party":

Three hours ago he stumbled up the trench;
Now he will never walk that road again:
He must be carried back, a jolting lump
Beyond all need of tenderness and care.

He was a young man with a meagre wife
And two small children in a Midland town;
He showed their photographs to all his mates,
And they considered him a decent chap
Who did his work and hadn't much to say,
And always laughed at other people's jokes
Because he hadn't any of his own.

That night when he was busy at his job
Of piling bags along the parapet,
He thought how slow time went, stamping his feet
And blowing on his fingers, pinched with cold.
He thought of getting back by half-past twelve,
And tot of rum to send him warm to sleep
In draughty dug-out frowsty with the fumes
Of coke, and full of snoring weary men.

He pushed another bag along the top,
Craning his body outward; then a flare
Gave one white glimpse of No Man's Land and wire;
And as he dropped his head the instant split
His startled life with lead, and all went out.

The moment of the soldier's death is shifted only slightly from the mundane routine by the use of "instant" in the penultimate line; the shift, however, is sufficient to indicate a qualitative difference. With such typical economy in the use of figurative language, Sassoon restores to it something of the force it originally had; when he gives it free rein in "Everyone Sang," the impression is almost that of a totally new discovery.

Since his prewar background had been leisured and pleasant, Sassoon was all the more alert to the contrasts provided by the conditions of life at the front. Where Owen's compassion was Christian and undifferentiated, the older poet was more likely to particularize; "Dreamers," for example, uses the human paraphernalia of civilized life to nice ironic effect:

> Soldiers are dreamers; when the guns begin
>   They think of firelit homes, clean beds and wives.
> I see them in foul dug-outs, gnawed by rats,
>   And in the ruined trenches, lashed with rain,
> Dreaming of things they did with balls and bats,
>   And mocked by hopeless longing to regain
> Bank-holidays, and picture shows, and spats,
>   And going to the office in the train.

There is the dramatist's mode of achieving effect through character and setting (in such poems as "The Hero") and the way he names protagonists:

> When Dick was killed last week he looked like that,
> Flapping along the fire-step like a fish,
> After the blazing crump had knocked him flat. . . .[31]

> Young Hughes was badly hit; I heard him carried away,
> Moaning at every lurch; no doubt he'll die today.[32]

The contrast between the soldier as a civilized human being and his environment of mechanized savagery provides Sassoon with much material for irony. Equally pertinent is the contrast between the soldier facing the fact of death and the noncombatant safely at home with only the idea of death. "How to Die," for example, is more

parody than satire—but it is a parody grimly underpinned
with reality:

> Dark clouds are smouldering into red
>   While down the craters morning burns.
> The dying soldier shifts his head
>   To watch the glory that returns;
> He lifts his fingers toward the skies
>   Where holy brightness breaks in flame;
> Radiance reflected in his eyes,
>   And on his lips a whispered name.
>
> You'd think, to hear some people talk,
>   That lads go West with sobs and curses,
> And sullen faces white as chalk,
>   Hankering for wreaths and tombs and hearses.
> But they've been taught the way to do it
>   Like Christian soldiers; not with haste
> And shuddering groans; but passing through it
>   With due regard for decent taste.

Sassoon's skepticism about the relevance of such
abstractions as "glory," "holy brightness," and the other
loosely metaphorical expressions which characterize the
work of his lesser contemporaries is refreshing, particularly in view of his prewar (and, to some extent, his post-
war) skill in handling metaphor for its own sake. It is
unlikely that he had read Synge's 1908 pronouncement,
"It is may almost be said that before verse can be human
again it must learn to be brutal,"[33] but, perhaps out of
instinct, he described the war as it was, and not as
dreamers would have had it. Emotive abstractions such
as "glory" had lost their value through overuse; even
"God" (sometimes spelled "Gott") was more of a rhetorical convenience than anything else. And no amount of
rhetoric, be it ever so comforting, could palliate the strains
to which the infantry were subjected in this war. Largely
because of Staff ignorance of the novel war-making machinery with which the war came to be fought, the men

were exposed too long to conditions of extreme stress. The result was mental collapse.[34] But few commanders were psychologists; unless a man were visibly wounded or unconscious, he was considered fit to fight—or, at best, in need of a rest:

No doubt they'll soon get well; the shock and strain
   Have caused their stammering, disconnected talk.
Of course they're "longing to go out again,"—
   These boys with old, scared faces, learning to walk.
They'll soon forget their haunted nights; their cowed
   Subjection to the ghosts of friends who died,—
Their dreams that drip with murder; and they'll be proud
   Of glorious war that shatter'd all their pride . . .
Men who went out to battle, grim and glad;
Children, with eyes that hate you, broken and mad.[35]

The concluding couplet of "Survivors" drops the satirical tone of the preceding lines to make a direct and unambigious statement. When the satire is unrelieved by such a tonal shift, the effect is not always satisfactory. "Does It Matter?" slips from satire into sarcasm in its last stanza, seemingly because Sassoon, intent on making his point, overconcentrates the irony:

Do they matter?—those dreams from the pit? . . .
You can drink and forget and be glad,
And people won't say that you're mad;
For they'll know you've fought for your country
And no one will worry a bit.

The previous stanza, by dropping the ironical stance to make a shrewd pictorial observation, is much more effective:

Does it matter?—losing your sight? . . .
There's such splendid work for the blind;
And people will always be kind,
As you sit on the terrace remembering
And turning your face to the light.

Here the subject is left to carry its own burden of meaning; the sardonic poet is absent, and the juxtaposition of the compassionate observation with the preceding irony makes the bitter point without intrusive bitterness.

The art of pointed juxtaposition—so necessary if the satiric poems are to extend themselves into areas of moral concern—is Sassoon's most typical device. "Suicide in the Trenches" shows the economy with which his two most obsessive contrasts could be made—but it also, in the last stanza, shows his weakness for rhetorical oversimplification:

> I knew a simple soldier boy
> Who grinned at life in empty joy,
> Slept soundly through the lonesome dark,
> And whistled early with the lark.
>
> In winter trenches, cowed and glum,
> With crumps and lice and lack of rum,
> He put a bullet through his brain.
> No one spoke of him again.
>
> .   .   .   .
>
> You smug-faced crowds with kindling eye
> Who cheer when soldier lads march by,
> Sneak home and pray you'll never know
> The hell where youth and laughter go.

Stanzas 1 and 2 are unsentimental and to the point: even the compliant sanguinity of the most unreflective soldier is vulnerable to terror and privation. Granting Sassoon the credibility of his material, these two stanzas are an effectively understated horror story, sufficient in themselves. But he wished to use the contrast between the soldier and the suicide (and its implications) as a single term in yet another contrast—hence the typographical separation between stanzas 2 and 3. The third stanza, which oversimplifies rather than understates, shows something of the overt propaganda which occasionally diminishes the value of Sassoon's poetry. "Sneak home . . ." is an instance of anger over-riding art, a making of a point by insult instead of observation. Sassoon's anger at civilian complacency is justifiable—and, at times, insult may be called for—but the rhetoric of scorn here prevents the poem from doing its own work. Our attention is drawn away from the material of the poem to the poet, to *his* reaction: we are being *told*.

A more successfully worked contrast between human values and the abstract values of a nation at war is "Lamentations," in which Sassoon, by adopting a *persona*, allows the poem to make its own point without his editorial intrusion:

> I found him in the guard-room at the Base.
> From the blind darkness I had heard his crying
> And blundered in. With puzzled, patient face
> A sergeant watched him; it was no good trying
> To stop it; for he howled and beat his chest.
> And, all because his brother had gone west,
> Raved at the bleeding war; his rampant grief
> Moaned, shouted, sobbed, and choked, while he
>   was kneeling
> Half-naked on the floor. In my belief
> Such men have lost all patriotic feeling.

The extent to which Sassoon "used" the materials of this poem for satirical purposes may be seen by comparing the poem with a prose account of the actual occurrence. Returning to the front in February 1917, he was obliged to spend a night at the Fifth Infantry base depot at Rouen. After reporting in, he went in search of the store-room for blankets:

> After groping about in the dark and tripping over tent ropes I was beginning to lose my temper when I opened a door and found myself in a Guard Room. A man, naked to the waist, was kneeling in the middle of the floor, clutching at his chest and weeping uncontrollably. The Guard were standing around with embarrassed looks, and the Sergeant was beside him,

patient and unpitying. While he was leading me to the blanket store I asked him what was wrong. "Why, sir, the man's been under detention for assaulting the military police, and now 'e's just 'ad news of his brother being killed. Seems to take it to 'eart more than most would. 'Arf crazy, 'e's been, tearing 'is clothes off and cursing the war and the Fritzes. Almost like a shell-shock case, 'e seems. It's his third time out. A Blighty one don't last a man long nowadays, sir." As I went off into the gloom I could still hear the uncouth howlings.[36]

Though "Lamentations" is a successful thrust at the prototypical patriotism of bishops, politicians, and newspapermen, the prose passage is the more moving account of despair reduced by extremity to madness. By subordinating the inherent pathos of the situation to his satiric intention, Sassoon makes his point—but misses a much larger one. It is a characteristic limitation, one from which Owen was free: a failure of poetic sensibility at a crucial moment in order to score most obviously off the public ignorance and cupidity which Sassoon found so oppressive and so omnipresent.

This is not to say that Sassoon constantly diminishes the poetic value of experience simply to make a point; "Attack" and "Dreamers" are just two examples of his ability to forget his audience and keep his eye on the subject. And it would be purblind aestheticism to lament the force of the social concern which, to the occasional detriment of art, found its way to the surface in his work. The poem "They," for example, can be taken as an amusing satire on the limitations inherent in any institutionalized religion; but it can also be read as an expression of angry despair over the Church's abdication of humanitarian responsibility. Few poets would have even bothered with the theme; Sassoon did:

The Bishop tells us: "When the boys come back
"They will not be the same; for they'll have fought

"In a just cause: they lead the last attack
"On Anti-Christ: their comrades' blood has bought
"New right to breed an honourable race,
"They have challenged Death and dared him face to face."

"We're none of us the same!" the boys reply.
"For George lost both his legs; and Bill's stone blind;
"Poor Jim's shot through the lungs and like to die;
"And Bert's gone syphilitic; you'll not find
"A chap who's served that hasn't found *some* change."
And the Bishop said: "The ways of God are strange!"

The implications of the poem go beyond the ironic; the bishops may have been easy targets, but they had the public ear, and what they had to say was usually more patriotic than Christian. In a sermon which made the point that killing in war is not the "killing" forbidden in the sixth commandment of the Decalogue, the Reverend Robert F. Horton demonstrated a peculiarly "moral" position:

> When a great country . . . has to defend herself against the invasion of a foe, or when a great country has to vindicate her honour—which may be more precious to a country, as to a man, than life itself—the individual citizen cannot stand aside and say that that is no concern of his. We are all bound as citizens of a great State to take our part in the defence of our country and the vindication of her honour, and the only exception I know to that principle is this: that supposing the country demands of us what we believe to be contrary to the law of God; if, for example, the country passed a law that we should all habitually commit adultery. . .[37]

The clergyman's moral discriminations were not unusual in his profession. The Right Reverend A. F. Winnington-Ingram, Bishop of London, demonstrated the English version of the *Gott mit uns* syndrome in a sermon on "The Conditions of Victory." How, he asks, may the world emerge once more from darkness into light? The answer, it appears, is really rather simple:

> That the nations which are to be the instruments of God's judgments are worthy to be weapons in His hands. That is why we have these days of penitence and prayer. As God reaches down His hand to His quiver to find the weapon for the bow which He has made ready, He must find a weapon which He can use. Are we, as a nation, such a weapon? That is the question for us to-day.[38]

The Bishop's bellicose rhetoric was as irrelevant to the war as were the poems of Jessie Pope and Katherine Hale; even where men of the cloth could have contributed to the spiritual welfare of men at the front, they failed miserably. Robert Graves, among others, mentions the conspicuous absence from the fighting areas of the Anglican chaplains, though they were always available with patriotic exhortations in regimental rest areas. (The criticism did not, however, apply to Roman Catholic chaplains, who stayed with their troops even in the most dangerous areas, administering extreme unction to the dying and—in at least one case—assuming military command of a sector when all the other officers had been killed or wounded.)[39] Sassoon, in a poem which uses church bells as a symbol of irrelevance, "What means this metal in windy belfries hung / When guns are all our need?", states the case with some irritation:

> Bells are like fierce-browed prelates who proclaim
> That "if our Lord returned He'd fight for *us.*"
> So let our bells and bishops do the same,
> Shoulder to shoulder with the motor-bus.[40]

In a way which was, unfortunately, beyond the comprehension of the Church's spokesmen, Christ *was* fighting in the trenches. Wilfred Owen was to express it most cogently, but Sassoon, in a poem entitled "The Redeemer," developed a pictorial image of unmistakable pathos and relevance—a context within which even the soldier's casual blasphemy assumes a moral dimension:

> I turned in the black ditch, loathing the storm;
> A rocket fizzed and burned with blanching flare,
> And lit the face of what had been a form
> Floundering in mirk. He stood before me there;
> I say that He was Christ; stiff in the glare,
> And leaning forward from His burdening task,
> Both arms supporting it; His eyes on mine
> Stared from the woeful head that seemed a mask
> Of mortal pain in Hell's unholy shine.
>
> No thorny crown, only a woollen cap
> He wore—an English soldier, white and strong,
> Who loved his time like any simple chap,
> Good days of work and sport and homely song;
> Now he has learned that nights are very long,
> And dawn a watching of the windowed sky.
> But to the end, unjudging, he'll endure
> Horror and pain, not uncontent to die
> That Lancaster on Lune may stand secure.
>
> He faced me, reeling in his weariness,
> Shouldering his load of planks, so hard to bear.
> I say that He was Christ, who wrought to bless
> All groping things with freedom bright as air,
> And with His mercy washed and made them fair.
> Then the flame sank, and all grew black as pitch,
> While we began to struggle along the ditch;
> And someone flung his burden in the muck,
> Mumbling: "O Christ Almighty, now I'm stuck!"[41]

Sassoon's clear-eyed vision of the Son of Man in man may be compared with the civilian-generated myth of the "Angels of Mons"[42] as a further instance of the curative value of his art. His "realism," even more than Owen's, was intended to destroy an obscurantism which, from the artist's point of view, sapped the strength of poetry at the same time as, on a wider scale, it insulated men from the truth about a world in which they were condemned to live and die.

Sassoon's impulse toward realism has, of course, some aesthetic disadvantages. In poetically rendering the nightmare of war-induced neurasthenia, he is generally less effective than Owen, whose artistic sensibility had more affinities with Keats than with such poets as Masefield. With some notable exceptions, Sassoon's control of images becomes unsure outside the area of tangible, reportable "reality"; consequently, he has only limited success in conveying the nature of a world which is so cruelly "imaginative" without ever being abstract. Owen's most horrifying—and convincing—neurasthenic image is that of a world drenched in blood:

> . . . on their sense
> Sunlight seems a blood smear; night comes blood-black;
> Dawn breaks open like a wound that bleeds afresh.[43]

Sassoon, on the other hand, when he attempts to capture poetically his own experience of neurasthenia, turns to images which are auditory and experiential rather than visual and symbolic. He buttresses this technique in "Repression of War Experience" with the dramatic device of interior dialogue, in which the language is deliberately simple, almost childlike: "Books . . . / . . . Which will you read? / Come on; O *do* read something; they're so wise." There is no irony in "they're so wise"; Sassoon is fearfully in earnest:

> I tell you all the wisdom of the world
> Is waiting for you on those shelves; and yet
> You sit and gnaw your nails, and let your pipe out,
> And listen to the silence. . . .

He has seen a moth fluttering close to a candle flame; the simple fact of its danger is what starts the dialogue:

> No, no, not that,—it's bad to think of war,
> When thoughts you've gagged all day come back
>   to scare you;

And it's been proved that soldiers don't go mad
Unless they lose control of ugly thoughts
That drive them out to jabber among the trees.

Now light your pipe; look, what a steady hand.
Draw a deep breath; stop thinking; count fifteen,
And you're as right as rain . . .
                           Why won't it rain? . . .

His dramatic form allows Sassoon to use the actual
moment of breakdown as the point of maximum poetic
intensity; whereas Owen builds tension through a sequence of images, Sassoon builds it through a dramatic
interplay of voices:

You're quiet and peaceful, summering safe at home,
You'd never think there was a bloody war on! . . .
O yes, you would . . . why, you can hear the guns.
Hark! Thud, thud, thud,—quite soft . . . they never
     cease—
Those whispering guns—O Christ, I want to go out
And screech at them to stop—I'm going crazy;
I'm going stark, staring mad because of the guns.

By 1917, Sassoon had no patriotic illusions about
the war. He went back to the front after each hospitalization—even after Craiglockhart, where his anti-war statement had sent him—but not in search of glory, not to
destroy the Bishop's Anti-Christ. Like Owen he went
back out of loyalty to the men in the trenches, men who
had no voice to tell of their wrongs, who died mutely
and daily and in their millions. In one of his most moving poems, he speaks both for them and for himself:

I am banished from the patient men who fight;
They smote my heart to pity, built my pride.
Shoulder to aching shoulder, side by side,
They trudged away from life's broad wealds of light.
Their wrongs were mine; and ever in my sight
They went arrayed in honour. But they died,—

Not one by one: and mutinous I cried
To those who sent them out into the night.

The darkness tells how vainly I have striven
To free them from the pit where they must dwell
In outcast gloom convulsed and jagged and riven
By grappling guns. Love drove me to rebel.
Love drives me back to grope with them through hell;
And in their tortured eyes I stand forgiven.

"Banishment" is not a great poem—but it is, I think, adequate to its subject. The last three lines are particularly rich, and even in the first stanza the juxtaposition in lines 5 through 7 of honorific image and brutal reality shows Sassoon's ability to rescue an otherwise platitudinous expression ("went arrayed in honour") and give it once more some significant meaning.

To do critical justice to the unique relationship which existed between infantry officers and their men in the Great War would require a volume in itself. Both Owen and Sassoon offer convincing poetic testimony to the strength of this mutual loyalty, but perhaps the most direct statement of its nature was that of a Scottish poet and officer who was killed in action in November 1917:

Oh, never shall I forget you,
    My men, who trusted me:
More my sons than your fathers'—
    For they could only see
The little helpless babies,
    Or the young men in their pride:
They could not see you dying
    Or hold you, while you died.

Happy and young and gallant
    They saw their first-born go;
But not the strong limbs broken,
    And the beautiful men laid low,
And the piteous writhing bodies
    That screamed: "Don't leave me, sir!"

> For they were only your fathers,
>   And I was your officer.[44]

Sassoon is more clipped and satiric in "Twelve Months After"; but in the nightmarish "Sick Leave" the ghosts of the soldiers he has watched die gather around his convalescent bed to ask the emotionally-loaded question:

> "When are you going out to them again?
> Are they not still your brothers through our blood?"

Sassoon did go out again, this time to the Middle East, where he was promoted to captain. He returned to the western front in May 1918; but, after suffering a head wound (ironically enough, it was inflicted by one of his own trigger-happy sentries as Sassoon returned from a skirmish with a German machine-gun post), he was safely out of the war. His convictions had not changed; "Reconciliation" and "Aftermath" show the same sober and ironical disquietude as the best of the 1917 trench poems. But he was free. And in April 1919 the fact became poetry. Sassoon described the occasion in *Siegfried's Journey:*

> One evening in the middle of April I had an experience which seems worth describing for those who are interested in methods of poetic production. It was a sultry spring night. I was feeling dull-minded and depressed, for no assignable reason. After sitting lethargically in the ground-floor room for about three hours after dinner, I came to the conclusion that there was nothing for it but to take my useless brain to bed. On my way from the arm-chair to the door I stood by the writing-table. A few words had floated into my head as though from nowhere. In those days I was always on the look-out for a lyric—I wish I could say the same for my present self—so I picked up a pencil and wrote the words on a sheet of note-paper. Without sitting down, I added a second line. It was as if I were remembering rather than thinking. In this mindless, recollecting manner I wrote down my poem

119

in a few minutes. When it was finished I read it through, with no sense of elation, merely wondering how I had come to be writing a poem when feeling so stupid. I then went heavily upstairs and fell asleep. . . .[45]

The poem which made this spontaneous entry into the world was "Everyone Sang," a lyric which expresses exultation and release through two of Sassoon's richest lyric images, song and the songbird. In *Heart's Journey* (first published in 1927), he was to explore the potentialities of these two images as metaphors for the human soul, and with them evolve his own lyric symbology. "Everyone Sang" was the starting point for this lyric search, just as it was the culmination of his poetic involvement in the Great War:

Everyone suddenly burst out singing;
And I was filled with such delight
As prisoned birds must find in freedom,
Winging wildly across the white
Orchards and dark-green fields; on—on—and out of
  sight.

Everyone's voice was suddenly lifted;
And beauty came like the setting sun:
My heart was shaken with tears; and horror
Drifted away . . . O, but Everyone
Was a bird; and the song was wordless; the singing
  will never be done.

The correspondences established by the poem have a lyric intensity and a figurative validity comparable to those of Wordsworth and Blake. Although Sassoon would never again achieve such visionary power, he has, in this one lyric, made true poetry out of the fact of his physical, emotional, and spiritual survival.

He did, in sum, survive the war, and as a poet. It remains to consider a man whose poetic vision was both deeper and more intense than Sassoon's, but to whom survival was denied: Wilfred Owen.

5

THE POETICS OF RESPONSIBILITY

Wilfred Owen

18 March 1893 - 4 November 1918

The mind of man has two kinds of shepherds; the poets who rouse and trouble and the poets who hush and console.

W. B. Yeats

But Art may tell a truth
Obliquely, do the thing shall breed the thought,
Nor wrong the thought, missing the mediate word.
So may you paint your picture, twice show truth,
Beyond mere imagery on the wall,—
So, note by note, bring music from your mind,
Deeper than ever e'en Beethoven dived,—
So, write a book shall mean beyond the facts,
Suffice the eye and save the soul beside.
Browning, "The Ring and the Book," XII. 859–67.

When the First World War broke out in August 1914, Wilfred Owen was in France, working as a tutor. From the seclusion of Bordeaux, he wrote his first war poem, a reflective sonnet which treated the event in self-consciously "universal" terms:

> War broke: and now the Winter of the world
> With perishing great darkness closes in.
> The foul tornado, centred at Berlin,
> Is over all the width of Europe whirled,
> Rending the sails of progress. Rent or furled
> Are all Art's ensigns. Verse wails. Now begin
> Famines of thought and feeling. Love's wine's thin.
> The grain of human Autumn rots, down-hurled.
>
> For after Spring had bloomed in early Greece,
> And Summer blazed her glory out with Rome,
> An Autumn softly fell, a harvest home,
> A slow grand age, and rich with all increase.
> But now, for us, wild Winter, and the need
> Of sowings for new Spring, and blood for seed.[1]

For the production of a twenty-one-year-old Englishman in time of war, "1914" is remarkably restrained, both in imagery and movement. One need only compare it with contemporary verses on the same subject by Brooke, Sassoon, Sorley, and Nichols—to say nothing of the rhetorical outpourings from such poetic pensioners as Alfred Noyes, Stephen Phillips, and Sir Henry Newbolt—to notice its unrancorous maturity. Artistically it is unimpressive; the Keatsian elements are barely assimilated, and the form is strained at times ("Love's wine's thin," for example) to contain its fairly bulky material. Its chief value is as a point of departure. Like Sassoon's first war poems, it shows a response limited by an outworn convention; a young poet's innocent attempt to turn the stuff of experience into the stuff of art. Nonetheless, its imagery is both relevant and under control. The use of only two end-rhymes in the octave shows technical determination; and the last two lines, particularly the final image, suggest a poetic consciousness unafraid to create its own metaphors.

Unlike most of the young poets mentioned in earlier chapters, Owen had no university education, his family being unable to afford the expense. After he left Shrewsbury Technical School, he spent almost two years in a curacy in Oxfordshire—the Church being the only avenue which might possibly have gained him entrance to the University. He was a serious and idealistic youth, however, and became strongly dissatisfied with the Anglican-pastoral version of Christianity represented by the Reverend Wigan, under whom he was preparing himself for orders. In August 1913 he took a post as an English tutor in the Berlitz School in Bordeaux, leaving this to become a private tutor in July 1914. He was troubled by the outbreak of war, but served out his contract with the Léger family, returning to England in September 1915. On 21 October 1915 he enlisted in the Artists' Rifles.

Biographical information about Owen is still rather sparse. Although there is a three-volume memoir by his brother Harold, it adds very little of value to the material available in Sassoon's *Siegfried's Journey,* Edmund Blunden's *Memoir* (appended to the *Collected Poems*), and C. Day Lewis's introduction to the 1963 edition of the poems. These sources also contain relevant excerpts from Owen's letters, which were compiled and published in 1967.

Since he was born in a working-class, nonliterary milieu and did not survive the war in which he came to poetic maturity, Owen never received that kind of contemporary notice which subsequently provides the critic with a background against which to set his work. Such lack of secondary information is, of course, not entirely a disadvantage. The most important fact for the literary critic, as for the general reader, is the poetry; and this, thanks to Sassoon, Blunden, and the Sitwells, has been preserved.

I would like, at the outset, to indicate those characteristics which set Owen's poetry apart from that of his contemporaries. The following comparison, therefore, between Owen's "Anthem for Doomed Youth" and Brooke's sonnet IV: "The Dead," is intended more as a demonstration of a radical difference in approach to the subject (which in each case is the same) than as a demonstration of which is the better poem. The grounds for comparison are certainly tenable: both poems are elegiac sonnets; both attempt to render the pathos of untimely death; both are formally acceptable variants of the Elizabethan sonnet.[2] In both style and thought Brooke exhibits what I wish to call a "conventional" response, while Owen exhibits a "radical" response.

To indicate this difference before venturing on a closer examination of the poems, it may suffice to draw attention to a certain similarity in the resolutions of the two poems. Owen's soldiers are to be remembered, not by the traditional candles before a church altar, but by the light in the eyes of youth: "Not in the hands of boys, but in their eyes / Shall shine the holy glimmers of goodbyes." For Brooke death—represented by frost—leaves "a white / Unbroken glory, a gathered radiance, / A width, a shining peace, under the night." The similarity, slight though it is, results mainly from both poets' use of light as a metaphor. The difference, which extends throughout the poems, is in the particularity with which the metaphor is realized in relation to its correlative.

In "The Dead," Brooke's response to his subject is generalized and poetically conventional; it may, with some reservations, be called a lyric response. The burden of the octave, expressed in largely abstract terms, is that life is good and is made up of positive responses to pleasant stimuli. Only in the last line does Brooke use concrete terms, and here he achieves some of the poignancy that makes "The Great Lover" such a fine poem:

> These hearts were woven of human joys and cares,
>   Washed marvellously with sorrow, swift to mirth.
> The years had given them kindness. Dawn was theirs,
>   And sunset, and the colours of the earth.
> These had seen movement, and heard music; known
>   Slumber and waking; loved; gone proudly friended;
> Felt the quick stir of wonder; sat alone;
>   Touched flowers and furs and cheeks. All this is ended.

By capping the list with "All this is ended," Brooke stirs us a little—but only a little. For this is the furthest extent of his response: death itself will be approached only through a metaphor—the metaphor which makes up the sestet. It is not unfair to say of the octave that, rather than achieving universality with such generalizations as "These had seen movement, and heard music," the poem has lost touch with the particular, and we see not men but, if anything, a shadowy everyman. The "These" of the poem are not sufficiently defined by their context—as they so profoundly are in Owen's sonnet—to awaken our sympathy.

The pitfalls of such abstraction become all too evident in the sestet, which is "poetic" in a peculiarly unsatisfactory way:

> There are waters blown by changing winds to laughter
> And lit by the rich skies, all day. And after,
>   Frost, with a gesture, stays the waves that dance
> And wandering loveliness. He leaves a white
>   Unbroken glory, a gathered radiance,
> A width, a shining peace, under the night.

Here the subject (soldiers who have fallen in battle) is removed from the realm of experience into the realm of its metaphor. Brooke, beautifully able to work out and justify the *metaphor* on the level of aesthetics, by implication justifies the *experience* on the level of ethics. This is a practice which the critic rightly holds suspect—though it should be recognized for what it is, rather than set aside with, "the sestet describes water which has frosted over, and seems to have nothing to do with the octave."[3] The irrelevance to which Enright here refers is too significant to be dismissed with a shrug; it is an irrelevance which Brooke only just manages to evade in the octave, and it is the most obvious symptom of moribund Romanticism: the fault of metaphoric abstraction.

For men who suffer and die are not water which sparkles briefly in the sun only to be frozen to stillness by the inevitable winter. In his too easy reliance on the metaphor, and on the similar abstractions of the octave, Brooke betrays the reality of his subject. Though frost may indeed leave "a white / Unbroken glory, a gathered radiance, / A width, a shining peace, under the night," this is not to say (nor even honestly to suggest) that death itself leaves something analogous in the world of men—but this, certainly, is what the reader is left to infer.

Unlike Owen's "Anthem," which is continuously and vitally infused with the poet's compassion and anger, Brooke's sonnet is grounded in a twilight determinism, a too ready resignation to all that must be. This determinism underlies (and, if accepted, justifies) the entire sestet, which uses the water metaphor to remove the experiences of suffering and death to the region of natural, inexorable—and hence acceptable—phenomena. In the process, too many questions are begged, and too much of life is ignored or transmuted into a pale and inconsequential form of art.

Owen, on the other hand, opens his poem with a

question which in its imageric* immediacy and relevance could never have occurred in the decayed Tennysonian mode to which Brooke had retreated: "What passing-bells for these who die as cattle?"—not a comfortable way to begin a commemorative poem. Abrupt in form and disturbing in content, it is far from the pleasant reassurances and even tone of "The Dead." The second line supplies the answer to the question and establishes the direction of the poem, a direction at once elegiac and unconsolatory: "Only the monstrous anger of the guns."

The answer is as important for what it denies as for what it affirms. It refuses access to the ritualized abstractions we normally use to palliate the thought of death and, by keeping the reader's attention on the *condition* of the death process, effectively prevents that still further abstracting encouraged by Brooke: that use of language which would cloak the fact of death in a metaphor. The octave maintains this explicit denial of figurative substitution by firmly centering attention on the engines of death, building them into the framework of a religious ceremony which Owen finds inadequate as a response to the fact of this kind of death:

> Only the stuttering rifles' rapid rattle
> Can patter out their hasty orisons.
> No mockeries now for them; no prayers nor bells,
> Nor any voice of mourning save the choirs,—
> The shrill, demented choirs of wailing shells;
> And bugles calling for them from sad shires.

In a world where heaven is literally the "highway for a shell,"[4] the use of symbolic abstractions may be worse than irrelevant; it may be criminally misleading.

Owen's elegy is unrelenting in its concentration on the actual condition—the *experience*—to be rendered as

---

* I apologize for forcing this apparently unusual word on the reader. It occurs only in contexts where the adjective closest to the noun "image" seems to me necessary.

128

verse. This is what I would term a poetically radical, rather than a poetically conventional, response. The "These" of Owen's poem are "these who die as cattle," while Brooke's "had seen movement, and heard music." If we are to judge them as war poems, there can be little question as to which is the more successful evocation of relevant fact.

The sestet maintains the tension of the octave's search for an appropriate response while achieving a resolution far transcending that of "The Dead" in its fidelity to its subject. The only valid response to death is awareness of it. The poem denies the value of "candles," "pall," and "flowers," and in their place puts human reactions:

> What candles may be held to speed them all?
>   Not in the hands of boys, but in their eyes
> Shall shine the holy glimmers of good-byes.
>   The pallor of girls' brows shall be their pall;
> Their flowers the tenderness of patient minds,
> And each slow dusk a drawing-down of blinds.

This replacing of objects by actions once more focuses attention on the immediate, the significant human fact, rather than on the symbol. There is no metaphoric escape in Owen's sestet; in what one could call a reversal of the conventional process of poetic image-making, he replaces "flowers" with the "tenderness of patient minds," and "candles" with the shining eyes of boys.

Geoffrey Hill has criticized this poem in a way which, it seems to me, reveals Owen's compassion while attempting to demonstrate an internal contradiction:

> The fact that Owen employs irony in this poem cannot alter the fact that he takes thirteen lines to retreat from the position maintained by one. If these men really do die as *cattle*, then all *human* mourning for them is a mockery, the private and the public, the inarticulate and true as much as the ostentatiously-false.[5]

Were Hill's point valid, it would deny mourning to all except those who died in the most dignified, and ritualized, circumstances. Though his intention is to stress the uselessness of mourning, it seems merest callousness to deny its existence as a human reaction. Surely a sense of human value would indicate that the conditions of a man's death could never dispel the feeling of loss which underlies what we call mourning. Indeed, the more futile the manner of his death, the more intense would be the sense of loss; one need only read Owen's "Futility" to appreciate the power and essential humanity of "mourning."

All may be vanity, as Hill and Ecclesiastes would have us believe, but there are degrees of uselessness; one hesitates to dismiss compassion on the grounds that it is less final than death. "Anthem for Doomed Youth" remains true to what we know of human nature. The poem refuses palliative symbols, and anchors grief in its actual manifestations—not brutally, but with a delicacy and restraint which permits the last line to carry its full weight of sadness while suggesting that even grief must finally rest.

As an example of elegy in an age of mechanized warfare, the poem is admirable. Its internal movement is the search for a suitable response to the fact of brutalized death, and its imagery shows a tough-minded refusal to compromise that fact with irrelevant metaphor. The poem answers the questions posed by its own rhetoric, honestly requiting its own plea for honesty.

Both "Anthem for Doomed Youth" and sonnet IV: "The Dead" are viable elegies; each is a successful example of its method. It is evident, however, that one method is more effective in conveying the actuality of experience than the other. If we judge our poetry by its success in rendering human experience in images drawn directly from the sensory fact of that experience, rather than from a stock of analogues which may—or may not—parallel the world perceived by the senses, then Owen's sonnet is the superior. By refusing to take flight into the fantasy world of metaphor-manipulation, Owen created a poem out of images which represent reality, rather than out of images which are born—and have their only relevance—in the graceful world of metaphor. The result is immediacy, which was his intention.

This kind of poetic immediacy is not simply fidelity to fact; were that the case, prose would be as adequate a vehicle for communication. In its imaginative transmutation of the stuff of experience into the stuff of art, such poetry renders the *essence* of the fact—"shall mean beyond the facts," as Browning had it—without ever losing sight of the fact. A convenient example, which may clarify this point, is Owen's "The Sentry." I have interpolated sections of the poem, in sequence, with sections of a letter Owen wrote to his mother on 16 January 1917. Both poem and letter describe the same incident:

> I have not been at the front. I have been in front of it.
> I held an advanced post, that is, a "dug-out" in the middle of No Man's Land. We had a march of 3 miles over shelled road, then nearly 3 along a flooded trench. After that we came to where the trenches had been blown flat out and had to go over the top. It was of course dark, too dark, and the ground was not mud, not sloppy mud, but an octopus of sucking clay, 3, 4, and 5 feet deep, relieved only by craters full of water. Men have been known to drown in them. Many stuck in the mud and only got on by leaving their waders, equipment, and in some cases their clothes. High explosives were dropping all around, and machine-guns spluttered every few minutes. But it was so dark that even the German flares did not reveal us. Three-quarters dead, I mean each of us ¾ dead, we reached the dug-out and relieved the wretches therein. I then had to go forth and find another dug-out for a still more advanced post where I left 18 bombers. I was responsible for other posts on the left, but there was a junior officer in charge. My dug-out held 25 men tight packed. Water filled it to a depth of 1 or 2 feet, leaving say 4 feet of air. One entrance had been blown in and blocked. So far, the other remained. The Ger-

131

mans knew we were staying there and decided we
shouldn't.[6]

We'd found an old Boche dug-out, and he knew,
And gave us hell, for shell on frantic shell
Hammered on top, but never quite burst through.
Rain, guttering down in waterfalls of slime,
Kept slush waist-high and rising hour by hour,
And choked the steps too thick with clay to climb.
What murk of air remained stank old, and sour
With fumes of whizz-bangs, and the smell of men
Who'd lived there years, and left their curse in
 the den,
If not their corpses. . . .

Those fifty hours were the agony of my happy life.
Every ten minutes on Sunday afternoon seemed an
hour. I nearly broke down and let myself drown in
the water that was now slowly rising over my knees.
Towards 6 o'clock, when, I suppose, you would be
going to church, the shelling grew less intense and
less accurate; so that I was mercifully helped to do my
duty and crawl, wade, climb, and flounder over No
Man's Land to visit my other post. It took me half an
hour to move about 150 yards. I was chiefly annoyed
by our own machine-guns from behind. The seeng-
seeng-seeng of the bullets reminded me of Mary's
canary. On the whole I can support the canary better.
In the platoon on my left the sentries over the dug-out
were blown to nothing. One of these poor fellows was
my first servant whom I rejected. If I had kept him he
would have lived, for servants don't do sentry duty. I
kept my own sentries half-way down the stairs during
the more terrific bombardment. In spite of this one
lad was blown down and, I am afraid, blinded.

There we herded from the blast
Of whizz-bangs, but one found our door at last,—
Buffeting eyes and breath, snuffing the candles,
And thud! flump! thud! down the steep steps came
 thumping
And sploshing in the flood, deluging muck—

The sentry's body; then, his rifle, handles
Of old Boche bombs, and mud in ruck on ruck.
We dredged him up, for killed, until he whined
"O sir, my eyes—I'm blind—I'm blind, I'm blind!"
Coaxing, I held a flame against his lids
And said if he could see the least blurred light
He was not blind; in time he'd get all right.
"I can't," he sobbed. Eyeballs, huge-bulged like
      squids',
Watch my dreams still; but I forgot him there
In posting Next for duty, and sending a scout
To beg a stretcher somewhere, and flound'ring about
To other posts under the shrieking air.

> This was my only casualty. The officer of the left
> platoon has come out completely prostrated and is in
> hospital. I am now as well, I suppose, as ever.

Those other wretches, how they bled and spewed,
And one who would have drowned himself for good,—
I try not to remember these things now.
Let dread hark back for one word only: how
Half listening to that sentry's moans and jumps,
And the wild chattering of his broken teeth,
Renewed most horribly whenever crumps
Pummelled the roof and slogged the air beneath—
Through the dense din, I say, we heard him shout
"I see your lights!" But ours had long died out.

The difference of effect between poem and letter is so evident that it needs no exegesis. But it is worth noting that the difference does not depend on any rhetorical excess in the poem. The letter—a typical war-letter—is factually detailed and descriptive, organized as a narrative: prosaic in the most obvious sense. The poem, on the other hand, has edited and reorganized the facts with considerable economy into a sequence of images which are qualified and heightened by their poetic context. The interaction among these images (all of them, as the letter substantiates, directly related to the experienced facts)

133

reveals, in its total effect, much more of significance about the experience than does the more thoroughly-detailed letter.

Owen's developing sophistication in control of images can be illustrated by comparing "The Sentry" with the superficially similar "Dulce et Decorum Est," written some thirteen months earlier. "Dulce et Decorum Est" is quite overt in its rhetorical use of anger; the last stanza turns directly, almost commandingly, to its audience with "If in some smothering dreams you too could pace / Behind the wagon that we flung him in." Here Owen's attention is, to some extent, outside the subject of the poem; his intention—certainly an admirable one—is to "show" the horror to an all-too-uncomprehending audience on the home front. It is not irrelevant that, of the four existing drafts of the poem, two are subscribed *To a certain Poetess* and another is subscribed *To Jessie Pope etc.*[7] It would be insensitive to condemn the poem as simple propaganda, unless one were also to dismiss Donne's "The Canonization," Marvell's "To His Coy Mistress," and countless other poems which make persuasive use of a second-person address.

Most of the critical disapproval engendered by the poem seems to be related to a sense of uneasiness at the unrelieved piling-up of horrific images in the last stanza. Johnston attacks the poem for its "negative, cynical attitude"[8]—ignoring the tone of the poem in order to make a point about the details of imagery. It is urgency, rather than cynicism, which prompts this particular display of horror; in his rudimentary table of contents Owen listed "Indifference at Home" as the "Motive" for this poem. Despairing of ever breaking through that indifference, Owen had at one time considered a much more direct approach, as Frank Nicholson, librarian of Edinburgh University, recalled:

> . . . it was then that I got a hint of the effect that the horrors he had seen and heard of at the Front had made upon him. He did not enlarge upon them, but

they were obviously always in his thoughts, and he wished that an obtuse world should be made sensible of them. With this object he was collecting a set of photographs exhibiting the ravages of war upon the men who took part in it—mutilations, wounds, surgical operations, and the like. He had some of these photographs with him, and I remember that he put his hand to his breast-pocket to show me them, but suddenly thought better of it and refrained. No doubt he felt that the sight of them would be painful to me, and perhaps also that such methods of propaganda were superfluous in my case.[9]

Owen was recuperating from shell shock at the time he met Nicholson. There is no evidence that he ever used the photographs he had accumulated; as a matter of fact, considering his sensitivity and deference in company, it is unlikely that he ever did so.

The important point is, however, that the anguish of "Dulce et Decorum Est" is carried for the most part by vividly-realized visual images. Images of a distinctive kind: as in "The Sentry," the most nightmarish passages take place in an unnatural, seemingly underwater setting. The brief "action" of the earlier poem is this:

But someone still was yelling out and stumbling
And flound'ring like a man in fire or lime . . .
Dim, through the misty panes and thick green light,
As under a green sea, I saw him drowning.

In all my dreams, before my helpless sight,
He plunges at me, guttering, choking, drowning.

There is a similarly claustrophobic microcosm in "The Sentry":

Rain, guttering down in waterfalls of slime,
Kept slush waist-high and rising hour by hour,
And choked the steps too thick with clay to climb.
. . . .
Eyeballs, huge-bulged like squids',
Watch my dreams still; but I forgot him there

> In posting Next for duty, and sending a scout
> To beg a stretcher somewhere, and flound'ring about
> To other posts under the shrieking air.[10]

The similarities and differences of these two passages are instructive. Both events seem to be barely assimilable by the poet's rational consciousness, and both give rise to haunting dreams; but in "The Sentry" Owen does not make the event so dramatically central to the poem. Our attention—and Owen's—is pulled away from the blinded man by the need for further action; his responsibilities as an officer must displace for the moment his compassion for the suffering individual. (The effect of this necessity on Owen as a person—unstated in the poem, but underlying much of his work—can be estimated from the memoirs of those who knew him, and who testified to his intense sensitivity to others' pain.) Artistically, the result of the poem's movement away from the specific event, the focal point of suffering, is to extend rather than diminish the nightmare. Whereas in "Dulce et Decorum Est" "flound'ring" describes the soldier who is literally drowning, in "The Sentry" it describes the speaker himself as he struggles, though no longer in the flooded underground chamber, to carry out his duties "under the shrieking air."

The last section of "The Sentry" is a dramatically conceived attempt to establish an adequate narrative distance from the events of the battlefield. The deliberately reductive "Those other wretches, how they bled and spewed," with its implication that horror has become meaningless through repetition, prepares the way for the narrative intrusion, "I try not to remember these things now." The pathos of this simple statement is reinforced by the use of the word "dread" as a synonym for "memory" in the next line: horror has now drawn too close to be safely visualized or used as a basis for outrage. It seems almost as if the limits of sanity themselves require the poet to maintain a distance from his material, as if they are what govern the cautious and almost mono-syllabic "Let dread hark back for one word only," as if it is they which ensure the complete absence of visual imagery in what follows. The final limitation to auditory imagery not only modulates the horror of the continuing bombardment (our lexicon of horror is largely—though not exclusively—made up of visual images), but it suc-ceeds magnificently in its imageric isolation of the sen-try's pathetic cry, "'I see your lights.'" For those who can see, sight is a maddening burden; for the blinded man it is, paradoxically, a link with sanity. There is no angry propaganda here, only a restrained and artistic rendering of frightful experience, all the more frightful for the seeming calm with which it is narrated.

The possibilities for imageric antithesis and paradox are demonstrated in "Spring Offensive," a complex poem (even the title has paradoxical overtones) which may be taken as the definitive example of that type of poetry which deals imaginatively with fact (as opposed to that type of poetry which deals imaginatively with fancy). The poem's images, gradually evolving from a sensitive and low-keyed descriptive opening, gather momentum as the poem progresses:

> Halted against the shade of a last hill,
> They fed, and lying easy, were at ease
> And, finding comfortable chests and knees,
> Carelessly slept. But many there stood still
> To face the stark, blank sky beyond the ridge,
> Knowing their feet had come to the end of the world.

The opening is cinematically accurate and spare; the subtlety of "last hill" in the first line is such that it ini-tially passes as straightforward description—an interpre-tation reinforced by the fact that not until line five does another "weighted" image occur: "the stark, blank sky beyond the ridge." Only with line six, "Knowing their feet had come to the end of the world," is the elegiac note definitively sounded; the stanza which follows is effectively static:

Marvelling they stood, and watched the long grass swirled
By the May breeze, murmurous with wasp and midge,
For though the summer oozed into their veins
Like an injected drug for their bodies' pains,
Sharp on their souls hung the imminent line of grass,
Fearfully flashed the sky's mysterious glass.

The image of summer as a drug is, and is not, akin to the "drowsy numbness" of Keats's "Ode to a Nightingale"; the particularity of "injected" and the deliberate subordination of the simile to the dread of the "imminent line of grass" indicate the precariousness—and, for these men, the artificiality—of a moment Keats had been able to prolong. Nature and her beauties are hardly more than ironic facts in this paradoxical interlude of relaxation before certain nightmare; it is not anthropomorphism, but the heightened awareness of the condemned, which notices how

the buttercup
Had blessed with gold their slow boots coming up,
Where even the little brambles would not yield,
But clutched and clung to them like sorrowing hands. . . .

Within this partial context, "buttercup" might seem too typically Georgian and precious; but within the context of the whole poem, it becomes an image of profound and ironic bitterness. When the soldiers finally race and plunge over the ridge

instantly the whole sky burned
With fury against them; earth set sudden cups
In thousands for their blood; and the green slope
Chasmed and steepened sheer to infinite space.

An earlier draft of the poem had the weaker and more obvious line "and soft sudden cups / Opened in thousands for their blood"[11] instead of "earth set sudden cups / In thousands for their blood." The revision not only shows Owen's skillful control of images, it sounds a Hardyan note of nature's impartiality, which qualifies the Romantic richness of the earlier passages.

The transition from the Arcadian atmosphere of shelter to the fully-expected horror of an infantry attack is handled in a way which both describes and demonstrates the unflamboyant heroism so incomprehensible on the home front:

> They breathe like trees unstirred.
>
> Till like a cold gust thrills the little word
> At which each body and its soul begird
> And tighten them for battle. No alarms
> Of bugles, no high flags, no clamorous haste—
> Only a lift and flare of eyes that faced
> The sun, like a friend with whom their love is done.
> O larger shone that smile against the sun,—
> Mightier than his whose bounty these have spurned.

The attitude described in these last four lines escapes simple definition. It is not stoicism, not surly defiance; yet neither is it the willful self-dramatization of Alan Seeger's

> I have a rendezvous with Death
> On some scarred slope of battered hill,
> When Spring comes round again this year,
> And the first meadow-flowers appear.[12]

It is an attitude better described than defined; profoundly unsentimental and selfless, its pathos external and observed rather than—as in Seeger—internally cultivated for exhibition. It is possible that the last two comparative lines ("larger . . . / Mightier . . ."), echo the religious dilemma dealt with more overtly in "At a Calvary near the Ancre" and "Le Christianisme," though, as

D. S. R. Welland's fine and consistent interpretation of the poem shows, the primary mode of alienation has resulted from a breakdown in the "rich organic unity of man and nature."[13]

The infantryman's well-founded dread of exposure, already evoked by several references to the blankly inhospitable sky, is superbly rendered by the caesura in the fifth stanza:

> So, soon they topped the hill, and raced together
> Over an open stretch of herb and heather
> Exposed. And instantly the whole sky burned
> With fury against them. . . .

"Open stretch of herb and heather" concludes a seemingly innocuous descriptive couplet. But the syntactically isolated word "Exposed" marks the soldiers' transition into a world bitterly and unremittingly hostile. The stanza, and the first section of the poem, ends with ". . . earth set sudden cups / In thousands for their blood; and the green slope / Chasmed and steepened sheer to infinite space." "Green slope / Chasmed . . ." is an image Owen has imaginatively transferred (somewhat in the manner of Sassoon's "Counter-Attack") from the realm of subjective experience of death itself to the realm of objective description. The tumbling disorientation of explosion and endless falling is modulated into a source of irony, horror, and compassion in the second half of the poem. Here Milton's Satan, cast down from heaven, finds his innocent modern counterpart in men who deliberately seek hell:

> Of them who running on that last high place
> Leapt to swift unseen bullets, or went up
> On the hot blast and fury of hell's upsurge,
> Or plunged and fell away past this world's verge,
> Some say God caught them even before they fell.
>
> But what say such as from existence' brink
> Ventured but drave too swift to sink,

The few who rushed in the body to enter hell,
And there out-fiending all its fiends and flames
With superhuman inhumanities,
Long-famous glories, immemorial shames—
And crawling slowly back, have by degrees
Regained cool peaceful air in wonder—
Why speak not they of comrades that went under?

The "last hill" of the first stanza is now "that last high place," Calvary. The tonal shift indicates the elegiac gravity which provides a counterbalance to the dislocation and confusion of the anonymous deaths verbally rendered by "Leapt," "went up," "plunged," and "fell away." Owen's use of the cosmic dimension in "Chasmed and steepened sheer to infinite space" broadens the context of the poem to permit the religious references an inevitability not only traditional but also figurative. But the poem subtly underscores Owen's doubt about the validity of God in such a context. The "Some" who can so easily assimilate the fact of the soldiers' deaths are not those who were there as witnesses; those who have survived hell by "out-fiending . . . / With superhuman inhumanities" remain significantly silent. The final questioning line casts a deep shadow over the whole poem. It is a question which implicates any treatment of war as a "subject": "In what *possible* context," the poem seems to ask, "can this experience be placed?" The question is not simply rhetorical. As in the earlier poem "Asleep," Owen is aware that he is creating a context in which to speak of "comrades that went under." A partial understanding of the boundaries of that context, and of Owen's conception of poetic honesty, can be obtained from a footnote to an unfinished draft of "Spring Offensive" he sent Sassoon: "Is this worth going on with? / I don't want to write anything to which a soldier would say No Compris!"[14]

The footnote is significant not only for its echoes of Wordsworth's "language that men use" but for the way in which it extends Owen's prefatory disclaimer "Above

141

all I am not concerned with Poetry." The men who lived
and died in the world Owen distilled into his work
were, if not his audience, his witnesses—witnesses that
he spoke truth as well as poetry. He knew that he was
the speaker among them; while waiting to return to the
front for his last tour of duty, he had expressed his sense
of vocation in this definitive stanza:

> For leaning out last midnight on my sill
> I heard the sighs of men, that have no skill
> To speak of their distress, no, nor the will!
> A voice I know. And this time I must go.[15]

The "skill / To speak" was not that of the propagandist.
By this time Owen was aware of his growing artistic
powers. The knowledge was expressed with typical modesty in a letter he wrote to his mother in May 1918: ". . .
nowadays my head turns only in shame away from these
first flickers of the limelight. For I am old already for a
poet, and so little is yet achieved."[16]

What was achieved may have been little in quantity
but, in many of the poems, he transcended the factual
limitations of his subject in a way characteristic of the
finest poetry. This part of his poetry is wider than the
war; in effect, it validates the war as a human experience, while showing its truly intolerable nature. The
poet's ability to universalize, to make valid in the widest
human sense, his subject, underlies C. K. Stead's enthusiastic endorsement of Yeats: an appraisal relevant here
because when he compares Yeats to the "war poets,"
Stead misses the point at the same time that he makes it:

> Yeats stands alone among English speaking poets of
> this century in his ability to assimilate a complex polit-
> ical event in the framework of a poem without distor-
> tion of the event or loss of its human character in
> abstraction. It will be worth keeping "Easter 1916" in
> mind when we come to consider the English poets
> of the First World War. Of them, the patriots are
> absurdly partisan, abstract and rhetorical; while the

disillusioned soldier poets—though more admirable than the patriots because their poems come from honest feeling and particular experience—are too closely involved in the destruction to be capable of transforming these things, as Yeats transforms them, into a universal image. It is . . . a matter of establishing a correct distance between the poet and his subject. The soldier poets stand too close to their subject, the patriots at too great a distance. Yeats' dramatic "mask" is a means of holding himself at a correct distance. He has pored long enough over the slow fires of his own and others' art, to know that death in itself is a commonplace; but that particular death, transformed in poetry to an object of contemplation, becomes a symbol—a way of understanding and expressing the human condition.[17]

There is critical worth in Stead's observation that to become the material of great poetry, particular events must be transformed into "universal" images. His admiration for Yeats, however, obscures his critical vision. It is an oversimplification to divide poets writing during the First World War into "patriots" and "disillusioned soldier poets." And the concept of "correct distance," useful as it is, may be a function of something other than simple artistic excellence; the division I have drawn between poetry of experience and poetry of contemplation is one attempt to deal with this problem. It is in no way necessary (though it may in cases be sufficient) that a great poem be, with Yeats, "cold and passionless as the dawn";[18] one need only refer to the rich tradition of lyric and elegiac poetry in English or any language to demonstrate that Stead's criterion for greatness is too exclusive.

On the contrary, it is frequently their closeness to their subject which makes the poetry of Owen and Sassoon so striking; their moral outrage is an inherent factor in the complex event called "poem." I have already referred to Owen's comment on Sassoon's "Counter-Attack": Sassoon's admitted intention was to shock the reader into some awareness of the morally indefensible realities of trench life and death yet—as should be evi-

143

dent by now—in so doing, he wrote some fine poetry. There is no necessary contradiction between the aesthetic value of a poem and its ability to evoke a moral or emotional response; even though the latter characteristic be part of the poet's intention, the former is determined by the style with which he incorporates this intention with the other elements of his art. As Susan Sontag says,

> If morality is so understood—as one of the achievements of human will, dictating to itself a mode of acting and being in the world—it becomes clear that no generic antagonism exists between the form of consciousness, aimed at action, which is morality, and the nourishment of consciousness, which is aesthetic experience.[19]

And a fixed idea of correct distance as a criterion of poetic greatness seems simple-minded in the case of "Spring Offensive," where the poet's distance from his material is varied deliberately within the poem as he interweaves the elegiac "meditative" approach with a narrative so close to the actual experience that he transposes the sensations of the falling, dying soldiers into a personal descriptive mode like that of Sassoon's "Counter-Attack."

For both Owen and Sassoon were capable of transforming their experience into poetry without "distortion of the event or loss of its human character in abstraction." It is worth keeping Stead's criticism in mind when we consider the manner in which a particular death is transformed into an object of contemplation both poetic and moral in Owen's "Futility":

> Move him into the sun—
> Gently its touch awoke him once,
> At home, whispering of fields unsown.
> Always it woke him, even in France,
> Until this morning and this snow.
> If anything might rouse him now
> The kind old sun will know.

Think how it wakes the seeds,—
Woke, once, the clays of a cold star.
Are limbs, so dear-achieved, are sides,
Full-nerved—still warm—too hard to stir?
Was it for this the clay grew tall?
—O what made fatuous sunbeams toil
To break earth's sleep at all?

Yeats may indeed have "pored long enough over the slow fires of his own and others' art, to know that death in itself is a commonplace"; there are other ways of achieving such knowledge, as the ten million commonplace deaths in the Great War might suggest. The subject of "Futility" is one of those deaths, or any of them, or all of them: it is an elegy. The tone of the poem is unashamedly tender, yet it is not sentimental; there is neither undue humility nor undue elevation, only a sure control which demonstrates the Aristotelian principle of poetic decorum. Perhaps an understanding of decorum is a more useful critical guide than poetic distance; it, at least, makes provision for estimating fitness of style in relation to a poem's subject, rather than in relation to an arbitrary concept of the poet's role.

"Futility" is a title appropriate to the several levels on which the poem simultaneously exists. Not only is it futile to try to wake the man (futility in the most immediate sense); the complex series of events which have shaped him "dear-achieved" and "Full-nerved" have now come to nothing (a more generalized futility); and, as the last three lines suggest, insofar as the man is typical of youth, his destruction represents a victory of chaos over order (futility in the most universal sense). J. H. Johnston comments:

> The final question implies a disillusionment far more profound than that associated with the reactions of the idealists and the humanitarians. The nature of that disillusionment reveals how deeply Owen had considered the problem of evil and its demands on both flesh

145

> and spirit. . . . He implies that the forces of evil can
> neither be reconciled with the principle of creativity
> nor interpreted in terms of Christian providence. For
> Owen the war is not merely a military struggle between
> Germany and England but a manifestation of the
> fundamental forces that shape or destroy human life.[20]

Owen's artistic control over the elements of hope, pathos, and despair is fully evident in this poem. By skirting the edge of sentimentality in "If anything might rouse him now / The kind old sun will know," he conveys grief sharpening to despair: a grief suddenly aware of the limits of sanity, and facing madness in order to subdue it. The outlet which the grief takes—the three questions—is a release justifiable both artistically and psychologically. Though the questions are asked in despair, there is in the last one a hint of the cathartic anger which indicates a return to bitter rationality.

The poem contains no reference to the manner of the soldier's death; indeed, it is only the totality of the poem which confirms the fact of death. Initially, there is an ambiguity permitted which is sufficient to draw the reader into momentarily entertaining the hopes of the speaker. Perhaps, after all, the man is only wounded, or sick, and would welcome the chance of lying in the sunlight. With the last two lines of the first stanza, however, the reader begins to sense the desperateness of what is happening; he has been misled into hope through the quality of the speaker's despair.

This despair, this hope, comes close to madness in the childlike simplicity of the appeal "Think how it wakes the seeds," a reference to an organic world whose values and processes, basic as they are, have become suddenly and terribly irrelevant. The speaker *knows* that the soldier is dead; it is some indication of Owen's sureness of touch that the line carries pathos rather than morbidity in its reversion to man's most primitive ideas about the source of life. The following line, separated by a dash, diverts this movement somewhat; its imagery is

more conventionally mature, more assimilable as metaphor. But the pause is brief. The succeeding two lines
are syntactically fragmented in a way which recalls the
analogous scene from *King Lear*, the grieving king
crouched over the body of his daughter: "Do you see
this? Look on her, look, her lips, / Look there, look
there!"

The last three lines modulate the pain into anger—
humanity asserting itself in the face of intolerable odds.
The poem as a whole is just such a gesture of assertion,
transcending its subject in the act of revealing it, making
experience into art. There are many factors simultaneously at work to this end: the contrast between the emotionally neutral command which opens the first stanza
and the corresponding line in the second stanza, the
pathos of the second appearance of the word "clay"; the
inescapable moral significance of the epithet in "what
made fatuous sunbeams toil . . . ," the tension induced by
juxtaposing half-rhyme with full rhyme—these and other
elements combine and recombine to create a poetic
transformation of battlefield death, death particular and
individual, into death as the absurd and ultimate denial
of the value of life.

A more basic, though nonetheless artistic, use of
images may be seen in "Greater Love," one of Owen's
earlier war poems.[21] Written before he had met Sassoon,
this poem shows Owen's technique of creating a context
within which ambivalent images, because of the moral
force of the context, become themselves the means of
expressing the disparity between the two fronts. Each of
the four stanzas uses the images of love to provide perspective on the fact of death; each uses a different characteristic of the loved one; each illuminates through that
characteristic a different aspect of the soldiers' sacrifice.

The first stanza draws on the imagery of conventional "romantic" love (painted lips, alluring eyes, the
game of courtship) to indicate without subtlety the con-

trasts which underlie the superficial similarity between "love" and the "greater love."

> Red lips are not so red
> As the stained stones kissed by the English dead.
> Kindness of wooed and wooer
> Seems shame to their love pure.
> O Love, your eyes lose lure
> When I behold eyes blinded in my stead!

As a statement, the stanza seems a little unfair—one would rather question Owen's need for such contrasts than deny their validity—but it could be maintained that he felt the necessity to outline the moral order within which the activities of the war could be most meaningfully viewed.

With the second stanza, moreover, the poem begins to justify itself artistically, despite the continuation of polemic. Even the simplistic contrasts cease to be statemental in nature; they are transformed into poetry because the images themselves have a life independent of their moral content:

> Your slender attitude
> Trembles not exquisite like limbs knife-skewed,
> Rolling and rolling there
> Where God seems not to care;
> Till the fierce love they bear
> Cramps them in death's extreme decrepitude.

In this stanza's use of the imagery of sexual love, there is perhaps an undertone of revulsion similar to that in some of Brooke's work, but it is firmly subordinated to artistic purpose: the image's observable characteristics must serve initially to obscure the differences which the statement is emphasizing. "Trembles not exquisite like limbs knife-skewed" is visualization coldly accurate in its reference to the extremities of passion both sexual and mortal, but the statement rejects the possibility of comparing them. The seeming contradiction between image and statement points up the specifically moral quality of the observation, but it is an observation rooted in a highly developed sense of aesthetic fitness—a "Poetics" not easily to be discriminated from an "Ethics."

The use of such a visually ambiguous image in order to deny its ambiguity is indicative of Owen's concentration on the war itself as a source for his poetry. Again, it is necessary to emphasize the aesthetic significance of his statement, "Above all I am not concerned with Poetry. My subject is War. . . ." In "Apologia Pro Poemate Meo," a poem similar to "Greater Love," he manipulates paradox in such a way as to allow exultation, beauty, and peace to be sensations intrinsic to the horrific experience of war, but he refuses to permit the transference of sensations from the sphere of war to any other sphere of human experience. It is no negative criticism to say that his poetry is defined by its subject—war; his world of images is drawn, almost centripetally, to the fact of war; to transfer images in the other direction would be—if I may use a pun seriously—to defy the gravity of the war itself.

"Greater Love" is ample illustration of this fact; the continuing movement of the poem shows how Owen subordinates all his available resources of imagery and poetic convention to one task, that of adequately rendering the experience of war in poetry. The third stanza continues to assimilate to war the images of love poetry. This time it is the qualities of the beloved's voice which are transferred:

> Your voice sings not so soft,—
>   Though even as wind murmuring through
>   raftered loft,—
> Your dear voice is not dear,
> Gentle, and evening clear,
> As theirs whom none now hear,
>   Now earth has stopped their piteous
>   mouths that coughed.

The moral use of paradox is here quite evident; but it is in the imagerically dense last stanza that the poem reaches its apotheosis. I have already commented on the potency of the image developed in the first two lines (see pp. 79–80); the remainder of the stanza shifts, with no artistic strain, to place both sexual love and the soldiers' agony in the context of Western civilization's most revered sacrifice. Here Eros and Thanatos are subsumed, transcended in a final statement of dignity and sublimity:

> Heart, you were never hot
>   Nor large, nor full like hearts made great with shot;
> And though your hand be pale,
> Paler are all which trail
> Your cross through flame and hail:
>   Weep, you may weep, for you may touch them not.

The reference to the cross is no passing one; "Christ is literally in no man's land," Owen wrote home on 2 May 1917; and of his role as an infantry officer he observed, "For 14 hours I was at work—teaching Christ to lift his cross by numbers, and how to adjust his crown . . ."[22] The last line of the poem is an unmistakable echo of a text that Owen, once a lay assistant to the vicar of Dunsden, must have known well: "Jesus saith unto her, Woman why weepest thou? . . . Touch me not."[23] The gulf which the war had created between the women who had to wait and the men who had to die is richly analogous to Magdalene's separation from Christ; this contrast between secular and sacrificial love is an essential element in Owen's increasingly moral vision of the activity of war. When he removes the redemptive Christian framework, as in the poem "Disabled," he successfully demonstrates the chilling pathos of a sacrifice which is nothing more or less than waste.

The figurative structure of "Disabled" is purely secular. Using the same social values as Housman's "To an

Athlete Dying Young," it makes its point by denying the young man the consummation of death in battle. The athlete lives on "Legless, sewn short at elbow":

> Now he will never feel again how slim
> Girls' waists are, or how warm their subtle hands;
> All of them touch him like some queer disease.

The overall tone of the poem is the blend of irony and compassion characteristic of Owen. But in the last two lines there is a sudden and highly dramatic shift to the consciousness of the cripple:

> Now, he will spend a few sick years in Institutes,
> And do what things the rules consider wise,
> And take whatever pity they may dole.
> To-night he noticed how the women's eyes
> Passed from him to the strong men that were whole.
> How cold and late it is! Why don't they come
> And put him into bed? Why don't they come?

The querulous tone of these last two lines is in marked contrast with the sports-field virility which characterized the young man before his body was smashed in war; although he has not lost his life, he has lost the ability to live it.

The most pitiful examples of suffering, the "men whose minds the Dead have ravished,"[24] are those whose bodies have survived at the highest cost of all: neurasthenic madness. "Mental Cases" is a nightmarish journey into insanity of the worst sort—perpetual horror—and it reaches its climax in a visual image that recurs significantly in Owen's attempts to render the extreme plight of violence-glutted senses, the image of light as blood. D. S. R. Welland has brilliantly examined the symbolic intensity and dual nature of blood imagery in Owen's poetry.[25] Little can be added to his account, except to note that there are occasions, as in "The Sentry," when

Owen deliberately avoids such visual imagery for reasons both psychological and aesthetic.

"Mental Cases" is a rudimentary dialogue. The first stanza opens with two questions, "Who are these? Why sit they here in twilight?" and draws much of its power from its close description of the deranged men *from an external vantage point*. Since the *fact* of madness is never visible (except as behavioral symptoms) the speaker's limitation—the limitation of those who have not shared "with them in hell the sorrowful dark of hell"—is also the reader's:

> Who are these? Why sit they here in twilight?
> Wherefore rock they, purgatorial shadows,
> Drooping tongues from jaws that slob their relish,
> Baring teeth that leer like skulls' teeth wicked?
> Stroke on stroke of pain,—but what slow panic,
> Gouged these chasms round their fretted sockets?
> Ever from their hair and through their hands' palms
> Misery swelters. Surely we have perished
> Sleeping, and walk hell; but who these hellish?

Contemporary attitudes toward neurasthenia, particularly contemporary military attitudes, were deplorable. "War is war, and soldiers are to fight" was the attitude of the General Staff and the doctors—both, needless to say, holding positions well behind the front line. Unless a man was visibly wounded, he was thought to be shirking his duty. Owen records one case in "The Dead-Beat" in which the doctor's comment on the soldier concerned was " 'That scum you sent last night soon died. Hooray.' " (The doctor's actual words were "That dirt you sent me down last night's just died. So glad!")[26] A less sprightly but more humane observation is that of the military historian, Leon Woolf:

> There were hundreds of cases referred to, often contemptuously, as shell-shocks, which in later years would be diagnosed not wholly in terms of reaction to artillery fire but as serious neuropathic disorders

resulting from a total experience beyond their capacity to assimilate. Such men, tramping stolidly back from No Man's Land along the ankle-deep duckboards, could not always be recognized as mental casualties unless they were crying uncontrollably, or giggling, or muttering under their breaths, or falling prone at every explosion or sharp command. Some were, in fact, outwardly quite normal. If you asked one his name he knew it, and if you told him rations were down he might very well wander off to meet them, and if you asked him his outfit he might tell you plainly. He would know where he was and did not seem too distressed. But he would be vaguely confused under more pointed questioning, and perhaps a little too anxious to leave; and as for further fighting he would be plainly far beyond that—perhaps even beyond defending himself.[27]

Robert Graves points out that an infantry officer's period of usefulness in the trenches coincided with his third or fourth week of duty ("unless he happened to have any particular bad shock or sequence of shocks"); and if he had not had recuperative periods away from the front, "after a year or fifteen months he was often worse than useless."[28] Sassoon, Owen, and Graves, all infantry officers, benefited from behind-the-lines technical courses. Other ranks, for obvious reasons, were less fortunate; and since neurasthenia was a psychological, rather than a physical, affliction, they suffered accordingly. Some were shot by their own officers for displaying cowardice in the face of the enemy; others went completely mad or committed suicide.[29]

By its very existence "Mental Cases" indicates a sensibility more comprehensive, more attuned to the subtler horrors of war, than the times would seem to have allowed. The second stanza extends the image of hell, already introduced in the first stanza, to answer the question "Who are these?" They are, in a very complex way, the damned:

—These are the men whose minds the Dead have ravished.
Memory fingers in their hair of murders,

Multitudinous murders they once witnessed.
Wading sloughs of flesh these helpless wander,
Treading blood from lungs that had loved laughter.
Always they must see these things and hear them,
Batter of guns and shatter of flying muscles,
Carnage incomparable, and human squander
Rucked too thick for these men's extrication.

The judicial and unemotional sixth line—"Always they must see these things and hear them"—carries a multivalent irony. The transference of guilt to these "witnesses" of sin, enforced by the ambiguous "must" in a context which deliberately recalls Dante (the first stanza ends: "Surely we have perished / Sleeping, and walk hell; but who these hellish?"), raises the question of responsibility—responsibility for evil, and also responsibility for the punishment of evil. Though the poem's images may echo traditional religious conceptions, the world within which it moves is unremittingly secular; the tension between the two factors is an indication of Owen's tortured speculation about a hell which men have designed, and in which men are condemned to suffer. But condemned by whom? The problem of evil underlying Owen's "Futility" is present here too; it reaches a pitch of intensity—and its inescapable resolution—in the last stanza:

Therefore still their eyeballs shrink tormented
Back into their brains, because on their sense
Sunlight seems a blood-smear; night comes blood-black;
Dawn breaks open like a wound that bleeds afresh.
—Thus their heads wear this hilarious, hideous,
Awful falseness of set-smiling corpses.
—Thus their hands are plucking at each other;
Picking at the rope-knouts of their scourging;
Snatching after us who smote them, brother,
Pawing us who dealt them war and madness.

If one recalls the values that sunlight, night, and dawn held for Owen—as, indeed, for most men—the extent of these soldiers' alienation from the world of "normal" sensory impression becomes all too clear. And Owen is unambiguous in assigning the greater guilt, the guilt of complicity in evil, to the reader and to himself. A letter he wrote at this time from a hospital on the Somme reflects his awareness of the only possible solution to such manifestations of evil, a solution the more unworkable for its simplicity and integrity:

> Already I have comprehended a light which never will filter into the dogma of any national church: namely, that one of Christ's essential commands was: Passivity at any price! Suffer dishonour and disgrace, but never resort to arms. Be bullied, be outraged, be killed; but do not kill. It may be a chimerical and an ignominious principle, but there it is. It can only be ignored; and I think pulpit professionals are ignoring it very skilfully and successfully indeed. . . .[30]

Passivity in the face of what Hardy called "demonic force"[31] may be the most difficult of all attitudes. As Bernard Bergonzi points out, in an age when mass extermination is a technique of warmaking, "not all wars might as well be lost as won."[32] Owen was confronting the problem of participating in public aggression at a time when what he called the "trek from progress" had not yet reached the stage to which Bergonzi refers; but his ethical insight is as appropriate—and perhaps as unworkable—today as it was in 1917. When he referred to himself in the same letter as "a conscientious objector with a very seared conscience,"[33] he indicated the profound agony of knowing that in a world of conflicting loyalties right action may be an impossibility.

Owen had no easy solution to offer. But he did have a consistent attitude, and it was significantly anthropocentric rather than idealistic. His prefatory distinction between "Poetry" and his "subject" is an implicit criticism of aesthetic idealism—a criticism inherent in his practice as a poet, as I have attempted to illustrate in the comparison between his "Anthem for Doomed Youth" and Brooke's sonnet IV: "The Dead." A further illustration is afforded by the poem "Asleep," in which what Susan Sontag has called "the *formal* function of subject-matter"[34] is brilliantly demonstrated. In this epistemological poem the subject is brought tentatively into focus from two distinct (and poetically conventional) viewpoints, each of which is formally viable, each of which is rejected. The rejection comes, however, not from any superficially "realistic" impulse, but from the poet's concern with the subject itself and its relevance in the largest, most humanly inclusive sense. Owen's answer to the question "What is to be our attitude toward this fact, in what metaphysical *form* can we render it?" is simply, and terribly, to sharpen the reader's focus on the experience within which the fact exists:

> Under his helmet, up against his pack,
> After the many days of work and waking,
> Sleep took him by the brow and laid him back.
> And in the happy no-time of his sleeping,
> Death took him by the heart. There was a quaking
> Of the aborted life within him leaping . . .
> Then chest and sleepy arms once more fell slack.
> And soon the slow, stray blood came creeping
> From the intrusive lead, like ants on track.
>
>   ❊   ❊   ❊
>
> Whether his deeper sleep lie shaded by the shaking
> Of great wings, and the thoughts that hung the stars,
> High pillowed on calm pillows of God's making
> Above these clouds, these rains, these sleets of lead,
> And these winds' scimitars;
> —Or whether yet his thin and sodden head
> Confuses more and more with the low mould,
> His hair being one with the grey grass
> And finished fields of autumns that are old . . .
> Who knows? Who hopes? Who troubles? Let it pass!
> He sleeps. He sleeps less tremulous, less cold
> Than we who must awake, and waking, say Alas!

It is as an artist, not as a philosopher, that Owen rejects the claims of ideas about reality ("Poetry") in favor of directly experienced reality ("subject" = "War"). The two ideological possibilities considered—the Christian's redemption and the materialist's dissolution—are firmly dismissed as irrelevant: "Who knows? Who hopes? Who troubles? Let it pass!" Owen's idea of relevance exists only in the comparison expressed in the last two lines—a comparison which concentrates attention on the quality of existence left to those who are not dead. Under conditions such as these, metaphysical speculation is out of place; the hierarchy of relevance starts with the life-condition of the living. The poem's ending finds the attractiveness of life compared negatively with that of death—after the latter has been denied any substantive possibilities—in order to demonstrate more effectively than would a direct statement the sheer intolerability of the soldiers' lives. When the dead man is characterized as "less cold" than the living, it is well to pause and reconsider not only the terms which we use to define experience, but the nature and desirability of experience itself.

Owen's imaginative transformation of experience into image—and here I use "experience" in contradistinction to "idea"—is consistent with the aesthetic viewpoint we may infer from the Preface. The seeming paradoxes he wields so skillfully in "Apologia Pro Poemate Meo" use the truths of experience to refurbish such conventional ideas as "love," "God," and "beauty" through the tension of antithesis. The figurative structure in the fifth and sixth stanzas,

> I have made fellowships—
> Untold of happy lovers in old song.
> For love is not the binding of fair lips
> With the soft silk of eyes that look and long,
>
> By Joy, whose ribbon slips,—
> But wound with war's hard wire whose stakes
> are strong;

Bound with the bandage of the arm that drips;
Knit in the webbing of the rifle-thong.

is not only a radical redefinition of the bonds of love; it
is a stringent critique of the praxis of style. The "binding
of fair lips / With the soft silk of eyes" exists solely as an
image; it is language bestowing significance on experience. An image such as "the bandage of the arm that
drips," however, is grounded in physical reality; here
experience, transformed by art into image, bestows significance on language.

The poem ends with an assertion of the primacy of
experience:

Nevertheless, except you share
With them in hell the sorrowful dark of hell,
Whose world is but the trembling of a flare,
And heaven but as the highway for a shell,

You shall not hear their mirth:
You shall not come to think them well content
By any jest of mine. These men are worth
Your tears. You are not worth their merriment.

If one grants the validity of Owen's redefinitions of such
concepts as love, world, and heaven—and most accounts
of life in the front line confirm what he says—the last
stanza, with its bitter *noli me tangere* implications, is
inevitable and just. There is no way for the reader, even
a sympathetic one, to share, and thereby comprehend,
the nightmare world of the soldier. As Rudolph Binding
observed, the war had created a gulf between soldiers
and civilians that no verbal communication could properly bridge. "Apologia" is Owen's most overt statement
of this separation between the two worlds of the war.
Although it renders the experience of war in a comprehensible set of images, it acknowledges at the same time
the limits of artistic re-creation: no reader will ever suffer neurasthenia from reading a poem.

The somber elegy "Strange Meeting" is Owen's most universal summation of the terrible significance of the war. Dramatically, it takes place beyond good and evil, beyond life itself: it is an elegy not so much for a generation as for a race whose achievements in technology have so noticeably outstripped its achievements in morality. The critical bugbear of "perspective" in war poetry is not applicable here; "Strange Meeting" shows Owen working with consummate skill in the meditative mode that characterizes traditional elegies. He is not dealing with physically immediate fact; he makes the point plain in the opening lines: "It seemed that out of battle I escaped / . . . no blood reached there from the upper ground, / And no guns thumped, or down the flues made moan."[35]

The imagery and movement of the poem are derived from warfare; but it is a warfare abstracted into moral terms. As D. S. R. Welland points out:

> Essentially a poem of trench warfare, realistically based on the First World War, it is a fine statement of Owen's moral idealism as well, but it is also a poem that shows his true relationship to the Romantic tradition as something much more positive and creative than his earlier aestheticism suggests.[36]

In his *Critical Study*, Welland has demonstrated the parallels between this poem and Shelley's *Revolt of Islam* (canto V, stanzas 9–13) and Keats's *Endymion* (book IV, lines 893–97); he has also emphasized the significance of Owen's recourse to the frequent Romantic image of the *Doppelgänger*. The enemy, the friend, the self that the speaker has killed rises to meet him, and in seven words reveals the source of the elegiac passion which had given rise to such poems as "Futility," "Anthem for Doomed Youth," "Asleep," and "Mental Cases." "Strange friend," says the poet in wonder, "here is no cause to mourn." The other answers (the italics are mine), "*None . . . save the undone years, / The hopeless-ness.*"

Almost all that follows—it is no slight to say so—is elaboration of this statement. But the elaboration is both densely textured and cumulative; so much so, in fact, that it is almost impossible to quote from the next twenty-four lines without destroying the necessary effect on each line of its immediate context. This is the statement and its development:

> "None," said that other, "save the undone years,
> The hopelessness. Whatever hope is yours,
> Was my life also; I went hunting wild
> After the wildest beauty in the world,
> Which lies not calm in eyes, or braided hair,
> But mocks the steady running of the hour,
> And if it grieves, grieves richlier than here.
> For of my glee might many men have laughed,
> And of my weeping something had been left,
> Which must die now. I mean the truth untold,
> The pity of war, the pity war distilled.
> Now men will go content with what we spoiled,
> Or, discontent, boil bloody, and be spilled.
> They will be swift with swiftness of the tigress.
> None will break ranks, though nations trek from
>   progress.
> Courage was mine, and I had mystery,
> Wisdom was mine, and I had mastery:
> To miss the march of this retreating world
> Into vain citadels that are not walled.
> Then, when much blood had clogged their
>   chariot-wheels,
> I would go up and wash them from sweet wells,
> Even with truths that lie too deep for taint.
> I would have poured my spirit without stint
> But not through wounds; not on the cess of war.
> Foreheads of men have bled where no wounds
>   were."

Owen wrote in his Preface, "All a poet can do today is warn." But in "Strange Meeting" he indicates what else the poet might have given his world: "For of my glee might many men have laughed, / And of my weeping something had been left, / Which must die now." This is by no means all, there is also the "truth untold," and—in one of the most delicately handled images in modern poetry—the poet's own perception of the quality of life itself: the "wildest beauty in the world," which "mocks the steady running of the hour." A quality denied to these ghosts who stand in hell, who can speak—but who are forever lost to the process of life.

With admirable economy "Strange Meeting" achieves a universality truer and far more profound than any epic equation of culture and hero; with no hint of self-glorification the soldier-poet is given the attributes of Christ Himself, who, if one must seek the hero in Owen's poetry, is always immanent. It is not necessary to provide a biblical gloss for the humility and dignity of:

Then, when much blood had clogged their
     chariot-wheels,
I would go up and wash them from sweet wells,
Even with truths that lie too deep for taint.
I would have poured my spirit without stint
But not through wounds; not on the cess of war.
Foreheads of men have bled where no wounds were.

This, surely, is heroism more palatable than the infantile posturings of an Achilles or the canny self-interest of a Ulysses.

It is all the more disappointing, given the implications of this—a well-known—poem, to find a critic such as J. H. Johnston ignoring the most elementary critical standards to comment,

> . . . Owen cannot shift his eyes from particulars that represent merely a part of an enormous complex of opposed human energies comprehensible only on the historic or tragic scale. Although he attempts to give these particulars a universal significance, his vision of pity frequently obscures rather than illuminates the whole; we are likely to lose sight of the historical real-

161

ity as well as the underlying tragic values that inspire the pity.[37]

I have already mentioned Johnston's somewhat pedestrian unwillingness to tolerate any poetic response (other than the conventionally structured epic) to the phenomenon of war. In his largely negative assessment of Owen's achievement, he quotes Yeats's dictum on "passive suffering" and the poet,[38] then makes this revealing case for the epic:

> The function of the epic narrative, of course, was to communicate that luminous effect; the epic poet, dealing with and illuminating great events, interpreted his tale in the light of heroic values. These values affected the form as well as the materials of the narrative; *the epic vision determined the attitude and technique of the poet as well as the motivations and actions of his characters.*[39]

Johnston evidently is both serious and approving in the above passage. But it is precisely the "determinative" quality he so admires which was rejected by the poets who fought in the war; their all-too-real confrontation with the phenomenon taught them that the imposition of predominantly aesthetic ideals of structure and motivation was, at best, a sign of imaginative failure, at worst, a sign of willful dishonesty. The experience of technological warfare demanded of its artists a new approach. The only soldier-poet who did write an epic, David Jones, was keenly aware of the problem and, as I have mentioned (Chapter 2), made explicit his reservations about his use of the form. There may be no artistic dilemma for critics, but one cannot doubt Jones's probity when he says,

> Some of us ask ourselves if Mr. X adjusting his box-respirator can be equated with what the poet envisaged, in
>
> "I saw young Harry with his beaver on."

and,

> For the old authors there appears to have been no such
> dilemma—for them the embrace of battle seemed one with
> the embrace of lovers. For us it is different.[40]

The second paragraph of Owen's Preface makes a
salutary discrimination between war and its traditional
attributes:

> This book is not about heroes. English poetry is not yet
> fit to speak of them.
> Nor is it about deeds, or lands, nor anything about
> glory, honour, might, majesty, dominion, or power,
> except War.[41]

By such refusals to impose traditionally sanctioned values on an experience which manifestly denied their
validity, such poets as Owen, and Sassoon, served their
art as well as they served truth: though Poetry was a
victim of the war, poetry itself survived.

I do not wish to subject "Strange Meeting" to close
textual analysis; John Middleton Murry, Edmund Blunden, and, more recently, D. S. R. Welland have provided
ample appreciations of its technical excellences. Like
most of Owen's poems, it is best left to speak for itself;
all the critic can do is direct the reader's attention and
hope for (rather than insist on) an intelligent appreciation of its moral and artistic integrity.

It is in this spirit that I submit the following two
stanzas of "Insensibility" that seem peculiarly relevant
in view of the Procrustean attempts of critics to perpetu-
ate modes of literary expression which, for better or for
worse, are no longer adequate to render the qualities of
a world with which the modern sensibility is faced. In
them Owen is contrasting the insensibility of those whose
lives have been violated by the war with the insensibility
of those to whom experience exists only in the realm of
idea. The rebuke is, shamefully, still deserved:

163

We wise, who with a thought besmirch
Blood over all our soul,
How should we see our task
But through his blunt and lashless eyes?
Alive, he is not vital overmuch;
Dying, not mortal overmuch;
Nor sad, nor proud,
Nor curious at all.
He cannot tell
Old men's placidity from his.

But cursed are dullards whom no cannon stuns,
That they should be as stones;
Wretched are they, and mean
With paucity that never was simplicity.
By choice they made themselves immune
To pity and whatever moans in man
Before the last sea and the hapless stars;
Whatever mourns when many leave these shores;
Whatever shares
The eternal reciprocity of tears.

6

AFTERMATH

It remains to be said, as usual, that the war ended on the eleventh hour of the eleventh day of the eleventh month of 1918. It had meant nothing, solved nothing, and proved nothing; and in so doing had killed 8,538,315 men and variously wounded 21,219,452. Of 7,750,919 others taken prisoner or missing, well over a million were later presumed dead; thus the total deaths (not counting civilians) approach 10,000,000. The moral and mental defects of the leaders of the human race had been demonstrated with some exactitude. One of them (Woodrow Wilson) later confessed that the war had been fought for business interests; another (David Lloyd George) had told a newspaperman, "If people really knew, the war would be stopped tomorrow, but of course they don't—and can't know. The correspondents don't write and the censorship wouldn't pass the truth. The thing is horrible, and beyond human nature to bear, and I feel I can't go on any longer with the bloody business."

Leon Woolf, war historian

Have you forgotten yet? . . .
Look down, and swear by the slain of the War that

you'll never forget.
Siegfried Sassoon, war poet

Wilfred Owen was killed by enemy machine-gun fire on 4 November 1918, as he tried to get his company across the Sambre Canal in an operation botched, like so many others, in the planning stage. He had gone back to the front because of his men: "to help," he said, "—directly by leading them as well as an officer can; indirectly, by watching their sufferings that I may speak of them as well as a pleader can. I have done the first."[1] In his death as a man, and in his life as a poet, he gave example of the end of man's most pernicious myth: the glory of death in battle.

Owen was a hero, if bravery and leadership be the criteria. But they are not sufficient; there must also be suitable conditions in which the hero can demonstrate his qualities. These conditions existed, if at all, rarely on the western front. In a poem which uses the dramatic device of a telephone conversation with a dead officer, Sassoon demonstrated the pathetic and unepical nature of the war; this is the final stanza:

> Good-bye, old lad! Remember me to God,
>   And tell Him that our Politicians swear
> They won't give in till Prussian Rule's been trod
>   Under the Heel of England . . . Are you there?
> Yes . . . and the War won't end for at least two years;
> But we've got stacks of men . . . I'm blind with tears,
>   Staring into the dark. Cheero!
> I wish they'd killed you in a decent show.[2]

The final line is the key to the quality of the First World War—perhaps to any war in which technology reduces man to a machine operator. A poem by Ian Gordon, explicitly entitled "For Us No More in Epic Encounter," makes the same point with admirable simplicity:

> We who are heroes
> Not by choice but by mere chronology
> Lug the machine gun to the dismal beach
> And await the onset of a heroic age.[3]

The age which found its military expression in the First World War may well be characterized as a heroic age—but only if "heroism" is redefined. For the kind of heroism demonstrated by soldiers such as Wilfred Owen was not the stuff out of which subsequent artists could make a national myth. The culture in which he was born and died did commemorate Owen—but instead of an epic, his artistic memorial is a Christian requiem mass which combines the *Missa pro Defunctis* with his own elegies in a work of great nobility and gravity.[4] That his monument should be a religious affirmation of man's mortality, rather than a secular celebration of deeds in war, is of more than passing significance. The war was a lesson in humility, not an exercise in cultural style: death came unseen and from a distance, and the inoffensive ex-clerk in an ill-fitting uniform who dutifully placed shell after shell in the breechblock of a gun which pointed only at the sky never knew if heroes or cowards or corpses awaited dismemberment in the distance. Men died asleep or playing cards, eating breakfast, writing letters, quarreling, picking lice from their clothes and hair. They died praying or cursing, weeping or dumb with horror, comforting each other or fighting for shelter. It was pitiable, but it was war.

It was a war in which men released machines against each other, and learned to organize their armies as subordinate elements of the new technology. There was no longer a place for Ulysses or for Achilles; the men who directed battles sat far away over maps, and the men who fought battles stood nervously behind thin white tapes and waited for their officer's watch to indicate that the time had come for them to step forward. The technology of warfare now extended far behind the battlefield; nations were mobilized and underwent thereby radical changes. One professional soldier, a brigadier-general from one of England's most honored fighting families, noted the implications of this irreversible change:

> It is perfectly clear to me that in the future, if a rumour of war is ever hushed or noised around, the peoples of the world must all rise up and say "No," with no uncertain voice: not because they are now denied any chance of real victory in the field which soldiers have been able to promise with reasonable certainty in the past, prior to 1914—in that respect, "the game is up"; but because of the havoc which is created in the ramifications of daily life among the young and innocent. A gamble in war might be excusable if only the players stood to suffer; but no man or nation has a right to gamble on the breakup of the moral fibres of society or of civilization itself.[5]

But in the trenches the new kind of heroism was most obviously manifest; the hero of the First World War was each man who took upon himself the act of sacrifice and walked, on command, out into No Man's Land.

It is this omnipresent hero whose agony and nobility are celebrated in Owen's elegies. They can hardly be called "lyrics," if the term is to retain any value. As a matter of fact, one critic has gone so far as to say, "Owen's point of view is essentially *epic* in its scope and manner of treatment."[6] Although Daiches's point (that the "personal note" is subordinated to the demands of fact and value) is sound insofar as it removes Owen's poetry from the category of the lyric, it may not be necessary to extend it to the extreme of redefining the poetry in terms of epic. But if one may do some salutary violence to the traditional concept of the epic hero and his modes of self-manifestation, then Daiches is justified

169

in his use of the word. Perhaps rightly, he considers the "epic" ability to be that which can penetrate to the "inner reality" of the war, and Owen had this

> ability to relate these particular facts to the rest of human experience, to the life of men and women in cities and fields, to see war in relation to all this, to appreciate just what this activity meant—what it meant as a whole and what particular aspects of it meant—in a world which was already old before the war, where happiness and suffering were no new phenomena, where men had lived diversely and foolishly and richly and gone about their occupations and were to do so again when all this was over.[7]

And Siegfried Sassoon, himself a thoroughly competent lyricist, found little in Owen's work to fit the lyric category: "There was," he said, "a slowness and sobriety in [Owen's] method, which was, I think, monodramatic and elegiac rather than leapingly lyrical."[8]

For both Owen and Sassoon the Great War was defined by their experience of the western front, where there was little troop mobility and hence little opportunity for the kind of activity which characterized the older, nontechnological practice of warfare in which a representative hero could perform deeds sufficiently isolated for epic treatment. There are, it hardly need be said, certain criteria to be satisfied if a hero is to embody the traditional values of the epic. These myth-bounded criteria are implicit in Stephen Gilman's observation: "The major theme of all epic poetry is heroism itself, heroism as the perilous mythification of man. . . ."[9] And although it lies outside the bounds of this study there was, in 1914–1918, available both opportunity for epic action and an epic hero to bring it to fruition.

None of the critics who have called for an epic of the Great War, for a hero for our times, have acknowledged the obvious: not only was there a hero in the grand tradition—a man who, in manifesting his own nobility, endured hardships as cruel as those of Ulysses—

but he even wrote his own epic. Yet this man, worshipped as a god by the armies he so brilliantly directed and led, would seek the protection of obscurity—and ultimately death—after the war was over. His epic heroism was socially useful only until the moment of victory; thereafter, he and the ideals he embodied became an embarrassment to the political and industrial leaders of a political and industrial war. There was no processional triumph in the West for the man who mortified his heroism by choosing the role of airman Shaw.

Critical neglect of T. E. Lawrence is not simply due to the fact that he fought Western civilization's first Great War on a non-European front; his epic heroism is so unlikely an act of the twentieth century that most general histories of the war and its literature mention him, if at all, in a footnote. Yet *Pillars of Wisdom,* as Hugh MacLennan noted some years ago, stands as a monument to epic heroism in that moment in Western history between the pre-Freudian and the post-Freudian climates of opinion.[10] Once the popular imagination learned Freud's name, and made minor mythologies out of such concepts as compulsion and neurosis, the simpler mythological equation of man and hero became the first target for criticism. *Heroes' Twilight,* Bernard Bergonzi's somewhat uneven survey of the literature of the Great War, exhibits the popular critical ambivalence towards epic heroism as a desirable ideal but a dubious practice. After lamenting the lack of a traditionally-populated First World War epic, Bergonzi includes one paragraph on T. E. Lawrence in his chapter on autobiography. He concludes, "One is uncomfortably aware of his [Lawrence's] domineering personality, with its scarcely concealed pressures towards self-advertisement."[11] (One is presumably aware of Ulysses' essential modesty, scarcely concealed beneath his magnificent epic boasting.) Once such terms as "domineering personality" and "scarcely concealed pressures" become critics' commonplaces, the

171

"perilous mythification of man" which is the epic hero becomes perilous in a new and uncomfortable sense.

But the epic is there, and its hero, if anyone wishes to make an act of faith in the traditional categories.

Heroism was also the theme of Owen's poetry, but it was heroism observed, not heroism abstracted into social myth. If there was to be mythic value in the manner of life and death in the war, it would come out of the fact, not before the fact: both Owen and Sassoon knew better than to fit experience to arbitrary abstractions—a sense of caution not always evident in the works of poets on the home front. Poems such as "Grey Knitting" and "To the First Gun" illustrate the danger of loosely applying traditional abstract standards to a real situation about which the poet knows nothing.

But one cannot dismiss traditional values out of hand; long-standing myths should be explored for their relevance, and if they fit, they should be used. One twentieth-century English poet who was acutely conscious of the value of myth did, in fact, stage a confrontation between myth and reality in a "war" poem of unmistakable value to lovers of the epic tradition. T. S. Eliot waited until 1931 to voice his reaction to the war; there can be little doubt that he had the necessary artistic distance. Yet the *Triumphal March* from "Coriolan" is no celebration of mythic resonance, even though it includes the technical machinery of modern warmaking, the hero-worshippers waiting for the Hero, and the Hero himself. The roadside crowd is Eliot's proletariat, complete with stools and sausages, waiting eagerly and gossiping in awe as thousands of airplane engines, army wagons, field kitchens, and other paraphernalia are dragged past, followed by the predictable and almost endless stream of civic groups, Boy Scout troops, and councilmen. When the leader finally does appear, he is a satiric patchwork of attributes from the still points of Eliot's various turning worlds: "perilous mythification" indeed.[12]

No poet has been more thoughtful than Eliot in the search for a satisfactory myth; no poet is more aware of the virtues of authority; no poet's work is so littered with the fragments of philosophies tried and found wanting—yet forever absent from any position of approbation is the Caesar figure: the epic leader who, because he is victorious in war, compels society's admiration.

It is, however, such a hero who is inevitably at the center of that most ambitious of narrative poems, the epic—although we may note, in passing, the peculiar violence done to the image of the central figure in *The Dynasts* and *In Parenthesis*. Who, among the soldiers who fought in the Great War, could be chosen as the mythic personification of the heroic mode? The generals, whose criminal bungling sent thousands of unknowing troops to their deaths? Those soldiers whose acts of real heroism in the face of despair earned them recognition in the form of medals, usually awarded posthumously? Or that most pathetic of all modern symbols of depersonalization, the Unknown Soldier?

Modern warfare is too diffuse in nature, too mechanical and sordid in operation, to allow of any representative hero-figure whose more-than-human exploits would serve as a summation, or quintessence, of a national *Geist*. C. S. Lewis, whose appreciation of the epic form needs no elaboration here, went to the war like Sassoon, with his ideals and illusions intact. The first bullet he heard at the front, "so far from me that it 'whined' like a journalist's or a peacetime poet's bullet," occasioned the thought, "This is War. This is what Homer wrote about." But he refers to this insight as "an imaginative moment." The war (with a small *w*) that he experienced was a confusion of

> ... the frights, the cold, the smell of H.E., the horribly smashed men still moving like half-crushed beetles, the sitting or standing corpses, the landscape of sheer earth without a blade of grass, the boots worn day and night till they seemed to grow to your feet. . . .[13]

173

When the presence of fact calls into question the structures of idealism, it may be time to reexamine idealism. The alternative is to retreat from the world of fact, which no responsible poet is willing or able to do.

Owen and Sassoon emphasized the *fact* of war in their poetry. But it would be critical obtuseness to thereby regard them simply as myth-destroyers—even though this is an honorable and necessary function for a poet in any age. One need only read "Strange Meeting" to become aware of the implicit myth to which both poets held—a myth which evolved from their confrontation with the war.

Their myth was a faith in the endurance of man's humanity: a myth rich and valid, but perilous as any other, as history demonstrates. Its vulnerability is the vulnerability of any humanistic ethic, and may be satisfactorily illustrated by a poem which draws on Owen's "Insensibility" for more than simply rhetorical structure. It was written by a poet who survived the first World War as an infantry officer only to see the carnage renewed and refined a generation later. Besides the poem's other virtues, it is a graceful—and at the same time, unhappy—tribute to Owen's selfless love for his fellowman. It is section 5 of Herbert Read's "Ode, written during the Battle of Dunkirk, May 1940":

> Happy are those who can relieve
> suffering with prayer
> Happy those who can rely on God
> to see them through.
>
> They can wait patiently for the end.
>
> But we who have put our faith
> in the goodness of men
> and now see man's image debased
> lower than the wolf or the hog—
>
> Where can we turn for consolation?[14]

Read's question is unanswerable, except in personal terms. It is possible that the myth which sustained Owen and Sassoon will be judged as socially no more relevant than the ancient myths they called into question. Only by its affirmation can it exist, and history has called Christian humanism into question equally with the myth of the epic hero. But Owen and Sassoon were witnesses to its existence; and, since it is a myth whose possibilities are embodied in every man, perhaps it is renewable and justifiable as well as vulnerable. These men were humanists, and poets, and they were involved in the war. It was their faith in humanity which caused them to try to communicate, through their art, their awareness of the new possibilities for evil which technology was providing for an unprepared race. As poets and men of conscience, they realized that it was time to sound a warning about where the old myths, whether cynically mishandled or simply misunderstood, were leading man in an age of scientific industrialism.

Their poetry, in form as in content, was an adequate response to the fact of modern warfare—warfare which, in its technical sophistication, was more of a threat to human values than war had ever been before. As a warning it may have failed; as art it succeeds in once more demonstrating the inseparability of experience and ideals.

Seven days after Owen was killed, the war collapsed. The men who survived straggled back out of their experience into a world which would call them heroes and try to forget why it had forced heroism on them. There was one living poet who was able to render the moment's significance in a way Owen would have understood and approved. Thomas Hardy wrote what may rest as the last word:

> Calm fell. From Heaven distilled a clemency;
> There was peace on earth, and silence in the sky;
> Some could, some could not, shake off misery:
> The Sinister Spirit sneered: "It had to be!"
> And again the Spirit of Pity whispered, "Why?"[15]

Notes

NOTES TO CHAPTER 1

1. Wilfred Owen, Preface to *The Collected Poems of Wilfred Owen,* ed., with Intro. and Notes by C. Day Lewis, and with a Memoir by Edmund Blunden (New York: New Directions, 1964), p. 31. All quotations of Owen's poems are from this edition, hereafter cited as *CP.*
2. From the prayer by Charles Wesley: *"Gentle Jesus, meek and mild, / Look upon this little child, / Pity my simplicity, / Suffer me to come to Thee. Amen."* Hymm 444 in *The Methodist Hymnal* (1935).
3. Quoted by Hugh D. Ford, *A Poet's War: British Poets and the Spanish Civil War* (Philadelphia: University of Pennsylvania Press, 1965), p. 214.
4. Preface to *CP,* p. 31.
5. Ernest Hemingway, ed., *Men at War: the Best War Stories of All Time* (New York: Crown Publishers, 1942), pp. xiv–xv.
6. See, for example, John H. Johnston, *English Poetry of the First World War: A Study in the Evolution of Lyric and Narrative Form* (Princeton: Princeton University Press, 1964); Bernard Bergonzi, *Heroes' Twilight: A Study of the Literature of the Great War* (London: Constable, 1965); and Christian Karlson Stead, *The New Poetic* (London: Hutchinson University Library, 1964).
7. Robert Langbaum, *The Poetry of Experience: The Dramatic Monologue in Modern Literary Tradition* (New York: W. W. Norton, 1957), pp. 35–36.
8. Cited above, n. 6.
9. Langbaum, *Poetry of Experience,* p. 134.
10. Preface to *CP,* p. 31.
11. "In Tenebris, II," in Thomas Hardy, *Collected Poems* (London: Macmillan & Co., Ltd., 1960). All quotations of Hardy's poetry are from this edition.
12. William Wordsworth, *The Prelude* (1850 ed.), XIV. 103–109.
13. Ibid., VI. 737–38.
14. Langbaum, *Poetry of Experience,* p. 38.
15. *Prelude,* XII. 126.
16. Langbaum, *Poetry of Experience,* p. 46.
17. Hanson W. Baldwin, *World War I: An Outline History* (New York: Harper & Row, 1962), p. 54.
18. Quoted in *CP,* p. 176.

19. John Dewey, *Art as Experience* (New York: G. P. Putnam's Sons, Capricorn Books, 1958), p. 54.
20. "Insensibility."
21. "Dulce et Decorum Est."
22. "Insensibility."
23. "Fight to a Finish," in Siegfried Lorraine Sassoon, *Collected Poems, 1908–1956* (London: Faber & Faber Ltd., 1961), p. 77. All quotations of Sassoon's poems are from this edition, hereafter cited as *Collected Poems*.
24. Quoted in *CP*, pp. 174–75.
25. An expression not traceable to any definite source, but current throughout the war years. See Frank Swinnerton, *The Georgian Literary Scene, 1910–1935* (London: J. M. Dent & Sons, Ltd., 1938), p. 258.
26. Douglas Jerrold, *The Lie about the War: a Note on some Contemporary War Books* (London: Faber & Faber Ltd., 1930), p. 9. The sixteen novels are *A Farewell to Arms* (Hemingway); *All Quiet on the Western Front* (Remarque); *Death of a Hero* (Aldington); *Good-Bye to All That* (Graves); *Le Feu* (Barbusse); *Red Cavalry* (Bebel); *Rough Justice* (Montague); *Squad* (Wharton); *The Case of Sergeant Grischa* (Zweig); *The Enormous Room* (Cummings); *The Path of Glory* (Blake); *The Secret Battle* (Herbert); *The Spanish Farm Trilogy* (Mottram); *The Storm of Steel* (Junger); *These Men Thy Friends* (Thompson); and *War Birds* (Anon).
27. Wyndham Lewis, *Blasting & Bombardiering* (London: Eyre & Spottiswoode, 1937), p. 306.
28. Jerrold, *Lie about the War*, p. 8.
29. Jerrold, *Lie about the War*, pp. 22–24.
30. I am indebted for this figure to Jacques Barzun's article "Truth and Poetry in Thomas Hardy," *The Southern Review*, 6, no. 1 (1940): 183–84.

NOTES TO CHAPTER 2

1. David Jones, *In Parenthesis* (New York: Chilmark Press, 1962), pp. 176–77.
2. Ibid., pp. 175–76.
3. Ibid., p. 28.
4. Letter to Osbert Sitwell, 4 July 1918. Quoted in *CP*, p. 23.
5. "The Dream."
6. Preface to Jones, *In Parenthesis*, pp. xiv–xv.
7. Ibid., p. xiv.
8. Ibid., p. ix.
9. Geoffrey Hill, "I in Another Place: Homage to Keith Douglas," *Stand*, 6, no. 4 (1964), 6–13.
10. Leon Woolf, *In Flanders Fields: The 1917 Campaign* (New York: Viking Press, 1958), pp. 252–53.
11. Ibid., pp. 259, 261–62.
12. F. P. Crozier, *A Brass Hat in No Man's Land* (New York: Jonathan Cape & Harrison Smith, 1930), p. 38 (my italics).

13. Quoted in Barbara W. Tuchman, *The Guns of August* (New York: Dell Publishing Co., 1965), p. 68.
14. Raymond Aron, *The Century of Total War* (Boston: Beacon Press, 1954), p. 18.
15. Ibid.
16. Tuchman, *Guns of August*, p. 42.
17. Woolf, *In Flanders Fields*, p. 254.
18. B. H. Liddell Hart, *The Real War: 1914–1918* (Boston: Little, Brown & Co., 1930), pp. 127–28.
19. British at the Somme, 1 July 1916. Baldwin, *World War I*, p. 79.
20. Reginald Pound, *The Lost Generation of 1914* (New York: Coward-McCann, 1965), pp. 248–49.
21. Frederick S. Oliver, *Ordeal by Battle* (New York: Macmillan Co., 1916), pp. 367–68n.
22. Quoted in Pound, *Lost Generation*, p. 179.
23. Lewis, *Blasting & Bombardiering*, p. 205.
24. Ibid., p. 140.
25. Ibid., pp. 28–29.
26. Ibid., p. 81.
27. William H. Owen, *Journey from Obscurity: Wilfred Owen, 1893–1918. Memoirs of the Owen Family* (London: Oxford University Press, 1963–65), 3:162.
28. "The Call." Jessie Pope, *Jessie Pope's War Poems* (London: Grant Richards Ltd., 1915), p. 38.
29. "A Cossack Charge," ibid., p. 24.
30. Quoted in *CP*, p. 27.
31. "The Next War."
32. Robert Underwood Johnson, "To the First Gun," *Toronto Globe*, 23 July 1917.
33. "On being asked for a War Poem," *The Variorum Edition of the Poems of W. B. Yeats*, ed. Peter Allt and Russell K. Alspach (New York: Macmillan Co., 1957), p. 359.
34. Quoted in Pound, *Lost Generation*, p. 113.
35. From the Author's Note, dated West Flanders, 13 June 1916, Rudolph Binding, *A Fatalist at War*, trans. Ian F. D. Morrow (Boston: Houghton Mifflin Co., 1929).
36. Ernst Lissauer, "Hymn of Hate," trans. Barbara Henderson, in *Armageddon: The World War in Literature*, ed. Eugene Löhrke (New York: Jonathan Cape & Harrison Smith, 1930), pp. 101–2.
37. Quoted in J. P. Bang, *Hurrah and Hallelujah: The Teaching of Germany's Poets, Prophets, Professors and Preachers*, trans. from the Danish by Jessie Bröchner (New York: George H. Doran Co., 1917), pp. 118–19. The Geibel quotation Rump refers to is: "Und es mag am deutschen Wesen / einmal noch die Welt genesen."
38. Johnston, *English Poetry of the First World War*, p. 16.
39. Letter to his aunt, 16 September 1916, *War Letters of Fallen Englishmen*, ed. Laurence Housman (New York: E. P. Dutton & Co., 1930), pp. 317–18.
40. Binding, *Fatalist at War*, p. 35.

41. Ibid., p. 19.
42. Bang, *Hurrah and Hallelujah,* p. 76.
43. Binding, *Fatalist at War,* p. 43.
44. Ibid., p. 61.
45. Owen's "Apologia Pro Poemate Meo," stanzas 8 and 9.

NOTES TO CHAPTER 3
1. Christopher Hassall, *Rupert Brooke: A Biography* (New York: Harcourt, Brace & World, 1964), p. 531.
2. Robert H. Ross, *The Georgian Revolt, 1910–1922: Rise and Fall of a Poetic Ideal* (Carbondale: Southern Illinois University Press, 1965), p. 117.
3. *Prefatory note to 1st ed.* (London: The Poetry Bookshop, 1918).
4. Quoted in Ross, *Georgian Revolt,* p. 119.
5. Ibid., p. 118.
6. *Georgian Poetry, 1911–1912,* p. 16.
7. See Hassall, appendix, *Rupert Brooke,* pp. 535–39.
8. Brooke to Sidgwick, 20 September 1911, quoted in Hassall, *Rupert Brooke,* p. 287.
9. Rupert Brooke, *The Collected Poems of Rupert Brooke, with a Memoir* (London: Sidgwick & Jackson, Ltd., 1920). All quotations of Brooke's poetry are from this edition.
10. Sassoon, "To My Brother."
11. Hassall, *Rupert Brooke,* p. 354.
12. Tennyson, *Maud,* III, 29–33.
13. Quoted in Hassall, *Rupert Brooke,* p. 455.
14. Quoted in ibid., p. 459.
15. Quoted in ibid., p. 243. Brooke's criticism of the role of the artist under socialism is worth keeping in mind when he is taken to be an example of the artist under imperialism. The speech was subsequently reprinted. See Rupert Brooke, *Democracy and the Arts* (London: Rupert Hart-Davis, 1946).
16. Ross, *Georgian Revolt,* p. 118.
17. For this information, and for the linking of the two poems, I am indebted to Christopher Hassall. See *Rupert Brooke,* p. 468.
18. Hassall, *Rupert Brooke,* p. 472.
19. Quoted in ibid., p. 472.
20. D. J. Enright, "The Literature of the First World War," *Pelican Guide to English Literature,* vol. 7, *The Modern Age,* ed. Boris Ford (Baltimore: Penguin Books, 1961), p. 155.
21. Quoted in Enright, "Literature of the First World War," p. 157.
22. Thomas Hardy, "The Pity of It," dated April 1915.
23. "Absolution," dated 1915.
24. Brooke, sonnet IV: "The Dead."
25. Sassoon, "Absolution."
26. Sassoon, "France."
27. Bergonzi, however, acknowledges Edmund Blunden's appraisal of it. See *Heroes' Twilight,* p. 45.

28. Quoted, approvingly, by Johnson, *English Poetry of the First World War,* p. 29.
29. Quoted in Hassall, *Rupert Brooke,* p. 232.
30. Quoted in ibid., p. 519–20.
31. Charles Hamilton Sorley, *Marlborough and Other Poems* (Cambridge: Cambridge University Press, 1916), pp. 25–26. All quotations of Sorley's poems are from this collection. "Return" is dated 18 September 1913.
32. See, for example, "Autumn Dawn," dated 16 September 1913.
33. Sonnet I: "Peace," from the "1914" sequence, ll. 2–6.
34. These are stanzas 6, 11, 12, and 13.
35. Letter to the Master of Marlborough dated 20 February 1914, in Charles Hamilton Sorley, *The Letters of Charles Sorley, with a Chapter of Biography* (Cambridge: Cambridge University Press, 1919), p. 97.
36. Letter to A. J. Hopkinson, October [?] 1914, Sorley, *Letters,* p. 232.
37. Letter to A. E. Hutchinson, 14 November 1914, ibid., pp. 240–41.
38. This poem is undated.
39. *Marlborough and Other Poems,* p. 133.
40. Ibid., p. 132.
41. Jones, *In Parenthesis,* p. ix.
42. Stanza 1, ll. 1–4.
43. XXII, stanza 3, ll. 9–12.
44. Ibid., stanza 3, ll. 1–8.
45. This poem is undated.
46. Letter to his mother from Aldershot dated 28 April 1915, in Sorley, *Letters,* p. 263.
47. Sonnet IV is analyzed below. Cf. pp. 125–31.
48. Enright, "Literature of the First World War," p. 156.
49. The poem is dated 12 June 1915.
50. See "When You See Millions of the Mouthless Dead," quoted below.
51. Letter to Arthur Watts, dated 26 August 1915, in *Marlborough and Other Poems,* p. 139 (my italics).
52. See Chapter 4.
53. *The Modern Age,* p. 157.
54. Letter to the Master of Marlborough dated 5 October 1915, in *Marlborough and Other Poems,* p. 141.

NOTES TO CHAPTER 4

1. Siegfried Sassoon, *Memoirs of a Fox-Hunting Man* (London: Faber & Faber Ltd., 1930), p. 306.
2. Ibid., p. 305.
3. Sassoon, *Memoirs of a Fox-Hunting Man,* p. 307.
4. Ibid., p. 319.
5. Quoted in *CP,* p. 171. The letter is dated November 1917.
6. "Counter-Attack," ll. 7–12.
7. "Absolution," l. 4.

8. Quoted in Sassoon, *Memoirs of an Infantry Officer* (London: Faber & Faber Ltd., 1930), p. 308.
9. Robert Graves, *Goodbye to All That,* rev. ed. (London: Cassell & Co., Ltd., 1957), pp. 154–55 (my italics).
10. See, for example, Siegfried Sassoon, *Siegfried's Journey, 1916–1920,* (London: Faber and Faber Ltd., 1945), pp. 37, 55, and 69.
11. With reference to the "epic" vs. the "lyric" response to the war, see *Siegfried's Journey,* pp. 70–71, passim, where Sassoon speaks of describing the war in a "comprehensive" way to "broaden and vitalize" his account so that he could write "on a bigger scale." He obviously has the epic mode in mind, since he refers to Hardy's *Dynasts* as a model. But, he continues, "Short poems are my natural means of expression, and for sustained description I have come to prefer prose."
12. Sassoon, *Siegfried's Journey,* pp. 17–18.
13. Graves, *Goodbye to All That,* p. 210.
14. Sassoon, *Siegfried's Journey,* p. 78.
15. Ibid., p. 79. The lines from *The Dynasts* occur in Sir Francis Burdett's speech in part III, act 5, scene 5.
16. Ibid., p. 193.
17. "I had lost my temper with the man who had shot Kendle; quite unexpectedly, I found myself looking down into a well-conducted trench with a great many Germans in it." *Memoirs of an Infantry Officer,* p. 91.
18. Ibid., p. 326.
19. David Perkins in *English Romantic Writers* (New York: Harcourt, Brace & World, 1967), p. 390.
20. Bergonzi, *Heroes' Twilight,* p. 97.
21. Graves, *Goodbye to All That,* p. 206.
22. Reginald Farrar, *The Void of War: Letters from Three Fronts* (New York: Houghton Mifflin Co., 1918), p. 28.
23. "Smile, Smile, Smile."
24. Lt. the Hon. Gerald William Grenfell (killed in action 30 July 1915) to his mother, 20 July 1915, in Housman, ed., *War Letters,* p. 117.
25. Sassoon, *Siegfried's Journey,* pp. 14–15.
26. Ibid., pp. 14–15.
27. Sassoon acknowledged the influence of Hardy's *Satires of Circumstance;* see *Siegfried's Journey,* p. 29.
28. Blunden used the expression as the title of his war memoirs. See Edmund Blunden, *Undertones of War* (New York: Doubleday, Doran & Co., 1929).
29. *A Treasury of War Poetry: British and American Poems of the World War 1914–1919,* 2nd ser. (New York: Houghton Mifflin Co., 1919), p. 313. Katherine Hale (Mrs. John W. Garvin) was one of the *Toronto Globe*'s roster of war poets.
30. D. H. Lawrence, letter to Catherine Carswell dated 11 June 1916, quoted in Vivian de Sola Pinto, *Crisis in English Poetry, 1880–1940* (London: Hutchinson University Library, 1958), p. 157.

31. "The Effect," ll. 13–15.
32. "Wirers," ll. 11–12.
33. Quoted in D. S. R. Welland, *Wilfred Owen: A Critical Study* (London: Chatto & Windus, 1960), p. 13. Hemingway, who in his best period did much to restore concreteness to literary language, demonstrated a similar aversion to abstraction. In *A Farewell to Arms* Henry observes, "I was always embarrassed by the words sacred, glorious, and sacrifice and the expression in vain. We had heard them, sometimes standing in the rain almost out of earshot, so that only the shouted words came through, and had read them, on proclamations that were slapped up by billposters over other proclamations, now for a long time, and I had seen nothing sacred, and the things that were glorious had no glory and the sacrifices were like the stockyards at Chicago if nothing was done with the meat except to bury it. There were many words you could not stand to hear and finally only the names of places had dignity. Certain numbers were the same way and certain dates and these with the names of the places were all you could say and have them mean anything. Abstract words such as glory, honor, courage, or hallow were obscene beside the concrete names of villages, the number of roads, the names of rivers, the numbers of regiments and the dates." Ernest Hemingway, *A Farewell to Arms* (New York: Charles Scribner's Sons, 1957), p. 191.
34. For comments on neurasthenia, see Chapter 5.
35. "Survivors." The ellipsis is Sassoon's.
36. Sassoon, *Memoirs of an Infantry Officer*, p. 168.
37. Basil Mathews, ed., *Christ: And the World at War; Sermons Preached in War-Time* (London: James Clarke & Co., 1917), p. 77.
38. Ibid., p. 135.
39. Graves, *Goodbye to All That*, pp. 168–69, passim.
40. "Joy-Bells," stanza 3.
41. "The Redeemer," stanzas 2–4.
42. See Chapter 2, p. 51.
43. "Mental Cases," ll. 20–21, and see Chapter 5.
44. Poem by Ewart Alan Mackintosh of the Seaforth Highlanders (killed in action 21 November 1917), quoted in Pound, *Lost Generation*, pp. 201–2.
45. Sassoon, *Siegfried's Journey*, p. 140.

NOTES TO CHAPTER 5
1. "1914." One of Owen's drafts titles it, perhaps more effectively, "The Seed" (*CP*, p. 129n.).
2. Brooke's rhyme scheme is *abab cdcd eefgfg* and Owen's is *abab cdcd effegg*, though each uses an octave resolved in a sestet rather than quatrains.
3. Enright, "Literature of the First World War," p. 156.
4. "Apologia Pro Poemate Meo."
5. Hill, "I in Another Place," *Stand*, 6, no. 4 (1964), 7.

6. The letter is quoted by Blunden in his Memoir, reprinted in *CP*, pp. 158–60.
7. *CP*, p. 55n. For Jessie Pope, see Chapter 2, above.
8. Johnston, *English Poetry of the First World War*, p. 174.
9. *The Poems of Wilfred Owen*, ed. Edmund Blunden (New York: Viking Press, 1961), pp. 134–35.
10. "The Sentry," ll. 3–5, 22–26.
11. *CP*, p. 53n.
12. Alan Seeger, "I Have a Rendezvous With Death," ll. 11–14, in *Poems* (New York: Charles Scribner's Sons, 1917), p. 144.
13. Welland, *Wilfred Owen*, p. 83.
14. Quoted in *CP*, p. 53n.
15. "The Calls," stanza 7.
16. Quoted by Blunden in Memoir, *CP*, p. 173.
17. C. K. Stead, *The New Poetic* (London: Hutchinson & Co., 1964), pp. 39–40.
18. W. B. Yeats, "The Fisherman," ll. 39–40.
19. Susan Sontag, *Against Interpretation* (New York: Farrar, Straus & Giroux, 1966), pp. 24–25.
20. Johnston, *English Poetry of the First World War*, p. 188.
21. Welland's tentative dating is May 1916.
22. C. Day Lewis's Introduction, *CP*, p. 23.
23. John, 20 : 15, 17.
24. "Mental Cases," l. 10.
25. Welland, *Wilfred Owen*, chap. 4.
26. *CP*, p. 73n.
27. Woolf, *In Flanders Fields*, p. 228.
28. Graves, *Goodbye to All That*, p. 143.
29. Ibid., p. 155; Owen's "The Chances" and Sassoon's "Survivors"; Owen's "S.I.W." and Sassoon's "Suicide in the Trenches."
30. Quoted by Blunden in Memoir, *CP*, p. 167.
31. Hardy, "We Are Getting to the End," l. 13.
32. Bergonzi, *Heroes' Twilight*, p. 19.
33. Quoted by Blunden in Memoir, *CP*, p. 167.
34. Sontag, *Against Interpretation*, p. 20.
35. "Strange Meeting," ll. 1, 12–13.
36. Welland, *Wilfred Owen*, p. 99.
37. Johnston, *English Poetry of the First World War*, p. 205.
38. "A 'pleader' for the sufferings of others necessarily makes those sufferings his own; 'withdrawn into the quicksilver at the back of the mirror,' he loses his objectivity and his sense of proportion: 'no great event becomes luminous in his mind.'" Johnston, ibid., quoting Yeats, p. 206.
39. Ibid., pp. 206–7 (my italics).
40. Jones, *In Parenthesis*, pp. xiv, xv respectively.
41. Preface to *CP*, p. 31.

NOTES TO CHAPTER 6

1. Letter to his mother, 4 or 5 October 1918, quoted by Blunden in Memoir, *CP*, p. 178.
2. "To Any Dead Officer."
3. Quoted by William van O'Connor, *Sense and Sensibility in Modern Poetry* (Chicago: University of Chicago Press, 1948), p. 9.
4. Benjamin Britten, *War Requiem*, Opus 66.
5. Crozier, *Brass Hat in No Man's Land*, p. 155.
6. David Daiches, *New Literary Values: Studies in Modern Literature* (London: Oliver & Boyd, 1936), p. 62.
7. Ibid., p. 60.
8. Sassoon, *Siegfried's Journey*, p. 62.
9. Quoted by Roy H. Pearce, *The Continuity of American Poetry* (Princeton: Princeton University Press, 1961), p. 61.
10. *The Montreal Star*, 18 May 1962, suppl., p. 4.
11. Bergonzi, *Heroes' Twilight*, p. 169.
12. The reader who wishes to compare the original is referred to T. S. Eliot, *Collected Poems, 1909–1962* (New York: Harcourt, Brace & World, 1963), pp. 125–26.
13. C. S. Lewis, *Surprised by Joy: the Shape of My Early Life* (New York: Harcourt Brace & Co., 1955), p. 196.
14. Herbert Read, *A World Within a War* (London: Faber & Faber Ltd., 1944), p. 17.
15. Hardy, "And There Was a Great Calm," stanza 9.

Index

Arthur E. Lane, assistant professor of English, California State University, Northridge, did his undergraduate work at the Royal Military College of Canada (1959). He received his M.A. from the University of Montreal (1962) and his Ph.D. from the University of California, San Diego (1967). Professor Lane is a frequently published poet. An Adequate Response is his first critical work. The manuscript was edited by Aletta Biersack. This book was designed by Joanne Kinney. The typeface for the text is Linotype Caledonia designed by W. A. Dwiggins about 1938; and the display face is Perpetua designed by Eric Gill about 1925. The text is printed on Napco Book offset paper and the book is bound in Columbia Mills' Bayside Linen over binders' boards. Manufactured in the United States of America.

NONVERBAL COMMUNICATION

NONVERBAL COMMUNICATION:

THE STATE
OF THE ART

ROBERT G. HARPER
ARTHUR N. WIENS
JOSEPH D. MATARAZZO
Department of Medical Psychology
University of Oregon Health Sciences Center
Portland, Oregon

A WILEY-INTERSCIENCE PUBLICATION

JOHN WILEY & SONS, New York · Chichester · Brisbane · Toronto

Library of Congress Cataloging in Publication Data:

Harper, Robert Gale, 1944–
    Nonverbal communication.

    (Wiley series on personality processes)
    "A Wiley–Interscience publication."
    Bibliography: p.
    Includes indexes.
    1. Nonverbal communication. I. Wiens, Arthur N.,
joint author. II. Matarazzo, Joseph D., joint author.
III. Title. [DNLM: 1. Nonverbal communication.
2. Spatial behavior. 3. Eye movements. HM258.H295n]
P99.5.H37   001.56   77–19185
ISBN 0–471–02672–7

Printed in the United States of America

10 9 8 7 6 5 4

Series Preface

This series of books is addressed to behavioral scientists interested in the nature of human personality. Its scope should prove pertinent to personality theorists and researchers as well as to clinicians concerned with applying an understanding of personality processes to the amelioration of emotional difficulties in living. To this end, the series provides a scholarly integration of theoretical formulations, empirical data, and practical recommendations.

Six major aspects of studying and learning about human personality can be designated: personality theory, personality structure and dynamics, personality development, personality assessment, personality change, and personality adjustment. In exploring these aspects of personality, the books in the series discuss a number of distinct but related subject areas: the nature and implications of various theories of personality; personality characteristics that account for consistencies and variations in human behavior; the emergence of personality processes in children and adolescents; the use of interviewing and testing procedures to evaluate individual differences in personality; efforts to modify personality styles through psychotherapy, counseling, behavior therapy, and other methods of influence; and patterns of abnormal personality functioning that impair individual competence.

IRVING B. WEINER

Case Western Reserve University
Cleveland, Ohio

Preface

This review attempts to delineate the current "state of the art" in the major areas of nonverbal communication research, taking into account the most important recent studies and the methodological principles involved. Though some of the individual findings may have immediate practical significance, the main value of this review is to individuals interested in the research aspects of nonverbal behavior. Specifically, the material has been organized and presented to give the reader a reasonably specific idea of *how* findings were obtained, in addition to what the findings were. This is important because the field is still in its infancy, and despite the rapid proliferation of studies, the full complexity of this area is difficult to appreciate.

A number of prominent researchers in nonverbal communication have written introductory texts on the subject (e.g., Argyle, 1975; Harrison, 1974; Kleinke, 1975; Knapp, 1972; and Weitz, 1974) that have been very helpful in the preparation and organization of this manuscript. These works generally provide a description of the different areas of nonverbal research and then present selected studies illustrating how nonverbal behaviors are important in social interaction. In contrast, the goal of this book is to review as many studies as possible and organize them into sections on the various channels of communication, starting with a discussion of methodological considerations. As such, we expect this book to be harder reading than many sources but also, we hope, rewarding work for those wanting a single source providing access to a large number of the references in the field. In attempting such a goal we are aware that important omissions can occur. Some readers may also feel that we may have glossed over flaws or weaknesses in some of the studies described or failed properly to acknowledge many of the significant contributions of individual researchers. We hope that the number will be few, but the important point is that there is ultimately no substitute for reading the relevant original sources and imposing one's distinct critical judgments on the work. With this forewarning, we can turn to a brief description of the basic organization of the book.

In the introductory chapter we identify and discuss some of the many different definitions and classification systems that researchers have proposed. The most important aspect of all of the systems is the notion that nonverbal behaviors convey information that, although in some cases redundant to spoken language, often provides additional information to that from verbal channels. Information concerning the attitudes and affective state of a speaker and his interpersonal relationship to his conversational partner is the most important example. In addition, many nonverbal behaviors serve to regulate the flow of conversation and, as such, exercise some control over the rate of transmission of verbal material. Also discussed in the introduction are models of communication including Dittmann's important theory on the communication of emotion, in which he applies the mathematical model of communication and with it such important concepts as communication channels, communicative specificity, information, and "noise."

The two basic types of research strategies—the *structural* approach, which is observational-descriptive, nonexperimental and nonstatistical in nature, and the experimental *external variable* approach—are described. Next, the important but often disregarded distinction between nonverbal behaviors and nonverbal communication is considered. In a strictly technical sense nonverbal behavior cannot be considered communicative unless certain important conditions are met. Indeed, much of the research pertains to the indicative or informative aspects of nonverbal behavior, which provide cues (if not communicative codes) as to the nature of an interaction or an individual's emotional state. Finally, the five basic areas of nonverbal research to be covered are identified: (a) paralanguage and temporal characteristics of speech, (b) facial expressions, (c) kinesic behavior of body movements, (d) visual behavior, and (e) proxemics, or the use of space and distance.

Paralinguistic phenomena include nonlanguage sounds (moans, yells, etc.) and nonwords such as "uh-huh" and such variables as pitch, tempo, intensity, and range. To study these phenomena researchers have employed various methodological techniques to separate out the verbal content, most recently using electronic filters to "muffle" speech while maintaining its sequence or a randomized splicing technique that "scrambles" the words but still permits analysis of paralinguistic variables that are unrelated to the sequencing of speech. The bulk of research on paralanguage has consisted of attempts to identify personality correlates or to relate them to emotional or attitudinal states. Efforts to identify personality correlates have included ratings of these vocal characteristics in terms of inferred personality dimensions and comparisons between paralinguistic behaviors of different personality types. In general, studies relating emotion and attitudes to paralinguistic variables have yielded stronger or more consistent results, which should not be surprising given the more "direct" physical-anatomical relationship between speech and emotion.

Speech disturbances have been another focus of study by researchers. In particular, disturbances of speech *not* including "ah" sounds (i.e., sentence corrections, repetitions, stutters, tongue slips, and the like) appear to be a reasonably sensitive indicator of anxiety. Speech can also be characterized by its temporal aspects, which are strongly influenced by the speech behavior of the other conversational partner and the social context. Verbal productivity (e.g., rate of speech) has, in addition, been related to anxiety, but in a relatively complex and not fully understood fashion that involves consideration of both momentary situational and dispositional or trait anxiety. In addition, it has been studied in relation to mood states (e.g., depression) and self-disclosure in psychotherapy. A relatively neglected area has been the study of silence, particularly those "interactive silences" that are longer than the typical hesitation and pauses that are related to anxiety and/or speech encoding processes. Finally, we have ended this review with consideration of a new focus to research; the role that paralinguistic behaviors play in the regulation of conversation, especially turn-taking.

As our review suggests, the face and *facial expression* may be the most important area of the body in nonverbal communication. In particular, several theories of emotional and facial expression are based on the notion that the two are intimately related on a neurophysiological level and that, perhaps, our proprioception of the pattern of facial muscle contractions may be the first component of the experience of emotion. Historically, facial expression research has been conducted along two parallel lines: some psychologists have attempted to identify various dimensions in which facial expressions can be classified; others have focused on more discrete categories of emotion (e.g., happiness, anger, sadness). Investigators employing the latter approach have produced the more consistent findings, whereas dimensional researchers have been unable to agree as to the basic dimensions or a theoretical model and, most important, have been unable to reduce the facial expression phenomena to a few common dimensions.

Despite some early negative findings, it is now well established that observers can accurately identify facial expressions. Indeed, the most recent research has focused on differences in this ability and the role that separate facial areas play in contributing to accurate emotion judgments. Important advances in accurately scoring facial components and in obtaining "emotion predictions" have been made. Other recent research has centered on the relative contribution made by facial expression when the situational context is considered.

Perhaps of greatest theoretical importance are those studies that suggest that facial expressions of emotion categories are universal and not culture-specific phenomena. Ekman has led the research in this field, and his theory of facial expression of emotion is a major contribution to the literature. Particularly important is his notion of display rules—socially learned, culture-specific rules that govern when and what emotions can be expressed facially.

In our concluding section on facial expression, we attempt to provide the reader with a selection of the more recent research in which facial expressions were employed as either dependent or independent variables. Particularly intriguing are the suggestions that facial expressions may in some situations be more reliable measures of emotion than self-report or physiological indices. Finally, a summary is presented of the major methodological considerations that one should be aware of before attempting to undertake research in this exciting but difficult area.

Kinesics as we have defined it refers to all discriminable bodily movements excluding facial expression and eye movements, which are considered as separate, if related, phenomena. Structural theorists such as Birdwhistell have employed a much broader definition of kinesic behavior. More important, they insist that each behavior be considered in relation to both all other behaviors occurring and the total context to obtain the "meaning" of the behavior. Birdwhistell has proposed a notation system for kinesic behavior similar to linguistic theories on the structure of grammar. Just as there are phonemes and morphemes, so does Birdwhistell postulate kinemes, kinemorphs, and the like. Despite his pioneering work and irrefutable contributions, we conclude that the "linguistic-kinesic analogy" is not the appropriate model for research in this field.

Employing the external variable approach, individual kinesic behaviors can alternatively be examined in relation to other psychological variables (e.g., mood state, personality characteristics) as either communicative or indicative phenomena. Following a classification scheme developed by Ekman and Friesen, body movements may theoretically be described in terms of their usage, origin, and coding. Based on this system, various nonverbal behaviors may be identified: *emblems,* communicative movements that have direct verbal translation; *illustrators,* speech-related movements that often "illustrate" what is being said; *regulators,* movements that monitor and regulate conversational behavior; and *adaptors,* movements with no communicative or interactive purpose that are nonetheless frequently indicative of an individual's inner thoughts and immediate emotional experience.

Information that we may withhold verbally and fail to display in our facial expressions may be "leaked" through movements of our hands, legs, feet, and so forth, which are less under our conscious control and more likely to reflect our emotional state at the moment. Many research investigations in clinical settings have focused on bodily movements in relation to verbal content, dynamic themes, and the therapeutic process. Several "structural" researchers have investigated microkinesic behavior, movements that occur so rapidly that they cannot be seen by the naked eye. Using special slow-motion photography, these researchers have observed a "synchrony" of movement that occurs between patient and therapist. Research following the external variable approach has shown that kinesic behavior may be reflective of a patient's mood state and diagnostic category or the status of the patient in treatment (e.g., admission vs. discharge). Psychotherapy researchers have also focused on therapist characteristics, personality type, and relationship variables.

Other studies have been devoted to the close relationship between body movements (especially hand movements) and the encoding of speech. Many kinesic behaviors provide important cues to a speaker's intention to continue talking, to yield the floor to a listener, and the like. Finally, we have reviewed a large number of studies relating kinesic phenomena to such external variables as anxiety, "perceived persuasiveness" in communication, psychological differentiation (e.g., field-dependence–independence) and interpersonal attitudes (e.g., positive, negative, affiliative), to name a few. Together these findings indicate the many functions and information value of nonverbal body movements in human interaction.

Visual behavior has become a separate area of nonverbal research, given the fundamental significance that interpersonal gaze plays in human interaction and communication. Indeed, looking signals a readiness to communicate and an awareness of another person. Research on visual behavior has been fraught with special methodological problems. Studies have been conducted on the acuity of observers judging shifts in gaze direction and the role observer distance and angle play in the reliability and validity of eye contact between two interactants. Mutual gaze, one-sided look, eye-gaze, face-gaze, and gaze avoidance have all been proposed as terms describing visual behavior other than eye contact. Whether one interactant's gaze is kept constant or if both interactants' gaze varies "naturally" may determine the operational definition of looking behavior.

Despite the methodological problems, much meaningful research on visual behavior has been accomplished. Various studies have demonstrated looking and gaze aversion as crucial elements in the initiation and maintenance of communication. The eyes are also of obvious importance in monitoring speech, providing feedback, signaling understanding, and regulating speaker-listener turn-taking. Typically, whites look more when listening than speaking, but this is not true of other racial groups (e.g., blacks). Considerable research on interpersonal attraction has shown the frequency and duration of looking to be an important dependent measure of positive interpersonal regard. One important theory of intimacy posits that looking is directly related to interpersonal distance; that is, the farther the interaction distance, the more we look in order to compensate for the reduction in intimacy produced by the distance.

As an independent variable, visual behavior has a demonstrable "interactive influence": prolonged looking (staring) reliably produces flight or avoidance responses in strangers. Researchers have also studied the interpersonal attributions made by observers about an individual's looking behavior in various contexts. Finally, individual differences in visual behavior have been reliably associated with sex differences, patient diagnostic status (e.g., depression), and personality differences (e.g., extraversion, introversion, and dominance). Recently, studies have focused on the direction of gaze while thinking (i.e., left- or right-gaze), which seems related to a variety of individual characteristics, including hemispheric dominance.

Lastly, in our section on visual behavior, we briefly review the research on pupillary dilation. Although for technical reasons it might well be excluded from consideration as a nonverbal behavior, so much controversy and so many studies have been conducted on the pupil that we have attempted to identify and summarize some of the most recent research in that area.

The final area of nonverbal communication pertains to how we structure, use, and are affected by space in our interactions with others. Research in this area has been generally labeled as the study of *proxemics*. Edward Hall, an anthropologist, first investigated this phenomenon systematically. Hall identified important cultural differences in proxemic behavior as well as the social functions served by various interpersonal distances, which he identified as intimate, personal, social, and public. Another important concept, *personal space,* describes a stable hypothetical boundary that we each employ in interpersonal interactions. In the experimental research various methodologies have been employed in the study of proxemics, ranging from having one or both interactants approach another up to a "comfortable" distance, to observing their behavior when "intruded" upon, to measuring the distance at which subjects space figures representing humans on a form board. Each approach has important weaknesses and limitations; moreover, they do not appear to be consistently correlated to one another, which suggests that they are not measuring the same psychological construct.

As might be expected, there are individual differences in personal space and interpersonal distance, including sex, racial, and cultural differences. Age is also a factor, as are personality and psychiatric diagnosis. Much proxemic research has also been focused on personal space in relation to interpersonal variables such as familiarity, interpersonal similarity, and liking and the relationship between distance and eye contact in the regulation of intimacy. The effect of interpersonal distance on impression formation has also been studied.

Seating distances have been employed as dependent measures of positive or negative social experiences. Seating arrangements have also been related to leadership and status roles and the counseling or psychotherapeutic situation. "Invasions" of personal space have been manipulated by seating experimental confederates uncomfortably close to other students in the study of territorial behavior. In addition to variations of interpersonal distance, environmental variables such as density, crowding, social confinement, and the like have been important influences on individuals' behavior that often interact with the individual difference behaviors noted earlier. Indeed, living arrangements may affect our general social behavior in situations away from that setting.

Though long neglected by researchers, touching behavior has begun to attract attention, and important sex differences are emerging. Some research suggests that even unobtrusive momentary touches can measurably affect our perceptions. Finally, the remaining portion of this section is devoted to some of the recent theories that attempt to conceptualize how we use space. Though by no means comprehensive, they offer the beginnings of a solid conceptual base on which to organize many diverse findings.

Although these chapters cover the major channels of nonverbal communication, other special topic areas are emerging such as "multichannel communication" and "encoding and decoding" of nonverbal behavior, which are not specifically focused on in this work. These points and other issues for future research are considered in a final brief epilogue to this work.

ROBERT G. HARPER
ARTHUR N. WIENS
JOSEPH D. MATARAZZO

Portland, Oregon
August, 1977

REFERENCES

Argyle, M. (1975). *Bodily communication.* London: Methuen.

Harrison, R. P. (1974). *Beyond words: An introduction to nonverbal communication.* Englewood Cliffs, NJ: Prentice-Hall.

Kleinke, C. L. (1975). *First impressions: The psychology of encountering others.* Englewood Cliffs, NJ: Prentice-Hall.

Knapp, M. L. (1972). *Nonverbal communication in human interaction.* New York: Holt, Rinehart, and Winston.

Weitz, S. (Ed.) (1974). *Nonverbal communication: Readings with commentary.* New York: Oxford University Press.

Contents

NONVERBAL COMMUNICATION

CHAPTER 1

Introduction to Nonverbal Communication Research

OVERVIEW

This review covers much of the world's literature in English on nonverbal communication and organizes it in a fashion useful for three purposes: (a) to provide a current overview of "the state of the art"; (b) to map out the current "domains" of research in nonverbal communication and the most promising directions for future research, both theoretical and applied; and (c) to provide a conceptual base and up-to-date summary of findings into which new findings may be integrated. This has been no small task, given the many different disciplines represented in the nonverbal communication literature, and thus some work undoubtedly has been missed. Anthropologists, linguists, and communication specialists, as well as psychiatrists and social and clinical psychologists, have all contributed to the ever-growing body of findings. Although we have reviewed many of the important contributions of these other disciplines, this review covers the literature contributed primarily by persons trained in psychological research methods. Our own research interests have resulted in our focusing in greater detail on the experimental, psychological research, at the expense of other studies that utilize more of an ethological or descriptive method of investigation.

An attentive reader who scans the bibliography of this manuscript will observe that most of the references are quite recent. In a review of the nonverbal communication literature, Harrison, Cohen, Crouch, Genova, and Steinberg (1972) noted that:

Sharp changes have taken place in the nonverbal communication literature, in the past decade, and in particular, in the last two years. A decade ago, few books existed; and the early works tended to be speculative, anecdotal, and tentative. Recently, a flurry of popular books have caught the attention of the layman. Perhaps somewhat unfortunately, these books have drawn largely on the early anecdotal state of knowledge. But behind this popular fad is a growing body of solid

1

research literature. Major works are now emerging which, on the one hand, organize and synthesize the existing data from a variety of fields. Research programs extending over a number of years are now culminating and the results are becoming available. Theoretical issues have become clarified, and a range of active theories vie for support. Finally, methodological problems are being examined—and, frequently they are being solved. . . . The amount of knowledge has now reached a "critical mass"—and a general availability—so that even more exciting things may be ahead. (pp. 473–474)

In this introduction we consider the major theoretical, conceptual, and research issues in the nonverbal communication field. As will be seen, there has been a variety of approaches employed in the study of nonverbal communication and, as yet, there is no real consensus as to its exact definition, the domain that it encompasses, or what the best research approaches are. Thus before the many hundreds of individual studies can be reviewed intelligently, it is especially important to develop some conceptual framework into which they can be organized.

NONVERBAL COMMUNICATION: AN ATTEMPT AT DEFINITION

Definitions of nonverbal communication abound, ranging from very broad to very narrow, rigorous statments. In a recent article Knapp (1972), a scholar for many years in nonverbal communication, stated:

Traditionally, educators, researchers, and laymen have used the following definition when discussing nonverbal communication: Nonverbal communication designates all those human responses which are *not* described as overtly manifested words (either spoken or written). (p. 57)

Similarly, Harrison (1973) commented:

The term nonverbal communication has been applied to a broad range of phenomena: everything from facial expression and gesture to fashion and status symbol, from dance and drama to music and mime, from flow of affect to flow of traffic, from the territoriality of animals to the protocol of diplomats, from extrasensory perception to analog computers, from the rhetoric of violence to the rhetoric of topless dancers. (p. 93)

Key, a linguist, noted that "human communication is a body movement. Movement of the vocal apparatus results in *speech,* the verbal act, *or paralanguage,* a nonverbal act" (1972, p. 1). In contrast to these very broad definitions, Wiener, Devoe, Rubinow, and Geller (1972) insisted upon a very specific and methodologically rigorous definition of nonverbal communication that we consider in greater detail later.

This very diversity in definition, although indicative of the interdisciplinary effort and excitement this topic area has generated, "also reflects a lot of intellectual confusion, particularly when researchers try to move from speculation to investigation" (Harrison and Knapp, 1972, p. 343). In part, this problem stems from a lack of agreement on the boundary between verbal and nonverbal and the distinction between communicative or non-communicative behavior. For example, as we discuss, Wiener, Devoe, Rubinow, and Geller (1972) viewed nonverbal behavior that is communicative as a subset of the larger domain of specifiable nonverbal acts. In contrast, Barker and Collins (1970) stated:

There has been a tendency to use the term *nonverbal communication* synonymously with the term *nonverbal behavior*. However, nonverbal communication is much broader than nonverbal behavior. A room devoid of behaving, living things communicates atmosphere and function. Static clothing communicates the personality of the wearer. (p. 344)

There are sound reasons to disagree with this latter definition, but some consideration should first be given to some of the phenomena that different researchers have subsumed under the rubric of nonverbal communication.

Consistent with their broad view of nonverbal communication, Barker and Collins (1970) classified 18 nonverbal communication forms: (a) animal and insect; (b) culture; (c) environmental surroundings; (d) gestures, facial expression, bodily movement, and kinesics; (e) human behavior; (f) interaction patterns; (g) learning; (h) machine; (i) media; (j) mental processes, perception, imagination, and creativity; (k) music; (l) paralinguistics; (m) personal grooming and apparel; (n) physiological; (o) pictures; (p) space; (q) tactile and cutaneous; and (r) time. Obviously, this classification describes an area too broad for anyone interested primarily in interaction between two or more humans. Concerning human interaction, Poyatos (1974) proposed a broad classification of nonverbal phenomena according to the sensorial channels involved (acoustic, visual, olfactory, and tactile); the classes of verbal-vocal, nonverbal-vocal, and nonverbal-nonvocal; and whether they are interactional or noninteractional in nature. That his classification system is "total" should be evident when one considers some of the examples cited: in the area of "acoustic body communication" is included "intestinal gas expelled through the anus, or stomachic one lets out by the mouth" (p. 3); olfactory body communication encompasses "body secretions" including perspiration and "the odors from somebody—adaptors, such as clothes, tobacco, and drinks" (p. 4).

A psychologist, Argyle (1969), listed the following as nonverbal behaviors: bodily contact, posture, physical appearance, facial and gestural movement, direction of gaze, and the paralinguistic variables of emotional tone, timing, and accent. Knapp (1972) identified the following: body motion or kinesic behavior, facial expression, physical characteristics, eye behavior, touching behavior, paralanguage, proxemics, artifacts, and environmental factors. Duncan's (1969) list of "nonverbal modes" included body movement or kinesic behavior, paralanguage, proxemics, olfaction, skin sensitivity to temperature and touch, and the use of artifacts. Scheflen (1968) described kinesic and postural behaviors and tactile, odorific, territorial, proxemic, and artifactual categories as "nonlanguage modalities" in addition to the nonlexical vocal modalities of paralinguistic behaviors.

These authors classified nonverbal behaviors or modalities primarily in terms of body area (face, eyes) or body activities (gestures, motor approach-avoidance). Other communication researchers have considered nonverbal behavior in somewhat more abstract terms. Reusch and Kees (1972), for example, described nonverbal communication in terms of "action language," "sign language," and "object language." Harrison (1973) subsumed various combinations of nonverbal behavior under the following categories: "performance codes" based on bodily actions, "artifactual codes" (e.g., the use of clothing, jewelry), "mediational codes" involving manipulation of the media, and "contextual codes" (e.g., employment of nonverbal signs in time and space).

In summary, what is meant by the terms nonverbal communication, nonverbal modality, nonverbal sign, nonverbal act, or nonverbal behavior, and how they are used and classified by different authors are real problems in this area of research. Although there is no consensual definition at present, we arbitrarily limit our consideration of nonverbal phenomena to those that are most important in the structuring and occurrence of interpersonal communication and the moment-to-moment regulation of the interaction. This includes some consideration of spatial (proxemic) aspects of the physical setting of interactions, insofar as these affect interpersonal communication. However, we do not consider such phenomena as dress, use of artifacts, and physical characteristics (e.g., appearance, body odor) in this review.

FUNCTIONAL CLASSIFICATIONS OF NONVERBAL COMMUNICATION

Several authors have defined functions of nonverbal phenomena from the perspective of a communication system. Harrison (1973), for example, proposed that "nonverbal signs" function at three different levels:

1. Nonverbal signs define, condition, and constrain the system; e.g., time, place, and arrangement may provide cues for the participants as to who is in the system, what the pattern of interaction will be, and what is appropriate and inappropriate communication content.

2. Nonverbal signs help regulate the system, cueing hierarchy and priority among communicators, signaling the flow of interaction, providing metacommunication and feedback.

3. Nonverbal signs communicate content, sometimes more efficiently than linguistic signs but usually in complementary redundancy to the verbal flow. (p. 94)

The reader should note that Harrison's descriptions incorporate several phenomena (e.g., architecture, human artifacts) that we do not consider to be forms of nonverbal communication for the purpose of our interests. Scheflen (1968), a pioneer in nonverbal research in the tradition of Birdwhistell, also considered nonverbal behavior in the context of a human communications systems approach. Without going into detail concerning this rather complicated approach, we should note that Scheflen (1968) considered the context, interaction, and flow of interactive behavior as essentially inseparable aspects of "behavioral programs." Specifically, he cautioned, "You must not be satisfied to isolate bits of behavior and merely measure or count them. It is the relations of the elements or events, the configuration, the patterns we are after" (p. 44). Scheflen described "three orders of integration" in communication. The first is first-order communication, which is the simple coordination of activities that do not require utilization of language or signals. Work routines, lovemaking, and many other social activities occur almost automatically, without special attention or communication being necessary. At this level, nonverbal behaviors serve no particular function other than being part of essentially "automatic" behavior programs.

However, Scheflen's second-order communication level requires the utilization of integrational signals. These signals serve to modify and integrate activities when ambiguities occur in behavioral sequences. Examples would include *pacing signals,* such as head-nods, which regulate the speed of performance; *identification signals,* including both "indicators of categorical membership," such as skin color (racial identification), sex (gender identification), and age; and "indicators of state," which communicate the interest, awareness, and mood of the participant. Other second-order communications include *social integration signals* which serve to monitor inattention, interpersonal distance, and inappropriate relationships, and *references to contexts,* which may influence the mode of performance. Scheflen noted that second-order communications may modify particular enactments within a behavioral program, but do not modify the program itself. Indeed, the significance of the signals cannot be ascertained until the basic programs have been identified and explicated in detail.

Finally, Scheflen defined third-order communication as metacommunication or "communication about communication." Nonverbal metacommunications can be as simple as a smile during a wrestling match which indicates that the activity is friendly play involving no physical danger. In contrast to second-order communications, metacommunications do function to identify the nature of the particular behavioral program being enacted. A major problem with Scheflen's system of analysis, from our point of view, is that one must first learn the behavioral program being enacted in interpersonal interaction situations before the function of the nonverbal behavior can be identified. This can be tremendously time consuming for, as Scheflen warned, "It is when you have watched the stream of behavior 30, 50, or more times that the pattern will begin to be evident" (p. 45).

Rather than viewing nonverbal behavior and its functional properties in the context of an abstract and complicated communication system, some researchers have chosen to consider it directly in relation to spoken or verbal communication. For example, Key (1972) pointed out:

> The occurrence of the nonverbal acts in the interaction between human beings and the resultant effect on syntax have been too long passed over by linguists. Recent thinking in linguistic theory, however, would indicate that linguists are moving closer to acknowledging the dependence of meaning to syntax. If syntax is, indeed, undecipherable without reference to meaning, then we must consider that the understanding of meaning is also undecipherable without reference to the nonverbal component of the communication item. One senses a merging of syntax and semantics in the description of language, and concomitantly a merging of verbal and nonverbal. (p. 2)

Whereas many researchers would view nonverbal behavior as functioning in a supportive role to verbal communication, Key contended that a communicative expression may or may not include verbal behavior but that "some nonverbal element is always present. When the verbal act occurs, the nonverbal may be in accordance with, or contradictory to the verbal, but it is an obligatory correlate to the total behavioral event" (p. 3). For example, a person may communicate awareness of the rain by uplifting his face to the sky and holding his hands out to catch drops, with or without the accompanying statement, "I think it's beginning to rain." Thus, according to Key, in some instances nonverbal communication can serve as verbal communication, and in all instances of interpersonal communication it contributes to the syntax.

Speer (1972) described a fourfold classification of nonverbal and verbal communications, each serving to convey cognitive or affective information. Specifically, he described Type A communication as purely verbal-cognitive such as didactic information-giving, Type C communication as nonverbal acts that can substitute for Type A communication (e.g., headshaking, pointing), Type B communications as verbal expressions of affect states, and Type D communications as nonverbal expressions of emotion (e.g., facial grimaces, fist-clenching). Speer emphasized, in particular, that Type D communication always accompanies Type A, B, and C communications and "is essentially a continuous, universal form of information-about-self communication" (p. 411). He employed the term, introduced by Watzlawick, Deavin, and Jackson (1967), "analogic communication," to describe Type D communications as conveying information about the interpersonal relationship existing at the time of communication.

Perhaps the most widely cited description of the various roles that nonverbal behaviors play in human communication was provided by Ekman and Friesen (1969). They specified five general functions that nonverbal behavior serves in relation to spoken communication. The most obvious is perhaps *repetition*, as when a baseball umpire may signal "out" with his thumb while simultaneously verbalizing. Verbal and nonverbal behaviors may also *contradict*, as in the case of a verbal praise given in a sarcastic tone of voice. Nonverbal behaviors may also *complement* verbal behavior: praise can be given with a smile or pleasant tone of voice. In addition, they can even *accent* spoken words. One can lean forward or touch the other interactant in both a verbal and nonverbal display of affection. Finally, as we see in later sections, nonverbal behavior is employed to *regulate* human interaction and communication, especially through the use of eye contact and gestures.

In summary, then, in addition to kinds of nonverbal behavior and communication, one can identify various functional properties of nonverbal phenomena within the context of somewhat esoteric and complicated communication system approaches, or one can attempt to specify how nonverbal behaviors interrelate with accompanying verbal behaviors. The latter approach at present appears to us the more useful in the planning and conduct of experimental research, whereas the former is primarily suited to observational studies.

NONVERBAL COMMUNICATION: METHODOLOGICAL CONSIDERATIONS

Thus far in our description of the field of nonverbal communication we have attempted to show examples of the definitions given to nonverbal communication and the functions they serve in communicative behavior. We have reviewed the rather formidable variety of phenomena that have been included by various researchers in the "domain" of nonverbal phenomena. In particular, we have noted a variety of terms (e.g., nonverbal communication, nonverbal behavior, nonverbal cues or signs), which have sometimes been used as if they were interchangeable, though they are not. Nonverbal communication refers to the whole process of communication between two or more persons. In contrast, nonverbal behaviors are simply behaviors or physical acts that may or may not have a particular "meaning." The term nonverbal cue or sign implies that the behavior has some referential meaning beyond the act itself, but whether it is communicative or merely indicative depends upon the model of communication subscribed to and certain methodological considerations to which we now turn.

Models of communication

Although research in nonverbal communication is still in its infancy, a number of attempts have been made to apply theoretical models of communication to the analysis of nonverbal behavior. Unfortunately, the problems of definition of nonverbal communication also apply to communication itself. As Barnlund (1968) stated, "When one attempts to discover precisely what is meant by 'communication' one finds it surrounded by vagueness and ambiguity" (p. 4). Nevertheless, it is still possible to identify certain aspects of models of communication that provide some basis for the development of a conceptual framework for nonverbal research. In the development of models (Barnlund, 1968), communication has been conceptualized "structurally" in terms of sender-message-receiver; "functionally" in terms of encoding-decoding processes, based on intent of message (expressive-instrumental); and in terms of "channel" (mode of transmission). The models of communication developed included, originally, *structural-linear* models descriptive of the flow of communication from sender to receiver. Later "circular" models were proposed, which incorporate the notion of "feedback" to modify message transmission. Other models have emphasized the functional aspects of communication, of encoding-decoding.

Fortunately, for our purposes, Dittmann (1972) recently produced a book in which he attempted to apply communication theory to the interpersonal communication of emotions. Since nonverbal behavior probably contributes more heavily to the communication of emotion than even verbal behavior, Dittmann's model is worth considering in some detail. As an introduction to models of communication, he described a verbal interaction situation to illustrate a structural model of communication in a social situation:

The sending person (source), having an idea to get across, transforms his idea into linguistic forms (source encoding); . . . he shapes these linguistic forms by means of his vocal apparatus and articulators into sounds (channel encoding). . . . The receiving person hears the sounds through the air between them (channel) and groups them together into linguistic forms (channel decoding), which he finally translates centrally (user decoding) into the idea the sending person had wished to communicate, thus understanding what was said (user). (p. 22)

Schematically, this process can be diagrammed as follows:

Source → source encoder → channel encoder → channel →
channel decoder → user decoder → user

In developing his model of emotional communication, Dittmann identified four important aspects of a mathematical theory of communication: (a) the information contained in a message; (b) the coding process that takes place in a message transmission, both encoding and decoding; (c) the channels employed in transmission, their capacities, and the limitations they impose upon transmitting messages; and (d) the effects of noise on accurate transmission of information.

The concept of "information" is elusive, even more so when applied to human interaction. Basically, the amount of information contained in a message is a function of its scarcity or lack of redundancy in relation to other elements. For example, a momentary frown on the part of a person who is otherwise laughing and smiling carries a great deal of information in comparison to each smile or utterance of laughter. The concept of coding is important in that this describes the process whereby messages are represented in some form, be it spoken language, gestures, or facial expression. Unfortunately, here Dittmann made no explicit distinction between encoding and decoding processes that involve different activities (e.g., body movement in encoding, perceptual–cognitive-language processes in decoding). He did, however, isolate some important "structural characteristics" of a message that are related to the extent of coding. "Communicative specificity" is a term used by Dittmann to define a communication continuum, with the most communicative message, *language,* on the one end and the least communicative messages (e.g., self-manipulations), *expression,* on the other. In between are facial expression and paralinguistic cues, which generally convey less information than spoken words but are more highly coded than gross body movements. Dittmann was careful to note that this dimension is not analogous to either a verbal-nonverbal or a conscious-unconscious dimension. Some nonverbal behaviors (e.g., emblematic hand movements representing sign language) are fully communicative even though most tend towards the expressive side of the continuum.

Two other structural characteristics of messages are the *level of awareness* and *intentional control.* By level of awareness, Dittmann referred to two dimensions extending from aware to repressed and from aware to subliminal, respectively. A person can repress a message or be fully conscious of it, or a message may be so weak (subliminal) that it does not draw his attention even though there are no psychodynamic factors interfering with reception of the message. Intentional control refers to the degree to which emotional messages are allowed to be expressed or communicated versus controlled. Though he did not describe these characteristics in these terms, level of awareness would appear primarily relevant to decoding processes and intentional control to encoding processes. Table 1-1 summarizes the various characteristics of messages outlined by Dittmann.

In discussing *channels* of communication, Dittmann addressed himself to a term frequently used in nonverbal communication, but one which has been rarely defined. He adopted a definition of channel given by Wiener and Mehrabian (1968): "*Channel* will define any set of behaviors in a communication which has been systematically denoted by an observer *and* which is considered by that observer to carry information which can be studied (in principle at least) independently of any other co-occurring behaviors" (Wiener and Mehrabian, 1968, p. 51). Channels can be classified as discrete or continuous categories that can be related to communicative specificity. The closer a message to the communication end of the dimension (e.g., spoken words, each of which has a distinct meaning), the more probable it will be discrete. Expressive messages such as hand-rubbing or

Table 1-1.   Aspects of Messages (Adapted from Dittmann, 1972)

All messages may vary:

A.   In terms of Sender or Encoder:

Message may vary in intentional control; how much control sender exercises in communicating message

B.   In terms of Receiver or Decoder:

Awareness of message: message may be subliminal and not perceived, or perceived and repressed (kept out of awareness)

C.   In terms of message information value:

Continuum of communicative specificity

D.   In terms of the channel of communication:

Communicative . . . .*Expressive*
                 Language   Facial expression   Vocalizations   Body movements
Discrete . . . .*Continuous*
Greatest channel capacity   Least channel capacity needed
needed (highest message   (lowest message information value and
information value and   least decoder attention required)
most decoder attention
required)

posture shifts, in turn, are likely to be continuous. Nonverbal behaviors generally are expressed through continuous channels whereas spoken language, with high communicative specificity, can be considered a discrete channel. Channels defined by Dittmann include audible channels (short- and long-term spoken language, vocalizations) and visual channels (facial expression, body movement, and psychophysiological responses such as blushing).

An additional way of describing channels is in terms of the "memory" they possess. Dittmann described a "constant channel . . . characterized by freedom of choice as to which message element may be sent now, regardless of the ones that have preceded it" (1972, p. 127). In contrast, the channel with memory, the next message element is partially determined by those elements which precede it.

Finally, Dittmann suggested that channels can be measured and understood in terms of their *capacity*, perhaps their most important characteristic. Channel capacity refers to the amount of information a channel may convey at any moment in time. This concept is important because channels vary in their capacity. The discrete, audible channel of spoken language, with its high communicative specificity, can be used to convey a much larger number of messages than the visual, continuous channel of body movement, which consists of relatively few "expressive" acts that convey emotion. Both speed of transmission and information value determine channel capacity. Highly codable (i.e., discrete) messages increase channel capacity by providing high information value. Thus emotions can be conveyed very accurately through spoken language whereas body movements, being messages toward the expressive end of the dimension, only convey a general idea that is vague as to feeling state. In contrast, in some instances very rapid shifts in facial expression can convey (emotional) messages of higher information value than can spoken language in a comparable period of time.

A final comment to be made on Dittmann's work concerns his use of the term "noise." In communication theory, "noise" basically consists of "random" stimuli that interfere with communication transmissions or mask message elements. "Random noise" in interpersonal communication might consist of a person brushing a fly from his face, this action thus distracting his friend from noticing that he just smiled. Dittmann conceded that interferences in human communication cannot all be attributed to "random" events. However, in dealing with the concept of noise and communication theory strategies for combatting it, his thinking led him to several useful tactics to combat some interferences with emotional communication. One tactic specified by his communication theory is to employ coding in which messages are made more discrete. Dittmann pointed out that as a rule, the higher the message is in communicative specificity, the more demanding it is of attention. Listening to speech is a very attention-absorbing task, more so than noting postural changes. Thus a way to insure communication of positive affect (i.e., to avoid interference in communication transmission) is to verbalize the feeling rather than express it through a postural shift.

A second way to reduce "noise" in human communication concerns a characteristic of the "receiver." Here, Dittmann called not upon communication theory but upon D. E. Broadbent's filter theory (Broadbent, 1958). Broadbent conceived the human central nervous system as a channel with a limited capacity for processing information. Incoming messages initially pass through perceptual "channels" (i.e., vision, hearing, smell, the tactile senses) and then through a selective filter that determines which messages get through and which do not. Message transmission can be facilitated by increasing either the physical intensity of the message (e.g., loudness of voice) or its novelty or information value, or by stimulating drive states that sensitize the person to particular messages. Perhaps the most important aspect of Broadbent's theory was his emphasis on the limitation in the channel capacity in the central nervous system. The implication of this notion is that presentation of communications by way of several channels (e.g., visual, audible) can result in *interference between channels* and a loss of message transmission through one of the channels. Complicated verbal messages may take up so much of one's channel capacity that they mask less highly coded nonverbal behavior. Conversely, there are situations where messages transmitted through several channels can increase the redundancy of information and thus the accuracy of communication.

Dittmann was the first to concede that his theory of emotional communication is just that, and that there are places where the "fit" between mathematical communication theory and interpersonal behavior is not good or is lacking in empirical support. What he did provide was a conceptualization of human communication that included both verbal and nonverbal behavior and dimensions within which one may categorize interpersonal behavior that is considered in the realm of communication. His structural characteristics of communicative specificity, awareness, intentional control of channels, and channel capacity are needed concepts in nonverbal communication research. As this review shows, however, the research, in most instances, unfortunately does not reflect the sophistication of this theory. Even so, Dittmann's theoretical framework can be very useful in attempts to organize diverse findings into a meaningful whole.

Research strategies

Duncan (1969) summarized the research in nonverbal communication historically as consisting of "three interlocking phases." Initial research in nonverbal communication involved primarily the development of transcription systems for categorizing nonverbal behaviors. These involved the efforts of linguists, such as Trager (1958), who schematized paralanguage as consisting of vocalizations and voice qualities; or ethologists, such as Birdwhistell (1952), who developed a transcription system for almost every form of human movement. Hall (1963) similarly developed a notation system for proxemic behaviors. The development and utilization of these transcription systems led to a series of descriptive *studies* where interpersonal behaviors were transformed into units of analysis.

Duncan identified two broad research strategies that have been employed. In the first, the *structural approach,* nonverbal communication is studied as "a tightly organized and self-contained social system like language. . . . [which] operates according to a definite set of rules" (1969, p. 121). The second or *external variable* approach strategy has been to study the relationship between nonverbal behaviors and other variables, such as the interactants. An important difference in the two approaches lies in the use of statistics. Structuralists have not concerned themselves with whether individual elements occur together; if they are natural elements of a communication structure, they will be present every time. Questions asked by structuralists include: "(a) Out of all behaviors which are possible to perform, which ones actually occur in communication in a given situation in a given culture? (b) Do these selected communicative behaviors occur in characteristic sequences or clusters with other behaviors in the same or a different modality?" (Duncan, 1969, p. 121). Typically, structural studies have involved descriptions of minute behavior sequences (e.g., Crystal and Quirk, 1964; Scheflen, 1966). In some respects this approach would appear tedious and unproductive, but Duncan emphasized that both approaches were "complementary and mutually facilitating. . . . [and] should be vigorously pursued" (1969, p. 121). Indeed, he stated, "It is clear that extensive research on the function of nonverbal behaviors in communication and on their personality and situational concomitants will be unnecessarily encumbered until larger structural units, perhaps analogous to known linguistic units, can be discovered" (1969, p. 122). That such an approach can yield valuable information is seen in the classic study by Condon and Ogston (1967) in which analysis, "over many months," of a 5-second portion of sound film produced their notion of "self-synchrony" (in an individual) and "motion flow synchrony" between interactants.

Despite such actual and potential contributions, the inherent limitations of this type of structural research have led most investigators of nonverbal communication to favor the external variable approach. Ekman and Friesen (1968) classified studies of this type into *indicative* and *communicative* studies. Indicative studies focus upon the association of psychological states with nonverbal behaviors that are indicative of those states. Communicative studies focus upon observers accurately interpreting the "meaning" of given nonverbal behaviors in terms of particular psychological states. Certain hand movements may correlate with and be indicative of anxiety; if observers interpret the movements as reflecting anxiety, then we can say that the behavior also is communicative.

Ekman and Friesen noted five implicit and interrelated assumptions why nonverbal behaviors are studied (from an external-variable approach). First, nonverbal behavior can function as a *relationship language*, "sensitive to, and the primary means of, signalling changes in the quality of an ongoing interpersonal relationship" (1968, p. 180). Second, nonverbal behavior is "the primary means of expressing or communicating emotion" (1968, p. 180). Third, "body language" may convey in some instances symbolic messages concerning a person's attitudes towards himself or others. Fourth, nonverbal behaviors can serve metacommunicative functions in regulating human disclosure, such as through regulation of speaking and listening. A fifth, final assumption, especially relevant to Ekman's research but also applicable to research investigation of psychotherapy, is that certain nonverbal behaviors are less susceptible to attempts at censorship of communication.

Ekman and Friesen (1968) also described five indicative research methods. Indicative studies measure statistical relationships between specific nonverbal behaviors and other variables (e.g., spoken language, personality characteristics, or other nonverbal measures). First, *rate measures,* or frequency of nonverbal behaviors over time, can yield information concerning the characteristics of the sender (e.g., sex or race) or the sender's emotional state (angry, guilty). Second, rate measures can also be related to *situational or role context,* such as location of interaction (e.g., hospital vs. home) or the fact that the person is the interviewer rather than the interviewee. Third, frequency of nonverbal behaviors can be related to the other interaction participant's behavior or characteristics. Fourth, nonverbal behavior can be related to other nonverbal behavior in terms of frequency of sequential or co-occurrence. Finally, nonverbal behavior can be related to spoken language (i.e., verbal content).

In discussing communicative methods, Ekman and Friesen (1968) identified four. As we noted, communicative studies are concerned with the meanings attributed by observers to various nonverbal behaviors. One method is to use selected or complete samples of nonverbal behavior in a judgment task concerning the observed person's characteristics or situation (e.g., was the film taken at the patient's time of admission or at discharge). A second communicative method evaluates differential communication from different sources of nonverbal behavior (hands, face, etc.). Third, a single nonverbal act (e.g., static facial expression, a posture) can be presented and judgments obtained as to its meaning. Finally, different channels or modes of behavior can be examined as to their relative information value (e.g., script vs. audio vs. video vs. audio-visual modes of presentation).

To summarize, Ekman and Friesen's categorization of communicative studies really described studies that involve decoding of nonverbal behaviors presented to observers. Mehrabian (1972) noted a number of advantages of decoding studies:

Such a method is advantageous since it allows a comparison of the effects of a number of cues, singly or in combination, on inferred attitudes. It also allows the investigation of the relative effects of these cues for various communicator and addressee groups (e.g., different sex or personality). Finally, possible confounding effects of communications in other channels (e.g., facial expressions, verbalizations, or gestures) can be eliminated. A decoding method yields considerable information because it makes possible the systematic control of a large number of variables. (p. 154)

In contrast, encoding studies, as described by Mehrabian, are those in which subjects are placed in situations that elicit different attitude-related behaviors, which are then measured. Mehrabian has often favored role-playing in his encoding studies, where a person would assume an attitude (e.g., like-dislike). An encoding study does not permit the systematic study of interactions among communication cues. Although with an encoding method one is limited to the study of interaction between one cue, addressee, and communicator characteristic, there is, however, no limit to the number of nonverbal behaviors that can be studied this way. Mehrabian, in particular employed multiple regression or discriminant analysis to assess the relative information value of different encoded nonverbal cues. Decoding methods, while permitting factorial designs with multiple interactions, are limited by the fact that only so many variables (nonverbal behaviors) can be included in a factorial design before it becomes unmanageable.

Mehrabian also described a third procedure where encoded nonverbal behaviors were presented to subjects who were asked to indicate which they would prefer to use in various social situations. In a sense, subjects were choosing among forms or combinations of behavior to be used to communicate various attitudes. This procedure permits use of factorial designs, as in decoding studies, with analysis of the independent and interactive effect of encoded behaviors in communicating attitudes. It additionally permits the investigator easily to test out nonverbal behaviors that he thinks communicate certain messages, without requiring special knowledge necessary to prepare appropriately encoded messages for a decoding study. In summary, Mehrabian (1972) noted that "Whereas encoding methods are appropriate in the beginning stages of communication research, the proposed encoding-decoding method is appropriate for intermediate stages, and decoding methods are appropriate during the highly developed phases of such research" (p. 156).

Nonverbal Behavior versus Nonverbal Communication

Finally, in our review of methodology, consideration must be given to the important article by Wiener, Devoe, Rubinow, and Geller (1972) that deals with the issue we have thus far skirted, that of nonverbal *behavior* versus nonverbal *communication*. These authors began with the basic paradigm of human communication: a person (encoder) who transmits behavior (code) that is understood by another person (decoder). Nonverbal behavior consists of signs and communications. The term "nonverbal communication" implies "(a) a socially shared signal system, that is, a code; (b) an encoder who makes something public via that code; and, (c) a decoder who responds systematically to that code" (1972, p. 186). In contrast, a "nonverbal sign" implies only that a decoder has made an inference concerning a behavior or has attached some "significance" to a behavior. Nothing is implied about what goes on at the encoding end. Unfortunately, in nonverbal "communication" research most studies have involved decoding paradigms where inferences are made concerning certain behaviors, following which the inferred meanings of the behaviors are taken as "communications." Wiener and his co-authors were especially critical of psychoanalytically oriented investigators who consider all behaviors as communications of "unconscious encodings of experience." They argued that there was no justifiable basis for calling any nonverbal behavior "communicative" unless both encoding and decoding processes are taken into account. An experimental method limited to decoding only, therefore, does not permit differentiation of nonverbal signs from nonverbal communications.

According to Wiener, Devoe, Rubinow, and Geller (1972), before a behavior can be considered "communicative," encoding on the part of the sender must be demonstrated. Implicit in the term "encoding" is the use of a code. A code "is taken to be a set of behaviors which have referents other than themselves" (1972, p. 201). Unfortunately, as these authors pointed out, most investigators have not specified referents to behaviors that they consider communicative and instead have "fallen back on the conscious intentions of the subject as the criterion for considering a behavior to be communicative" (1972, p. 202). This latter criterion presents methodological problems in that an observer cannot always determine a subject's intention and a subject's self-report could be a lie or a mistake in addition to being the truth. They criticized Ekman and Friesen's recent attempt (Ekman and Friesen, 1969) to define nonverbal communication as lacking an explicit concept of code to aid in the sign-communication distinction.

Wiener, Devoe, Rubinow, and Geller defined a code as follows:

If a set of behaviors will be considered to constitute a code, it must be demonstrated both that the behaviors have referents and that the referents of the behavior are known and used by a group; that is, used by at least two persons who emit (encode) the behavior to stand for the agreed-on referent and take (decode) the emitted behavior of the other to stand for the agreed-on referent. (1972, p. 204).

To them, the key to demonstrating nonverbal communication was code usage. They stated:

Code usage will be posited on the basis of a set of interrelated predicted findings when manipulation of the experiences to be made public, of the forms available to the addressor, or of the responsiveness of the addressor to communication conditions results in the predicted effect on the emitted behaviors as a function of such manipulations. (1972, pp. 205–206)

They specified a plan by which code usage can operationally be demonstrated. First, it is necessary to begin by specifying behaviors that obviously represent instances of code usage (e.g., verbal language). Second, behaviors associated with verbal language behaviors are identified, and their patterns of occurrence are noted. Third, it is then necessary to show that as variations in the use of language occur so do variations in the associated behaviors, and that the predictable nonverbal behaviors will occur when verbal behaviors are constrained. Fourth, it must be demonstrated that use of these nonverbal languages in the place of language does not produce changes in decoding behavior known to be indications of understanding or valid decoding. Finally, if it can be shown that since these nonverbal behaviors are presented predictably they do not modify significantly decoding indicators; thus, the nonverbal behaviors can be considered substitutes for verbal forms and hence, instances of nonverbal communication.

Wiener, Devoe, Rubinow, and Geller proposed some behaviors that appear to meet the criteria outlined in their steps for demonstrating code usage. For example, they specified several "semantic modifying relational gestures" (such as a "palms up" gesture) that "seem to serve the function of specification and modification served by adjectives and adverbs in the verbal channel" (1972, p. 211). They summarized:

The chief communicative functions of the gestural channel appear to be to specify the referent of an ambiguous verbal statement, to specify the addressor's relationship to his verbal communication, and to indicate intensity or emphasis by introducing redundancy into the message. (1972, p. 211)

It will become apparent to the reader in the following chapters that, in general, research has been rather primitive, theoretically and methodologically, when compared to the model of communication offered by Dittmann and the methodology outlined by Wiener and his co-workers. It is encouraging to note, however, that efforts are being made to provide a solid conceptual base for the proliferating nonverbal research.

OUTLINE OF CHAPTERS

Despite the many different classifications of nonverbal phenomena that we noted earlier, there are basically five ways one can communicate nonverbally. Excluding "communication" via the sense of smell or autonomic nervous reactions such as blushing, perspiration, and the like, one can convey information nonverbally through the use of the voice, facial expressions, and body movements and gestures. Nonverbal aspects of voice are generally defined as paralinguistic phenomena and temporal characteristics of speech. Body movements are considered part of the study of kinesics. One can also vary his direction of gaze in interaction. "Eye contact" is a fundamental aspect of many communications. Finally, the physical distance between interactants is an important feature of communication which is considered part of the study of proxemics. Most of the experimental literature can be classified and organized into these five topic areas, which together define the domain of nonverbal phenomena to be considered in this review: (a) paralanguage and formal characteristics of speech, (b) facial expression, (c) kinesics, (d) visual behavior, and (e) proxemics.

REFERENCES

Argyle, M. (1969). *Social interaction.* New York: Atherton.

Barker, L. L., and N. B. Collins (1970). Nonverbal and kinesic research. In P. Emmert and W. D. Brooks (Eds.), *Methods of Research in communication.* Boston: Houghton Mifflin. Pp. 343–371.

Barnlund, D. C. (Ed.) (1968). *Interpersonal communication: Survey and studies.* Boston: Houghton Mifflin.

Birdwhistell, R. L. (1952). *Introduction to kinesics: An annotation system for analysis of body motion and gesture.* Louisville, KY. University of Louisville. (Now available in microfilm only from University Microfilms, Inc., 313 North First Street, Ann Arbor, Michigan.)

Broadbent, D. E. (1958). *Perception and communication.* Oxford: Pergamon Press. (Dittmann, A. (1972). *Interpersonal messages of emotion.* New York: Springer. Pp. 156–161.)

Condon, W. S., and W. D. Ogston (1967). A segmentation of behavior. *Journal of Psychiatric Research,* **5,** 221–235.

Crystal, D., and R. Quirk (1964). *Systems of prosodic and paralinguistic features in English.* The Hague: Mouton. (Duncan, S. D., Jr. (1969). Nonverbal communication. *Psychological Bulletin,* **72,** 118–137.

Dittmann, A. T. (1972). *Interpersonal messages of emotion.* New York: Springer.

Duncan, S. D., Jr. (1969). Nonverbal communication. *Psychological Bulletin,* **72,** 118–137.

Ekman, P., and W. V. Friesen (1968). Nonverbal behavior in psychotherapy research. In J. M. Shlien, H. F. Hunt, J. D. Matarazzo, and C. Savage (Eds.), *Research in psychotherapy,* Vol. 3. Washington, D.C.: American Psychological Association. Pp. 179–218.

Ekman, P., and W. V. Friesen (1969). The repertoire of nonverbal behavior: Categories, origins, usage, and coding. *Semiotica,* **1,** 49–98.

Hall, E. T. (1963). A system for the notation of proxemic behavior. *American Anthropologist,* **65,** 1003–1026.

Harrison, R. P. (1973). Nonverbal communication. In I. de Solo Pool, W. Schramm, N. Maccoby, F. Fry, E. Parker, and J. L. Fein (Eds.), *Handbook of communication.* Chicago: Rand McNally. Pp. 93–115.

Harrison, R. P., A. A. Cohen, W. W. Crouch, B. K. L. Genova, and M. Steinberg (1972). The nonverbal communication literature. *Journal of Communication,* **22,** 460–476.

Harrison, R. P., and M. L. Knapp (1972). Toward an understanding of nonverbal communication systems. *Journal of Communication,* **22,** 339–352.

Key, M. R. (1972) *The relationship of verbal and nonverbal communication.* Paper presented at Proceedings of the 11th International Congress of Linguists, Bologna.

Knapp, M. L. (1972). The field of nonverbal communication: An overview. In C. J. Stewart and B. Kendall (Eds.), *On speech communication: An anthology of contemporary writings and messages.* New York: Holt, Rinehart, and Winston. Pp. 57–71.

Mehrabian, A. (1972). Nonverbal communication. In J. K. Cole (Ed.), *Nebraska Symposium on Motivation, 1971.* Lincoln: University of Nebraska Press. Pp. 107–161.

Poyatos, F. (1974). *The challenge of "total body communication" as an interdisciplinary field of integrative research.* Paper presented at the meeting of the International Congress of Semiotic Sciences, Milan.

Reusch, J., and W. Kees (1972). *Nonverbal communication: Notes on the visual perception of human relations,* 2nd ed. Berkeley: University of California Press.

Scheflen, A. E. (1966). Natural History method in psychotherapy: Communication research. In L. A. Gottschalk and A. H. Auerbach (Eds.), *Methods of research in psychotherapy.* New York: Appleton-Century-Crofts. Pp. 263–289.

Scheflen, A. E. (1968). Human communication: Behavioral programs and their integration in interaction. *Behavioral Science,* **13,** 44–55.

Speer, D. C. (1972). Nonverbal communication of affective information: Some laboratory findings pertaining to an interactional process. *Comparative Group Studies,* **3,** 409–423.

Trager, G. L. (1958). Paralanguage: A first approximation. *Studies in Linguistics,* **13,** 1–12.

Watzlawick, P., J, Deavin, and D. Jackson (1967). *Pragmatics of human communication.* New York: W. W. Norton. (Speer, D.C. (1972). Nonverbal communication of affective information: Some laboratory findings pertaining to an interactional process. *Comparative Group Studies,* **3,** 409–423.)

Wiener, M., S. Devoe, S. Rubinow, and J. Geller (1972). Nonverbal behavior and nonverbal communication. *Psychological Review,* **79,** 185–214.

Wiener, M., and A. Mehrabian (1968). *Language within language: Immediacy, a channel in verbal communication.* New York: Appleton-Century-Crofts.

CHAPTER 2

Paralanguage and Formal Characteristics of Speech

PARALANGUAGE AND FORMAL CHARACTERISTICS OF SPEECH

We have chosen these terms to describe those aspects of verbal behavior not associated with language itself, that is, measures of speech that are content free. Harrison (1973) noted that the term "extralinguistic" has occasionally been used instead of paralanguage, but we will not become immersed in problems of definition concerning "extralinguistic," "paralinguistic," or "metalinguistic" phenomena. Indeed, Mehrabian argued:

In its narrow and more accurate sense, "nonverbal behavior" refers to actions as distinct from speech. It thus includes facial expressions, hand and arm gestures, postures, positions, and various movements of the body or the legs and the feet. . . . In the broader sense in which the concept has been used traditionally, however, the term "nonverbal behavior" is a misnomer, for a variety of subtle aspects of speech frequently have been included in discussions of nonverbal phenomena. These include paralinguistic or vocal phenomena such as fundamental frequency range and intensity range, speech errors or pauses, speech rate and speech duration. . . . In our discussions, we shall refer to these vocal qualities as "implicit" aspects of speech. (1972, pp. 1–2)

The relationship between language and paralanguage was nicely described by Trager (1958):

When language is used it takes place in the setting of an act of *speech*. Speech ("talking") results from activities which create a background of *voice set*. This background involves the idiosyncratic, including the specific physiology of the speakers and the total physical setting; it is in the area of prelinguistics. . . . Against this background there take place three kinds of events employing the vocal apparatus: language; variegated other noises, not having the structure of language—*vocalizations;* and modifications of all the language and other noises. These modifications are the *voice qualities.* The vocalizations and the voice qualities together are being called *paralanguage.* (pp. 3–4)

Voice set, a "prelinguistic" phenomenon, refers to the organismic characteristics of the speaker such as age, sex, state of health (e.g., fatigue, illness), status in a group, or higher social organization. Though we do not focus on this aspect of speech, it must be kept in mind "who the speaker is" who is being studied. *Voice qualities* noted by Trager include the following: "pitch range, vocal lip control, glottis control, pitch control, articulation control, rhythm control, resonance, tempo" (1958, p. 5). These are all characteristics of speech that accompany it and are identifiable by a listener. Trager defined three kinds of vocalizations: (1) *Vocal characterizers* include nonlanguage sounds that might be arranged along continua such as laughing, giggling, snickering, whimpering, sobbing, and crying. Other vocal characterizers would include yelling, muttering, muffled sounds, and whispering; moaning and groaning; yawning and belching; whining and voice breaking. (2) *Voice qualifiers* are similar to voice qualities, but Trager identified them separately because of their role in regulating or "qualifying" portions of language material. He describes intensity, pitch height, and extent as the vocal qualifiers. (3) *Vocal segregates* include such "non-words" as "uh-huh" and "uh-uh," which stand for affirmation and negation, respectively.

Though Trager's description of paralinguistic behavior provided a structural base for subsequent research, we do not elaborate in detail or follow his terminology exactly in reviewing the empirical studies done in this area. Indeed, a frequent problem in understanding the research in this area is determining exactly what paralinguistic aspects were actually studied. Nor have we attempted to review the various transcription systems developed by authors who have followed Trager (e.g., Crystal and Quirk, 1964; Pittenger, Hockett, and Danehy, 1960; Pittenger and Smith, 1957). These have been employed in essentially structural-descriptive linguistic studies which, however important, do not utilize experimental methodologies and statistical techniques.

A second major way content-free speech may be conceptualized is in terms of its temporal characteristics, that is, in terms of the variables of duration of utterance, interruptions (including simultaneous speech), and reaction time latency (Matarazzo and Wiens, 1972). Other content-free measures include quantity of speech, verbal productivity, and rate of speech. Silences, including hesitations and pauses, can also be described as "nonverbal" speech phenomena that are important aspects of interpersonal communication. All these aspects of speech can be considered *temporal* characteristics of speech in that they are defined in terms of units per time interval. Disturbances of speech and dysfluencies are the remaining kinds of content-free speech that are considered.

RESEARCH ON PARALINGUISTIC VARIABLES

Research interests in the paralinguistic characteristics of speech have primarily centered on the relationship of these paralinguistic variables to either the more enduring personal qualities and personality traits and attributes or the more transient, situationally based emotional and attitudinal states. Though the categorization of paralinguistic phenomena just presented would seem to offer an ideal outline to follow in this section, such an approach is not feasible given the nature of the studies conducted to date. Most of the early studies in this area unfortunately did not differentiate the various paralinguistic aspects of speech from one another. In particular, when one looks at the literature and the definitions of extralinguistic phenomena employed, the methods used, and the methodological problems involved in the research, there is little consistency and much confounding of these variables. Before considering these studies we thus need to review some of the problems of definition that are confusing as well as the related methodological difficulties encountered in the research.

Problems of Definition

A basic distinction to make in this research is between those content-free sound characteristics of speech that are directly related to the sequence of speech in a linguistic sense (i.e., those vocal characteristics that accompany speech sequencing but which can be considered paralinguistic) and those that accompany speech but which can be separated from the sequential aspects of speech. First, there are several identifiable, content-free aspects of speech that must still be considered "linguistic phenomena" (Dittmann and Wynne, 1961). These include, as shown in Table 2-1, junctures, stress, and pitch, all of which are related to the grammatical organization of language when analyzed in terms of phonemes (a phoneme is the basic sound unit in linguistics, consisting of speech sounds that have the same meaning to native speakers of a language.) *Junctures* are dividing points between speech clauses; *stress* is the increase and decrease in loudness within a clause; and *pitch* is the rise and fall of fundamental frequency within a clause. Each of these consists of several different identifiable varieties.

Paralinguistic phenomena that are associated with the sequence of speech include Trager's *vocal qualifiers,* described by Dittmann and Wynne (1961) as "extra increase or decrease in loudness, pitch, and duration beyond what are needed to convey juncture, pitch, and stress patterns" (p. 202). What becomes confusing in this formulation is consideration of the voice qualities of "register range" and "intensity range," which are *unrelated* to speech sequence. All of these are derivatives of two basic vocal variables, ampli-

Table 2-1. Linguistic and Paralinguistic Variables (Adapted
from Dittmann and Wynne, 1961)

Linguistic	
Junctures	Related to semantic structure
Stress	Related to semantic structure
Pitch	Related to sequence of speech
Paralinguistic	
Vocal qualifiers	
Loudness	Unrelated to semantic structure
Pitch	Related to sequence of speech
Voice qualities	
Register range	Unrelated to semantic structure
Intensity range	Unrelated to sequence of speech

tude and fundamental frequency, but only the last variables (register range and intensity range) can be measured independent of the sequence of words. Thus when one sees the terms "pitch" or "loudness" in studies, it is important to consider whether these terms refer to stress or pitch, vocal qualifiers, voice qualities, or all of these lumped together. The method of measurement is important in this respect, as we shall see. Many of the studies to be reported, however, appear not to have taken these basic differences into account.

Methodological Considerations

Notwithstanding the problems of definition mentioned above, when one is interested in studying such voice qualities as pitch and loudness, which are functions of frequency and amplitude, direct physical measurement of these variables is possible and they can be related to such external variables as independently assessed personality characteristics, known encoded attitudinal or emotional state, intentions, and the like. A problem occurs with decoding studies where one is interested in inferred meaning of voice qualities and vocalizations as determined by consensus among judges. Obviously, the first step is to remove the effect that different semantic content might have in influencing the judgments made of speakers. Scherer (1971) recently reviewed the methods employed. These have included attempts to control the content of speech by (1) having speakers recite meaningless content (such as letters of the alphabet) or read standard constant content; (2) use of foreign language speech or speech played backward on a tape recorder;

and (3) electronic low-bypass filtering or randomized splicing of taped speech. Each of these methods has its limitations, however.

The most common method employed in studies of voice and personality, that of *constant content,* involves speakers reading a standard passage following which listeners rate the speaker. This procedure entails a potential interaction between the speaker and verbal content such that some might find certain content easier to read. Speakers can also develop "microphone fright" due to heightened self-consciousness over recording their speech unnaturally. A third problem with this technique is that listeners are still exposed to speakers all reading the same content but with individual differences in "rate of speech, nonfluencies, hesitation pauses, intonation contours, accents and or dialects" (Scherer, 1971, p. 156), and speech-related paralinguistic sequence phenomena that can be confounded with voice qualities. A more important objection, however, is that personality characteristics such as dominance, extraversion, etc. may not be present in such standardized single-person situations but are only manifested in a two-person interaction situation where the speakers are not restricted in their content of speech and can respond naturally to each other.

One technique that permits variability in content is the use of electronic *low-bypass filters,* which mask high-frequency sounds (voice frequencies above 400–600 Hz) that are most important to our correct identification of words. Speech thus masked comes across to a listener as virtually indistinguishable sounds, similar to "mumbling through a wall." The exact frequency ranges to be filtered out so as to make the speech unintelligible depend on the particular speaker's voice (Rogers, Scherer, and Rosenthal, 1971). Although Mahl (1964) and Starkweather (1967) argued that the lower frequencies are important in the communication of emotional content, Kramer (1963) noted that "the upper as well as the lower overtones of speech contribute to the personal tone or timbre of a person's voice" (p. 416). Kramer also noted that this filtering method produces differences in voice ratings compared to ratings of unmasked speech as judged by naive listeners. In addition, repeated exposure to content-filtered speech will lead to recognition of that speech unless the frequency cutoff point is very low (Kramer, 1964). Perhaps the most important objection to this method is that it attenuates frequency and amplitude while leaving unaffected variables associated with the sequence of speech such as rate of speech, pausing, rhythm, intonation contours, stress patterns, and the like. While these variables are all content-free aspects of speech, they are related to speech more closely than voice quality variables such as register, intensity, and the variations in each.

A method that permits isolation of the voice qualities of pitch, amplitude, and the variations in each without a deliberate confounding of the aforementioned suprasegmental paralinguistic speech phenomena is that of *randomized splicing,* developed by Scherer (1971). Scherer described his technique as follows:

Basically the technique consists of cutting a stretch of recording tape into pieces and splicing them back together in random order. However, certain precautions must be taken. First, silent pauses of all kinds must be removed from the speech sample to be masked by physically cutting out the respective pieces of tape and by splicing the remaining pieces together, producing a continuous sequence of sound. The stretch of recording tape is cut into pieces about 2 in. long (at a recording speed of 7.5 m./sec.). The length of these pieces should vary to some extent with the rate of speech of the respective speaker—if the tempo is extremely high, they should be approximately 1 in. long. These pieces of recording tape are then arranged in random order (care has to be taken that the track—on half- or quarter-track tape recorders—remains in right position) and spliced back together with splicing tape. (1971, pp. 156–157)

He also described a variation of this procedure that he called "randomized copying" which does not require splicing, and even a computerized approach that eliminates the laborious aspects of the first two methods. Scherer reported good results with this method in evaluating emotion (Scherer, 1972) and inferred personality characteristics (Scherer, 1971, 1972), and higher interrater reliability in ratings of emotions in comparison to the electronic filtering technique (Scherer, Koivumaki, and Rosenthal, 1972).

Concerning the *reliabilities* of various vocal measures, Dittmann and Wynne (1961) studied specifically the paralinguistic voice qualities identified by Trager (1958) by having various conversations coded for the paralinguistic phenomena according to linguistic notation developed by Trager. Selected segments of the conversation were classified by three coders once and then again after six months. Interrater reliability figures were obtained by tallying the number of identical codings made by the coders for the same portion of speech at each of the two time intervals. Similar ratings were made for linguistic phenomena with some differences in scoring. The results showed good agreement between coders and, over time, for the linguistic variables (e.g., interrater agreements for stress and pitch were 76% and 87%, respectively). There was, however, considerable disagreement among coders in their attempts to classify voice qualities and vocal qualifiers.

In contrast, Markel (1965) obtained reliabilities of ratings of pitch, loudness, and tempo (following Trager's definitions for vocal qualifiers) in a much different fashion. Raters who had two years of study in linguistics were asked to judge standard-content statements given by 56 speakers on a 7-point scale with the dimensions high-low for pitch, soft-loud for loudness, and slow-fast for tempo. An important aspect of the rating procedure was the very detailed description given these three characteristics of speech and their precise anchoring on the scale. Interrater reliability scores were obtained in addition to test-retest reliability over a 10-day interval. An initial group of raters included the author and four of his students in a paralanguage class; a second group consisted of three undergraduates "trained" with a 90-minute tape. Both groups obtained reliabilities in excess of .80, suggesting that these three aspects of voice can be accurately identified and may, therefore, be considered phenomena appropriate for study. Duncan (1965) and Duncan and Rosenthal (1968) also reported adequate reliabilities for "loudness, pitch, and tempo." A question that arises, however, is, to what extent did the linguistic variables of pitch and stress, the corresponding paralinguistic vocal qualifiers, or the voice qualities of "register" and "intensity" each contribute to the ratings? As we noted earlier, the first set of variables is not technically paralinguistic, the second is related to speech, and the third is supposedly independent of it. Despite the expertise of the raters and the care with which they were instructed, the possibility remains that linguistic and paralinguistic variables were confounded. It would be interesting to see whether such high reliabilities as those reported by Markel and by Duncan and his associates could be obtained with listeners rating a tape recording modified by randomized splicing.

Now that some methodological points have been made, it is possible to turn to the research relating these attributes of speech to other variables. In general, they have been related primarily to either personality attributes of the speaker or inferred emotional states.

PARALANGUAGE AND PERSONALITY

In a review on "nonverbal aspects of speech," Kramer (1963) considered attributions, based on voice, of personality traits, personality adjustment and psychopathology, and global personality characteristics. Although he concluded that there was a relationship between voice and personality, he noted "a lack of adequate independent criteria for the success of vocal judgments [that was a result of] . . . the lack . . . of an adequate criteria for describing voice" (p. 410). Kramer reported judgments of dominance from voice to be related significantly to criterion measures based on the Allport A-S Reaction Study (Allport and Cantril, 1934) and nonsignificantly to the Maslow Social Personality Inventory (Maslow, 1937). Some early attempts failed to relate introversion-extraversion or sociability to voice (Fay and Middleton, 1941, 1942). However, Moore (1939) did find that "breathy" tone of voice was related directly to dominance and inversely to introversion as defined by the Bernreuter Personality Inventory. Mallory and Miller (1958) similarly were able to relate dominance and introversion to several rated vocal characteristics (loudness, resonance, low pitch). Stagner (1936) obtained a positive relationship between aggression and a negative relationship between nervousness and "flow, noise, and clearness" in speech.

A number of early researchers attempted to have raters match general personality descriptions with voice samples. Some positive findings emerged (Allport and Cantril, 1934; Wolff, 1943), but other investigators employing the same methodology could find no relationships (Starkweather, 1955, 1956; Taylor, 1934). Early studies relating voice variables to psychopathology include that by Duncan (1945) where the voice characteristic "monotonism" was associated with low adjustment scores on the Bell Adjustment Inventory. Other similar efforts attempted to relate ineffective communication of mood to emotional disturbance, with success (Goldfarb, Braunstein, and Lorge, 1956; Ramm, 1946) and without (Cohen, 1961).

In a slightly more recent study, Hunt and Lin (1967) found that student judges rated individuals from their voice samples similarly to these individuals' ratings of themselves. While large individual differences in accuracy were noted among judges, there was a similarity among ratings regardless of lexical content of the voice sample. In general, there was greater accuracy for affective-connotative personality attributes than for attributes describing behavioral physical characteristics.

Addington (1968) also had judges rate the standard-content speech of two male and two female speakers, who also simulated seven voice characteristics (tense, thin, flat, breathy, throaty, nasal, and orotund), three variations of speaking rate (normal, fast, and slow), and pitch variation (normal and above and below normal). Ratings were made of perceived personality characteristics as selected from a list of 40 bipolar adjectives on 7-point scales. Good interrater reliability scores were obtained on the vocal characteristics of a single speaker, ranging from .75 for tense to .99 for rate of speech. Interrater reliability coefficients for perceived personality characteristics ranged from .94 for feminine-masculine to a low of .64 for extraverted-introverted. Some additional findings suggested that changes in male voices affected personality perception differently than changes in female voices. A factor analysis of the rated personality characteristics suggested that the male personality was perceived in terms of physical and emotional power, the female in terms of social faculties. Analysis of individual voice characteristics and personality dimensions yielded many more significant correlations than could be obtained by chance, making possible descriptions of the perceived attributes of the different voice characteristics. For example, increased breathiness in male voices was associated significantly with ratings of youngness and artistic ability; females using increased vocal tension were perceived as being younger, less intelligent, more emotional, feminine, and high strung. Although Addington was investigating "vocal stereotypes" rather than personality itself (as measured by some inventory), his findings are still important to the extent that raters appeared to agree on some personality characteristics associated with voice qualities. How reliably one is perceived (and related to) is important, even if the perceptions are not completely valid.

In a study that nicely demonstrates the relationship that some voice characteristics may have to personality, Friedman, Brown, and Rosenman (1969) found that a "voice analysis" task measuring "explosive vocal intonations" correctly identified 84% of normal subjects and 76% of coronary heart patients who exhibited a "Type A" profile. [A "Type A" personality profile is characterized "by an interplay of certain personality traits consisting chiefly of excessive drive, ambition, and aggressiveness with the environment" (Friedman, Brown, and Rosenman, 1969, p. 828).] The authors had subjects read a standard passage depicting an officer exhorting his men into battle, first in a normal tone of voice (as if the subject were alone at home) and then as if he were the officer actually before his troops. This latter "hortatory speech" instruction was designed to interact with the "Type A" individual's predisposition to respond to a challenge (in this instance to read the passage convincingly) and elicit his or her characteristic aggressive mode of expression.

A judgment task of the diagnostic category was used by Markel, Meisels, and Houck (1964) to differentiate schizophrenic from nonschizophrenic patients by voice. Patients classified as schizophrenic or nonschizophrenic by two psychiatrists recorded standard-content passages. These recordings were then rated by college students on a semantic differential scale of activity, potency, and evaluative factors. Schizophrenics were rated as being "more potent" than the nonschizophrenics. In addition, patients (schizophrenic and nonschizophrenic) perceived by the raters as being schizophrenic were rated as being both more potent and more active.

In another study, Markel (1969) obtained ratings of pitch, loudness, and tempo of samples of standard-content speech of 78 psychiatric patients. Patients were assigned to one of three voice-defined groups (peak-pitch, peak-loudness, and peak-tempo) based on the voice characteristic that was most elevated for the patient. As in his earlier study (Markel, 1965), satisfactory interrater and test-retest reliabilities were obtained for judges trained in the rating procedure. Markel found that these three voice-defined groups of patients were significantly different in their mean MMPI profiles and on several scales (e.g., Hs, Hy, and Si). In particular, the peak-pitch patients showed a "best fit" profile of 2-8, which typically is believed to be descriptive of a diagnosis of psychosis, poor prognosis, and poor interpersonal relations. In contrast, the peak-loudness group generated a "3-2-1" profile, most commonly interpreted as a psychoneurotic personality and good prognosis.

In contrast to studies using standard-content passages, Scherer (1971, 1972) reported only modest success in relating voice variables (with content masked by randomized splicing of tape recordings) to several personality characteristics. Scherer (1972) worked with both American and German subjects whose voices were recorded while participating in a mock jury trial, a procedure designed to elicit their emotional involvement which in turn would facilitate their natural expressiveness and reduce their self-consciousness. Independent personality ratings were obtained on a 5-dimension scale and a 35-item adjective checklist that the speaker, two peers of the speaker, and American and German voice raters all filled out. Verbal content was masked by the randomized splicing technique. For the personality measures there was only modest interrater reliability. In particular, there were no significant correlations between speakers' self-ratings and judges' ratings of personality characteristics. However, Scherer did obtain some surprisingly high correlations between the voice ratings by unfamiliar judges and peer ratings of the subject speakers. For example, voice ratings by American judges of American speakers correlated .61 with peer ratings for extraversion; similar relationships were noted for dominance ($r = .85$) and emotional stability ($r = .79$) with German speakers. Scherer additionally noted that listener-judge interrater reliabilities of voice tended to be higher for American speakers than German speakers, a finding that he speculated might be due to possible different functions that the paralinguistic cues may serve in the two languages.

Several recent studies have specifically investigated vocal intensity in relation to personality. Welkowitz, Feldstein, Finkelstein, and Aylesworth (1972) examined vocal intensity patterns in conversational partners. In an interesting manipulation, the conversational interactants were told either that prior psychological testing had revealed they were paired because they were similar or that they were paired on a random basis. Interactions obtained on the first and third one-hour meeting of the dyads were then analyzed in terms of the mean amplitude of speech. Statistical analysis revealed that for the dyads believing they were similar there was a much greater congruence in vocal intensity than for those subjects ostensibly paired on a random basis.

Following on this research, Natale (1975) studied the congruence of vocal intensity over time in dyadic interaction. He first trained an interviewer to interact verbally in a standardized manner with naive subjects. Visual cues were eliminated by having the interviewer communicate from a separate room. Electronic modification of the interviewer's speech permitted accurate restriction of vocal intensity to three levels, which were varied over interviews. Analysis of the subjects' vocal intensities showed that they tended to converge with changes in the interviewer's vocal intensity. In a second study involving three one-hour unstructured interactions between two subjects, the subjects' vocal intensities showed a marked tendency to converge over time; in addition, the degree to which this occurred was related to the individual subject's propensity to act in a prescribed social manner, as measured by the Marlowe–Crowne Social Desirability Scale. As we note later, similar findings were reported by Matarazzo and Wiens (1972) in their own research for temporal speech measures (e.g., reaction time latency and speech interruptions).

Recently, considerable research has focused on differences in the degree of control that individuals feel they have over their environment. In an interesting study, Bugenthal, Henker, and Whalen (1976) hypothesized that individuals who have an external locus of control (i.e., who perceive that they have little control over their environment) would exhibit very strong displays of assertiveness on a verbal level compared to individuals who believe they control their environment. On a nonverbal level, however, they predicted that vocal, internally controlled individuals would show greater assertiveness while individuals with an external locus of control would "leak" their low expectations of personal influence. Verbal behavior is considered "a high awareness channel" (i.e., we are quite aware of what we say) whereas vocal behavior is viewed as a "low awareness" channel (i.e., we tend to monitor and modify our paralinguistic behavior much less than verbal behavior). First-year students in a counseling program were audiotaped while interacting in three-member groups in spontaneous conversation and while role-playing as a supervisor. Undergraduates were trained to rate verbal transcripts and content-filtered portions of the interactions for assertiveness. As predicted, subjects with internal locus of control were more assertive in this vocal than the verbal channel while externally oriented subjects were most assertive in their verbal behavior. Interestingly, these findings were consistent with earlier research (Bugenthal and Love, 1975) that showed that parents of difficult-to-control children tended to detract from their verbal assertions by weak voices when attempting to exert control, and that in turn such parents were more likely to be ignored by their children (Bugenthal, 1972). The authors concluded:

Vocal intonation, which is not easily self monitored, mirrors an individual's personal beliefs about his effectiveness as a source of influence, while verbal content reflects his beliefs about how much assertion is required for effectiveness. (Bugenthal, Henker, and Whalen, 1976, p. 12)

In summary, then, several recent studies have successfully related some vocal characteristics to personality. Relationships have been demonstrated between selected qualities and *inferred personality characteristics* (e.g., Addington, 1968), between personality type and voice (e.g., Friedman, Brown and Rosenman, 1969; Markel, 1969; Markel, Meisels, and Houck, 1964), and between *personality characteristics* (e.g., dominance) and paralinguistic cues. The probable reasons for the greater relative success of the more recent studies include a more rational and specific selection of voice characteristics to be studied (e.g., Addington, 1968; Friedman, Brown, and Rosenman, 1969; Markel, 1969); more reliable and valid methods for describing personality (e.g., the MMPI, independent psychiatric ratings, reliable diagnostic interview, and aggregate peer ratings as opposed to self-ratings); and improved methodologies (e.g., use of trained speakers or an emotionally involving task to obtain recordings of standard-content speech or content-masked recordings).

PARALANGUAGE, EMOTION, AND ATTITUDE

Researchers have long theorized that the verbal content of speech provides "semantic information" whereas the vocal qualities of speech convey primarily emotion (Soskin, 1953). Studies correlating emotional states to voice characteristics have generally consisted of two types: those that have attempted to identify whether or not a speech passage contained emotional content, and those that have involved actor encoding of several distinct emotions followed by a decoding task matching emotion types with vocalizations.

Voice and Emotion

Early studies linking emotional states to vocal characteristics, while suffering from the same methodological limitations as those noted previously in the studies of personality and voice, still were somewhat more successful in demonstrating such a relationship (perhaps because of the greater ease in manipulating and demonstrating a transitory emotional state than a presumably more enduring personality variable). Thompson and Bradway (1950) simulated a therapy interview in which the conversation consisted of numbers spoken with appropriate inflections to communicate feelings. Listeners were subsequently able to match the voice recordings to descriptions by the speakers of the feelings they expressed. Kauffman (1954) examined listeners' ratings of an actor's speech when the actor's emotional expression was either congruent or incongruent with the words. Comparisons between listener ratings of the content-filtered speech recordings were made with written typescripts. When the actor's emotional expression was incongruent with the verbal content, listener ratings were more heterogeneous, presumably reflecting the greater ambiguity of the messages. Black and Dreher (1955) found that judges could identify accurately phrases consisting of five syllables as being spoken with an attitude of certainty or uncertainty. In an interesting study, Starkweather (1955, 1956) had 12 clinical psychologist judges evaluate content-filtered samples of speech produced by Senator Joseph McCarthy and attorney Welch in the famous McCarthy-Army trial. Despite a lack of confidence in their own ratings, there was good interjudge agreement among the raters as to emotional content. Subsequent evaluations of the unfiltered speakers' speech showed general agreement that Welch's voice was more pleasant and appropriate to the verbal content whereas McCarthy's voice lacked variation in emotion. Jurich and Jurich (1974) correlated self-report, observer ratings, and finger sweat-print measures of anxiety with female subjects' nonverbal behavior during an anxiety-arousing interview (i.e., a discussion of sexual attitudes). "Tone of voice" correlated significantly with the finger sweat-print measure ($r = .56$) and observers' "global" rating of anxiety ($r = .67$) but not with subjects' own self-report measure of anxiety. Unfortunately, the authors did not specify which tone qualities were important in contributing to the impression of anxiety. These findings nonetheless appear sufficiently promising to warrant replication.

In none of the above studies was there an attempt to sort out the various vocal characteristics contributing to perceptions of emotional expression. As was mentioned earlier, Dittmann and Wynne (1961) found the classification of vocal aspects of speech into paralinguistic categories of vocal qualifiers and voice qualities, as shown in Table 1-1, to be too unreliable for research purposes, even though nonlinguistic vocal characteristics were more closely related to emotional expressions than the linguistic variables. Friedhoff, Alpert, and Kurtzberg (1962), however, were successful in relating differences in the spoken intensity of words to emotional arousal. Subjects were instructed to respond with the statement "no" to words that were visually presented to them. Subjects tended to deviate upward from their baseline vocal intensity to neutral stimuli when presented with those presumably arousing emotion. However, this finding could be obtained only when a masking noise was introduced so subjects could not perceive their speech and regulate their tone of voice. In a subsequent publication (Alpert, Kurtzberg, and Friedhoff, 1963) these authors reported that the major change in intensity occurred for the low-frequency band of the voice spectrum.

A number of studies have focused on clinical interviews. Starkweather (1967) reported correlations across six interviews between predictions of patients' mood ratings based on voice spectrum analysis and clinically judged mood ratings for depressed patients. The correlations ranged from .81 to .77 for three depressively retarded patients. Starkweather further reported that "the vocal measures of timing, energy, mean pitch, and number of words per interview distinguish depressed from recovered interviews for the retarded patients" (1967, pp. 261–262).

Rubenstein and Cameron (1968) adopted the novel approach of recording portions of therapy interviews in which the therapist felt that nonverbal communication of emotion was particularly evident. The therapist then had the patients subsequently read aloud the written transcriptions of those interview segments. Comparisons of the patients' spoken repetitions of therapist-designated "loaded" and "unloaded" passages on a sonogram (a device for measuring sound frequency, amplitude, and duration) revealed systematic differences between the two communications. Emotionally loaded statements were represented by significantly higher frequency excursions. In this study, changes in frequency were the most sensitive indicators of emotion, whereas changes in amplitude differentiated loaded and unloaded statements for some but not all patients. This finding in particular suggests that the method of masking speech with high frequency filters may eliminate "information" important to nonverbal communication of emotion.

Rice, Abrams, and Saxman (1969) compared psychiatric patients having "flat" affect as their prominent symptom to carefully matched control patients. Recordings were obtained of patients first reading a nonemotional passage and then making up a story in response to a Thematic Apperception Test card. Physiological measures (electromyographic readings of the frontalis muscle, finger blood volume, Galvanic Skin Response, and heart rate) and measures of body movement (obtained from a recording device attached to the chair) were obtained in addition to oscillograph readings of speech. During the "emotional" storytelling procedure, "flat affect" patients showed a decrease in their fundamental frequency-level measures of speech that was paralleled by decreases in body movement and heart rate. Exactly the opposite relationship obtained for control patients when they read emotional passages, whereas no differences were observed among groups for readings of neutral passages. The authors concluded that "the diminished affective and physiological responses of 'flat' affect patients may be 'selective' to emotional stimuli" (1969, pp. 571–572). Finally, Duncan (1966) studied the paralinguistic characteristics of therapy hours judged by the therapist to be either particularly good or poor. Raters analyzed the phonemic clauses of therapists' and patients' speech for variations in energy level and pitch as well as for other characteristics (e.g., dysfluencies). Different types of stress clauses were associated with peak and poor psychotherapy sessions. For example, low energy and low pitch ratings of client speech were reliably related to peak therapy hours, whereas the combination of low energy-normal pitch in therapist phonemic clauses was associated with poor therapy sessions.

Voice and Attitudes

In addition to vocal characteristics of emotion, nonverbal vocal characteristics of attitudes have also been studied. Duncan subsequently conducted several studies examining the subtle cues that experimenters might give subjects in "biasing" their performance on experimental tasks (Duncan, Rosenberg, and Finkelstein, 1969a, 1969b; Duncan and Rosenthal, 1968). The speech of experimenters was analyzed for differences in suprasegmental phoneme variables (stress, pitch, and juncture) and such paralinguistic variables as intensity, drawl-clipping, and vocal segregates. Through a complex scoring analysis it was possible to score experimenters' communications for a positive or negative bias for a person perception task. Experimenters' "differential vocal emphasis" correlated significantly with subjects' subsequent performance ($r = .72$). (Interestingly, deliberate attempts to create biases in experimenters by giving them positive or negative expectancies were not related to subjects' performance; only experimenters' vocal characteristics were influenced.) This relationship was most manifest in subjects who were high in "evaluation apprehension," a characteristic that evidently sensitized them to subtle intonations in experimenters' voices of which they were apparently unaware. These findings were consistent with those of a study by Cameron and Anderson (1968), who manipulated tonal phrasing of poll questions to produce "changes in opinion" of approximately 13%. Most recently, however, Burkhart (1976) reported findings that seriously undermine the apparent significance of the experimenter bias research. In a replication of the earlier research, he found essentially the opposite pattern of results: subjects low in evaluation apprehension showed a bias in their ratings in the direction specified by the experimenters' paralinguistic cues, while those high in evaluation apprehension responded in the opposite fashion. These findings attest to the importance of multiple replications of highly "significant" popular experiments.

Addington (1971) studied voice characteristics enacted by trained speakers in relation to judges' attributions of three dimensions of "source credibility": competence, trustworthiness, and dynamism. Vocal characteristics judged least credible included throaty, "denasal", tense, nasal, monotone, and breathy. Mehrabian and Williams (1969) had subjects transmit messages encoding varying degrees of intended persuasiveness. Two voice characteristics were significantly related to perceived persuasiveness: speech volume ($r = .46$) and vocal activity ($r = .51$). The latter measure was based on a weighted combination of fundamental-frequency measure and intensity range. Packwood (1974) more specifically examined the role that loudness has in relation to verbal persuasiveness. Three independent judges rated for persuasiveness 900 counselor statements and subsequent client responses that were recorded during 35 actual counselor interviews. The 24 highest- and 15 lowest-rated persuasive statements were analyzed by a graphic level recorder. Analysis of the relative sound levels showed that the more persuasive statements were louder than the less persuasive statements. Packwood noted, however, that if an expression is too loud it may be perceived as more hostile than persuasive, so that there are undoubtedly limits to this relationship.

Weitz (1972) examined interracial attitudes, tone of voice, and social behaviors of whites who were led to believe they would be interacting with a black. Voice ratings were obtained from recordings of subjects rehearsing the experimental instructions they were to deliver to their co-subject before and after they received a description of him (as being white or black). Judges rated the voice recordings on the following qualities: "loud-soft, warm-cold, admiring-condescending, pleasant-unpleasant, and personal-businesslike." Subjects' attitudes were measured by conventional paper-and-pencil tasks and by specific behavioral measures. The latter were based on subject choices of experimental task (of varying intimacy), chair placement, whether or not the subject was willing to wait together or apart from the other subject, and the like. For 80 "liberal" white college males, Weitz reported that: "A general pattern of overt friendliness and covert rejection was found" (1972, p. 14). Specifically, friendliness shown in subjects' verbal content was *negatively* related to friendliness of rated voice tone and attitudinal behavior exhibited toward them. In contrast, voice tone and attitudinal behavior were positively related.

Mehrabian (1972) recently proposed a formula for assessing attitudes:

$$[A \text{ total} = 0.07A \text{ verbal} + 0.38A \text{ vocal} + 0.55A \text{ facial.}]$$

He concluded: "When there is inconsistency between verbally and implicitly expressed attitude, the implicit portion will dominate in determining the total message" (p. 108). The results of several of Mehrabian's other studies evaluating various aspects of social behavior and voice characteristics revealed the following positive relationships: affiliative behavior and pleasantness of vocal expressions (Mehrabian, 1971b); ingratiation and pleasantness of vocal expression (Mehrabian and Ksionsky, 1972); and "responsiveness to other" and vocal activity and speech volume (Mehrabian, 1971b; Mehrabian and Ksionsky, 1972).

Encoding of Specific Emotions

A second general area of focus in the research on communication has been the study of specific kinds of emotions as expressed through vocal cues. Dusenbury and Knower (1939) instructed speech students to encode "emotions" by reciting letters of the alphabet. These different alphabet letter recitations were subsequently matched with the correct emotions on a bet-ter-than-chance basis. Knower (1941) repeated this experiment with enco-ders speaking in a whisper to eliminate the fundamental frequency of the voice. Even so, recognition of the emotions was significantly greater than chance. Pollack, Rubenstein, and Horowitz (1960a, 1960b) masked en-actment of emotions in "meaningless content" speech with increasing signal : noise ratios. Under these interference conditions, emotions were still bet-ter recognized than the verbal content. This was true even if the fundamen-tal frequency of voice was eliminated by the sentences being whispered. Fairbanks and his colleagues employed experienced student actors to enact emotions by reading constant-content passages. Portrayals of emotions by some actors were easier to identify than others, and differences in pitch (Fairbanks and Pronovost, 1939) and duration of phrases (Fairbanks and Hoaglin, 1941) were also noted among the various emotions. Kramer (1963), however, noted that the task of expressing the same passage in different emotional styles may have produced exaggerations in pitch and duration not ordinarily found in natural emotional expressions.

Perhaps the most prolific researcher on emotional components of vocal expressions has been Davitz. Davitz and Davitz (1959) used speakers recit-ing 10 different letters each in a manner to represent a different emotion. In addition to demonstrating that judges could match a list of emotions to the different voice recordings, they noted wide individual differences in en-actment ability of speakers (ranging from 23 to 50 percent accuracy in communication) and in decoding ability of listeners (ranging from 20 to 50 percent). Some emotions were easier to identify than others: for example, expressions of anger, nervousness, sadness, and happiness were easiest to judge, whereas fear, love, and surprise were among those emotions hardest to identify. In a subsequent study, Davitz (1964) examined auditory corre-lates of speech and dimensions of emotional meaning of 14 emotions ex-pressed in constant-content speech. The 14 feelings expressed included ad-miration, affection, amusement, anger, boredom, cheerfulness, despair, disgust, dislike, fear, impatience, joy, satisfaction, and surprise. Meanings of emotions were evaluated on Osgood's Semantic Differential Scale mea-suring valence, strength, and activity factors. These were related to judges' ratings of voice characteristics of loudness, pitch, timbre, and rate of speech. The pattern of vocal characteristics across emotional expressions did not change as a function of sex. Mean rank orderings of the emotions by dimensions were generally as might be expected. For example, joy and affection were rated most positive in valence whereas anger was rated the least. The primary finding of his study was that the auditory vocal cues (loudness, etc.) were consistently related positively to the dimensions of activity but not to the dimensions of strength or valence.

Davitz (1964) also studied personality, perceptual, and cognitive corre-

lates of sensitivity to vocal emotional communications. None of the personality correlates was related to subjects' emotional sensitivity (i.e., their accuracy in identifying emotional expressions of standard-content speech). Perceptual and cognitive correlates included tests of auditory discrimination
(the Seashore Measures of Musical Talents test, measuring auditory discrimination of pitch, loudness, timbre, and tune), abstract symbolic ability
(Raven Progressive matrices), verbal intelligence (a vocabulary test), and
knowledge of vocal characteristics. This last test required subjects to describe what a voice sounds like when expressing different emotions. A multiple correlation coefficient relating these variables to the criterion of emotional sensitivity was highly significant ($r = .60$). The following beta
weights were obtained for each of the predictor variables: verbal intelligence, .19; abstraction ability, .13; auditory ability, .18; knowledge, .35.
The test of word knowledge itself correlated .50 with emotional sensitivity
and was the best predictor. This should not be surprising, since the test
directly measured for knowledge thought to be important for the decoding
task of emotional sensitivity.

Though Davitz and his colleagues employed methods that were subsequently criticized on methodological grounds (e.g., enacted expressions of
emotions using meaningless content or standard-content speech may confound speakers' conceptions of vocal stereotypes of emotion with true expression), their work is still the most systematic to date, and his book
should be read carefully by anyone intending to do research in this area.
Other findings reported in his book include relationships between sensitivity to vocal expressions of emotions and sensitivity to other communication
modes as music and art (Beldoch, 1964), differences in emotional sensitivity
among different patient groups (e.g., psychotics vs. nonpsychotics), and
ability to express emotions vocally (Levy, 1964).

Costanzo, Markel, and Costanzo (1969) had students read five different
paragraphs (indicating anger, indifference, contempt, love, and grief) in
which the same "test" passage was included. Speakers were only asked to
"assume the role of an actor" in reading the paragraphs, a procedural variation of being directly asked to simulate an emotion artificially by reading a
neutral passage. Judges subsequently rated the test passage for peak tempo,
pitch, and loudness according to the procedure (described earlier) developed by Markel (1965). Voices rated highest on peak-pitch were judged as
portraying love and grief, while peak loudness was associated with anger
and contempt and peak tempo with ratings of indifference. The authors
hypothesized that these three voice orientations might reflect the following
"stable modes of interpersonal orientation": "moving towards others"
(peak pitch), "moving against others" (peak loudness), and "moving away
from others" (peak tempo).

Thus far in the research reported, studies on the identification of emotions from voice have employed the technique of meaningless-content or standard-content passages. The disadvantages with this technique have been noted earlier. In contrast, Scherer, Koivumaki, and Rosenthal (1972) employed high-frequency filtering and randomized splicing techniques to eliminate listener perception of the spoken content of passages (from *Death of a Salesman*) chosen to depict expressions of anger, grief, sadness, happiness, and matter-of-factness. Listeners rated the spoken passages on a semantic differential scale measuring the dimensions of activity, evaluation, and potency. Unfortunately, these listener ratings were not correlated with the emotional content of the different passages because the authors did not feel that the judges' ratings of the emotional value of each passage were sufficient criteria. However, they did find that the random-spliced voice recordings were more reliably rated by listeners on the semantic differential scale than were content-filtered recordings. They interpreted the overall findings to "reaffirm the earlier assertion . . . that the lower frequencies of the voice spectrum are sufficient to communicate the affective state of the speaker" (1972, p. 282). There also appeared to be a systematic trend for random-spliced voice recordings to be rated more positively than content-filtered ones. In this study the authors hoped to demonstrate a relationship between the following voice characteristics and semantic differential dimensions: evaluation and pitch, activity versus pitch and amplitude variation, and potency and amplitude. Support was found for this last hypothesized relationship.

In another study, Scherer (1974) employed a Moog synthesizer to vary pitch level and variation, amplitude level and variation, tempo, and signal duration in a factorial design. Listener subjects then rated the artificially created sounds on dimension scales of pleasantness, evaluation, activity, and potency. In addition, they were asked to judge whether the sound resembled any of the emotions of interest, sadness, fear, happiness, disgust, anger, surprise, elation, and boredom. Scherer found support for the hypothesized relationships between auditory variables and the activity, potency, and evaluative dimensions. He also reported that there was above-chance agreement among raters in matching sound combinations to emotional labels. Scherer concluded on this exciting note: "Judging from recent evidence . . . supporting Darwin's theory of innate mechanisms in emotional expression, . . . one may be justified in speculating about the existence of unlearned neural programs for the vocal expression and recognition of emotion (1974, p. 108). The precise control that this method allows in combining acoustic cues suggests it as a promising device for future research. In particular, artificial synthesis of sounds offers a methodology that seems to avoid entirely the problem of decoding which voice cues are segmental, or suprasegmental, paralinguistic, or linguistic variables.

Relationship of Voice to Behavior

Thus far we have noted studies concerned primarily with demonstrating that vocal characteristics of speech do communicate emotional states to listeners. Before turning to the next section, we report on two studies investigating some practical aspects of this relationship. Hornstein (1967) recruited 62 pairs of female freshman college roommates at the beginning of the academic year before they had become well acquainted. Each was asked to try to communicate eight emotions to the other via meaningless content (alphabet letters); the other, in turn, was to write down which emotion she thought was being expressed. This procedure permitted measurement of each subject's "emotional sensitivity" to her roommate's communication. Measurements of emotional sensitivity were obtained at the beginning and at the end of 3 months. Also at that time, compatibility ratings were obtained, based upon roommates' responses to a questionnaire indicating liking and the degree to which they wanted to engage in various activities with their roommate. Hornstein reported that, as a group, roommates became more sensitive to each other's communications over time. Compatibility between roommates *after 3 months* was not related to the initial measurement of their emotional sensitivity to each other but rather to their emotional sensitivity ratings after 3 months. Further, the more compatible roommates showed a greater positive change than the less compatible pairs. An additional measure of general sensitivity to emotional expression failed to predict compatibility between roommates. Analysis of error patterns of some incompatible roommates suggested that they were differentially sensitive to negative emotional communications. The reader should not conclude, however, that emotional sensitivity facilitated roommate compatibility. Rather, compatibility probably facilitated or was covariant with emotional sensitivity.

Another study (Milmoe, Rosenthal, Blane, Chafetz, and Wolf, 1967) related physicians' attitudes and their experience on an alcoholic service in diagnosing and referring patients. What was novel about the experiment was that the attitudes were elicited in an open-ended interview approximately one year *after* the alcoholic patient program. Interview variables based on male and female judges' ratings of normal speech, content only, and content-filtered speech were related to the proportion of patients seen by the physician who subsequently followed the referral recommendation for treatment. Interview variables rated were anger, sympathy, anxiety, and matter-of-factness. Because of the small samples involved, very high correlations were required for significance. Despite modest reliabilities in ratings within sex and between sex, "suggestive" ($p \leq .10$) correlations were found between referral effectiveness and normal speech ratings of anxiety ($r =$

.62) and tone-only ratings of anger ($r = -.65$). While the exact meaning of these correlations can only be speculated upon, it is particularly notable that the content-only ratings yielded no suggestive findings.

In a subsequent "pilot" study, Milmoe, Novey, Kagan, and Rosenthal (1968) interviewed mothers concerning their children after a series of mother-child interactions had been observed and rated for various child behaviors. As in the previous study, ratings were made of normal speech, content only, and content-filtered speech. Despite very small samples, a large number of significant relationships emerged between filtered and unfiltered voice ratings, the former in some cases being more "postdictive." For example, ratings of anxiety and anger in mothers' voices were associated with signs of irritability and insecurity in children. Ratings of warmth and pleasantness of voice, in filtered voice conditions only, were related to indexes of child's attention to a human voice at 13 months.

Summary

Summarizing briefly, studies relating vocal phenomena to emotional-attitudinal states have been more consistently successful than those focusing on personality. This should not be surprising, given the obvious effect that physiological (i.e., emotional) arousal can have on the organs of speech. From this perspective it is understandable that many "personality trait" factors will not be highly related to paralinguistic variables unless they are predictably related to emotional behaviors in some way. The study by Friedman, Brown, and Rosenman (1969) that evaluated certain affectively toned behaviors as manifestations of personality trait ("Type A" personality) is a good example of how emotional arousal may be an intervening variable relating paralinguistic phenomena to personality. What is required, however, are more sophisticated experimental manipulations that can be predicted to evoke emotion in one personality type but not another.

DISTURBANCES IN SPEECH

Mahl (1956) was perhaps the first researcher to study systematically this content-free measure of speech in relation to his interest in indices of anxiety in psychotherapy interviews. He concluded:

In the therapeutic interchange, the intensity of the patient's anxiety may fluctuate markedly during the course of a single interview. Continuous change must also be anticipated in most of the variables with which one would wish to correlate patient anxiety, such as physiological measures, various categories of therapist behavior, patient-content categories, or other linguistic measures. As a result, procedures giving only single measures of anxiety for large segments of interviews or for entire sessions taken as the units might obscure more precise covariations that inevitably would be of interest. It seems that the most generally useful procedure would involve the measurement of some relatively continuous aspect of the patient's behavior. (p. 1)

Mahl hypothesized that "the most valid linguistic measures of anxiety will be those based on the behavioral or 'expressive' aspects of speech rather than those based on manifest verbal content analysis" (1956, p. 1). He proposed as a unit of analysis the "speech disturbance ratio," which he defined as the number of speech disturbances divided by the total number of spoken words. Disturbance categories, as shown in Table 2-2, included the following: "ah" sounds, sentence corrections (construed as an interruption in the word-to-word sequence by a listener), sentence incompletions, repetitions, stutters, intruding, incoherent sounds, tongue slips, and omissions. Reliability coefficients for trained judges using written transcripts were obtained, the mean reliability coefficient being .94.[1] Mahl subsequently created two categories of speech disturbance, the "ah" and "non-ah" ratios (Mahl, 1959b). The latter measure consisted of the sum of all speech disturbance categories minus "ahs" divided by the total number of words. As subsequent research has shown, the "ah" ratio seems to serve a different function than the "non-ah" ratio. Though Mahl's measures have been by far the most popular, others have been proposed (Boomer, 1963; Dibner,

Table 2-2.   Speech Disturbance Categories (After Mahl, 1956)

Category	Definition
Sentence correction	Correction in form or content perceived by listener as interruption or word sequences
Sentence incompletion	Interrupted expression with communication continuing without correction
Stutter	Stutter
Intruding incoherent sound	Unrecognizable sound that does not alter the form of the expression
Tongue slip	Neologisms, transposition of words from correct sequences, substitution of unintended for intended word
Omission	Words or parts of words omitted; generally terminal syllables of words
Filled pauses, repetition	Unnecessary serial repetition of one or more words
Ah	Definite occurrence of "ah" sound

1956; Krause and Pilisuk, 1961). In particular, the category "filled pause" (usually consisting of "ahs" or repetitions) has been considered a dysfluency. We consider this phenomenon further in our section on silence, which includes hesitations and pauses, both filled and unfilled.

In his 1956 study, Mahl employed a content analysis of two patients' speech to determine defensive and conflicted phases of the psychotherapy interviews (the former postulated as being less anxiety arousing) and found corresponding differences in the speech disturbance ratios. His procedure in this experiment required an intimate understanding of the patient's personal dynamics. Panek and Martin (1959) examined two of Mahl's speech disturbance categories, "ahs" and repetitions, in relation to fluctuations in patients' Galvanic Skin Response (GSR) readings. Short-term fluctuations in patients' GSRs were significantly associated with their speech disturbances, consistent with Mahl's hypothesis relating anxiety to speech disturbances. Interestingly, analysis of 5-minute segments of high and low GSR did not show significant association with speech disturbance measures, suggesting that the latter reflect more transient fluctuations in arousal. Boomer (1963) examined Mahl's "non-ah" disturbance ratio (i.e., the quotient of all speech disturbances except "ahs" over the total number of words) in relation to "nonpurposive body movements." The latter constituted his observable index of anxiety. Both measures were taken separately from a series of interviews of a single patient. Boomer obtained a significant correlation of .42 between the two measures, both of which were assumed to be reflective of the patient's anxiety.

Krause and Pilisuk (1961) studied "speech disruption" measures of Mahl (1956) and Dibner (1956) in an experiment in which subjects were exposed to either neutral or stressful stimuli. Anxiety was thus experimentally manipulated. Subjects' reports of their subjective experiences were evaluated for speech disruptions. The speech disturbance category "intrusive sounds," in particular laughs and sighs, was the most accurate predictor of stressful interviews. One problem in the study was the apparent differential effectiveness of stress stimuli with different subjects which may have made the manipulations less effective. It is also interesting to note that these intrusive sounds seem to correspond to Trager's paralinguistic "vocal characterizers."

Kasl and Mahl (1965) manipulated anxiety experimentally in an interview by introducing various anxiety-arousing topics based on their knowledge of the subject obtained from a neutral interview and the subject's MMPI profile. Analysis of tape recordings of the interviews for various speech disturbance measures showed highly significant increases in all but the "ah" speech disturbance category during the anxiety-arousing interview. Palmar sweat measures showed a corresponding increase in the anxiety interview. The "ah" measure was not sensitive to the anxiety manipulation per se, but there was a marked increase in "ahs" for subjects who were shifted from an experimenter-present situation to an experimenter-absent (communicating from behind a one-way mirror) interview, whereas the other speech disturbance measures were not so affected. The authors speculated that the lack of visual feedback may have caused subjects to employ pauses (filled with "ahs") more. Kasl and Mahl also examined subjects' speech disturbance profiles (based upon the pattern of relative frequencies of the different types of disturbances), which are generally stable across situations. Those who showed "unstable profiles" over the two interviews had higher scores on their Manifest Anxiety scores. Interestingly, there was a highly significant negative relationship between palmar sweat and profile instability (biserial correlation $= -.68, p < .0001$). That is, those with stable profiles showed the most labile palmar sweat indexes. The authors concluded: "This relationship suggests that palmar sweat and disruption of fluent speech may be alternate ways in which each subject reacted to anxiety fluctuations which occurred during the experiment" (1965, p. 443). Kasl and Mahl also noted that "ahs" seem to be differently related to speech than the other speech disturbance measures, a finding that prompted them to employ separate "ah" and "non-ah" ratios in their analysis. In a study mentioned earlier investigating interview anxiety and nonverbal behavior, Jurich and Jurich (1974) found articulation errors (similar to the speech disturbance measure) correlated significantly ($r = .37, p < .05$) with sweatprint measures of anxiety, despite low observer reliability ($r = .53$) in rating this type of nonverbal behavior.

Pope, Siegman, and Blass (1970) examined "ah" and "non-ah" speech disturbance ratios in two interviews in which the topic was held constant. In the second interview, however, anxiety was aroused in subjects by their being given information that there was a "psychological disturbance" in their families. Whereas a control group receiving no anxiety induction showed a significant decrease in "non-ah" ratios (reflecting an adaptation to the experiment), the anxiety group subjects showed no such decrease, which the authors interpreted to be due to the effect of anxiety. A predicted significant increase in rate of speech was noted. As in the study by Kasl and Mahl, the "ah ratio" was not significantly affected by the anxiety induction and thus seemed functionally independent of the "non-ah" ratio. These findings were also consistent with other studies by the authors relating anxiety to an increase in verbal productivity and speech disruptions (Pope, Blass, Siegman, and Raher, 1970; Siegman and Pope, 1965a). Finally, Siegman and Pope (1972) compared segments of interviews of psychiatric patients on days judged anxious and nonanxious by nurses. As expected, "non-ah" speech disturbances were significantly more frequent on high-anxious days. Table 2-3 summarizes the results of these studies on anxiety and speech disturbances.

Siegman and Pope (1972) also reported a series of experiments investigating the relationship of ambiguity as well as anxiety to interviewee behavior. The authors noted that in previous studies (Brenner, Feldstein, and Jaffee, 1965; Maclay and Osgood, 1959; Pope and Siegman, 1962) ambiguous interviewer probes or more difficult English passages, both of which create "verbal uncertainty," tended to be associated with increased verbal dysfluencies. For example, Brenner, Feldstein, and Jaffee (1965) obtained a curvilinear relationship between subjects' speech disruptions and the degree of "semantic uncertainty" of passages they were given to read. To Siegman and Pope, then, an important question was how interview ambiguity related to disturbances in speech as reflected in Mahl's "non-ah" speech disturbance ratios. A variety of manipulations was employed in the experiments by asking subjects highly specific or nonspecific questions, the latter presumably being more ambiguous. In addition, in several experiments the "relationship" was made more "ambiguous" by separating interviewer and interviewee with a screen or by having the female interviewees sit facing away from the interviewer so that they could not see him. In all cases there was no relationship between "non-ah" speech disturbance ratios and the degree (high-low) of ambiguity, though there were significant relationships between interview ambiguity and other variables (to be mentioned elsewhere). In several of these studies, the authors also manipulated anxiety by asking questions dealing with personal information as well as impersonal matters. In those instances, there was a significant increase in subjects' speech disturbance ratios, which were presumably associated with an increase in their anxiety. However, no relationship was noted between interviewees' Manifest Anxiety Scale scores and their speech disturbance ratios.

Siegman and Pope further varied interviewer attractiveness and status by having a warm-cold or high-low status interviewer interact with subjects. For highly ambiguous questions, interviewees were more dysfluent when talking to the cold versus the warm interviewer; interviewees showed an increase in dysfluencies when discussing family relations with low status interviewers but not with those with high status. These studies thus systematically documented that ambiguity in an interview per se is not associated with "non-ah" speech disturbances but that anxiety-arousing questions are. The relationship between interviewer qualities (warm-cold vs. high-low status) and interviewee verbal behavior was less clear but not inconsistent with previous findings. Without detracting from the value of these studies, it would have been interesting if additional measures of anxiety (i.e., interviewee self-report or physiological recordings) had been obtained to de-

Table 2-3.   Summary of Anxiety—Speech Disturbance Research

Study	*Procedure*	*Findings*
Mahl (1956)	Compared defensive versus conflicted speech of patients	Speech disturbance ("ahs" and "non-ahs") more frequent with conflicted (anxiety-arousing) speech segments
Panek and Martin (1959)	Compared patients' GSR fluctuations with speech disturbances	Speech disturbances ("ahs" and repetitions) were associated with increased GSR fluctuations
Boomer (1963)	Nonpurposive body movements employed as index of anxiety	"Non-ah" ratio correlated .42 with body movement measure
Krause and Pilisuk (1961)	Subjects described their probable reaction to stressful and nonstressful situations	Intrusive sounds more frequent during stressful interviews
Kasl and Mahl (1965)	Discussion of stressful topics	Increase in "non-ah" ratio during discussion of anxiety-arousing topics
Seigman and Pope (1965a)	Low and high anxiety-arousing topics discussed	"Non-ah" speech disturbances increased with anxiety-arousing topics
Siegman, Pope, and Blass (1970)	Discussion of anxious and nonanxious interview topics	"Non-ah" ratio failed to decrease during anxiety-arousing interview compared to neutral interview
Pope, Blass, Siegman, and Raher (1970)	Examined high and low anxiety monologues of patients	High-anxiety monologues had more "non-ah" disturbances
Siegman and Pope (1972)	Interview behavior of psychiatric patients on anxious and nonanxious days	Patients evidenced more "non-ah" speech disturbances on nonanxious days

termine whether the ambiguity manipulations were, in fact, not as anxiety-arousing as might be supposed.

The studies just reported generally show a clear relationship between anxiety and "non-ah" speech disturbances. It is interesting to note that in studies where anxiety presumably was evoked in subjects there was an associated increase in speech errors. For example, in a series of studies reported by Mehrabian (1971a), interviewees, when experimentally manipulated into being deceitful, tended to make more speech errors. In a study that looked at the *effect* of dysfluencies on listeners, McCroskey and Mehrley (1969) demonstrated that speech dysfluencies occuring in well organized messages significantly limited listener attitude change to a level comparable to that attained by subjects listening to poorly organized messages. In addition, the credibility of the speakers delivering the message was significantly lowered by dysfluencies. This was apparently a more important factor than whether or not the message was well organized. Finally, in an important study, Beekman (1975) studied sex differences in two-person interaction situations. Forty-four male and forty-four female graduate students engaged in 7-minute conversations with partners of the same and the opposite sex. The videotape of the final 5 minutes of each conversation was analyzed by a coder for a large number of nonverbal behaviors (e.g., kinesics, gaze, paralinguistic variables). Beekman found that males and females differed in their nonverbal behaviors although the sex of the subject's partner generally had no significant effect. One of Beekman's findings was an interesting difference for males and females in filled pauses in dyadic conversations. Specifically, male subjects emitted many more "ahs," "ums," "ers," and so forth while engaged in interaction with the same or the opposite sex; the rate of filled pauses correlated significantly with males' self-descriptions on the Gough Adjective Checklist for counseling readiness (.46), abasement (.31), heterosexuality ($-.45$), and dominance ($-.34$), and with the Thorndike Dimensions of Temperament Scale measures of sociability and ascendence. Interestingly, no such relationships were found for females. Beekman speculated that because the traditional male role requirement is to be assertive and dominant, the interaction may have been more stressful for males, especially for those naturally less dominant.

TEMPORAL CHARACTERISTICS OF SPEECH

It is easily recognized that there are very different rates (timing) of speech among people or even within a given individual at different times (depending on motivational state) and under different circumstances. In fact, individuals who are mismatched in speech rates may have a difficult time communicating with each other and may even have a tendency not to like each other. An oft-quoted example of the importance of timing in speech is that actors may take a short play, play it first as a tragedy and then, using the same words, play it as a comedy. Here the language is seen as unimportant, and the timing is the factor that makes the difference in its effect on the audience (Chapple and Arensberg, 1940, p. 33).

Matarazzo and Wiens and their colleagues for many years conducted empirical research concerned with the reliability and validity of inferences based on temporal dimensions of speech. Specifically, they studied the frequency and duration of single units of speech and silence in dyadic interaction. Three major speech variables were studied in many different interview situations: duration of utterance (DOU), reaction time latency (RTL), and percentage of interruptions (INT). The mean speech duration (DOU) is defined as the total time that the interviewee (or interviewer) speaks divided by his total number of speech units. The mean speech latency (RTL) is defined as the total latency time (the period of silence separating two different speech units) divided by the number of units of interviewee (or interviewer) latency. The percentage of interruptions (INT) is defined as the total number of times the interviewee (or interviewer) speaks divided into the number of these same speech units that were interruptions of his partner. Other temporal speech measures were also defined (e.g., Initiative Time Latencies, Percentage Talk Time, etc.), but are not reviewed here. Detailed definitions of all of these temporal speech measures are presented in Matarazzo and Wiens (1972).

Because the focus in this research was on temporal speech measures, the interviewers were asked to standardize some aspects of their speech and interview style to allow comparison across subjects and studies. Interviewers were asked to speak in utterances of 5 seconds' duration, to respond to the interviewees with less than 1-second response latencies, and not to interrupt the interviewee. The interviewer was also asked to use open-ended questions and a nondirective interviewing style, that is, to follow the discussion topics as the interviewee introduces them. In clinical research, however, the general topic areas (e.g., "family . . . occupation . . . education") were constant across interviews. Observers who watched both these experimental interviews and real-life interviews that form the basis for clinical decisions were unable to discern the particular interviewer behaviors that have been standardized.

During the initial years, this research (summarized in Saslow and Matarazzo, 1959) centered on assessing the reliability and stability of interviewee speech patterns defined in this way. Interviewees were re-interviewed by the same and different interviewers at time intervals of 5 minutes, 1 week, 5 weeks, and 8 months. These studies showed that the temporal verbal interaction measures employed reflected stable and invariant behavior characteristics under the real-life, minimally standardized interview conditions in which these subjects were studied. It was also apparent that there were wide individual differences in subjects' speech, silence, and interruption characteristics.

Modifiability of Temporal Speech Characteristics

In follow-up studies it was revealed that, despite this high reliability over time, if the interviewer systematically changed his own speech characteristics this would produce striking corresponding changes in the speech behavior of the interviewees. These planned interviewer changes included increases and decreases in his average DOUs, increases and decreases in his RTLs, and increases and decreases in his speech interruptions.

In one series of experiments (Matarazzo, Weitman, Saslow, and Wiens, 1961) it was found that, by doubling or halving the duration of each of his own single speech units (from a mean of 5.3, 9.9, and 6.1 seconds, respectively, in each of the three 15-minute periods of a 45-minute interview), the interviewer was able to influence the mean DOU of interviewees in the three comparable periods of the interview (24.3, 46.9, and 26.6 seconds, respectively; $p < .01$). The positive results of this study were cross-validated in two follow-up experiments in which the interviewer unobtrusively controlled his single speech-unit durations to approximately 10-5-10 seconds and 5-15-5 second durations in the three parts of his planned interview.

Planned changes in the interviewer's own RTL, utilizing preplanned interviewer RTLs of 1-1-1-, 1-5-1, 5-1-5, 1-10-1, and 1-15-1 seconds in separate experiments (Matarazzo and Wiens, 1967), also produced the predicted increases and decreases in the corresponding RTLs of the interviewee. The frequency of an interviewer's interruption of the interviewee likewise revealed that, with surprising regularity, the interviewee's interruption rate was covariant with that of the interviewer (Wiens, Saslow, and Matarazzo, 1966).

Other speech modifiability studies employed head-nodding (Matarazzo, Saslow, Wiens, Weitman, and Allen, 1964) and saying "mm-hmm" (Matarazzo, Wiens, Saslow, Allen, and Weitman, 1964) during the experimental periods of a standardized interview, and demonstrated that these are powerful tactics which can increase interviewee DOUs. In another study (Allen, Wiens, Weitman, and Saslow, 1965), an experimentally induced set, in which an interviewee was led to believe that he would talk to either a "cold" or "warm" interviewer, was found to influence markedly the interviewee's RTL (i.e., a longer RTL with the "cold" set).

Other studies have suggested that such interviewer-control effects may not be limited to face-to-face interviews. Matarazzo, Wiens, Saslow, Dunham, and Voas (1964) demonstrated that the DOUs of an orbiting astronaut correlated with changes in the DOUs of ground communicators. Ray and Webb (1966) showed that how much or how little President Kennedy talked in response to a reporter's questions in his 1961–1963 series of press conferences correlated with the length of questions posed by the reporter. Clearly, such effects are out of the realm of conscious awareness.

In another publication, Matarazzo, Wiens, Matarazzo, and Saslow (1968) reported the temporal verbal interaction patterns of three psychotherapists and seven patients (for a total of seven patient-therapist pairs) over an extended series of interviews. These interviews were entirely unstructured and the interviewers preplanned neither the content of their comments nor their temporal characteristics. The results of this research revealed a synchrony, or tracking, over the sessions in the speech behavior of the two speakers. That is, each person's RTLs showed not only sizeable differences from one session to the next but also a remarkable correlation with increases and decreases in the RTL of his/her interview partner. Frequency of interrupting behavior likewise showed such synchrony across the numerous psychotherapy sessions of the therapist-patient pairs. However, there was a lack of synchrony over therapy sessions between the mean duration of utterance of the two members of the therapy dyad. In fact, if anything, there tended to be negative correlations. The authors suggested that this lack of synchrony for DOU may have been a function of the "therapeutic set" of their therapists—that is, this therapeutic set might have led them, in the free clinical situation, to talk more (thus hoping to stimulate the patient in those therapy sessions when their patient was talking little), and conversely, to talk less in those therapy sessions when the patient was talking in longer average DOUs.

Individual Differences Among Groups

One of the early questions in this research program was whether the highly reliable average DOUs for each interviewee could be useful for differential diagnosis. This question was examined in a study (Matarazzo, Wiens, and Saslow, 1965) of the interviewee speech behaviors of five different groups of interviewees who were ordered along a gross mental health continuum: chronic psychotic state hospital patients, neurotic and acute psychotic inpatients and outpatients in a general hospital, outpatient clinic neurotics, and two groups of normals (applicants for sales positions in two large department stores in different cities). The median value for DOUs increased steadily from the presumably sickest group (chronic state hospital patients) to the acute psychotic and neurotic inpatient group, the outpatient neurotics, and finally the presumably healthiest two normal groups. Although the variability in each group was too large to allow accurate individual diagnosis by DOU alone, the results do seem to offer encouragement to investigators who wish to develop nonverbal temporal speech characteristics as indices to aid in differential diagnosis.

Wiens (1976) followed up this interest in individual diagnosis and assessment of personality characteristics with a discussion of the interview as an assessment procedure. Temporal speech characteristics and various other nonverbal communication signals were reviewed for their potential usefulness in behavioral assessment. A central underlying assumption in this publication was that both participants share actively in the process of interviewing and are influenced by each other, the end product of the interview being a result of this interaction (mutual feedback).

In another study, Wiens, Matarazzo, Saslow, Thompson, and Matarazzo (1965) interviewed groups of staff nurses, head nurses, and supervising nurses. In these interviews the nurses were asked to describe nursing activities on a typical working day. Again, the interviewer was asked to make his comments nonchallenging, open-ended, and limited to the interviewee's past comments or to some new general topic that followed naturally from her past comments. The supervising and head nurses did not differ significantly from each other in their temporal speech characteristics. The staff nurses, however, differed significantly from both these groups. They interrupted the interviewer fewer times, spoke in shorter DOUs, and used less of the total interview time for their own speech. This research did not answer the questions whether the differentiating temporal interaction characteristics were inherent in the individual nurses and had led to some of them being appointed to administrative positions and others not, or whether the appointment to an administrative position stimulated the development of the verbal interaction patterns that characterized the supervising and head nurses. In a second study with nurses, Molde and Wiens (1967) investigated the temporal speech characteristics of two groups of nurses (psychiatric and surgical) who were assumed to be engaged in widely different work settings. As was predicted, the psychiatric nurses had a greater verbal output in the standardized interview than did the surgical nurses. The latter were found to interrupt the interviewer more frequently and to exhibit a shorter RTL in responding to the interviewer's comments than did their psychiatric counterparts. Occupational demands on the nurses' verbal behavior may help to account for these differences, although it is not clear what interrelationships exist between innate or idiosyncratic factors and environmental influences on speech behavior, or how they interact.

Surprisingly, little direct attention has been paid to sex differences. In the study by Beekman (1975) cited earlier (see p. 46) a number of sex differences emerged in temporal speech behaviors. Specifically, males engaged in longer periods of talk and longer utterances during the 7-minute conversations than females. This was especially true for male-male dyads, who because of their longer utterances had fewer speaking turns than any other type of dyad (i.e., male-female, female-female). In addition, Beekman found that the duration of utterances for males correlated positively with subject self-descriptions on the Gough Adjective Checklist for autonomy and aggression, and negatively with nurturance and affiliation. For women, duration of talking turns was positively related to self-ratings of aggressiveness. These findings appear to reflect the traditional male interpersonal style oriented towards dominance and self-assertion as opposed to the more affiliative orientation of females.

Matarazzo, Wiens, and Saslow (1966) explored the effects of training in psychotherapy skills on the actual performance of student interviewers in an interview-therapy setting. They observed a 100% increase in the RTLs of student interviewers between a "naive" first series of interviews and a second series given after they had received 8 weeks of intensive instruction in psychotherapy skills. Inasmuch as this change was accompanied by a gross drop in the mean percentage interruption units by the student interviewers, it seems reasonable to conclude that their interviewing training dramatically affected the temporal interaction characteristics of their speech.

VERBAL PRODUCTIVITY

Various indices have been employed to measure the amount of speech a person produces as an indicator of variations in his psychological state. Anxiety has been perhaps the single variable most frequently related to verbal productivity. Fortunately, a recent review by Murray (1971) covered a considerable amount of literature in relating various measures of speech productivity to anxiety. Murray described verbal productivity as being most commonly measured by verbal quantity and speech rate (silence, a negative correlate of verbal productivity, is considered in a subsequent section, as are other findings relating verbal productivity to additional psychological variables.)

Measures of Verbal Productivity

The most commonly used measures of verbal quantity include the time spent talking, number of words, number of interactions, number of clause units, and duration (total time talking divided by the number of interactions). Matarazzo, Holman, and Wiens (1967) presented evidence that time spent talking, number of clause units, and number of words were very highly correlated. In contrast, the numbers of interactions and clause units were significantly negatively correlated and the number of clause units was only moderately correlated with speech duration of utterance. Speech rate has typically been measured as the number of words divided by period of time, which is positively related to verbal quantity and both are negatively related to pauses.

In actuality, there are other measures of speech rate possible. Webb (1969) described two types of speech rate measures: phonation rate, the number of syllables (or words) of an utterance divided by the phonation time used to speak that utterance; and verbal rate, the number of syllables (or words) per unit time in a complete utterance. The latter corresponds to the most typical measures of speech rate employed in research, but differs from the former in the important respect that it includes pauses between words as well as phonation times. This phonation rate appears similar to the "articulation rate" measure employed by Siegman and Pope (1972) with the exception that for the articulation rate measure silent pauses of only 2 seconds or more are subtracted from the total response time. Differences have been noted in the research literature between the two measures (e.g., Webb, 1969), but because of the ease of measuring verbal rate and the infrequent use of other rate measures in studies of interest to us, we do not expound further on this distinction. Since the main measures of verbal productivity (in relation to speaker anxiety) have been based on verbal quantity measures of time of talking, number of words, and speaking rate, we do not separately report which of the indices were used since they were all reasonably correlated.

Anxiety

Anxiety has been related to verbal productivity through experimental manipulations of situational anxiety and by measurement of either test-described personal dispositions for anxiety or concurrent signs of anxiety. In his review, Murray (1971) classified a number of types of experimental manipulations employed to create situational anxiety. For example, experimenters evaluated speakers' verbal productivity as a function of public speaking situations involving positive or negative audience approval (Cervin, 1956; Miller, 1964; Miller, Zavos, Vlandis, and Rosenbaum, 1961; Vlandis, 1964), differences in the size of the audience (Levin, Baldwin, Gallwey, and Paivio, 1960), individual differences in fear of speaking before others (Geer, 1966), and overt versus covert recordings of speech (Sauer and Marcuse, 1957). Stressful topics were employed to create anxiety (Kanfer, 1959, 1960; Siegman and Pope, 1965a, 1966; Pope and Siegman, 1967). Manipulation of warm or cold interviewer attitudes (Pope and Siegman, 1968; Reece, 1964; Reece and Whitman, 1962) was another method of anxiety induction; others included inducing stimulus deprivation with social isolation (Oyamada, 1966; Suedfeld, Vernon, Stubbs, and Karlins, 1965), use of electric shock (Kanfer, 1958a, 1958b), or naturalistic observation of individuals under stress such as just before a parachute jump (Fenz and Epstein, 1962). Dispositional anxiety was studied through the use of paper-and-pencil tests, the most commonly employed one being the Taylor Manifest Anxiety Scale (Benton, Hartman, and Sarason, 1955; Cervin, 1956; Eisenman, 1966; Kanfer, 1960; Matarazzo, Matarazzo, Saslow, and Phillips, 1958; Preston and Gardner, 1967; Sauer and Marcuse, 1957; Siegman and Pope, 1965b). Studies utilizing concurrent signs of anxiety have employed physiological measures (pupil dilation: Bernick and Oberlander, 1968; GSR: Pope and Siegman, 1964; blood pressure: Innes, Miller, and Valentine, 1959; heart rate: Kanfer, 1958a; number of eyeblinks: Kanfer, 1960), and "non-ah" speech disturbance ratios (Krause, 1961; Mahl, 1959b; Pope and Siegman, 1962, 1964, 1966, 1968; Siegman and Pope, 1965a). In particular, intercorrelations between verbal quantity and speech disturbance measures ranged from .50 to .24; verbal rate was measured in only two instances (Krause, 1961; Mahl, 1959b), where the correlations were .35 and .32 respectively. The study by Jurich and Jurich (1974), which provides a measure of situation-specific (interview) anxiety, showed significant correlations between speech rate and finger sweat-print (.39) and speech rate and observers' "global" ratings of anxiety (.64).

Without further going into detail into Murray's review (1971), it is possible to note his conclusion based on the pattern of findings:

There is a strong tendency for verbal quantity to be positively related to dispositional and concurrent anxiety, but negatively related to situational anxiety. . . . These results, plus studies showing verbal quantity first rising and then falling as stress increases, appear to indicate a U-curve relationship between anxiety and verbal productivity. (p. 244)

That is, the studies employing dispositional and concurrent measures of anxiety were seen as utilizing relatively low ranges of anxiety in subjects whereas the situational stress manipulations were generally considered more arousing (especially for those high in dispositional anxiety). Thus an *inverted U* relationship is hypothesized whereby at low levels of stress verbal productivity will increase with stress, but as anxiety or stress increases, verbal productivity will diminish. Since only a few of the studies reviewed above employed speech rate measures, application of this interpretation to that measure must be considered more tentative.

Several studies, not described by Murray, additionally related anxiety to verbal productivity. Siegman and Pope (1972) reported that anxiety-arousing content produced higher verbal quantity. In yet another study (referred to earlier) in which Pope, Siegman, and Blass (1970) kept the topic constant but induced anxiety by suggesting a psychological disturbance in subjects' families, anxiety produced an increase in subjects' verbal productivity but with no significant changes in speech rate. However, in an additional study they examined patients' verbal behavior on anxious and nonanxious days, and speech rate was significantly greater on high anxious days (Siegman and Pope, 1972). Mehrabian (1971a) reported a series of experiments in which subjects engaged in deceitful behavior that was presumably anxiety arousing. The duration of speech (analogous to verbal quantity) decreased when subjects were communicating mistruths. In addition, though speech rate decreased significantly with deceitful communications in one of his experiments, an increase was noted in another study. Interestingly, Mehrabian postulated a U-shaped relationship between anxiety level and speech rate, the opposite relationship of that hypothesized by Murray (1971). In summary, Murray's hypotheses have not been consistently supported by subsequent research. This state of affairs only reinforces Murray's conclusion:

For the future, research is needed using four or more levels of stress arousal, and four or more levels of dispositional anxiety, since studies with dichotomized variables often mask curvilinear relationships. Studies of concurrent anxiety, with verbal samples collected under low, moderate, and high stress conditions would be informative. (1971, p. 258)

Interpersonal Influence

In addition to anxiety, it is possible to relate several other variables to speech rate and verbal quantity. Mehrabian (1972) recently reported on several experiments (Mehrabian, 1971b; Mehrabian and Ksionzky, 1972) examining the affiliative behavior of an experimental subject and a confederate in a waiting room. The confederate's behavior was carefully rehearsed to be either slightly positive or slightly negative. Subjects' behavior during the interaction was correlated with measures of their affiliative tendencies obtained at the end of the experiment. Based on a factor analysis of the findings, Mehrabian found the following variables were positively related to affiliative behavior: total number of statements per minute, number of declarative statements per minute, and percent duration of subject and confederate's speech. A second factor pertaining to the subject's responsiveness to the confederate was positively related to speech rate.

Mehrabian (1972) also reported a series of experiments (Mehrabian and Williams, 1969) investigating the relation of nonverbal behavior to persuasiveness in communication of messages. Subjects were asked to convey messages to an experimental confederate in a neutral, moderately persuasive, or highly persuasive manner. Judges who were unaware of the instructions given to subjects rated their behaviors by how persuasive the communications were. Significant correlations were noted between several ratings of perceived persuasiveness and speech rate ($r = .41$). This finding is in contrast to Addington's study (Addington, 1971), in which it was found that speaking rate was not related to judgments of speaker credibility. Subjects in that study listened to carefully prepared standard-content passages, whereas in Mehrabian's experiment subjects were asked to behave persuasively in a more natural situation.

A number of studies have also investigated rate of speech in group interaction situations. Stang (1973) had female subjects judge female confederates in three-person groups who talked either 50, 33.3, or 16.7% of the time. Females with the highest talking rate (50%) were judged most positively on leadership qualities whereas those exhibiting medium (33.3%) amounts of talking were rated highest on a measure of liking. More recently, Kleinke, Lenga, Tully, Meeker, and Staneski (1976) extended this research in five studies involving subjects of the same or opposite sex in two-person interactions with confederates engaging in talk 20, 50, or 80% of the time. The confederates' speech was recorded and electronically filtered for content, with amount of talking and temporal characteristics controlled by reading of standardized scripts. Ratings of these tapes by undergraduate subjects revealed that persons talking 80% of the time were seen as outgoing and domineering but also as impolite, inattentive, and inconsiderate. Persons talking 50% were rated as less dominant and most liked, whereas 20% talkers were judged as extremely submissive and introverted and were liked only moderately. Interestingly, persons in same-sex interactions were judged as more intelligent when they talked more.

Sorrentino and Boutiller (1975) investigated the effect of quantity and quality of verbal interaction on group member ratings of leadership ability. Confederates were trained to interact with four-member problem-solving groups, varying the quantity as well as the quality of interaction. The quality of interaction corresponded to the number of correct solutions that the confederate provided to the group. The quantity of a confederate's verbal participation was positively related to other members' perceptions of him as competent, confident, interested, influential, and having socioemotional and task leadership ability; the quality of interaction was only related to perceptions of his contribution (i.e., success in solving problems). The authors argued that quantity of verbal interaction is perceived as a motivational factor (reflective of one's investment in the group) and that in the absence of verbal quantity, a person who is competent (i.e., provides correct answers) will not be perceived as a socioemotional leader.

Interview Ambiguity

We noted earlier that ambiguity in the interview situations created by Siegman and Pope (1972) was unrelated to speech disruption measures. In that study, ambiguity was created by employing high- and low-specific (i.e., high-ambiguous or low-ambiguous) questions and by placing a screen between the interviewer and interviewee, or by having the interviewee face away from the interviewer. High-ambiguous questions produced an increase in interviewee productivity (defined as the number of words per response), whereas it decreased with elimination of visibility between interviewer and interviewee. Verbal productivity was also less when interviewees were questioned by a low-status as opposed to a high-status interviewer. Speech rate, in contrast, decreased significantly in response to ambiguous questions.

Personality

Several studies have also related speech productivity measures to personality, particularly in certain diagnostic categories. In a study of "person perception," Addington (1968) reported that listeners evaluating various vocal characteristics of standard-content speech associated speaking rate with extraversion. Aronson and Weintraub (1972) reported that number of words spoken and speaking rate in a 10-minute interview significantly differentiated impulsive, depressed, compulsive-ritualistic, and delusional patient groups. In particular, impulsive patients showed a relatively high verbal rate whereas compulsive-ritualistic patients were relatively high in total number of words spoken. Depressed patients were relatively low in both categories. In a subsequent study, however, Weintraub and Aronson (1974) found no differences in speaking rate or number of words between groups of compulsive and normal control subjects.

In a study cited earlier, Matarazzo, Wiens, and Saslow (1965) found that duration of utterances appeared to define a gross mental health continuum, with chronic psychotics, acute psychotics, neurotic inpatients, neurotic outpatients, and medical inpatients and outpatients showing increasingly longer mean DOUs. Hinchliffe, Lancashire, and Roberts (1971) also reported that depressed patients showed a lower rate of speech (i.e., words per minute), and Starkweather (1964) observed that number of words per interview was different for nonagitated depressed patients at time of illness and recovery. In addition to finding "explosive speech intonations" in Type A patients, Friedman, Brown, and Rosenman (1969) also noted that Type A patients' speech rates were faster than those of Type B patients when reading the "hortatory passage." Finally, Axtell and Cole (1971) found that "repressors" talked significantly less about themselves, regardless of negative or positive content or verbal feedback, compared to sensitizers or subjects who obtained scores in the middle of the Byrne Repression-Sensitization scale. Sensitizers, as predicted, increased in their verbal productivity with interviewer feedback. These findings were interpreted as being consistent with the general notion of repression as an avoidance behavior.

Psychotherapy

Beyond the use of measures of verbal productivity as indices of emotional, behavioral, or motivational states or of personality traits, researchers have been interested in verbal productivity in the interview situation as a variable in the psychotherapeutic process. After all, language is the medium of the communication exchange in psychotherapy. Indeed, in a study differentiating novice from experienced psychotherapists, the latter were found to employ more words per statement in relating to patients (Ornston, Cicchetti, Levine, and Fierman, 1968), this being one of the major differences observed. In particular, a number of studies have investigated verbal productivity and measures of empathy in an interview situation. Strupp and Wallach (1965) employed practicing psychotherapists as subjects whose task was to dictate their verbal responses to comments of two patients shown on film. Independent ratings of therapist empathy, as based on the dictated verbal responses, showed a modest correlation between the number of words and rated empathy. Truax (1970) utilized his own empathy scale and found total therapist talk time also to be modestly related to empathy. Caracena and Vicory (1969) noted a similar association for independently judged empathy for interviewers interviewing undergraduates. Other researchers, however, have reported less consistent support for this relationship (e.g., Hargrove, 1974; Staples, Sloane, and Cristol, 1976; Welkowitz and Kue, 1973; and Wenegrat, 1974). Matarazzo and Wiens (1977) recently completed a review of these findings in relation to temporal speech measures and concluded that the evidence is suggestive but not definitive for an empathy-talk relationship.

Interestingly, of the studies cited above, only Staples, Sloane, and Cristol (1976) reported a significant relationship between interviewee talk time and rated therapist empathy. They also noted that patient outcome appeared to be related negatively to therapist talk time and positively to patient total talk time. Pope, Nudler, Vonkorff, and McGhee (1974) compared interviewee (female college student) productivity with novice and professional interviewers. Contrary to the prediction that the professional interviewer would elicit greater interviewee productivity, no differences were observed. However, productivity between novice interviewers and interviewees was positively related to, and also correlated with, the warmth and empathy (as measured by the Truax scale) of the student interviewer. The warmer the student interviewer, the more "synchronous" or mutually productive the exchange. In contrast, interviewer productivity was negatively correlated with interviewee productivity for the "professional" interviewers and uncorrelated with ratings of interviewer warmth (a finding that was not replicated). The lack of synchrony for professional therapists and interviewees was interpreted as reflecting a "role differentiation" where the professional follows a strategy of saying little if the interviewee is productive and talking actively if he is silent. This observation is consistent with a similar conclusion of Matarazzo, Wiens, Matarazzo, and Saslow (1968), who noted a tendency toward negative correlations between durations of utterance of experienced therapist and patient over successive therapy interviews. Their suggestion was that the therapeutic set of the therapists was to talk more when the patient was silent, hoping to stimulate the patient, and less when the patient was talking more. It may be that therapist or interviewer experience acts as a moderator variable in this empathy-talk relationship; clearly, however, more research is needed.

Self-Disclosure

Some studies have suggested that verbal productivity (i.e., duration of talk on a particular item of information) may serve as an index of self-disclosure, an important interview variable recently reviewed in depth by Cozby (1973). In one study (Vondracek, 1969), duration of disclosure correlated modestly with intimacy ($r = .42$). Similarly, Doster and Strickland (1971) obtained a significant correlation ($r = .50$ $p < .01$) between productivity and self-disclosure to "private" and "public" topics. Jourard and Jaffee (1970) demonstrated that increases in interviewer disclosure time prior to discussion of a topic led to increases in subject disclosure on the topic. Most recently, Taylor and Kleinhans (1974) found that disclosure time (time spent talking on a particular topic) was greatest for "medium intimacy" topics, followed by low intimacy and high intimacy items. Although the exact relationship between disclosure time and intimacy is thus not clear, they concluded:

Studies have consistently demonstrated that duration of self-disclosure is a reliable aspect of the interpersonal process. While it is fairly easy to assess interpersonal openness by having experimental subjects engage in overt self-disclosing behaviors, the unobtrusive measure of disclosure duration offers additional advantages. Time spent talking can be easily measured with a simple pocket stop watch. Subjects are not aware that the length of their disclosures is being tapped; hence it is impossible for them to distort deliberately their responses either to please or disrupt the experimenter's purposes. The stability of findings across studies using this measure attests to its sensitivity and usefulness. Future research will undoubtedly demonstrate this measure to be as useful and effective in assessing interpersonal behaviors as is spatial distance. (p. 7)

In contrast to these positive findings, Scher (1975) did not find client-counselor verbal activity to be related to therapeutic success. Interestingly, Kaplan (1967) found that while "sensitizer" interviewers took a more active role than "repressor" or "normal" interviewers, their verbal activity had the effect of diminishing the total talk time of their interviewees. No differences in speech content were noted, however. The exact circumstances in which verbal productivity is a positive feature of therapy thus require further clarification.

Experimental Manipulation of Verbal Productivity

Finally, a number of researchers have focused on interviewer methods to increase interviewee speech. Siegman (1972) recently reviewed a number of studies in which social reinforcement was employed. One experimental approach was to contrast warm versus cold interviewer behavior. Following up on an earlier study (Heller, Davis, and Myers, 1966) in which a warm-cold interviewer manipulation had no effect, Heller and Jacobson (cited in Heller, 1972) found that personality factors of the interviewee were important. Specifically, independent but not dependent males increased in speaking time as a function of warm interviewer behavior; females showed an increase regardless of personality variables. Subsequently, Heller (1972) had interviewers vary warm versus reserved behavior with psychiatric patients, who showed increased verbal productivity during the warm interview segments. Pope and Siegman (1968) trained interviewers to smile, nod, and speak "warmly," or to refrain from smiling and nodding and speak in a cold or "drab" tone of voice. Female interviewees were significantly more verbally productive (in terms of total words spoken in response to each question) during the warm interview. However, this was only true for a warm-cold interview sequence; when the cold interview occurred first, subjects maintained their reserve during the second (warm) interview.

More recently, Siegman (1972) evaluated the interaction between subjects' expectations of a warm and cold interviewer and the actual interviewer's behavior. Siegman found that male subjects' expectancies interacted with the interviewer's behavior in influencing productivity. Specifically, males expecting a warm but interacting with a cold interviewer were the least verbally productive, whereas those expecting a cold but receiving a warm interview were less productive than those expecting and receiving a warm interview. Interviewee expectations thus had an inhibiting effect on male subjects' verbal productivity when their expectations were violated. In contrast, females were more productive in the cold than the warm interviews. However, a simple comparison of males expecting and receiving cold or warm interviews was not significant, despite clear evidence that the warm interviewer was perceived as warmer and more attractive.

To evaluate more specifically the effect of the noncontingent reinforcements for speech employed in the above studies, Siegman (1972) had interviewers vary verbal reinforcement with nonreinforcement during interview segments. Subjects tended to give longer responses during the nonreinforced segments. In particular, subjects were more productive during a period of verbal reinforcement. To evaluate whether this nonreinforcement effect was perceived by subjects as a sign of displeasure (a cue for more information), Siegman (1972) next had liked and disliked interviewers give agreeing, disagreeing, or neutral responses. As predicted, interviewees were most verbally productive following disagreements, regardless of whether the interviewer was liked or disliked. On the basis of these studies, he concluded:

The assumption that the best strategy for maximizing interviewee productivity is for the interviewer to be warm and accepting, and that the more of this the better, is an assumption which we now know is naive, simplistic, and incorrect. . . . We probably have underestimated the potential value of negative reinforcers, such as interviewer disagreements for eliciting longer responses. (Siegman, 1972, p. 30)

Apropos of this point, Doster and Strickland (1971) reported that their subjects were more verbally productive when interacting with an "impersonal" rather than a "personal" interviewer.

In an attempt to further clarify these results, Siegman (1976) conducted several additional studies. In the first, a male interviewer conducted interviews with females while seated in a back-to-back position to eliminate visual cues. The interview was divided up into the following two segments for each subject where mm-hmm responses were administered on an intermittent schedule to avoid reinforcing a particular response class: no-response–response, response–no-response, response-response, no-response–no-response. These sequences provided both a between- and a within-subjects design that allowed evaluation of the effect of interviewer response sequence and changes in interviewee behavior over time. The results showed that interviewee verbal productivity increased in the response–no-response and no-response–no-response conditions. In contrast, subjects failed to increase their verbal behavior for the no-response–response sequence, which should have occurred if noncontingent "mm-hmm" responses were indeed reinforcing. In his second study Siegman employed both male and female interviewers interacting with same-sex subjects with normal face-to-face seating arrangement. No significant changes were observed in verbal productivity for any response sequences despite evidence from interviewee ratings of the interviews that the "mm-hmm" responses were viewed as socially reinforcing.[2]

SILENCE

Bruneau (1973) observed in a recent publication:

Silence is to speech as the white of this paper is to this print. Physiologically, silence appears to be the mirror image of the shape of discernible sound for each person. Speech signs, created by necessity or will, appear to be mentally imposed *figures* on mentally imposed *grounds* of silence. Mind creates both. . . . The entire system of spoken language would fail without man's ability to both tolerate and create sign sequences of silence-sound-silence units. In other words, significations of speech signs are possible because of their interdependence of imposed silence. It follows, then, that significations of various loci, intensities, durations, and frequencies of imposed silences are possible because of their interdependence with speech. (p. 18)

As with certain paralinguistic phenomena, it is necessary to distinguish several kinds of silence that have been identified and to note those that are related most directly to verbal processes. "Hesitation phenomena" (Duncan, 1969) consist of a variety of pauses serving different functions. Pauses have been described as either unfilled or filled, the latter being "filled" with an utterance such as "um," "ah," or "er," repetition, etc. Filled pauses have often been considered a type of speech disturbance or dysfluency, and indeed, this type of "gap" in speech has been associated with anxiety (e.g., Boomer, 1963; Boomer and Dittmann, 1964; Duncan, 1965; Panek and Martin, 1959). Filled pauses, however, can be associated with psychological phenomena other than anxiety. In fact, a major function of hesitation phenomena is their relationship to grammatical encoding-decoding processes. Though consideration of these processes in a sense is a departure from nonverbal phenomena into the verbal area, it is necessary to consider this issue briefly in order to understand better the nonverbal aspects of silence. Bruneau (1973) described one kind of silence as "psycholinguistic"—hesitations related to the encoding and decoding of speech. Hesitations of these sorts (including filled and unfilled pauses) enable the encoder to process mental thought into the proper words and grammatical form to be spoken. Boomer (1965), for example, took his finding that filled and unfilled pauses occurred most frequently at the beginnings of phonemic clauses to be "evidence in support of the theory that speech encoding at a grammatical level operates with units larger than the word" (p. 155). Studies by Boomer and Dittmann (1962) showed a differential ability of listeners to judge hesitation pauses over juncture pauses. In addition, several other studies (Dittmann and Llewellyn, 1967, 1968, 1969) further implicated the phonemic clause as a basic unit in encoding and decoding speech and illustrated the functions that hesitations, vocalizations (e.g., "mm-hmm") and body movements (e.g., head nods) serve in regulating the transmission and reception of speech. Goldman-Eisler (1967, 1968), Henderson, Skarbek

(1965), and others (e.g., Cook and Lalljee, 1970; Howell and Vetter, 1969; Martin, 1967, 1970; Martin and Strange, 1968a, 1968b) all related pauses to the encoding and decoding of speech in terms of its semantic complexity. For example, Goldman-Eisler (1967) reported that relatively longer hesitations were followed by relatively longer or more complex periods of speech. In fact, she observed a temporal or "cognitive rhythm" consisting of a regular structure of speech and silence durations, both in readings and simultaneous speech, in those instances in which 30% of the utterance time was pausing time. Martin (1968) gave subjects Thematic Apperception Test cards to respond to either freely or in only one sentence. When speech was restricted, pauses occurred more often within clauses before high information words, whereas unrestricted speakers tended to pause more often between clauses. Those in the restricted group seemed to choose their words carefully. In contrast, speakers who could talk freely employed pauses at clause boundaries, reflecting a lesser concern over the exact words used. Beyond noting these findings we do not belabor the hesitation phenomena associated with psycholinguistic silences other than to mention Duncan's caveat that "there seems to be a clear danger in studying pauses without regard to their linguistic context" (1969, p. 128).

In addition to distinguishing psycholinguistic silences, Bruneau outlined a category that he called "interactive silences." These tend to be longer than psycholinguistic silences, the latter being typically quite short pauses and hesitations. However, in some cases, psycholinguistic silences can be of longer durations, especially when a person is in the process of engaging in higher-order speech encoding. Bruneau noted: "Interactive silences differ from psycholinguistic silence mainly in each participant's conscious recognition of the degree and manner in which he is expected to participate in communicative exchange" (1973, p. 28). Interactive silences can be associated with making the decision as to who will assume the burden of speaking; lengthy interactive silences can signify that one is cautious or careful in appraisal of another; they can signify an emotionally close relationship, or an interpersonal snub if the interactants are not familiar. Silences can be used as a form of social control, as when social norm violators are given the "cold treatment" by others. In some contexts the initial burden of breaking a silence falls to the subordinate in the relationship; in other instances, it may be a sign of deference to remain or become silent in the presence of a superior. Deep emotions are often "expressed" most significantly by the absence of expression, or silence. Interpersonal embarrassment is generally accompanied by uncomfortable periods of silence and occasional attempts at laughter to "fill" or "prevent" the silence. Silences, depending on the situational context, can also maintain or alter interpersonal distance. These are but a few examples of the different "kinds" of silence that punctuate interpersonal interaction.

Despite the many meanings that silence can assume given the interpersonal context, the research literature to date has ignored such distinctions as offered by Bruneau. Rather, silence has been defined only in terms of free moments in speech and not in terms of true situational context. For example, Mahl's "silence quotient" consists of the number of seconds of silence divided by the number of seconds available for the individual to talk (Mahl, 1956). In his study, Mahl noted that periods of greater relative silence were accompanied by more dysfluencies both of which occurred during conflicted phases of the psychotherapy session. Reaction time latency—the period of time before a person speaks after a completed utterance—is another commonly employed measure of silence. This measure is typically correlated positively with pauses that are measured as the hesitations during speech. Generally, pauses over and under 1 second have little relationship to each other (Levin and Silverman, 1965), while the number of pauses and total time pausing are significantly correlated (Levin, Silverman, and Ford, 1967). As Murray (1971) summarized, pauses and verbal quantity measures are negatively correlated, as are reaction time and verbal quantity.

The great majority of studies of silence (with the exception of those involved with "psycholinguistic silences") have considered it in relation to anxiety. Most of the studies reviewed by Murray (1971) and noted in our section on verbal productivity also employed measures of silence either based on pauses or latency measures. Murray (1971) concluded, based on his review, that "silence tends to be related negatively to dispositional, but positively to situational and concurrent anxiety" (p. 244). Thus with the exception of personality measures based on somewhat questionable scales (e.g., the Manifest Anxiety Scale), silence has been consistently associated with anxiety. In their series of research investigations cited earlier, Siegman and Pope (1972) reported that patients had higher silence quotients on high-anxiety than low-anxiety days. However, their anxiety-arousing topic manipulation did not affect their subjects' silence quotients. In addition, a filled pause ratio (number of hesitation phenomena divided by total number of words) did not vary as a function of high-low anxiety days or anxiety topic. Further, in only one of two studies on message ambiguity was a silence quotient associated with greater ambiguity. The status of interviewer manipulation had no consistent effect. Most recently, Jurich and Jurich (1974) found that filled pauses were correlated with finger sweat-print measures ($r = .42$) and observer ratings of interviewee anxiety ($r = .68$).

With respect to personality variables, Aronson and Weintraub (1972) added up all speech-free interview segments greater than 5 seconds to obtain composite measures of silence. This measure significantly differentiated their impulsive, delusional, depressed, and compulsive patients. However, Hinchliffe, Lancashire, and Roberts (1971) found no significant differences in their measure of silence for depressives compared to controls, nor did Weintraub and Aronson (1974) for their compulsive patients. Ramsay (1966) varied tasks requiring differing levels of semantic complexity while measuring for very brief intervals of silence. Although he found (as predicted by Goldman-Eisler, 1968) that task semantic complexity was associated with longer silences, extraverts spent more time talking than introverts who had a lower total ratio of sound to silence.

Finally, a number of studies employed silence measures as indices of the status of therapy. Duncan (1966) reported a disproportionate number of hesitations and pauses in his "poor" as opposed to "peak" therapy hours. Cook (1964) studied the percentage of client-terminated silences and found successful therapy cases to have higher percentages than unsuccessful cases. Pierce and Mosher (1967) found that subjects judged interviewers who responded to interviewees' completed utterances with an inappropriate silence (i.e., delayed response) as being less empathetic. And in an interesting study, Fischer and Apostal (1975) found that a simulated audiotape of a client-counselor session was judged high in self-disclosure when there were more unfilled pauses. They concluded: "The presence of unfilled pauses over that of filled pauses and minimum pauses indicates to a counselor that the message which ensues is revealing more about the counselee and that the counselee is more willing to disclose this material" (p. 95).

PARALANGUAGE AND THE REGULATION OF CONVERSATIONAL BEHAVIOR

Recently researchers have begun to study nonverbal behaviors that serve to regulate the communication process. Duncan (1972, 1974), in particular, described a number of "turn taking signals" for conversation. He stated:

The question may be asked, again rhetorically, how participants in a conversation can avoid continually bumping into each other in a verbal sense. The thesis of this paper is that there is a regular communication mechanism in our culture for managing the taking of speaking turns in face to face interaction . . . Through this mechanism, participants in an interaction can effect the smooth and appropriate exchange of speaking turns. (1972, p. 299)

Based on "meticulous transcriptions" of speech and body-motion behaviors during two videotaped 19-minute dyadic interviews, Duncan identified three paralinguistic signals that reliably indicate that a speaker is ready to yield to the listener: (a) "intonation changes." A common sequence of phonemic clauses involves clauses ending on an intermediate pitch level that is maintained without rising or falling. Any deviation from this (i.e., a rising or falling in pitch level at the terminal juncture of a phonemic clause), in contrast, is a turn-yielding signal; (b) "paralinguistic drawl" on the last syllable or stressed syllable in a clause; (c) "drop in paralinguistic pitch or loudness" in association with a stereotyped ("sociocentric") statement such as "you know," "or something." (This is typically perceived as a "trailing off" of speech.)

In addition to turn-yielding cues, Duncan (1974) described listener "back channel signals," those "cues" which are feedback to a speaker that a listener is following the conversation. One such cue is the vocal segregate "mm-hmm," which occurs typically during the earlier portions of a speaker's utterance and most commonly between juncture clauses (Dittmann and Llewellyn, 1967).[3] In particular, Duncan found strong associations between turn-yielding cues and subsequent auditor turn-taking attempts.

Finally, several researchers have investigated the role voice intensity plays in regulating conversation in those instances where both interactants are talking. In an important study, Meltzer, Morris, and Hayes (1971) studied the role of vocal amplitude in determining the outcome of interruptions (i.e., who gains the floor). Sixty all-male dyads engaged in problem-solving discussions for 40 minutes. Bone-conduction microphones permitted each subject's speech to be separately recorded. An analogue-to-digital converter sampled subjects' vocal amplitude. The authors found that, irrespective of the average vocal amplitude of each speaker, the raising during an interruption of a speaker's voice relative to that of his conversational partner primarily determined the outcome of the interruption. However, this strategy was generally effective only for the person holding the floor, not for the listener. In addition, the longer the interruption, the less effective a defense this was (e.g., for a 3-second interruption a relative rise in the speaker's voice was only 50% effective).

More recently, Feldstein, Alberti, BenDebba, and Welkowitz (1974) investigated whether personality factors play a role in the occurrence of simultaneous speech. They distinguished two types: *interruptive simultaneous speech,* defined as "a segment of speech that begins while the participant who has the floor is talking but ends after he has stopped" (p. 2); and *noninterruptive simultaneous speech,* in which one person's speech segment begins and ends while the other has been talking. Twenty-four female college students were assigned to groups of four to engage in separate dyadic conversations of half an hour with each of her three fellow group members. Electronic analysis of sound and silence patterns revealed that individuals who could be described on Cattel's Sixteen-Factor Personality Questionnaire as easygoing, relaxed, conciliatory, complacent, secure, and insensitive to the approbation or disapprobation of others more frequently initiated simultaneous speech. Subjects initiated more simultaneous speech with partners "described as good natured, cooperative, attentive to people, emotionally mature, realistic, talkative, cheerful, and socially group dependent"

(p. 7). However, the outcome of simultaneous speech (i.e., whether it was interruptive or noninterruptive) was unrelated to the personality factors. In addition, the authors also found that the frequency with which individuals engage in interruptive and noninterruptive speech is consistent across conversational topics and conversational partners (Feldstein, BenDabba, and Alberti, 1974). Finally, Friedman (1975) has studied simultaneous speech in groups of Type A businessmen and found that those who engaged in more interruptions were at lower risk for coronary heart disease than those who seldom interrupted. Simultaneous speech correlated positively with relaxation, complacency, security, and independence, and negatively to apprehension, self-reproach, tension, and frustration as measured by Cattell's Sixteen-Factor Personality Questionnaire. In both Feldstein's and Friedman's studies, the presence or absence of specific turn-taking cues was not investigated. However, one might expect, especially with Type A individuals (cf. Friedman, Brown, and Rosenman, 1969), that voice amplitude changes may have been used.

NOTES

[1]Mahl's classifications were made from typewritten transcripts with simultaneous audio recordings. Using this procedure, Krause and Pilisuk (1961) obtained interrater reliabilities ranging from .71 to .93 for many of Mahl's categories. In contrast, Siegman and Pope (1972) and Boomer (1963) reported lower interscorer agreement (74 and 45%, respectively) for "non-ah" ratios. Boomer noted that only "ahs" and repetitions could be scored reliably from the tape alone. A recent study by Butterfield (1970) suggests that without extensive training only "ahs" can be reliably measured in clinical observation sessions.

[2]Siegman's findings are in contrast to the report by Matarazzo, Wiens, Saslow, Allen, and Weitman (1964) that interviewer "mm-hmms" significantly increase interviewee DOUs. Several possibly significant differences can be identified in the studies completed in these two laboratories. First of all, in the Siegman experiments the interviewer's reinforcements (mm-hmms) were being delivered during silent pauses in the interviewee's speech; in the Matarazzo studies the interviewer repeated "mm-hmm" practically throughout the whole of each of the interviewee's single utterances (i.e., while the interviewee was speaking). One possible difference in the two study formats is that silence versus speech was being reinforced. Second, in Siegman's studies the interviewee explicitly signalled the end of an utterance; in those of Matarazzo the interviewer judged that the interviewee had completed his utterance, and responded with his own next comment within 1 second (the average interviewer RTL was 0.4 seconds). Third, in the Siegman experiments there could have been significantly more explicit cognitive interviewee determination of the length of an interviewee utterance, and hence less susceptibility to the reinforcement value of the interviewer's "mm-hmm." That is, by instructing subjects specifically to signal when they had finished speaking, Siegman may have explicitly negated the prompting effect that "mm-hmms" have in normal conversation as an auditor back-channel signal (Duncan, 1974).

[3]Dittmann (1972) recently investigated "listener responses" in relation to age. Surprisingly, listener responses (paralinguistic and kinesic) were virtually absent in children, not appearing until adolescence and adulthood. These findings have been taken as evidence suggestive that complete comprehension of speech and development of social roles (i.e., the ability to appreci-

ate and recognize a speaker's need for feedback) may take longer to develop than researchers have thought.

REFERENCES

Addington, D. W. (1968). The relationship of selected vocal characteristics to personality perception. *Speech Monographs, 35,* 492–503.

Addington, D. W. (1971). The effect of vocal variation on ratings of source credibility. *Speech Monographs, 38,* 242–247.

Allen, B. V., A. N. Wiens, M. Weitman, and G. Saslow (1965). Effects of warm-cold set on interviewee speech. *Journal of Consulting Psychology, 29,* 480–482.

Allport, G., and H. Cantril (1934). Judging personality from voice. *Journal of Social Psychology, 5,* 37–55.

Alpert, M., R. L. Kurtzberg, and A. J. Friedhoff (1963). Transient voice changes associated with emotional stimuli. *Archives of General Psychiatry, 8,* 76–79.

Aronson, H., and W. Weintraub (1972). Personal adaptation as reflected in verbal behavior. In A. W. Siegman and B. Pope (Eds.), *Studies in dyadic communication.* New York: Pergamon Press. Pp. 265–278.

Axtell, B., and C. W. Cole (1971). Repression-sensitization response mode and verbal avoidance. *Journal of Personality and Social Psychology, 18,* 133–137.

Beekman, S. J. (1975). *Sex differences in nonverbal behavior.* Paper presented at the meeting of the American Psychological Association, Chicago.

Beldoch, M. (1964). Sensitivity to expression of emotional meaning in three modes of communication. In J. R. Davitz (Ed.), *The communication of emotional meaning.* New York: McGraw-Hill. Pp. 31–42.

Benton, A. L., C. H. Hartman, and I. G. Sarason (1955). Some relations between speech behavior and anxiety level. *Journal of Abnormal and Social Psychology, 51,* 295–297.

Bernick, N., and M. Oberlander (1968). Effect of verbalization and two different modes of experiencing on pupil size. *Perception and Psychophysics, 3,* 327–330.

Black, J. W., and J. J. Dreher (1955). *Nonverbal messages in voice communication.* Report No. NM001 104 500.45. U.S. Naval School of Aviation Medicine Research. (Kramer, E. (1963). Judgment of personal characteristics and emotions from nonverbal properties of speech. *Psychological Bulletin, 60,* 408–420.)

Boomer, D. S. (1963). Speech dysfluencies and body movement in interviews. *Journal of Nervous and Mental Disease, 136,* 263–266.

Boomer, D. S. (1965). Hesitation and grammatical encoding. *Language and Speech, 8,* 148–158.

Boomer, D. S., and A. T. Dittmann (1962). Hesitation pauses and juncture pauses in speech. *Language and Speech, 5,* 215–220.

Boomer, D. S., and A. T. Dittmann (1964). Speech rate, filled pause, and body movement in interviews. *Journal of Nervous and Mental Disease, 139,* 324–327.

Brenner, M. S., S. Feldstein, and J. Jaffee (1965). The contributions of statistical uncertainty and test anxiety to speech disruption. *Journal of Verbal Learning and Verbal Behavior, 4,* 300–305.

Bruneau, T. J. (1973). Communicative silences: Forms and functions. *Journal of Communication, 23,* 17–46.

Bugenthal, D. B. (1972). Inconsistency between verbal and nonverbal communication patterns: Its interpretation and effects. In P. Zimbardo (chairman), *Consistency as a process and a problem in psychology.* Symposium paper presented at the meeting of the International Congress of Psychology, Tokyo.

Bugenthal, D. B., B. Henker, and C. K. Whalen (1976). Attributional antecedents of verbal and vocal assertiveness. *Journal of Personality and Social Psychology, 34,* 405–411.

Bugenthal, D. B., and L. Love (1975). Nonassertive expression of parental approval and disapproval and its relationship to child disturbance. *Child Development, 46,* 747–752.

Burkhart, B. R. (1976). Apprehension about evaluation, paralanguage cues, and the experimenter–bias effect. *Psychological Reports, 39,* 15–23.

Butterfield G. (1970). Interjudge reliability for formal aspects of interviewee communication. *Perceptual and Motor Skills, 31,* 311–316.

Cameron, P., and J. Anderson (1968). Effects of introductory phrases and tonal-facial suggestion upon question-elicited responses. *Psychological Reports, 22,* 233–234.

Caracena, P. F., and J. R. Vicory (1969). Correlates of phenomenological and judged empathy. *Journal of Counseling Psychology, 16,* 510–515.

Cervin, V. (1956). Individual behavior in social situations: Its relation to anxiety, neuroticism, and group solidarity. *Journal of Experimental Psychology, 51,* 161–168.

Chapple, E. D., and C. M. Arensberg (1940). Measuring human relations: An introduction to the study of the interaction of individuals. *Genetic Psychology Monographs, 22,* 3–147.

Cohen, A. A. (1961). Estimating the degree of schizophrenic pathology from recorded interview samples. *Journal of Clinical Psychology, 17,* 403–406.

Cook, J. J. (1964). Silence in psychotherapy. *Journal of Counseling Psychology, 11,* 42–46.

Cook, M., and M. Lalljee (1970). The interpretation of pauses by the listener. *British Journal of Social and Clinical Psychology, 9,* 375–376.

Costanzo, F. S., N. N. Markel, and P. R. Costanzo (1969). Voice quality profile and perceived emotion. *Journal of Counseling Psychology, 16,* 267–270.

Cozby, P. C. (1973). Self-disclosure: A literature review. *Psychological Bulletin, 79,* 73–91.

Crystal, D., and R. Quirk (1964). *Systems of prosodic and paralinguistic features in English.* The Hague: Mouton.

Davitz, J. R. (Ed.). (1964). *The communication of emotional meaning.* New York: McGraw-Hill.

Davitz, J. R., and L. J. Davitz (1959). The communication of feelings by content-free speech. *Journal of Communication, 9,* 6–13.

Dibner, A. S. (1956). Cue-counting: A measure of anxiety in interviews. *Journal of Consulting Psychology, 20,* 475–478.

Dittmann, A. T. (1972). Developmental factors in conversational behavior. *Journal of Communication, 22,* 404–423.

Dittmann, A. T., and L. G. Llewellyn (1967). The phonemic clause as a unit of speech decoding. *Journal of Personality and Social Psychology, 6,* 341–349.

Dittmann, A. T., and L. G. Llewellyn (1968). Relationship between vocalizations and head nods as listener responses. *Journal of Personality and Social Psychology, 9,* 79–84.

Dittmann, A. T., and L. G. Llewellyn (1969). Body movements and speech rhythm in social conversation. *Journal of Personality and Social Psychology, 11,* 98–106.

Dittmann, A. T., and L. C. Wynne (1961). Linguistic techniques and the analysis of emotionality in the interview. *Journal of Abnormal and Social Psychology, 63,* 201–204.

Doster, J. A., and B. R. Strickland (1971). Disclosing of verbal material as a function of information requested, information about the interviewer, and interviewee differences. *Journal of Consulting and Clinical Psychology, 37,* 187–194.

Duncan, M. H. (1945). An experimental study of some of the relationships between voice and personality among students of speech. *Speech Monographs, 12,* 47–60.

Duncan, S. D., Jr. (1965). Paralinguistic behaviors in client-therapist communication in psychotherapy. Unpublished doctoral dissertation, University of Chicago. (Duncan, S. D., Jr. (1969). Nonverbal communication. *Psychological Bulletin, 72,* 118–137.)

Duncan, S. D., Jr. (1966). Paralinguistic analysis of psychotherapy interview. Summary in *Proceedings of the 74th Annual Convention of the American Psychological Association.* Washington, D.C.: American Psychological Association. Pp. 191–192.

Duncan, S. D., Jr. (1969). Nonverbal communication. *Psychological Bulletin, 72,* 118–137.

Duncan, S. D., Jr. (1972). Some signals and rules for taking speaking turns in conversations. *Journal of Personality and Social Psychology, 23,* 283–292.

Duncan, S. D., Jr. (1974). On the structure of speaker-auditor interaction during speaking turns. *Language in Society, 2,* 161–180.

Duncan, S. D., Jr., M. J. Rosenberg, and J. Finkelstein (1969a). Nonverbal communication of experimenter bias. Summary in *Proceedings of the 77th Annual Convention of the American Psychological Association.* Washington, D.C.: American Psychological Association. Pp. 369–370.

Duncan, S. D., Jr., M. J. Rosenberg, and J. Finkelstein (1969b). The paralanguage of experimenter bias. *Sociometry, 32,* 207–219.

Duncan, S. D., Jr., and R. Rosenthal (1968). Vocal emphasis in experimenters' instruction reading as unintended determinant of subjects' response. *Language and Speech, 11,* 20–26.

Dusenbury, D., and F. H. Knower (1939). Experimental studies on the symbolism of action and voice: II. A study of the specificity of meaning in abstract tonal symbols. *Quarterly Journal of Speech, 25,* 67–75.

Eisenman, R. (1966). Birth order, anxiety, and verbalizations in group psychotherapy. *Journal of Consulting Psychology, 30,* 521–526.

Fairbanks, G., and L. W. Hoaglin (1941). An experimental study of the duration characteristics of the voice during the expression of emotion. *Speech Monographs, 8,* 85–90.

Fairbanks, G., and W. Pronovost (1939). An experimental study of the pitch characteristics of the voice during the expression of emotion. *Speech Monographs, 6,* 87–104.

Fay, P. J., and W. C. Middleton (1941). The ability to judge sociability from the voice as transmitted over a public address system. *Journal of Social Psychology, 13,* 303–309.

Fay, P. J., and W. C. Middleton ((1942). Judgement of introversion from the transcribed voice. *Quarterly Journal of Speech, 28,* 226–228.

Feldstein, S., L. Alberti, M. BenDebba, and J. Welkowitz (1974). *Personality and simultaneous speech.* Paper presented at the meeting of the American Psychological Association, New Orleans.

Feldstein, S., M. BenDebba, and L. Alberti (1974). *Distributional characteristics of simultaneous speech in conversation.* Paper presented at the meeting of the Acoustical Society of America, New York.

Fenz, W. D., and S. Epstein (1962). Measurement of approach-avoidance conflict along a stimulus dimension by a thematic apperception test. *Journal of Personality, 30,* 613–632.

Fischer, M. J., and R. A. Apostal (1975). Selected vocal cues and counselors' perceptions of genuineness, self-disclosure, and anxiety. *Journal of Counseling Psychology, 22,* 92–96.

Friedhoff, A. J., M. Alpert, and R. L. Kurtzberg (1962). An effect of emotion on voice. *Nature, 193,* 357–358.

Friedman, E. R. (1975). Simultaneous speech and coronary risk. *Psychosomatic Medicine, 37,* 90.

Friedman, M., A. E. Brown, and R. H. Rosenman (1969). Voice analysis test for detection of behavior pattern. *Journal of the American Medical Association, 208,* 828–836.

Geer, J. H. (1966). Effects of fear arousal upon task performance and verbal behavior. *Journal of Abnormal Psychology, 71,* 119–123.

Goldfarb, W., P. Braunstein, and I. Lorge (1956). A study of speech patterns in a group of schizophrenic children. *American Journal of Orthopsychiatry, 26,* 544–555.

Goldman-Eisler, F. (1967). Sequential temporal patterns and cognitive processes in speech. *Language and Speech, 10,* 122–132.

Goldman-Eisler, F. (1968). *Psycholinguistics: Experiments in spontaneous speech.* New York: Academic Press.

Hargrove, D. S. (1974). Verbal interaction analysis of empathetic and unempathetic responses of therapists. *Journal of Consulting and Clinical Psychology, 42,* 305.

Harrison, R. P. (1973). Nonverbal communication. In I. de Solo Pool, W. Schramm, N. Maccoby, F. Fry, E. Parker, and J. L. Fein (Eds.), *Handbook of communication.* Chicago: Rand McNally. Pp. 93–115.

Heller, K. (1972). Interview structure and interviewer style in initial interviews. In A. W. Siegman and B. Pope (Eds.), *Studies in dyadic communication.* New York: Pergamon Press. Pp. 9–28.

Heller, K., J. D. Davis, and R. A. Myers (1966). The effects of interviewer style in a standardized interview. *Journal of Consulting Psychology, 30,* 501–508.

Henderson, A., F. Goldman-Eisler, and A. Skarbek (1965). The common value of pausing time in spontaneous speech. *Quarterly Journal of Experimental Psychology, 17,* 343–345.

Hinchliffe, M. K., M. Lancashire, and F. J. Roberts (1971). Depression: Defense mechanisms in speech. *British Journal of Psychiatry, 118,* 471–472.

Hornstein, M. (1967). Accuracy of emotional communication and interpersonal compatibility. *Journal of Personality, 35,* 20–30.

Howell, R. W., and H. J. Vetter (1969). Hesitation in the production of speech. *Journal of General Psychology, 81,* 261–276.

Hunt, R. G., and T. K. Lin (1967). Accuracy and judgments of personal attributes from speech. *Journal of Personality and Social Psychology, 6,* 450–453.

Innes, G., W. M. Miller, and M. Valentine (1959). Emotion and blood pressure. *Journal of Mental Science, 105,* 840–851.

Jourard, S. M., and P. E. Jaffee (1970). Influence of an interviewer's disclosure on the self-disclosing behavior of interviewees. *Journal of Counseling Psychology, 17,* 252–257.

Jurich, A. P., and J. A. Jurich (1974). Correlations among nonverbal expressions of anxiety. *Psychological Reports, 34,* 199–204.

Kanfer, F. H. (1958a). Effect of a warning signal preceding a noxious stimulus on verbal rate and heart rate. *Journal of Experimental Psychology, 55,* 73–80.

Kanfer, F. H. (1958b). Supplementary report: Stability of a verbal rate change in experimental anxiety. *Journal of Experimental Psychology, 56,* 182.

Kanfer, F. H. (1959). Verbal rate, content, and adjustment ratings in experimentally structured interviews. *Journal of Abnormal and Social Psychology, 58,* 305–311.

Kanfer, F. H. (1960). Verbal rate, eyeblink, and content in structured psychiatric interviews. *Journal of Abnormal and Social Psychology, 61,* 341–347.

Kaplan, M. F. (1967). Interview interaction of repressors and sensitizers. *Journal of Consulting Psychology, 31,* 513–516.

Kasl, S. V., and G. F. Mahl (1965). The relationship of disturbances and hesitations in spontaneous speech to anxiety. *Journal of Personality and Social Psychology, 1,* 425–433.

Kauffman, P. E. (1954). An investigation of some psychological stimulus properties of speech behavior. Unpublished doctoral dissertation, University of Chicago, (Kramer, E. (1963). Judgment of personal characteristics and emotions from nonverbal properties of speech. *Psychological Bulletin, 60,* 408–420.)

Kleinke, C. L., M. R. Lenga, T. B. Tully, F. B. Meeker, and R. A. Staneski (1976). Effect of talking rate on first impressions of opposite-sex and same-sex interactions. Paper presented at meeting of the Western Psychological Association, Los Angeles.

Knower, F. H. (1941). Analysis of some experimental variations of simulated vocal expressions of the emotions. *Journal of Social Psychology, 14,* 369–372.

Kramer, E. (1963). Judgment of personal characteristics and emotions from nonverbal properties of speech. *Psychological Bulletin, 60,* 408–420.

Kramer, E. (1964). Elimination of verbal cues in judgements of emotion from voice. *Journal of*

Abnormal and Social Psychology, **6,** 390–396.

Krause, M. S. (1961). Anxiety in verbal behavior: An intercorrelational study. *Journal of Consulting Psychology,* **25,** 272.

Krause, M. S., and M. Pilisuk (1961). Anxiety in verbal behavior: A validation study. *Journal of Consulting Psychology,* **25,** 414–429.

Levin, H., A. L. Baldwin, M. Gallwey, and A. Paivio (1960). Audience stress, personality, and speech. *Journal of Abnormal and Social Psychology,* **61,** 469–473.

Levin, H., and I. Silverman (1965). Hesitation phenomena in children's speech. *Language and Speech,* **8,** 67–85.

Levin, H., I. Silverman, and B. L. Ford (1967). Hesitations in children's speech during explanation and description. *Journal of Verbal Learning and Verbal Behavior,* **6,** 560–564.

Levy, P. (1964). The ability to express and perceive vocal communication of feeling. In J. R. Davitz (Ed.), *The communication of emotional meaning.* New York: McGraw-Hill. Pp. 43–55.

Maclay, H., and C. E. Osgood (1959). Hesitation phenomena in spontaneous English speech. *Word,* **15,** 19–44.

Mahl, G. F. (1956). Disturbances and silences in the patients' speech in psychotherapy. *Journal of Abnormal Social Psychology,* **53,** 1–15.

Mahl, G. F. (1959a). Exploring emotional states by content analysis. In I. D. Pool (Ed.), *Trends in content analysis.* Urbana: University of Illinois Press. Pp. 89–130.

Mahl, G. F. (1959b). Measuring the patient's anxiety during interviews from "expressive" aspects of his speech. *Transactions of the New York Academy of Science,* **21,** 249–257.

Mahl, G. F. (1964). Some observations about research on vocal behavior. In D. McK. Rioch (Ed.), *Disorders of communication.* Proceedings of ARNMD, Vol. 42. Baltimore: Williams and Wilkins. Pp. 466–483. (Scherer, K. R., J. Koivumaki, and R. Rosenthal (1972). Minimal cues in the vocal communication of affect: Judging emotions from content-masked speech. *Journal of Psycholinguistic Research,* **1,** 269–285.)

Mallory, E. B., and V. R. Miller (1958). A possible basis for the association of voice characteristics and personality traits. *Speech Monographs,* **25,** 255–260.

Markel, N. N. (1965). The reliability of coding paralanguage: Pitch, loudness, and tempo. *Journal of Verbal Learning and Verbal Behavior,* **4,** 306–308.

Markel, N. N. (1969). Relationship between voice-quality profiles and MMPI profiles in psychiatric patients. *Journal of Abnormal Psychology,* **74,** 61–66.

Markel, N. N., M. Meisels, and J. E. Houck (1964). Judging personality from voice quality. *Journal of Abnormal and Social Psychology,* **69,** 458–463.

Martin, J. G. (1967). Hesitations in the speaker's production and listener's reproduction of utterances. *Journal of Verbal Learning and Verbal Behavior,* **6,** 903–909.

Martin, J. G. (1968). Two psychological mechanisms specified by hesitation in spontaneous speech. Summary in *Proceedings of the 76th Annual Convention of the American Psychological Association.* Washington, D.C.: American Psychological Association. Pp. 17–18.

Martin, J. G. (1970). On judging pauses in spontaneous speech. *Journal of Verbal Learning and Verbal Behavior,* **9,** 75–78.

Martin, J. G., and W. Strange (1968a). Determinants of hesitations in spontaneous speech. *Journal of Experimental Psychology,* **76,** 474–479.

Martin, J. G., and W. Strange (1968b). The perception of hesitation in spontaneous speech. *Perception and Psychophysics,* **3,** 427–438.

Maslow, A. H. (1937). Dominance-feeling, behavior, and status. *Psychological Review,* **44,** 404–429.

Matarazzo, J. D., D. C. Holman, and A. N. Wiens (1967). A simple measure of interviewer and interviewee speech durations. *Journal of Psychology,* **66,** 7–14.

Matarazzo, J. D., G. Saslow, A. N. Wiens, M. Weitman, and B. V. Allen (1964). Interviewer head nodding and interviewee speech durations. *Psychotherapy: Theory, Research, and Practice,* **1,** 54–63.

Matarazzo, J. D., M. Weitman, G. Saslow, and A. N. Wiens (1961). Interviewer influence on durations of interviewee speech. *Journal of Verbal Learning and Verbal Behavior,* **1,** 451–458.

Matarazzo, J. D., and A. N. Wiens (1967). Interviewer influence on durations of interviewee silence. *Journal of Experimental Research in Personality,* **2,** 56–69.

Matarazzo, J. D., and A. N. Wiens (1972). *The Interview: Research on its anatomy and structure.* Chicago: Aldine-Atherton.

Matarazzo, J. D., and A. N. Wiens (1977). Speech behavior as an objective correlate of empathy and outcome in interview and psychotherapy research. *Behavior Modification,* **1,** 453–480.

Matarazzo, J. D., A. N. Wiens, R. G. Matarazzo, and G. Saslow (1968). Speech and silence behavior in clinical psychotherapy and its laboratory correlates. In J. Shlien, H. Hunt, J. D. Matarazzo, and C. Savage (Eds.), *Research in psychotherapy,* Vol. 3. Washington, D.C.: American Psychological Association. Pp. 347–394.

Matarazzo, J. D., A. N. Wiens, and G. Saslow (1965). Studies in interview speech behavior. In L. Krasner and L. P. Ullmann (Eds.), *Research in behavior modification: New developments and implications.* New York: Holt, Rinehart, and Winston. Pp. 179–210.

Matarazzo, J. D., A. N. Wiens, G. Saslow, B. V. Allen, and M. Weitman (1964). Interviewer mm-hmm and interviewee speech durations. *Psychotherapy: Theory, Research, and Practice,* **1,** 109–114.

Matarazzo, J. D., A. N. Wiens, G. Saslow, R. M. Dunham, and R. B. Voas (1964). Speech durations of astronaut and ground communicator. *Science,* **143,** 148–150.

Matarazzo, R. G., J. D. Matarazzo, G. Saslow, and J. S. Phillips (1958). Psychological test and organismic correlates of interview interaction patterns. *Journal of Abnormal and Social Psychology,* **56,** 329–338.

Matarazzo, R. G., A. N. Wiens, and G. Saslow (1966). Experimentation in the training and learning of psychotherapy skills. In L. K. Gottschalk and A. A. Auerbach (Eds.), *Methods of research in psychotherapy.* New York: Appleton-Century Crofts. Pp. 597–635.

McCroskey, J. C., and S. Mehrley (1969). The effects of disorganization and nonfluency on attitude change and source credibility. *Speech Monographs,* **36,** 13–21.

Mehrabian, A. (1971a). Nonverbal betrayal of feeling. *Journal of Experimental Research in Personality,* **5,** 64–73.

Mehrabian, A. (1971b). Verbal and nonverbal interaction of strangers in a waiting situation. *Journal of Experimental Research in Personality,* **5,** 127–138.

Mehrabian, A. (1972). *Nonverbal communication.* Chicago: Aldine-Atherton.

Mehrabian, A., and S. Ksionzky (1972). Categories of social behavior. *Comparative Group Studies,* **3,** 425–436.

Mehrabian, A., and M. Williams (1969). Nonverbal and concomitants of perceived and intended persuasiveness. *Journal of Personality and Social Psychology,* **13,** 37–58.

Meltzer, L., W. N. Morris, and D. P. Hayes (1971). Interruption outcomes and vocal amplitude: Explorations in social psychophysics. *Journal of Personality and Social Psychology,* **18,** 392–402.

Miller, G. R. (1964). Variations in the verbal behavior of a second speaker as a function of varying audience response. *Speech Monographs,* **31,** 109–115.

Miller, G. R., H. Zavos, J. W. Vlandis, and M. E. Rosenbaum (1961). The effect of differential reward on speech patterns. *Speech Monographs,* **28,** 9–15.

Milmoe, S., M. S. Novey, J. Kagan, and R. Rosenthal (1968). The mother's voice: Postdictor of aspects of her baby's behavior. Summary in *Proceedings of the 76th Annual Convention of the American Psychological Association.* Washington, D.C.: American Psychological Association. Pp. 463–464.

Milmoe, S., R. Rosenthal, H. T. Blane, M. E. Chafetz, and I. Wolf (1967). The doctor's voice: Postdictor of successful referral of alcoholic patients. *Journal of Abnormal Psychology,* **72,** 78–84.

Molde, D. A., and A. N. Wiens (1967). Interview interaction behavior of nurses with task versus person orientation. *Nursing Research,* **17,** 45–51.

Moore, W. E. (1939). Personality traits and voice quality deficiencies. *Journal of Speech Disorders,* **4,** 33–36.

Murray, D. C. (1971). Talk, silence, and anxiety. *Psychological Bulletin,* **75,** 244–260.

Natale, M. (1975). Convergence of mean vocal intensity in dyadic communication as a function of social desirability. *Journal of Personality and Social Psychology,* **32,** 790–804.

Ornston, P. S., D. V. Cicchetti, J. Levine, and L. B. Fierman (1968). Some parameters of verbal behavior that reliably differentiate novice from experienced psychotherapists. *Journal of Abnormal Psychology,* **73,** 240–244.

Oyamada, T. (1966). Studies on sensory deprivation. V. Part 5. The effects of sensory deprivation on the performance of the projective test (3). *Tohoku Psychologica Folia,* **25,** 19–53. (Murray, D. C. (1971). Talk, silence, and anxiety. *Psychological Bulletin,* **75,** 244–260.)

Packwood, W. T. (1974). Loudness as a variable in persuasion. *Journal of Counseling Psychology,* **21,** 1–2.

Panek, D. M., and B. Martin (1959). The relationship between GSR and speech disturbances in psychotherapy. *Journal of Abnormal and Social Psychology,* **58,** 402–405.

Pierce, W. D., and D. L. Mosher (1967). Perceived empathy, interviewer behavior, and interviewee anxiety. *Journal of Consulting Psychology,* **31,** 101.

Pittenger, R. E., C. F. Hockett, and J. J. Danehy (1960). *The first five minutes.* Ithaca, N. Y.: Martineau.

Pittenger, R. E. and H. L. Smith, Jr. (1957). A basis for some contributions of linguistics to psychiatry. *Psychiatry,* **20,** 61–78.

Pollack, I., H. Rubenstein, and A. Horowitz (1960a). Communication of verbal modes of expression. *Language and Speech,* **3,** 121–130.

Pollack, I., H. Rubenstein, and A. Horowitz (1960b). *Recognition of "verbal expression" over communications systems.* Paper delivered at the meeting of the Acoustical Society of America. (Kramer, E. (1963). Judgment of personal characteristics and emotions from nonverbal properties of speech. *Psychological Bulletin,* **60,** 408–420.)

Pope, B., T. Blass, A. W. Siegman, and J. Raher (1970). Anxiety and depression in speech. *Journal of Consulting and Clinical Psychology,* **35,** 128–133.

Pope, B., S. Nudler, M. Vonkorff, and J. P. McGhee (1974). The experienced professional interviewer versus the complete novice. *Journal of Consulting and Clinical Psychology,* **42,** 680–690.

Pope, B., and A. W. Siegman (1962). The effect of therapist verbal activity and specificity on patient productivity and speech disturbance in the initial interview. *Journal of Consulting Psychology,* **26,** 489.

Pope, B., and A. W. Siegman (1964). An intercorrelational study of some indices of verbal fluency. *Psychological Reports,* **15,** 303–310.

Pope, B., and A. W. Siegman (1966). Interviewer-interviewee relationship and verbal behavior of interviewee in the initial interview. *Psychotherapy: Theory, Research, and Practice,* **3,** 149–152.

Pope, B., and A. W. Siegman (1967). Interviewer warmth and verbal communication in the initial interview. Summary in *Proceedings of the 75th Annual Convention of the American*

Psychological Association. Washington, D.C.: American Psychological Association. Pp. 245–246.

Pope, B., and A. W. Siegman (1968). Interviewer warmth in relation to interviewee verbal behavior. *Journal of Consulting and Clinical Psychology,* **32,** 588–595.

Pope, B., A. W. Siegman, and T. Blass (1970). Anxiety and speech in the initial interview. *Journal of Consulting and Clinical Psychology,* **35,** 233–238.

Preston, J. M., and R. C. Gardner (1967). Dimensions of oral and written language fluency. *Journal of Verbal Learning and Verbal Behavior,* **6,** 936–945.

Ramm, K. (1946). Personality maladjustment among monotones. *Smith College Studies of Social Work,* **17,** 264–284.

Ramsay, R. W. (1966). Personality and speech. *Journal of Personality and Social Psychology,* **4,** 116–118.

Ray, M. L., and E. J. Webb (1966). Speech duration effects in the Kennedy news conference. *Science,* **153,** 899–901.

Reece, M. M. (1964). Climate and temporal verbal reinforcement. *Journal of Clinical Psychology,* **20,** 284–286.

Reece, M. M., and R. N. Whitman (1962). Expressive movements, warmth, and verbal reinforcement. *Journal of Abnormal and Social Psychology,* **64,** 234–236.

Rice, D. G., G. M. Abrams, and J. H. Saxman (1969). Speech and physiological correlates of "flat" affect. *Archives of General Psychiatry,* **20,** 566–572.

Rogers, P. L., K. R. Scherer, and R. Rosenthal (1971). Content filtering human speech: A simple electronic system. *Behavior Research Methods and Instrumentation,* **3,** 16–18.

Rubenstein, L., and D. E. Cameron (1968). Electronic analysis of nonverbal communication. *Comprehensive Psychiatry,* **9,** 200–208.

Saslow, G., and J. D. Matarazzo (1959). A technique for studying changes in interview behavior. In E. A. Rubenstein and M. B. Parloff (Eds.), *Research in psychotherapy,* Vol. 1. Washington, D.C.: American Psychological Association. Pp. 125–159.

Sauer, R. E., and F. L. Marcuse (1957). Overt and covert recording. *Journal of Projective Techniques,* **21,** 391–395.

Scher, M. (1975). Verbal activity, counselor experience, and success in counseling. *Journal of Counseling Psychology,* **22,** 97–101.

Scherer, K. R. (1971). Randomized splicing: A note on a simple technique for masking speech content. *Journal of Experimental Research in Personality,* **5,** 155–159.

Scherer, K. R. (1972). Judging personality from voice: A cross-cultural approach to an old issue in interpersonal perception. *Journal of Personality,* **40,** 191–210.

Scherer, K. R. (1974). Acoustic concomitants of emotional dimensions: Judging affect from synthesized tone sequences. In S. Weitz (Ed.), *Nonverbal communication: Readings with commentary.* New York: Oxford University Press. Pp. 105–111.

Scherer, K. R., J. Koivumaki, and R. Rosenthal (1972). Minimal cues in the vocal communication of affect: Judging emotions from content-masked speech. *Journal of Psycholinguistic Research,* **1,** 269–285.

Siegman, A. W. (1972). *What makes interviewees talk or how effective are social reinforcers in facilitating interviewee productivity?* Paper presented at a colloquium given at the University of Maryland, Catonsville.

Siegman, A. W. (1976). Do noncontingent interviewer mm-hmms facilitate interviewee productivity? *Journal of Consulting and Clinical Psychology,* **44,** 171–182.

Siegman, A. W., and B. Pope (1965a). Effects of question specificity and anxiety-producing messages on verbal fluency in the initial interview. *Journal of Personality and Social Psychology,* **2,** 522–530.

Siegman, A. W., and B. Pope (1965b). Personality variables associated with productivity and verbal fluency in the initial interview. In B. E. Compton (Ed.), *Proceedings of the 73rd Annual Convention of the American Psychological Association.* Washington, D.C.: American Psychological Association. Pp. 273–274.

Siegman, A. W., and B. Pope (1966). The effect of interviewer ambiguity-specificity and topical focus on interviewee vocabulary diversity. *Language and Speech,* **9,** 242–249.

Siegman, A. W., and B. Pope (Eds.). (1972). *Studies in dyadic communication.* New York: Pergamon Press.

Sorrentino, R. M., and R. G. Boutillier (1975). The effect of quantity and quality of verbal interaction on ratings of leadership ability. *Journal of Experimental Research in Personality,* **11,** 403–411.

Soskin, W. F. (1953). *Some aspects of communication and interpretation in psychotherapy.* Paper presented at the meeting of the American Psychological Association, Cleveland. (Kramer, E. (1963). Judgment of personal characteristics and emotions from nonverbal properties of speech. *Psychological Bulletin,* **60,** 408–420.)

Stagner, R. (1936). Judgments of voice and personality. *Journal of Educational Psychology,* **27,** 272–277.

Stang, D. J. (1973). Effect of interaction rate on ratings of leadership and liking. *Journal of Personality and Social Psychology,* **27,** 405–408.

Staples, F. R, R. B. Sloane, and A. H. Cristol (1976). Truax variables, speech characteristics, and therapeutic outcome. *Journal of Nervous and Mental Disease,* **163,** 135–140.

Starkweather, J. A. (1955). *The communication value of content-free speech.* Paper presented at the meeting of the Midwestern Psychological Association, Chicago. (Kramer, E. (1963). Judgment of personal characteristics and emotions from nonverbal properties of speech. *Psychological Bulletin,* **60,** 408–420.)

Starkweather, J. A. (1956). Content-free speech as a source of information about the speaker. *Journal of Abnormal and Social Psychology,* **52,** 394–402.

Starkweather, J. A. (1964). Variations in vocal behavior. In D. McK. Rioch and E. A. Weinstein (Eds.), *Disorders of communication.* Baltimore: Williams and Wilkins. Pp. 424–449.

Starkweather, J. A. (1967). Vocal behavior as an information channel of speaker status. In K. Salzinger and S. Salzinger (Eds.), *Research in verbal behavior and some neurophysiological implications.* New York: Academic Press. Pp. 253–265.

Strupp, H. H., and M. S. Wallach (1965). A further study of psychiatrists' responses in quasi-therapy situations. *Behavioral Science,* **10,** 113–134.

Suedfeld, P., J. Vernon, J. T. Stubbs, and M. Karlins (1965). The effects of repeated confinement on cognitive performance. *American Journal of Psychotherapy,* **7,** 493–495.

Taylor, D. A., and B. Kleinhans (1974). *Beyond words: Other aspects of self-disclosure.* Paper presented at the meeting of the American Psychological Association, New Orleans.

Taylor, H. C. (1934). Social agreement on personality traits as judged from speech. *Journal of Social Psychology,* **5,** 244–248.

Thompson, C. W., and K. Bradway (1950). The teaching of psychotherapy through content-free interviews. *Journal of Consulting Psychology,* **14,** 321–323.

Trager, G. L. (1958). Paralanguage: A first approximation. *Studies in Linguistics,* **13,** 1–12.

Truax, C. B. (1970). Length of therapist response, accurate empathy, and patient improvement. *Journal of Clinical Psychology,* **26,** 539–541.

Vlandis, J. W. (1964). Variation in the verbal behavior of a speaker as a function of varied reinforcing conditions. *Speech Monographs,* **31,** 116–119.

Vondracek, F. W. (1969). Behavioral measurement of self-disclosure. *Psychological Reports,* **25,** 914.

Webb, J. T. (1969). Subject speech rates as a function of interviewer behavior. *Language and Speech,* **12,** 54–67.

Weintraub, W., and H. Aronson (1974). Verbal behavior analysis and psychological defense mechanisms: VI. Speech pattern associated with compulsive behavior. *Archives of General Psychiatry*, **30**, 297–300.

Weitz, S. (1972). Attitude, voice, and behavior: A repressed affect model of interracial interaction. *Journal of Personality and Social Psychology*, **24**, 14–21.

Welkowitz, J., S. Feldstein, M. Finklestein, and L. Aylesworth (1972). Changes in vocal intensity as a function of interspeaker influence. *Perceptual and Motor Skills*, **35**, 715–718.

Welkowitz, J., and M. Kue (1973). Interrelationships among warmth, genuineness, empathy, and temporal speech patterns in interpersonal interaction. *Journal of Consulting and Clinical Psychology*, **41**, 472–473.

Wenegrat, A. (1974). A factor-analytic study of the Truax Accurate Empathy Scale. *Psychotherapy: Theory, Research, and Practice*, **11**, 48–51.

Wiens, A. N. (1976). The assessment interview. In I. B. Weiner (Ed.), *Clinical methods in psychology*. New York: Wiley-Interscience. Pp. 3–60.

Wiens, A. N., J. D. Matarazzo, G. Saslow, S. M. Thompson, and R. G. Matarazzo (1965). Interview interaction behavior of supervisors, head nurses, and staff nurses. *Nursing Research*, **14**, 322–329.

Wiens, A. N., G. Saslow, and J. D. Matarazzo (1966). Speech interruption behavior during interviews. *Psychotherapy: Theory, Research, and Practice*, **3**, 153–158.

Wolff, W. (1943). *The expression of personality*. New York: Harper. (Kramer, E. (1963). Judgment of personal characteristics and emotions from nonverbal properties of speech. *Psychological Bulletin*, **60**, 408–420.)

CHAPTER 3

Research on Facial Expression

INTRODUCTION

In many respects the face may be the single most important body area and "channel" of nonverbal communication. In his overview on nonverbal communication, Knapp (1972) noted:

The face is rich in communicative potential. It is the primary site for communicating emotional states; it reflects interpersonal attitudes; it provides nonverbal feedback on the comments of others; and some say that, next to human speech, it is the primary source of giving information. For these reasons and because of its visibility, we pay a great deal of attention to what we see in the faces of others. (pp. 68–69)

Dittman (1972) remarked: "Facial expressions of emotion are very specific. . . . In this sense these expressions lie towards the communicative end of the scale" (p. 79). As Ekman, Friesen, and Ellsworth (1972) pointed out, "Although there are only a few words to describe different facial behaviors (smile, frown, furrow, squint, etc.), man's facial muscles are sufficiently complex to allow more than a thousand different facial appearances; and the action of these muscles is so rapid, that these *could* all be shown in less than a few hours time" (p. 1). In her recent book of selected readings on nonverbal communication, Weitz (1974) described research on the face as follows: "Facial expression is perhaps the area in nonverbal communications research that comes closest to the more traditional concerns of psychology. The question of nature versus nurture as the origin of behavior is very much present here" (p. 11).

Thus several reasons why the face is an important nonverbal channel include the amount of information it can convey (especially in a short period of time) and the kind of information (e.g., emotional, attitudinal) conveyed. Of perhaps broader theoretical import is the relevance of facial behavior to the nature-nurture question as noted by Weitz: there is a growing and, by now, well documented body of research suggesting that facial expressions may be an innate characteristic of man, cutting across cultures

77

(unlike most other aspects of human behavior, which are largely culture-bound). With Darwin's 1872 work, *The Expression of the Emotions in Man and Animals,* came the notion that emotions were expressed in similar ways among species. Darwin theorized that expressive behaviors have survival value and are thus selected much as physical structures and characteristics. Recent work by ethologists who have studied man (e.g., Blurton-Jones, 1972; Eibl-Eibesfeldt, 1971) as well as animals (e.g., Goodall, 1971) has substantiated this idea. We do not review this work or Darwin's theory in detail, inasmuch as our concern is on human research that is suitable to laboratory investigations and statistical measurement. Fortunately for our purposes, a number of researchers (e.g., Ekman, 1972, 1973; Izard, 1971), applied psychological research techniques to this cross-cultural question. In doing so, they additionally noted the contribution of cultural influences on the *control* of emotional expression, thus providing a persuasive model that seems to explain the diverse phenomena in the nature-nurture controversy. This cross-cultural research is an important subject of a topic area to be covered later.

In addition to the intriguing idea that facial expressions are innate is the related notion that the face is the primary site of our emotions. Specifically, Tomkins (1962; Tomkins and McCarter, 1964) reintroduced the James–Lange theory of emotion—that the physiological state precedes, and is the basis for, the experience of emotion. Tomkins argued that for each emotion there are particular patterns of neural firings and associated facial muscle movements, and that this proprioceptive feedback provides the basis for our experience of emotion.[1] Gellhorn (1964) posited two physiological processes underlying emotion, one of which he described as follows:

the facial contraction patterns which are characteristic for the expression of particular emotion. These contractions set up complex proprioceptive patterns which arouse the diffuse hypothalamic–cortical system while the sensorimotor area in the cortex is excited via the specific afferent system from tactile and proprioceptive facial receptors. (p. 468)

The implication of Tomkins' theory for psychological research is that in studying facial expressions we are, in fact, studying "emotion itself," whereas the traditional reliance upon introspective reports, self-report devices, or only grossly accurate, nonspecific measures of physiological (autonomic) arousal may be in contrast to the more indirect measures. Izard (1971) built upon many of these notions in arriving at his theory of emotion: specifically, emotion is considered to consist of three interrelated components. These include "neural activity, striate muscle or facial-postural activity, and subjective experience" (p. 195). In particular, the feedback provided by the facial muscle contractions is seen as a crucial aspect of our immediate experience of the emotion.

In reviewing the literature on facial expressions we continue to focus primarily on experimental, psychological research rather than research based on a structural approach (Duncan, 1969); the latter is perhaps best represented by Birdwhistell (1970). In particular, Birdwhistell argued against the notion of universal facial expression and maintained that all body movement is learned and communicative. In his own research he reportedly isolated 32 distinct movements or "kinemes" in the face and head area (others have proposed fewer or greater numbers). Birdwhistell (1970) contended that meaningful statements could be made about the face alone and that it could only be understood as part of a larger system of body movement. Despite the debatable validity of this contention, one advantage of the structural approach in facial expression research is that facial behaviors are considered in relation to other nonverbal phenomena. Facial "stress markers" (Birdwhistell, 1959) frequently occur in relation to speech. For example, an elevation of the eyebrows typically occurs in conjunction with a rise in pitch at the end of a sentence as a means of changing a statement into an interrogative.

In his review on nonverbal communication, Harrison (1973) categorized researchers on the face into "those who are primarily interested in emotion and those who are interested in other factors, e.g., the face as a regulator (Vine, 1970)" (p. 100). Those who are interested in facial affect can be further subdivided into those who employ a "dimensional approach" (Frijda, 1969) and those who take a "category approach" (Ekman, Friesen, and Ellsworth, 1972). Although we focus almost entirely on facial affect research and spend some time regarding the dimensional approach, the bulk of this review constitutes a summary of the work done by Ekman and his colleagues, who have followed the category approach. Though Tomkins and Izard made invaluable contributions to the study of facial behavior, no one has elevated research in this area to its present state of scientific respectability as much as Ekman. Indeed, as Harrison, Cohen, Crouch, Genova, and Steinberg (1972), in their review of the nonverbal communication literature, stated:

The Ekman, Friesen, and Ellsworth volume, *Emotion in the Human Face: Guidelines for Research and an Integration of Findings,* might well have been titled: "All you ever wanted to know about facial research, and never would have thought to ask." . . . it is a must reading for any modern researcher who would study facial expressions. And it is an instructive reference book for any scholar with a general interest in nonverbal communication. (pp. 467–468)

Much of this chapter is based upon the conceptual framework and the literature provided by that one book. The serious student of facial research should not, however, neglect Izard's 1971 book, *The Face of Emotion,* which places a greater emphasis on emotion per se and perhaps a broader perspective of facial research in relation to psychology in general. Vine (1970) has an excellent chapter summarizing research on "facial visual signals."

Though research on facial expression of emotion is currently one of the most important and promising areas in nonverbal communication research, this has only recently been the case. Though many researchers in the first half of the 20th century pursued the notion that the face accurately communicates emotion, most of their research investigations resulted in failure. These unsuccessful efforts led Hebb to conclude: "These studies have led to the conclusion that an emotion cannot be accurately identified by another observer" (1946, p. 90). Following these early efforts, most researchers left the study of the face as an unproductive venture and turned to other areas. During the 1950s little attention was given to facial research, though Harold Schlosberg continued the interest that he developed in the face while a student of Woodworth and subsequently developed a "dimensional approach" to the study of emotions (Schlosberg, 1954). This line of research has been continued to the present by several researchers whose work we consider in the next section. In actuality, only in the last 10 years has there been increased interest in the communicative aspects of facial behavior, in part due to the search for behavioral measures for psychotherapy research (e.g., Beier, 1966): Tomkins' theory of emotion, Ekman's seminal contributions, and the development of the communication field of "semiotics" (literally, the study of signs).

Research on facial expressions can be organized in the form of various questions. The first must necessarily concern what is meant by the term emotion. Unfortunately, the area of emotional experience and behavior is still most confused and ill defined in psychology. Much of the early work on emotion and facial expression dealt with attempts to identify and define either distinct categories of emotion, such as happiness or sadness, or dimensions (e.g., pleasant-unpleasant) that were posited to underlie various emotion categories. Assuming that such categories or dimensions can be identified, the next question is, can these be accurately identified in the face? Related to this question is the issue of whether facial components are differentially important in expression of feelings. Since most real-life judgments about the face are made in social situations, the contribution of contextual cues must be considered. Finally, since facial expressions can be controlled, one must evaluate the extent to which censorship of facial affect is important since this will influence the utility of studying facial expressions. This question leads directly into Ekman's theory of facial behavior, which provides a convenient introduction for his work on the cross-cultural expression of emotion. This work firmly established the study of facial affect in psychological research. Accordingly, some examples of studies using facial expression as independent and dependent variables are presented, as well as the future direction that research in this area may take. Finally, we briefly review the main methodological considerations that must be undertaken before research can be fruitfully conducted in this area.

FACIAL EXPRESSION AND THE DIMENSIONAL APPROACH

If facial expressions are to be considered communicative of emotions, the first experimental task is to demonstrate that observers can reach an agreement on the meaning of a particular facial expression. Ekman, Friesen, and Ellsworth (1972) called this task "establishing the vocabulary which can be utilized by observers of facial behavior" (p. 67). Dittmann (1972) similarly described this as "the alphabet of emotional communication" (p. 59). One approach has been to have observers consider facial behaviors in terms of traditional emotion labels or categories (happy, sad, fearful). An alternative approach is to assume that behind these categories are some "primary" dimensions on which judgments of emotions are based. Frijda (1969) noted:

Recognition of emotion can be conceived of as a process of multidimensional placement rather than as placement in one of a number of unrelated categories. Moreover, the multitude of emotions as distinguished in the language appears to be reducible to combinations of a far smaller number of dimensions. (p. 176)

That is, emotions such as sad, happy, angry, and so on can be located on a small set of continuous scales or dimensions (each of which is presumably applicable to other emotion categories). One advantage of this approach is the use of ordered or interval data analysis procedures made possible by dimensional scale representation in contrast to the nominal measurement techniques dictated by the category approach. A second attraction of this approach to many researchers was noted by Osgood (1966), namely that dimensions can be employed that represent connotative meaning (as do his three semantic differential factors obtained from his verbal work), which may be more relevant to facial expressions than the denotative emotion categories.

Obviously, the dimension researcher's task is to attempt to define the fewest number of dimensions needed to describe adequately the facial reactions depicted. Two experimental approaches have typically been employed in dimensional studies. One method requires observers to rate facial expressions on experimentally preselected scales; the other, known as the similarity approach, requires judges to rate the similarity between pairs of faces. Factor-analytic techniques frequently are then employed to obtain the dimensions from the rating scales. Schlosberg (1954) can be credited as being the first researcher to conceptualize emotions in terms of several dimensions originally proposed by Woodworth (1938). Based on earlier work, Schlosberg (1954) proposed three dimensions that could be depicted in circular form: pleasant-unpleasant, attention-rejection, and sleep-tension. With this schema, emotion categories can be graphically plotted within the dimensional scheme such that the contribution of each dimension to each category is clearly visible. For example, according to Schlosberg's scheme, the emotion categories fear and anger are rated higher in activation than disgust or contempt. Schlosberg's summary of his rationale for his dimension of sleep-tension illustrates some of the attractions of a dimensional approach:

The activation theory of emotion brings together many of the theories and facts of emotion, at least as far as the intensive dimension is concerned. Instead of treating emotion as a special state, differing qualitatively from other states, the theory locates emotional behavior on a continuum that includes *all* behavior. This continuum, general level of activation, has its low end in sleep, its middle ranges in alert attention, and its high end in the strong emotions. Any one of a number of physiological processes may be taken as an index of general level of activation, but electrical skin conductance has certain advantages for the purpose. It is sensitive, easy to measure, and varies in a manner consistent with expected changes in level of activation. It promises to be equally useful in work on skills and efficiency, as well as on emotions. (1954, p. 87)

Unfortunately, Schlosberg's enthusiasm for physiological measurement as a technique, as well as his posited dimensions, has probably not been supported by research findings.

As was noted, the importance of a dimensional approach lies in identifying the fewest essential variables needed to define emotions. In his research, Schlosberg showed good agreement among observer subjects for his three-dimensional scheme (Engen, Levy, and Schlosberg, 1958). Triandis and Lambert (1958), using Greek subjects, obtained similar agreement. However, Thompson and Meltzer (1964), employing live subjects instead of still photographs of trained actors (as did Schlosberg), failed to demonstrate the circularity of the scale. In addition, they found that only 5 of 6 emotion categories proposed by Schlosberg could be accounted for. Abelson and Sermat (1962) employed 13 facial stimuli from the Lightfoot series of pictures (Engen, Levy, and Schlosberg, 1957) and found agreement with the pleasant-unpleasant dimension, but discovered that the attention-rejection and sleep-tension dimensions were redundant. Gladstones (1962) obtained three dimensions, only two of which were clearly identifiable. Nummenmaa and Kauranne (1958) and Kauranne (1964) employed a similarities and a semantic differential method respectively and obtained support for only two of Schlosberg's dimensions (pleasant-unpleasant and attention-rejection).

Other studies, based on a variety of different methodologies, showed some overlap in dimensions but also considerable variation as well. Osgood (1955, 1966) employed live performances instead of photographs and obtained pleasant-unpleasant, quiet-intense, quiet-active (or "control"), and interest dimensions from a factor analysis of observer ratings. Hastorf, Osgood, and Ono (1966) utilized still photographs of one stimulus person and a factor analysis of 12 rating scales, and obtained three dimensions (pleasant-unpleasant, control, and interest). Frijda and Philipszoon (1963) used a set of 30 pictures in which an actress portrayed a wide variety of emotions and obtained four dimensions from a factor analysis. The first, third, and fourth factors corresponded to pleasant-unpleasant, expressiveness-control, and active attention-disinterest dimensions, but the second could not easily be defined. In two subsequent studies, Fridja (1968, 1969) obtained six and seven factors respectively.

Finally, Dittmann (1972) recently used a dimensional approach with motion picture segments (rather than still photographs) of two interview participants. "An Affect Checklist of 17 categories developed from a thorough search of the literature both on perception of emotion and of feeling and emotion generally" was employed (Dittmann, 1972, p. 67). Sixteen judges rated each of 25 three-second movie segments using the Adjective Checklist. A factor analysis yielded four dimensions including pleasant-unpleasant, activation, trust-mistrust, and a fourth, unidentifiable one.

As can be seen from this sample array of dimension studies, there is little agreement on the exact number of dimensions (the studies cited suggest anything from two to seven) or the labels. Ekman, Friesen, and Ellsworth (1972) suggested that three dimensions are probably common to most studies (pleasant-unpleasant, attentional activity, and intensity-control), but that at least one more and perhaps two or three more may be necessary to account for the emotions studied. The problem with these findings is that the original utility value of the dimensional approach was to reduce the number of meanings necessary to understand emotion to a smaller number than provided for by the category approach. Another problem is the lack of agreement on a model. Schlosberg, Frijda, and Osgood, the three main proponents of dimensional research, all contended that their dimensions were related to emotion categories. However, Frijda proposed a hierarchial model (where emotion categories were independent but shared the dimensional qualities), whereas Osgood and Schlosberg attempted to relate emotion categories within geometric dimensional models. In addition, Frijda believed the dimensions should relate to action tendencies, whereas Osgood favored the dimensions from his verbal semantic differential model. Many of the differences between studies may thus have been due to differences in the choices among scales.

In addition to differences in the dimension models and choice of dimensions, Ekman, Friesen, and Ellsworth (1972) noted a number of methodological inadequacies common to most of these studies (with the exception of Dittmann, 1972). One major problem has been the use of only a few stimulus persons who might have had particular idiosyncratic expressions that limited the generality of ratings. This problem may be further compounded by the use of posed expressions and still photographs rather than filmed or videotape recordings of spontaneous facial expressions. In summarizing the research on the dimensional approach, the authors stated:

It seems doubtful that consistent findings about dimensions of emotion will be found until investigators utilize stimuli which have been shown by other means to represent a number of different emotion categories, . . . until they sample the behavior of many different persons, and until they select scales which systematically represent all or, at least, many of the aspects of emotion which might be judged from the face—appearance, feeling, action, consequences, etc. (Ekman, Friesen, and Ellsworth, 1972, p. 74)

FACIAL EXPRESSIONS AND EMOTION CATEGORIES

In contrast to a dimensional approach, one can simply make the assumption that there is a set of *basic* emotions, and that once identified, these categories cannot be profitably reduced any further. The following passage by Ekman, Friesen, and Ellsworth (1972) provides a nice summary of the category approach to studying emotion in the face:

Some theorists have postulated a set of basic emotion categories, or primary affects. Each of these categories includes a set of words denoting related emotions which may differ in intensity, degree of control, or, in minor ways, in denotative meaning. While the principal of inclusion is not always explained, the words within a category are held to be a lot more similar than the words across categories. Presumably different facial behaviors are associated with each of these emotion categories, although no theorist has ever fully explicated the exact nature of such differences in facial components. (p. 57)

Allport first proposed a set of emotion categories in 1924, though Woodworth (1938) was the first to research this question systematically. The typical research strategy has been to obtain samples of emotional behavior and then have observers label each. Woodworth employed one person enacting 10 emotions for photographs. Observers then rated these photographs using 10 emotion words supplied them (those most commonly used from a much larger list of emotion words). Correlations between the poser's intended expression and observer judgment constituted the basis for selection of the particular categories. As a result of his work, Woodworth proposed the following categories or sets of categories: love, mirth, happiness; surprise; fear; suffering; anger; determination; disgust; and contempt. More recent investigators proposed the emotion categories shown in Table 3-1:

Table 3-1. Postulated Emotion Categories (Adapted from Ekman, Friesen, and Ellsworth, 1972)

Pluchick (1962)	Tomkins and McCarter (1964)	Osgood (1966)	Frijda (1968)
Coyness, happiness, joy	Enjoyment, joy	Compacency, quiet, pleasure, joy, glee, worried laughter	Happy
Surprise, amazement, astonishment	Surprise, startle	Surprise, amazement, bewilderment, awe	Surprise
Apprehension, fear, terror	Fear, terror	Fear, horror	Fear
Pensiveness, sorrow, grief	Distress, anguish	Despair, boredom, dreamy sadness Acute sorrow, despair	Sad
Annoyance, anger, rage	Anger, rage	Sullen anger, rage, stubbornness, determination	Anger
Tiresomeness, disgust, loathing	Disgust, contempt	Annoyance, disgust, contempt	Disgust
Attentiveness, expectancy, anticipation	Interest, excitement	Expectancy, interest	Attention
Acceptance, incorporation	Shame, humiliation	Pity, distrust, anxiety	Calm
			Bitter
			Pride
			Irony
			Insecure
			Skepticism

In obtaining his emotion categories, Plutchik (1962) photographed two stimulus persons instructed to move their facial muscles in every conceivable way rather than to pose emotions. In contrast, Tomkins and McCarter (1964) used a larger number of stimulus persons (11) who were also photographed portraying various emotions. Osgood (1966) had observers rate different subjects posing a total of 40 different labels for feeling states. Fifty subjects were given a list of 5 feeling states to enact such that each feeling state was enacted by 5 different persons. Observers thus had a wide selection of emotion vocabulary words to choose from. Cluster analysis and factor-analytic techniques were employed to extract the emotion categories. Finally, Frijda (1968) also utilized factor analysis in evaluating observer ratings of still photographs of two persons posing an unspecified number of emotions. It is interesting that even though observers had 100 emotion category words from which to choose, Frijda still obtained seven major categories.

Despite variations in emotion words within categories and some differences in the number of categories obtained, considerable agreement can be seen from these results. As Ekman, Friesen, and Ellsworth (1972) noted: "It is a tribute to the robustness of the phenomena that, despite the span of time over which this research was done and the very different theoretical viewpoints of the investigators, the results are by and large consistent" (pp. 60–61). Based on their own and previous investigations, Ekman, Friesen, and Ellsworth (1972) proposed happiness, surprise, fear, sadness, anger, disgust-contempt, and interest as the seven major primary affect categories. In addition, they identified a number of methodological reasons why the findings might be inconsistent. To adequately identify facial expression categories a sufficient sample of facial behavior must be studied. In reviewing these studies, Ekman, Friesen, and Ellsworth (1972) noted that few employed more than a small number of stimulus persons and most judgments were based only on photographs of posed stimuli. Furthermore, observers were generally limited in their response to pictures to the number of descriptive verbal categories provided by authors, which varied greatly from study to study. What facial stimuli the observers rate is also obviously important. For example, pain, while not an emotion (even though it is associated with a discriminable facial appearance), may be a component expressed in some of the stimuli rated by observers (Ekman and Friesen, 1967). Indeed, Boucher (1969) demonstrated that stimuli previously labeled in terms of Woodworth's categories of fear and suffering or in Tomkins and McCarter's categories of distress and anguish could be judged as either fear, sadness, or pain, or a combination of two of the terms.

"Confusion" among observers in rating facial expressions may also lead to discrepant findings. In particular, some emotions may be frequently confused for one another. Tomkins and McCarter (1964) described these errors as being "common confusions," where a minority of judges are consistent in their rating of facial expression (and where a majority of observers use another emotion category). For example, fear, surprise, and interest appear related to each other, given that surprise is frequently mistaken for interest and fear for surprise (though fear and interest are rarely confused). Similarly, anger and disgust-contempt are often confused.

A real possibility for many confusions, however, lies in the presence of *affect blends* which may occur in facial expressions. This important point was illustrated in a recent study (Kiritz and Ekman, 1971). Observers who were allowed to indicate an affect blend did so for stimuli which, in other studies, had yielded approximately a 60–40% distribution of judgment responses (divided between the two categories making up the blend). Interestingly, Kiritz and Ekman found that when the proportion of judgment responses became more skewed (i.e., 80–20), most observers were unable to perceive a blend (even when the judgment process allowed for it), and there was a consistent minority of observers who showed "uncommon shared confusions." Ekman's identification of affect blends is particularly important for category research because categories (other than the basic seven proposed here) may represent secondary-affect categories based on blends of primary affects. He noted:

For example, it may be that the term "smugness" would be used to describe specific facial behavior when observers are given a free choice to use any word in their vocabulary, and that this same facial behavior would be described as both *angry* and *happy* when observers are limited to choosing among the seven categories but allowed multiple choices. (Ekman, Friesen, and Ellsworth, 1972, p. 64)

STUDIES ON THE RECOGNITION OF FACIAL EXPRESSION

One of the hindrances to research on facial expression was the finding, reported in several early studies (e.g., Landis, 1924, 1929; Sherman, 1927), that observers could not identify facial expressions accurately beyond what would be expected by chance. Subsequent influential reviews of the literature (Bruner and Tagiuri, 1954; Tagiuri, 1968), noting these negative findings, tended to discourage further research along these lines. Recently, Ekman and his colleagues carefully reviewed the early research on facial expression and noted important methodological faults that tend to discredit these studies with negative results. We do not attempt to summarize their points beyong agreeing with their conclusion that "the Landis and Sherman experiments, with their questionable negative findings, have, in our opinion, had unmerited influence in the investigation of judgment of emotion from facial behavior" (Ekman, Friesen, and Ellsworth, 1972, p. 89).

More recent studies investigating observer accuracy in recognition of facial expression have employed various stimuli in the judgment task, including candid photos, posed emotions, and filmed spontaneous behavior. In an early study, Munn (1940) employed candid magazine photographs of individuals in spontaneous poses. An immediate problem of any study of this sort concerns the criteria for accuracy. That is, when a person says a facial expression is sad, how do we know he is correct? Munn's answer was to present some observers only the photographs of the face and others the whole picture (face and social context), the latter judgments serving as the criteria for the accuracy of the former. A second criterion employed was his own "expert" judgment of the photographed facial expression. Though observers were able to label accurately the facial expressions at a level beyond chance, these accuracy criteria can be criticized on the grounds that (a) Munn's own judgments were not based on his personally witnessing the photographed event, and (b) there was no test to evaluate for the contribution that the face made in the face-alone versus full-photograph situation. Indeed, in all three ratings, the facial expression was present, and thus none of the judgments can be considered independent of one another.

To demonstrate an alternative approach, Ekman, Friesen, and Ellsworth (1972) took the photographs employed by Munn and two other researchers who employed candid photographs (Hanawalt, 1944; Vinacke, 1949) and made up verbal descriptions of the situations. These were then submitted to one set of raters who selected from a list of emotion category responses that which they thought best fitted the situation. Descriptions for which there was at least 50% agreement as to what emotion was being expressed were compared with observers' ratings of the corresponding photographs. Accuracy, as determined in this fashion, was obtained for photographs rated as depicting happy, surprised, fearful, and sad facial expressions; anger and disgust-contempt stimuli could not be consistently rated. Though the criterion for accuracy employed in this approach can hardly be considered absolute, verbal description is free of the confounding effect of facial expression that cuts across Munn's judgment procedures.

A second way in which accuracy has been studied in the judgment of facial expressions has been through the use of posed or enacted emotional expressions, either in still photographs or, in some cases, in motion pictures or videotapes. The use of posed or enacted emotional expressions has been criticized because they are obviously not necessarily representative of unposed or spontaneous emotional expressions, but they are experimentally advantageous in that the instructions to enact an emotion in a sense "defines" the criterion of accuracy. Where actors are not employed, however, there remains the question of how well the expression was enacted. Several early studies (Dusenbury and Knower, 1938; Kanner, 1931; Woodworth, 1938) employed this procedure, and above-chance accuracy in identifying emotions was obtained. More recently, Thompson and Meltzer (1964) had 50 untrained subjects enact 10 emotions live before four judges, who attempted to decode the subjects' facial expressions. Accuracy ranged from 38 to 76%, with happiness, fear, love, and determination being more accurately recognized than disgust, contempt, and suffering. Thompson and Meltzer noted "considerable individual differences" in enactment ability among subjects, an important finding resulting from the large number of encoders used. Contrary to their expectations, no personality correlates of enactment ability were obtained, as based on administration of the California Personality Inventory.

Levitt (1964) obtained filmed reactions of 50 persons enacting different emotions which were then judged by 24 observers. Accuracy was above chance, happiness being the easiest to recognize, followed by sadness, anger, fear, disgust/contempt, and surprise. Subsequently, Ekman and Friesen (1965) asked six psychiatric patients to describe before a camera how they were feeling. Though not exactly a posed-emotion situation, patients' descriptions of their affect states were regarded as the criteria for accuracy. High agreement was obtained for patient description and observer judgments of happiness and sadness and low agreement for fear and disgust-contempt. In his study noted earlier, Osgood (1966) obtained above-chance accuracy for recognition of all emotions, though for some reason accuracy was only 16% for fear and 19% for sadness categories (not above chance). With the goal of replicating the experiment by Thompson and Meltzer (1964), Drag and Shaw (1967) had 48 subjects attempt to communicate facially 10 emotions to 4 judges. Again, happiness was found the easiest to communicate, followed by surprise and fear, whereas sadness, anger, and disgust-contempt were less accurately recognized. In addition, females were found easier to judge than males when conveying happiness, love, fear, and anger. A measure of situational anxiety did not appear related to communication accuracy. Most recently, Zuckerman, Lipets, Koivumaki, and Rosenthal (1975) photographed male and female subjects enacting six emotions (i.e., anger, happiness, sadness, fear, surprise, disgust). Subjects were given a card containing each emotion word embedded in an appropriate sentence. Each sentence also contained the word "really" (e.g., "I am really sad") and all subjects were photographed while saying that word. Females tended to be better expressers than males. The positive emotions, happiness and surprise, were the easiest for observers to judge, compared to the "negative" emotions of fear, sadness, anger, and disgust.

These findings of sex differences were recently extended to racial differences. Kozel and Gitter (1968) employed black and caucasian actresses to express emotions via motion picture. Blacks were more accurately perceived in the expression of anger and sadness; whites more accurately communicated happiness and fear. Gitter, Black, and Mostofsky (1972) employed 10 white and 10 black actors, male and female, who were photographed expressing happiness, anger, surprise, fear, disgust, pain, and sadness. One hundred and sixty observers of both races and sexes judged the photographs. Blacks were less accurately judged than whites, while females communicated their emotions better than males. In particular, white expressers were judged more accurately on all six emotions except for pain, where blacks appeared to be more expressive. Females were more accurately judged on anger, surprise, and fear, while males were better in expressing sadness, pain, and disgust.

Finally, a number of judgment studies have utilized samples of spontaneous behavior, generally obtained through some experimental manipulation. Compared to studies of posed emotions, experiments of this type have been generally limited to judgments of positive and negative emotional states rather than specific emotion categories. The reason for this is that it is difficult to devise situations that can predictably elicit specific emotions. Indeed, a weakness in this approach is that one cannot always guarantee that the subject's reaction will be the intended one. Nevertheless, studies of this kind are the only ones in which "natural" reactions can be elicited and where some control over the eliciting circumstances is possible.

In these studies, the observer was usually asked to identify the emotion aroused, which was compared with the hypothesized effect of the experimental manipulation (e.g., to make the subject fearful) or the subject's self-report. In other instances, the observer was asked to name the actual eliciting circumstance, based on the subject's facial cues. The main exceptions to this approach are two early studies by Ekman (Ekman and Bressler, 1964; Ekman and Rose, 1965), which used as their accuracy criterion expected differences in mood states of psychiatric patients (depressives) during acute and remitted phases of a psychotic disorder. Ratings of the patients' expressions on a pleasant-unpleasant scale were reliably associated with the patient illness course.

In another series of studies, Ekman (1965) employed an experimental manipulation in an interview situation. Interviewees were submitted to "stress" and "catharsis" interview experiences during which a series of photographs was taken, some of which were randomly selected for rating. Observers were to rate the photographs in terms of Schlosberg's dimensions of pleasant-unpleasant, attention-rejection, and sleep-tension, accuracy being judged in terms of the two stimulus situations. Observer ratings of photographs from stress and catharsis situations reflected above-chance accuracy for the pleasant-unpleasant dimension. In a similar approach, Jorgensen and Howell (1969) and Howell and Jorgensen (1970) took motion pictures of females subjected to pleasant and unpleasant interview situations. Two-minute film segments of 8 interviewees during the stress and relief phases were judged by observers. In their first study, accuracy was measured by the agreement between the interviewees' semantic differential ratings of their own emotion and the observers' ratings on the same scale. In the second study, observers simply indicated whether the interviewee seemed to be experiencing an unpleasant or pleasant emotion, the criterion for accuracy being the actual stimulus situation for the interviewee. In addition to finding greater overall observer accuracy on judgments from visual (i.e., facial) cues as opposed to written transcripts, the authors found that unpleasant emotions were less accurately judged than pleasant emotions and that stimulus subjects differed considerably in their transmissions of affective cues.

Several studies followed an ingenious paradigm first developed to study communication in monkeys (Miller, Banks, and Ogawa, 1962). Gubar (1966), for example, exposed two separated human subjects to a shock-avoidance situation where one subject was given information and the other the avoidance response. To successfully prevent shock, the second subject had to discriminate the other's facial reaction to reward (nonshock) and punishment (shock trial) signals. In his study, Gubar found that subjects who first had an opportunity to learn the discrimination avoidance task (i.e., they were presented the signal and allowed to make a response) were subsequently able to benefit from their partner's facial cues and avoid the shock on a better-than-chance basis when they were denied direct information. Lanzetta and Kleck (1970) secretly videotaped subjects receiving signalled shock and nonshock trials who later were presented with the videotapes of themselves and other subjects with the task of identifying shock and nonshock trials. Significant accuracy was demonstrated, though some subjects gave more distinct facial cues than others. Facial expressiveness, interestingly, was negatively related to physiological reactivity.

In a series of studies, Buck and his colleagues (Buck, Miller, and Caul, 1974; Buck, Savin, Miller, and Caul, 1969, 1972) presented subjects with a series of "emotionally loaded" slides arranged in five categories: sexual, scenic, maternal, unpleasant, and unusual. Each subject viewed the slide for 10 seconds and then verbally described his response. At the same time, an "observer" subject viewing the "sender" through closed-circuit TV (video but no audio) judged what category of slide was being presented and the sender's emotional reaction in terms of pleasantness-unpleasantness. Statistically significant "communication" was demonstrated. Females appeared to be better senders (i.e., more facially expressive as judged by the experimenter) than males. In addition, for male senders, skin conductance correlated $-.74$ ($p < .01$) with communication accuracy (Buck, Miller, and

Caul, 1974). These authors subdivided the subjects into two groups based upon their "communication accuracy" (agreement of sender and receiver on each's pleasantness scale ratings) and physiological skin conductance response. One group was identified as internalizers, the other as externalizers. Internalizers tended to be male and physiologically more reactive to the slides, but were less facially expressive and more impersonal in their descriptions of their feelings. On various personality measures they were also lower in self-esteem and higher in introversion and in sensitization scores on the Byrne R-S scale. Though these findings at present require much additional investigation to be fully understood, it is gratifying to note that a number of potentially important personality correlates are emerging from studies such as these.

ANALYSIS OF FACIAL COMPONENTS

To date almost all of the research on facial expression has been directed towards demonstrating that facial expressions do reliably communicate emotional states. Having demonstrated this, investigators have begun to ask whether specific components of facial expression (i.e., particular facial areas) are differentially important in communicating emotional states. Ekman described component studies as follows:

In component studies facial behavior is the dependent variable or response measure, rather than the independent variable or stimulus as it is in judgement studies. We are not attempting to determine what observers can say about faces, but what the measurement of facial components can indicate about some aspect of a person's experience. (Ekman, Friesen, and Ellsworth, 1972, p. 109)

Ekman also noted, however, that:

There have been remarkably few component studies, [which is probably] due to the difficulty in deciding what to measure in the face. At this point there is still no accepted notion of the units of facial behavior, nor any general procedure for measuring or scoring facial components. (Ekman, Friesen, and Ellsworth, 1972, p. 109)

Recently, several techniques have been developed. Two are based on an ethological approach (Blurton-Jones, 1969; Grant, 1969); neither has been experimentally validated. A third approach (FAST, or Facial Affect Scoring Technique), developed by Ekman, Friesen, and Tomkins (1971), has received some validation and is the focus of this section.

Excluding from consideration some early facial component studies (Fulcher, 1942; Landis and Hunt, 1939; Thompson, 1941; these are reviewed in Ekman, Friesen, and Ellsworth, 1972) and notwithstanding a study employing schematic drawings (Harrison, 1965), only three have been reported in the last decade prior to the development of the FAST system. Leventhal and Sharp (1965), for example, studied the facial features of women in pre-childbirth labor. "Comfort" and "distress" signs were derived from Birdwhistell's coding system and systematic observations were made during four time periods of labor. Observations were made of the forehead, brow, eyelids, nose, eye, and mouth area. The data revealed a significant and systematic decrease in facial comfort signs and an increase in distress signs for the forehead, brow, and eyelid indices as labor progressed. In addition, self-report measures of predispositional anxiety were positively associated with greater signs of distress, and women with prior childbirth experience showed fewer facial signs of distress and more comfort signs than the primigravidae. Just what specific emotions accompanied these changes was not ascertained.

In another study, Trujillo and Warthin (1968) attempted to relate signs of frowning (specifically the number of vertical furrows) to peptic ulcer patients. The authors tested their hypothesis by asking 100 diagnosed duodenal ulcer patients and 100 control patients to frown, during which time the number of vertical furrows appearing within 1.5 centimeters of the midline was counted. Ninety-five of the control patients had two or less vertical furrows whereas 87 of the 100 duodenal ulcer patients had three or more and 64 had four or more. A replication sample yielded a 77% incidence of three or more vertical furrows in ulcer patients and a 6% rate for controls. Despite the interesting nature of this finding, this particular brow sign has been associated with anger, fear, and sadness as well as pain, and it cannot be regarded as giving any specific information about the emotional experience of those patients. Finally, Rubenstein (1969) reported an interesting procedure whereby depressed patients' smiles before and after ECT were photographed. Through a complicated technique involving photographing of facial silhouettes from different angles, he was able to show that 14 of 16 post-ECT patients showed a greater facial displacement when smiling after ECT. The information value and potential utility of this procedure were not discussed. However Schwartz (1974; Schwartz, Fair, Greenberg, Mandel, and Klerman, 1975) made use of EMG facial readings to achieve a form of "invisible" component analysis in several studies that are described later.

In 1971 Ekman, Friesen, and Tomkins published a report on their Facial Affect Scoring Technique (FAST), which can be used for evaluating either fixed facial expressions or "live" (e.g., videotaped) facial expressions. The FAST technique requires that coders view separate areas of the face (the brows/forehead area; eyelids; lower face including cheeks, nose, and mouth) for observable facial movements which are then compared to FAST still-photographic examples. Coders are first trained in the application of the technique consisting of a careful discussion of each FAST photograph item (the important discriminations to make, etc.), followed by supervised scoring of practice photographs. The photographic items employed in FAST are carefully selected "to define each of the movements within each area of the face which, theoretically, distinguish among six emotions: happiness, sadness, surprise, fear, anger, and disgust" (Ekman, Friesen, and Ellsworth, 1972, p. 114). Whereas other scoring approaches consist of only a verbal description, FAST does not:

> Instead of describing a movement as "the action of the frontalis muscle which leads to raising of both brows in a somewhat curved shape, with horizontal wrinkles across the forehead," FAST utilizes a picture of just that area of the face in that particular position to define that scoring item. (Ekman, Friesen, and Ellsworth, 1972, p. 114)

Ekman further described FAST as follows:

> FAST is applied by having independent coders view each of three areas of the face separately, with the rest of the face blocked from view. It should be emphasized that the FAST measurement procedure does *not* entail having the coder judge the emotion shown in the face he is coding. Rather, each movement within a facial area is distinguished, its exact duration determined with the aid of slowed motion, and the type of movement classified by comparing the movement observed with the atlas of FAST criterion photographs. (Ekman, Friesen, and Ellsworth, 1972, p. 114)

Eight FAST atlas photographs are provided for the brows/forehead area, 17 for the eyes/lids, and 45 for the lower face.

In scoring any facial movement, the judgments of more than one independent observer are used to derive an emotion prediction based upon the FAST items selected. This exact but very time-consuming[2] procedure yields a series of duration scores for each of the seven emotion categories and the three separate facial areas. The frequency of occurrence or the duration of each emotion sign within each facial area can be utilized alone, or composite scores can be obtained for the entire face that can show a single emotion or blend of emotions.

In an initial test of their FAST system (Ekman, Friesen, and Tomkins, 1971), pictures of full facial expressions considered to reflect a single emotion were chosen from photograph sets developed by other investigators such as Frois-Wittmann (1930), Frijda, Izard, Nummenmaa, Schlosberg, and Ekman. Fifty-one such pictures (of 28 different persons) were shown to 82 observers who were permitted to choose two emotions from six available categories. Each photograph was scored by the FAST procedure by coders working independently. An emotion was assigned to each photograph based upon the most frequent emotion category assigned to the three separate facial areas. Comparisons were made between the FAST ratings and whole-face judgments by other observers. Agreement was obtained on 45 of the 51 photographs including perfect agreement for surprise and anger categories, one disagreement each on sadness, happiness, and disgust pictures, and four on fear. Application of more complex decision rules than the simple majority-rule criterion increased agreement to 49 of the 51 photographs.

In a careful review of earlier component studies (e.g., Coleman, 1949; Hanawalt, 1944; Nummenmaa, 1964; Plutchik, 1962), Ekman, Friesen, and Ellsworth (1972) noted considerable inconsistency among the findings. Based on their analysis, they concluded:

We believe this confusion is due to an oversimplified view of how facial components might be related to emotion, based on an unwarranted assumption that different facial areas are independent, and a questionable assumption that there is one movement in one facial area for each emotion. . . . Instead, we believe that for *each* emotion there may be a number of alternative movements within *each* facial area. (p. 125)

Complicating this matter are facial movements which are completely irrelevant to emotion, such as facial gestures and instrumental actions. Thus Ekman, Friesen, and Ellsworth stated:

The facial areas probably differ in terms of the ratio of nonaffective movements to affect-specific components which can occur. The brows/forehead probably have a smaller number of nonaffective movements and also of affect-specific components than the lower face. (1972, pp. 125–126)

In another study, Ekman, Friesen, and Malmstrom (1970), in association with Averill, Opton, and Lazarus (1969) at the University of California, Berkeley, had Japanese and American subjects view stressful and neutral films while a videotape was secretly obtained of their facial behavior. FAST-derived scores from three-minute video film segments revealed tremendous differences in subjects' facial behaviors for the two situations. In addition, Ekman and his colleagues were able to identify more FAST-defined facial expressions of surprise, sadness, disgust, and anger during the stress film (a film on sinus surgery). The neutral film (on autumn leaves) showed more facial behavior measured by FAST as happiness. In addition to providing further validity for the FAST system, the findings show that for any individual even in a short time span more than one facial emotion may be elicited by a particular stimulus.

Decoders in judgment tasks of filmed behavior may thus be faced with a number of different facial cues. A disadvantage of filmed segments of facial behavior is thus that the expressions can change quickly over time, and exactly what cues a decoder has utilized may be impossible to determine without the aid of special slow motion equipment. Indeed, different judgments by decoders may reflect accurate perceptions of different facial cues. In addition, self-reports by subjects of their emotional experience may not be accurate criteria for their facial behavior unless they are obtained in close association with the actual facial behavior that is occurring.

Most recently, Boucher and Ekman (1975) reported an evaluation of their hypothesis that facial areas are differentially involved in emotional expression. Subjects were presented 32 photographs of six persons showing emotion poses of happiness, anger, sadness, disgust, fear, and surprise. An important procedure in the selection of photographs was the requirement that there be 70% agreement among judges that the posed emotion was the only emotion present. The photographs meeting this criterion were then cut into various sections with each section to be shown alone to student judges or combined with a complementary section of a neutral facial expression. Except for happiness and disgust poses, division of the photographs into parts was based upon the anatomical independence of facial musculature. Subject raters were required to rate each facial area on all six emotion categories, giving an intensity value for each. A facial area was considered to contribute to an accurate judgment of the hypothesized emotion if the subject rated that emotion highest in intensity. As predicted, the following results (percentage of correct judgements) were obtained:

1. Fear was best predicted (67%) from the eyes/eyelid area.
2. Sadness was best judged (67%) from the eyes/eyelids.
3. Happiness was seen in the cheeks/mouth (98%) and eyes/eyelids with cheeks/mouth (99%).
4. Surprise was predictable from all of the three facial areas (brow/forehead, 79%; eyes/eyelids, 63%; cheeks/mouth, 52%).

Contrary to predictions, anger was not best judged from the cheeks/mouth and brows/forehead areas. Instead, anger was identified with only about 30% accuracy from the cheeks/mouth, brows/forehead, and eyes/eyelids areas, suggesting that "anger differs from the other five facial expressions of emotions in being ambiguous to the viewer unless the anger is registered in at least two and usually three areas of the face" (Boucher and Ekman, 1975, p. 27). Interestingly, the accuracy of emotion predictions based on judgments of facial areas was comparable to agreement obtained for the photographs of the entire face. The results of this study thus provide strong support for the differential importance of facial areas in the expression of emotion. In addition, they provide a ready explanation why earlier investigators who were unaware of the importance of different facial areas were not more successful in their research.

FACIAL EXPRESSIONS AND THE SITUATIONAL CONTEXT

In real life we always observe others' facial expressions in some situation. Though the research has demonstrated that above-chance accuracy judgments from facial cues in isolation can be made, it is important to consider how much information facial expression does provide when the situation is also known. An especially important question is, what does an observer judge about a person's emotion when his facial behavior is inconsistent as well as with the situation? Fernberger in 1928 hypothesized that the situational context would dictate what emotion was judged rather than the person's facial expression. Bruner and Tagiuri (1954) suggested that information from both sources would yield more accurate judgments than from either alone.

An example of a study investigating the relative contribution of facial and situational cues to emotion judgments was conducted by Frijda (1969). Frijda had observer subjects rate facial photographs and written situation descriptions independent of each other on a 7-point bipolar scale. A week later the same subjects then rated the photographs combined with the situation description. Emotion ratings of each type of cue judged alone and together were obtained. In addition, some situation-description–facial-expression combinations were inconsistent with each other, the judgments on these combinations permitting a test of the relative contribution of the type of cue. Frijda found that information from the face dominated observer-subject judgments of discordant cue combinations. In several further experiments, Frijda found that the particular emotion associated with each cue was important in determining the weight given each in discordant cue situations. When a sad story was presented with a happy face, verbal context tended to dominate; however, when a sad face was paired with a happy story, the face clearly influenced the judgment. Generally, Frijda's findings indicated that facial cues were the more important, contrary to what Fernberger (1928) or Bruner and Tagiuri (1954) had predicted. Employing a different approach, Thayer and Schiff (1969) compared facial expressions and motion cues shown in an animated film presentation. Various sets of facial expressions (e.g., happy, angry) were shown in various combinations of approach-withdrawal from each other. In general, facial cues tended to dominate the judge's interpretation of the social situation. For example, an angry face combined with any motion cue still resulted in an interpretation of an "angry encounter."

In their book, Ekman, Friesen, and Ellsworth (1972) pointed to a number of important variables generally not considered in studies of context and facial cues. Specifically, the *source clarity* of a facial or situational cue must be taken into account. Source clarity refers to the kind and magnitude of information that either a facial or contextual cue supplies about emotion to observers. A cue may vary in its source clarity as a function of its *ambiguity* (e.g., as reflected in the magnitude of agreement among observers as to the meaning of a facial cue), its *complexity* (e.g., a single emotion versus a blend of emotions in a facial expression), and its *strength* (as measured by an observer's intensity rating). As Ekman, Friesen, and Ellsworth (1972) noted, no studies up to the time of their book had controlled for these source clarity variables. However, Watson (1972) recently did control for one aspect of source clarity (i.e., ambiguity) in facial and contextual cues by selecting and using only stimulus materials for which there was high observer agreement as to the emotion category or dimension rating of each cue. These stimuli were then presented to other subjects in concordant and discordant combinations. Watson found facial expressions were more salient in the judgment process than contextual information. Only when neutral facial expressions were paired with sad situational context did the observer judgments favor the context.

Thus in two recent experiments facial cues seemed *more* important than the verbal situational description. However, since the context cues were provided in written form while the facial cues were from photographs and hence possibly more "real" to observers, it is possible that those sets of cues differed in their credibility. Further experimentation (perhaps with nonwritten visual contextual cues) is necessary to answer the question concerning the relative importance of the type of cues. In addition, Ekman, Friesen, and Ellsworth (1972) noted that it will be important "to investigate the nature of those occasions when the face provides more information than the context, when the context provides more information. . . . [and] the particular cognitive mechanisms employed [by observers] to resolve discrepant information between the face and context" (p. 150). Indeed, Shapiro (1968) observed that some individuals tend to favor linguistic cues whereas others favor facial cues, and that these tendencies appear to be reliable.

EKMAN'S THEORY OF FACIAL EXPRESSION: UNIVERSALS AND CULTURE-BOUND ASPECTS

Having considered many of the findings related to judgments of emotion from the face and/or facial components, we come to the important question concerning the *generality* of facial expressions of emotion. That is, to what extent a person in one culture recognizes the emotions of a person from another culture from that person's facial expression? Darwin (1872) was the first to propose universal facial behaviors for each emotion. Allport (1924), Asch (1952), Tomkins (1962), Izard (1971), and Ekman (1972) wrote in support of this view, whereas Birdwhistell (1963) and LaBarre (1947, 1962), for example, argued that facial expressions are "culture bound." In particular, Birdwhistell espoused this view:

When I first became interested in body motion . . . I anticipated a research strategy which could first isolate universal signs of feeling that were species specific. . . . As research proceeded, and even before the development of kinesics, it became clear that this search for universals was culture bound. . . . There are probably no universal symbols of emotional state. (1963), p. 126).

Today, however, there is considerable evidence that facial expressions of emotion themselves are "universal" though specific cultural norms may dictate differently how and when they are expressed. The evidence referred to is largely based on the research of Paul Ekman and his associate Wallace Friesen, who, with some early guidance from Silvan Tomkins, developed their theory of facial expression of emotion which will be the subject of this section. Earlier we recommended as "must" reading Ekman, Friesen, and Ellsworth's 1972 book on *Emotion in the Human Face*. For this section in which cross-cultural research is considered and his theory is fully elaborated, an essential reference is his article, "Universals and cultural differences in facial expression of emotion" (Ekman, 1972).

Ekman described how early in his work he became persuaded that different facial behaviors were both universal and culture-bound. Describing a visit by Silvan Tomkins, who viewed a film on two preliterate cultures, he wrote:

We showed him some short samples of the facial behavior from each of the two cultures, providing him with no information about either of the cultures. Tomkins inferred many aspects of the differences between the two cultures in child rearing, marital practices, and adult–adult interaction, which we knew to be correct from information provided by Gajdusek and Sorenson. Tomkins showed us how he thought he made his inferences, based upon the frequency of occurrence of specific facial expressions of emotions, sequences of emotional expressions, the context in which facial expressions were shown, etc. Equally important, he pointed out some of the specific facial muscular movements upon which he based his interpretations. . . . These experiences convinced us that there must be both universal and culture-specific facial expressions. (1972, p. 211)

Ekman (1968, 1972) and Ekman and Friesen (1967, 1971) proposed a "neurocultural theory of facial expressions of emotion":

Universals occur through the operation of a facial affect program which specifies the relationship between distinctive movements of the facial muscles and particular emotions, such as happiness, sadness, anger, fear, etc. Cultural differences in facial expression occur (a) because most of the events which through learning become established as the elicitors of particular emotions will vary across cultures, (b) because the rules for controlling facial expressions in particular social settings will also vary across cultures, and (c) because some of the consequences of emotional arousal will also vary with culture. (Ekman, 1972, p. 212)

Ekman's theory of facial affect expressions consists of *elicitors* that evoke the innate *facial affect program,* which is in turn modified by cultural *display rules,* resulting in certain *behavioral consequences.* Elicitors of facial expression can, in some cases, be unlearned, such as a disgust expression in response to a bad smell or taste, or surprise expressions to a sudden loud sound or unexpected event. However, most elicitors of emotional reactions are learned and a majority are interpersonal in nature and, as such, tied to the culture. Though the facial expression will have the same meaning across cultures, the stimulus that elicited it may differ from culture to culture. A common fault in cross-cultural research has been the assumption that the same stimulus or event will elicit the same emotional reaction in two different peoples. For example, one might erroneously assume that a New Orleans black's facial expression of a sadness at a funeral is what we would consider a smile, when in truth their cultural response to death is not sadness but instead joy and happiness for the deceased, which is quite consonant with the smiling seen at the funeral.

While the eliciting events for the same emotions vary from one culture to another, given cultural norms, individual expectations, social learning histories, and so forth, "what is universal in facial expressions of emotion is the particular set of facial muscular movements triggered when a given emotion is elicited" (Ekman, 1972, p. 216). Ekman (1972) reviewed a number of theories that attempt to explain the development of a linkage between certain facial expressions and different emotions. We will not review them here beyond noting again that Ekman posited seven primary emotions (happiness, anger, surprise, fear, disgust, sadness, interest), each associated with distinct neural affect programs which are universal. In addition to the primary affects, it is important to recognize that secondary, blend, or multiple emotions can occur from combinations of primary affects. Blends can theoretically occur in four ways: (a) as a rapid sequence of two primary emotions which to an observer may be perceptually fused into a blend, (b) one area of the face may show one emotion and another part a second emotion, (c) the right and left sides of the face may show different emotions, (d) a blend can be the muscular movement resulting from activation of different primary emotions. Ekman noted that only the second type of blend has really been studied while the others, though predictable from theory, have not been experimentally demonstrated. But, he stated, "Without postulating the existence of blended expressions which present various mixtures of the primary emotions, we would not be able to account for the host of complex facial expressions of emotions and of emotion words, which far exceed the small list of primary emotions" (1972, p. 222). Blends may occur when a stimulus event elicits more than one emotion, as when winning a lottery may produce both surprise and happiness. In some circumstances we may try to disguise a primary emotion with another one. Finally, we may react to our own feelings: a subassertive person may become frightened (e.g., show fear) of his own feeling of anger. As can be noted from the above examples, affect blends are probably subject to more cultural variability than are the primary emotions.

When an eliciting event occurs, it is usually subject to some "cognitive processing" by the individual prior to activation of the facial affect program. For example, when a football player scores a touchdown we must first identify his team before we can react emotionally with sadness or happiness. The more complex the eliciting circumstance (i.e., the more social learning involved), generally, the more cognitive processing is involved. Following this, the facial appearance may be modified either by voluntary decision and control of facial muscles or by more or less "unconscious," automatic habits (which Ekman called display rules) that modify or alter facial expression in accordance with the social situation. Socially learned (culture-specific) *display rules* can modify facial expression in the following ways:

1. A display rule can require intensification of the felt emotion. In some cultures, especially Mediterranean, grief (sadness) responses are exaggerated.

2. Deintensification of the emotion may be appropriate—the British are noted for their "understatement" of emotion.

3. Neutralization of the emotion may be called for, as in the case of sadness and fear in public situations for middle-class white males in the United States.

4. Masking an emotion with a different one may be dictated in some situations. For example, a beauty contest runner-up is supposed to show happiness for the winner rather than sadness over her own disappointment. Morsbach (1973) noted that the Japanese often employ laughing and smiling to cover up anger, sorrow, or disgust.

Display rules are typically learned during childhood and become habits (i.e., learned to the point of being automatic and outside of normal awareness, though not ordinarily unconscious in a Freudian sense. Depending upon the eliciting circumstance and amount of intervening cognitive processing occurring between it and the activation of the facial affect program, a display rule might interrupt a facial expression after it has occurred, or it could prevent it from occurring. The former instance is most likely when the elicitor is an unlearned, noninterpersonal event that "naturally" arouses an emotion.

The identification of display rules that act upon emotional expression is a major contribution of Ekman in clarifying previous confusion in cross-cultural research:

In comparisons across cultures, investigators must be wary of interpreting evidence as showing a basic difference in the muscles involved in an emotional expression, when that difference could be due to the application of different display rules in the cultures being compared. (Ekman, 1972, p. 227)

Ekman specifies two approaches in cross-cultural research that are necessary in separating out display rules from the true emotional expressions. One is to inquire of a member of a culture what emotional reactions would be shown to varying situations. Display rules generally derive from the following factors (Ekman, 1972): (a) invariant personal characteristics, such as sex, age, body size; (b) unchanging social characteristics (e.g., a long-term vs. a new social relationship, a military inspection vs. a party); (c) variable personal characteristics (e.g., roles assumed, attitudes); (d) transient interaction requirements (e.g., talking vs. listening, greeting vs. saying goodbye). By employing different combinations of the above personal and situational characteristics, it should be possible to sort out some of the culture-specific display rules for regulating facial affect expressions.

Rather than have individuals enact behaviors to descriptions of hypothetical situations, one could attempt to directly measure facial expressions in the various possible situations. For example, analysis of micromomentary facial expressions is possible (Haggard and Isaacs, 1966), and one can detect attempts to conceal emotions or "aborted expressions" (interrupted muscular movements). Ekman (1972), for example, suggested that control of the facial muscles is best around the mouth and lower face rather than the eyes; display rules are thus more likely to be modifying the lower face area. Measurement of facial expression for their modification by display rules is probably best when the elicitor is unlearned, that is, it "naturally" evokes an emotional response, such as an unpleasant odor. When the display rule is likely to precede and thus completely inhibit the emotional expression, then the first technique described is probably more desirable.

The final aspect of Ekman's theory of facial affect expressions is the behavioral consequence of emotional arousal, which is a function of the interaction between the eliciting event, facial affect program, and the display rule. Six consequences are considered possible:

1. It is possible for the facial affect program to occur without modification by a display rule. In these instances we can say the emotional expression is "universal," that is, it would be "understood" in any culture.

2. The facial affect expression can be masked by a display rule.

3. We can experience and display feeling in reaction to an elicited emotion, which may be masked or blended with our reactive feeling (a feeling about a feeling).

4. Motor-adaptive behavior can occur, involving the face, body, or both. These behaviors can either serve to cope with the emotion (e.g., a sign of relief following surprise) or the eliciting circumstance (running from something fearful).

5. Emotional arousal may consequate in verbal behavior.

6. Emotional arousal may produce physiological change such as increased heart rate, blood pressure, respiration, etc.

Ekman thus summarized his theory as follows:

Our view then is that most of the immediate behavorial consequences of an emotion—the masking facial behavior, the reactive facial behavior, the verbal-vocal behavior, and the motor adaptive patterns—are socially learned ways of coping with emotion and emotion-eliciting events. They will vary across as well as within cultures. The physiological changes which accompany emotion may be less socially programmed, although some may be subject to interference by learned habits or instituted solely by learning. And the facial expressions of emotion, we have argued, distinguish among emotions and are universal, but they can be interfered with by display rules, and elicited by culturally variable events. (1972, p. 231)

In obtaining support for his pancultural theory of emotional expression, Ekman, Friesen, and Ellsworth (1972) produced a review of impressive evidence. We do not attempt to cover all of the studies cited (e.g., Dickey and Knower, 1941; Triandis and Lambert, 1958; Vinacke and Fong, 1955) beyond noting a common technique employed by many of the studies to test the question of cultural relativism versus universality of facial expression. That is, if the same pictures are shown to persons belonging to different cultures, it is possible to compute the degree of agreement among emotion categories assigned to each particular stimulus for the two cultures. Using this approach, Izard (1969) and Ekman and Friesen (1972, cited in Ekman, Friesen, and Ellsworth, 1972, pp. 157–159) found substantial agreement among literate individuals from the United States, England, Germany, Sweden, France, Greece, Africa, Japan, Brazil, Argentina, and Chile.[3]

Employing a different approach, Cuceloglu (1970) employed 60 cartoon-like drawings of facial expressions resulting from the combination of four eyebrow, three eye, and five mouth types. American, Japanese, and Turkish subjects rated these stimuli on 40 emotion name scales. A factor analysis of these scales yielded three dimensions (pleasantness, irritation, and nonreceptivity) and evidence of considerable agreement in ratings among the three cultures.

Concerning the studies just noted, Ekman, Friesen, and Ellsworth (1972) recognized that "these data could be interpreted as evidence that culturally variable learning is the sole basis for the association of facial behaviors with emotions. On the ground that there was some shared visual input among the cultures compared, it could be argued that everyone had learned to recognize the same set of conventions" (p. 159). To answer this potential criticism, Ekman, Sorenson, and Friesen (1969) used the same facial photographs they had employed earlier, but with two preliterate cultures on Borneo and New Guinea. The members of these two cultures, however, did have some contact with Western culture. An appropriate story was told to these natives in which only one emotion was involved; their task was to pick one of three pictures depicting the correct emotion. In support of Ekman's theory, their choice was highly similar to those of Americans. In a subsequent report, Ekman (1972) showed videotapes of these individuals (who were filmed enacting primary emotions) to American observers, who were highly accurate in their identification of facial affect.

In another study cited earlier, Ekman, Friesen, and Malmstrom (1970) studied the facial expression of native Japanese and American students to a stress-inducing and also a neutral film. Based on previous research (Averill, Opton, and Lazarus, 1969), the authors had determined the eliciting event (a sinus surgery film) to be stressful for both groups. Utilization of the FAST procedure to film segments of the facial behavior of American and Japanese subjects permitted an analysis of the repertoire of facial behavior for the two cultures, which Ekman hypothesized would be quite similar for the emotion (stress) film. Indeed, the rank order correlation between the emotion categories shown by the two groups was .88 based on FAST measurements of the whole face, .86 for the brows/forehead area, .95 for the eyes/lids, and .96 for the lower face area. In addition, the authors noted that these relationships were obtained in a situation where activation of display rules was unlikely because subjects were unaware they were being observed and filmed. However, based on a subsequent personal interview, they found that "when display rules should apply, the Japanese appear to have engaged in masking by showing happy faces when their Japanese interviewer asked them about their experience, while the Americans typically did not cover signs of negative affect when they talked with their American interviewer" (Ekman, Friesen, and Ellsworth, 1972, p. 165).

The results of these studies point out strong support for Ekman's theory that primary emotions are represented by the same facial expressions across cultures.[4] In particular, the last study cited nicely supports this point, in addition to which it demonstrates the importance of Ekman's notion of culture-specific display rules which may modify the expression of facial affect.

SOME EXAMPLES OF RESEARCH UTILIZING FACIAL EXPRESSIONS

Even prior to the recent research on facial expressions and emotion, investigators have speculated on the potential value of the face in psychological research. Mandler, for example, noted the following some 15 years ago:

It is rather surprising that facial expression has rarely been used in controlled studies of emotion, that is as a dependent variable in conjunction with some of the other emotional variables . . . if people can make such reliable judgements [about the face], then psychologists also should be able to do so and to use expressive behavior more consistently in the laboratory. We might then have a reliable and useful dependent variable for the study of the whole emotional complex. (1962, p. 307)

The studies we review in this section have been purposefully selected to exemplify use of facial expressions as both independent and dependent variables in the research.

Thus far we have only made some passing reference to special measurement techniques for studying facial expression. One important aspect of facial behavior that requires special measurement techniques is what Haggard and Isaacs (1966) have described as "micromomentary facial expressions." This phenomenon was discovered by the authors when viewing some psychotherapy films for nonverbal behavior:

During such explorations, for instance, we noted that occasionally the expression on the patient's face would change dramatically within three to five frames on film (as from smile to grimace to smile), which is equivalent to a period of from one-eighth to one-fifth of a second. We were not able to see these expression changes at the normal rate. (Haggard and Isaacs, 1966, p. 154)

In applying this technique to the analysis of psychotherapy sessions they noted that rapid changes of facial expressions seemed to occur most during phases of general expressiveness except when the patient was in conflict concerning feelings and impulses. During periods of conflict, micromomentary facial expressions appeared to be inconsistent with the verbal content and adjacent facial expressions. Heimann (1967) measured the facial movements of his patients for symmetry by comparing the static positions of the face every tenth frame. For schizophrenic patients, the index of symmetry of right-left facial movements was considerably different from normals.

Reduced symmetry was also noted for subjects receiving LSD and experiencing mental stress.

Several other techniques employ electromyographic measurement of the facial muscles. Sumitsuji, Matsumoto, and Kaneko (1965) described a procedure utilizing five stainless steel wire electrodes, implanted in the facial muscle, which "gave the subjects practically no pain" (p. 269). A more recent technique reported by Schwartz (1974) requires surface attachment of electrodes to four facial muscles (the corrugator, frontalis, depressor anguli oris, and masseter). Schwartz instructed subjects simply to "think" of sad, happy, or angry experiences. Even though no visible changes could be detected, evaluation of the physiological readings did permit differentiation of the joyful, angry, and sad thoughts.[5] More recently, Schwartz, Fair, Greenberg, Mandel, and Klerman (1975) employed this technique to the study of clinically depressed patients. Specifically, they found that depressed patients showed attenuated facial EMG patterns to happy (but not sad or angry) imagery, and their facial muscle pattern during a resting state was one of sadness (as compared to matched normals). Of interest, however, was the finding that facial EMG parallelled clinical response to drug therapy, "with the largest EMG increases in the happy affect conditions occurring in those patients showing the best improvement" (p. 82).

Schwartz's measurement approach is within the domain of biofeedback phenomena. That is, it should be theoretically possible to give individuals feedback when their facial muscle pattern approximates the facial expression associated with the emotion state "happiness." Assuming for a moment that Tomkins' application of the James–Lange theory is correct (i.e., that the facial expression precedes the subjective experience), and that the correlated changes (e.g., hormonal or biofeedback changes) might occur as a result, a biofeedback treatment approach for affective disorders is not unthinkable. Providing some support for this idea on a psychological level are the results of a study by Laird (1974). Laird had subjects contract various facial muscles until they exhibited a frown or a smile (though they were not told to do either). The results showed that subjects who were "smiling" rated cartoons as being more humorous and themselves as more happy than when they were "frowning," at which time they reported feeling more angry. Laird's interpretation of this finding was in terms of self-attribution theory (e.g., "I feel as I act"), but it is possible to speculate that biological changes could also occur.

Draughton (1973) recently reported an interesting study in which she investigated subjects' ability to duplicate facial expressions. Following up on an approach of Frieda Fromm-Reichmann (who would literally take the physical stance of the patient to introspect what she could not understand verbally), Draughton speculated that "facial expression duplication could be an important addition to the training of clinicians (and others) to use these nonverbal cues better in their work with people" (p. 140). Draughton presented pictures of facial expressions to subjects whose task was to attempt to match them with their own facial expression. At the same time, observers compared the subject's attempt at duplication with the photographed facial expression. Subjects were given a series of duplication trials with and without the aid of a mirror. The results showed that subjects improved in their ability to duplicate facial expressions when allowed to use a mirror. In contrast, their performance deteriorated without a mirror. However, this was true primarily for low-anxious subjects (based on their ratings of how they felt at the beginning of the experiment); high-anxious subjects tended to do better without the mirror than with it. Though these findings are interesting, they have apparently not been followed up with any practical application (e.g., in a clinical situation).

A number of studies have investigated facial behavior as an independent variable in interpersonal interaction situations. Shapiro, Foster, and Powell (1968) looked at Truax's measures of empathy, genuineness, and warmth in relation to facial expressions. Subjects trained in Truax's rating system and untrained observers rated photographs of counselors previously selected as being high, medium, or low on empathy, genuineness, and warmth. The photographs were presented so that, in some cases, the face was masked, the body was masked, or the whole picture was shown. Correlations between the untrained observer's ratings and the ratings of trained observers as criterion measures showed that the face but not the body provided cues for those counselor characteristics.

Bayes (1972) examined observers' global ratings of interpersonal warmth in relation to specific behaviors occurring within a videotaped interview. Specific behaviors evaluated included positive verbal statements about self, others, or the surroundings, speech rate, body and head movement, hand movements, and smiles. Rate of smiling correlated highest with interpersonal warmth ($r = .67$), followed by number of positive statements about others. Bayes concluded that "the finding that smiling is the best single predictor of warmth supports the repeated suggestions in the literature" (p. 337). Rosenfeld (1966) examined "instrumental affiliative acts," that is, the facial and gestural expressions of subjects motivated to seek or avoid approval of another subject. The frequency of smiles and gesticulations best differentiated between the two groups. Rosenfeld also found that need for social approval (Marlowe–Crowne scale) was positively correlated with smiling in the dyadic interview situation.

In a recent study, Hackney (1974) examined the effect of listeners' nonverbal behaviors on speakers' expression of feelings (i.e., frequency of self-references and affect statements). Female subjects were instructed to engage in a 5-minute monologue addressed to "listeners." The "listener" was actually a TV videotape of a male or a female engaging in one of the following behaviors: no expression, head nods, smiles, or head nods and smiles. The results showed that the female subjects made more self-reference and affect statements as a function of "listener" head-nods, smiles, and head-nod–smile combination. However, this was true only when the listener was female. When the male was "listening" and smiling, this decreased the females' affect responses and self-references. Hackney speculated, "Possibly the female subjects are more uncertain about the meaning of a male's nonverbal behavior when that behavior includes a smile or a combination of nonverbal responses which include a smile" (p. 177).

Efran and Cheyne (1974) studied facial behavior as a dependent measure of the invasion of conversational space of two other persons. Specifically, experimental subjects were given a request that required them, in one instance, to cut in between two conversational partners in a narrow hallway or, in another, merely to pass by them. During these times, subjects' expressive behaviors were secretly filmed. In addition, subjects filled out self-report mood scales. Subjects required to intrude showed more agonistic facial behaviors (e.g., grimaces) and less positive mood than when they were not required to intrude on the conversational space of others.

Facial behavior in interaction situations has also been related to sex differences. In the study by Beekman (1975; see p. 46) in which male and female same-sex and opposite-sex dyads were observed in interaction, she found that females tended to laugh and smile more than males. Males who laughed and smiled most described themselves as more sociable, friendly, and affiliative. In contrast, smiling for females appeared primarily related to feelings of discomfort with the interview and self-ratings of deference and abasement. Since laughing and smiling are socially approved behaviors for females in interaction situations, those most uncomfortable with the situation may have reacted in a more stereotyped fashion whereas Beekman hypothesized, those behaviors may have reflected a more genuinely affiliative response in males.

Several studies investigated subjects' facial behaviors when engaging in honest versus deceptive communications. Mehrabian (1971) found that "negative affect-inducing cues" (e.g., speech errors, less talk and smiles) were more common in deceptive communications. In addition, high-anxious subjects showed less facial pleasantness during role-played deceit whereas low-anxious or extraverted subjects displayed the opposite pattern. However, Knapp, Hart, and Dennis (1974) found no difference in the number of smiles between deceivers and nondeceivers. Ekman and Friesen (1974) had nurses frankly describe their feelings when viewing a pleasant film and conceal their negative feelings and simulate pleasant feelings when viewing an unpleasant one. Nurses' ability to deceive facially (i.e., based on an observer's inability to decode them) significantly correlated with their rated effectiveness in working with patients as judged by their supervisors during the following academic year. As the authors noted, "This finding suggests that how subjects behaved in this experiment, as measured from their nonverbal behavior, was not irrelevant to the rest of their life, but instead was predictive of their subsequent career" (1974, p. 287).

Finally, as a further example of the relevance of nonverbal behaviors, we note a report of a study by Harrison in his review on nonverbal communication: "The following is an example of a finding from a study in which affect was judged. Young boys who were judged to look happy and aroused while watching television violence engaged in significantly more postviewing aggression" (Ekman, Liebert, Friesen, Harrison, Zlatchin, Malmstrom, and Baron, 1972).

METHODOLOGICAL CONSIDERATIONS

Before closing this chapter on the face, it is important to review and consider carefully the particular research problems posed by this challenging area of investigation. As in other sections of this chapter, Ekman, Friesen, and Ellsworth (1972) have contributed heavily to the notions presented here.

The first consideration concerns the goal of the research. Basically, two kinds of designs have been used. *Judgment* studies require a decision from an observer on (a) the particular emotion category associated with a facial expression, (b) the nature of the emotion that a subject is experiencing, and (c) the particular eliciting circumstance that the subject is faced with. In judgment studies, the face is treated as a stimulus; in *component* studies the facial expression is treated as a response related to an emotion or particular eliciting circumstance. An important assumption necessary for a component study is that there should be agreement among observers that the facial behaviors do reliably differ with the particular emotion or eliciting circumstance. If observer agreement that whole facial expressions differ cannot be demonstrated, then hypotheses about the relationship of certain emotions or circumstances to differences among *parts* of the face cannot be logically tested.

However, if there is no observer agreement, one cannot necessarily assume that no information is given from the facial expression. For example, assume that still photographs are used in a task in which observers are to match faces with emotion categories. A lack of observer agreement could be due to the presence of facial affect blends and the absence of appropriate response choices for observers (e.g., the ability to select more than one emotion category for each given stimulus). If a particular stimulus reflects a 60–40 blend of fear and anger and observers can pick only one emotion category to describe the face, then disagreement should occur. If a film or videotape is employed and observers are to match emotion descriptions with the film segment, disagreement could occur as a function of observers using different facial cues as a basis for their judgments. If observers cannot agree that a subject in an eliciting circumstance is not displaying a hypothesized emotion, this could be for any of the reasons noted above or because a display rule served to mask facial expression in that particular circumstance. Finally, if the observer's judgment is in terms of the eliciting circumstance, the experimenter must somehow demonstrate that the circumstances do indeed elicit the hypothesized emotional arousal or particular emotional facial response.

Thus, in designing an experiment, the researcher must carefully consider how encoding of facial behavior is to be achieved and then how decoding shall occur. Errors at either part may account for an inconclusive experiment. In choosing an eliciting circumstance, one must be able to show that the eliciting circumstance is relevant to emotion (and, presumably, to facial behavior), that simulation or arousal of an emotion does occur, and that the facial behavior is recorded at the time of arousal or simulation. Simulation or posing of emotions has been popular because this eliciting circumstance is clearly relevant to facial behavior and the instructions to pose tend to remove display rules that otherwise might modify facial expressiveness. Emotional arousal, however, does not occur as it does "naturally." On the other hand, spontaneously elicited emotional reactions suffer from the limitation that they are often accompanied by modified facial expressions due to activation of display rules (which the posing task minimizes).

Whatever the eliciting circumstances chosen, it is important that more than one be employed so that idiosyncracies about a particular experimental manipulation are minimized. Especially if observer accuracy is crucial to the experiment, eliciting circumstances that reliably evoke a variety of different emotions should be employed. Some emotions are easier to recognize (e.g., happiness), whereas others (e.g., fear and sadness) are more similar in the arrangement of their facial components. Thus two studies on the information value of facial expression that used happy-sad or angry-fearful stimuli would be expected to differ in their outcome, the latter showing poorer accuracy among observers.

In most instances, eliciting circumstances will not always evoke the same emotional reaction or facial display for every person or consistently over time. Thus, the issue of sampling behaviors becomes important, since as a rule only segments of subjects' reactions can be presented to observers. As Ekman, Friesen, and Ellsworth (1972) noted, "Unless the sampling procedures have been specified the . . . question of *how often* the face provides accurate information . . . cannot be answered" (p. 41).

Precisely what information is preserved for the observer-decoder depends on the recording technique. Still photographs provide consistent stimuli across observers, but background facial features (e.g., wrinkles due to a static facial characteristic) may be confounded with facial movements and expressions (wrinkles caused by muscle contractions). In contrast, motion picture or videotape films preserve the natural flow of changes in expression but observers are presented with multiple stimuli. In the case of videotaped or filmed expressions, a particular facial expression cannot be linked to an emotion unless observers agree on the facial cues used. For example, the cue used to differentiate subjects exposed to different eliciting situations might be a gesture or some other cue unrelated to facial affect expression. In that case, for either photograph or film recording techniques, it is necessary to demonstrate in some fashion (e.g., self-report, physiological monitoring) that the emotion did occur at the same time as the facial expression.

Careful specification of the decoding task is important. As mentioned earlier, the kinds of responses an observer can make are crucial to the judgment process. Free responses or a wide range of responses are required if the question is the "meaning" of a particular facial behavior (especially when affect blends are likely). However, if the question concerns what eliciting circumstance or specific quality of emotional experience (pleasant vs. unpleasant) can be judged, inclusion of additional choices may not be indicated and may increase error variance arising fom the judgment process.

Finally, a variable just emerging as an important factor in facial affect studies is the sampling of subjects, both encoders and decoders. A range of encoders is important not only to control for the effect of idiosyncratic physiognomies but also to control for differences in encoding ability. As noted earlier (Buck, Miller, and Caul, 1974; Buck, Savin, Miller, and Caul, 1969, 1972; Lanzetta and Kleck, 1970; also see Snyder, 1974), individual differences in encoding abilities are now a focus of research. Ekman, Friesen, and Ellsworth (1972) also noted that individuals may vary in their ability to encode certain emotions. Further investigation will undoubtedly reveal differences in decoding abilities, as already suggested by reports of Lanzetta and Kleck (1970), Ekman and Friesen (1974), and Zuckerman, Lipets, Koivumaki, and Rosenthal (1975).

In particular, some important tools for future research investigations are found in two publications by Ekman and his colleagues. One, *Unmasking the Face* (Ekman and Friesen, 1975), has practical implications since it is designed to make clinicians as well as researchers more sensitive to the recognition of facial expression through the use of written discussion, pictorial examples, and exercises. The other publication will consist of a "Facial Atlas"—the first of its kind—by which a researcher should be able to measure precisely facial expressions on the basis of comparison of facial components with Atlas photographs. Emotion predictions are then possible from the composite ratings, much as has been accomplished with the FAST system. In particular, when this latter publication is made available sophisticated research on the face will become a real possibility for more and more researchers.

NOTES

[1]In an intriguing study, Schwartz (1974) reported taking electromyograph readings of specific facial muscles of subjects who were instructed to engage only in happy and sad thoughts. Though no observable changes in facial expression occurred, reliable changes in EMG readings were noted. Though this cannot be construed as direct support of Tomkins' theory, it does suggest a very close and important association between the face and experience of emotion.

[2]Ekman (1972) reported that 3 hours of scoring time are required for each minute of facial behavior.

[3]Izard (1971) did note that some differences do occur in the identification of particular emotions. For example, differences were noted between Americans and Europeans versus Japanese in identifying faces depicting disgust-contempt, shame, anger, and fear. However, in subsequent research, he was able to demonstrate that these differences were probably related to cultural differences in *attitudes* towards certain emotions. For example, shame and fear are rated as the most dreaded emotions in Western cultures; for the Japanese, it is disgust-contempt. Thus differences in attitudes towards emotion and the labeling of emotion probably account for the above variation rather than differences in facial expression per se. Izard concluded: "While each fundamental emotion has a transcultural core meaning, it may also have some culture-specific meanings or emotion-related cognitions of significance for intercultural understanding and communication" (1971, p. 281).

[4]There is some additional research that we do not consider but which also suggests an innate component to facial expression of emotions. Specifically, a number of studies have been conducted demonstrating that blind children show facial expressions similar to normals. Izard (1971) reviewed much of this research in his book.

[5]Interestingly, Ring (1967) earlier conducted a study in which 214 interviewers classified 1869 West German adults as having the corners of their mouths either upturned, horizontal, or lowered. Those with lifted corners were judged by interviewers (and, indeed, rated by themselves) as happier than persons whose mouth corners were lowered.

REFERENCES

Abelson, R. P., and V. Sermat (1962). Multidimensional scaling of facial expressions. *Journal of Experimental Psychology,* **63**, 546–554.

Allport, F. H. (1924). *Social psychology.* Boston: Houghton Mifflin.

Asch, S. E. (1952). *Social psychology.* Englewood Cliifs, NJ: Prentice-Hall.

Averill, J. R., E. M. Opton, Jr., and R. S. Lazarus (1969). Cross-cultural studies of psychophysiological responses during stress and emotion. *International Journal of Psychology,* **4**, 88–102.

Bayes, M. A. (1972). Behavioral cues of interpersonal warmth. *Journal of Consulting and Clini-*

cal Psychology, **39,** 333–339.

Beekman, S. J. (1975). *Sex differences in nonverbal behavior.* Paper presented at the meeting of the American Psychological Association, Chicago.

Beier, E. G. (1966). *The silent language of psychotherapy: Social reinforcement of unconcious processes.* Chicago: Aldine-Atherton.

Birdwhistell, R. L. (1959). *Frames in the communication process.* Paper presented at the meeting of the Americal Society for Clinical Hypnosis. (Vine, I. (1970). Communication by facial-visual signals: A review and analysis of their role in face to face encounters. In J. H. Crook (Ed.), *Social behavior in birds and mammals: Essays on the social ethology of animal and man.* New York: Academic Press. Pp. 279–353.)

Birdwhistell, R. L. (1963). The kinesic level in the investigation of emotions. In P. Knapp (Ed.), *Expression of the emotions in man.* New York: International Universities Press. Pp. 123–139.

Birdwhistell, R. L. (1970). *Kinesics and context.* Philadelphia: University of Pennsylvania Press.

Blurton-Jones, N. G. (1969). Criteria used in describing facial expressions. Unpublished manuscript. (Available from the Department of Growth and Development, University of London, London, England.) (Ekman, P., W. V. Friesen, and P. Ellsworth (1972). *Emotion in the human face: Guidelines for research and an integration of the findings.* New York: Pergamon Press.)

Blurton-Jones, N. G. (Ed.) (1972). *Ethological studies of child behavior.* Cambridge, U.K.: Cambridge University Press.

Boucher, J. D. (1969). Facial displays of fear, sadness, and pain. *Perceptual and Motor Skills,* **28,** 239–242.

Boucher, J. D., and P. Ekman (1975). Facial areas of emotional information. *Journal of Communication,* **25,** 21–29.

Bruner, J. S., and R. Tagiuri (1954). The perception of people. In G. Lindzey (Ed.), *Handbook of social psychology,* Vol. 2. Reading, MA: Addison-Wesley.

Buck, R. W., R. E. Miller, and W. F. Caul (1974). Sex, personaility, and physiological variables in the communication of affect via facial expression. *Journal of Personality and Social Psychology,* **30,** 587–596.

Buck, R. W., V. J. Savin, R. E. Miller, and W. F. Caul (1969). Nonverbal communication of affect in humans. Summary in *Proceedings of the 77th Annual Convention of the American Psychological Association.* Washington, D.C.: American Psychological Association, pp. 367–368.

Buck, R. W., V. J. Savin, R. E. Miller, and W. F. Caul (1972). Communication of affect through facial expressions in humans. *Journal of Personality and Social Psychology,* **23,** 362–371.

Coleman, J. C. (1949). Facial expressions of emotion. *Psychological Monographs,* **63,** 1 (Whole No. 296). Pp. 1–36.

Cuceloglu, D. M. (1970). Perception of facial expressions in three different cultures. *Ergonomics,* **13,** 93–100.

Darwin, C. (1872). *The expression of the emotions in man and animals.* London: Murray. (Dittmann, A. (1972). *Interpersonal messages of emotion.* New York: Springer.)

Dickey, E. C., and F. H. Knower (1941). A note on some ethological differences in recognition of simulated expressions of the emotions. *American Journal of Sociology,* **47,** 190–193.

Dittmann, A. T. (1972). *Interpersonal messages of emotion.* New York: Springer.

Drag, R. M., and M. E. Shaw (1967). Factors influencing the communication of emotional intent by facial expressions. *Psychonomic Science,* **8,** 137–138.

Draughton, M. (1973). Duplication of facial expressions: Conditions affecting task and possible clinical usefulness. *Journal of Personality,* **41,** 140–150.

Duncan, S. D., Jr. (1969). Nonverbal communications. *Psychological Bulletin,* **72**, 118–137.

Dusenbury, D., and F. H. Knower (1938). Experimental studies of the symbolism of action and voice: I. A study of the specificity of meaning in facial expression. *Quarterly Journal of Speech,* **24**, 424–435.

Efran, M. G., and J. A. Cheyne (1974). Affective concomitants of the invasion of shared space: Behavioral, physiological, and verbal indicators. *Journal of Personality and Social Psychology,* **29**, 219–226.

Eibl-Eibesfeldt, I. (1971). Transcultural patterns of ritualized contact behavior. In A. H. Esser (Ed.), *Behavior and environment: The use of space by animals and men.* New York: Plenum Press. Pp. 297–312.

Ekman, P. (1965). Communication through nonverbal behavior: A source of information about an interpersonal relationship. In S. S. Tomkins and C. E. Izard (Eds.), *Affect, cognition, and personality.* New York: Springer. Pp. 390–442.

Ekman, P. (1968). *The recognition and display of facial behavior in literate and non-literate cultures.* Paper presented at the symposium "Universality of the Emotions" of the American Psychological Association. (Ekman, P. (1972). Universal and cultural differences in facial expressions of emotions. In J. K. Cole (Ed.), *Nebraska symposium on motivation* (Vol. 19). Lincoln: University of Nebraska Press. Pp. 207–283.)

Ekman, P. (1972). Universal and cultural differences in facial expressions of emotions. In J. K. Cole (Ed.), *Nebraska symposium on motivation, 1971.* Lincoln: University of Nebraska Press. Pp. 207–283.

Ekman, P. (Ed.). (1973). *Darwin and facial expression: A century of research in review.* New York: Academic Press.

Ekman, P., and J. Bressler (1964). In P. Ekman, Progress report to National Institute of Mental Health, Bethesda, Maryland. (Ekman, P., W. V. Friesen, and P. Ellsworth (1972). *Emotion in the human face: Guidelines for research as an integration of the findings.* New York: Pergamon Press.)

Ekman, P., and W. V. Friesen (1965). Progress report to National Institute of Mental Health, Bethesda, Maryland. (Ekman, P., W. V. Friesen, and P. Ellsworth (1972). *Emotion in the human face: Guidelines for research and an integration of the findings.* New York: Pergamon Press.)

Ekman, P., and W. V. Friesen (1967). *Origin, usage, and coding: The basis for five categories of nonverbal behavior.* Paper presented at the Symposium on Communication Theory and Linguistic Models, Buenos Aires. (Ekman, P., W. V. Friesen, and P. Ellsworth (1972). *Emotion in the human face: Guidelines for research and an integration of the findings.* New York: Pergamon Press.)

Ekman, P., and W. V. Friesen (1971). Constants across cultures in the face and emotion. *Journal of Personality and Social Psychology,* **17**, 124–129.

Ekman, P., and W. V. Friesen (1974). Detecting deception from the body or face. *Journal of Personality and Social Psychology,* **29**, 288–298.

Ekman, P., and W. V. Friesen (1975). *Unmasking the face: A guide to recognizing emotions from facial clues.* Englewood Cliffs: Prentice-Hall.

Ekman, P., W. V. Friesen, and P. Ellsworth (1972). *Emotion in the human face: Guidelines for research and an integration of the findings.* New York: Pergamon Press.

Ekman, P., W. V. Friesen, and E. J. Malmstrom (1970). Facial behavior and stress in two cultures. Unpublished manuscript. (Available from the Langley Porter Neuropsychiatric Institute, San Francisco, California.) (Ekman, P., W. V. Friesen, and P. Ellsworth (1972) *Emotion in the human face: Guidelines for research and an integration of the findings.* New York: Pergamon Press.)

Ekman, P., W. V. Friesen, and S. S. Tomkins (1971). Facial affect scoring technique: A first validity study. *Semiotica,* **3**, 37–58.

Ekman, P., R. M. Liebert, W. V. Friesen, R. P. Harrison, C. Zlatchin, E. Malmstrom, and R. A. Baron (1972). Facial expressions of emotion while watching televised violence as predictors of subsequent aggression. In G. A. Comstack, E. A. Rubinstein, and J. P. Murray (Eds.), *Television and social behavior, reports and papers.* Vol. 5, *Television's effects: Further explorations.* Rockville, Maryland: National Institute of Mental Health. Pp. 22–58.

Ekman, P., and D. Rose (1965). In P. Ekman, Progress report to National Institute of Mental Health, Bethesda, Maryland. (Ekman, P., W. V. Friesen, and P. Ellsworth (1972). *Emotion in the human face: Guidelines for research and an integration of the findings.* New York: Pergamon Press.)

Ekman, P., E. R. Sorenson, and W. V. Friesen (1969). Pan-cultural elements in facial displays of emotion. *Science,* **164**, 86–88.

Engen, T., N. Levy, and H. Schlosberg (1957). A new series of facial expression. *American Psychologist,* **12**, 264–266.

Engen, T., N. Levy, and H. Schlosberg (1958). The dimensional analysis of a new series of facial expressions. *Journal of Experimental Psychology,* **55**, 454–458.

Fernberger, S. W. (1928). False suggestion and the Piderit model. *American Journal of Psychology,* **40**, 562–568.

Frijda, N. H. (1968). *Emotion and recognition of emotion.* Paper presented at the Third Symposium on Feelings and Emotions, Loyola University, Chicago. (Ekman, P., W. V. Friesen, and P. Ellsworth (1972). *Emotion in the human face: Guidelines for research and an integration of the findings.* New York: Pergamon Press)

Frijda, N. H. (1969). Recognition of emotion. In L. Berkowitz (Ed.), *Advances in experimental social psychology,* Vol. 4. New York: Academic Press. Pp. 167–223.

Frijda, N. H., and E. Philipszoon (1963). Dimensions of recognition of emotion. *Journal of Abnormal and Social Psychology,* **66**, 45–51.

Frois-Whitmann, J. (1930. The judgment of facial expression. *Journal of Experimental Social Psychology,* **13**, 113–151.

Fulcher, J. S. (1942). "Voluntary" facial expression in blind and seeing children. *Archives of Psychology,* **38**, N. 272, Pp. 1–49.

Gellhorn, E. (1964). Motion and emotion: The role of proprioception in the physiology and pathology of the emotions. *Psychological Review,* **71**, 457–472.

Gitter, A. G., H. Black, and D. Mostofsky (1972). Race and sex in the communication of emotion. *Journal of Social Psychology,* **88**, 273–276.

Gladstones, W. H. (1962). A multi-dimensional study of facial expression of emotion. *Australian Journal of Psychology,* **14**, 95–100.

Goodall, J. L. (1971). *In the shadow of man.* Boston: Houghton Mifflin.

Grant, E. C. (1969). Human facial expression. *Man,* **4**, 525–536.

Gubar, G. (1966). Recognition of human facial expressions judged live in a laboratory setting. *Journal of Personality and Social Psychology,* **4**, 108–111.

Hackney, H. (1974). Facial gestures and subject expression of feelings. *Journal of Counseling Psychology,* **21**, 173–178.

Haggard, E. A., and K. S. Isaacs (1966). Micromomentary facial expressions as indicators of ego mechanisms in psychotherapy. In L. A. Gottschalk and A. H. Auerbach (Eds.), *Methods of research in psychotherapy.* New York: Appleton-Century-Crofts. Pp. 154–165.

Hanawalt, N. G. (1944). The role of the upper and the lower parts of the face as a basis for judging facial expressions: II. In posed expressions and "candid camera" pictures. *Journal of General Psychology,* **31**, 23–36.

Harrison, R. P. (1964). Pictic analysis: Towards a vocabulary and syntax for the pictorial code, with research on facial communication. Doctoral dissertation, Michigan State University. *Dissertation Abstracts,* **26**, (1965), 519. (Vine, I. (1970). Communication by facial-visual signals: A review and analysis of their role in face to face encounters. In J. H. Crook (Ed.), *Social behavior in birds and mammals: Essays on the social ethology of animal and man.* New York: Academic Press. Pp. 279–354.)

Harrison, R. P. (1973). Nonverbal communication. In I. de Solo Pool, W. Schramm, N. Maccoby, F. Fry, E. Parker, and J. L. Fein (Eds.), *Handbook of communication.* Chicago: Rand McNally. Pp. 93–115.

Harrison, R. P., A. A. Cohen, W. W. Crouch, B. K. L. Genova, and M. Steinberg (1972). The nonverbal communication literature. *Journal of Communication,* **22**, 460–476.

Hastorf, A. H., C. E. Osgood, and H. Ono (1966). The semantics of facial expressions and the prediction of the meanings of stereoscopically fused facial expressions. *Scandinavian Journal of Psychology,* **7**, 179–188.

Hebb, D. O. (1946). Emotion in man and animal: An analysis of the intuitive processes of recognition. *Psychological Review,* **53**, 88–106.

Heimann, H. (1967). Die qualitative Analyse mimischer Bewegungen und ihre Anwendungsmöglichkeiten. Bericht über den 22. Kongress der Deutschen Gesellschaft für Psychologie, Göttingen. (Izard, C. E. (1971). *The face of emotion.* New York: Appleton-Century-Crofts.)

Howell, R. J., and E. C. Jorgensen (1970). Accuracy of judging unposed emotional behavior in a natural setting: A replication study. *Journal of Social Psychology,* **81**, 269–270.

Izard, C. E. (1969). The emotions and emotion constructs in personality and culture research. In R. B. Cattell (Ed.), *Handbook of modern personality theory.* Chicago: Aldine-Atherton.

Izard, C. E. (1971). *The face of emotion.* New York: Appleton-Century-Crofts.

Jorgensen, E. C., and R. J. Howell (1969). Judging unposed emotional behavior. *Psychotherapy: Theory, Research and Practice,* **6**, 161–165.

Kanner, L. (1931). Judging emotions from facial expressions. *Psychological Monographs,* **41**, 3 (Whole No. 186).

Kauranne, U. (1964). Qualitative factors of facial expression. *Scandinavian Journal of Psychology,* **5**, 136–142.

Kiritz, S. A., and P. Ekman (1971). The deviant judge of affect in facial expression: Affect-specific errors. Unpublished manuscript. (Available from the Langley Porter Neuropsychiatric Institute, San Francisco, California). (Ekman, P., W. V. Friesen, and P. Ellsworth (1972). *Emotion in the human face: Guidelines for research and an integration of the findings.* New York: Pergamon Press.

Knapp, M. L. (1972). The field of nonverbal communication. An overview. In C. J. Steward and B. Kendall (Eds.), *On speech communication: An anthology of contemporary writings and messages.* New York: Holt, Rinehart, and Winston. Pp. 57–72.

Knapp, M. L., R. P. Hart, and H. S. Dennis (1974). The rhetoric of duplicity: An exploration of description as a communication construct. Unpublished manuscript. (Available from the Communication Research Center, Purdue University, Lafayette, Indiana).

Kozel, N. J., and A. G. Gitter (1968) *Perception of emotion: Differences in mode of presentation, sex of perceiver, and race of expressor.* Communication Research Center Report No. 18, Boston University.

LaBarre, W. (1947). The cultural basis of emotions and gestures. *Journal of Personality,* **16**, 49–68.

LaBarre, W. (1962). *Paralanguage, kinesics, and cultural anthropology.* Report for the Interdisciplinary Word-Conference on Paralanguage and Kinesics. Bloomington: Indiana University, Research Center in Anthropology, Folklore, and Linguistics. (Ekman, P., W. V. Friesen, and P. Ellsworth (1972). *Emotion in the human face: Guidelines for research and an integration of the findings.* New York: Pergamon Press.)

Laird, J. D. (1974). Self attribution of emotion: The effects of expressive behavior on the quality of emotional experience. *Journal of Personality and Social Psychology, 29*, 475–486.

Landis, C. (1924). Studies of emotional reactions: II. General behavior and facial expression. *Journal of Comparative Psychology, 4*, 447–509.

Landis, C. (1929). The interpretation of facial expression in emotion. *Journal of General Psychology, 2*, 59–72.

Landis, C., and W. A. Hunt (1939). *The startle pattern.* New York: Farrar. (Ekman, P., W. V. Friesen, and P. Ellsworth (1972). *Emotion in the human face: Guidelines for research and an integration of the findings.* New York: Pergamon Press.)

Lanzetta, J. T., and R. E. Kleck (1970). Encoding and decoding of nonverbal affect in humans. *Journal of Personality and Social Psychology, 16*, 12–19.

Leventhal, H., and E. Sharp (1965). Facial expressions as indicators of distress. In S. Tomkins and G. E. Izard (Eds.), *Affect, cognition, and personality.* New York: Springer. Pp. 296–318.

Levitt, E. A. (1964). The relationship betwen abilities to express emotional meanings vocally and facially. In J. R. Davitz (Ed.), *The communication of emotional meaning.* New York: McGraw-Hill. Pp. 87–100.

Mandler, G. (1962). Emotion. In *New directions in psychology: I.* New York: Holt, Rinehart, and Winston. Pp. 267–343.

Mehrabian, A. (1971). Nonverbal betrayal of feeling. *Journal of Experimental Research in Personality, 5*, 64–73.

Miller, R. E., J. H. Banks, and N. Ogawa (1962). Communication of affect in cognitive conditioning of rhesus monkeys. *Journal of Abnormal and Social Psychology, 64*, 343–348.

Munn, N. L. (1940). The effects of knowledge of the situation upon judgment of emotion from facial expressions. *Journal of Abnormal and Social Psychology, 35*, 324–338.

Nummenmaa, T. (1964). *The language of the face.* Jyvaskyla studies in education, psychology, and social research. Jyvaskyla, Finland: Jyvaskylan Yllopistoyhdistys. (Ekman, P., W. V. Friesen, and P. Ellsworth (1972). *Emotion in the human face: Guidelines for research and an integration of the findings.* New York: Pergamon Press.)

Nummenmaa, T., and U. Kauranne (1958). *Dimensions of facial expression.* Report No. 20, Department of Psychology, Institute of Pedagogics (now University of Jyvaskyla), Jyvaskyla, Finland. (Ekman, P., W. V. Friesen, and P. Ellsworth (1972). *Emotion in the human face: Guidelines for research and an integration of the findings.* New York: Pergamon Press.)

Osgood, C. E. (1955). Fidelity and reliability. In H. Quastler (Ed.), *Information theory in psychology: Problems and methods.* Glencoe, IL: The Free Press. Pp. 374–390.

Osgood, C. E. (1966). Dimensionality of the semantic space for communication via facial expressions. *Scandinavian Journal of Psychology, 7*, 1–30.

Plutchik, R. (1962). *The emotions: Facts, theories, and a new model.* New York: Random House.

Ring, E. (1967). Ausdrucksbeobachtungen in der Demoskopie. *Psychologie und Praxis, 11*, 1–11. (Izard, C. E. (1971). *The face of emotion.* New York: Appleton-Century-Crofts.)

Rosenfeld, H. M. (1966). Instrumental affiliative functions of facial and gestural expressions. *Journal of Personality and Social Psychology, 4*, 65–72.

Rubenstein, L. (1969). Facial expressions: An objective method in the quantitative evaluation of emotional change. *Behavior Research Methods and Instruments, 1*, 305–306.

Schlosberg, H. (1954). Three dimensions of emotion. *Psychological Review, 61*, 81–88.

Schwartz, G. E. (1974). Facial expression and depression: An electromyogram study. *Psychosomatic Medicine, 36*, 458.

Schwartz, G. E., P. L. Fair, P. S. Greenberg, M. R. Mandel, and G. L. Klerman (1975). Facial expressions and depression. II: An electromyographic study. *Psychosomatic Medicine, 37*, 81–82.

Shapiro, J. G. (1968). Responsivity to facial and linguistic cues. *Journal of Communication, 18*,

11–17.

Shapiro, J. G., C. P. Foster, and T. Powell (1968). Facial and bodily cues of genuineness, empathy, and warmth. *Journal of Clinical Psychology, 24,* 233–236.

Sherman, M. (1927). The differentiation of emotional responses in infants: I. Judgments of emotional responses from motion picture views and from actual observation. *Journal of Comparative Psychology, 7,* 265–284.

Snyder, M. (1974). Self-monitoring of expressive behavior. *Journal of Personality and Social Psychology, 30,* 526–537.

Sumitsuji, N., K. Matsumoto, and Z. Kaneko (1965). A new method to study facial expression using electromyography. *Electromyography, 5,* 269–272.

Tagiuri, R. (1968). Person perception. In G. Lindzey and E. Aronson (Eds.), *The handbook of social psychology,* 2nd ed., Vol. 3. Reading, Mass: Addison-Wesley.

Thayer, S., and W. Schiff (1969). Stimulus factors in observer judgment of social interaction: Facial expression and motion pattern. *American Journal of Psychology, 82,* 73–85.

Thompson, D. F., and L. Meltzer (1964). Communication of emotional intent by facial expression. *Journal of Abnormal and Social Psychology, 68,* 129–135.

Thompson, J. (1941). Development of facial expression of emotion in blind and seeing children. *Archives of Psychology, 37,* N. 264. Pp. 5–47.

Tomkins, S. S. (1962). *Affect, imagery, consciousness,* Vol. 1: *The positive affects.* New York: Springer.

Tomkins, S. S. and R. McCarter (1964). What and where are the primary affects? Some evidence for a theory. *Perceptual and Motor Skolls, 18,* 119–158.

Triandis, H. C., and W. W. Lambert (1958). A restatement and test of Schlosberg's theory of emotion with two kinds of subjects from Greece. *Journal of Abnormal and Social Psychology, 56,* 321–328.

Trujillo, N. P., and T. A. Warthin (1968). The frowning sign multiple forehead furrows in peptic ulcer. *Journal of the American Medical Association, 205,* 218.

Vinacke, W. E. (1949). The judgment of facial expressions by three national-racial groups in Hawaii: I. Caucasian faces. *Journal of Personality, 17,* 407–429.

Vinacke, W. E., and R. W. Fong (1955). The judgment of facial expressions by three national-racial groups in Hawaii: II. Oriental faces. *Journal of Social Psychology, 41,* 185–195.

Vine, I. (1970). Communication by facial-visual signals: A review and analysis of their role in face-to-face encounters. In J. H. Crook (Ed.), *Social behavior in birds and mammals: Essays on the social ethology of animal and man.* New York: Academic Press. Pp. 279–354.

Watson, S. E. (1972). Judgment of emotion from facial and contextual cue combinations. *Journal of Personality and Social Psychology, 24,* 334–342.

Weitz, S. (Ed.) (1974). *Nonverbal communication: Readings with commentary.* New York: Oxford University Press.

Woodworth, R. S. (1938). *Experimental psychology.* New York: Henry Holt.

Zuckerman, M., M. S. Lipets, J. H. Koivumaki, and R. Rosenthal (1975). Encoding and decoding nonverbal cues of emotion. *Journal of Personality and Social Psychology, 32,* 1068–1076.

CHAPTER 4

Kinesics

INTRODUCTION

Most researchers in nonverbal communication consider body movements, or kinesics, as a basic area of nonverbal research. Knapp (1972), in his book *Nonverbal Communication in Human Interaction,* stated that "body motion, or kinesics behavior, typically includes gestures, movements of the body, limbs, hands, head, feet, and legs, facial expressions (smiles), eye behavior (blinking, direction and length of gaze, and pupil dilation) and posture" (p. 5). This definition is in general agreement with those of other major nonverbal communication researchers (e.g., Birdwhistell, 1970; Duncan, 1969).

However, we would make several distinctions for the purposes of our discussion. First, though facial expression, as reviewed in the last chapter, is incontestably a part of body movement or kinesic behavior, we have treated it in a separate chapter for two reasons: (a) because of the large volume of work conducted on facial expressions alone; (b) because facial expressions are thought to deal with expressions of emotions, perhaps direct expression (i.e., neural affect program), a possibility which gives them a slightly different status than other forms of body movement. A second distinction we make is to treat visual behavior separately. The study of direction and length of gaze have become a specific area of research, and eye contact (two persons looking at each other) is such an important psychological phenomenon that this behavior requires separate treatment in itself. In addition, we question whether pupillary dilation belongs with kinesic behavior. From a physiological standpoint, pupillary dilation is essentially not under voluntary control, not "communicative" (except perhaps in a very special and restricted sense to be discussed later), and it is not entirely clear what meaning can be given to the behavior. Finally, although postural behaviors are important in regulating interpersonal distance and hence might best be considered a part of proxemic behavior, we shall consider them as basically kinesic phenomena.

These distinctions leave us with the following behaviors that are considered here: movements of the head (excluding facial expressions and change in gaze direction of or eye contact), hands, feet and limbs (arms and legs), and body trunk. The most common physical actions representing these body areas probably include head-nods and head-turning, gestures (hands and arms), and postural shifts. As we see later, movements can serve different purposes and functions and can have different meanings.

Kinesic behavior or body movements fall on the expressive end of the communicative specificity dimension described by Dittmann (1972b). With the exception of movements such as head-nods and certain well understood gestures, few body movements can be considered discrete, most being continuous in nature. As such, given the expressive nature of movements, kinesics as a channel of communication possesses relatively low channel capacity (compared to speech and facial expression). These characteristics should not, however, belittle the role that body movements play in the total communication process.

Earlier we noted the various functions that kinesic behavior may play in an interpersonal communication situation: repeating, contradicting, substituting, complementing, accenting, and relating and regulating. Pointing in the same direction as one is describing verbally would be an example of the repetitive function of nonverbal communication. A person who moves about in intense and jerky movements would be nonverbally contradicting any concurrent verbal claim that he was not upset. A person who holds his hand out palm up as it begins raining may substitute that action for the comment, "It's beginning to rain." One can complement the threat, "I'm going to hit you," by drawing back one's fist. Pointing to or grasping different fingers in sequence with the other hand can serve to accent a spoken list of terms. Finally, regulation of verbal communication is accomplished by many body movements. For example, nodding is one of the most important ways in which a conversational partner's speech is reinforced (Matarazzo, Saslow, Wiens, Weitman, and Allen, 1964).

In reviewing the literature on kinesics, we have found it useful to group the studies into several sections. First, one may consider the relatively large number of investigations of body movement in the therapy or clinical interview situation. Use of nonverbal cues in this context began literally with psychotherapy as it was created by Freud. Following this, there are studies in which body movement that accompanies speech is analyzed. Dittmann has been a pioneer in investigating this area. Finally, there is the growing number of empirical investigations of body movement stimulated by the resurgence of interest in this field. An important guide to the research on body movement is the book by Davis (1972), which is an annotated bibliography of more than 900 references.

Before this research is considered, however, we must make the distinction between two basic strategies in nonverbal communication research: the *structural* and the *external variable* approaches (Duncan, 1969). Up until now, we have made only limited reference to Birdwhistell's approach to the study of nonverbal behavior. Though our main focus is on external variable research, it would be unfair and unrepresentative not to consider Birdwhistell's contributions, especially to research on kinesics. In considering his research, the important limitations of the structural approach are noted, and the characteristics of the external variable approach, perhaps best represented by Ekman and his colleagues, are identified. Consideration of the strengths and limitations of these two approaches should give the reader a better context in which to consider the research to be reviewed. Some of the research is based on a structural approach (e.g., Scheflen); most, however, is conducted with the external variable approach.

BIRDWHISTELL AND THE STRUCTURAL APPROACH

Birdwhistell is an anthropologist who has devoted his research career to the study of human communication. He first elaborated his theories in 1952 with the publication *Introduction of Kinesics: An Annotation System for Analysis of Body Motion and Gestures,* although, for many years thereafter, he studied body movement in relative isolation since few other researchers were interested in that field. However, it is largely due to his contributions that there has been a resurgence of interest in kinesics and nonverbal communication, and any criticisms of his approach should be tempered with this realization. Birdwhistell's influence has been greatest in the nonexperimental areas of psychiatry and communications research, though, as with Freud, many of his naturalistic observations later became subject matter for empirical investigation. Until recently, few of his writings were in print because most of his work was communicated at professional meetings. His 1970 book, *Kinesics and Context,* edited by Barton Jones, provides a review of his work. Important reviews of this work were written by Kendon (1972) and Dittmann (1971).

Birdwhistell has taken an ethological or essentially descriptive approach to studying human communications. As Kendon (1972) noted, Birdwhistell views communication as a system with a structure that can be described independently of the behavior of the particular participants. This is a "systemic" view of communication and it assumes that all interpersonal behavior, that is, behavior that occurs and is detectable by another person, must be presumed to be socially learned and communicative until proven otherwise. Verbal and nonverbal communication are integral and inseparable parts of the total communication system. Knapp (1972) quoted Birdwhistell as saying that "studying nonverbal communication is like studying noncardiac physiology" (p. 3). In other words, it is not meaningful or useful to talk about a distinction between verbal and nonverbal communication. From this point of view, one cannot focus on one part of the total pattern of verbal and nonverbal interaction and expect to understand the significance, for example, of individual movements. A person's orientation to another (e.g., facing towards or away) is as important or "communicative" as the exact words being spoken (e.g., "I really think a lot of you"), and the significance of each is partially dependent on the other.

To Birdwhistell, the context in which certain body movements occur was crucial as they could not be understood in isolation. Kendon (1972) described an example of a man with a raised fist. Unless the whole communicational context were known, we could not decide whether that action represented a greeting, a sign of anger, accompanied a verbal description of another person as "tightfisted," or represented a political symbol of "power." Whereas others might try to learn the "meaning" of this particular behavior, Birdwhistell sought to determine the different environments in which the behavior occurred (i.e., its range of use), from which one could begin to determine the function of the movement within the total communication situation.

The method of study chosen by Birdwhistell was nicely summarized by Kendon (1972):

> The focus, then, is on what behaviors people characteristically engage in when they interact. Since we do not know what these behaviors are, we must look and see. Most often, an investigator with this orientation will seek to gather records on film or video tape of occasions when people are present to one another and then, by patient and detailed watching, he will try to describe the elements of behavior that occur and the way these elements are patterned to one another. Gradually, as he accumulates examples, he will be able to state the contexts within which the elements he has isolated may be found, and from such statements specify the ways in which these elements function in the communication system he is studying.
>
> The most rigorously developed methodology consonant with this approach is that of descriptive linguistics. (p. 443)

Knapp (1972) provided a good analysis of the *"linguistic-kinesic analogy"* that underlies Birdwhistell's methodology. As linguistic study can be divided up into descriptive and historical linguistics, kinesic study can be broken up into prekinesics, microkinesics, and social kinesics. Prekinesics concerns the study of physiological determinants and limits of movements. Microkinesics deals with the identification of units of movements, and social kinesics is the study of units and patterns of movement in the social situation (context) where their function can be determined. As there are paralinguistic phenomena, one can also identify parakinesic variables. These include motion or activity qualifiers such as the degree of muscular tension for each movement, the time, and the range of movement.

Birdwhistell determined that the study of kinesics should begin with derivation of the basic units of analysis, the units of measurements. Determination of the units of analysis is microkinesic analysis. The basic kinesic unit with discriminable meaning is the *kine.* Those kines or movements which may have the same *differential* meaning are called *allokines.* The analysis of body movement into these units required slow-motion film analysis by Birdwhistell:

In terms of duration, kines have been recorded in sequences that ranged from 1/50 of a second (significant lid, finger, hand, lip, and head movements faster than this *seem* to be allokinic within a range from as fast as 1/100 of a second to as long as a full second) to over 3 seconds. (1970, pp. 101–102)

For example, all those kines that consist of raising the eyebrows are also allokines in that they can be substituted for one another without changing their meaning. Together, a group of allokines make up a *kineme,* the smallest set of body movements with differential meaning, which is analogous to the linguistic unit, the phoneme. (Differential meaning is determined by asking subjects in an experimental setting whether a particular movement or position has a "different meaning" to them compared to another movement or position.)

In studying body movements in American culture, Birdwhistell hypothesized approximately 50 or 60 kinemes. The significance of this list can readily be appreciated by considering the following:

Physiologists have estimated that the facial musculature is such that over twenty thousand different facial expressions are somatically possible. At the present state of investigations, we have been able to isolate thirty-two kinemes in the face and head area. (1970, p. 99)

Kinemes, the basic movements that have structural meaning, "are combined into orderly structures of behavior in the interactive sequence . . . [contributing] to social meaning" (Birdwhistell, 1970, p. 99). Kinemorphs are the next higher unit, consisting of combinations of kinemes. Birdwhistell noted that kinemorphs were "further analyzable into kinemorphic classes which behave like linguistic morphemes" (1970, p. 101). He developed a lengthy pictorial notation system for coding kines, called kinegraphs. In this system the body is divided into eight different areas and movement in each body area is transcribed in a different type of kinegraphic symbol. An observer trained in this system can easily record the movements quickly without the use of mechanical equipment.

The social meaning of kinesic units is determined, as mentioned earlier, by observing them in different social contexts. An example of what this method of context analysis can yield comes from Birdwhistell's identification of *markers.* These are defined as "particular movements that occur regularly in association with or in substitution for certain syntactic arrangements in American English speech" (Birdwhistell, 1970, p. 103). Hand gestures are a most common form of marker.

Birdwhistell (1968) transcribed conversations verbally and kinesically, later excluding all kinesic activity which did not accompany speech. Certain of the remaining movements were then discovered to accompany specific verbal behaviors such as statements and questions. Similarly, Birdwhistell identified other kinesic behaviors important to speech:

During the same period that research was delineating these semantically bound markers, systematic observation revealed that a second series of behaviors, previously discussed as speech effort behavior, were regular and orderly. Slight head nods and sweeps, eye blinks, small lip movements, chin thrusts, shoulder nods and sweeps, thorax thrusts, hand and finger movements, as well as leg and foot shifts proved to be allokines of a quadripartite kinesic *stress* system. (1970, pp. 103–104)

These included *primary stress, secondary stress, unstressed* movements, and *destressed* movements. A primary kinesic stress is a strong movement normally occurring with loudest linguistic stress. Secondary stress is a weaker movement that occurs in association with the primary stress and can be contrasted with unstressed or normal movements accompanying speech. Destressed allokines represent reductions of movements below the normal flow during phrases and clauses.

The above description of kinesic speech markers and stress movements exemplifies only part of the productivity of Birdwhistell's system of analysis. In a fascinating discussion, "Masculinity and femininity as display" (Birdwhistell, 1970), he identified several gender-related kinesic behaviors in American cultures. The importance of identifying such behaviors follows from Birdwhistell's reasoning: "My work in kinesics leads me to postulate that man and probably a number of other weakly dimorphic species necessarily organize much of gender display and recognition at the level of position, movement, and expression" (1970, p. 42). Birdwhistell noted that in peoples of eight different cultures "both male and female informants distinguished not only typically male communicational behavior from typically female communicational behavior, but when the opportunity presented itself, distinguished 'feminine' males and 'masculine' females" (1970, p. 43). Differences in male and female movements were noted in "intrafemoral angle and body angle" and pelvic position. A more subtle difference was also identified:

Informants often describe particular lid and eye behavior as masculine or feminine. However, only careful observation and measurement reveal that the structural components of circumorbital behavior are related, in closure of the lid in males, to prohibiting movement of the eyeballs while the lids are closed. Comparably, the communicative convention prescribes that unless accompanying signals indicate sleepiness or distress, males should close and open their lids in a relatively continuous movement. (Birdwhistell, 1970, p. 44)

To date, Birdwhistell's research has largely been limited to the study of the units of kinesic analysis. Scheflen, a psychiatrist influenced by Birdwhistell, went beyond the units of kinesic analysis and attempted to specify *behavioral programs,* movement patterns much larger than kinemorphic constructions. Scheflen's work is not described here because it was reviewed briefly in Chapter 1; some of his work in psychotherapy is described later. Suffice it to say here that Scheflen's method of contextual analysis is essentially the same as Birdwhistell, and both share the same aversion to "atomistic" psychological research following the external variable approach.

In evaluating Birdwhistell's contributions, we should note that he has not claimed to have provided all the answers to the study of body movement. As Kendon (1972) noted in his book review:

We do not get a well-worked map of the territory. Despite some reviewers, however, I see no reason why we should have expected such a map. It is only within the last five years that anyone other than Birdwhistell himself, besides a mere handful of workers, has even begun to take the field seriously. (1972, p. 441)

Nevertheless, it is possible legitimately to criticize Birdwhistell's research on a number of grounds. Weitz (1974) pointed out that "kinesic analysis is very much like literary analysis: one can impose one's own structure on the material and never really be certain that this is the best fitting model or the 'correct' one" (p. 130). From a more practical standpoint, the method of analysis is extremely time-consuming and the recording system (i.e., use of kinegraphs) is not readily adaptable to typewriters or for use with computers. In addition, there are only verbal descriptions of the kines, kinemorphs, and pictorial symbols in the observation system; no pictures are provided to exemplify what the precise movements are. Birdwhistell's system does not provide for sampling behavioral sequences; it requires an entire event.

The most important criticism of this method, however, is the assumption of an analogy between kinesic behavior and language. Dittmann (1971), in his review, concluded that "the basic hypothesis of kinesics as a communication system with the same structure as spoken language is not a viable one" (p. 341). He pointed out that words were discrete information sources but that only certain movements that were discrete might be classified as kinemes, analogous to phonemes. However, the bulk of movements are more continuous in nature or, if discrete, cannot be considered kinemes. As such, too few movements in kinesic analysis probably exist to justify such an analogy. More importantly, "there is no evidence that movement elements are assembled into groupings based upon any set rules internal to the movements themselves" (p. 341). With language there are discrete, reliable units of analysis and readily discernable rules for their combination such that new utterances (consisting of units not previously combined) can be understood. No such rules exist for body movement behavior. Wiener, Devoe, Rubinow, and Geller (1972) thus concluded: "Although we can understand how to proceed with a structural analysis after a communication system has been designed, we do not know how to discover a communication system by analysis of the smallest common units of a modality" (p. 197).

In summary, we agree with Dittmann's assessment of Birdwhistell's work and the structural approach:

> Birdwhistell's initial inpact was to spur a number of workers to look at these [kinesic] phenomena, using whatever methods were available. . . . The way one conceives of the basic data for his research determines the methods he may use to examine those data. If the basic hypothesis of kinesics had been accepted by all investigators interested in the communicative aspects of body movement, their research would have been limited to linguistic methods which are really not appropriate to research in this area, and the chances are that we would not know as much about these phenomena as we know today. Communication by means other than language is a field of a number of diverse topics and the types of information encountered by the research are also diverse. . . . Theories and methods appropriate to all these different kinds of information are needed. Birdwhistell has given a theory, resting on untenable premises, which would confine investigators to only one method. (1971, pp. 341–342)

We now return to a research approach more in accord with our own thinking, that of the external variable approach demonstrated by Ekman and his colleagues.

EKMAN AND THE EXTERNAL VARIABLE APPROACH

In describing the difference between Birdwhistell's structural approach and Ekman's research, Weitz (1974) noted:

> Ekman . . . is not trying to establish a grammar of body language or even to study the communication process per se, as Birdwhistell is. Rather, his concern is the relationship of nonverbal behavior to inner feeling states and to the decoding of

these states by others. . . . Ekman also does not integrate the verbal and nonverbal spheres, a primary goal of the Birdwhistell school. Ekman is concerned with the psychological problem of the communication of emotional state, rather than the structural one of the nature of the communications system itself. (p. 131)

Birdwhistell began his research with a strong commitment to a theoretical model that did not always fit with subsequent research. In contrast, Ekman began on an experimental basis and developed his theory based on empirical findings: "We were antitheoretical when we began our work measuring body movements, blaming the sorry state of this field of research on an over-abundance of theory with too few facts" (Ekman and Friesen, 1972, p. 355). Ekman's research followed the external variable approach (Duncan, 1969), which consists of indicative and communicative studies. As described in Chapter 1, indicative studies examine the relationship between nonverbal variables and other variables; communicative studies investigate the meaning of nonverbal behaviors by observers. Ekman employed as his "unit of observation" for nonverbal behavior the *nonverbal act/position*. An act is a clear movement observable to another person, without aid of special equipment, that has a distinct beginning and end. A still position occurs when there is not movement. Ekman and Friesen (1968) explained:

Our level of analysis is thus geared to what can be observed and is distinctive to the unaided eye, although reliability in determining both the boundaries and classification of the unit is aided by repetition, magnification and slowed motion routines. . . . The classification of acts and positions is thus based upon what is easily recognizable to any observer. The classificatory scheme is built directly from the acts and positions found in the film records, rather than derived from a priori notions. No notational system or series of measurements is needed to distinguish between movements or to recall types of acts or positions; instead a simple verbal label is utilized, with filmed examples of each act or position type readily retrievable by use of a series of search tags. (pp. 193–194)

In their 1968 paper, Ekman and Friesen distinguished their unit of analysis from microkinesic analysis (used by other researchers such as Loeb, 1968), which requires slow motion analysis of body movements—movements that are not ordinarily visible. However, in a later paper they reported: "Our interest in the experience of the individual when alone has led to including such micro-events, while our interest in how nonverbal behavior functions in social interaction has required our examining molar units of behavior" (Ekman and Friesen, 1972, p. 354).

In the basic exposition of their position, Ekman and Friesen (1969b) described the usage, origin, coding, and classification of nonverbal behavior. We review the main aspects of this theory, outlined in Table 4–1, excluding their empirical findings for later comment.

Table 4-1. Ekman-Friesen Classification of Nonverbal Behavior

Types of Nonverbal Behavior	*Characteristics of Nonverbal Behaviors*

1. Emblems: movements that are communicative substitutes for words	1. Usage
	   External conditions
	   Relationship to verbal behavior
	   Awareness/intentionality of person engaging in nonverbal act
	   External feedback
	   Type of information conveyed

2. Illustrators: movements that accompany speech and accent, modify, punctuate it, etc.	
3. Regulators: movements that maintain or signal a change in listening/speaking role	

4. Adaptors: self- or object-manipulations related to individual need or emotional state	Idiosyncratic encoded meaning
	      Informative
	      Communicative
	      Interactive

5. Affect displays: facial expressions (see Chapter 3)	2. Origin
	      Innate response
	      Culturally learned
	      Socially learned

	3. Coding
	      Extrinsically coded acts
	      Arbitrarily coded acts
	      Iconically coded acts
	      Intrinsically coded acts

Usage

Ekman and Friesen defined usage as the "regular and consistent circumstances surrounding the occurrence of a nonverbal act" (1969b, p. 53). Usage includes *external conditions* that occur at the same time as the body movement, such as the physical setting, role situation, or emotional atmosphere. The *relationship of the nonverbal act to verbal behavior* is an aspect of usage that involves both the temporal relationship and the meaning of both verbal and nonverbal behavior. *Awareness* is an aspect of usage that concerns the person's conscious or unconscious knowledge about the behavior being performed. *Intentionality* is an important feature of nonverbal behavior and includes behavior that the performer is conscious of and desires to communicate. *External feedback* is the information that the performer of the nonverbal behavior receives, indicating that his behavior is being received and evaluated.

Finally, the *type of information* conveyed "refers to a basic distinction between idiosyncratic and shared information, and definitions of *informative, communicative,* and *interactive* nonverbal behavior" (1969a, p. 54). A nonverbal act has idiosyncratic meaning if the behavior is emitted or can be understood only in relation to a particular inidvidual. An act with idiosyncratic encoded meaning is emitted under particular circumstances by only one individual. If a nonverbal behavior is received and understood by only one person, then it has idiosyncratic decoded meaning. Nonverbal acts with shared meaning are those which a number of persons would describe similarly. Nonverbal acts can thus be analyzed in terms of the "layers of meaning" (idiosyncratic and shared) and type of meaning (encoded or decoded). Many acts have both idiosyncratic and shared meaning depending on how they are classified by observers.

A nonverbal behavior is informative if it has a shared *decoded meaning,* even if observers are not accurate about the correct meaning of the behavior. Communicative nonverbal behavior involves those acts that are consciously encoded to transmit a given message to a receiver. *Communicative nonverbal acts* may have idiosyncratic or shared meaning, but they are not necessarily informative. Finally, *interactive nonverbal behaviors* are acts by one person that influence or modify the behavior of another person or persons. Interactive behaviors can be informative and communicative as well, or they can be idiosyncratic in their meanings. Justifying the use of this somewhat complex terminology, Ekman and Friesen stated:

We have developed this terminology in order to clarify our own thinking and illuminate possible differences between our approach and those of Birdwhistell, of Scheflen, and of Mahl. Birdwhistell and Scheflen have applied a communication framework to nonverbal behavior, based largely upon the argument that much of the nonverbal behavior they observe influences the behavior of the other interactants. We believe that their use of the term "communicative" is too broad; it fails to distinguish among that behavior which has a shared decoded meaning (informative), that which influences the other person's interaction (interactive), and that which is intended to transmit a message (communicative). Many nonverbal behaviors may have interactive affects, but not be intended to communicate nor best be considered as analogous to verbal communication. Similarly, nonverbal behavior with a shared decoded meaning may not be intended to communicate, nor be best considered as analogous to linguistic phenomena. (1969b, p. 57)

Origin

By *origin of nonverbal behavior,* Ekman and Friesen meant the source of the action. An inborn reflex action is a source of some nonverbal behavior. Some nonverbal behavior can be considered common to a species even if not inborn, having its origin, for example, in the common experience that food is delivered to the mouth by the hands. Finally, many nonverbal behaviors originate from culture-specific instrumental tasks or social interaction. They may be formally taught, imitated, or the result of incidental learning.

Coding

Finally, it is possible to describe nonverbal behaviors in terms of their coding: how meaning is attached to the act. An act that is *extrinsically coded* is one that signifies something else; the meaning of the act cannot be seen from the action itself. Some extrinsic acts are *arbitrarily coded* and bear no resemblance to their meaning: the raised fist gives by itself no information concerning an intention to convey a "power to the people" message. An *iconically coded* extrinsic act, however, does resemble what it means, as when a person makes a throat-cutting movement with the index finger. In contrast, an act that is *intrinsically coded* "stands for itself:" the meaning of the act is seen in the action itself. If one were to substitute a karate chop movement for the words, "He gave John a 'karate chop,'" this would be an example of an intrinsically coded act. Nonverbal acts can also be *pictorial* (drawing a square in the air to depict your attitude about another person), *spatial* (hands held apart to demonstrate length of a fish), *rhythmic* (a conductor leading an orchestra), *kinetic* (the iconic throat-cut movement or the intrinsically coded karate chop), or *pointing* movements. Pictorial, rhythmic, and spatial movements are by definition iconically coded; kinetic movements may be iconic or intrinsically coded; pictorial movements are always intrinsically coded.

In introducing their categories of nonverbal behavior, Ekman and Friesen (1969b) noted:

Nonverbal behavior is not a single, unified phenomenon with but one type of usage, one origin and one form of coding. Instead, facial and body behavior involve a number of quite different kinds of behavior which will be described in terms of five categories distinguished by the particulars of usage, origin and coding. (pp. 62–63)

Emblems, their first category of behavior, are those movements that have a "direct verbal translation" well known to others. Typically, an emblem can be replaced by one or two words that can take its place in a conversation without substantially modifying it. In addition to having a shared decoded meaning, they have a shared encoded meaning and are communicative acts (i.e., their usage is intentional and conscious). Emblems are interactive and generally result in external feedback, given that they originate through social learning. In particular, decoders of emblems assume that they are deliberately communicated and that the sender assumes responsibility for the communication. Most acts are extrinsically (arbitrarily and iconically) coded, though intrinsic coding is considered possible. Examples of emblems would include shaking a fist, waving as for a greeting, or tracing a body of a woman (an iconic-pictorial emblem). Because they have a specific agreed-upon meaning they are most easily understood, but as such they generally carry less personal or idiosyncratic meaning than other nonverbal behaviors. Ekman and Friesen considered the study of emblems important in cross-cultural research:

Peculiarities in the environmental conditions in which communication occurs, and the state of development of the technology of communication might lead to the production of a large number of emblems for a specific message domain in one culture but not in another. For example, a warring society which conducts guerilla warfare but which lacks the technology for quiet verbal communication among its members, and where the terrain permits line-of-sight observation over fairly long distance, might develop a large number of emblems to convey information back and forth between warriors as they approach their prey. (1969b, p. 66)

Illustrators are defined as those movements that are directly related to speech and illustrate what is verbalized (e.g., extending the hands apart to demonstrate the length of a fish). Like emblems, they are generally intentional and informative (with shared decoded meaning) and often communicative and interactive as well. They are socially learned through imitation and thus can vary across cultures. Most are iconically coded, though some are intrinsically coded. Efron (1941) provided six terms descriptive of illustrators: (a) *batons:* movements that are in synchrony with the pace or tempo of speech; (b) *deictic or pointing movements;* (c) *spatial movements* descriptive of spatial relationships; (d) *ideographic or movements tracing a line of thought;* (e) *kinetographic movements* depicting a bodily action; (f) *pictographs,* which outline the picture of the verbal referent.

Regulators are nonverbal behaviors which maintain and regulate speaking and listening between two interactants, such as head nods and small postural shifts. Since they have become ingrained habits, regulators are not communicative in the sense of interactants being aware of or intending to control each other's behavior, though they are always considered interactive and informative. Ekman and Friesen were unsure of the coding of regulators, but it seems clear that they are importantly related to the environmental setting and to the social class, race, and culture of individuals. Credit is given to Scheflen (1963, 1964, 1966) for identifying, from structural analysis of social interaction, three important kinds of regulators: *points* (movements of the head, neck, or eyes occurring usually after utterances of several sentences); a *position* (several points, including a posture, that represent a conversational attitude); a *presentation,* or the totality of movements within an interaction. Presentations include body posture and distance, which define interpersonal intimacy, or postural similarity (an indication of status or conversational congruence) and body orientation (towards vs. away), which identifies the type of interaction (transmission of feeling or impersonal information).

Affect displays involve primarily facial expressions, which are covered in detail in Chapter 3. Here we note that they are often informative and sometimes interactive and communicative, though in many instances facial expressions occur without intention or awareness. Facial behaviors generally receive more external feedback than the other categories. Because of the uncertainty surrounding the origin of facial expressions (i.e., are they innate or learned), Ekman and Friesen warned that: "The coding of facial affect displays is not at all obvious" (1969b, p. 78). Affect displays give more personal information than illustrators and most emblems, and often possess idiosyncratic meaning when affect blends occur in individuals. Affect displays include a facial expression that in turn is followed by a behavioral consequence. This is some body movement that coincides with or follows the facial expression that "copes" with the facial display of affect. Ekman and Friesen classified behaviors such as these as adaptors.

Adaptors are the most theoretical part of their classification scheme and yet the most important in terms of the meaning they convey about individuals. Rarely are they communicative (i.e., occur with conscious intention), though many are informative (possess shared decoded meaning) and interactive. All are coded iconically or intrinsically but not arbitrarily. Adaptors are described as early-learned (often in childhood) acts that were once parts of efforts to manage body needs, emotions, or interpersonal interaction, or to learn instrumental behaviors. Once they were part of a sequence of goal-directed acts, but subsequently they have become automatic habitual acts that occur during adulthood outside normal awareness. Self-adaptors are acts that involve some manipulation of a part of the body (e.g., head-scratching, licking the lips, rubbing hands) whose meaning often can be inferred by considering the original adaptive act (fulfilling some personal or body need) that they may have served. Picking at one's face in the absence of a skin irritation may represent, for example, a form of personal attack. Alter-directed adaptors consist of movements originally related to prototypic interpersonal contacts (e.g., giving-taking, fight-flight, sexual flirtation). Folding the arms across the body can be interpreted as a protective move designed to fend off attack; leg movements may be "residues of kicking aggression, sexual invitation or flight" (1969b, p. 89). Finally, object-adaptors are sequences of movements learned for some instrumental purpose, such as smoking, driving, a golf swing, etc. Unlike self- and alter-adaptors, object-adaptors are more often within awareness and more socially acceptable. Self- and alter-adaptors are many times socially taboo (e.g., self-stimulation behavior), though they may become manifest during times of emotional arousal or disorgainzation.

Nonverbal Betrayal of Affect

One of the most interesting hypotheses of Ekman and Friesen (1969a), which relates categories of nonverbal behavior to each other, concerns their notion of "nonverbal" betrayal of affect. Freud once said: "He that has eyes to see and ears to hear may convince himself that no mortal can keep a secret. If his lips are silent, he chatters with his finger tips, betrayal oozes out of him at every pore" (Freud, 1905, p. 94). Given that in our culture, and others, people are most aware of facial affect expressions that are inhibited through socially learned display rules, they are not always representative of an individual's emotions. In contrast, body movements are not typically subject to display rules and are normally outside our awareness (and hence less subject to censorship). Ekman and Friesen (1969a) thus postulated that when an individual was engaging either in self-deception (ego-deception) or deception of another person (alter-deception) the body would provide more accurate cues of deception than the face. These cues that the body would provide in the form of an increase in adaptors, or awkward or inappropriate emission of emblems, illustrators, or regulators, were called *"nonverbal leakage."* Leg and foot movements were considered the most likely sources of leakage, followed by the hands and face, which were increasingly subject to awareness and voluntary inhibition. Some of Ekman's most exciting work (to be discussed shortly) involved tests of this hypothesis.

In summary, it is difficult not to be impressed with the conceptualization of nonverbal behavior offered by Ekman and Friesen. While both Ekman and Birdwhistell began with careful analysis of nonverbal behavior and the sequence and context of nonverbal acts, the latter's insistence on *never* considering any behavior in isolation or in relation to specific external variables, in our opinion, imposed a tremendous methodological handicap. Though Birdwhistell's approach might seem more encompassing or broader by beginning with the assumption that "all behavior is communicative," his findings and those of his structuralist colleague, Scheflen, can actually be subsumed into Ekman's classification scheme.

One possible criticism of Ekman and Friesen's classification scheme might be that the different categories are not always clearly defined in terms of their usage, origin, or coding. Indeed, Wiener, Devoe, Rubinow, and Geller (1972) criticized their system on the grounds that it lacks an "explicitly stated code" necessary for nonverbal communication to be demonstrable (see p. 17). Specifically, they suggested a method for demonstrating nonverbal communication and proposed several categories of be-havior that would seem to meet their requirement. Interestingly, this method for demonstrating communication and the behaviors proposed as communicative by these authors would seem to fit easily within Ekman's system as a special set of nonverbal behaviors. In the final analysis, it is this flexibility that makes this work and the method of investigation more pow-erful and meaningful than the structural approach of Birdwhistell.

EMPIRICAL RESEARCH

Thus far we have discussed two different conceptual and methodological approaches typified by two of the major contributors to kinesic research. In this section we consider some of the empirical research on kinesics, begin-ning with research in the clinical interview situation.

Clinical Research: Structural Approach

Much of the structural research has been conducted in the interview situa-tion. Because of the intricate "systemic" nature of this kind of research, it is difficult to summarize it briefly. The reader is thus encouraged to refer to the original articles for a firsthand knowledge of how the findings were obtained.

Scheflen, a psychiatrist, followed Birdwhistell's approach analysis but attempted to look at larger units of behavior. Scheflen (1966) defined a structural unit as "a regular organization or complex of components occur-ring in specific situations or contexts. A structural unit, then, has: (1) a given set of component parts; (2) a definite organization; and (3) specific location in a larger system" (p. 271). In an important paper, Scheflen noted:

One of these regular structures that invariably appeared in psychotherapy included behaviors like those found in American courtship. The ethics of psychotherapy have traditionally proscribed sexual behavior, and most of the therapists we studied were unaware that they behaved in ways which could be identified as sexual in therapy sessions. (1974, p. 182)

His method of observation was described as follows:

Briefly, the many elements of behavior are examined to find their structural co-nfigurations as they appear in a stream of behavior. (This practice is very different from the usual approach in the psychological sciences, where this or that a priori decision is made about what elements of behavior will be selected or which qualities will be abstracted for study as variables). Then, when a unit has been identified, each recurrence of it is examined in the contexts in which it occurs. By contrasting what happens when it does and does not occur, its function in the larger systems—and, therefore, its significance or meaning—is derived. (Scheflen, 1974, pp. 183–184)

Using this approach with films of therapeutic encounters, in addition to business encounters and conferences, Scheflen described a set of "quasi-courtship behaviors." *Courtship readiness* behaviors include a combination of high muscle tone, reduced eye-bagginess and jowl-sag, decreased slouch, and less stomach- and shoulder-sag. Postural *positioning cues* include torso, arm, and leg positions oriented towards one person and serving to reduce interaction with others. *Preening behaviors* are acts that include hair-stroking, tie-straightening, reapplying make-up, etc. Finally, there are *actions of appeal or invitation* such as flirtatious glances, leg-crossing to expose a thigh, and the like.

In a series of studies, Condon and Ogston (1966, 1967) exhaustively studied body movement in relation to speech articulation and listening behavior of normal and pathological individuals. Analyzing speech and film segments frame by frame, they noted "harmonious or synchronous organizations of change between body motion and speech in *both* intra-individual and interactional behavior. Thus, the body of the speaker dances in time with his speech. Further, the body of the listener dances in rhythm with that of the speaker!" (Condon and Ogston, 1966, p. v 338). Without going into detail about the speech-related syncrony, their observation of *motion-flow dyssyncrony* among disturbed patients is of particular clinical interest. A description of a paranoid schizophrenic patient talking with her physician is illustrative of the findings of Condon and his associates:

Her eyes, in the film, displayed some micro strabismus. There was also a temporal dyssynchrony in the way the body parts moved in relation to each other as contrasted with the normal, temporal organization of movement. Her left arm, with the hand held flexed and limp, moved slowly in a sustained direction for approximately ⅓ of a second and was disharmonious with the rhythm of her speech. While the left arm was moving in this fashion the right arm was moved and changed in harmony with the speech. (Condon and Brosin, 1969, p. 830)

Observations such as this were particularly notable among schizophrenic subjects who showed different parts of the body moving "out of cycle" with the rest, or at a different tempo. In a particularly fascinating study, Condon, Ogston, and Pacoe (1969) reported an analysis of films of the different personalities of the patient who was depicted in the motion picture "The Three Faces of Eve." A "microtransient strabismus" was noted in the patient's different personalities, with Eve Black, the most unstable personality, exhibiting five times as many strabismic occurrences as the other two personalities. Interestingly, analysis of a film of "Jane II," a more stable personality that emerged several years later, showed no microstrabismus, suggesting that this was somehow associated with the course of the illness. Similar changes were observed in some of their schizophrenic patients during acute and remission phases of illness.

Charny (1966) examined structural and thematic vocal behavior and body motion of a patient and therapist in a filmed interaction. He found a significant association between upper-body "mirror congruent" postures of patient and therapist and positive, interpersonal-oriented speech content. (Mirror congruent postures occur when each person's posture behavior is the mirror image of the other.) Charny summarized:

The content themes coincident with mirroring were principally centered upon critical awareness of the significance of events in the patient's previous day and attempts to effect therapeutic gain by examining the patient's reaction to them. In contrast, the content themes of the noncongruent periods were highly self-oriented, self-contradictory, and frequently negational or non-specific. (1966, p. 314)

Postural congruence was proposed as a "naturally occurring interactive unit indicative of a state of therapeutic rapport or relatedness" (1966, p. 314). Loeb (1968), employing similar slow motion analysis of a psychotherapy film, identified a micromomentary fistlike movement in the patient that occurred "in contexts containing lexical expressions which are known to be regularly associated with the conscious content 'anger'" (p. 611). In this micromomentary study, expressive body movements were related to the interpretation of unconscious and conscious verbal behaviors of a patient. In another study, Loeb, Loeb, and Ross (1972) identified "mechanically purposeless grasp like movements in space" made by patients. Verbal content analysis revealed that these particular movements were associated with need themes of getting close to or away from such objects as mother, milk, breast, or food. Films of these grasping and nongrasping movements were then shown to naive experimental subjects who more frequently attributed to the grasping movements (than nongrasping movements) the same general kinds of meanings that were interpreted from the patient's speech. These grasping movements were further seen as being similar to nursing movements made by infants, and the verbal content was ideationally related to the feeding situation. This interesting method appears particularly appropriate for investigations concerned with psychoanalytic theory and analysis of unconscious or preconscious material.

Clinical Research: External Variable Approach

All the previous research essentially followed the structural approach in that sequences of behavior were analyzed in verbal and situational contexts. None of these studies related body movement to "external variables." In contrast, Dittmann (1962) selected psychotherapy film segments during which a patient's various moods were in evidence. Selection of each film segment was based on the mood expressed directly by the patient (e.g., "I'm jittery this morning") and analysis by two judges of audio recordings of the patient's speech to insure that the mood reflected in the patient's voice was consistent with his verbal statements. Analysis of the film segments revealed an association between the patient's mood states and body movements. In particular, different patterns of movements were noted as a function of mood state. For example, many head and leg but few hand movements occurred when the patient was expressing anger, whereas few movements of the head and hand, but many leg movements, were noted during the depressed mood state.

Using the same psychotherapy interview earlier studied by Dittmann, Boomer (1963) examined the relationship between the patient's body movements and speech disturbances, both hypothesized to be measures of anxiety. As mentioned in Chapter 2, the frequency of nonpurposive body movement correlated significantly ($r = .42, p < .01$) with Mahl's non-ah speech disturbance measure. To rule out the alternative possibility that speech disturbances and body movement covaried with speech rate, Boomer and Dittman (1964) had volunteer subjects spontaneously increase their speech rate under presumably nonarousing conditions. No increase in body movement was noted, suggesting that the body movement observed in Boomer's study (Boomer, 1963) was not related to a patient's rate of speech.

Ekman and Friesen (1968) reported examining a patient's filmed body movements for differences on admission and discharge. Particular body movements (e.g., the feet, hands) were observed for frequency and type of movement. This constituted an indicative measure. Observers then separately made ratings on an adjective checklist of films of the particular body areas obtained during admission. These ratings, in contrast, were based on the communicative method. Differences in the frequency and type of movement were noted between admission and discharge, and observer ratings of the body movements were consistent, indicating their "communicative" value. For example, repetitious foot sliding was the most common behavior on admission, whereas more varied and active foot behavior could be noted on discharge. Analysis of hand movements by type, frequency, and concurrent speech revealed consistent associations between particular movements and verbal content. For example, the movement "hand-shrug rotation" was consistently accompanied by verbal themes of uncertainty or confusion; hand-tosses accompanied comments about the patient's inability to control behavior. Adjective checklist ratings based on judgments of the behavior in isolation were compared with adjective ratings made from complete film presentation. Judges' ratings were in agreement for the various hand acts, each of which communicated different information—suggesting, in turn, that each had distinct "communicative value."

In another study, Ekman and Friesen (1969a) examined the value of head and body cues in detecting deception in patients. They showed observers a film segment of an interview of a depressed woman who, at the time, was motivated to simulate normalcy in order to gain discharge and the freedom to commit suicide. Head-only, body-only, and head-and-body films were rated by different observers on an adjective checklist. By comparing the frequencies of adjectives checked in association with head- and body-only film presentations, the results, in general, supported their contention that head cues would transmit the patient's intended message of "being well" while the body movements conveyed information that she was actually still disturbed. Similar analysis of other film segments of the same patient at a time when she appeared unaware of her hysterically seductive behavior revealed that this behavior was communicated by body movements rather than facial cues.

In a more recent study, (Kiritz, Ekman, and Friesen, in preparation), Kiritz, a student of Ekman, hypothesized that hand illustrator activity would vary with patient mood on admission and discharge. As predicted, psychotic depressives showed fewer illustrators on admission than neurotic depressives and schizophrenics and significantly more illustrators on discharge. Mood ratings by psychiatrists of patients shown on sound films on admission and discharge yielded negative correlations between illustrator activity and ratings of depressive mood, motor retardation, blunted activity, and emotional withdrawal. Total self-adaptor activity on admission and discharge was positively correlated with an "upset" factor (obtained from a factor analysis of the rating scale), and picking or scratching adaptors were correlated with a hostility or suspiciousness factor. The results of this study thus further demonstrated that a nonverbal act has both indicative meaning (i.e., is associated with admission or discharge status) and communicative meaning (i.e., is decoded consistently by observers, or has shared decoded meaning).

Subsequently, Hinchliffe, Hooper, Roberts, and Vaughan (1975) video-taped interactions between depressed patients and their spouses, during the psychiatric hospitalization and, following their discharge, when they were recovered. Surgical patients and their spouses served as a control group. In addition to findings that negative verbal expressions were more frequent in the hospitalized depressed patients, there was a tendency for patients' rate of body-focused hand movements (hand movements analogous to adaptors) and postures to become more similar or congruent to their spouses during the second post-treatment interview. In addition, for the depressed patients who initially spoke fewer than 160 words per minute, object-focused hand movements (the equivalent of illustrators) increased significantly following discharge. Interestingly, during an interview with a stranger that was also recorded at the time of their hospitalization, the slower-speaking depressed patients showed significantly more object-focused hand movements than when talking with their spouse. This led the authors to emphasize the potential situational factors that may affect non-verbal behavior:

The classic view of depression which supposes that the clinician's observations are of some entity lying within the patient is obviously challenged by these data. If the clinician believes he is solely an observer of a depressed patient he will fail to perceive that the depression is a function of a system of which the patient is only one part. (1975, p. 171)

Finally, Waxer (1976) showed observers videotape segments of admission interviews of 12 depressed and 8 nondepressed patients. Observers were to rate the depression for severity and then indicate the cues used to do so. Observer ratings of depression from the nonverbal behaviors correlated .58 with the MMPI D-scale scores. Even when a group of subjects were not given an experimental set to look for depression they were able to discriminate degree of depression ($r = .37$ with the MMPI-D scale). Cues identified by observers included downward angling of head and infrequency of hand movements, in addition to downward lip-contractions and poor eye-contact.

Mahl is another researcher who has made major contributions to the study of gestures in an interview situation. In one experiment, Mahl (1968) put his formidable clinical skills to the test by observing, without sound, interviews between patients and therapists. During such times he dictated his observations of the nonverbal behavior in the interviews, including occurrences of several kinds of body movements. Interviews of eight males and seven females were judged in this fashion. A number of sex-related gestures were noted. For example, only the males made pointing-out gestures whereas females more commonly held or clasped hands together, folded their arms across their waist, or patted their hair. Mahl also compared his recorded interpretations of the nonverbal behavior with interview content and information from the patient's clinical record. Thirty-six of Mahl's 43 personality inferences were supported. One of Mahl's findings was that many gestures or body movements may be anticipatory of later verbalizations in psychotherapy. A classic example of this occurred during an interview with a patient who fiddled with her wedding ring while discussing her symptoms. Subsequent investigation revealed that her real problem was marital in nature.

In an interesting investigation of the expressive versus communicative function of autistic behaviors, Mahl (1968) also compared back-to-back with typical face-to-face interview situations. Autistic actions were defined by Mahl as idiosyncratic actions on the part of the patient that were thought to be expressions of internal states; they would be considered self-adaptors by Ekman and Friesen. As predicted, Mahl found an increase in autistic behaviors on the part of patients who were seated back-to-back to the interviewer compared to those seated face-to-face. In addition, there was a decrease in communicative gestures in the back-to-back situation, both findings supporting the hypothesis that autistic behaviors would be disinhibited by removing the "visual channel" from the interview communication situation.

Most recently, Gottschalk and Uliana (1976) explored the relationship between lip caressing and speech content from the psychoanalytic perspective that nonverbal behavior is related to mentation. Male and female college student subjects in an analogue of a clinical interview were instructed to either keep their hands at their side or to caress their lip with one hand. For those subjects who were relatively lower in assessed social assets there was a relationship between hopefulness expressed in their verbal content and lip caressing. The complexity of other findings suggests that further study of this relationship is needed. Nonetheless, the findings support Ekman and Friesen's hypothesis that adaptor behaviors are reflective of emotional and need states and Mahl's observations concerning autistic behaviors as percursors to speech.

Freedman and Hoffman (1967) investigated body movements in two patients during "altered clinical states." Two 10-minute videotape segments were taken of patients at different points in time (e.g., acutely psychotic versus relatively compensated) when their clinical status had changed according to independent therapist judgments. Empirical analysis of the body movements yielded two distinct categories of movements, body-focused and object-focused. Body-focused movements appear analogous in significance to Ekman and Friesen's self-adaptors and Mahl's autistic gestures; object-focused movements closely resemble Ekman's hand illustrator categories. Observation revealed that virtually all (95%) of the object-focused movements were related to speech and 85% of the body-focused movements were independent of speech. Analysis of one patient's body movements, especially object-focused movements, suggested the hypothesis to the authors "that clinical improvement may be defined in part as the internalization of dissociated movement patterns into verbally articulated form" (1967, p. 539). Specifically, a shift from motor primacy movements (a class of object-focused movements associated with unverbalized thought) to speech primacy movements (an object-focused movement accompanying articulated speech) was observed as the patient improved. In another paper, Freedman (1972) noted that object-focused movements were more prevalent among paranoid patients and body-focused movements more prevalent in depressives. The relative absence of object-focused movements was interpreted as signifying the reduction in "communicative intent" characteristic of depression.

Grand, Freedman, Steingart, and Buchwald (1975) videotaped interviews with nonparanoid schizophrenic patients, half of whom had been identified as being prone to future hospitalization and half as "nonprone." Body-focused and object-focused hand movements were coded by observers. While no significant differences occured in object-focused hand movements between "prone" and "nonprone" schizophrenic patients, the prone patients engaged in significantly more continuous self-stimulation, whereas the nonprone patients showed more discrete body-focused hand movements. In addition, total continuous self-stimulation hand movements correlated .54 with a measure of the patients' propensity for social isolation and .60 with the measure of hospital proneness. It was considered that the isolation and hyperarousal seen in chronic (i.e., hospital-prone) schizophrenics is also accompanied by stereotyped motor activity, which serves "to regulate attentional processes via proprioceptive feedback," enabling such patients better to maintain their focus of attention during the interview.

Clinical Research: Therapist Behavior

In addition to studies of nonverbal patient behavior, there are a number that investigate therapist variables in the interview situation. Fretz (1966) recorded body movements of counselors and clients during the first, third, and sixth interviews. Following the third and sixth interviews, both clients and counselors completed the Barrett–Lennard Relationship Inventory, which was employed as a criterion measure of the therapeutic relationship. Vertical hand movements were the best indicator of satisfaction for both clients and counselors as indicated by their inventory ratings. Counselors' hand clasping was the best indicator of counselors' inventory ratings of relationship variables (e.g., positive regard, empathy and unconditional regard, etc.), while clients' leaning forward and backward was the best indicator of clients' relationship variables. Hand movements and smiles and laughing correlated positively with the relationship variables. Counselors used significantly more positive head-nods and total movements than clients. From these findings, Fretz hypothesized that hand movements, smiles, and laughing would be the best indication of a positive relationship.

Strong, Taylor, Bratton, and Loper (1971) videotaped experienced counselors interviewing a confederate client, in one instance in an animated, active manner with many nonverbal body movements, in the second instance with little body movement. Ratings of the counselors by observers showed that the interviewer was judged more positively when active than when still in the interview. "Active counselors" were described as warm, more casual, agreeable, and energetic, whereas "still counselors" were judged as more logical, cold, and analytic. Haase and Tepper (1972) showed videotape segments of an interview to observers, with the interviewer displaying varying combinations of eye contact, trunk-lean, and body orientation and distance while giving a verbal message of a predetermined value of empathy. Comparisons of observer ratings of the videotapes in terms of judged empathy of the interviewer showed that the nonverbal variables accounted for twice the variance as compared to the verbal message. A forward trunk-lean was one of the most important nonverbal behaviors in addition to maintenance of eye contact and a close distance. D'Augelli (1974) had eight subjects meet together. Each subject was asked to disclose a personal concern and to engage in a helping interaction with another when he was disclosing. Trained observers rated each subject's nonverbal behaviors when engaged in helping. Subjects also rated each other as helpers. Observer's ratings of helpers showed a significant relationship between judged effectiveness and frequency of smiling and nodding. Helper-rated understanding and warmth correlated significantly with the frequency of head nods by the helper. LaCrosse (1975) also recently reported that smiles and gesticulations were among the prime cues used in making ratings of counselor attractiveness and persuasiveness.

Smith (1972) investigated postural and gestural communication of A and B "therapist types." A-type individuals have been described as socially cautious, inhibited, intropunitive, and desiring of social approval, whereas B-type males are seen as socially affiliative, risk-taking, and extropunitive. Male college students were selected as extremes on the A-B therapist scale and dyads were formed of every possible combination of interviewer (A or B)-interviewee (A or B). One subject was instructed to interview the other for approximately 12 minutes while several observers recorded the postural and gestural behavior of both. Other observers rated the interview participants on a number of interaction variables (e.g., ease of responding, liking one another, etc.). As predicted, A-type persons were more variable than Bs in their use of several nonverbal behaviors (number of negative head-nods, time spent in trunk-side position and arm-crossed position). In addition, these behaviors, which are considered to be more "disjunctive" (i.e., less affiliative than such behaviors as forward lean, positive head nods, etc.), indeed were negatively related to those observer ratings of positive interaction variables. For example, "trunk side" movements were negatively correlated with "like other" ratings for interviewers.

Body Movements and Speech

As Birdwhistell (1970) noted, many gestures and body movements are related to speech. In their study of synchrony, Condon and Ogston (1966) observed:

As a person talks, "blending phone into syllable into word," his body moves in a series of configurations of change which are precisely correlated with that serial transformation of "phone into syllable into word" of speech. Kinesic segmentation in general seems to coincide with *etic* segmentations of speech. (p. 339)

By "etic" the authors were referring to physical aspects of the articulation process, as opposed to "emic" segmentations, which are classes of sounds involved in language. Kendon (1970) studied interactional synchrony between speaker and listener and observed it to occur even when the listener could not observe the speaker. He concluded:

The coordination of the listener's movements with the behavior of the speaker is brought about through the listener's response to the stream of speech. . . . The precision with which the listener's movements are synchronized with the speaker's speech means that the listener is in some way able to anticipate what the speaker is going to say. (p. 164)

Kendon speculated that in listening, as in speaking, body movements are coordinated with the cognitive processes that occur with those activities. He remarked that "It would be interesting to know if the listener marks in movement differentially the size of the unit of speech he is processing" (1970, p. 123). Kendon further noted that listener movements in processing speech may be an important source of feedback to the speaker that he is being understood and properly "tracked."

Dittman has studied body movements in relationship to speech perhaps more systematically than other investigators of nonverbal behavior. Dittmann and Llewellyn (1967) proposed the phonemic clause as the basic unit in speech decoding. The phonemic clause has been defined as "a string of words, averaging five in length, in which there is one and only one primary stress and which is terminated by a juncture, a barely perceptible slowing of speech, often with slight intonation changes at the very end," (Dittmann and Llewellyn, 1969, p. 99). Phonemic clauses typically are bound by pauses and hesitations that occur during the encoding process. Dittmann and Llewellyn (1967) first examined vocalizations of listeners' responses to speakers who were visually isolated from them. Listener responses such as, "I see," "mm-hmm," etc. (indicators that the listener is following the speaker) occurred primarily at the end of the phonemic clause. Their interpretation of this phenomenon was that the phonemic clause was the main unit of decoding speech and the "listener must wait until an entire phonemic clause has been uttered before he can discriminate the main lexical item from the other material in the group. Until he has made that discrimination he has not, in effect, heard what the speaker has said during that time" (Dittmann and Llewellyn, 1967, p. 343).

In a subsequent study, Dittmann and Llewellyn (1968) extended their analysis of listener responses to vocalizations and head-nods of two visually interacting subjects. As predicted, both vocalizations and head-nods occurred primarily at the end of a phonemic clause. When they co-occurred, head-nods usually preceded vocalization. Further analysis of the speech content suggested that these behaviors served a social function. Head-nods plus vocalizations seemed to be a signal that the listener was going to, or wanted to, say something. Single occurrences of either generally appeared to be listener feedback to the speaker. Another observation has been that head-nods are a listener tactic encouraging the speaker to continue. This observation was directly and experimentally verified by Matarazzo, Saslow, Wiens, Weitman, and Allen (1964). They asked their interviewers to employ head-nodding during the experimental period of a standardized interview. The effect of this interviewer tactic was to increase significantly interviewee durations of utterance during the experimental period.

This line of investigation was further expanded to include hand and feet movements (Dittmann and Llewellyn, 1969). Again, all movements were found to occur at positions at the start of a phonemic clause more often than would be expected by chance. In addition, hand and foot movements conformed more closely to the speech rhythm than head movements, although all three were related. An important observation was the range of total movements in a conversation, which, in some cases, varied "astonishingly" between individuals. The significance of these body movements to speech was explained as follows:

Our explanation of the movement-speech rhythm relationship is mainly concerned with the process of speech encoding . . . Forming one's thoughts or ideas into words is an astonishing accomplishment, and the complications of performing the task are shown by the many hesitations and slips in speech. . . . Among the reasons behind these difficulties are the complexity of the idea to be expressed; the impression the speaker is trying to make on the hearer; wishes or fears which the speaker might have about the subject matter. . . . Whenever factors like this intervene, tension builds up within the speaker. The most direct reflection of this tension is the hesitation, and next are the other forms of influency. . . . In some cases the tension may spill over into the motor sphere, producing movements of the type we have been studying here. (Dittmann and Llewellyn, 1969, pp. 104–105)

One very important implication of this finding was subsequently pointed out by Dittmann (1972a):

If our interest is in fidgetiness as an expression of emotional states, . . . then we should develop some way of eliminating those encoding-related movements from further consideration, for they contribute too much redundancy to the measurement system. . . . in future studies of frequencies of body movements, we shall be feeding the outputs of accelerometers into counters for machine processing. We can capitalize on our knowledge that pauses make up the largest category of nonfluencies by detecting pauses and gating the counters to omit those movements which occur at the same time as the pauses, or just following them. (p. 150)

Using a different approach, Hoffman (1969) examined object-focused hand movements (hand movements related to speech). Subjects made up TAT stories, recalled them from memory, or responded to Rorschach cards. It was hypothesized that those tasks requiring more ideation would produce more hand movements associated with greater cognitive activity. As predicted, there were more hand movements when subjects responded to Rorschach cards than TAT cards and when making up stories to TAT cards than when recalling stories. In addition, more fluent subjects showed more hand movements than less fluent subjects and movements decreased when visual contact was eliminated. Restraining subjects' hand movements had little affect on their fluency but increased talking time. Wolff and Gutstein (1972) found that gestural movements may affect speech content. Subjects were required to engage either in circular and linear hand movements or to observe such movements while making up a story or listing words belonging to a particular category (i.e., naming objects found in a kitchen). Analysis of the story protocols by raters showed that the type of movement could be inferred from the story content, especially in the stories of subjects who observed gestural movements. However, word productions were not affected by subjects' performance or observance of gestures, suggesting that the effect occurred at an ideational level of production (i.e., stories).

Subsequently, Freedman, Blass, Rifkin, and Quitkin (1973) related Freedman's categories of object- and body-focused movements to "verbal encoding of aggressive affect." The authors' rationale for this study was that "kinetic manifestations linked to speech are more likely to be indicative of an ability to encode . . . hostile promptings into the verbal content" (pp. 73–74). Subjects were exposed to a warm-cold or cold-warm interview sequence where the interviewer was alternatively friendly and responsive (warm) or disinterested and impatient (cold). The researchers then analyzed subjects' verbal and kinesic behavior in the warm interview when it followed the cold interview (it was assumed the cold-warm interview sequence would arouse hostility in the cold interview which might be subsequently expressed in the warm interview). The authors hypothesized that verbally overt expression of hostility would be associated with object-focused movements. Overt-covert hostility was scored by a content analysis from the audiotapes, while videotapes were utilized to measure kinesic behavior. As predicted, speech-primacy and representational motor-primacy movements (both object-focused movements) were significantly associated with overt expressions of hostility ($r = .49$ and $.36$, respectively). Conversely, hand-to-hand body-focused movements were correlated with covert expressions of anger ($r = .52$). Continuous or discrete body-touching, another category of body-focused movements, was not associated with verbal aggression. Two additional observations were noted. First, when the expressions of anger were particularly blatant, there were few, if any, object-focused movements. Second, as in the earlier mentioned study by Mahl (1968) it appeared to the authors from a sequence analysis of the verbal and kinetic behavior that the movements preceded the verbal expressions of hostility: "Gestures appear to be instrumental in paving the way for the encoding of the hostile promptings. Kinetic expressions may then help the person to build up to a pitch so that the stirred affect can be articulated" (p. 80).

Several studies have related hand movements to physiological variables. Kimura (1973a, 1973b) observed hand movements during speech (as opposed to nonspeech activities) among subjects who were left hemisphere-dominant for speech function, as determined by a dichotic listening task. Such subjects showed significantly more right-handed movements (the side controlled by the left hemisphere). Left-handed subjects did not show the same bias for asymmetrical hand movements, suggesting that speech functions are bilaterally represented for these individuals. In a fascinating study, with many implications for further research, Condon and Sander (1974) expanded their research on interactional synchrony to infant neonates and adult speech. Examination of micromomentary movements by the infants showed synchrony with the adult speech. This was true whether the adult speaker was present or if speech consisted of an audiotape of American or even Chinese voice sounds. However, disconnected vowel and tapping sounds had no such effect. Condon and Sander hypothesized:

If the infant, from the beginning, moves in precise, shared rhythm with the organization of the speech structure of his culture, then he participates developmentally through complex, sociobiological entrainment processes in millions of repetitions of linguistic forms long before he later uses them in speaking and communicating. By the time he begins to speak, he may have already laid down within himself the form and structure of the language system of his culture. (1974, p. 101)

In addition to hand movements being related to speech encoding processes, it is also true that gestures serve an interpersonal communicative function. For example, Cohen and Harrison (1973) demonstrated that subjects will engage in more illustrator activity when communicating with another person face-to-face compared to communication over an intercom where the other interactant could not see.

Finally, Duncan (1972, 1973, 1974; Duncan and Niederehe, 1974) examined nonverbal cues for turn-taking in conversation. Several activities were identified as important in monitoring a conversation between two interactants: turn-yielding, when a speaker signals to a listener he is going to stop talking; attempt-suppressing signals, signals that the speaker intends to continue talking despite any yielding cues being concurrently displayed; and back-channel communication, or listener responses that acknowledge or accompany the speaker. Back-channel communications can also be used by a listener to avoid taking a turn. Nodding at the end of a speaker's utterance can serve as a cue to "continue speaking" even when the speaker is displaying yielding signals. In addition to various paralinguistic behaviors, various body movements were cues for the regulation of conversation. For example, cessation of hand gesticulations (excluding body-focused movements or self-adaptors) by the speaker is a "floor yielding" cue, while movement of one and particularly both hands is an attempt-suppressing cue that serves to "maintain the floor" for the speaker. Back-channel communications by the listener include head-nods in addition to vocal signals such as "mm-hmm." Table 4–2 summarizes Duncan's turn-taking signals.

Table 4-2. Conversation Turn-Taking Signals (Adapted from Duncan, 1972, 1974)

Speaking-turn signals

1. Speaker-turn signal (cue to listener that it is permissible to speak)

    a. Speaker head-turn towards listener (at end of completed utterance)
    b. Relaxation of speaker foot from marked dorsal flexion
    c. Termination of hand gesticulation or relaxation of hand tension by speaker

2. Speaker gesticulation signal

    Illustrator behavior will maintain speaker state and will negate any previous speaker-turn signal

3. Speaker-state signal (cue that listener is to become speaker)

    a. Shift in head direction away from direct orientation towards speaker
    b. Initiation of gesticulation

Speaker-listener behaviors within speaking turns

1. Auditor back-channel signal (i.e., listener feedback to speaker)

    a. Head-nod
    b. Head-shakes

2. Speaker-within-turn signal

    Speaker head-turn towards listener at end of grammatical clause and often followed by auditor back-channel behavior and/or speaker continuation signal

3. Speaker continuation signal
    Head turn-away from listener at beginning of new clause

Detailed empirical analysis of several videotape conversations (Duncan, 1972) revealed that turn-taking by the listener predictably increased as a function of speaker-yielding cues, whereas display by a speaker of an attempt-suppressing cue virtually insured that the listener kept silent. The majority of those occasions when the listener and speaker engaged in simultaneous turns was due to the speaker ignoring his own yielding cue. For one of the speakers, relaxation of the foot from a marked dorsal flexion was found to be a reliable floor-yielding cue.

Subsequently, Duncan (1974) evaluated auditor back-channel signals, speaker-within-turn signals, speaker continuation signals, and all listener speaker behaviors that occur *during* speaking turns. With respect to auditor back-channel behaviors, Duncan found that speaker gesticulations (in contrast to their suppressing effect on auditor turn-taking signals), had no effect on back-channel behaviors such as head nods and paralinguistic "mm-hmms." Whereas auditor-turn claims occurred almost always at the end of speech units (the phonemic clause), back-channel behaviors were distributed more evenly, as might be expected. Back-channel behavior between units and those occurring late within the units were almost perfectly correlated with speaker cues ($r = .99$), reflecting the listener's acknowledgment that the speaker had not yet yielded. Early back-channel behaviors (nods and "mm-hmms") significantly increased the probability of speaker continuation signals. Finally, speaker-within-turn signals (which occur typically at the ends of units of speech) were strongly related ($r = .96$) to speaker continuation signals at the beginning of the next speech unit. This was true specifically for the speaker-state cue, head turned away from listener, but did not apply for initiation of a gesticulation. These detailed analyses, based upon careful study of videotape segments, are examples of the complex but precise interrelationships between nonverbal behaviors in the regulation of conversation.

An important final illustration of this point was provided in the study conducted by Knapp, Hart, Fredrich, and Shulman (1973), who examined the "verbal and nonverbal correlates of human leave taking" (i.e., saying good-bye). These authors videotaped 80 5-minute interviews between dyads, of which the behaviors during the last 45 seconds were studied intensively. Their observations and prior theory yielded a large number of verbal and nonverbal behaviors used in terminating an interaction. Interestingly, those behaviors utilized by the subjects did not vary as a function of status difference or degree of acquaintance, and the authors noted that "behavior regularity attends leave-taking" (p. 193). Without going into detail about all of their findings we can note some, especially those related to body movement:

For this study, "proper" leave-taking seems to consist primarily of a combination of Reinforcement, Professional Inquiry, Buffing [short words serving to change the discussion, e.g., "ah," "er"], and Appreciation on the verbal level, and the non-verbalisms of Breaking Eye Contact, Left Positioning, Forward Lean, and Head Nodding. (p. 194)

In addition, the authors found that the timing of these behaviors was significant in that the peak of activity occurs during the 15 seconds immediately prior to standing (except for handshake and left-positioning, which occur most frequently at the end). They observed: "In the light of such patterns, it is easy to see why we often become frustrated if we are not 'released' after rising. Such an interpersonal denial means that we must go through the whole routine again!" (1973, p. 196).

MISCELLANEOUS EXTERNAL VARIABLE RESEARCH

In addition to those studies already mentioned, many others have recently been conducted in which body movement was employed as an independent or dependent variable in relation to psychological or social-psychological variables. Body movements were measured as indices of individual difference variables, that is, psychological states or psychological characteristics; the effect of body movements on others' interpersonal behaviors was investigated; finally, the meanings of certain body movements or the information conveyed therein were studied. The sheer diversity of studies makes organization for ease of reading virtually impossible; however, the number of studies reviewed should give the reader a reasonably full appreciation of empirical research on body movements.

Personality Variables

Jurich and Jurich (1974) sought to establish the relationship between two traditional measures of anxiety, subject self-report and physiological response (finger sweat-print), to various nonverbal behaviors including body movement. Anxiety was experimentally manipulated by the experimenter interviewing female subjects about their premarital sexual attitudes. Finger sweat-prints were obtained prior to and following the interview, at which time the subject also reported her anxiety. Videotapes of the interview were subsequently rated for nonverbal behavior. Head-touch movements, degree of postural relaxation, and posture shifts were scored by raters with reliabilities exceeding $r = .90$. Self-report anxiety was correlated poorly with the other variables, probably reflecting the subjects' defensiveness about the interview. Postural relaxation and posture shifts did correlate significantly with sweat-print (r = .58 and .43, respectively) and the observers' global rating of anxiety (r = .69 and .45, respectively). Hand movements correlated only with observers' global rating (r = .35). Other significant relationships were obtained between tone of voice and postural relaxation (.32), postural shifts (.46), and hand-to-head movement (.38); percent gaze-aversion and posture (.64), postural shifts (.45), and hand movements (.41); speech errors and postural relaxation (.57), postural shifts (.68), and hand movements (.55); "editorial errors" and posture (.62), postural shifts (.61), and hand movements (.54). Also related were immediacy of verbal content and postural relaxation (.43) and filled pauses and postural shifts (.68), and hand movements (.54). In addition, posture and articulation errors were modestly but significantly related (.33). These findings suggest that measures of posture, postural relaxation, and posture shifts seem to provide a relatively reliable and objective measure of anxiety, at least when obtained using trained observers. Unfortunately, the direction of many of the relationships (i.e., positive or negative) is unclear from the published results.

In an interesting study Blazer (1966) examined leg position in relation to psychological characteristics of women. One thousand women were given the Wechsler Adult Intelligence Scale; the Allport, Vernon, and Lindzey Study of Values Test; and the Edwards Personal Preference Schedule. The most common method of leg-crossing shown by each subject was determined by observation during an interview for two modes of dress ("dressy" and "casual"). Following the interview women were asked directly to demonstrate their favorite leg position. Despite the fact that statistical analyses were not employed, each leg position was associated with particular personality characteristics. For example, a majority of the women who typically sit with their knees and feet together with legs extended generated the following personality description: "Desire for neatness and orderliness in work, likes to make plans, doesn't like change and uncertainty, organizes life according to a rigid schedule, appreciates the orderliness of each experience" (p. 11).

Herb and Elliott (1971) examined the personality variable of authoritarianism in relation to body movement. High- and low-authoritarian subjects were exposed to experimental situations in which they were placed in subordinate and superordinate role-positions by two experimental confederates ostensibly working with the subject on a group task. As predicted, high-authoritarian subjects showed a more rigid body posture (i.e., less movement) across the two situations than low-authoritarian subjects. In addition, when the confederates attempted to make the high-authoritarian subjects play a subordinate role, they tended to lean forward more often than low-authoritarian subjects while remaining more rigid (moving less). This was interpreted as a tendency on the part of high-authoritarian subjects to embrace the leadership role in the face of a challenge from others.

Hetherington (1972) compared, with male interviewers, the nonverbal behavior of girls who were daughters of divorced or widowed mothers. Analysis of their body movements showed that daughters without fathers showed more self-manipulations than girls with fathers. Daughters of divorcees showed more forward lean, more arm and leg openness, and more smiling with the male interviewer, reflecting their positive reaction to him. In contrast, daughters of widows were more uncomfortable and less interactive, engaging in more backward-leaning, less direct orientation, and less arm openness, with their hands being folded in their laps and their legs together. These differences were even more pronounced for girls whose separations occurred early in their life. For example, the daughters of divorcees exhibited more than three times as many gesticulations or expressive hand movements as girls who lost their fathers before the age of five. These findings were part of impressive evidence that absence of the father in a family has a definite effect on adolescent daughters in their development of heterosexual relationships.

Physical Differences

Kleck (1968) studied interactions between physically normal and physically "stigmatized" individuals to examine if the latter group faced a different interpersonal environment. An experimental confederate was placed in a special wheelchair designed to simulate a left-leg amputation. A measure of motoric activity was obtained by filming the subject in front of a wall painted in a checkerboard pattern with six squares. Head-turns of more than 45° and movements greater than 6 inches were scored. In addition to predicted differences in impression formation (e.g., an exaggerated positive impression of the "disabled" confederate), subjects were inhibited in their movements when listening (but not talking) to their stigmatized conversational partner. Kleck noted: "This result fits an earlier finding that Ss are more emotionally aroused and the arousal may serve to inhibit movement, particularly when the arousal may be generated by uncertainty as to how to interact" (1968, p. 26).

Cognitive Variables

Several studies have investigated the role of posture in relation to cognitive functioning. Berdach and Bakan (1967) tested the psychoanalytic hypothesis that lying down in a relaxed posture facilitates memory recall during free association. Two groups of subjects were asked to recall memories, one while sitting up, the other while lying down, during a 20-minute period. Memories were divided into memory-age intervals of 3 years, corresponding to the subject's age at which that memory occurred. Subjects who were lying down tended to have more memories, except in the case of the most recent memories where the trend was reversed (but not significantly so). Memory recall was a negatively accelerated function of time, more memories being recalled during the first 5 minutes, particularly early memories. A comparison of earliest memories (age 0–3) showed that significantly more were recalled from the lying-down position. Rand and Wapner (1967) examined postural status as a factor in memory in a verbal learning situation. It was hypothesized that posture would be an important contextual factor in early stages of learning and recall, but less so during the later stages of learning. Subjects were given nonsense syllables to learn and relearn either under "positive congruent" (e.g., sitting upright or supine during learning and relearning) or "positive incongruent" (e.g., supine, upright; or upright, supine postures). When posture remained the same there was a significant saving in relearning which, as predicted, was manifested primarily during the early stages of recall. The authors concluded:

When . . . one examines the individual at an early stage in the learning process, i.e., where the "work" of language and/or memory is "in progress," the contribution of these general organismic variables becomes more apparent. Consider, for example, the activity of the hands, the contortions of the face, the bobbing of the torso as if to place oneself in different poses, etc., when trying to recall a name. The triviality of this small experiment becomes all too apparent when juxtaposed with these universal and compelling experiences. (1967, p. 271)

Considering these more recent findings, it is interesting that Beigel (1952) observed and commented much earlier on the effect of postures in his patients' performance on a projective test, the Thematic Apperception Test:

The hypothesis is formulated that body position exerts considerable influence on apperception, thinking, and emotions. The reclining position has a tendency to remove these processes from reality considerations and consequently allows greater complacency. It favors expansion of suggestions and associations, but inhibits the tendency towards action. More room is given to the exploration of relevant and irrelevant factors. In the standing position the energies are stimulated toward action and emotions express themselves more forcefully. At the same time the field tends to be narrowed and the influx of new suggestions is partly blocked. Situations are not scrutinized as carefully and surrounding circumstances and possibilities are not sufficiently examined. Decisions come faster and are more vigorous. (p. 198)

The above studies related a form of kinesic behavior (posture) as an independent variable to cognitive functions. Other studies investigated cognitive factors and their influence on gestures (a dependent variable in such cases). Baxter, Winters, and Hammer (1968) obtained measures of subjects' "verbal category differentiation" as measured by Kelly's Role Construct Repertory Test. These subjects were given familiar or unfamiliar topics to speak about. The primary findings were that the more highly differentiated subjects showed more body movement activity, especially during discussion of the more familiar topics. The predominant movements were vigorous extensor-arm/hand movements, which appeared to serve a supplementary rather than a substitutive and complementary function.

Freedman, O'Hanlon, Oltman, and Witkin (1972) studied gestural behavior in relation to two independent variables: the cognitive variable of field-dependence–independence and the "communicative context." Communicative context was manipulated by utilizing warm-cold or cold-warm interview sequences during which the interviewer was either friendly and responsive while listening to the subject (warm), or was disinterested and impatient (cold). Kinetic behaviors were categorized into object-focused movements and body-focused movements, as described earlier by Freedman and Hoffman (1967). Among the many findings reported, field-dependent subjects, when talking without interruption for 5 minutes, engaged in more continuous body-focused (hand-to-hand movement) activity than field-independent subjects. This was true for warm and cold interview situations. In addition, during a conversation period with the warm interviewer, field-dependent subjects showed more object-focused motor-primacy gestures. The authors summarized:

For the individual with more limited differentiation, the motor rather than the verbal channel becomes the significant vehicle for representation. The F-D S is more likely to use gestures in the description of external events or inner feelings, and they frequently employed pointing and groping movements when words seemed unavailable. Their motor expression is relatively devoid of those articulatory maneuvers which punctuate or qualify what is being uttered. (1972, p. 249)

Field-independent subjects, who displayed more speech-primacy movements during the conversation period, showed an increase in motor-primacy movements when faced with the increased demand of having to talk uninterrupted for 5 minutes.

A major additional finding was that the "cold" interview treatment produced an increase in body-focused movements, particularly body-touching. These behaviors were unrelated to psychological differentiation and appeared to be a generalized reaction to the negative encounter, which indeed continued to be evident even during the warm interview in those instances when it followed the cold interview. Further analysis showed that the field-independent subjects showed increased gaze-aversion and body-focused movements during the cold interview but not the warm interview. This behavior suggested that field-independent subjects made an appropriate discrimination between the two situations. In contrast, field-dependent subjects showed increased gaze-aversion and body-focused movements during the warm interview when it followed the cold interview. It was as if they had failed to discriminate between situations.

Sex Differences

Interestingly, there has been little research specifically focusing on sex differences in kinesic behaviors. Beekman (1975) was one of the few authors to report a number of sex differences in body movements. In her study (see p. 46) of male and female subjects engaged in same- and opposite-sex dyadic interaction, male subjects engaged in significantly more seat-position shifts than women. In addition, for men the duration of their longest gesture, time spent moving feet, average duration of foot movement, and duration of longest foot movement decreased from the first to second interview (irrespective of the sex of the conversational partner), while the reverse was true for women. Beekman speculated that males may have exhibited their greater discomfort with the first interview with increased movement, whereas females may become more inhibited in accordance with their conception of stereotyped "ladylike" behavior.

Social Behaviors

Other research involving measurement of body movement has dealt with social behaviors. In one of his books, Mehrabian (1972) summarized many of the findings of earlier studies which included postural variables. Without going into detail into each of this researcher's very complex experiments and findings, we may note that his method involved either decoding of posed behaviors (Mehrabian, 1968a) or encoding of interpersonal attitudes (e.g., liking, status relationships) by role-playing (Mehrabian, 1968a, 1968b; Mehrabian and Friar, 1969). In Mehrabian (1968a), standing postures were encoded; in two subsequent studies (Mehrabian, 1968b; Mehrabian and Friar, 1969) seated positions were employed. Mehrabian (1969, 1972) summarized his research on liking and status and the postural and position cues relevant to those variables. A forward lean was consistently associated with degree of liking. A seated-sideways lean was considered an index of relaxation, and moderate degrees were judged indicative of positive interpersonal attitudes. Males exhibited the least sideways-lean and least body relaxation with intensely disliked males, whereas females showed the most sideways-lean with intensely disliked males or females. Use of the arms and legs in an open posture for seated females (but not for males) conveyed a positive attitude to younger and older but not to same-aged individuals. An arms akimbo position was more likely with low-status individuals than high-status persons, as were a raised head, relaxation of the hands and trunk, and sideways lean while sitting. Based on the previous studies, Mehrabian (1969) proposed a set of cues for a relaxation dimension that he related to liking and status variables. Relaxation was defined by arm-position asymmetry, sideways-lean, openness of arm position, leg-position asymmetry, and higher rates of gesticulation.

In a subsequent experiment, Mehrabian and Williams (1969) hypothesized that message persuasiveness was related to the degree to which the communicator was liked by a listener. In one (encoding) study, subjects were instructed to attempt to show varying degrees of persuasiveness in delivering messages and, in a second study, to deliver either persuasive or informative messages. In a third, decoding study, observers rated actors for their nonverbal persuasiveness while enacting degrees of relaxation. In the two encoding experiments the authors found the predicted relationship between intended and perceived persuasiveness. Increased facial activity and gesticulation, reduced reclining angles, increased head-nodding, and reduced self-manipulation were related to intended and perceived persuasiveness. Increased facial activity was not predicted and seemed to convey an increase in the communicator's responsivity to the target of communication, which was related to persuasiveness and message impact. Head-nodding, decreased self-manipulation, and reduced reclining angles were also found to convey liking. In addition, when the listener was receptive, increased self-manipulation by the speaker was related to greater perceived persuasiveness. A relaxation factor was studied in the third decoding experiment. For male communicators, slightly tense positions were judged less persuasive than relaxed postures. This finding did not hold for female communicators, suggesting that slight degrees in tension for females may be considered socially appropriate.

Mehrabian (1971a) additionally studied nonverbal behaviors of subjects performing deceitful communications. In one experiment subjects were required to convey truthfulness while communicating arguments contrary to their actual beliefs. In a second, subjects were asked to role-play or engage in actual deceit, and in a third study they were experimentally induced into lying. It was hypothesized that negative affect would be induced by the deceitful behavior and conveyed nonverbally. Indeed, subjects nodded less, gesticulated less, showed fewer leg and foot movements, smiled more, and assumed a less immediate position (e.g., less forward-lean) when being deceitful.

Finally, Mehrabian (1971b) and Mehrabian and Ksionzky (1972) examined the nonverbal correlates of affiliative behavior of two strangers in a waiting situation. In both studies one of the individuals was an experimental confederate trained to be slightly negative or slightly positive towards the experimental subject. Various nonverbal behaviors of naive subjects were recorded by observers during a 2-minute interaction period. Subjects also provided self-report measures of their affiliative tendency, sensitivity to rejection, and achieving tendency. Factor analysis of the nonverbal behaviors yielded various results. An affiliative behavior factor was identified and positively related to number of head-nods per minute and hand and arm gestures per minute. A relaxation factor was negatively related to leg and foot movements per minute and rocking movements per minute and positively related to (sideways) body-lean. In general, subjects reciprocated the degree of affiliative behavior shown by confederates, especially the highly affiliative subjects. These relationships were replicated again in an experiment by Mehrabian and Ksionzky (1972). In addition, an ingratiation factor was isolated, that was positively related to self-manipulations per minute. A behavioral distress factor (reflecting interpersonal discomfort) was related positively to duration of walking, object manipulations per minute, and arm position asymmetry.

Mehrabian's research is in contrast to many of the studies described earlier because of his heavy reliance on enacted or role-played behaviors and his attempts to identify combinations of nonverbal cues important in defining certain behavioral factors. From his research, Mehrabian proposed three salient dimensions in human interaction, each of which involved various nonverbal behaviors reported in this and other chapters. These included positiveness (or liking/affiliative behavior), responsiveness (activity level), and relaxation (related to dominance/submission). Mehrabian's interest was thus to identify clusters of nonverbal behaviors related to social-psychological phenomena rather than to study the significance of specific nonverbal behaviors or special categories of nonverbal behaviors that others (e.g., Ekman, Freedman) have chosen to study.

Rosenfeld is another researcher who has studied nonverbal behavior extensively, also in relation to interpersonal influence processes. In one study, Rosenfeld (1966b) manipulated need for approval in female subjects by instructing them to act as if they wanted to get to know or avoid contact with another person (in actuality a confederate). Motivation to behave in these ways was enhanced with the message that the other subject would rate them on their affiliative behavior. Gestural behaviors observed included positive and negative head-nods, smiles, gesticulations, self-manipulations, and postural changes. Of these, smiles and gesticulations were related to approval-seeking behavior. A second experiment with two uninstructed subjects suggested that gestures by one subject tended to be reciprocated by the other.

In a second study, Rosenfeld (1966a) instructed one set of subjects to seek or avoid intimacy in dyadic conversation with the subjects they were paired with, who were completely uninstructed. Approval-seeking males engaged in significantly more head-nods and smiles than approval avoiding males. For females, an increase in gesticulations was significantly related to approval seeking. Ratings on interpersonal attractiveness of the approval-avoiding subjects by the naive subject revealed that positive head-nods were positively related to attraction ($r = .70$). The number of self-manipulations was negatively related to ratings of attractiveness ($r = -.70$). Possibly the general negative interpersonal attitude assumed by the approval-avoiding subjects enhanced the saliency and meaning of these particular behaviors.

To further elucidate the notion that many nonverbal behaviors indicating approval are typically reciprocated in free social interactions, Rosenfeld (1967) next instructed interviewers either to react positively, negatively, or not at all to responses from 9th-grade interviewees. As expected, positive nonverbal approval of responses (smiles and positive head-nods, specifically) by interviewers were reciprocated by interviewees, who also showed fewer self-manipulations and non-ah speech disturbances than interviewees in the negative or neutral feedback conditions. Later, Breed (1972) employed confederates to engage in high-, medium-, and low-intimacy nonverbal behaviors by systematically varying their eye contact and forward-lean. In support of Rosenfeld's reciprocity hypothesis, subjects interacting with confederates increased their forward-lean as confederate intimacy increased. In addition, subject attitudes became more positive towards the confederate with increasing intimacy. Interestingly, although subject self-reports for confederate females indicated greater liking, their nonverbal behavior displayed less intimacy (e.g., fewer forward-leans, more posture changes).

Dabbs (1969) had one subject mimic another's gestures to investigate the attitudinal effect of physical similarity. In one study, an actor mimicked one of two other subjects (e.g., the actor mirrored the subject's posture, leg-crossing, and hand gestures). Although mimicry did not affect liking of the actor, mimicked subjects viewed themselves as more similar to the actor. They also viewed the actor as more persuasive (i.e., their opinions on issues being discussed were viewed as being more congruent). A second experiment utilized untrained confederates instructed to mimic or engage in the opposite behaviors. Mimicked subjects reported that they were more similar in their posture to the confederate and that the confederate would impress others more favorably. Initial perceived similarity interacted with mimicry such that mimicked subjects who viewed themselves as similar to the untrained confederates reported that they liked them more. In contrast, subjects who saw themselves as initially similar to the confederate instructed to "antimimic" rated those confederates as especially low on liking measures. Dabbs (1969) noted:

When two people are trying to communicate, similarities between them may improve communication. Their attitudes, moods, and expressive behaviors may even become more similar as a result of communication. But this similarity can provide a background of rapport without necessarily being noticed. Dissimilarity, on the other hand, is more intrusive. It can be jarring, as when one person reveals a prejudice his partner finds distasteful, or employs an inappropriate gesture, or pronounces a word in an unexpected manner. Such a discrepancy may be more noticeable and intrusive when the two people initially believe they are similar to one another. (p. 338)

Dabbs' study showed that initial perceived similarity was an important factor in predicting how nonverbal behavior would affect another. McCaa (1972) measured the interpersonal orientation of subjects and found that those least interpersonally oriented were affected more positively by warm experimenter behaviors (e.g., including nods, gesticulations, body-lean). Holstein, Goldstein, and Bem (1971) investigated need for social approval, sex differences, and the effect of nonverbal expressiveness on liking. A male confederate who was assigned the role of interviewee was trained to emit high or low amounts of eye contact and smiles and low amounts of gesticulations for positive expressiveness, and low eye contact, smiles, and frequent finger-drumming on the table for negative expressiveness. Verbal content of interviewee speech was held constant during the interview. In each experimental session, one subject (male or female) was assigned the role of interviewer, while a second observed the interaction from behind a two-way mirror. Positive expressive behaviors generally induced favorable ratings of liking but individual differences and sex of subject were important factors. Males high in need for social approval liked the confederate more regardless of the amount or kind of expressiveness. This was true whether the subjects were observing or actually participating in the interview. In contrast, females high in need for approval liked the confederate less than females low in need for approval, especially when in the observer role. However, females who participated in the interviews and were high in need for approval reacted more strongly to the positive and negative expressive cues than low-need approval females, who actually preferred the negatively expressive confederate. Actual participation in the interview resulted in greater liking than observation alone, and subjects hearing the interaction showed no distinction between expressive conditions.

Washburn and Hakel (1973) examined impression formation processes in observers of interviews. The interviews consisted of two subjects, one assigned to be an interviewer, the other a job applicant. Interviewers were instructed to be enthusiastic or unenthusiastic and to emit high or low amounts of gestures as well as eye-contact and smiling. Observer subjects then made ratings of the interviewer. The enthusiastic interviewer was perceived as being younger and more youthful, liking his job better, being more enthusiastic, easily approached, more interested, considerate, and intelligent. Even though the "applicant" subjects were given no special instructions, they too tended to be rated more favorably, probably the result of their response to the interviewer. Chaikin, Sigler, and Derlega (1974) manipulated teacher expectancies of students by describing them as bright or dull. As predicted by the earlier much-publicized study by Rosenthal and Jacobson (1968), student tutors were more responsive to a 12-year-old when labeled bright than dull. In particular, teachers gave more positive head-nods and forward-leans to the "bright" student in addition to more smiles and eye contact. Female subject tutors leaned forward less and smiled more than the males.

London (1973) studied persuasion and attitude change and postulated that confidence expressed by a persuader was an important factor in changing a persuadee's attitude. After demonstrating that persuader confidence was an important variable in producing persuasion, London then tested "kinesically expressed confidence" in an ingenious experiment with body movement as an independent variable. An actor recorded a speech advocating a particular position in a court case while role-playing an advanced law student. Subsequently, the actor portrayed three degrees of confidence in his body posture (high, moderate, and low) while "mouthing" the words. Later, the single audiotape was combined with the three films, providing audiovideo films in which verbal content and paralinguistic variables were constant while kinesic behavior varied as experimentally manipulated. Experimental subjects read a prepared case and then heard and viewed one of the three prepared films. As predicted, there was a strong, indeed linear, relationship between subject-film-actor agreement and the actor's degree of confidence expressed in his body movements. More recently, McGinley, Lefevre, and McGinley (1975) presented films of a female discussing her beliefs while assuming a body-open (limbs-outward position) or a body-closed (limbs-inward) position. Subjects who viewed the body-open film showed a significant shift in attitude towards the communicator's viewpoint. The body-open position was also associated with ratings of being more active, evaluatively positive, and more potent.

Decoding Body Movements

Earlier in this chapter we described Ekman's categories of nonverbal behaviors and some of his clinical research. In addition to his work with clinical populations, much of Ekman's work was done with experimental interview situations in which observer subjects would decode nonverbal behaviors shown to them. One experimental manipulation involved subjects receiving stress and catharsis interviews. Photographs of subjects during each phase were shown to observers for various ratings. In one study Ekman (1965) hypothesized that head cues primarily provided information about the particular affect (e.g., happiness, anger) while intensity was expressed by body cues. Subjects rated face-only, body-only, and whole photos of interviewees on Schlosberg's pleasant-unpleasant and sleep-tension dimensions. The former dimension was considered related to emotion while sleep-tension was thought to reflect intensity. As predicted, observer judgments for sleep-tension were more consistent for the body than the face, whereas judgments of pleasant-unpleasant were more consistent for the face than the body.

In a subsequent study, Ekman and Friesen (1967) repeated their experimental procedure, but this time judgments of the face and body cues were made in terms of emotion categories. As predicted, there was more agreement for head than body cues for the emotion categories.[1] Further analysis of the body-only photographs revealed that judges showed higher agreement as to emotion category when the photograph showed an apparent act (movement) rather than a static position. This finding led to a reformulation of their affect-intensity relationship. Specifically, they proposed that emotions can be judged from head cues and body acts whereas body positions and head orientation convey gross affective states. Further, the intensity of affect can be conveyed through head and body cues. Body acts generally convey moderate to high intensity ranges of emotion while body positions can reflect a full range of intensity.

As was noted earlier, facial expressions can convey the full range of intensity though they are often inhibited by display rules. This last hypothesis was put directly to the test in the recent study by Ekman and Friesen (1974). In this study nurses viewed pleasant and unpleasant films. During the unpleasant film they were required to simulate pleasant feelings while withholding their unpleasant feelings. Observers were then shown face-only or body-only videotapes of these nurses in the two situations. Half the observers were first shown a sample of each nurse engaged in an honest communication and then a second videotape segment that they were to judge as being either a deceptive or an honest communication by the nurse. The remaining observers were not given a "familiarization videotape" sample of honest behavior. As predicted, facial rather than body cues were identified more often by observers as the behavior to be modified when engaging in deception. More importantly, subjects viewing the body only videotapes were more accurate in identifying deception than subjects viewing only the face. However, this was only true when they had the benefit of a familiarization videotape of the nurse-subjects engaging in honest behavior.

Additional analysis of the nurses' body movements (reported in Ekman and Friesen, 1972) revealed a change in the frequencies of various hand movements during the deception session. Specifically, nurses engaged in more hand-shrug emblems, fewer illustrators, and more face-play adaptors.

In particular, the rate of self-adaptors was highly correlated ($r = .75$) with judgments of deception. Further, the frequency of self-adaptors during the deception session was negatively correlated ($r = -.54$) with the nurses' combined clinical and academic grades one year later. In summary, the ability to simulate positive affect in a negative affect-inducing situation was reflected in an absence of anxious body movements and was directly related to the nurses' ability to function in their professional role. Knapp, Hart, and Dennis (1974) also observed an increase in the duration of adaptor movements of Vietnam veterans when making statements about VA educational benefits counter to their true beliefs about such benefits.

Recently, Ekman extended his empirical analysis of hand movements to emblems. In particular, Johnson, Ekman, and Friesen (1975) studied emblems in the American culture and formulated a number of important research questions:

There are a number of questions about emblems which should be of interest to students of nonverbal communication or semantics. What is the ontogeny of emblems, at what point do different emblems become established in the infant's repertoire, and how does the acquisition of emblems interlace with the acquisition of verbal language? How are emblems utilized in conversation, are there regularities in which messages are transmitted emblematically, and do these emblems substitute, repeat or qualify the spoken messages? Are there any universal emblems, can we explain instances in which the same message is performed with a different motor action in two cultures? (pp. 3–4)

In conducting their research on American emblems, three methodological steps were employed. First, subjects were asked to encode various emblems from definitions given to them (e.g., "be silent," "nice figure," etc.), with instructions to display only those actions that they knew were used in ordinary conversation (i.e., no pantomime movements). Second, these behaviors were videotaped and performance of the particular emblems was compared by the authors across encoders. Those emblems that were not similarly enacted by at least 70% of the encoders were not further considered. The selected behaviors were then enacted by one of the investigators on videotape. The third step involved showing this videotape to decoders whose task was to write down the message conveyed by the behavior and to make ratings of "message certainty" (how sure they were about their decoding of the emblem) and "usage certainty" (i.e., how natural or artifical the behavior seemed). By employing these three steps the researchers obtained a final list of emblems for which (a) the decoder interpretation closely matched the definition of the particular emblem in at least 70% of the cases, and (b) at least 70% of the decoders judged the action pattern natural in usage. This method thus provided a means of systematically evaluating the relative degree to which each emblem was known and used in the particular culture. Emblems meeting this criteria were considered "verified emblems." Examples of verified emblems would be hand signals depicting the words "come here," "get lost" (interpersonal directions); "a close shave," "tastes good," "it's hot" (descriptions of own physical state); "the hell with you" (personal insults); "okay," "I don't know" (replies); and the like. Based on lesser degrees of usage certainty and decoding accuracy, lists of probably and ambiguous emblems were compiled as well. Interestingly, a comparison between these American emblems and those derived for Colombians and Sicilians showed considerable overlap. This most probably reflected basic cultural similarities, since comparison of American emblems and those used by Japanese showed less overlap. Currently, the authors are preparing a report comparing U.S., Japanese, Iranian, and Israeli emblems.

Employing a different approach in investigating the meaning of hand movements, Gitin (1970) investigated gestural expressions by utilizing 36 photographs of manual expression which were presented to subjects. Ratings were made of each photograph on 40 semantic differential scales, following which a factor analysis was performed (the method employed was thus generally similar to the dimensional analysis performed on facial expression described in the previous chapter.) Four distinct factors emerged, corresponding to activation, evaluation, dynamism, and control dimensions. A second factor analysis yielded four "concept factors" that were correlated with the dimensional factors. For example, a "grip factor" correlated most highly with the activation dimensional factor (Factor I) and was based on pictures depicting gripping hands. Similarly, Factor II (evaluation) was correlated with a "droop factor," based on pictures of hands bent downwards. The third concept factor, a "cup" factor, was associated to some extent with hands in that position and with dimensional scale ratings of weak, submissive, and shy (Factor III). Finally, a "push" factor concept correlated with dimensional Factor IV (control); pictures of hands pushing away was most highly related to this factor concept and were rated as being immature, impulsive, and uncontrolled. These findings clearly suggest that observers do attach consistent meanings to gestures, even those depicted in isolation on photographs. Stephano (1971) compared untrained observer responses to hand gestures shown by a human model or a stick figure. More accurate judgments were obtained with human models. Although the author concluded that stick figures could be used, positive gestures received stronger semantic differential ratings than the negative gestures.

Special Subject Populations

Finally, it is appropriate to consider how body movements differ with groups of people as a function of social or cultural variables. Michael and Willis (1968) investigated transmission and interpretation of gestures for children of different age, social class, and education levels. The gestures studied all corresponded to Ekman and Friesen's emblems: gestures signifying such messages as "go away," "come here," "how many," and the like. The children were first asked to transmit (encode) all the gestures, and then to interpret (decode) them when the interviewer performed them. The results showed that middle-class children were more accurate in transmitting and interpreting the gestures than were lower-class children. Children with one year of school were better than children with no prior school, and boys were more accurate than girls. Unfortunately, age and differences in verbal intelligence and race were not evaluated, thus not ruling out the possibility that these findings were possible covariates of these unstudied variables.

Michael and Willis (1969) replicated their experiment using native German children and American children who were living on military bases or in the German community. As they had shown previously, socioeconomic differences and educational experience (one year of school vs. none) were related to skill in transmission and interpretation of gestures. However, the pattern of cultural differences was not as predicted: skill with gestures was greatest for Americans living off post, followed by German children, and American living on post (the last group initially had been hypothesized to be the most skillful). In addition, no sex differences were noted. Again, failure to control for verbal intelligence, race, and age by the authors presented problems of interpretation for the data.

Despite the importance that race relations have assumed in the past decades, relatively little research has been conducted on nonwhite populations in the United States. One of the few authors to do research in this area is Johnson (1971), who has written a fascinating paper on black kinesics in which he describes many nonverbal behaviors that would have no meaning among whites. A black who assumes a limp stance with lowered head when receiving a reprimand is not communicating distress or submission; rather, this posture signifies that he has "tuned out" the speaker. Frankel and Frankel (1970) took observations of white and black surgical patients while they were being interviewed by a 24-year-old white female interviewer about their hospital care. Patients were unobtrusively observed for different gestures and the frequency, "force," radius (expansiveness or distance of movements from the body), and expressiveness (speech-related movements) of their body movements. The black patients were significantly less expressive and more restricted in the range of their communicative gestures, suggesting an inhibition in their general expressiveness. In addition, blacks showed a preponderance of "palms up" hand movements and hand-clasp movements compared to whites, these behaviors reflecting uncertainty and helplessness, and inhibition, respectively. LaFrance (1974) studied conversational management in blacks who were observed during a 10-minute interview. Among a number of paralinguistic and eye contact differences between black and white turn-taking behaviors in conversation, LaFrance noted that black speakers, like whites (as Duncan, 1972, noted), cease gesticulating when about to yield the floor, and that the listeners begin to move about during the last part of the speaker's utterance. She also noted that many of the nonverbal cues were different, as well as differently organized.

Most of the research on cultural differences in nonverbal behaviors has been based upon naturalistic observation and conducted by anthropologists and semanticists rather than psychologists. Hamalian (1965), for example, is an English professor who has reported his observations of communication by gestures among Middle Eastern people. More recently, however, Morsbach (1973), a psychologist, has published a very interesting description of the significance of nonverbal communication in Japan. Though neither study described any "empirical" research, many of their observations could easily be put to the test. For example, making a circle with one's thumb and index finger while extending the others in American is emblematic of the word "OK"; in Japan it signifies "money" (okane), and among Arabs this is a gesture usually accompanied by a baring of teeth and together these gestures signify extreme hostility. The need for further research in this area is obvious.

Body Movements and Aesthetics

One important set of research contributions that we do not describe in detail but should acknowledge is the work recently published by Spiegel and Machotka (1974) in their book, *Messages of the Body*. Rather than study live human interactions, the authors have chosen to investigate body movement and postures represented in famous paintings or depicted by mannequins. Much of the work reported reflects Machotka's interest in aesthetics. A number of experiments are reported in which the judgmental process of observers is studied in relation to their perception of various postures. A reader interested in kinesics and the arts will find this book interesting reading.

Comments

As we noted earlier, the diversity of these studies on kinesics has made difficult the organization and presentation of this material in a review. One should remember, however, that in Dittmann's terms (see p. 11) most body movements are primarily expressive. As communication channels they are continuous rather than discrete, and as messages they are low in communicative specificity. Behaviors of this sort are thus most suitable for indicative studies, where one hopes to correlate body movements with a psychological state or psychological characteristic. Unfortunately, most researchers have studied body movement in relation to the particular psychological variables they are interested in, rather than attempting to identify psychological variables in relation to designated body movements. Ekman, Duncan, Dittmann, and Freedman and their colleagues, who have focused directly on body movements as their primary interest, are the exceptions. Their research clearly stands out as having more organization and continuity compared to others engaged in external-variable research. The importance of such organized, continuing research projects is especially evident when one deals with nonverbal behaviors that cannot be readily decoded into discrete, specific messages.

NOTES

[1]Recently, Shapiro (1972) employed still photographs of counselors in an interview situation and obtained judges' ratings on several dimensions (e.g., empathy, active-passive, etc.) for face-only, body-only, and whole photographs. Shapiro found that there was less interjudge variance for the body-only photograph judgments than for the face-only stimuli. Shapiro proposed that this finding showed higher agreement for body than facial cues, the opposite relationship of that proposed by Ekman and Friesen. However, his photographs did not represent a sampling of distinct affective states (i.e., from stress vs. catharsis situations) and his dimensions were different than those used by Ekman. In addition, Shapiro used variances as a measure of agrement rather than a concordance measure. It may be that the judges were more conservative in their ratings of body cues, which are generally used less than facial cues. Thus the lower variance for the body cues could reflect a restricted range in judgment, not greater agreement. For these reasons, we regard Shapiro's findings with some reservation.

REFERENCES

Baxter, J. C., E. P. Winters, and R. E. Hammer (1968). Gestural behavior during a brief interview as a function of cognitive variables. *Journal of Personality and Social Psychology,* **8**, 303–307.

Beekman, S. J. (1975). *Sex differences in nonverbal behavior.* Paper presented at the meeting of the American Psychological Association, Chicago.

Beigel, H. G. (1952). The influence of body position on mental processes. *Journal of Clinical Psychology,* **8**, 193–199.

Berdach, E., and P. Bakan (1967). Body position and the free recall of early memories. *Psychotherapy: Theory, Research, and Practice,* **4**, 101–102.

Birdwhistell, R. L. (1952). *Introduction to kinesics: An annotation system for analysis of body motion and gesture.* Louisville, Kentucky: University of Louisville.

Birdwhistell, R. L. (1968). Communication without words. In *L'aventure humaine.* Encyclopedia des sciences del'Homme. Geneva: Kister S. A. Paris: De La Grange Batelière S. A. Vol 5, Pp. 157–166. (Barker, L. L., and N. B. Collins (1970). Nonverbal and kinesic research. In P. Emmert and W. D. Brooks (Eds.), *Methods of research in communication.* Boston: Houghton Mifflin. Pp. 343–371.)

Birdwhistell, R. L. (1970). *Kinesics and context.* Philadelphia: University of Pennsylvania Press.

Blazer, J. A. (1966). Leg position and psychological characteristics in women. *Psychology,* **3,** 5–12.

Boomer, D. S. (1963). Speech disturbance and body movement in interviews. *Journal of Nervous and Mental Disease,* **136,** 263–266.

Boomer, D. S., and A. T. Dittmann (1964). Speech rate, filled pause, and body movement in interviews. *Journal of Nervous and Mental Disease,* **139,** 324–327.

Breed, G. R. (1972). The effect of intimacy: Reciprocity or retreat? *British Journal of Social and Clinical Psychology,* **11,** 135–142.

Chaikin, A. L., E. Sigler, and V. J. Derlega (1974). Nonverbal mediators of teacher expectancy effects. *Journal of Personality and Social Psychology,* **30,** 144–149.

Charny, E. J. (1966). Psychosomatic manifestations of rapport in psychotherapy. *Psychosomatic Medicine,* **28,** 305–315.

Cohen, A. A., and R. P. Harrison (1973). Intentionality in the use of hand illustrators in face to face communication situations. *Journal of Personality and Social Psychology,* **28,** 276–279.

Condon, W. S. and H. W. Brosin (1969). Micro linguistic-kinesic events in schizophrenic behavior. In D. V. Siva Sankar (Ed.), *Schizophrenia: Current concepts and research.* Hicksville, NY: PJD Publications. Pp. 812–837.

Condon, W. S., and W. D. Ogston (1966). Sound film analysis of normal and pathological behavior patterns. *Journal of Nervous and Mental Disease,* **143,** 338–347.

Condon, W. S., and W. D. Ogston (1967). A segmentation of behavior. *Journal of Psychiatric Research,* **5,** 221–235.

Condon, W. S., W. D. Ogston, and L. V. Pacoe (1969). Three faces of Eve revisited: A study of transient microstrabismus. *Journal of Abnormal Psychology,* **74,** 618–620.

Condon, W. S., and L. W. Sander (1974). Neonate movement is syncronized with adult speech: Interactional participation and language acquisition. *Science,* **183,** 99–101.

Dabbs, J. M., Jr. (1969). Similarity of gestures and interpersonal influence. Summary in *Proceedings of the 77th Annual Convention of the American Psychological Association.* Washington D.C.: American Psychological Association. Vol. 4, pp. 337–338.

D'Augelli, A. R. (1974). Nonverbal behavior of helpers in initial helping interactions. *Journal of Counseling Psychology,* **21,** 360–363.

Davis, M. (1972). *Understanding body movement: An annotated bibliography.* New York: Arno Press.

Dittmann, A. T. (1962). The relationship between body movements and moods in interviews. *Journal of Consulting Psychology,* **26,** 480.

Dittmann, A. T. (1971). Review of *Kinesics and context* by R. L. Birdwhistell. *Psychiatry,* **34,** 334–342.

Dittmann, A. T. (1972a). The body movement-speech rhythm relationship as a cue to speech encoding. In A. W. Siegmen and B. Pope (Eds.), *Studies in dyadic communication.* New York: Pergamon Press. Pp. 135–151.

Dittmann, A. T. (1972b). *Interpersonal messages of emotion.* New York: Springer.

Dittmann, A. T., and L. G. Llewellyn (1967). The phonemic clause as a unit of speech decoding. *Journal of Personality and Social Psychology,* **6,** 341–349.

Dittmann, A. T., and L. G. Llewellyn (1968). Relationship between vocalizations and head nods as listener responses. *Journal of Personality and Social Psychology,* **9,** 79–84.

Dittmann, A. T., and L. G. Llewellyn (1969). Body movements and speech rhythm in social conversation. *Journal of Personality and Social Psychology,* **11,** 98–106.

Duncan, S. D., Jr. (1969). Nonverbal communication. *Psychological Bulletin,* **72,** 118–137.

Duncan, S. D., Jr. (1972). Some signals and rules for taking speaking turns in conversations. *Journal of Personality and Social Psychology,* **23,** 283–292.

Duncan, S. D., Jr. (1973). Toward a grammar for dyadic conversations. *Semiotica,* 9, 29–46.

Duncan, S. D., Jr. (1974). On the structure of speaker-auditor interaction during speaking turns. *Language in Society,* 2, 161–180.

Duncan, S. D. Jr., and G. Niederehe (1974). On signalling that it's your turn to speak. *Journal of Experimental Social Psychology,* 10, 234–247.

Efron, D. (1941). *Gesture and environment.* New York: Kings Crown Press.

Ekman, P. (1965). Differential communication of affect by head and body cues. *Journal of Personality and Social Psychology,* 2, 726–735.

Ekman, P., and W. V. Friesen (1967). Head and body cues in the judgment of emotion: A reformulation. *Perceptual and Motor Skills,* 24, 711–724.

Ekman, P., and W. V. Friesen (1968). Nonverbal behavior in psychotherapy research. In J. M. Shlien, H. F. Hunt, J. D. Matarazzo, and C. Savage (Eds.), *Research in psychotherapy,* Vol. 3. Washington, D.C.: American Psychological Association. Pp. 179–218.

Ekman, P., and W. V. Friesen (1969a). Nonverbal leakage and clues to deception. *Psychiatry,* 32, 88–106.

Ekman, P., and W. V. Friesen (1969b). The repertoire of nonverbal behavior: Categories, origins, usage, and coding. *Semiotica,* 1, 49–98.

Ekman, P., and W. V. Friesen (1972). Hand movements. *Journal of Communication,* 22, 353–374.

Ekman, P., and W. V. Friesen (1974). Detecting deception from the body or face. *Journal of Personality and Social Psychology,* 29, 288–298.

Frankel, S. A., and E. B. Frankel (1970). Nonverbal behavior in a selected group of Negro and white males. *Psychosomatics,* 11, 127–132.

Freedman, N. (1972). The analysis of movement behavior during the clinical interview. In A. Siegman and B. Pope (Eds.), *Studies in dyadic communication.* New York: Pergamon Press. Pp. 153–175.

Freedman, N., T. Blass, A. Rifkin, and F. Quitkin (1973). Body movements and verbal encoding of aggressive affect. *Journal of Personality and Social Psychology,* 26, 72–85.

Freedman, N., and S. P. Hoffman (1967). Kinetic behavior in altered clinical states: Approach to objective analysis of motor behavior during clinical interviews. *Perceptual and Motor Skills,* 24, 527–539.

Freedman, N., J. O'Hanlon, P. Oltman, and H. A. Witkin (1972). The imprint of psychological differentiation on kinetic behavior in varying communicative contexts. *Journal of Abnormal Psychology,* 79, 239–258.

Fretz, B. R. (1966). Postural movements in a counseling dyad. *Journal of Counseling Psychology,* 13, 335–343.

Freud, S. (1959). Fragment of an analysis of a case of hysteria (1905). *Collected papers,* Vol 3. New York: Basic Books. Pp. 13–146. (Knapp, M. L. (1972). *Nonverbal communication in human interaction.* New York: Holt, Rinehart, and Winston.)

Gitin, S. R. (1970). A dimensional analysis of manual expression. *Journal of Personality and Social Psychology,* 15, 271–277.

Gottschalk, L. A., and R. L. Uliana (1976). A study of the relationship of nonverbal to verbal behavior: Effect of lip caressing on hope and oral references as expressed in the content of speech. *Comprehensive Psychiatry,* 17, 135–152.

Grand, S., N. Freedman, I. Steingart, and C. Buckwald (1975). Communicative behavior in schizophrenia. *Journal of Nervous and Mental Disease,* 161, 293–306.

Haase, R. F., and D. T. Tepper, Jr. (1972). Nonverbal components of empathic communication. *Journal of Counseling Psychology,* 19, 417–424.

Hamalian L. (1965). Communication by gesture in the Middle East. *ETC: Review of General Semantics,* 22, 43–49.

Herb, T. R., and R. F. Elliott, Jr. (1971). Authoritarianism in the conversation of gestures. *Kansas Journal of Sociology,* **7** (3), 93–101.

Hetherington, E. M. (1972). Effects of father absence on personality development in adolescent daughters. *Developmental Psychology,* **7,** 313–326.

Hinchliffe, M., D. Hooper, F. J. Roberts, and P. W. Vaughan (1975). A study of interaction between depresed patients and their spouses. *British Journal of Psychiatry,* **126,** 164–172.

Hoffman, S. P. (1968). *An empirical study of representational hand movements.* Doctoral dissertation, New York University. [*Dissertation Abstracts,* **29** (1969), 4379B. University Microfilms No. 69–7960.]

Holstein, C. M., J. W. Goldstein, and D. J. Bem (1971). The importance of expressive behaviors, involvement, sex, and need-approval in induced liking. *Journal of Experimental Social Psychology,* **7,** 534–544.

Johnson, H. G., P. Ekman, and W. V. Friesen (1975). Communicative body movements: American emblems. *Semiotica,* **15,** 335–353.

Johnson, K. R. (1971). Black kinesics: Some nonverbal communication patterns in the black culture. *Florida Foreign Language Reporter,* Spring–Fall, 17–20.

Jurich, A. P., and J. A. Jurich (1974). Correlations among nonverbal expressions of anxiety. *Psychological Reports,* **34,** 199–204.

Kendon, A. (1972). Review of *Kinesics and context: Essays on body motion* by R. L. Birdwhistell. *American Journal of Psychology,* **85,** 441–445.

Kendon, A. (1970). Movement coordination in social interaction: Some examples described. *Acta Psychologica,* **32,** 100–125.

Kimura, D. (1973a). Manual activity during speaking: I. Right handers. *Neuropsychologica,* **11,** 45–50.

Kimura, D. (1973b). Manual activity during speaking: II. Left handers. *Neuropsychologica,* **11,** 51–55.

Kiritz, S. A., P. Ekman, and W. V. Friesen. Hand movements and psychopathology. In preparation. (Ekman, P., and W. V. Friesen (1974). Nonverbal behavior and psychopathology. In R. J. Friedman and M. M. Katz (Eds.), *The psychology of depression: Contemporary theory and research.* Washington, D.C.: Winston and Sons.)

Kleck, R. E. (1968). Physical stigma and nonverbal cues emitted in face-to-face interaction. *Human Relations,* **21,** 19–28.

Knapp, M. L. (1972). *Nonverbal communication in human interaction.* New York: Holt, Rinehart, and Winston,

Knapp, M. L., R. P. Hart, and H. S. Dennis. The rhetoric of duplicity: An exploration of description as a communication construct. Unpublished manuscript. (Available from the Communication Research Center, Purdue University, Lafayette, Indiana.)

Knapp, M. L., R. P. Hart, G. W. Fredrich, and G. M. Shulman (1973). The rhetoric of good-bye: Verbal and nonverbal correlates of human leave-taking. *Speech Monographs,* **40,** 182–198.

LaCrosse, M. B. (1975). Nonverbal behavior and perceived counselor attractiveness and persuasiveness. *Journal of Counseling Psychology,* **22,** 563–566.

LaFrance, M. (1974). *Nonverbal cues to conversational turn taking between Black speakers.* Paper presented at the meeting of the American Psychological Association, New Orleans.

Loeb, F. F., Jr. (1968). The microscopic film analysis of the function of a recurrent behavioral pattern in a psychotherapeutic session. *Journal of Nervous and Mental Disease,* **147,** 605–618.

Loeb, L. R., F. F. Loeb, Jr., and D. S. Ross (1972). Grasping as an adult communication signal. *Journal of Nervous and Mental Disease,* **154,** 368–386.

London, H. (1973). *Psychology of the persuader.* Morristown, NJ: General Learning Press.

Mahl, G. F. (1968). Gestures and body movements in interviews. In J. M. Shlien, H. F. Hunt, J. D. Matarazzo, and C. Savage (Eds.), *Research in psychotherapy*, Vol. 3. Washington, D.C.: American Psychological Association. Pp. 295–346.

Matarazzo, J. D., G. Saslow, A. N. Wiens, M. Weitman, and B. V. Allen (1964). Interviewer head nodding and interviewee speech durations. *Psychotherapy: Theory, Research, and Practice,* 1, 54–63.

McCaa, B. B. (1971). *A study of some factors mediating unintended experimental effects upon subjects in psychological experiments.* Doctoral dissertation, Washington University, St. Louis, MO. [*Dissertation Abstracts International,* 32 (1972), 5338A. University Microfilms No. 79–9355.]

McGinley, H., R. Lefevre, and P. McGinley (1975). The influence of a communicator's body position on opinion change in others. *Journal of Personality and Social Psychology,* 31, 686–690.

Mehrabian, A. (1968a). Inference of attitudes from the posture, orientation, and distance of a communicator. *Journal of Consulting and Clinical Psychology,* 32, 296–308.

Mehrabian, A. (1968b). Relationship of attitude to seated posture, orientation, and distance. *Journal of Personality and Social Psychology,* 10, 26–30.

Mehrabian, A. (1969). Significance of posture and position in the communication of attitude and status relationships. *Psychological Bulletin,* 71, 359–372.

Mehrabian, A. (1971a). Nonverbal betrayal of feeling. *Journal of Experimental Research in Personality,* 5, 64–73.

Mehrabian, A. (1971b). Verbal and nonverbal interaction of strangers in a waiting situation. *Journal of Experimental Research in Personality,* 5, 127–138.

Mehrabian, A. (1972). *Nonverbal communication.* Chicago: Aldine-Atherton.

Mehrabian, A., and J. T. Friar (1969). Encoding of attitude by a seated communicator via posture and position cues. *Journal of Consulting and Clinical Psychology,* 33, 330–336.

Mehrabian, A., and S. Ksionzky (1972). Categories of social behavior. *Comparative Group Studies,* 3, 425–436.

Mehrabian, A., and M. Williams (1969). Nonverbal concomitants of perceived and intended persuasiveness. *Journal of Personality and Social Psychology,* 13, 37–58.

Michael, G., and F. N. Willis, Jr. (1968). The development of gestures as a function of social class, education, and sex. *Psychological Record,* 18, 515–519.

Michael, G., and F. N. Willis, Jr. (1969). The development of gestures in three subcultural groups. *Journal of Social Psychology,* 79, 35–41.

Morsbach, H. (1973). Aspects of nonverbal communication in Japan. *Journal of Nervous and Mental Disease,* 157, 262–277.

Rand, G., and S. Wapner (1967). Postural status as a factor in memory. *Journal of Verbal Learning and Verbal Behavior,* 6, 268–271.

Rosenfeld, H. M. (1966a). Approval-seeking and approval-inducing functions of verbal and nonverbal responses in the dyad. *Journal of Personality and Social Psychology,* 4, 597–605.

Rosenfeld, H. M. (1966b). Instrumental affiliative functions of facial and gestural expressions. *Journal of Personality and Social Psychology,* 4, 65–72.

Rosenfeld, H. M. (1967). Nonverbal reciprocation of approval: An experimental analysis. *Journal of Experimental Social Psychology,* 3, 102–111.

Rosenthal, R., and L. Jacobson (1968). *Pygmalion in the classroom.* New York: Holt, Rinehart, and Winston.

Scheflen, A. E. (1963). Communication and regulation in psychotherapy. *Psychiatry,* 26, 126–136.

Scheflen, A. E. (1964). The significance of posture in communication systems. *Psychiatry,* 27, 316–331.

Scheflen, A. E. (1966). Natural history method in psychotherapy: Communication research. In L. A. Gottschalk and A. H. Auerbach (Eds.), *Methods and research in psychotherapy.* New York: Appleton-Century-Crofts. Pp. 263–289.

Scheflen, A. E. (1974). Quasi-courtship behavior in psychotherapy. In S. Weitz (Ed.), *Nonverbal communication: Readings with commentary.* New York: Oxford University Press. Pp. 182–198.

Shapiro, J. G. (1972). Variability and usefulness of facial and body cues. *Comparative Group Studies, 3*, 437–442.

Smith, E. W. L. (1972). Postural and gestural communication of A and B "therapist types" during dyadic interviews. *Journal of Consulting and Clinical Psychology, 39*, 29–36.

Spiegel, J. P., and P. Machotka (1974). *Messages of the body.* New York: The Free Press, MacMillan Publishing Co.

Stephano, P. J. (1971). An investigation of hand gesture as nonverbal communication. *Journalism Abstracts, 9*, 193.

Strong, S. R., R. G. Taylor, J. C. Bratton, and R. G. Loper (1971) Nonverbal behavior and perceived counselor characteristics. *Journal of Counseling Psychology, 18*, 554–561.

Washburn, P. V., and M. D. Hakel (1973). Visual cues and verbal content as influences on impressions formed after simulated employment interviews. *Journal of Applied Psychology, 58*, 137–141.

Waxer, P. (1976). Nonverbal cues for depth of depression: Set versus no set. *Journal of Clinical and Consulting Psychology, 44*, 493.

Weitz, S. (Ed.). (1974). *Nonverbal communication: Readings with commentary.* New York: Oxford University Press.

Wiener, M., S. Devoe, S. Rubinow, and J. Geller (1972). Nonverbal behavior and nonverbal communication. *Psychological Review, 79*, 185–214.

Wolff, P., and J. Gutstein (1972). Effects of induced motor gestures on vocal output. *Journal of Communications, 22*, 277–288.

CHAPTER 5

The Eye and Visual Behavior

INTRODUCTION

In this chapter we consider the role of the eyes and visual behavior in nonverbal communication. Visual behavior and, in particular, gaze-encounter or eye contact are unique, nonverbal phenomena in their social, physiological, even psychological significance. As Heron (1970) stated, "The most fundamental *primary* mode of interpersonal encounter is the interaction between two pairs of eyes and what is mediated by this interaction. For it is mainly here, throughout the wide ranges of social encounter, that people actually *meet* (in the strict sense)" (p. 244). References to the significance of eyes abound in the literature: Emerson wrote, "One of the most wonderful things in nature is a glance of the eye; it transcends speech; it is the bodily symbol of identity" (cited in Champness, 1970, p. 309). George Simmel noted, "By the glance which reveals the other, one discloses himself . . . the eye cannot take unless at the same time it gives. What occurs in this direct mutual glance represents the most perfect reciprocity in the entire field of human relationship" (cited in Champness, 1970, p. 309). From his extensive research on visual behavior, Exline (1972) cited an instance where prolonged eye contact by an experimenter with a rhesus macaque monkey could stimulate a "program" of avoidance, threat, and attack behaviors by the animal.

Ellsworth (1975) listed three characteristics of the gaze: saliency, arousal, and involvement. She described *saliency* as follows:

A direct gaze is a salient element in the environment. Unlike many nonverbal behaviors having a potential cue-value which is rarely realized, such as foot movements, changes in pupil size, and subtle facial or postural changes, a direct gaze has a high probability of being noticed. For a behavior that involves no noise and little movement, it has a remarkable capacity to draw attention to itself even at a distance. . . . People often use a direct gaze to attract another person's attention in situations where noise or gesticulation are inappropriate. The fact that we expect others to be responsive to our gaze is illustrated by our exasperation when dealing

171

with people who have learned immunity to the effects of a stare, such as waiters. (pp. 5–6)

Visual behavior also has *arousal* properties in those instances when two persons make eye contact, as subsequent empirical research shows. Finally, it results in interpersonal involvement as a result of the arousal stemming from the personal and psychological contact that gaze-encounter permits.

Ellsworth and Ludwig (1972) published an excellent review of visual behavior in which they identified and organized much of the empirical research on visual behavior in interpersonal situations. They stated:

Visual behavior appears to provide information at several different communicational levels in social interaction. As a dependent variable, it has been used to measure stable individual and group differences, the regulation of the flow of conversation, and the search for feedback in an interaction. As an independent variable, it has been shown to influence emotional responses and cognitive attributions. (p. 375)

Ellsworth herself has been especially productive in studying the social-psychological significance of visual behavior as an independent variable. Cranach (1971), a German researcher, specialized in the study of its function in social interaction and its role in the behavioral repertoire of the sender and the receiver. Most recently, Argyle and Cook (1975) produced a book, *Gaze and Mutual Gaze,* that should serve the serious researcher well.

VISUAL BEHAVIOR: DEFINITIONS AND MEASUREMENT

Cranach (1971) offered a number of definitions of "looking behavior" to describe the various findings in the research literature. As shown in Table 5-1, one can first identify a *"onesided look"* as a gaze by one person in the direction of another's face, typically centered at the region of the other's eyes. Though Cranach did not make this distinction, it is also possible to differentiate an *eye-gaze* from a *face-gaze,* depending on the specificity the researcher wishes to attribute to the target (i.e., face vs. eyes) of a person's visual attention. A *mutual look,* by definition, occurs when two persons gaze at the other's face, typically in the direction of each other's eyes. *Eye contact* describes a situation where "both partners look into the other's eyes, most probably into one eye only, and both partners are aware of the mutual look" (Cranach, 1971, p. 220). Eye contact, in particular, is a term that has been carelessly used in the literature (in some cases, to describe even a onesided look). *Gaze avoidance* occurs when one avoids looking at the person who is interacting with him, especially when the other is looking at him, so that eye contact does not occur. The intention to avoid eye contact distinguishes gaze avoidance from *gaze omission,* which describes a situation where one partner is not looking at the other without intentionally avoiding eye contact. Additional terms important in describing visual behavior are gaze direction, eye or gaze *movement,* and *duration* of glances, eye contact, or mutual looking.

When one reads through the literature on visual behavior, it is thus important to know which of the various visual phenomena are really being described. As there is yet no established terminology for visual behavior, this is often possible only through consideration of the methodology of the particular study. In most experiments, the visual behavior of one of the interactants is controlled, that is, his gaze is either fixed on the other's eyes or face throughout the entire period of observation or for specified intervals. In the former instance, that of constant fixation (which is obviously atypical for most normal interactions), it is possible to say that a "mutual look"' has occurred when the other interactant's gaze (which is free to vary) makes contact with the eyes or face of the instructed participant. In the latter circumstance, variable eye-gazing, one can safely conclude only that a "onesided look" has occurred and not a "mutual look" unless there are observers rating both of the interactants' gaze directions, or unless the instructed interactant is programmed to return all onesided looks from the other. Typically, only the visual behavior of the uninstructed interactant is measured. According to Cranach's definition it should not be possible to conclude with full certainty that eye contact has occurred unless there is evidence that both interactants are aware that this is taking place. Clearly then, in uninstructed, spontaneous interactions, "eye contact" cannot necessarily be assumed. This emphasis on awareness should not be taken light-

Table 5-1.   Definitions of Visual Behavior (After von Cranach, 1971)

Term	Definition
Onesided look	Gaze by one person in direction of another's face.
Face-gaze	Directing of one person's gaze at another's face.
Eye-gaze	Directing of one person's gaze at another's eyes.
Mutual look	Two persons gaze at each other's face.
Eye contact	Two persons look into each other's eyes and are aware of each other's eye gaze.
Gaze avoidance	Avoidance of another's eye gaze.
Gaze omission	Failure to look at another without intention to avoid eye contact.

ly considering that there are instances where there is mutual looking with little arousal or involvement, and obviously other instances (of eye contact) where salience, arousal, and psychological involvement are high. Finally, in addition to being wary of the use of the term "eye contact," one must take care to distinguish a researcher's use of the terms face-gazing and eye-gazing. Technically, use of the latter term should involve some evidence that gaze fixation was actually on the eyes. As we see later, many of these problems may be more apparent than real in natural interaction situations. (Nonetheless, where "eye contact" appears in quotes, this will signify the particular author's definition of the term and not necessarily our own.)

Notwithstanding problems of definition, a second consideration in reviewing any study of visual behavior is the reliability and validity of the measure of visual behavior. This is obviously of crucial importance where the visual behavior is a dependent measure that varies among subjects. Exline (1963) reported interobserver reliabilities in excess of .90 for two observers rating "eye gazing" by a sender to one of two receivers. In this study, observers were positioned at an angle to the sender and receiver, which somewhat reduced observer accuracy. In later studies (e.g., Exline, Gray, and Schuette, 1965; Strongman and Champness, 1968) where the observer was situated directly behind the receiver, reliabilities in the vicinity of .90 and higher were reported. In other studies, Fugita (1974) obtained interobserver reliabilities of .98 and .99 for judgments of time looking and number of looks across 72 subjects, and Libby (1970) obtained reliabilities in the vicinity of .90 or better for her measures of eye-gaze, breaking of eye-gaze, and vertical and horizontal gaze-aversions.

In addition to total gaze or number of looks the degree of overlap in recorded glances may be measured since two techniques are the use of either pen recorders to judge time or an Interaction Chronograph (Wiens, Matarazzo, and Saslow, 1965). Exline (1963) found 81% interobserver agreement when the amount of overlap was measured in 2-second intervals, whereas Vine (1971) obtained 70–74% agreement. As might be expected, when shorter intervals for overlap are specified, lower reliabilities are obtained: Vine (1971) reported 66–69% agreement for .25-second intervals. Rubin (1970) and Exline (1972) computed the percentage of total time for which observers agreed and obtained percentages in the 90s.

The above reliabilities were based upon real-time observations. With videotape, slow-motion analysis of facial closeups is also possible. In our own laboratories we have employed time-addressing of videotapes whereby a digital time is electronically affixed to each videoframe (90 per second). Coders view a closeup of the subject's face as produced by a videocamera positioned over the shoulders of an interviewer in slow motion ($\frac{1}{7}$ normal speed). For subject face-gaze at the interviewer, average error per face-gaze look was $2/10$ second and overall agreement for total face-gazing over a 10-minute interval was 99%.

In contrast to the above findings, Mehrabian and Williams (1969) obtained only a reliability of .50 for observers rating total gaze. This finding was mitigated somewhat by the fact that ratings were made from videotapes (where observers were not positioned behind the sender and receiver). However, Stephenson and Rutter (1970) positioned observers behind a sender who varied his gaze from the eye to the ear or shoulder of the receiver. They found that as the distance between sender and receiver increased, observers increasingly tended to mistake ear- and shoulder-gaze for eye-gazing. Depending on the varying distances, the reliability correlations obtained ranged from $-.17$ to .85, with an overall mean of .43. A further disturbing finding was reported by White, Hegarty, and Beasley (1970) who examined the effect that observer training has on reliability scores. They found that advising subjects of the probable findings prior to the rating task systematically affected whether the observers judged increases or decreases in eye-gazing when the distance between sender and receiver was increased. Vine (1971), summarizing many of these discrepant findings, stated: "If judgment of gaze direction (GD) is typically poor, then the results of a rapidly growing body of research are in doubt, for as yet this has relied on observer judgments in monitoring the gazing variables" (p. 320).

In actuality, most studies measuring gaze-direction have relied on the findings of several experiments in which psychophysical measurements of gaze-direction were taken. Gibson and Pick (1963) had a sender fix his gaze on a receiver stationed 200 centimeters away on various points on or near the face of the receiver. The judgment task for the receiver was to determine whether the sender was gazing into his eyes, and if not, to judge the location of gaze. In addition to changes in gaze-direction, the sender's head-orientation was also varied (straight-on vs. a 30° angle). Gibson and Pick found that when the sender's head was pointed directly at the receiver, the receiver/s judgments of gaze-direction variations approached the limits of normal visual acuity. However, when the sender's head-orientation was away from the receiver, receivers tended consistently to *underestimate* deviations in gaze-direction away from their eyes.

Cline (1967), using slightly different measurement techniques, essentially replicated Gibson and Pick's findings concerning acuity of discrimination and the effect of sender head-orientation. In particular, he found that head-position and gaze-direction interacted such that the perceived gaze-direction fell between the head- and eye-positions. Further, he noted that "for most head-positions, the line of regard directed into S's eyes is discriminated with greater accuracy than all other lines of regard. The mutual glance is a unique experience and there are unique judgments coördinated with it'" (Cline, 1967, p. 50). Anstis, Mayhew, and Morley (1969) had a sender projected via a television screen. These authors discovered that as the sender-receiver axis was varied from a direct orientation (accomplished by rotating the TV screen), gaze-direction judgments reflected a consistent *overestimation* that was proportional to the deviation in sender-receiver axis. Head-turning increased this effect, though to a reduced degree, given receivers' tendencies to underestimate shifts in gaze produced by head movements. They next utilized an artificial eyeball set in a diaphram to evaluate systematically the effect of sender head-direction and sender-receiver axis on gaze-direction judgments. They found that the perceived portion of the iris in the eye was an important cue for observers, and consideration of the amount of white visible on either side of the iris could explain in geometric terms the overestimation and underestimation effects they obtained.

These studies (particularly the first two) have been widely cited as evidence that receivers can very accurately perceive whether someone is looking at their eyes. However, a more recent series of studies utilizing a sender, receiver, *and* observer has cast some doubt on these findings. Kruger and Huckstedt (1968) had senders vary their fixation points on seven target points (including the eye) on the receiver's face. Receiver judgments of eye contact were only 35% accurate at an 80-centimeter sender-receiver distance, this being reduced to 10% for a 2-meter distance. Ellgring (1969) later replicated this study with accuracy ratings of 50% and 30%, respectively, for the two distances. Kruger and Huckstedt (1968) also varied the head-orientation of the sender and his gaze-fixation to points outside the face. They found that receivers judged accurately most gazes directed at their faces but also frequently misjudged gazes directed beyond their faces. Head-orientation and increased sender-receiver distance tended to increase judgment errors. Further, observers were considerably less accurate than receivers in judging gaze-direction, especially when their orientation was oblique to the sender-receiver pair.

Cranach and Huckstedt (unpublished data cited in Cranach, 1971) then investigated the effect of having the sender make eye movements before fixating on a spot on and beyond the receiver's face. Sender eye movements alone did not improve receiver judgment accuracy for face-gazes. However, when the sender moved his eyes to a position toward, but not at, the receiver's face, receivers tended to misjudge the fixation point as a spot on their face. Extraverted receivers, interestingly, showed this bias to a greater degree for the larger angles of gaze. Subsequently, Cranach, Huckstedt, Schmid, and Vogel (1969, cited in Cranach, 1971) varied head-orientation and head movements in addition to eye movements and sender-receiver distance. The authors found that as sender-receiver distance increased, so did the frequency of misjudgments between face-gazes and nonface-gazes.

As a result, with increasing distance, head-orientation became relatively more important as a cue for receivers in making judgments. Head and eye movements actually tended to reduce discrimination accuracy. In particular, head movements tended to reduce the number of face-gaze responses for receivers and also observers (for the latter, only at a sender-receiver distance of 300 centimeters). Observers again were less accurate in their judgments than receivers. An additional finding was that extraverted subjects were less influenced by variations in head-position than introverts, and were more accurate.

Finally, Ellgring and Cranach (1972) investigated the effect of training in judging gaze-direction. Receivers were given feedback on the correct fixation targets of senders (within or outside the receiver's face) over a series of 500 judgment trials. Accuracy of recognition of gaze-direction improved over time (reflecting learning), but accuracy in recognition of direct eye-gazes did not. Apparently, the ability to detect eye-gazes was already "overlearned," whereas training was beneficial for accurate recognition of other gaze-directions. Personality factors (e.g., extraversion, neuroticism) and visual acuity did not play a role in the learning process. Nevertheless, individual differences in discrimination ability were noted which were maintained throughout the learning process.

While the results of these last studies were not directly comparable to the previous ones given differences in the methodologies, the conclusions of Cranach (1971) seem supported by his findings:

We come to the conclusion that, in this particular experimental condition, the receiver's judgment of the gaze behavior of the sender is influenced by various stimuli, the combined effects of which are dependent on the special conditions of the social situation. In special cases, judgments may reach a high degree of accuracy, while, in other cases, gazes directed at the face are not recognized or nonexisting gazes are erroneously perceived. Eye contact, in the sense of our definition, is not a measurable variable that can be regarded as a social signal. It should be replaced by the variable "mutual look." (pp. 223–224)

In addition to the variables identified above that may affect measurement of visual behavior, Vine (1971) noted that the judgment task given to observers or receivers is important. Where multiple-choice decisions about the target of gaze-fixation are required (e.g., Ellgring, 1969; Kruger and Huckstedt, 1968), there will be high judgment uncertainty and underestimation biases may occur, with too many eye-gaze responses being judged as a result. Where the judgment choice is simpler, "overestimation biases may apply when GDs [gaze directions] are angled substantially to the sender-receiver axis" (Vine, 1971, pp. 326–327). In his review of this topic, Vine (1971) concluded:

It is evident that accurate judgment of whether a gaze is actually an EG [eye gaze] or even an FG [face gaze] must depend upon the distance involved between sender and receiver or sender and observer. It is also evident that discrepancies between gaze and head orientations lead to errors, so that judging GD [gaze direction] in natural social interactions, especially where there are also movements of the eyes and head of the senders, will be much less accurate than the earliest experiments suggested. (p. 327)

Despite these apparently contradictory or discouraging findings, there is reason to believe that satisfactory measurement of visual behavior is possible in an experimental situation. The main assumption behind this premise is that in natural, social interactions, when we look at another person, we look at his eyes, as opposed to some other location. Assuming this is true, then the judgment task for an observer is only as difficult as the face-gaze versus nonface-gaze discrimination, for which the observer judgments are reasonably accurate. For example, Exline (1972), Exline, Gray, and Schuette (1965), and Goldberg, Kiesler, and Collins (1969) compared observer ratings against accuracy criteria of receiver judgments of amount of looking and number of looks during "normal" interaction (i.e., where one sender is not systematically varying gaze in finite increments). They obtained correlations ranging from .88 to .99. Using sender observer agreement for amount and number of looks as a criterion, Rutter, Morley, and Graham (1972) and Rutter and Stephenson (1972a) obtained agreements from 68 to 94%, with the majority in the vicinity of 90%. These findings, however, are based upon the assumption that sender and receiver judgments about looking are wholly accurate, which as Cranach (1971) has noted is only partially true.

In a more direct resolution of the findings of the psychophysical studies versus the natural interaction research, Vine (1971) conducted the following two experiments. First, he filmed two experimental confederates seated across from each other at a table. When one subject was giving a constant eye-gaze, the other was moving his eyes in a prescribed pattern of fixation points on his partner's face. Each of the subjects was filmed in the two roles (fixed vs. variable gaze) while assuming different postures (leaning forward and leaning backward). Two cameras were used, each positioned at different angles (25 vs. 15°) from the sender-receiver axis. Two observers made independent ratings of eye-gaze versus noneye-gaze from the films. Neither had been instructed in any shared measurement strategy that might spuriously raise the reliability measure. When the criterion for observer disagreement was set as a duration discrepancy of more than .25 second, observer agreements for the two film transcriptions were 66% and 69%. When the observer discrepancy criterion was shifted to 2 seconds (Exline, 1963), observer agreements were still only 70% and 74%. Since the observer ratings also had been made over two viewings 4 days apart, reliabilities over time could be computed, which were 76% for both observers. However, when the validity of observer judgments was computed by comparing the observer ratings against an actual transcript of the programmed visual behavior of the senders, only 76% of eye-gazing was correctly judged, with 18.5% of the gazes not directed at the receiver's face being misclassified as eye-gazes. Even allowing for some loss in accuracy due to use of films, Vine concluded that these findings were very modest.

However, Vine next had observer ratings made of films of two uninstructed subjects in spontaneous social interactions. Although no programmed transcripts were obviously available as validity criteria (against which to judge true observer accuracy), interobserver agreement was quite high (94%), as was the reliability over time (92%). He thus concluded, "On the basis of the data which has been considered, we may conclude that we are not forced to disregard the findings of most studies where gazing during social interaction has been monitored" (1971, p. 330). However, Vine cautioned that observer training could spuriously affect the reliability measure, as could variations in distance between sender and receiver. In addition, Gitter, Mostofsky, and Guichard (1972) found that simply the presence of another person may influence observer judgments about an individual's gaze-direction. They had subjects rate the gaze-directions of individuals shown in still photographs when either alone or in the presence of another person. They found that when there was a second person in the photograph, the first person's gaze was judged as being more in the direction of the second person. In addition, the gaze was regarded as more focused, even though the gaze-direction for the individuals shown in both sets of photographs (alone or with a second person) was apparently identical. (Unfortunately, this study has not been replicated with live subjects.) Finally, Deutsch and Auerbach (1975) compared acuity in the direction of gaze when the gaze to be judged was fixed and unmoving and when there was some eye movement occurring during gaze-fixation. That is, when making "eye contact" we can look at a single spot on the other person's face or our gaze can shift slightly between two points of fixation. Without going into the rather complicated details of their methodology, Deutsch and Auerbach found that there was essentially no difference in perceptual acuity but that observers were more likely to judge that eye contact was made when a movement cue was available.

Though we may conclude that, despite methodological problems, observer ratings of gaze-direction may be reasonably accurate at ordinary social distances when the sender's head and eyes are aligned in the direction of the observer,[1] we are still left with the problem that observers cannot tell us whether the receiver (often the uninstructed interactant in the experiment) is *aware* that he is being looked at. Further, receiver self-report may not always be accurate. As Ellsworth and Ludwig (1972) noted:

> Subjects in a social interaction may not be able to describe the other's visual behavior accurately, even when it can be demonstrated that this behavior has had an effect on their behavior. . . . Ellsworth and Ross (1976), for example, found that subjects could tell whether their partners looked at them a lot or hardly at all, but they could not tell whether or not the eye contact was contingent upon their own behavior. Argyle and Williams (1969) found that subjects, when questioned, could not even discriminate between high- and low-looking confederates. Thus subjective report may not be a very good measure in social interaction, since it can be demonstrated that "unnoticed" visual behavior can have important psychological effects. (pp. 383–384)

As a final comment to this section on measurement we should note that several researchers have attempted to devise formulas for *expected mutual looking* (what most researchers have called eye contact) in dyads that might occur by chance. Deviations from that would presumably represent seeking or avoidance of gaze by the dyad. Strongman and Champness (1968) proposed that the percentage of eye contact expected by chance within a dyad was the product of the percentage of each individual's looking at the other. In other words, if each individual looked at the other 50% of the time, chance eye contact would occur .5 × .5 or 25% of the time. Subsequently, Argyle and Ingham (1972) proposed a different formula to account for the customary disparity between looking while listening and looking while talking:

$$EC = \frac{L_t(A) \times L_l(B)}{A's\ talking} + \frac{L_t(B) \times L_l(A)}{B's\ talking}$$

By this example, during the time that dyad member B is talking, the looking-while-talking of B would be multiplied by the looking-while-listening of A, this product then being divided by the time B talked. The value thus obtained would then be added to a similar value obtained during A's speech. By actually measuring mutual gaze and comparing it with expected values, Argyle and Ingham (1972) concluded that Strongman and Champness's formula tended to overestimate mutual gaze while their formula underestimated it to a lesser degree.

FUNCTIONS OF VISUAL BEHAVIOR IN INTERPERSONAL COMMUNICATION

Gaze as a Signal for Communication

Visual behavior plays a major role in interpersonal communication. As indicated at the opening of this chapter, one function is simply "the announcement of a readiness to communicate" (Cranach, 1971). Cranach (1971) described a "hierarchially ordered" sequence of orienting behaviors signalling readiness for communication: gaze, head, and body turned toward the individual to be communicated with. He noted that "in inhibited depressive patients, the increase in orienting reactions seems to announce improvement even before verbal interaction is resumed" (p. 227). Eibl-Eibesfeldt (1972) described a pattern of greeting behavior that is apparently universal. This pattern consists of a very brief (e.g., one third of a second) series of acts: the direction of gaze toward another person, a smile, eyebrow-lift, and a quick head-nod. This behavior apparently acts as a "releaser," that is, it elicits the same behavior from others. (Indeed, some have argued that this is an innate response.) Eibl-Eibesfeldt additionally describes a slow lowering of the eyelid which interrupts eye contact for about one-half second. This, he contends, serves an "appeasing function," and may possibly be a substitute for a low-intensity head-nod.

Cary (1974) studied visual signals given by seated females to male subjects as they entered a room. Both looked at each other as the males entered, but it was the second look by the female that decided whether a conversation would occur. Cary then looked for this behavioral sequence in a real barroom. There, females did not look directly at entering males but rather aligned themselves to see them approaching peripherally. This permitted them to eye males whom they found interesting. Cary further noted, "Inexperienced males can occasionally be seen to pick the most physically appealing females; the more experienced males seem to know better and try to join the females who look to them" (1974, p. 8).

Gaze and Interpersonal Influence

Jellison and Ickes (1974) hypothesized that gaze could also serve to facilitate interpersonal influence and control as well as communication per se. In their study, subjects were led to believe that they were to interview another subject whom they would subsequently face in either a cooperative or a competitive game situation. Half the subjects were given a choice of either seeing or not seeing their partner (cooperative game) or opponent (competitive game); the other half were given the choice whether or not they were to be seen. A majority of subjects chose to see their partner or opponent or be seen by their partner; in contrast, only 34% of the subjects in the competitive game situation chose to be seen by their opponent. Clearly, the ability to see another implied an increase in interpersonal information and control, which in a cooperative (but not competitive) situation was mutually desirable. Interestingly, many subjects who chose to be seen by an expected opponent revealed during debriefing that, for various reasons, they felt they could better influence their opponent to their advantage.

Purpose of Gaze Avoidance

Gaze avoidance or gaze omission behaviors signal either a desire not to communicate or an unreadiness to communicate. Hutt and Ounsted (1966) dramatically illustrated gaze avoidance in their description of childhood autism. In particular, Hutt and Vaizey (1966) experimentally crowded a small room with subgroups of normal, brain-damaged, and autistic children. Aggressive behavior increased with room density in all children but the autistic ones, who, though essentially helpless, did not experience an increase in attacks. Hutt and his colleagues related this apparent effect of gaze avoidance to what ethologists have described as appeasement gestures in animals. However, Cranach (1971) perhaps more conservatively concluded, "It can be stated that there are too few reliable findings on the meaning of gaze avoidance or gaze omission; these behaviors probably indicate communication avoidance. Gaze avoidance seems to be accompanied by conscious body movements or postures in most cases" (p. 229).

In addition to communicating an unwillingness to communicate, gaze-aversion may be indicative of emotional arousal. Jurich and Jurich (1974), for example, asked anxiety-arousing questions of females and found that "percent of no eye contact" correlated very highly with subjects' sweat-prints ($r = .86$) and an observer's rating of anxiety ($r = .79$) as well as measures of speech dysfluencies. Exline, Gray, and Schuette (1965) conducted an experiment in which subjects were interviewed by a steadily gazing interviewer who covered either innocuous, personal, or embarrassing subject matter. Subjects asked personal or embarrassing questions tended to look less at the interviewer. Exline, Gray, and Schuette (1965) interpreted this behavior as a "perhaps unconscious" signal of a desire to maintain psychological distance from the interviewer whose questions were threatening the nature of their composure.

More recently, Modigliani (1971) developed a theory of embarrassment that he defined as "a special short-lived, but often acute, loss of self-esteem" (p. 16). Modigilani exposed subjects to success and failure on their portion of a group task, experienced in public or private. As predicted, subject self-esteem was least in the publicly experienced failure situation, and eye contact with a confederate was decreased compared to other conditions. Unfortunately, subjects' gaze-aversion may have been due to their dislike of the confederate who had criticized them for their failure rather than a sign of social inferiority. An interesting aspect of the study was the manner in which eye contact was studied: by confederates themselves operating a foot pedal connected to a marking device whenever subjects met their gaze.

Kleck (1968) and Kleck, Buck, Goller, London, Pfeiffer, and Vukcevic (1968) reported studies in which subjects interacted with a physically stigmatized individual: a confederate made to appear as an amputee. In neither instance, despite the experimenter's beliefs that such interaction would be arousing to subjects, was subjects' looking at the "stigmatized" confederate reduced. The authors speculated that the need for information from the confederate (regarding what he was like or how he was responding to the subjects) may have counteracted the tendency for gaze aversion.

Knapp, Hart, and Dennis (1974) had Vietnam veterans give arguments in favor of or against the position that educational benefits to veterans be increased. The latter task (speaking against) obviously involved making counterattitudinal or "deceitful" statements, which presumably was somewhat arousing. In addition to differing in other ways, "deceiving" subjects showed less looking duration than nondeceiving subjects. However, the number of looks at the interviewer did not differ for the subjects in the two conditions. Some evidence that subjects were more nervous in the counterattitudinal communication situation was seen in the increase in the duration of self-adaptors during the "deception" situation.

As reviewed in Chapter 3, Efran and Cheyne (1974) created an experimental situation where it was necessary for subjects to "intrude" on the conversational space of two confederates. Although no physiological differences in arousal were noted for intruding and nonintruding subjects, intruders did report less positive mood ratings. Specifically, "in describing their feelings subjects used words such as awkward, embarrassed, unpleasant, and uncomfortable" (1974, p. 224). More importantly, they exhibited many agonistic facial gestures (including an increased frequency and duration of negative mouth gestures) and the following measures of gaze-aversion: increased frequency and duration of head and gaze down and eyes closed, and increased frequency and duration of partial eye closure. In addition to being associated with subjects' emotional arousal, the authors speculated that these findings were similar to the apparently innate appeasing gestures that primates display in regard to dominance and territorial arrangements.

In contrast to the above studies in which arousal was manipulated as a function of the social-interactive context, Fromme and Schmidt (1972) studied subjects' nonverbal behaviors when they were role-playing different affective states. After a period of friendly discussion with the experimenter to minimize their self-consciousness, subjects were instructed to approach a confederate and to role-play a situation involving expression of various emotional states. The affective arousal conditions included the following emotions: neutral, fear, anger, and sorrow. Though other nonverbal behaviors varied as a function of enacted emotional state, differences in "eye contact" with the confederate obtained only for the enactment of sorrow. Subjects showed half as much eye contact in that condition as in the other conditions, suggesting that gaze-aversion was viewed as a reliable concommitant of the emotion of sadness, but not of the other emotions studied.

Gaze Regulation of Interaction

Beyond these general functions that eyes serve in signalling communication or communication avoidance, visual behavior provides information and feedback that are central to the regulation of speech, perhaps the most important aspect of social interaction. Goffmann (1964) described the importance of mutual looking in the initiation and maintenance of speech. Nielsen (1962), in observing sound-film recordings of two-person interactions, noted that interactants primarily looked at the other when listening rather than talking. He remarked: "Each particular visual act may have a number of functions. It may be a matter of observing, orientation, inspection, a rhetorical device, an example of expressive behavior, a concealment response, an avoidance of distraction or a search for pacification" (1962, p. 158).

Following up on Nielsen's observations, Kendon (1967) systematically analyzed segments of sound film recordings of 7 two-person conversations. Because of the extensive nature of his analysis, we note his findings in some detail. First, Kendon found that there were wide individual differences in looking time among the individuals, ranging from 28 to 70% for his sample. The pattern of looking, as Nielsen noted, was greatest when listening and least when speaking. Mutual gazes in the interactions occurred only for very brief time periods (rarely for more than 1 second). Individuals who gazed at their partners for longer periods tended to have lower rates of gaze-shift. The rate of gaze-shift was modestly correlated with the person's average duration of gaze avoidance. However, Kendon's most important finding, concerning the looking behavior of the two interactants, was the very strong association between the visual behavior of the two participants. A perfect rank-order correlation was obtained between rate of gaze-shifts, and there was a correlation of .81 between participants' length of gaze. Kendon commented: "It seems as if each dyad comes to a kind of 'agreement' whereby each looks at the other for a particular length of time, on the average, though for how long at a time each looks at the other depends upon the dyad" (1967, p. 30).

In relation to visual behavior and the occurrence of speech, Kendon found that during long utterances (5 seconds or longer), speakers would look away at the beginning and often in advance of their utterance, generally looking back at the other at the end of their utterance. This latter act appeared to serve as a cue for the listener to make a response. Indeed, listener response latencies were significantly longer when the speaker did not look at them than when he did. Further analysis showed that speech rate was higher when the speaker was looking at the listener during the utterance. A phrase-by-phrase analysis suggested that this was related to fluency and speech encoding. That is, while the individual is speaking freely during the phrase, he may be looking at the listener as a check that he is following and comprehending the speaker. Then, at the end of the utterance (where there is typically a hesitation while further encoding is occurring in preparation for the next utterance), the speaker will look away. This gaze avoidance facilitates concentration and also signals to the listener that the speaker intends to continue speaking.

With respect to shorter utterances (less than 5 seconds), Kendon identified the several types that are typically interspersed between longer utterances and which are not necessarily part of a speaker's "floor-holding" conversation. First, there are *accompanying signals* that can include *attention signals* (such as the comment "mm-hmm") or *agreement signals* (e.g., "that's true"). Specifically, Kendon found that most attention signals were associated with looking while agreement signals were most associated with gaze-aversions. Looking also tended to co-occur with several other accompaniment signals, short questions, and laughter. Interactants tended to look at the other when making positive exclamatory comments whereas they tended to look away when the comments were negative. In general, comments or questions dealing with negative affect were associated with gaze-aversion. Kendon also looked at instances of mutual gazing and gaze avoidance as indicators of emotional approach or withdrawal. In an analysis of one two-person interaction, Kendon used smiling as an index of interactant emotionality and, as hypothesized, as the level of smiling increased, the time spent in mutual looking decreased.

Kendon summarized the above findings on visual behavior in social interaction by categorizing it into *monitoring, regulatory,* and *expressive* functions. Monitoring occurs when the speaker looks at the listener for cues on which to base his future behavior, such as at the end of long utterances (to see if the listener wants to speak) or at the end of phrases (to insure that he is being followed). A speaker can regulate conversation with his eyes by looking away (to maintain the floor) or by giving the listener a prolonged look at the end of his utterance to signal that a response is desired. Nielsen (1962) described this behavior as "visual rhetoric," and Weisbrod (1965) found that in a discussion group of seven persons it was the person last looked at by the speaker who was most likely to gain the floor. Finally, looking towards or away can serve an expressive function by signalling positive or negative affect, and gaze-aversion is a powerful "cutoff act" that can reduce the emotional arousal in the interpersonal situation. Indeed, as was mentioned earlier by Kendon, the length of mutual looking essentially depended upon how much only one of the participants was looking.

In their paper on nonverbal communication, Wiener, Devoe, Rubinow, and Geller (1972) identified these visual "regulators" as nonverbal behaviors that are associated with spoken language. As such, they seem to satisfy one of their requirements of code usage. Argyle, Lalljee, and Cook (1968) had one subject interview another in one of four "visibility conditions": when each wore masks and only the eyes were visible; when each had on dark glasses hiding the eyes but not the face; when a screen hid their heads but not their bodies; when they could only hear each other. Speech pauses were more frequent when the face was visible than when there was no vision; the fewest pauses were when only the bodies or eyes were visible. More interruptions occurred when vision was completely obscured; the fewest occurred when the participants could view each other's eyes. Thus, consistent with another contention of Wiener, Devoe, Rubinow, and Geller (1972), constraints placed on nonverbal communicative behavior did produce some modifications in some other speech-related behaviors.

Argyle, Lalljee, and Cook (1968) also obtained evidence concerning the monitoring functions of the eyes. In a separate experiment they imposed the same visibility limitations on only one person in the interview dyad. Analysis of several rating scales revealed that the personal discomfort of subjects, and ratings of the difficulty of communication, increased as visibility of their interaction partner was reduced. Eliminating visibility of the face appeared to produce the greatest ratings of distress. Interestingly, when both participants were treated the same, the above findings did not obtain.

These findings were congruent with the social skill model of Argyle and Kendon (1967) that an individual relies on verbal and nonverbal cues from others as feedback to modify his social behavior. Argyle, Ingham, Alkema, and McCallin (1973) repeated an earlier experiment where one person's view of another was prevented by a one-way screen. They found that the person who could see looked 67% of the time, compared to 23% for the subject without visibility. The authors concluded that looking served to obtain information in the visual channel. (Interestingly, the subject who could not see accompanied his glances with nods, smiles, and eyebrow-raises, thus showing an intent to send information.) Further, when the seeing interactant engaged in a monologue looking decreased to 49%, probably because there was no need to engage in speech synchronization with the listener as in ordinary conversation.

Several other researchers have investigated the role of eye movements in conversational management. As was noted earlier, Kendon (1967) found that speakers would look away at the beginning of their utterance and they looked at the listener upon completion of the utterance. However, Levine and Sutton-Smith (1973) found that looking occurred at both the beginning and end of utterances; interestingly, this was true for adults but not for children. Whether subjects were encoding speech (looking away) in Kendon's study and monitoring it (i.e., seeking feedback) in Levine and Sutton-Smith (1973) is unclear. Steer and Lake (1972) found that when a dyad changed tasks there was more looking at the juncture point in their activity and in that instance a monitoring or feedback function seemed to be in operation. Duncan (1972), for example, in an analysis of conversation between two individuals identified a head-turn in the direction of the listener (which probably corresponds to Kendon's shift in gaze-direction) as one of six nonverbal "turn-yielding signals." Subsequently, Duncan and Niederehe (1974) described four "speaker-state signals," one of which is a head-turn by the listener away from the speaker that occurs within speaking turns, indicating the auditor's intention to initiate speech. The amount of looking that occurs during conversation also varies as a function of listener or speaker role. Argyle and Ingham (1972) reported a nearly 2 : 1 ratio of looking while listening to looking while speaking. This appears to be a reliable finding, at least for white speakers in dyadic conversation. However, Weisbrod (1965) earlier noted the reverse relationship in a group situation where the individual members looked 70% of the time while speaking and only 47% of the time while listening.

Such a pattern may also vary for dyads of different cultural groups, the study by Mayo and LaFrance (1973) being an important example. A naive black graduate student was filmed conversing for 10-minute periods with a white corporation executive and a black institutional administrator. Using the same method of scoring employed by Kendon (1967), the authors found that, in the black-black conversational dyad, there was a complete reversal of speaker-listener eye behaviors. The black speakers both tended to look at the listener while talking whereas the listener generally looked away while attending to the speaker. During the interracial conversation, the authors noted the following:

At several . . . pauses with sustained gaze on the black speaker's part, the white began to speak and both found themselves talking at once. In the obverse situation, the white speaker directing his gaze at the black listener often did not succeed in yielding the floor by this means alone and resorted to verbal repetition and direct query.

In interaction among whites, a clear indication of attention by the listener is that he looks at the speaker; thus if the speaker gazes at the listener in order to determine how he is being received, he more often than not finds the listener looking back. Blacks do not look while listening, presumably using other cues to communicate attention. When Blacks and Whites interact, therefore, these differences may give rise to communicational breakdowns. The White may feel he is not being listened to while the Black may feel he is being unduly scrutinized. Further, exchanges of listener-speaker roles become disjunctive leading to generalized discomfort in the encounter. (Mayo and LaFrance, 1973, p. 7)

Interestingly, mutual gazes during the interracial conversation were significantly longer than for the black-black conversation, most likely due to the combination of gaze behaviors (i.e., the black looks while talking and the white while listening). Mayo and LaFrance (1973) commented eloquently on the possible implication of this finding:

We do not merely register that someone is directing a sustained gaze at us; we assign psychological dispositions on the basis of these acts. We experience the other as aggressive or intrusive. . . . Misreading of subculture communicational differences helps to sustain stereotypic interpersonal judgements and contribute to conflict in interracial encounters. (p. 8)

In a subsequent study of conversational turn-taking between black speakers, LaFrance (1974) confirmed her earlier finding that blacks look while speaking and during turn-taking, whereas they look away before and during turn-taking while listening.

In addition to regulating the beginning and ending of speech, gaze obviously serves to initiate and terminate social interaction. Kendon and Ferber (1973) filmed greetings at a social gathering (birthday party). A "distance salutation" was identified as guest and hostess first saw one another. While approaching the hostess the guest averted gaze until a second mutual gaze occurred just before the handshake or embrace. With greetings between guests, mutual gaze would not necessarily lead to social contact unless one of the guests signalled a readiness to interact, such as returning the initial mutual gaze or orienting towards the other.

Finally, we should briefly note the study by Knapp, Hart, Fredrich, and Shulman (1973), who examined the role nonverbal behaviors play in terminating a conversation (i.e., the "goodbye ritual"). Without going into the details of the study (which is reported more fully in Chapter 4), we can note that "breaking eye contact" was observed to be an important nonverbal act that reliably occurred as individuals were in the process of completing an interview. Steer and Lake (1972), however, noted that when one member of a dyad of friends was asked to go to another room, there was more mutual looking at the end of their interaction than for an unacquainted dyad.

INTERPERSONAL RELATIONS AND VISUAL BEHAVIOR

Considerable evidence has accumulated that looking behaviors are related to the nature of the interpersonal relationship, especially interpersonal attraction. With some exceptions and qualifications, the research to date shows a direct relationship between looking and positive interpersonal sentiment. A number of investigators have attempted to study looking in the context of naturally or spontaneously occurring positive relationships. Kendon and Cook (1969) had 11 subjects interact with each of 4 other subjects. Those who engaged in longer but less frequent gazes were better liked than those who interacted with short, frequent looks. Rubin (1970) developed a paper-and-pencil scale to measure "romantic love." Couples who scored high on this scale spent significantly more time looking at each other than couples scoring lower. Subsequently, White (1975) attempted to replicate Rubin's findings with a population of 45 dating and engaged college student couples. Each couple was videotaped during a 3-minute conversation and also completed Rubin's scale of romantic love as well as a measure of intimacy. No significant correlations occurred between measures of gaze and romantic love, contrary to Rubin's findings. For females only, mutual eye-gaze and mutual eye-focus (i.e., percent of total time gazing less mutual eye-gaze and separate gazing by either partner alone) were positively correlated with ratings of intimacy. White noted that in contrast to Rubin's study, subjects were aware of being videotaped and that Rubin's findings only held for those who rated themselves strongly in love.

Many studies have reported experimental manipulations to induce positive interpersonal sentiment, with looking behavior as the dependent variable. Exline and Winters (1965) exposed subjects to positive and negative evaluations with an interviewer. All subjects were initially interviewed in a neutral fashion for 5 minutes to obtain a baseline measure of looking. Then the interviewer gave the subjects either positive or negative feedback as to their perceived intelligence, following which the subjects' visual behavior in subsequent interaction was compared to their baseline measure of looking. Throughout the experiment the interviewer kept a constant gaze directed at the speaker. As expected, subjects who received the positive feedback looked more while those getting negative appraisals of their intelligence looked less. In a subsequent study, subjects were asked to choose which of the two confederates they were interacting with they liked the most. Subsequent interaction with the chosen confederate showed that they increased their liking of the chosen confederate and that this was associated with increased looking by the subjects. Specifically, males increased in looking while listening, whereas females increased in their looking while speaking to the confederate.

Breed (1970) created high-, medium-, and low-intimacy situations for subjects by varying a confederate's looking behavior and posture. The more intimate the condition, the more positively the confederate was rated. In particular, less subject looking occurred in the low-intimacy condition than in the medium- or high-intimacy conditions. Murray and McGinley (1972) manipulated perceived similarity between a subject and one of two other individuals shown in a photograph. Subjects spent more time looking at the photograph of the person depicted as similar to them, presumably as a function of their greater interest in the person. In contrast to the above studies where visual behavior was the dependent variable, Stass and Willis (1967) found that subjects were more inclined to choose the confederate for their experimental partner when he had earlier looked at them rather than when he had avoided looking at them.

In an interesting study, Griffitt, May, and Veitch (1974) presented sexually arousing or neutral slides to groups of subjects. Not surprisingly, they found that sexually aroused subjects of both sexes tended to look more at opposite-sex than same-sex confederates in a subsequent interaction session. This was true primarily for subjects who were disposed to respond positively to sexual stimulation. These individuals also tended to evaluate opposite-sex targets more favorably, suggesting that interpersonal attraction was a mediating factor between the sexual arousal and consequent looking. Efran and Broughton (1966) manipulated subjects' expectancies for social approval by having them engage in a friendly conversation with one of two confederates prior to giving a 5-minute talk about themselves. Consistent with their hypothesis, their subjects looked more at the confederate whom they previously found socially reinforcing. Subsequently, Efran (1968) replicated the study with the addition that the status of the confederate was manipulated. Freshman subjects tended to look longer at approving confederates when they thought they were seniors than when they were freshman.

Other researchers have investigated the effect of role-playing liking for others. In a study by Gatton (1970) subjects looked more at a confederate when pretending to like him as opposed to disliking him. Similarly, Mehrabian (1968a) found that male subjects engaged in more looking towards an imaginary liked than to an imaginary disliked person. Subsequently, Mehrabian (1968b) employed five degrees of liking towards a hypothetical addressee. Gaze was lowest for most disliked addressees, maximal for neutral, and slightly less for intensely liked addressees. Mehrabian interpreted these findings that gaze decreases with degree of unfamilarity and decreases with dislike. Mehrabian and Friar (1969) also found gaze to be related to communication of positive attitude. In yet another study, Mehrabian (1971) had two subjects, a confederate and a naive subject, interact as strangers in a waiting room situation. The confederate's behavior was programmed to be slightly positive or slightly negative (though looking by the confederate remained the same). Among other nonverbal behaviors by the subject, percentage duration of looking at the confederate was positively related to an affiliative behavior factor. Mehrabian and Ksionzky (1972) then had confederates react slightly positively to subjects while waiting in the same situation, and obtained the same relationship. Pellegrini, Hicks, and Gordon (1970) instructed subjects to act toward a nonspeaking confederate as if their initial impression of the confederate were positive, negative, or neutral. Subjects acting as if they had a positive initial impression engaged in more frequent and longer looking than subjects in the other two conditions. Lefebvre (1975) assigned male subjects the task of inducing a female cosubject (actually a confederate) to participate in an additional 5 minutes' discussion at the end of the experiment. During a free association task prior to the subject's planned request to the confederate to stay longer, the subjects displayed more gaze (i.e., a higher percentage and longer and more frequent gaze) at the confederate than in a control condition where no such requirement for additional discussion was present.

Despite considerable evidence in support of a "liking-looking" relationship, a number of other studies suggest that more complex relationships are also possible. Breed and Porter (1972), for example, assigned subjects to positive, negative, and no-attitude (control) role-playing conditions. All subjects interacted with an experimental accomplice who looked for 2 minutes at the subject at either the beginning or the end of the 4-minute experimental interaction. Subjects role-playing a positive attitude looked at the accomplice less often when he began the interaction with a 2-minute look than when he ended the interaction by looking. Exactly the opposite pattern obtained for negative and no-attitude subjects. All subjects' ratings of their attitude towards the accomplice increased in a positive direction for the accomplice when he looked during the last 2 minutes as opposed to the first 2 minutes. The authors argued that when the accomplice shifted from not looking to looking, this was an acceptance behavior, whereas a shift from looking to not looking implied rejection. Further, they noted:

A rejecting friend would be an object of greater concern and attention than an accepting friend. Thus, subjects in the positive role playing condition . . . looked into the accomplice's eyes more frequently when he adopted the looking pattern of rejection than did the subjects who interacted with the accomplice when he adopted the looking pattern of acceptance. An accepting enemy would . . . be an object of greater attention than a rejecting enemy. Thus, subjects in the negative role playing condition . . . looked less frequently into the accomplice's eyes when he adopted a rejecting looking pattern than did the subjects when he adopted the accepting looking pattern. (Breed and Porter, 1972, pp. 215–216)

In other research, Ellsworth and Carlsmith (1968) found an interaction between "eye contact" and favorableness of message. Subjects were interviewed by an interviewer instructed to give positive or negative messages while making eye contact or not looking (gazing at the subject's ear). When the verbal content was positive, the gazing interviewer was rated more favorably. In contrast, gazing increased subjects' negative evaluation of the interviewer when the verbal content was negative. Here the visual behavior was an independent variable, and interpersonal attraction was the dependent variable. More recently, Scherwitz and Helmreich (1973) conducted a series of experiments varying confederate "eye contact" and verbal content as independent variables in relation to interpersonal attraction. "Eye contact" was defined as amount of confederate gaze at the subject. In one study, increasing eye contact was associated with greater liking by subjects when the verbal content of the interview was negative; with positive content, liking and eye contact were inversely related. A second study showed that with impersonal positive content, liking increased with eye contact, whereas with personal positive content, low eye contact produced the most liking by subjects. Finally, the authors found in a third experiment that the variables of physical attractiveness and eye contact were positively related to measures of subject liking. This was true, however, for subjects rated low and medium but not high in social competence. It should be noted that while the results of the first study are the opposite of the Ellsworth and Carlsmith (1968) study, Scherwitz and Helmreich (1973) used televised dyadic interactions whereas the earlier findings were based on live interactions.[2]

The above studies manipulated positive and negative information related to subjects. In contrast, Paradis (1972) gave subjects positive and negative bogus feedback about their personality test performance. Subsequently, subjects disclosed their good and bad feedback experiences to a confederate who made either high or low eye contact with the subjects. Regardless of the information transmitted by subjects, they liked the confederate who looked more. Finally, Fugita (1974) induced high and low social anxiety in subjects by having them interact with pairs of either high- and low-status confederates who gave subjects approving or nonapproving feedback on their intelligence and personality. When interacting with low-status confederates, they looked equally at the approving and nonapproving ones. However, when subjects were interacting with high-status confederates, they tended to look more at the approving one by increasing the duration of their glances while keeping the frequency of glances constant. The duration of glances to nonapproving confederates stayed the same but was reduced in frequency.

Some research suggests that the nature of the interaction will also qualify the liking-looking relationship. Kleinke and Pohlen (1971) had male subjects play a Prisoner's Dilemma Game against a confederate who emitted constant gaze or no gaze and played with 100 or 90% cooperativeness or 100% competitiveness. Confederate cooperation affected ratings of liking but confederate gazing did not. More specifically, however, subjects interacting with the gazing-100% competitive and nongazing-100% cooperative confederates rated themselves as feeling friendly and cooperative, whereas subjects interacting with the gazing-100% cooperative or nongazing-100% competitive confederates experienced feelings of hostility and competitiveness. Looking may also reflect status relationships in addition to interpersonal attraction. Burroughs, Schultz, and Autrey (1973) had a confederate present high-quality or low-quality arguments in a group discussion with two naive subjects. More "leadership votes" were given to the confederate when she presented high-quality arguments and subjects looked more at her. The correlation between looking behavior and leadership votes across conditions was $r = .69$.

Finally, there are some negative findings for a liking-looking relationship. For example, McCaa (1972) found no differences in looking time by subjects interviewed by confederates trained in various degrees of warmth (reflected in looking, gesticulating, nodding, smiling, etc.). This was true even though the interviewers were clearly perceived as more or less positive. Kleinke, Staneski, and Berger (1975) increased male subjects' gaze towards a female confederate who engaged in 100%, 50%, or no gaze. This was done by "reinforcing" subjects' gaze with a green light (which subjects were told reflected a positive evaluation of their physiological response) or punishing gaze-aversion with a red light. Neither rate of subject gazing nor confederate looking behavior was related to rated liking of the confederate, though confederates who looked more were judged as being more attentive. In another study, Kleinke, Staneski, and Pipp (1972) had male-female dyads spend 15 minutes getting acquainted. The females were accomplices who emitted 90 or 10% gaze. Gazing was related to ratings of attentiveness but not male liking. Instead, males liked the females best who were most attractive and were talking at a low level. In these two studies which reported negative findings for gazing behavior and interpersonal liking, it is interesting to note that the confederates were female while the subjects were male. In addition, the above negative findings were for gaze behavior employed as an independent variable, which may have imposed artificial or unnatural limitations on confederates' behaviors. Further, it may be that looking is more a consequence of liking and a less important factor in inducing liking. This possibility is supported by a study (Carter, 1970) in which female subjects were recruited to act as interviewers of other female subjects who were actually confederates. In the interviews, confederate interviewees emitted high or low amounts of smiling. Smiling confederates' interviewees were rated more positively than those of nonsmiling confederates, but no differences in interviewer gazing were obtained. However, when a subsequent group of interviewer-subjects was additionally instructed to act friendly or impersonal, differences in interviewer gazing were noted. Carter concluded that "while smiling and verbal evaluations depended mostly upon confederate smiling behavior, gazing seemed to be primarily a function of properties of the interviewer role" (p. 4015).

Goldberg and Mettee (1969) had female subjects communicate to two female confederates hidden behind a one-way mirror. Subjects were told that they could be either seen or not seen. This situation was designed to evaluate Exline's hypothesis (Exline and Winters, 1965) that individuals who were "emotionally involved" would send glances versus Efran's contention (Efran, 1968) that interpersonal attraction motivated a person to look for signs of social approval. Prior to this, subjects had engaged in friendly interaction with one of the confederates to induce more liking towards that confederate. Following the experimental communication session, subjects answered a series of questions that provided an estimate of subjects' liking towards the confederates. Subjects who thought they could be seen engaged in more looking than subjects who thought they could not be seen, but they did not look more at the better-liked confederates. The results thus failed to support Exline's hypothesis. The authors concluded that "both the desire to communicate and the desire to obtain information may motivate looking in face to face interaction, with the latter desire the one usually responsible for the liking-looking relationship" (Goldberg and Mettee, 1969, p. 278).

Gaze and Power Relationships

Gaze may also vary as a function of power or status relationships. Exline (1972) reported on the effect of dominance on power relationships. In one study, Exline (1972) employed ROTC cadets of officer and enlisted rank as subjects. Replicating this study, Ellyson (1973), a student of Exline, had cadet officers assign rewards for performance in a discussion task, either as instructed to benefit disproportionately themselves or the low power subject, or on the basis of their own discretion. As hypothesized, the low-power subjects looked significantly more when listening than when speaking compared to high-power cadet officer subjects. The general conclusion was that lesser visual attention was indicative of a higher power relationship. Interestingly, the amount of looking by cadet officers was subsequently found to be negatively correlated with actual leadership ratings made by active duty officers during the cadets' ROTC summer camp. Those who most exhibited a superior role also looked less at the subordinate subject during the experiment.

ARGYLE–DEAN AFFILIATIVE CONFLICT THEORY

An important early study by Argyle and Dean (1965) generated considerable research concerning affiliative behavior. In their paper they postulated that "eye contact" serves the following functions: "information seeking," "signalling that the channel is open," "concealment and exhibitionism," and "establishment and recognition of social relationship" (pp. 291–292). Their affiliative conflict theory specifies that approach and avoidance forces operate to determine whether eye contact will occur. Affiliative need and desire for (positive) visual feedback are the approach forces, whereas avoidance stems from a fear of being seen, of revealing one's inner feelings, or of perceiving negative feedback. Interaction of these approach-avoidance factors can be analyzed according to Miller's approach-avoidance conflict analysis to determine the level of eye contact displayed. Other behaviors also influence the degree of intimacy experienced in an interpersonal interaction. These include physical proximity, topic intimacy, and affiliative facial behaviors such as smiling. All of these behaviors operate in an interpersonal encounter to determine an equilibrium level of intimacy. In particular, if one behavior increases to disturb the equilibrium level of intimacy, another may decrease to restore that equilibrium.

Argyle and Dean (1965) initially tested their equilibrium theory by having subjects position themselves in front of a photograph of Argyle and then Argyle himself, seated in a chair with his eyes closed or open. Subjects positioned themselves closer to the photograph, next closest to Argyle when his eyes were closed, and farthest away from him when his eyes were open. Argyle and Dean next seated subjects 2, 6, and 10 feet apart from each other with the task of jointly making up a story to a Thematic Apperception Test card. One subject was a confederate who gazed continuously at the other. As predicted, physical distance was directly related to the amount of subject gazing, increased gazing occurring at the greater distances. This effect was most magnified between opposite-sex pairs. In addition, subjects seated at 2 feet tried to lean backward to increase their distance while those seated at 10 feet tended to lean forward. Subject gazing was not eliminated in the 2-foot distance condition, but

Signs of tension were observed in all subjects, especially when facing each other directly. They tried to increase the distance—by leaning backwards—which was prevented by chairs in the main experiment. They engaged in various gestures apparently to reduce EC [eye contact] or to distract attention: looking down, shading the eyes with the hand, narrowing the eyes, scratching the head, . . . blowing the nose, etc. (Argyle and Dean, 1965, pp. 301–302)

Goldberg, Kiesler, and Collins (1969) reexamined the effect of social proximity on visual behavior by having subjects converse in a task (estimating peer's opinions on issues) "requiring very little cognitive activity" (p. 43) as compared to the story making task of Argyle and Dean (1965). Male subjects were seated 2½ or 6 feet from a male confederate and, as predicted, the former looked less at a confederate than those seated 6 feet away.

In contrast to these positive results are some equivocal findings. Baxter (1971) attempted to investigate the angle of shoulder orientation (direct vs. indirect) in relation to "eye contact" by changing seating arrangements of two subjects who were previously acquainted. Though some support was obtained in pilot data for the hypothesis that mutual gazing would increase with an indirect orientation, the results of the main experiment were inconclusive. McDowell (1972) evaluated the equilibrium hypothesis by having confederates interact for 6 minutes with subjects, at distances of 97 or 48 centimeters, the latter an uncomfortably close distance. No control over confederate looking was apparently imposed. Photographs taken at 1-minute intervals were later evaluated for "eye contact" and looking at the confederate. Females were judged to have more "eye contact" at the closer distances whereas the reverse was true for males. Looking by subjects at the confederate's face did not vary as a function of interpersonal distance. The fact that findings were based on six photographs per subject-confederate interaction raises questions of methodological adequacy, however.

A number of qualifications to equilibrium theory as originally proposed are suggested by other research. For example, the sex of interactants, social context, and kind of intimacy (i.e., varying physical distance, immediacy of verbal content, etc.) appear to be important variables. In one study on *sex differences,* body orientation and physical distance were both varied by Aiello (1972b), who also allowed confederate gaze to vary "naturally." Distances were 2, 6, and 10 feet; body orientation was 0° (directly across) or 90°. The only constraint placed upon confederates' behavior was that they talk 50% of the time. The findings were that subject looking increased linearly with physical distance for subjects when they were seated at right angles and for males seated face-to-face. However, this was true for females seated face-to-face only from 2 to 6 feet, but not 6 to 10 feet. The decrease in their looking at 10 feet was considered to be due to a sex difference in personal-space boundaries for the distance-looking equilibrium formula. In general, females looked more than males.

In an attempt to further clarify these boundaries, Aiello (1972a) varied interviewer looking (85 vs. 15%) and distance (2.5, 6.5, and 10.5 feet) while keeping observers at a constant distance from subjects. With distance as an independent variable, the dependent measure was total subject gaze (in the region of the interviewer's eyes), which was subdivided into the average length of glance, looking while listening and speaking, and the proportion of return gaze. As hypothesized, Aiello found that looking for males increased linearly with interpersonal distance, whereas for females there was the curvilinear relationship noted in his earlier study. Specifically, females looked more, showed longer glances, returned the interviewer's gaze more, and looked longer when speaking at the close and intermediate but not the far distance where males looked more. In addition, looking while listening and distance were inversely related for females. Females also returned the interviewer's gaze more at the closest distance, and looked more when the interviewer's gaze increased. These findings thus provided further support for the hypothesis that females and males have different distance "boundaries."

In addition to the above sex differences, the *composition of the dyad* (i.e., same- vs. opposite-sex) should be considered. Breed (1972) produced high, medium, and low levels of intimacy by having confederates respectively vary their body posture (forward, upright, backwards), shoulder-orientation (direct vs. a 45° angle), and "eye contact" (constant gaze, intermittent, two gazes) with the subject. Contrary to the equilibrium hypothesis, subject looking behavior increased with intimacy as did number of subject forward leans. However, male subjects interacting with female confederates did look less as intimacy increased. Though subject self-report measures indicated greater liking for the confederates as intimacy increased, Breed (1972) noted:

The attitudes expressed by the non-verbal behavior of the subjects towards the male and female confederates appear to be in contradiction to the attitudes expressed on the rating scales. . . . When interacting with the female, subjects sat more erect (fewer forward or backward leans), looked less, and faced her directly less often. (pp. 141–142)

It would thus appear that when increased intimacy produced some discomfort, compensatory changes in looking did occur as predicted. However, when intimacy increased liking (reflected in subjects' self-report measures for same-sex dyads), the predictable increase in looking occurred as well.

The social *context* may also modify the applicability of equilibrium theory. Patterson, Mullens, and Romano (1971) varied the "immediacy" of female confederates towards other male and female students seated in a library by having the confederate sit adjacent to, across from, and two and three seats adjacent. Confederates attempted to maintain a 30% glance rate at subjects. In response to these invasions, the library students exhibited an increasing number of compensatory "blocking" and body-posture movements. They also increased in their glances towards the confederate at the closer distances. This unexpected finding may have been the result of the students disliking the more intrusive (i.e., immediate) confederates, with looking reflecting the degree of dislike as shown earlier by Mehrabian (1968b).

A number of studies have also investigated changes in looking as a function of *verbal intimacy*. McDowell (1973) investigated "eye contact" and interaction distance in relation to subject speech. McDowell hypothesized that speech can reduce intimacy and a person receiving excessive eye contact could reduce intimacy by speaking more. Confederates were trained to interact with subjects at varying distances (97 vs. 48 centimeters) durations of eye contact (4 of 5 vs. 1 of 5 minutes, or "normal eye contact" for a stranger). Neither confederate distance from the subjects nor nonconfederate gazing time had an effect on subjects looking behavior, in contrast to the equilibrium theory. However, total subject speech was related to confederate looking time. McDowell interpreted this effect to be due to subjects perceiving high-gazing confederates as communicating interpersonal attraction, In turn, subjects' speech had the effect of reducing this "unnatural" intimacy, giving them more control in the situation. McDowell did not consider that looking accompanies listening behavior (Kendon, 1967), and that confederate gaze may have, in essence, been a cue to the subjects "to speak." Indeed, McDowell reported that confederate "eye contact" and speech were negatively related. Jourard and Friedman (1970), however, found that experimenter eye contact with male subjects had no effect on their self-disclosure (time spent talking), while females slightly reduced their total verbal output.

Hobson, Strongman, Bull, and Craig (1973) recently tested Argyle and Dean's Affiliative Conflict Theory by manipulating subject anxiety. This was accomplished by the use of negative verbal feedback given to one group of subjects while two other groups received positive and neutral feedback. A manipulation check revealed that the negative feedback group reported experiencing more anxiety compared to the other two groups, and they evidenced more non-ah speech errors. In addition, the authors studied a second group of subjects, high and low in Manifest Anxiety, who were interviewed by a disapproving confederate. In both experiments gaze aversion did not increase as a function of subject anxiety, contrary to what the authors predicted from the Argyle–Dean equilibrium theory.

Recognizing that the intimacy of verbal content may vary from subject to subject, Weiss and Keys (1975) allowed subjects to select their topics for discussion from a list of topics ranging in intimacy. Observers rated subjects during the discussion for "nonverbal involvement" as defined by forward-lean and amount of looking at each other. Subsequently, tape recordings of the discussion were rated by a trained experimental assistant for intimacy of self-disclosure. For the dyads which exhibited more forward leans and looking at their partner, there were more intimate self-disclosures. Rather than simply rejecting Argyle and Dean's equilibrium theory, Weiss and Keys suggested that when individuals can freely choose the content of discussion and where self-disclosures are reciprocated, then an increase in verbal intimacy may be complemented by an increase in nonverbal intimacy. When an increase in intimacy is perceived as an intrusion resulting in a disequilibrium in the interaction, compensatory nonverbal distancing may occur (e.g., less looking when interpersonal distance is decreased unilaterally).

Finally, Rohner and Aiello (1975) investigated the intimacy equilibrium hypothesis by having female subjects discuss either a magazine's intimate account of sexual fantasies or the neutral topic of television programs. A female confederate discussant was trained to interact with subjects while engaging in 70% gaze when listening and 40% when speaking. Gaze at both confederate and interaction distance was measured. Neither of the predictions of decreased gaze or increased interaction distance during topic discussion occurred; rather, subjects decreased their verbalizing and there was an increase in mutual facial regard noted. Though not the authors' explanation, what may have happened was that subjects sought to shift the burden of discussion to the confederate, by speaking less and looking at the confederate (mutual facial regard) as a turn-yielding cue. Certainly this study and others on the equilibrium hypothesis illustrate the complexity of behaviors involved in regulating the level of comfort in interpersonal communication.

Several other studies additionally attest to the potential complexity of the intimacy equilibrium hypothesis. In one study Russo (1975) examined two measures of looking behavior (percentage of time engaged in and mean length of eye contact) in relation to distance, sex, age of interactants, and friendship status. Subjects were same-sexed pairs of children from kindergarten, third, and sixth grades who interacted at 1, 3.5, and 6 feet. Observers rated "eye contact" after previous training in which they showed close agreement between their ratings and interactants' actual ratings of eye contact. The mean length of eye contact, considered to be the most sensitive measure of affiliative needs, was greater for friend than nonfriend pairs, but did not vary as a function of interpersonal distance. However, proportion of time spent in eye contact did increase with distance. Females showed more eye contact than males for both measures. Russo interpreted these findings as suggesting that factors other than intimacy may mediate the distance-looking relationship:

The data suggest that affiliative motivation is not the appropriate variable to explain the percentage of EC/distance relationship. What the appropriate explanatory variables are remain in the realm of speculation. It may be that the greater the distance between interactants, the greater the dependence on visual rather than nonvisual cues, for a variety of complex reasons. (1975, pp. 501–502)

Cranach, Frenz, and Frey (1968) instructed their subjects to seek the most comfortable distance to look at "social stimuli." They found that subjects showed a tendency to approach persons who looked at them as opposed to those who looked away. Castell (1970) also found that normal and disturbed children approached closer to looking than nonlooking adults. Cranach (1971) concluded, "These results, although contradicting those of Argyle and Dean, do not disprove their theory; we have to assume, however, their equilibrium model can be applied under special conditions only" (p. 226).

In addition to this qualifying or negative evidence, several other studies, based on methodological arguments, have brought Argyle and Dean's original finding into question. Stephenson and Rutter (1970) demonstrated that as the distance between interactants increased, observers tended erroneously to judge gaze directed at the ear and shoulder as "eye contact." Thus, judged increases in eye contact or looking with interpersonal distance could be an artifact of observer unreliability. Argyle (1970), in a rejoinder to these findings, argued that rarely "during social interaction [do] real people spend a significant proportion of the time looking at each others' ears, shoulders, or adjacent areas" (p. 395). Rather, he contended that people will look at another's eyes or will look distinctly away. Argyle and Ingham (1972) subsequently formulated a relationship between expected eye contact and distance for observer judgment error. They then obtained observer ratings of eye contact of two interactants conversing "normally" (3 feet) and at 10 feet, and at 6 and 8 feet. As interpersonal distance increased, so did individual gaze, mutual gaze, length of mutual gaze, and length of glance. According to their interpretation of observer bias, the measures of looking should have reached an asymptote rather than continuing to increase; thus, they argued the results supported the original Argyle–Dean findings. Further, the distance effect was shown at 3 and 6 feet, within a range where they argued one should not find observer judgement error. In addition, they noted that increased distance had its effect primarily on looking while listening rather than looking while talking.

Following up on these studies, Stephenson, Rutter, and Dore (1972) videotaped two interactants seated 2, 6, and 10 feet apart during a free conversation period. Use of videorecording permitted observers to rate subjects' visual behavior from split-screen monitor presentations that made each subject pair appear the same distance apart regardless of the actual experimental distance. Although neither the number nor duration of looks of the interactants was significantly affected by distance, measures of the duration of eye contact and "mutual focus" (defined as the proportion of dyad's looking which results in eye contact) did increase with distance. No differences were noted for these behaviors as a function of sex grouping as was noted by Argyle and Dean (1965) and Argyle and Ingham (1972). Stephenson, Rutter, and Dore argued that because Argyle's studies employed constant confederate gaze, his findings were based on frequency and duration measures of looking which were not significant in their study. They noted that in addition to subjects engaging in more looking as distance increased (consistent with equilibrium theory), they also spent more time in mutual focus, which they interpreted as concern that their looking be noticed by the other:

Thus the effect of distance is not simply to increase the time spent in eye-contact, but to increase the individual's concern that his Looking should be noticed by his partner. Increasingly with distance, the subject would be inclined to Look when his partner was Looking or about to Look, and not to break off a particular Look until his partner indicated a similar intention. . . . This pattern of behaviour is considerably more complex than that predicted by the Intimacy model. (Stephenson, Rutter, and Dore, 1972, p. 256)

Finally, Knight, Langmeyer, and Lundgren (1973) raised additional important methodological questions concerning equilibrium theory. That is, could the positive findings result from the fact that observers were simply overestimating eye contact at the greater distances? In one experiment observers were positioned a constant 10 feet behind a subject who interacted with a confederate who was either 2, 5, or 8 feet away. Consistent with equilibrium theory, subjects' gaze increased as the interaction distance became greater. In a second study, observer distance and subject-confederate interaction distances remained the same except that observers this time judged confederate eye contact. Despite the fact that confederate eye contact was standarized at all distances, observers judged increased eye contact at the greater interaction distances. This was true even though their distance from the confederate never varied. Apparently there exists poorly defined observer expectation of eye contact at different distances.

Despite the above methodological issues and negative or partially inconsistent evidence concerning the Argyle–Dean Theory, Patterson (1973a), in his excellent review of this topic, concluded that compensatory relationships do exist and reviewed much of the literature in support of his contention. Specifically, Patterson (1973b) reported negative relationships between "approach distance" and "eye contact" in two experiments ($r = -.52$ and $-.38$, respectively) and between "eye contact" and angle of orientation ($r = -.37$). Moreover, he noted that in several studies of immediacy behaviors (Patterson and Sechrest, 1970; Stewart and Patterson, 1973), confederates found it difficult to maintain eye contact or a direct orientation at close distances. Indeed, in the latter study involving forward-lean and eye contact in a projective test situation, "even when the interviewer was aware of the manipulation, her compensatory reactions were very difficult to modify and required many practice trials" (Patterson, 1973a, p. 245).

In summarizing, Patterson (1973a) concluded: "The clearest support for compensation appears to be in the relationships between eye contact and distance" (p. 245). However, more investigation is obviously needed to elucidate the social conditions under which this relationship may operate. Obviously, it does not when one person intrudes upon another (e.g., Patterson, Mullens, and Romano, 1971), and it may not be observed when there are increases in liking occurring in the situation which, as noted earlier, produce increases in eye contact and immediacy behaviors. The desire for more information in the visual channel may provide an alternative explanation for increased looking at greater distances. Attempts to manipulate intimacy and psychological distance through speech (i.e., self-disclosure, positive-negative feedback) have not led to support of equilibrium theory. In addition, personality variables may act as moderator variables. Fromme and Beam (1974) found that high-dominant males increased their approach distance in response to confederate gaze whereas low-dominant male subjects showed a decrease. Further, Aiello's research (1972a, 1972b) showed that sex differences were an important factor in equilibrium theory. Nonetheless, the number of studies generated by the Argyle and Dean theory attest to its heuristic value and its continuing importance in conceptualizing social relationships.

RESEARCH ON THE INTERACTIVE INFLUENCE OF VISUAL BEHAVIOR

With some exceptions, most of the research in previous sections has been on visual behavior as a dependent variable of some other psychological phenomenon such as speech, interpersonal attraction, or intimacy. It is also possible to examine how visual behavior can influence an interaction or another person's behavior by employing it as an independent variable. This was done in some of the research cited earlier. Here we consider those other studies of the "interactive influence" (Ellsworth and Ludwig, 1972) of looking behavior.

Arousal

One influence that looking may have is simply arousal, as we noted earlier (Ellsworth, 1975). McBride, King, and James (1965) discovered "a greater GSR response" in subjects looking at a person's eyes than when looking at their mouth. Nichols and Champness (1971) investigated the effect of staring on autonomic arousal. Male and female subjects were instructed to stare at a confederate who either looked to one side of the subject's head or returned his gaze. When confederates returned subjects' gaze by making eye contact there was a reliable increase in the frequency and amplitude of subjects' GSR. In a study mentioned earlier (Kleinke and Pohlen, 1971), subjects who were gazed at by the confederate had significantly higher heart rates than those not gazed at. Finally, Gale, Lucas, Nissim, and Harpham (1972) monitored subjects' "transoccipital EEGs" while they were looking at a male confederate who either smiled while returning gaze, returned gaze only, or averted his gaze. Comparison of the confederate gaze-aversion versus confederate looking and smiling conditions showed that the latter reliably altered subjects' EEGs, especially in the alpha frequency (8.5 – 11.5 Hz) and low frequency (2.0 – 4.5 Hz) range.

Though he did not obtain measures of arousal resulting from looking, Exline (1972) reported some interesting findings concerning preferences of gazes from others. He asked 500 American and British students to imagine "how comfortable they would be with another who, when speaking, listening, or sharing mutual silence, would look at the respondent 50% of the time, never, or always" (1972, p. 167). Subjects of both nationalities agreed that their greatest comfort would be with 50% looking and the least comfort with a nonlooking other. They also judged they would be most comfortable when the other was looking and someone was speaking, and least at ease when they were speaking and the other was not looking, or when both were silent and the other was looking. Subjects described a nonlooking listener as showing disinterest, whereas the silent starer was considered "queer" or deviant. However, men found silent looking the least objectionable when the person staring was female, whereas staring by an opposite-sex peer for females was less ameliorating. In Exline's words, "The impact of bedroom eyes would seem to be greater on the male of the species" (1972, p. 170). Interestingly, the most unpleasant ratings were for American females being looked at in silence by an older male of their father's generation or British females experiencing the silent attention of a woman of their mother's age.

Finally, Ellsworth, Friedman, Perlick, and Hoyt (1976) noted the importance of social context in determining the emotional impact of others' gaze. Subjects were placed in an experimental situation in which they anticipated encountering a large snake (fear arousal) or a series of embarrassing questions (embarrassment arousal). They were then joined by a confederate who was either to experience the same experimental situation or who was ostensibly not involved in the study. Confederate gaze was either 75% looking at the subject or gaze-aversion following a brief initial glance. Ellsworth, Friedman, Perlick, and Hoyt hypothesized that in the fear arousal condition subjects would be motivated to seek social comparison (i.e., feel comfortable and interact with other person) but not in the embarrassment condition. Confederate looking was thus hypothesized to a positive behavior for subjects desiring social comparison (i.e., in facilitating communication) and a negative stimulus to those expecting to be embarrassed. As predicted, subjects expecting to encounter a snake were less tense and better liked the gazing rather than nongazing confederate. In contrast, those subjects awaiting embarrassing questions (who thus were motivated to avoid social comparison) preferred the nongazing confederate. These findings were true only when the confederate was perceived as a fellow subject. The sophistication of this research and the complexity of the findings further attest to the importance of context in determining the impact of nonverbal visual behavior.

Effect of Staring

In addition to emotional arousal, eye contact, or looking may produce behavioral changes in the interaction situation. Several studies have investigated the effect of staring on individuals. Ellsworth, Carlsmith, and Henson (1972) noted:

One of the most frequently reported components of agonistic or threat displays in primates is a steady, direct gaze at the object of aggression. . . . Typically it occurs as a prelude to attack or as a substitute for it depending upon the reaction of the other animal. This reaction is usually flight, a submissive display, a return gaze, or a combination of these elements. (p. 302)

In a series of ingenious experiments, the authors studied the effect of staring in a variety of natural situations. Experimenters either stared or did not stare at people, pedestrians or drivers, stopped at a traffic light. The experimenter either stood at the street corner or was on a motorcycle; "experimental subjects" were automobile drivers or pedestrians. The dependent measure, time spent crossing the street, was significantly affected by the staring manipulation: the people stared at crossed the intersection much more rapidly. To test for the possibility that staring may have been simply one of many incongruous behaviors that might stimulate avoidance of others, in the last experiment an experimenter sat on the street corner and, without looking at drivers, idly tapped and picked at the pavement with a street hammer. This obviously incongruous behavior had no effect on drivers' crossing time: "Subjects who were stared at for less than 5 seconds drove off just as fast as those who were stared at for 18 seconds or more" (1972, p. 310). Rather, it was only the perception that one was being stared at that was necessary to elicit the full avoidance response in the situations studied: "The stare, in effect, is a demand for response, and in a situation where there is no appropriate response, tension will be evoked, and the subject will be motivated to escape the situation" (1972, p. 311).

Werner and Reis (1974) conducted two studies on the effects of staring. In one, experimenters sat on a New York subway engaging in combinations of continuous-, intermittent-, or no-stare, and smiling or not smiling. When the subway stopped, the experimenter dropped some papers, delaying for a second to allow others to help. They found that the number of stared at persons (regardless of kind of stare or smiling) who helped was much lower than the number of persons who helped when the experimenter was not staring. In a follow-up laboratory situation, the authors found that subjects complied with an experimental confederate's request to help work on a task (following completion of the experiment) much less often when the confederate had earlier stared at them. Werner and Reis (1974) concluded that there is a strong social norm against staring, violation of which produces significant intra- and interpersonal consequences for behavior.

Gaze and its Influence on Others' Behaviors

Davey and Taylor (1968) assessed the influence of "eye contact" on conformity behavior using an Asch conformity situation. It was hypothesized that the gazes of others would increase the pressure to conform. Although subjects did conform in the experimental condition, it made no difference whether or not confederates were looking. However, subjects in both groups reported that they felt observed. It thus appeared that other factors rather than eye contact were influential in determining subjects' behavior.

Ellsworth, Carlsmith, and Henson (1972; see p. 204) considered that their staring manipulation was salient, arousing, and also involving, in that it called for an interpersonal response that was not available to the recipients of the stare. Because of this, the situation was even more uncomfortable for the subjects who thus showed strong flight responses. Ellsworth (1975) emphasized, however, that while gazes are arousing, the social context is important for labeling the subject's arousal. That is, depending on the cues available for labeling arousal, eye contact can produce avoidance or arousal. Ellsworth and Langer (1976) tested this notion by creating different distress situations calling for intervention by a bystander. Ambiguity of the situation was varied by having a confederate advise the subjects that a girl behind the subject needed help finding a contact lens (no ambiguity), or that the girl simply looked ill and needed help (high ambiguity). Upon looking around subjects saw a female confederate leaning over, either looking at the subject or at the ground. It was predicted that when subjects received a clear message concerning the distressed person's needs, eye contact would stimulate an approach (assistance) response, whereas an ambiguous message combined with eye contact would make subjects uncomfortable, leading to avoidance. These predictions were borne out in the experiment, supporting Ellsworth's contention that "staring is not necessarily perceived as a threatening signal, and does not automatically elicit flight" (1975, p. 18).

Kleinke and Singer (1976) also examined the effect gaze would have in different situations of interpersonal influence. Two female and two male experimenters handed out leaflets with a demanding ("Take one") or a conciliatory ("Excuse me. Would you like one?") tone, or no verbalization. Experimenter gaze was either continuous at the passersby (subjects) as the request was made, or it was directed at the street. Gaze increased subjects' taking the leaflets, especially when the experimenter was a male. With gaze, the tone of request (demanding, conciliatory, or silent) had no effect. An absence of experimenter gaze led to less compliance when the experimenter was also silent.

Ellsworth and Carlsmith (1973) also studied the effect of gaze-aversion as an appeasement gesture in influencing aggressive behavior from an angered subject. In this study, confederates first motivated the subjects to friendliness or dislike by acting friendly or hostile towards the subject. Subsequently, subjects were given the opportunity to administer shocks to the confederate during a series of trials. During this time, confederates responded with eye contact, gaze-aversion, or a random sequence of eye contact and gaze-aversion. Contrary to expectations, angered subjects gave fewer shocks to confederates who consistently gazed at them than to subjects who consistently averted their gaze. Ellsworth and Carlsmith speculated that confederate gaze, which occurred just after subjects signalled a shock trial, was, in effect, "punishing" the subjects with their gaze and thus "conditioning'" them to giving fewer shocks (thereby avoiding the confederate gaze). However, when confederate gazes were alternated with gaze-aversion during random response sequence, subjects gave more shock when the confederate gazed than when he looked away. In this situation subjects presumably could punish the aversive confederate gazes with shock and reward gaze-aversion by not shocking. Debriefing of subjects confirmed the impression that confederate gaze was aversive. Thus, rather than gaze-aversion acting as an appeasement gesture, what motivated subjects' behavior was the aversive quality of confederate gaze. In this instance, it was the timing of the visual behavior rather than the social context that provided the interactive influence.

A number of studies have also shown that interviewer gaze can have an effect on subjects' verbal behavior. In one of his studies on self-disclosure, Jourard varied "distance" by having an interviewer present with constant gaze or by having the interviewer physically vacate the room (Jourard and Friedman, 1970). Consistent with their interpretation of equilibrium theory, female subjects decreased their self-disclosure with decreasing interpersonal distance when the male interviewer was present. Snow (1972, cited in Argyle and Cook, 1976) reported that increased interviewer gaze when asking questions resulted in interview subjects making more self-references. Argyle and Cook (1976) speculated: "This may be due to looking acting as a kind of printing combined with emphasis" (p. 120). In a more complicated study, Sodikoff, Firestone, and Kaplan (1974) employed constant gazing or gaze-averting interviewers who also varied their own self-disclosure. Although gaze-aversion had the effect of reducing subjects' own looking behavior and postural immediacy (as well as their liking of the interviewer), they nevertheless became increasingly more talkative, giving longer replies to questions as the interview progressed. In contrast to these findings, Ellsworth and Ross (1976) observed that either continuous or contingent interviewer eye contact was associated with more intimate interviewee speech. In this study, gaze had a reinforcing effect. In an interesting study, Bates (1975) trained children to interact with students serving as their teachers and either gaze at the teachers' face 75% of the time (with frequent smiles) or 25% of the time (and no smiles). Though the child confederate's nonverbal behaviors (eye and face cues) cannot be separated, it is reasonable to assume that the child's visual behavior was an influential cue. As predicted, the student teachers responded to the more positive child confederate behaviors by increasing their face-gaze, positive verbal expressions, and word rate. In addition, the teacher subjects' tone of voice and their rating of the more positive child's intellectual and social abilities were more positive. This study nicely complements the research on teacher expectations of students, demonstrating that students' nonverbal behavior is a very influential factor in the student-teacher relationship.

In summary, the results of the studies in which gaze and arousal were studied, or which involved looking behavior as an independent variable and subject behavior as the dependent measure, indicate clearly that complex situational and mediating cognitive factors are involved. At present, much more research is thus required before the "meaning" of any visual behavior can be accurately specified. Whatever the factors determining the influence of gaze behavior on individuals, we should note, as Ellsworth and Ludwig pointed out, that the arousal produced by gaze

Is probably not so general as to be easily attributed to *any* stimulus that happens to be present. . . . We believe that an interpersonal cause will be sought. While interpersonal attraction is not implied, interpersonal *involvement* is, and the subjects' interpretation of the arousal will almost always be focused on his relationship with the other person. (1972, p. 397)

RESEARCH ON INTERPERSONAL ATTRIBUTIONS FROM VISUAL BEHAVIOR

Ellsworth and Ludwig (1972) described the general purpose of the research we consider in this section as follows:

In studying visual behavior as a source of attribution, we are asking what the visual behavior tells the receiver (as opposed to the more general influence question: "how does the visual behavior affect the receiver?"). A person may attribute stable characteristics, or more transient moods, reactions, or attitudes to the other person on the basis of his visual behavior. He will rarely hold the other person accountable for information received in this manner, however, and he will usually assume that the other person did not deliberately intend to convey this type of information. (p. 390)

The Effect of Being Observed

One of the most common situations in which attributions occur is obviously when someone is looking at us. Surprisingly, little research has been conducted upon subjects in the role of observer or observed. Argyle and Williams (1969) examined the influence of subjects actually being in the role of the observer or the observed. In a series of experiments, subjects acted as interviewers or interviewees, both in lightened or darkened position; subjects reported their feelings of comfort in interacting with same-aged or older persons of both sexes; subjects were looked at by a confederate either 20% or 80%, or 10% or 90% of the time. They found that subjects (females more so than males) felt more observed when acting as an interviewee than as an interviewer. Subjects also felt more observed in opposite-sex encounters, especially females. The amount that confederates actually looked was not related to subjects' postexperimental ratings of feeling observed, whereas subjects' own looking behavior was inversely related to their feelings of being observed. Interestingly, the more a subject felt observed, the more the other felt he was the observer (perhaps a consequence of the former's looking behavior). The authors concluded from the latter finding that feeling observed must be due to a cognitive set held by an individual and not based upon a realistic assessment of the social situation. In reviewing this study, Ellsworth and Ludwig (1972) theorized that:

A person who feels himself an observer will interpret the other's visual behavior and other nonverbal cues as indicators of the other's stable dispositions or internally-motivated moods, while a person who feels himself observed will interpret the same cues as reactions to himself and as influences on his own behavior. (p. 392)

Some evidence pertaining to this attribution theory (based upon Jones and Nesbett, 1971) is provided in a study by Ellsworth and Ross (1976). The experiment included a speaker who was to discuss intimate personal material with a listener who, in turn, responded with low or high degrees of eye contact. An observer monitored the interaction without sound from behind a one-way mirror. When the interactants and observer were female everyone agreed in their rating that the high eye contact from the listener made the situation more intimate. However, when the three subjects were males both the listener and observer felt high eye contact made the situation less intimate, whereas the male speaker rated high eye contact as being more intimate. In sum, the speaker's ratings were consistent with the notion that their judgments about intimacy would depend upon the response of the listener to them. Thus when the listener responded with high eye contact, speakers judged the situation as more intimate.

Gaze as a Cue of Interpersonal Attraction

Many studies on interpersonal attribution have focused upon interpersonal attraction as a variable. Looking by another is generally a signal of attraction or interest. For example, Kleck and Rubenstein (1975) varied the attractiveness of female confederates by changing their hairstyle and make up and found, not surprisingly, that male subjects increased their gaze at attractive females. Coutts and Schneider (1975) had hidden observers rate the attractiveness of two subjects in a nonconversational waiting room situation and found that both females and males glanced more at attractive opposite-sex persons. Wiener and Mehrabian (1968) reported that when an interviewer spent more time looking at one of two interviewees, the subject looked at more judged the interviewer as more positive toward her than toward the other interviewee. Similarly, subjects in a study by Kendon (unpublished data, cited in Argyle and Kendon, 1967, p. 74) rated an interviewer who looked away from them during part of an interview as having lost interest in what they were saying. When opposite-sex encounters occur, however, the meanings of gaze may be modified. More recently, Kleinke, Bustos, Meeker, and Staneski (1973) gave subjects, who had engaged in a 10-minute dyadic interaction, *false feedback* concerning the amount they had gazed at their partner (i.e., either high, average, or low gazing) and the amount their partner had gazed at them. Following administration of the false feedback, subjects rated their conversational partners. Significant sex differences emerged: males rated females as being more attractive when told they had given them low levels of gaze, whereas females rated their male partners as being most attractive when told they gazed at a high level. When given false information about their partner's gazing behavior, males rated low-gazing females as least attractive whereas females rated high-gazing males as least attractive. Both males and females rated low-gazing partners as least attentive and sincere. In addition to providing some support for the notion that our perceptions of our behavior influence our attitudes, the complementary nature of the findings for males and females suggests that there are strong and commonly shared norms for gazing behavior (in communicating interpersonal attraction) that exist between the sexes.

Gaze and Judged Interpersonal Effectiveness

Most impression formation studies based on visual behavior have used observer judges rating interpersonal behavior or interactions of others. In such studies, increased gaze leads to stronger impressions of interpersonal influence and communication effectiveness. LeCompte and Rosenfeld (1971) found that observers who viewed videotapes of a speaker rated the speaker as less nervous and less formal when the speaker glanced at the observers than when he did not look up at all. Kleck and Nuessle (1968) had observer subjects rate filmed interviewers of a male confederate who either gazed at a male interviewer 80% or 15% of the time. Observer subjects were asked to give their impression of the interviewee and to estimate his reaction to the interview. In asking those two questions the authors stated they hoped to obtain information concerning both the "indicative" and "communicative" meanings of high and low gazing by the interviewee. As predicted, judges rated the speaker more attractive and less tense in the high-gaze condition. However, contrary to the authors' predictions, sex of judge had no effect (not surprisingly considering that two males were interacting). Analysis of adjective checklist items filled out by the judges revealed that high eye contact was rated more positively (i.e., friendly, self-confident, natural, mature, sincere) than low eye contact (rated significantly more often as cold, defensive, submissive, cautious, pessimistic, immature, indifferent, and sensitive). Female raters tended to see high eye contact as more potent, and were more accurate in judging the percent of gazing time of the interviewee in the two film conditions than were males.

Beebe (1974) found that as gaze towards an audience increased, a speaker was viewed as more skilled, informed, and experienced, and also more honest, friendly, and kind. LaCrosse (1975) trained confederates to role-play counselors and engage in "affiliative" and "nonaffiliative" behaviors, which included 80% and 40% eye contact, respectively. As predicted, subjects viewing videotapes of the confederate-counselors rated those displaying affiliative behavior as more attractive and persuasive, citing frequency of eye contact as a primary cue for affiliativeness. Hemsley and Doob (1976) studied the effect of gaze-aversion on credibility of courtroom testimony. Observer subjects viewed videotapes (with sound) of purported trial testimony in which the witness (an experimental confederate) was shown either looking directly towards his interrogator or slightly downward while testifying. Other subjects listened to audiotapes of the testimony. When gaze aversion during testimony was available as a cue, the confederate witness was judged less credible and the defendant more likely to be guilty. Interestingly, a postexperimental questionnaire revealed that observers were significantly more aware of the nonlooking witnesses' looking behavior than the witness who looked at his interrogator. This latter finding points to the importance of the social context in which looking or nonlooking occurs in determining the salience of gaze behavior.

The above studies used noninteracting observers rather than participant raters. In the experiment by Kleinke, Staneski, and Berger (1975) female interviewers gazed constantly, intermittently, or not at all towards male subject interviewees. The nongazing interviewers were rated by interviewees as least attentive. They received the shortest answers and were kept at a greater social distance by interviewees during a subsequent debriefing session. Interviewer attractiveness did not affect the dependent measures (interviewee ratings and behavior) except that nongazing–low-attractive interviewers were rated far less attentive than all other interviewers. Interestingly, interviewer gaze was not related to ratings of attractiveness, and changes in interviewee gaze (which was reinforced during the interview) had no effect on subjects' ratings of the interviewer. That actual participation in the experience may be important in making some judgments is suggested by findings reported by Holstein, Goldstein, and Bem (1971). Subjects who interviewed and then rated expressive (e.g., smiling, eye contact, gestures, etc.) or unexpressive interviewees showed more liking for the expressive interviewees, whereas observer subjects did not. Involvement in the interaction may be important for some attributions, in this case ratings of interviewee "likeability." Wiemann (1974) had subjects interview four confederates who gazed at them 100, 75, 25, or 0% of the time. As hypothesized, as confederate gaze towards the subjects decreased, they were rated as less friendly. Hypotheses that subjects would rate confederates as being less dominant, more potent, and less confident (as a function of decreasing gaze) were not supported.

A perhaps implicit assumption of most impression formation studies is that differences in gaze are "perceived" by observers who make the ratings.

A recent study suggests that this assumption cannot be automatically made. Cook and Smith (1975) employed confederates of both sexes engaging in a "normal" gaze pattern (not defined), continuous gaze, and averted-gaze pattern when interacting with male and female subjects. Semantic differential ratings were obtained from subjects as well as free descriptions. Female confederates were rated less favorably than males when both engaged in continuous gaze and more favorable than males in the averted-gaze condition. The amount of gaze itself did not significantly influence subjects' impressions of confederates but, interestingly, less than half of the subjects made any mention about subject gaze in their free descriptions. Of those who did mention gaze, subject ratings of confederate potency increased with confederate gaze; and confederates averting gaze were rated less liked, less potent, and less easy to interact with than normal gazing confederates. The free descriptions revealed that confederates who averted gaze were seen as less confident and more fearful and that there was a general linear relationship between amount of confederate gaze and their being perceived as pleasant. Despite the general findings that increased gaze is regarded more positively, Cook and Smith noted that the "amount of gaze does not have such a strong effect on impressions as we had been led to suppose, by popular stereotypes and by previous research" (1975, p. 23).

Gaze as a Cue to the Relationship

In addition to being an important basis for attributions of individuals, visual behavior also can provide important cues for making inferences about the *relationship* among individuals. Lim (1972) investigated whether subjects could infer social relationships from "photographically presented variations in eye contact and direction of gaze" (p. 152). Interpersonal distance and crowding were also varied. As predicted, observer-subjects showed significant agreement in their judgements as to the nature of the relationship. Scherer and Schiff (1973) reported that ratings of intimacy based on photographs were directly related to ratings of eye contact, and inversely related to physical distance.

Kleinke, Meeker, and Fong (1974) made videotapes of actors role playing as engaged couples being interviewed by a psychologist. Different videotapes showed the couples gazing at each other or not gazing, using each other's name or not using it at all, touching and not touching. Students viewing the videotapes rated the gazing couples most positively, this cue being more important than the others in facilitating judgments of interpersonal attraction. Thayer and Schiff (1974) filmed "actors" sitting at a desk reading during which time various combinations of gazing between the two were shown (unreciprocated versus reciprocated gaze; long versus short duration). Observer judgments as to the length of the relationship were generally related to the length of single gazes or the presence of reciprocated gazes (mutual looking). Sex was an important variable in that female actor pairs were generally judged to have the shortest relationship, and variations in their looking were unrelated to relationship judgments. Prolonged onesided looks by a female to a male suggested a long relationship, whereas the same behavior by a male to another male was apparently indicative of a brief relationship. Female judges tended to judge longer relationship durations regardless of cues, but were especially sensitive to duration of looking in male-female dyads. The authors concluded, "Females may read more affection and inclusion into social relationships than do males and may weight eye-contact cues of duration and reciprocity as stronger indicators of a more positive, extensive relationship" (Thayer and Schiff, 1974, p. 114).

In an interesting study Hillabrant (1974) varied the physical movement of one interactant towards another as well as the gaze-direction. Videotapes were made of one individual (A) either standing or moving toward another, with high- or low-gaze (156 vs. 44 seconds). The other individual (B) was always shown standing and always gazing for 44 seconds at the other. When A was looking at B for 156 seconds (compared to 44 seconds for B), A was judged as more dominant and attractive and B as slightly unattractive. Movement by A toward B was not related to dominance but the findings for the attractiveness ratings only occurred when the interactants were stationary. Because the judges had not participated in the interaction, Hillabrant argued this eliminated the influence of gaze as an "ingratiating tactic" including reciprocal liking in the gaze recipient. Possibly being perceived as dominant (a valued attribute) produced the ratings of attractiveness.

Other Findings

Several other studies have reported findings relating gaze to perceived power or dominance. Weisbrod (1965, cited in Kendon, 1967) found that the more a person was looked at by other group members, the more he felt valued and the greater his own and others' ratings of his power. Exline and Kendon (unpublished data, cited in Argyle and Kendon, 1967, p. 74) reported that a listener who does not look at a speaker tended to be perceived as more potent than a visually attentive listener. Thayer (1969) had subjects interact with a confederate in a 3-minute nonverbal interaction described as an "impression formation" task. In one condition, confederates looked at the subject for three continuous 58-second intervals separated by three 2-second glances away. In the other condition, the sequence of looking was reversed. The confederate giving 58-second looks was judged more dominant than when he gave 2-second looks. Interestingly, analysis of subjects' own looking time and frequency of looks in the two conditions showed no significant differences.

Finally, there are a few other studies we may note in which yet additional attributions have been made about subjects' visual behavior. Exline and Eldridge (1967) evaluated the influence of eye contact with an addressee on the authenticity of a spoken message. A confederate was trained to interact with subjects, giving them his generally positive impressions of them. One message was given with the confederate looking directly at the subject; for the other, the confederate averted his gaze. As predicted, subjects rated the message accompanied by direct gaze as more favorable. When the confederate made eye contact for the second message (after averting his gaze for the first message) he was judged by subjects as being more confident in the accuracy of his impression. Haase and Tepper (1972) showed experienced counselors videotape segments of "client-counselor" interactions in which various nonverbal cues were present or absent. Observers then made ratings of empathy of the videotaped "counselor." The nonverbal behaviors accounted for twice the variability in judged empathy as compared to the verbal messages. In particular, there was a significant main effect for eye contact which was the most important nonverbal cue, contributing independently to the empathy judgments.

The last study we will report is especially interesting because of its social implications. Baxter and Rozelle (1975) investigated the effects that crowding by a policeman might have on an individual's nonverbal expressiveness. A confederate was trained to role-play a police officer and interview subjects much as a real policeman might do (by asking general identification questions and then questions about the contents of the subject's wallet). The following interpersonal distances were employed by the "policeman" during the experimental interview (in order of occurrence): 4 feet, 2 feet, 8 inches, and a return to 2 feet. A "control" interview utilized 4-foot and then 2-foot distances. The frequency of gaze aversion increased dramatically during the "severe crowding" situation (8 inches) in comparison to the control distances (4 feet and 2 feet). The significance of this finding may be seen from the following excerpts from Baxter and Rozelle where they described the results of interviews with actual policemen concerning the nonverbal cues they considered important in their work:

The police officers interviewed tended to emphasize the importance of gaze aversion in gauging the other person's intention to try to withhold or misrepresent information (i.e., to deceive), presumably out of a sense of guilt. While such implications of gaze aversion may be valid, it is also possible that the interview process itself, which often includes close spatial interaction, may lead to heightened gaze aversion. (unpublished manuscript, 1975, p. 2)

It requires little imagination to speculate on the effect that an aggressive, dominant officer's own behavior might have in erroneously raising or even confirming some suspicions about a person's guilt or honesty.

INDIVIDUAL DIFFERENCES IN VISUAL BEHAVIOR

Having considered the many ways visual behavior is important in social interaction and the meanings we attribute to gazes by others, it is not surprising that researchers have attempted to identify individual differences. As we mentioned earlier, Kendon (1967) noted that different individuals' gaze during dyadic conversation varied from 28 to 70% of the time. Nielsen (1962) reported variations in looking ranging from 8 to 73% for stressful interviews. Despite this remarkable variation, Kendon and Cook (1969) reported that frequency and duration of gazes while listening and speaking were somewhat stable characteristics of individuals across conversational situations. To provide greater control over the observation of individual visual behavior, Libby (1970) had subjects respond to 54 questions with instructions to look at the interviewer when he was asking the question. Observers rated the following ocular responses of subjects when they were answering questions: maintaining eye contact, breaking eye contact, vertical and horizontal gaze-aversion. Observers showed high reliability in scoring the responses. More important, subjects showed consistency in their eye movements over time (the course of the interview) despite wide individual differences. On the average, subjects maintained their gaze in answering a question for only 15.5% of the time and tended to look up rather than down and to the left rather than the right. Daniell and Lewis (1972) observed subjects for "eye contact" when being interviewed by the same or a different interviewer on three occasions over a 3-week period of time. Subjects' eye contact was remarkably stable over time and across interviews, correlations ranging from .81 to .96. Patterson (1973b) observed "eye contact" of subjects across two interviews 25 minutes apart and after a 1-week interval and also found good stability of measures among subjects.

Cultural Differences

Earlier we noted racial differences in synchronization of speech. Most recently, LaFrance and Mayo (1976) extended their observations to natural settings. Trained raters observed gaze behavior of blacks, whites, mixed race, and mixed-sex combinations conversing at college cafeterias, hospitals, airports, and the like. Only dyads that were uninterrupted and were distinctly involved with each other were coded for looking while listening during three 60-second observations. As expected, all-black looked less than all-white dyads while listening, expecially black male pairs. However, male-female black pairs did not look significantly less than male-female white pairs. Female black pairs looked less than female white pairs but not less than white male pairs or white male-female pairs. Male-female interactions in both races thus had a modifying effect on same sex conversational behavior.

Watson (1970) has performed the most extensive study to date of cultural differences in gaze. Subject dyads consisting of foreign students were observed conversing in their native language. A coding system for gaze behavior showed that Arabs, Latin Americans, and Southern Europeans focused their gaze on the eyes or face of their conversational partner. In contrast, Asians, Indian-Pakistanis, and Northern Europeans tended to show "peripheral gaze" (orienting towards the other without looking directly at the face/eyes) or no gaze at all (i.e., they would look down or stare into space). Interestingly, there was no relationship between gaze behavior and time spent overseas, suggesting that gaze patterns are unlikely to change with environmental-social influences.

Sex Differences

"In research on visual behavior, sex differences are the rule rather than the exception" (Ellsworth and Ludwig, 1972, p. 379). Throughout the literature on visual behavior, sex differences have been observed. One common finding is that women have been observed to engage in more overall looking (Aiello, 1972a; Exline, Gray, and Schuette, 1965; Exline, Thibaut, Brannan, and Gumpert, 1966; Exline and Winters, 1965; Levine, 1972; Levy, 1973; Nevill, 1974; Rubin, 1970; Russo, 1975), more looking while listening (observed in Exline and Winters, 1965; but not in Exline, Gray, and Schuette, 1965 or Levine, 1972), and more looking while speaking (e.g., Exline, Gray, and Schuette, 1965; Exline, Thibaut, Brannan, and Gumpert, 1966; Levine, 1972; Libby, 1970; Libby and Yaklevich, 1973). In their study on equilibrium theory, Argyle and Dean (1965) observed trends similar to those noted above. Kendon and Cook (1969) also found a trend for women to look more and to be looked at more. Libby and Yaklevitch (1973) observed that their main sex difference was primarily due to greater mutual gaze among female-female pairs. In contrast, Christenson (1973) found no sex differences in looking between males and females when relating happy, sad, and angry experiences. In the study by Patterson (1973b), while a tendency was noted for greater "eye contact" in same sex pairs, no overall sex differences in looking behaviors were found. Argyle and Ingham (1972), however, reported that male-female pairs showed less "eye contact" than all male-male and all female dyads, females tending to show a slightly greater inhibition than males. Possibly the observation that females seem to use shifts in looking when talking as signals of liking whereas males use looking when listening, may have some bearing on this finding (Exline and Winters, 1965).

It is important to note that these apparent sex differences also appear to be generally consistent across age. Kagan and Lewis (1965) have noted that female infants attend to faces more at 6 months than male infants, leading to speculation that it may be an innate sex-related characteristic. Ashear and Snortum (1971) observed 90 children from 4 to 14 talking to a continuously gazing adult female interviewer and found that eye contact decreased with age. Levine and Sutton-Smith (1973) recorded gaze during dyadic conversation of males and females in four age groups: 4–6, 7–9, 10–12, and adult. Subjects interacted with a same-sex partner within one year of their age. Total subject gazing during conversation increased over the age range 4–9, decreased during the years 10–12, and reached a maximum for adult subjects. For mutual gaze and gaze while speaking, females looked more than males. It was felt that the decrement in looking for the 10–12-year-olds might have been due to subject self-consciousness, although "no single factor . . . seemed to account for all the age changes in gazing" (1973, p. 404).

More recently, Kleinke, Desautels, and Knapp (1976) varied the gaze of an adult towards 3- to 5-year-old children during a word game. As the children were describing a vocabulary word, the experimenter engaged in either 80% or 20% gaze at the children. As predicted, female children looked more at the experimenter than males and both gazed more at the high gazing experimenter. Interestingly, male children indicated greater liking for the low-gazing experimenter in contrast to the females, who liked the high-gazing one better. This latter finding parallels the findings obtained by Kleinke, Bustos, Meeker, and Staneski (1973) for adults. It was speculated that the girls may have interpreted high-gaze as an indication of adult approval whereas the boys may have regarded it as surveillance by an adult looking for them to do something wrong.

Thus while there is general support for sex differences with the bulk of the evidence being that females look more than men, there are some conflicting findings that require some consideration. Although Kendon and Cook placed no restraints on interactants' gaze and Exline used constant gaze for confederates, this methodological difference cannot alone account for the weaker findings of Kendon and Cook (1969). Libby and Yaklevich (1973), who obtained similar results, also employed an interviewer who gazed steadily at subjects during their response to questions. The best explanation suggested at this point by our literature review is that the sex differences in looking are probably due to the different influence need-affiliation or liking variables have on the sexes. In the study by Exline (1963), need-affiliation interacted with sex such that high need-affiliation females engaged in, by far, the greatest looking when the situation was noncompetitive and conducive for liking. Exline, Gray, and Schuette (1965) also noted that females were more affection and inclusion oriented. And while Gray (1971) reported that need-affiliation was not related to looking behavior of males or females, Levine (1972) (who also found sex differences in looking) did find liking and gaze positively correlated. Exline (1963) has suggested that because women are more sensitive to the "social field" they may be more sensitive to changes in social situations and may rely more on visual activity in obtaining information about the social situation they are in.

Recently, Coutts and Schneider (1975) pointed out that most research on visual behavior has involved "focused interaction" of two or more individuals, i.e., during conversation or participation in a task. In contrast, male and female subjects for their study were observed in a waiting room situation at two seating distances (two and seven feet) where talk was prohibited and thus the "interaction" was "unfocused." Contrary to the findings on focused interactions, females did not look more in general although female dyads engaged in the most glancing. Females did tend to attract more glances than males. The amount of mutual gaze was approximately 1% of the 3 minutes' time that subjects were together and not above chance as would be predicted by the Strongman–Champness (1968) formula (see p. 180). More individual gaze and mutual gaze did occur at the longer interaction distance.

A further way the sexes may differ in terms of visual behaviors is the feeling of being observed. Argyle, Lalljee, and Cook (1968) and Argyle and Williams (1969) both found that females were less comfortable than males when not able to see their conversational partner. Unlike males, females preferred to see their partners even when they could not be seen. Ellsworth and Ludwig (1972) concluded:

If females feel more observed than males, they may rely more on visual feedback; without such feedback they may feel unable to adjust their social performances in response to their audiences. In general, . . . in a neutral or positive interaction at a given level of intimacy, females engage in more eye contact and possibly depend more on visual feedback than do males. (p. 380)

Personality Differences

We have already noted that affiliative needs are an important variable that interacts with subject sex. With respect to individual differences in affiliative needs, however, the findings are rather inconclusive. Exline (1963) found that subjects high in need-affiliation looked at a steadily gazing confederate more; this was especially true for females (who looked more while speaking, whereas males looked more while listening). In addition, this effect reversed when the situation changed from friendly interaction to competitive interaction, where low need-affiliation subjects increased their eye contact. Exline, Gray, and Schuette (1965) employed Schutz's FIRO-B test and found that subjects high on the inclusion and affection scales looked more at an interviewer giving steady gaze. However, Kendon and Cook (1969), who observed freely interacting individuals, found no more significant correlations between the FIRO-B scales and looking behavior than could be expected by chance. Similarly, Gray (1971) found no relationship between FIRO-B measure of affiliation orientation and gaze directed towards an interviewer. Efran and Broughton (1966) measured need for social approval by the Marlowe–Crowne Social Desirability scale and found it related to looking, but Efran (1968) subsequently was unable to replicate this finding.

One of the major individual difference variables studied has been *dominance,* a key variable in animal social behavior. Strongman and Champness (1968) had 10 subjects interact with each other in all possible dyadic combinations. The individual in each pair who most often was the first to break eye contact was defined as the less dominant individual in the pair. As the authors hypothesized, a reasonably consistent dominance hierarchy could be specified from the many different interactions. In a study examining visual behavior of subjects aged 4 to adulthood, Levine (1972) reported finding a positive relationship between descriptive measures of dominance and total gazing. In contrast to these positive findings, Patterson (1973b) did not find dominance of subjects related to their visual behavior during an interview. Kendon and Cook (1969) found a negative correlation between "dominance given" and frequency of gaze, but this was suspected to be a chance finding. Argyle and Williams (1969) reported that dominant males (based on the "control wanted" scores of the FIRO-B scale) felt less observed than females or dependent males when interacting with same sex-interactants younger than they, and that dependent and insecure males reported feeling more observed with females than males, especially with same-aged females. However, in a college student population, dominant subjects reported feeling more observed by male and female peers. These findings are thus not completely consistent with Argyle's social skill model (Argyle, 1969) which posited that dominant subjects would tend to take the role of observer and engage in more eye contact with others.

Several studies by Exline suggest that subject dominance can interact with situational factors, especially the perceived power or influence of the other interactant. Exline and Messick (1967) employed a steadily gazing confederate who varied his reinforcement (e.g., smiles, head nods, affirmative comments) for subject eye contact at a high or low rate. Subjects were differentiated on the FIRO-B scale as being dominant (wanting control) or dependent (wanting to be controlled). Under conditions of low social reinforcement, dependent subjects increased their looking from 38% (high reinforcement) to 55%, whereas dominant subjects decreased in their looking time (43%, high reinforcement, to 33%, low reinforcement). These data failed to support a reinforcement model but were consistent with an information seeking interpretation that dependent subjects would seek more information from another under conditions of low social reinforcement.[3] Later, Exline (1972) reported a study in which subjects, high or low in "control wanted" (FIRO-B scale), interacted with a confederate who gazed 50% of the time at the subject when speaking and either 100 or 0% (no gaze) when listening. While there was a tendency for dominant subjects to look more at the confederates while speaking and listening, the differences were not significant. Instead, a more complicated set of findings emerged. When listening, dominant subjects were not particularly affected by gaze differences in confederates, whereas the low-dominant subjects looked more often at the inattentive confederate.[4] However, when speaking, the dominant subjects looked much less at the inattentive than the attentive confederate whereas the opposite was the case with the low-dominant subjects. In particular, dominant subjects rated the less attentive confederate as more potent. Exline concluded that "powerful people do not monitor less powerful people" (i.e., the 100% gaze-attentive confederate); but that "dominant men seem more impressed with the personal force of one who listens without looking and also seems more reluctant to look at those whom they perceive to be forceful" (i.e., the 0% gaze-inattentive confederate) (Exline, 1972, p. 192).

Subsequently, Ellyson (1974) selected subjects who were high and low in their desired control over others as measured by the FIRO-B scale (while being the same on control wanted from others). Using essentially the same method as described above in Exline (1972), Ellyson found that high-control subjects looked less while listening than low-control subjects by an average of 38 to 56% of the time when the other person was speaking. A *visual dominance behavior* index was proposed; this index is based on the ratio of looking while listening to looking while speaking, the lower ratio indicating the greater dominance. Based on this index, low-control subjects showed a ratio of 1.51 to .89 for high control subjects. Herb and Elliott (1971) reported that high authoritarian subjects, when forced by confederates into a subordinate role, looked less at others than when placed in a superordinate leadership role.

Finally, a recent study suggests that dominance may be related to sex differences. Fromme and Beam (1974) had high- and low-dominant male and female subjects approach a constant-gazing or nongazing confederate until they felt comfortable. (It was assumed that the steadily gazing confederate would evoke a dominance signal on the part of subjects.) The investigators found that dominant males expressed their dominance primarily by approaching the gazing confederate (with no change in their looking), whereas dominant females increased their gaze but did not vary their approach. The authors hypothesized that males may use personal space more than eye contact to signal dominance whereas women may use reciprocal eye contact more. An unexpected but interesting finding was that all subjects gave positive ratings to high levels of confederate gaze except low-dominant males, who reacted negatively.

Other studies have attempted to relate introversion/extraversion to visual behavior, generally showing a positive relationship between extraversion and looking. Kendon and Cook (1969) found that gaze while speaking correlated positively ($r = .65$) with extraversion (measured by the Maudsley Personality Inventory) and negatively with neuroticism ($r = -.73$). Mobbs (1968) also found extraverts used "eye contact" more than introverts both when looking and speaking. Indeed, a correlation of .73 between looking duration and Heron's sociability measure was obtained. Argyle and Williams (1969), however, found no relationship between extraversion (or neuroticism) and subjects' ratings of feeling observed. More recently, Rutter, Morley, and Graham (1972), using the Eysenck Personality Inventory, found that extraverts looked more frequently, especially while speaking, than introverts. However, differences in duration measures (the proportion of time spent in looking, "eye contact," or the mean length of looks) were not found. In addition, it was found that extraverts tended to speak more than introverts, which might explain the greater number of looks. Lastly, Argyle and Ingham (1972) observed a positive correlation between extraversion and measures of looking, particularly for mutual looking at the more intimate distance. Neuroticism also correlated positively with the measures of looking.

A number of other miscellaneous personality variables have been related to visual behavior. Exline, Thibaut, Brannan, and Gumpert (1966), for example, found that subjects high on Machiavellianism showed less of a decrease in eye contact than low-Machiavellian subjects when they were implicated in cheating. Another variable studied by Kendon and Cook (1969) was field dependence, which they found correlated negatively with the amount of gaze while speaking. Nevill (1974) experimentally aroused dependency in subjects by having an experimenter leave the room, terminating the help being given to subjects on a task. For female subjects this had the effect of increasing their field dependency which was also correlated with an increase in duration of looking. Lefcourt and Wine (1969) employed a confederate who either engaged in eye contact or avoided looking at subjects during an interview. Subjects high on Rotter's internal control dimension tended to look more at the "unusual" gaze avoiding confederate than the "normal" one, whereas the reverse was true for subjects high in external control. The researchers concluded that internally oriented individuals adopt an information seeking, vigilant approach of attention deployment when faced with a problematic situation (i.e., a gaze avoiding other). In a recent study investigating gaze in all-male, all-female, and opposite-sex dyads during conversation, Beekman (1975) found that for males, gaze while listening correlated positively with personality measures of friendliness and sociability. No such relationship was noted for females. However, both males' and females' gaze while speaking was greater in subjects high in self-control and low in spontaneity, who may have been more inclined to seek visual feedback from their partners. Levy (1973) studied repression/sensitization in an experimental situation where subjects received positive or negative feedback from an interviewer. No differences in subjects' gaze behavior were noted as a function of feedback and the repression-sensitization dimension.

Finally, it is also possible that visual behavior may reflect complex differences in individual personality structures. In his study on the effects of father absence on the psychosexual adjustment of adolescent girls, Hetherington (1972) observed for differences in looking behavior in girls who were fatherless due to divorce or death, compared to girls with fathers. Compared to daughters with fathers, daughters of widows looked less at the male interviewer when speaking, during silence, and when the interviewer was talking. In contrast, daughters of divorcees looked more than the other father-status groups in these situations. In addition, differences were also found as a function of time of separation: daughters of recent widows showed more looking than daughters of early widows, but less than daughters of divorced mothers. These results attest to the sensitivity of looking behavior as a dependent measure of an important developmental phenomenon: adolescent girls' adjustment towards males. In particular, the findings show the relative shyness of daughters of widows, and the aggressiveness of daughters of divorcees towards males.

Research with Psychiatric Patients

A number of researchers have conducted studies on the visual behavior of psychiatric patients. As we noted earlier, Hutt and Ounsted (1966) and Hutt and Vaizey (1966) documented that gaze aversion was a salient characteristic of autistic children's behavior that interestingly minimized the number of aggressive encounters they experienced in a free-play situation with normal children. These researchers hypothesized that the autistic children are in a high state of behavioral and physiological arousal and that gaze aversion to social stimuli served to reduce their arousal: "It is possible, then, that in those species in which the dominant receptor modality is vision, gaze aversion is a built-in biological component of high arousal—that is an unlearnt response occurring in all members of a species" (Hutt and Ounsted, 1966, p. 355). O'Connor and Hermelin (1967), however, demonstrated that psychotic children generally spend more time in nondirected gaze than normals. Using an "inspection box" in which children could view two simultaneously presented figures, they found that there was no special avoidance of pictures of the human face as opposed to other stimuli by psychotic children. Richer and Coss (cited in Coss, 1972) studied the reactions of 10 autistic children and matched controls to an experimenter who talked to them with continuous gaze. During this time the experimenter at random intervals fully covered his face with his hands, covered all his face but one eye, exposed both his eyes, or did not cover his face at all. When the entire face was covered (and to a lesser extent when only one eye was exposed) there was more looking by the autistic children and less flight or stereotyped autistic behavior than when the eyes were fully exposed. In addition, the autistic children engaged in only 4% gaze (compared to 63% of controls). It was concluded that the awareness of others looking at them apparently makes autistic children quite anxious. Bartak and Rutter (1971), interestingly, reported a reduction in gaze-aversion of 50 autistic children as they showed progress in treatment. Thus, whether gaze-aversion in these children is related to overstimulation per se or more specifically from social sources remains to be conclusively demonstrated.

It has been generally assumed that adult schizophrenics also show gaze aversion. For example, Harris (1968) recorded the frequency of "eye contact" of subjects while waiting in a room with his mother, father, a peer, and an authority figure. Compared to normal subjects, the schizophrenic patients engaged in less frequent looking. Lefcourt, Rotenberg, Buckspan, and Steffy (1967) studied "eye contact" in process and reactive schizophrenics with same- and opposite-sex interviewers. It was hypothesized that process schizophrenics would show more gaze-aversion than reactives. In addition, since Donovan and Webb (1965) found that process schizophrenics showed an aversion to female voices and reactive schizophrenics to male voices, a similar pattern of gaze-aversion was predicted. No support for the hypothesis was found for looking duration measures, although there was a general but nonsignificant tendency for reactives to look more often at the interviewers. For looking frequency, process patients did look significantly less at females than males, whereas reactive subjects did not show any marked preference. No significant differences between process and reactive patients in their frequency of looking were found, although a sub-analysis based upon subjects on the extremes of the process-reactive dimension did approach significance. Rutter (1973), however, criticized this study on the grounds that inadequate sampling of the subjects' behavior was employed in obtaining the data, which he felt rendered the results unreliable.

Lefcourt, Telegdi, Willows, and Buckspan (1972) reported that human movement responses (M) on the Rorschach Test are related to the process-reactive dimension. These M responses were regarded as a measure of social approach. They found that among poor premorbid schizophrenics, those with high M responses engaged in less frequent gaze and shorter-duration gazes, whereas among good premorbid schizophrenics, high M was associated with more frequent gaze. For the duration measures, lengthier looking was related to low M and good premorbidity. These findings, while more complex than anticipated, further suggest that "eye contact" is an important characteristic of the process-reactive dimension, and that it can be related to projective test measures. Indeed, using normal college student subjects, the authors replicated the relationship between high M and frequency of looking.

A number of studies have yielded negative results for schizophrenics and gaze-aversion, however. Exline, Gottheil, Paredes, and Winkelmayer (unpublished manuscript, no date) employed schizophrenics and normal subjects to relate happy, angry, and sad stories to an interviewer. The authors were interested in the percentage of time subjects' gazes were downcast versus direct during the sad and happy stories. It was predicted that the degree to which downcast gazes were more prevalent during sad than happy stories would be related to the ease with which observers could identify the stories subjects were telling (based on their nonverbal behavior). The hypothesis was confirmed but no differences were observed in the gazing behavior of schizophrenic and normal subjects. Although Argyle (1972) cited some unpublished research in which "chronic schizophrenics" evidenced less eye contact which occurred in the form of short, oblique glances, Argyle (personal communication, 1970, cited in Rutter, 1973, p. 195) also noted that many schizophrenics do not show gaze aversion. More recently, Rutter (1975, unpublished, cited in Argyle and Cook, 1976) had schizophrenics engage in an impersonal problem-solving task (Choice Dilemmas) with another patient and a nonpatient. No differences in the gaze of normals and patients were recorded, suggesting that reduced gaze seen in schizophrenics may occur primarily in interviews where the focus is on interpersonal interaction. This possibly is seen more clearly in the study by Williams (1974), who seated schizophrenics and normal controls opposite a TV set and a female experimental confederate, who after 3 minutes attempted to engage the subject in conversation. During this time the confederate engaged in 100% gaze and the TV set showed an animal program. As the confederate was attempting to engage the subjects, the schizophrenics looked at the TV more and the confederate less relative to controls. These findings suggest that schizophrenics are attempting to avoid social contact rather than stimulation per se.

Several English researchers have conducted research on depressive patients. Hinchliffe, Lancashire, and Roberts (1970) interviewed 14 inpatient depressives concerning their symptoms while staring continuously at them. Compared to a control group of surgical patients, depressives showed a lower frequency and duration of "eye contact." Subsequently, Hinchliffe, Lancashire, and Roberts (1971) compared the gaze behavior of recovered depressives to depressed patients during a standardized 7-minute interview. As before, interviewer gaze was continuously directed at the subjects. The total duration of speech was the same for both groups, an important methodological consideration. As expected, the clinically depressed patients showed less overall "eye contact," less "eye contact" during speech, and fewer instances of "eye contact."

In an important article, Rutter (1973) critically reviewed studies of visual interaction. Rutter identified a number of variables not controlled for, or procedures omitted, in many of the studies noted above. These included adequate description and specification of patient populations and patient clinical state; control for interview content and interviewer behavior; separate analysis of visual behavior during speech and listening; and inappropriate, or uneven, sampling of interview segments for analysis. In addition, he noted that most studies suffer from the problems of observation that we noted earlier. In a well controlled study, Rutter and Stephenson (1972a) studied the visual behavior of 20 schizophrenics and 20 depressives who were given a standardized interview within 48 hours following admission. The interviewer behavior consisted of looking down while reading standardized questions, then constantly gazing at patients while they were answering. Compared to matched normal controls (chest patients), both schizophrenics and depressives spent less total time looking at the interviewer. Although there were no differences in the frequency of looks, the schizophrenics did look in shorter glances than their controls and depressives. There were no differences in speaking and the reduced looking of patients occurred during speech and listening alike. In particular, Rutter (1973) noted that there was no marked pattern of gaze aversion in schizophrenics as other researchers have reported; indeed, "there was considerable variation among subjects, both across and within patient groups, and there was some degree of overlap between patients and controls" (p. 199).

Rutter and Stephenson (1972b) subsequently conducted a follow-up study (similar to the above in procedure) using psychiatric patients suffering from anxiety or alcoholic conditions. This was done to evaluate the possibility that the decreased looking in schizophrenics and depressives might be a generalized phenomenon among psychiatric patients, the results of being stigmatized by their psychiatric hospitalization. No such differences were observed. Thus the reduction in looking indeed appears to be a special characteristic of schizophrenic and depressive illnesses. More recently Waxer (1974) showed videotapes of admission interviews of depressed and nondepressed patients to psychology faculty, graduates, and undergraduates, who were asked to identify which patients were depressed and the cues they used to make their judgments. All judges were able to identify, with considerable accuracy, the depressed from nondepressed subjects, and they specified the mouth, eyes, and angle of head-orientation as salient nonverbal cue areas. Ratings of patients' "eye contact" from the films showed that the two groups did not differ in frequency of looks but they did differ in duration of glances.

Research on the Direction of Gaze

We have reserved this section to comment on some research emerging on the direction of gaze and its possible relationship to personality and brain functioning. In a popular article, Bakan (1971) noted that right or left eye movements ("conjugate-lateral eye movements"), that occur with mental activity appear to be stable characteristics of individuals. Day (1964) found that subjects asked "reflective questions" typically moved their eyes consistently to the right or left (approximately 75% of the time) while formulating an answer. The consistency was more apparent among men than women, but there appeared to be approximately equal numbers of such individuals in general. In his article and own research, Bakan identified a number of characteristics of "left- and right-movers" that he related to the relative dominance of the right and left hemispheres respectively. Left-movers, for example, tended to have higher hypnotic-susceptibility scores and more alpha waves (52 vs. 20%, true for men only), and they were better able to produce alpha waves with training. Right-movers appeared to have higher quantitative Scholastic Aptitude Test (SAT) scores whereas left-movers had higher verbal scores; left-movers were more fluent writers and tended to choose classical/humanist career areas, whereas right-movers tended to major in science and quantitative areas. Bakan (1971) further noted:

I have also found evidence that right-movers have more tics and twitches than left-movers, and that they spend less time asleep (males), pay more attention to the right side of their body (males), prefer cool colors and make career choices earlier. Left-movers tend to have more vivid imagery, and they are more sociable, more likely to be alcoholic (males), and report themselves as more musical and more religious. (p. 66)

Given that the left and right hemispheres have been associated with linguistic and visuo-spatial abilities, they have been described as "analytic" and "synthetic" or propositional and "appositional." Geffen, Bradshaw, and Wallace (1971) produced evidence that reaction time to nonverbal stimuli, such as faces, was faster when presented in the left visual field, compared to stimuli requiring verbal encoding, which were processed faster in the right visual field.

Kinsbourne (1972, 1974) recently investigated handedness and problem task in relation to eye movements. Given that right-handed individuals have distinctly represented speech (left hemisphere) and nonverbal (right hemisphere) functions, whereas left-handed persons have these functions more bilaterally represented, differences were predicted in their eye movements when solving verbal and nonverbal problems. As hypothesized, right-handers solving verbal problems looked to the right and when solving numerical or spatial problems they looked to the left, whereas left-handers were more equal in the frequencies of their eye movements. Galin and Ornstein (1974) attempted to extend these findings to individuals who differ in cognitive mode: lawyers (primarily verbal-analytic) and ceramists (who employ spatial analysis in their three-dimensional constructions). Contrary to expectations, no lateral-gaze differences were noted, although ceramists looked up more often and lawyers down. However, verbal questions did produce more right eye movements than spatial questions, as well as more upward looks. Subsequently, Kinsbourne (1974) pointed out that these findings could be disrupted by confrontation by the experimenter, the sound of his voice, or a set to respond other than looking straight ahead. In their study on direction of gaze during standardized questioning by an interviewer, Libby and Yaklevich (1973) measured these personality variables: nurturance, abasement, and intraception. An interesting finding was that persons high in abasement tended to look more to the left than to the right, whereas low-abasement subjects looked equally to the right and left. This effect was primarily apparent for females. The authors cautioned against any hard interpretations of the finding (especially since the exit to the experiment was to the subject's left, and thus the finding may have simply been related to the high-abasement subject's need to leave the situation).

Gur (1975) reported a series of findings that further qualify and elucidate these types. In one study Gur found that when facing an interviewer, subjects would move their eyes primarily in one direction, regardless of the question. However, with the questioner out of view (e.g., behind the subject), right handers tended to look to the left for spatial problems and to the right for verbal problems. Hiscock (1975) replicated these results with the additional finding that anxiety tended to disrupt the laterality effect. Interestingly, he found that when subjects made the "appropriate" eye movement, they were more often correct in their answer than when they looked in the opposite direction. In another study Gur (1975) found that sex and handedness were moderating variables between hypnotic susceptibility and right-hemisphere dominance. Specifically, right hemisphere activity and hypnotic susceptibility are moderately related, but for right-handers only and for males only. With both moderating variables considered, hypnotizability was related to right-hemisphere activity (left-looking) for right-handed males ($r = .68$), and to the left-hemisphere activity (right-looking) for left-handed females ($r = .58$). Some additional important correlates of left- and right-movers can be summarized as follows: (a) left-movers tend to employ denial, repression, and reaction formation as defenses, whereas right-movers will externalize conflicts and act out against the environment; (b) left-movers report more psychosomatic complaints, probably associated with repression; (c) left- and right-movers tended to prefer the right and left side, respectively, of the classroom for seating. These findings certainly point out the need for further research on correlates of these characteristics, given the apparent ease with which one can identify a right- and left-mover. Finally, Schwartz (1974) conducted some intriguing research relating hemispheric asymmetry and emotion to lateral eye movements. Schwartz tested the hypothesis that emotions and spatial organization were primarily represented in the right hemisphere, whereas verbal processing occurred in the left hemisphere. Right-handed subjects were unobtrusively observed for lateral gaze when being asked emotional, spatial, and verbal questions. While verbal questions were associated with comparable numbers of right and left looks, spatial questions produced a decrement in right looks (but no increase in left looks). Emotional questions produced, as predicted, a decrease in right looks and an increase in left looks. These findings were generally replicated using electroencephalograms (EEGs) as a dependent variable rather than gaze-direction. A particularly interesting finding was that, based upon their eye movements, females appeared to show a stronger "emotion effect" than males, whereas males showed a larger right-hemispheric "spatial" effect. Schwartz (1974) noted, "that this pattern of results fits the standard stereotype of sex differences seen in our culture cannot go unnoticed" (p. 11).

RESEARCH ON PUPIL DILATION

In 1960, Hess reported some research conducted in his laboratory in which pupil dilation measurements were taken of subjects' eyes (Hess and Polt, 1960). Presenting the subjects slides of male and female pinups and other stimuli, Hess found that male subjects' pupils dilated to female pinups while female subjects showed greater pupil dilation to male pictures. Initially, Hess concluded that pupil dilation was a reliable index of positive emotional arousal and interest, and pupil constriction was a sign of emotional aversion. Since then, however, numerous studies have been conducted that have stirred controversy and cast doubt on the simplicity of the initial propositions. Perhaps more important, they have shown that pupillary response is a complex phenomenon subject to many influences that necessitate very sophisticated research methods. In a sense, one might question whether changes in the pupil size are "communicative behavior," inasmuch as they are essentially involuntary and not always indicative, given the necessity for the observer being rather close to the person in order to notice changes. On the other hand, Hindmarch (1970) observed greater pupillary dilation in females looking at slides of newly born babies. Conversely, Fitzgerald (1968) demonstrated that social stimuli evoke pupillary dilation in 1-month-old infants, this response becoming more specific to the mother's face by 4 months. Finally, it is useful to note that women have long used the drug "belladonna" to dilate their eyes, thus enhancing their attractiveness towards members of the opposite sex. Recently, Stass and Willis (1967) experimentally demonstrated the efficacy of this tactic. Thus, there is evidence that the pupils can serve indicative, interactive, and even possible "communicative" functions.

Fortunately, for any novices considering this area of research, there are a number of very recent reviews written by experts in the field. These include articles by Hindmarch (1973), Goldwater (1972), and Hess himself (Hess, 1972). These articles provide a detailed description of measurement technique and procedures in addition to selected reviews of literature. Finally, Janisse (1973, 1974; Janisse and Peavler, 1974) has written scientific and popular reviews on pupillary phenomena and edited a book on *Pupillary Dynamics and Behavior* (1974) that should be an important reference in the field. We do not attempt to duplicate these excellent reviews but rather seek to provide an overview of the research in this area.

The greatest excitement surrounding pupillary research has stemmed from Hess' contention that pupillary behavior accurately reflects differences in interests, emotions, and attitudes, free from the effects of verbal response. The potential implications of this proposition, of course, have stimulated the advertising industry to invest huge sums of money in pupillometry and many others to conduct research on its practical utility as a diagnostic instrument. This latter interest derived from Hess' now classic study in which he reported that male homosexuals showed greater pupillary dilation to male pinups than female pinups, whereas heterosexual males showed the opposite pattern, and females responded most to a picture of a mother and her baby. Further presentation of the female pinup with dilated or nondilated eyes revealed that males evidenced a much greater pupillary response to the former than the latter (Hess, 1965).

Since then a large number of positive findings as well as numerous negative findings have emerged. For example, studies have related pupillary dilation or constriction of normal subjects to pictures of preferred or non-preferred political figures (Barlow, 1969), opposite-sex pictures (Simms, 1967), to hostile versus "control" Thematic Apperception Test cards (Tinio and Robertson, 1969), to emotional words (Collins, Ellsworth, and Helmreich, 1967; Guinan, 1967), and to affect-laden mental images (Bernick and Oberlander, 1968). Bernick, Kling, and Borowitz (1971) obtained significant correlations between pupillary dilation and verbal reports of male sexual arousal to pornographic films. In a well cited study, Atwood and Howell (1971) compared pupillary reactions of "female aggressing pedophiliacs" and normal controls to pictures of mature and immature females. Experimental subjects showed pupillary constriction to the pictures of adult females whereas dilation occurred in all other cases. Simms (unpublished data, reported in Hess, 1972, p. 515) recently obtained evidence that male homosexuals preferred pictures of females with small pupils, apparently finding the sexual connotations of females with dilated pupils somewhat aversive. Clark (1975) most recently studied the value of pupillary response in detecting deception. Subjects, role-playing a "secret agent," memorized a secret code which they were subsequently exposed to during a lie-detection session. More pupil dilation occurred following presentation of the secret code number than to neutral codes, yielding an 80% "hit rate" for detecting deception, which was significantly above chance. Galvanic Skin Response measurement was 85% accurate, while the two combined yielded 95% accuracy in detecting deception.

In contrast to employing pupil dilation as a dependent measure, Stass and Willis (1967) had subjects interact with two confederates, one of whose eyes was dilated. As predicted, the latter was chosen more often as a partner. Using multiple photographs of a woman with variously dilated eyes, Hicks, Reaney, and Hill (1967) found only that females preferred the picture with small pupils (males showed no preference). Subsequently, Jones and Moyel (1971) found that in ratings of pictures of male strangers whose irises were dark or light, or whose pupils were large or small, the only difference obtained was a preference for lighter irises. In an interesting follow-up of the Ellsworth and Ludwig (1972) study, Kidd (1975) had subjects administer shocks to confederates who directed or averted their gaze at subjects, and in addition, who displayed dilated or constricted pupils. While gaze of confederate had no significant effect, subjects looked less at, and administered fewer shocks to, confederates with dilated pupils. Pupil dilation may have been a nonverbal cue incompatible with the noxious prospect of receiving electric shock.

Concomitant with these positive findings, however, are many negative ones. Woodmansee (1965) found that even small shifts in gaze from one part of a picture to another could produce alterations in pupil size. In addition, he was unable to find pupillary constriction to pictures of Negroes among anti-Negro subjects. Subsequently, Woodmansee (1970) conducted research with olfactory and other aversive stimuli and found no evidence to support Hess' contention that pupillary constriction was a reaction to an aversive stimulus. Indeed, Nunnally, Knott, Duchnowski, and Parker (1967) found pupillary dilation in response to a painful tone stimulus. Other studies that failed to demonstrate the relationship hypothesized by Hess included an experiment by Scott, Wells, Wood, and Morgan (1967), who presented to males, females, and homosexual males pictures of clothed and naked men and women; and a study by Lawless and Wake (1968) using photographs of nude and clothed males and females. No differences in pupillary response were found in subjects to preferred and nonpreferred schoolmates (Koff and Hawkes, 1968); to high- or low-valued words (Vacchiano, Strauss, Ryan, and Hockman, 1968); to neutral versus double entendre words (Bernick, Altman, and Mintz, 1972); or to pleasant and unpleasant mentation (Schaefer, Ferguson, Klein, and Rawson, 1968). Particularly damaging to notions of pupil dilation as a diagnostic test were additional findings by Bernick, Kling, and Borowitz (1971) that (despite the positive findings cited earlier) many heterosexual males also showed increased pupil size to homosexual stimuli. Libby, Lacey, and Lacey (1968) reported pupillary response to stimuli as a function of their attention value but not their positive or negative emotional valence.

Recently, Janisse (1973), noting the above conflicting findings, proposed that pupillary dilation was related to the intensity, not valence of stimulation. A U-shaped function was proposed where extreme positive and negative affect produced pupillary dilation. Using subjects' reactions to nonsense syllables, Janisse obtained some evidence for his position. Recently, however, Hicks and LePage (1976) have followed up on the controversy concerning Hess' bi-directional hypothesis. Twenty-one subjects from two groups of 625 were selected as having extreme attitudes towards different ethnic groups (e.g., Arab, Black, Chinese, American Indian). Positive, neutral, and negative stimuli (e.g., slides of specific ethnic-group members) were presented to subjects. As predicted, subjects showed pupillary dilation to positive stimuli, little or no change to neutral stimuli, and constriction to negative stimuli. A correlation of .74 between pupil size and attitudinal valance was obtained, demonstrating strong support for Hess' theory.

Several other researchers have attempted to relate individual differences to pupillary response. Hutt and Anderson (1967), for example, found an inverse correlation between recognition threshold and pupil size for taboo words, a finding with implications for perceptual defense research. Good and Levin (1970), however, found only a weak trend for sensitizers to dilate more than repressors to neutral and affect-laden stimuli. Fredericks (1970), in contrast, reported that sensitizers dilated more to pleasant stimuli and repressors constricted more to unpleasant stimuli, in support of Hess' position.

One possible reason for the inconsistency in findings is the relatively large number of variables related to pupil response. In his review, Hindmarch (1973) noted that pupil size varied with perceptual-cognitive load, or mental activity (see for example, Bradshaw, 1968a; Kahneman and Beatty, 1967; Kahneman, Peavler, and Onuska, 1968). Bradshaw (1968b) showed that pupil dilation was related to stimulus uncertainty and Kahneman and Peavler (1969), Simpson and Hale (1969), and Colman and Paivio (1970) all suggested that pupil size varied with the task demands or "cognitive load," or arousal as shown by other autonomic measures. Indeed, in the study by Kahneman, Tursky, Shapiro, and Crider (1969) pupil size was found to be the most consistent index of arousal, compared to heart rate, blood pressure, etc. Hess (1972) himself noted differences in pupillary dilation orienting reactions by hysteric patients, who reacted stronger than normals, and schizophrenics, epileptics, and alcoholics, who reacted weaker than normals (Streltsova, 1965). Most recently, Janisse (1976) reviewed the literature on pupil size in relation to anxiety, sexual arousal, or stress (psychological and physical; e.g., noise or lifting a weight). In this review, Janisse concluded:

What we know at present is quite limited, but speculation and hypothesis abound. The thrust of the literature indicates that the pupillary reaction to anxiety, arousal, or a stressor is one of dilation. This dilation may occur before an expected stimulus, or during a prolonged and substantial stimulus presentation, or following an unexpected stimulus. The only evidence for "emotional" constriction responses emerges from the literature employing pictorial stimuli which, it has been argued, are singularly inapt for research of this kind on the pupil. (p. 41)

In his recent book Janisse (1974) identified problem areas for pupillary research. First, he described physical parameter effects including controlling for the brightness of the stimulus, relative brightness within parts of a stimulus, and individual differences in the light reflex. Second, Janisse noted that few researchers had considered baseline differences in pupil diameter, a fundamental consideration in research with other autonomic variables. Control slides offer a partial solution whereby comparisons are made between the change from experimental slides to control slides. Basically, however, statistical procedures that take into account the Law of Initial Values should be employed. The distance of the stimulus from the eye must also be controlled, given the tendency for the pupil to constrict for near versus far vision, even given constant illumination. Janisse also noted that persons with light irises had larger and more reactive pupils, and consideration of this factor in subject selection and generalization of the findings is important. Variability in pupil size over time is another problem, given natural diameter changes of 1% from second to second, and 19–20% changes over several seconds. Finally, the measurement of pupils is itself a problem: typically sequential (two per second) still photographs measuring the pupil diameter have been used, but whether it is the average size, peak size, variance, etc. has not been agreed upon. More recently, electronic scanning devices that permit estimation of the amount of light emitted or reflected by the iris or pupil (leading to a continuous estimate of pupil size) have been designed, television pupillometers being the most promising (Janisse, 1976). The expense of the equipment has undoubtedly restricted its widespread use, however. Goldwater (1972) also discussed a number of methodological considerations, and most recently Tryon (1975) described 26 variables that influence pupil size, including two relatively obscure factors: the darkness reflex and wavelength of light. Both articles are must reading for anyone planning to use pupillary response as a dependent measure.

In summary, despite the improved research and continuing optimism of Hess (1972) and Janisse (1973, 1974, 1976), we must agree with Hindmarch's conclusion: "Generalizing from the data . . . is difficult since so many researchers have provided evidence for effects and relationships which are then repudiated by other investigators. Some authors even change their minds, several times within the space of a year, depending upon the co-authorship" (1973, p. 315). The most obvious problem is the large number of variables that might confound the relationships being studied. Indeed, Chapman, Chapman, and Brelje (1969) presented evidence that even the relationship between subjects and the experimenter may affect the pupillary response. Thus, given the apparent necessary revision of Hess' earlier speculations concerning the meaning of dilation and constriction and the sensitivity of these phenomena to confounds, it is difficult to see how they can have as widespread application as researchers once hoped.

NOTES

[1]Cranach, however, cautioned:
In those cases in which the distance was small and the spatial position favorable, we can assume that the "look into the face" was actually assessed. For this reason, we should understand the results of these investigations in terms of the more or less undefined orienting behavior of the sender rather than in terms of looking behavior. (1971, p. 232)

[2]In addition, the duration of looking by the televised confederate varied from a virtual stare (99% looking) to gaze-aversion (1% looking), whereas Ellsworth and Carlsmith's experimenter "looked" (in both conditions) less frequently and at the end of their completed utterances. The

latter study thus provided a more "natural" sample of looking behavior. Given the many functions of looking and the powerful psychological "messages" a gaze can convey, the researcher must be especially careful in employing "eye contact" as an independent variable.

[3]This interpretation is consistent with a recent finding by Nevill (1974), who experimentally aroused dependency in subjects (who subsequently increased their looking at an experimenter).

[4]One might assume that when visual attention and social acknowledgment (e.g., head-nods, smiling) are withheld, subjects who have or feel they have less power or control may respond with more liking. This was the interpretation of Exline and Messick (1967). More direct support is seen in a study by Exline (1972), who gave one subject control over rewards with instructions to reward himself more than his partner (for completing a joint task). As predicted, the less powerful individual (who did not administer the rewards) looked more at his more powerful cohort. Indeed, this effect was increased when the power differential was legitimized by having an ROTC officer administer rewards to an ROTC private.

REFERENCES

Aiello, J. R. (1972a). *Male and female visual behavior as a function of distance and duration of an interviewer's direct gaze: Equilibrium theory revisited.* Doctoral dissertation, Michigan State University. [*Dissertation Abstracts International,* 33, (1973), 4482B–4483B. University Microfilms No. 73-5312.]

Aiello, J. R. (1972b). A test of equilibrium theory: Visual interaction in relation to orientation, distance, and sex of interactants. *Psychonomic Science,* 27, 335–336.

Anstis, S. M., J. W. Mayhew, and T. Morley (1969). The perception of where a face or television 'portrait' is looking. *American Journal of Psychology,* 82, 474–489.

Argyle, M. (1969). *Social interaction.* New York: Atherton Press.

Argyle, M. (1970). Eye-contact and distance: A reply to Stephenson and Rutter. *British Journal of Psychology,* 61, 395–396.

Argyle, M. (1972). *The psychology of interpersonal behavior.* Baltimore: Penguin Books.

Argyle, M., and M. Cook (1976). *Gaze and mutual gaze.* London: Cambridge University Press.

Argyle, M., and J. Dean (1965). Eye-contact, distance, and affiliation. *Sociometry,* 28, 289–304.

Argyle, M., and R. Ingham (1972). Gaze, mutural gaze, and proximity. *Semiotica,* 6, 32–49.

Argyle, M., R. Ingham, F. Alkema, and M. McCallin (1973). The different functions of gaze. *Semiotica,* 7, 19–32.

Argyle, M., and A. Kendon (1967). The experimental analysis of social performance. In L. Berkowitz (Ed.), *Advances in experimental social psychology,* Vol. 3. New York: Academic Press. Pp. 55–98.

Argyle, M., M. Lalljee, and M. Cook (1968). The effects of visibility on interaction in a dyad. *Human Relations,* 21, 3–17.

Argyle, M., and M. Williams (1969). Observer or observed? A reversible perspective in person perception. *Sociometry,* 32, 396–412.

Ashear, V., and J. R. Snortum (1971). Eye contact in children as a function of age, social and intellective variables. *Developmental Psychology,* 4, 479.

Atwood, R. W., and R. J. Howell (1971). Pupillometric and personality test score differences of female aggressing pedophiliacs and normals. *Psychonomic Science,* 22, 115–116.

Bakan, P. (1971). The eyes have it. *Psychology Today,* 4, 64–67, 96.

Barlow, J. D. (1969). Pupillary size as an index of preference in political candidates. *Perceptual and Motor Skills,* 28, 589–590.

Bartak, L., and M. Rutter (1971). Educational treatments of autistic children. In M. Rutter, *Infantile autism: Concepts, characteristics, and treatment.* Edinburgh and London: Churchill Livingstone. Pp. 20–32.

Bates, J. E. (1975). *Effects of children's nonverbal behavior upon adults.* Paper presented at the meeting of the American Psychological Association, Chicago.

Baxter, E. H. (1971). *Body orientation and looking behavior as threat and appeasement: A study of nonverbal communication.* Doctoral dissertation, University of Oregon. [*Dissertation Abstracts International,* 32, (1972), 6536A. University Microfilms No. 72-14, 713.]

Baxter, J. C., and R. M. Rozelle (1975). Nonverbal expression as a function of crowding during a simulated police–citizen encounter. Unpublished manuscript, 1975. (Available from the Department of Psychology, University of Houston, Cullen Boulevard, Houston, Texas.)

Beebe, S. A. (1974). Eye contact: A nonverbal determinant of speaker credibility. *The Speech Teacher,* 23, 21–25.

Beekman, S. (1975). *Sex differences in nonverbal behavior.* Paper presented at the meeting of the American Psychological Association, Chicago.

Bernick, N., F. Altman, and D. L. Mintz (1972). Pupil responses of addicts in treatment to drug culture argot: II. Responses during verbalization of visually presented words. *Psychonomic Science,* 28, 81–82.

Bernick, N., A. Kling, and G. Borowitz (1971). Physiological differentiation of sexual arousal and anxiety. *Psychosomatic Medicine,* 33, 341–352.

Bernick, N., and M. Oberlander (1968). Effect of verbalization and two different modes of experiencing on pupil size. *Perception and Psychophysics,* 3, 327–330.

Bradshaw, J. L. (1968a). Load and pupillary changes in continuous processing tasks. *British Journal of Psychology,* 59, 265–271.

Bradshaw, J. L. (1968b). Pupillary changes and reaction time with varied stimulus uncertainty. *Psychonomic Science,* 13, 69–70.

Breed, G. R. (1969). *Nonverbal communication and interpersonal attraction in dyads.* Doctoral dissertation, University of Florida. [*Dissertation Abstracts International,* 31, (1970), 1369A. University Microfilms No. 70-14, 857.]

Breed, G. R. (1972). The effect of intimacy: Reciprocity or retreat? *British Journal of Social and Clinical Psychology,* 11, 135–142.

Breed, G. R., and M. Porter (1972). Eye contact, attitudes, and attitude change among males. *Journal of Genetic Psychology,* 120, 211–217.

Burroughs, W., W. Schultz, and S. Autrey (1973). Quality of argument, leadership votes, and eye contact in three-person leaderless groups. *Journal of Social Psychology,* 90, 89–93.

Carter, R. D. (1969). *Gazing and smiling and the communication of interpersonal affect in a quasi-interview situation.* Doctoral dissertation, University of Michigan. [*Dissertation Abstracts International,* 30, (1970), 4014A–4015A. University Microfilms No. 70-4045.]

Cary, M. S. (1974). *Nonverbal openings to conversation.* Paper presented at the meeting of the Eastern Psychological Association, Philadelphia.

Castell, R. (1970). Physical distance and visual attention as measures of social interaction between child and adult. In S. J. Hutt and C. Hutt (Eds.), *Behaviour studies in psychiatry.* Oxford: Pergamon Press. Pp. 91–102.

Champness, B. G. (1970). Mutual glance and the significance of the look. *Advancement of Science,* 26, 309–312.

Chapman, L. J., J. P. Chapman, and T. Brelje (1969). Influence of the experimenter on pupillary dilation to sexually provocative pictures. *Journal of Abnormal Psychology,* 74, 396–400.

Christenson, M. A. (1973). *Aspects of visual behavior in relation to sex of subject and expression of affect.* Doctoral dissertation, Washington State University. [*Dissertation Abstracts International,* **33,** (1973), 3298B–3299B. University Microfilms No. 73-38.]

Clark, W. R. (1975). *A comparison of pupillary response, heart rate, and GSR during deception.* Paper presented at the meeting of the Midwestern Psychological Association, Chicago.

Cline, M. G. (1967). The perception of where a person is looking. *American Journal of Psychology,* **80,** 41–50.

Collins, B. E., P. E. Ellsworth, and B. I. Helmreich (1967). Correlations between pupil size and the semantic differential: An experimental paradigm and pilot study. *Psychonomic Science,* **9,** 627–628.

Colman, F., and A. Paivio (1970). Pupillary dilation and mediation processes during paired associate learning. *Canadian Journal of Psychology,* **24,** 262–270.

Cook, M., and J. M. C. Smith (1975). The role of gaze in impression formation. *British Journal of Social and Clinical Psychology,* **14,** 19–25.

Coss, R. G. (1972). Eye-like schemata: Their effect on behavior. Unpublished doctoral dissertation.

Coutts, L. M., and F. W. Schneider (1975). Visual behavior in an unfocused interaction as a function of sex and distance. *Journal of Experimental Social Psychology,* **11,** 64–77.

Cranach, M. v. (1971). The role of orienting behavior in human interaction. In A. H. Esser (Ed.), *Behavior and environment: The use of space by animals and men.* New York: Plenum Press. Pp. 217–237.

Cranach, M. v., H. G. Frenz, and S. Frey (1968). Die "angenehmste Entfernung" zur Betrachtung sozialer Objekte. *Psychologische Forschungen,* **32,** 89–103.

Cranach, M. v., and G. Huckstedt Der Einfluss der Blickbewegung auf das Erkennen von Blickrichtungen. Unpublished manuscript cited in Cranach, M. v., The role of orienting behavior in human interaction. In A. H. Esser (Ed.), *Behavior and environment: The use of space by animals and men.* New York: Plenum Press, 1971. Pp. 217–237.

Cranach, M. v., B. Huckstedt, R. Schmid, and M. W. Vogel (1969). *Some stimulus components and their interaction in the perception of gaze direction.* (Mimeographed). MPI für Psychiatrie, München, West Germany. Unpublished manuscript cited in Cranach, M. v., The role of orienting behavior in human interaction. In A. H. Esser (Ed.), *Behavior and environment: The use of space by animals and men.* New York: Plenum Press, 1971. Pp. 217–237.

Daniell, R. J., and P. Lewis (1972). Stability of eye contact and physical distance across a series of structured interviews. *Journal of Consulting and Clinical Psychology,* **39,** 172.

Davey, A. G., and L. J. Taylor (1968). The role of eye-contact in inducing conformity. *British Journal of Social and Clinical Psychology,* **7,** 307–308.

Day, M. E. (1964). An eye movement phenomenon relating to attention, thought, and anxiety. *Perceptual and Motor Skills,* **19,** 443–446.

Deutsch, R., and C. Auerbach (1975). Eye movement in perception of another person's looking behavior. *Perceptual and Motor Skills,* **40,** 475–481.

Donovan, M. J., and W. W. Webb (1965). Meaning dimensions and male-female voice perception in schizophrenics with good and poor premorbid adjustment. *Journal of Abnormal Psychology,* **70,** 426–431.

Duncan, S. D., Jr. (1972). Some signals and rules for taking speaking turns in conversations. *Journal of Personality and Social Psychology,* **23,** 283–292.

Duncan, S. D., Jr. and G. Niederehe (1974). On signalling that it's your turn to speak. *Journal of Experimental Social Psychology,* **10,** 234–247.

Efran, J. S. (1968). Looking for approval: Effects on visual behavior of approbation from persons differing in importance. *Journal of Personality and Social Psychology,* **10,** 21–25.

Efran, J. S., and A. Broughton (1966). Effect of expectancies for social approval on visual behavior. *Journal of Personality and Social Psychology, 4,* 103–107.

Efran, M. G., and J. A. Cheyne (1974). Affective concomitants of the invasion of shared space: Behavioral, physiological, and verbal indicators. *Journal of Personality and Social Psychology, 29,* 219–226.

Eibl-Eibesfeldt, I. (1972). Similarities and differences between cultures in expressive movements. In R. A. Hinde (Ed.), *Nonverbal communication.* Cambridge: Cambridge University Press. Pp. 297–312.

Ellgring, J. H. (1969). *Die Beurteilung des Blickes auf Punkte innerhalb des Gesichts.* München, West Germany. Unpublished manuscript cited in Cranach, M. v. The role of orienting behavior in human interaction. In A. H. Esser (Ed.), *Behavior and environment: The use of space by animals and men.* New York: Plenum Press, 1971. Pp. 217–237.

Ellgring, J. H., and M. v. Cranach (1972). Processes of learning in the recognition of eye signals. *European Journal of Social Psychology, 2,* 33–43.

Ellsworth, P. C. (1975). Direct gaze as a social stimulus: The example of aggression. In P. Pliner, L. Krames, and T. Alloway (Eds.), *Nonverbal communication of aggression.* New York: Plenum Press, Pp. 53–76.

Ellsworth, P. C., and J. M. Carlsmith (1968). Effects of eye contact and verbal content on affective response to a dyadic interaction. *Journal of Personality and Social Psychology, 10,* 15–20.

Ellsworth, P. C., and J. M. Carlsmith (1973). Eye contact and gaze aversion in an aggressive encounter. *Journal of Personality and Social Psychology, 28,* 280–292.

Ellsworth, P. C., J. M. Carlsmith, and A. Henson (1972). The stare as a stimulus to flight in human subjects: A series of field experiments. *Journal of Personality and Social Psychology, 21,* 302–311.

Ellsworth, P. C., H. S. Friedman, D. Perlick, and M. F. Hoyt. Some effects of gaze on subjects motivated to seek or avoid social comparison. In preparation.

Ellsworth, P. C., and E. J. Langer (1976). Staring and approach: An interpretation of the stare as a nonspecific activator. *Journal of Personality and Social Psychology, 33,* 117–122.

Ellsworth, P. C., and L. M. Ludwig (1972). Visual behavior in social interaction. *Journal of Communication, 22,* 375–403.

Ellsworth, P. C., and L. D. Ross (1975). Intimacy in response to direct gaze. *Journal of Experimental Social Psychology, 11,* 592–613.

Ellyson, S. L. (1973). Visual interaction and attraction in dyads with legitimate power differences. Unpublished master's thesis, University of Delaware. Cited in Exline, R. V., Ellyson, S. L., and Long, B. Visual behavior as an aspect of power role relationships. In P. Pliner, L. Krames, and T. Alloway (Eds.), *Nonverbal communication of aggression.* New York: Plenum Publishing, 1975. Pp. 21–51.

Ellyson, S. L. (1974). *Visual behavior exhibited by males differing as to interpersonal control orientation in one- and two-way communication systems.* Unpublished dissertation. University of Delaware. Cited in Exline, R. V., Ellyson, S. L., and Long, B. Visual behavior as an aspect of power role relationships. In P. Pliner, L. Krames, and T. Alloway (Eds.), *Nonverbal communication of aggression.* New York: Plenum Publishing, 1975. Pp. 21–51.

Exline, R. V. (1963). Explorations in the process of person perception: Visual interaction in relation to competition, sex, and the need for affiliation. *Journal of Personality, 31,* 1–20.

Exline, R. V. (1972). Visual interaction: The glances of power and preference. In J. K. Cole (Ed.), *Nebraska symposium on motivation, 1971.* Lincoln: University of Nebraska Press. Pp. 162–205.

Exline, R. V. (1974). Visual interaction: The glances of power and preference. In S. Weitz (Ed.), *Nonverbal communication: Readings with commentary.* New York: Oxford University Press. Pp. 163–205.

Exline, R. V., and C. Eldridge (1967). *Effects of two patterns of a speaker's visual behavior upon the perception of the authenticity of his verbal message.* Paper presented at the meeting of the Eastern Psychological Association, Boston.

Exline, R. V., E. Gottheil, A. Paredes, and R. Winkelmayer Gaze direction as a factor in the accurate judgements of nonverbal expressions of affect. Unpublished manuscript. (Available from the Department of Psychology, University of Delaware, Newark, Delaware.)

Exline, R. V., D. Gray, and D. Schuette (1965). Visual behavior in a dyad as affected by interview content and sex of respondent. *Journal of Personality and Social Psychology,* **1,** 201–209.

Exline, R. V., and D. Messick (1967). The effects of dependency and social reinforcement upon visual behavior during an interview. *British Journal of Social and Clinical Psychology,* **6,** 256–266.

Exline, R. V., J. Thibaut, C. Brannan, and P. Gumpert (1966). *Visual interaction in relation to Machiavellianism and an unethical act.* Technical Report No. 16, Contract No. Nonr-2285(02). Newark, DE: Center for Research on Social Behavior, University of Delaware.

Exline, R. V., and L. C. Winters (1965). Affective relations and mutual glances in dyads. In S. S. Tomkins and C. E. Izard (Eds.), *Affect, cognition, and personality,* New York: Springer. Pp. 319–350.

Fitzgerald, H. E. (1968). Autonomic pupillary activity during early infancy and its relation to social and non-social visual stimuli. *Journal of Experimental Child Psychology,* **6,** 270–282.

Fredericks, R. S. (1970). Repression–sensitization and the pupillary reflex to pleasant and unpleasant stimuli. Unpublished doctoral dissertation, Illinois Institute of Technology.

Fromme, D. K., and D. C. Beam (1974). Dominance and sex differences in nonverbal responses to differential eye contact. *Journal of Research in Personality,* **8,** 76–87.

Fromme, D. K., and C. K. Schmidt (1972). Affective role enactment and expressive behavior. *Journal of Personality and Social Psychology,* **24,** 413–419.

Fugita, S. S. (1974). Effects of anxiety and approval on visual interaction. *Journal of Personality and Social Psychology,* **29,** 586–592.

Gale, A., B. Lucas, R. Nissim, and B. Harpham (1972). Some EEG correlates of face-to-face contact. *British Journal of Social and Clinical Psychology,* **11,** 326–332.

Galin, D., and R. Ornstein (1974). Individual differences in cognitive style: I. Reflective eye movements. *Neuropsychologia,* **12,** 367–376.

Gatton, M. J. (1970). Behavioral aspects of interpersonal attraction. Unpublished doctoral dissertation, Purdue University.

Geffen, G., J. L. Bradshaw, and G. Wallace (1971). Interhemispheric effects on reaction time to verbal and nonverbal visual stimuli. *Journal of Experimental Psychology,* **87,** 415–422.

Gibson, J. J., and A. D. Pick (1963). Perception of another person's looking behavior. *American Journal of Psychology,* **76,** 386–394.

Gitter, A. G., Mostofsky, D., and Guichard, M. (1972). Some parameters in the perception of gaze. *Journal of Social Psychology,* **88,** 115–121.

Goffman, E. (1964). *Behavior in public places.* New York: The Free Press of Glenco.

Goldberg, G. N., C. A. Kiesler, and B. E. Collins (1969). Visual behavior and face-to-face distance during interaction. *Sociometry,* **32,** 43–53.

Goldberg, G. N., and D. R. Mettee (1969). Liking and perceived communication potential as determinants of looking at another. *Psychonomic Science,* **16,** 277–278.

Goldwater, B. C. (1972). Psychological significance of pupillary movements. *Psychological Bulletin,* **77,** 340–355.

Good, L. R., and R. H. Levin (1970). Pupillary responses of repressers and sensitizers to sexual and aversive stimuli. *Perceptual and Motor Skills,* **30,** 631–634.

Gray, S. L. (1971). Eye contact as a function of sex, race, and interpersonal needs. Doctoral dissertation, Case Western Reserve University. [*Dissertation Abstracts, 32*, (1971), 1842B. University Microfilms No. 71-22, 805.]

Griffitt, W., J. May, and R. Veitch (1974). Sexual stimulation and interpersonal behavior: Heterosexual evaluative responses, visual behavior, and physical proximity. *Journal of Personality and Social Psychology, 30*, 367–377.

Guinan, J. F. (1966). An investigation of the relationship between pupil size and emotional words. Doctoral dissertation, Michigan State University. [*Dissertation Abstracts, 27*, 9-B (1967), 3286–3287.]

Gur, R. R. (1975). *Lateral eye movement, cerebral asymmetry, and personality.* Paper presented at the meeting of the International Neuropsychology Society, Tampa, Florida.

Haase, R. F., and D. T. Tepper, Jr. Nonverbal components of empathic communication. *Journal of Counseling Psychology, 19*, 417–424.

Harris, S. E. Schizophrenic mutual glance patterns. Doctoral dissertation, Columbia University. [*Dissertation Abstracts, 29* (1968), 2202B.]

Hemsley, G. D., and A. N. Doob (1975). *Effect of looking behavior on perceptions of a communicator's credibility.* Paper presented at the meeting of the American Psychological Association, Chicago.

Herb, T. R., and R. F. Elliott, Jr. (1971). Authoritarianism in the conversation of gestures. *Kansas Journal of Sociology, 7* (3), 93–101.

Heron, J. (1970). The phenomenology of social encounter: The gaze. *Philosophy and Phenomenological Research, 31*, 243–264.

Hess, E. H. (1965). Attitude and pupil size. *Scientific American,* April, 212, 46–54.

Hess, E. H. (1972). Pupillometrics: A method of studying mental, emotional, and sensory processes. In N. S. Greenfield and R. A. Sternbach (Eds.), *Handbook of psychophysiology.* New York: Holt, Rinehart, and Winston. Pp. 491–531.

Hess, E. H., and J. M. Polt (1960). Pupil size as related to interest value of visual stimuli. *Science, 132*, 349–350.

Hetherington, E. M. (1972). Effects of father absence on personality development in adolescent daughters. *Developmental Psychology, 7*, 313–326.

Hicks, R. A., and S. LePage (1976). *A pupillometric test of the bidirectional hypothesis.* Paper presented at the meeting of the Western Psychological Association, Los Angeles.

Hicks, R. A., T. Reaney, and L. Hill (1967). Effects of pupil size and facial angle on preference for photographs of a young woman. *Perceptual and Motor Skills, 24*, 388–390.

Hillabrant, W. (1974). *The influence of locomotion and gaze direction on perceptions of interacting persons.* Paper presented at the meeting of the American Psychological Association, New Orleans.

Hinchliffe, M. K., M. Lancashire, and F. J. Roberts (1970). Eye-contact and depression, a preliminary report. *British Journal of Psychiatry, 117*, 571–572.

Hinchliffe, M. K., M. Lancashire, and F. J. Roberts (1971). A study of eye-contact changes in depressed and recovered psychiatric patients. *British Journal of Psychiatry, 119*, 213–215.

Hindmarch, I. (1970). Pupil size and non-verbal communication. Paper presented at Proceedings of the NATO Symposium on Non-verbal Communication, Oxford. Cited in Hindmarch, I. Eyes, eye-spots and pupil dilation in nonverbal communication. In I. Vine and M. v. Cranach (Eds.), *Social communication and movement.* New York: Academic Press, 1973. Pp. 299–321.

Hindmarch, I. (1973). Eyes, eye-spots and pupil dilation in nonverbal communication. In I. Vine and M. v. Cranach (Eds.), *Social communication and movement.* New York: Academic Press, Pp. 299–321.

Hiscock, M. (1975). *The examiner location effect on gaze laterality: What is the role of anxiety.* Paper presented at the meeting of the International Neuropsychology Society, Tampa, Florida.

Hobson, G. N., K. T. Strongman, D. Bull, and G. Craig (1973). Anxiety and gaze aversion in dyadic encounters. *British Journal of Social and Clinical Psychology,* **12,** 122–129.

Holstein, C. M., J. M. Goldstein, and D. J. Bem (1971). The importance of expressive behaviors, involvement, sex, and need-approval in induced liking. *Journal of Experimental Social Psychology,* **7,** 534–544.

Hutt, C., and C. Ounsted (1966). The biological significance of gaze aversion with particular reference to the syndrone of infantile autism. *Behavioral Science,* **11,** 346–356.

Hutt, C., and M. J. Vaizey (1966). Differential effects of group density on social behavior. *Nature,* **209,** 1371–1372.

Hutt, L. D., and J. P. Anderson (1967). The relationship between pupil size and recognition threshold. *Psychonomic Science,* **9,** 477–478.

Janisse, M. P. (1973). Pupil size and affect: A critical review of the literature since 1960. *Canadian Psychologist,* **14,** 311–329.

Janisse, M. P. (1974). Pupillometry: Some advances, problems and solutions. In M. P. Janisse (Ed.), *Pupillary dynamics and behavior.* New York: Plenum Press. Pp. 1–8.

Janisse, M. P. (1976). The relationship between pupil size and anxiety: A review. In I. Sarason and C. Spielberger (Eds.), *Stress and anxiety,* Vol. 3. Washington, D.C.: Hemisphere (Wiley). Pp. 27–48.

Janisse, M. P., and W. S. Peavler (1974). Pupillary research today: Emotion in the eye. *Psychology Today,* **7,** 60–63.

Jellison, J. M., and W. J. Ickes (1974). The power of the glance: Desire to see and be seen in cooperative and competitive situations. *Journal of Experimental Social Psychology,* **10,** 444–450.

Jones, E. E., and R. E. Nesbett (1971). The actor and the observer: Divergent perceptions of the causes of behavior. In E. E. Jones, D. E. Kanouse, H. H. Kelley, R. E. Nesbett, S. Valins, and B. Weiner (Eds.), *Attribution: Perceiving the causes of behavior.* Morristown, N.J.: General Learning Press. Pp. 79–94.

Jones, Q. A., and I. S. Moyel (1971). The influence of iris color and pupil size on expressed affect. *Psychonomic Science,* **22,** 126–127.

Jourard, S. M., and R. Friedman (1970). Experimenter-subject distance and self-disclosure. *Journal of Personality and Social Psychology,* **15,** 278–282.

Jurich, A. P., and J. A. Jurich (1974). Correlations among nonverbal expressions of anxiety. *Psychological Reports,* **34,** 199–204.

Kagan, J., and M. Lewis (1965). Studies of attention in the human infant. *Merrill-Palmer Quarterly,* **2,** 95–122.

Kahneman, D., and J. Beatty (1967). Pupillary responses in a pitch discrimination task. *Perception and Psychophysics,* **2,** 101–105.

Kahneman, D., and W. S. Peavler (1969). Incentive effects and pupillary changes in association learning. *Journal of Experimental Psychology,* **79,** 312–318.

Kahneman, D., W. S. Peavler, and L. Onuska (1968). Effects of verbalization and incentive on the pupil response to mental activity. *Canadian Journal of Psychology,* **22,** 186–196.

Kahneman, D., B. Tursky, D. Shapiro, and A. Crider (1969). Pupillary heart rate, and skin resistance changes during a mental task. *Journal of Experimental Psychology,* **79,** 164–167.

Kendon, A. Some functions of gaze-direction in social interaction. (1967). *Acta Psychologica,* **26,** 22–63.

Kendon, A., and M. Cook (1969). The consistency of gaze patterns in social interaction. *British Journal of Psychology,* **60,** 481–494.

Kendon, A., and A. Ferber (1973). A description of some human greetings. In P. M. Michael and J. H. Cook (Eds.), *Comparative ecology and behavior of primates.* London: Academic Press. Pp. 591–668.

Kidd, R. F. (1975). Pupil size, eye contact, and instrumental aggression. *Perceptual and Motor Skills,* **41,** 538.

Kinsbourne, M. (1972). Eye and head turning indicates cerebral lateralization. *Science,* **176,** 539–541.

Kinsbourne, M. (1974). Direction of gaze and distribution of cerebral thought processes. *Neuropsychologia,* **12,** 279–281.

Kleck, R. E. (1968). Physical stigma and nonverbal cues emitted in face-to-face interaction. *Human Relations,* **21,** 19–28.

Kleck, R. E., P. L. Buck, W. L. Goller, R. S. London, J. R. Pfeiffer, and D. P. Vukcevic (1968). Effect of stigmatizing conditions on the use of personal space. *Psychological Reports,* **23,** 111–118.

Kleck, R. E., and W. Neussle (1968). Congruence between the indicative and communicative functions of eye contact in interpersonal relations. *British Journal of Social and Clinical Psychology,* **7,** 241–246.

Kleck, R. E., and S. Rubenstein (1975). Physical attractiveness, perceived attitude similarities, and interpersonal attraction in an opposite sex encounter. *Journal of Personality and Social Psychology,* **31,** 107–114.

Kleinke, C. L., A. A. Bustos, F. B. Meeker, and R. A. Staneski (1973). Effects of self-attributed and other-attributed gaze on interpersonal evaluations between males and females. *Journal of Experimental Social Psychology,* **9,** 154–163.

Kleinke, C. L., M. S. Desautels, and B. E. Knapp (1976). Adult gaze and affective and visual responses of preschool children. Paper presented at the meeting of Eastern Psychological Association, New York.

Kleinke, C. L., F. B. Meeker, and C. L. Fong (1974). Effects of gaze, touch, and use of name on evaluation of "engaged" couples. *Journal of Research in Personality,* **7,** 368–373.

Kleinke, C. L., and P. D. Pohlen (1971). Affective and emotional responses as a function of other person's gaze and cooperativeness in a two-person game. *Journal of Personality and Social Psychology,* **17,** 308–313.

Kleinke, C. L., and D. A. Singer (1976). *Influence of gaze on compliance to demanding and conciliatory requests in a field setting.* Paper presented at the meeting of the Western Psychological Association, Los Angeles.

Kleinke, C. L., R. A. Staneski, and D. E. Berger (1975). Evaluation of an interviewer as a function of interviewer gaze, reinforcement of subject gaze, and interviewer attractiveness. *Journal of Personality and Social Psychology,* **31,** 115–122.

Kleinke, C. L., R. A. Staneski, and S. L. Pipp, (1975). Effects of gaze, distance, and attractiveness on males' first impressions of females. *Representative Research in Social Psychology,* **6,** 7–12.

Knapp, M. L., R. P. Hart, and H. S. Dennis (1974). An exploration of deception as a communication construct. *Human Communications Research,* 1974, **1,** 15–29.

Knapp, M. L., R. P. Hart, G. W. Fredrich, and G. M. Shulman (1973). The rhetoric of good-bye: Verbal and nonverbal correlates of human leave taking. *Speech Monographs,* **40,** 182–198.

Knight, D. J., D. Langmeyer, and D. C. Lundgren (1973). Eye contact distance and affiliation: The role of observer bias. *Sociometry,* **36,** 390–401.

Koff, R. H., and T. H. Hawkes (1968). Sociometric choice: A study in pupillary response. *Perceptual and Motor Skills,* **27,** 395–402.

Kruger, K., and B. Huckstedt (1968). *Die Beurteilung von Blickrichtungen.* (Mimeographed.)

MPI für Psychiatrie, München. Unpublished manuscript cited in Cranach, M. v. The role of orienting behavior in human interaction. In A. H. Esser (Ed.), *Behavior and environment: The use of space by animals and men.* New York: Plenum Press, 1971.

LaCrosse, M. B. (1975). Nonverbal behavior and perceived counselor attractiveness and persuasiveness. *Journal of Counseling Psychology,* **22,** 563–566.

LaFrance, M. (1974). *Nonverbal cues to conversational turn taking between black speakers.* Paper presented at the meeting of the American Psychological Association, New Orleans.

LaFrance, M., and C. Mayo (1976). Racial differences in gaze behavior during conversations: Two systematic observational studies. *Journal of Personality and Social Psychology,* **33,** 547–552.

Lawless, J. C., and F. R. Wake (1968). *Sex differences in pupillary response to visual stimuli.* Unpublished manuscript, National Defense Medical Centre, Ottawa, Canada.

LeCompte, W. F., and H. M. Rosenfeld (1971). Effects of minimal eye contact in the instruction period on impressions of the experimenter. *Journal of Experimental Social Psychology,* **7,** 211–220.

Lefcourt, H. M., F. Rotenberg, R. Buckspan, and R. Steffy (1967). Visual interaction and performance of process and reactive schizophrenics as a function of examiner's sex. *Journal of Personality,* **35,** 535–546.

Lefcourt, H. M., M. S. Telegdi, D. Willows, and B. Buckspan (1972). Eye contact and the human movement inkblot response. *Journal of Social Psychology,* **88,** 303–304.

Lefcourt, H. M., and J. Wine (1969). Internal versus external control of reinforcement and the deployment of attention in experimental situations. *Canadian Journal of Behavioral Science,* **1,** 167–181.

Lefebvre, L. M. (1975). Encoding and decoding of ingratiation in modes of smiling and gaze. *British Journal of Social and Clinical Psychology,* **14,** 33–42.

Levine, M. H. (1972). *The effects of age, sex, and task on visual behavior during dyadic interaction.* Doctoral dissertation, Columbia University. [*Dissertation Abstracts International,* **33** (1972,) 2325B–2326B. University Microfilms No. 72-28, 063.]

Levine, M. H., and B. Sutton-Smith (1973). Effects of age, sex, and task on visual behavior during dyadic interaction. *Developmental Psychology,* **9,** 400–405.

Levy, T. M. (1972). *Gaze behavior, repression-sensitization, and social approach and avoidance.* Doctoral dissertation, University of Miami. [*Dissertation Abstracts International,* **33** (1973), 4544B–4545B. University Microfilms No. 73-5826.]

Libby, W. L., Jr. (1970). Eye contact and direction of looking as stable individual differences. *Journal of Experimental Research in Personality,* **4,** 303–312.

Libby, W. L. Jr., B. Lacey, and J. I. Lacey (1968). *Pupillary and cardiac activity during visual stimulation.* Paper presented at the meeting of the Society for Psychophysiological Research, Washington, D.C.

Libby, W. L., Jr., and D. Yaklevich (1973). Personality determinants of eye contact and direction of gaze aversion. *Journal of Personality and Social Psychology,* **27,** 197–206.

Lim, B. (1972). Interpretations from pictures: The effects on judgments of intimacy of varying social context and eye contact. *Journalism Abstracts,* **10,** 152–153.

Mayo, C., and M. LaFrance (1973). *Gaze direction in interracial dyadic communication.* Paper presented at the meeting of the Eastern Psychological Association, Washington, D.C.

McBride, G., M. G. King, and J. W. James (1965). Social proximity effects of galvanic skin response in adult humans. *Journal of Psychology,* **61,** 153–157.

McCaa, B. B., Jr. (1971). *A study of some factors mediating unintended experimenter effects upon subjects in psychological experiments.* Doctoral dissertation, Washington University, St. Louis, MO. [*Dissertation Abstracts International,* **32** (1972), 5338A. University Microfilms No. 79-9355.]

McDowell, K. V. (1972). Violations of personal space. *Canadian Journal of Behavioral Science,* **4,** 210–217.

McDowell, K. V. (1973). Accommodations of verbal and nonverbal behaviors as a function of the manipulations of interaction distance and eye contact. Summary in *Proceedings of the 81st Annual Convention of the American Psychological Association,* Washington, D.C. American Psychological Association, **8,** pp. 207–208.

Mehrabian, A. (1968a). Inference of attitudes from the posture orientation, and distance of a communicator. *Journal of Consulting and Clinical Psychology,* **32,** 296–308.

Mehrabian, A. (1968b). Relationship of attitude to seated posture, orientation, and distance. *Journal of Personality and Social Psychology,* **10,** 26–30.

Mehrabian, A. (1971). Verbal and nonverbal interaction of strangers in a waiting room. *Journal of Experimental Research in Personality,* **5,** 127–138.

Mehrabian, A., and J. T. Friar (1969). Encoding of attitude by a seated communicator via posture and position cues. *Journal of Consulting and Clinical Psychology,* **33,** 330–336.

Mehrabian, A., and S. Ksionzky (1972). Categories of social behavior. *Comparative Group Studies,* **3,** 425–436.

Mehrabian, A., and M. Williams (1969). Nonverbal concomitants of perceived and intended persuasiveness. *Journal of Personality and Social Psychology,* **13,** 37–58.

Mobbs, N. A. (1968). Eye-contact in relation to social introversion/extraversion. *British Journal of Social and Clinical Psychology,* **7,** 305–306.

Modigliani, A. (1971). Embarrassment, facework, and eye-contact: Testing a theory of embarrassment. *Journal of Personality and Social Psychology,* **17,** 15–24.

Murray, R. P., and H. McGinley (1972). Looking as a measure of attraction. *Journal of Applied Social Psychology,* **2,** 267–274.

Nevill, D. (1974). Experimental manipulation of dependency motivation and its effects on eye contact and measures of field dependency. *Journal of Personality and Social Psychology,* **29,** 72–79.

Nichols, K. A., and Champness, B. G. (1971). Eye gaze and the GSR. *Journal of Experimental Social Psychology,* **7,** 623–626.

Nielsen, G. (1962). *Studies in self-confrontation.* Copenhagen: Munksgaard.

Nunnally, J. C., P. D. Knott, A. Duchnowski, and R. Parker (1967). Pupillary response as a general measure of activation. *Perception and Psychophysics,* **2,** 149–155.

O'Connor, N., and B. Hermelin (1967). The selective visual attention of psychotic children. *Journal of Child Psychology and Psychiatry,* **8,** 167–169.

Paradis, M. H. (1972). The effects of eye contact on posture and negative self-disclosure Doctoral dissertation, Washington State University. [*Dissertation Abstracts International,* **33** (1972), 2795B. University Microfilms No. 72-31, 292.]

Patterson, M. L. (1973a). Compensation in nonverbal immediacy behaviors: A review. *Sociometry,* **36,** 237–252.

Patterson, M. L. (1973b). Stability of nonverbal immediacy behaviors. *Journal of Experimental Social Psychology,* **9,** 97–109.

Patterson, M. L., S. Mullens, and J. Romano (1971). Compensatory reactions to spatial intrusion. *Sociometry,* **34,** 114–121.

Patterson, M. L., and L. B. Sechrest (1970). Interpersonal distance and impression formation. *Journal of Personality,* **38,** 161–166.

Pellegrini, R. J., R. A. Hicks, and L. Gordon (1970). The effects of approval-seeking induction on eye-contact in dyads. *British Journal of Social and Clinical Psychology,* **9,** 373–374.

Rohner, S. J., and J. R. Aiello (1975). *The effect of topic intimacy on interaction behaviors.* Paper presented at the meeting of the Eastern Psychological Association, New York.

Rubin, Z. (1970). Measurement of romantic love. *Journal of Personality and Social Psychology,*

16, 265–273.

Russo, N. F. (1975). Eye contact, interpersonal distance, and the equilibrium theory, *Journal of Personality and Social Psychology*, 31, 497–502.

Rutter, D. R. (1973). Visual interaction in psychiatric patients: A review. *British Journal of Psychiatry*, 123, 193–202.

Rutter, D. R., I. E. Morley, and J. C. Graham (1972). Visual interaction in a group of introverts and extraverts. *European Journal of Social Psychology*, 2, 371–384.

Rutter, D. R., and G. M. Stephenson (1972a). Visual interaction in a group of schizophrenic and depressive patients. *British Journal of Social and Clinical Psychology*, 11, 57–65.

Rutter, D. R., and G. M. Stephenson (1972b). Visual interaction in a group of schizophrenic and depressed patients: A follow-up study. *British Journal of Social and Clinical Psychology*, 11, 410–411.

Schaefer, T., J. B. Ferguson, J. B. Klein, and E. B. Rawson (1968). Pupillary responses during mental activities. *Psychonomic Science*, 12, 137–138.

Scherer, S. E., and M. R. Schiff (1973). Perceived intimacy, physical distance, and eye contact. *Perceptual and Motor Skills*, 36, 835–841.

Scherwitz, L., and R. Helmreich (1973). Interactive effects of eye contact and verbal content on interpersonal attraction in dyads. *Journal of Personality and Social Psychology*, 25, 6–14.

Schwartz, G. E. (1974). *Hemispheric asymmetry and emotion: Bilateral EEG and lateral eye movements.* Paper presented at the meeting of the American Psychological Association, New Orleans.

Scott, T. R., W. H. Wells, D. Z. Wood, and D. I. Morgan (1967). Pupil response and sexual interest re-examined. *Journal of Clinical Psychology*, 23, 433–438.

Simms, T. M. (1967). Pupillary response of male and female subjects to pupillary difference in male and female picture stimuli. *Perception and Psychophysics*, 2, 553–555.

Simpson, H. M., and S. M. Hale (1969). Pupillary changes during a decision-making task. *Perceptual and Motor Skills*, 29, 495–498.

Snow, P. A. (1972). Verbal content and affective response in an interview as a function of experimenter gaze direction. Unpublished masters thesis, Lakehead University, Thunder Bay, Ontario, Canada. (Argyle, M., and Cook M. *Gaze and mutual gaze.* Cambridge: University Printing House, 1976.)

Sodikoff, C. L., I. J. Firestone, and K. J. Kaplan (1974). *Distance matching and distance equilibrium in the interview dyad.* Paper presented at the meeting of the American Psychological Association, New Orleans.

Stass, J. W., and F. N. Willis, Jr. (1967). Eye contact, pupil dilation, and personal preference. *Psychonomic Science*, 7, 375–376.

Steer, A., and J. A. Lake (1972). *Nonverbal cues in the termination of encounters: An example of a transition point in social interaction.* Unpublished manuscript. (Available from the Department of Psychology, Birbeck College, London, England).

Stephenson, G. M., and D. R. Rutter (1970). Eye-contact, distance, and affiliation: A re-evaluation. *British Journal of Psychology*, 61, 385–393.

Stephenson, G. M., D. R. Rutter, and S. R. Dore (1972). Visual interaction and distance. *British Journal of Psychology*, 64, 251–257.

Stewart, D. J., and M. L. Patterson (1973). Eliciting effects of verbal and nonverbal cues on projective test responses. *Journal of Consulting and Clinical Psychology*, 41, 74–77.

Streltsova, N. I. (1965). The influence of some physiological and pharmacological factors on the pupillary orienting reflex. In L. G. Voronin, A. N. Leontiev, A. R. Luria, E. N. Sokolove, and O. S. Vinogradova (Eds.), *Orienting reflex and exploratory behavior.* Moscow: Academy of Pedagogical Sciences, RSFSR, 1958. Translated by V. Shmelev and K.

Hanes, D. B. Lindsley (Ed.). Washington, D.C.: American Institute of Biological Sciences.

Strongman, K. T., and B. G. Champness (1968). Dominance hierarchies and conflict in eye contact. *Acta Psychologica*, **28**, 376–386.

Thayer, S. (1969). The effect of interpersonal looking duration on dominance judgements. *Journal of Social Psychology*, **79**, 285–286.

Thayer, S., and W. Schiff (1974). Observer judgment of social interactions: Eye contact and relationship inferences. *Journal of Personality and Social Psychology*, **30**, 110–114.

Tinio, F., and M. Robertson (1969). Examination of two indices of hostility: Fantasy and change in pupil size. Summary in *Proceedings of the 77th Annual Convention of the American Psychological Association*. Washington, D.C.: American Psychological Association. Pp. 173–174.

Tryon, W. W. (1975). Pupillometry: A survey of sources of variation. *Psychophysiology*, **12**, 90–93.

Vacchiano, R. B., P. S. Strauss, S. Ryan, and L. Hockman (1968). Pupillary response to value linked words. *Perceptual and Motor Skills*, **27**, 207–210.

Vine, I. (1971). Judgement of direction of gaze: An interpretation of discrepant results. *British Journal of Social and Clinical Psychology*, **10**, 320–331.

Watson, O. M. (1970). *Proxemic behavior: A cross-cultural study*. The Hague: Mouton.

Waxer, P. (1974). Nonverbal cues for depression. *Journal of Abnormal Psychology*, **83**, 319–322.

Weisbrod, R. R. (1965). Looking behavior in a discussion group. Term paper submitted for Psychology 546 under the direction of Professor Longabaugh, Cornell University, Ithaca, New York.

Weiss, M., and C. Keys (1975). *The influence of proxemic variables on dyadic interaction between peers*. Paper presented at the meeting of the American Psychological Association, Chicago.

Werner, A. and H. Reis (1974). *Do the eyes have it? Some interpersonal consequences of the stare*. Paper presented at the meeting of the Eastern Psychological Association.

White, G. T. (1975). *The mating game: Nonverbal interpersonal communication between dating and engaged college couples*. Paper presented at the meeting of the Western Psychological Association, Sacramento.

White, J. H., J. R. Hegarty, and N. A. Beasley (1970). Eye contact and observer bias: A research note. *British Journal of Psychology*, **61**, 271–273.

Wiemann, J. M. (1974). *An experimental study of visual attention in dyads: The effect of four gaze conditions on evaluation of applicants in employment interviews*. Paper presented at the meeting of the Speech Communication Association, Chicago.

Wiener, M., S. Devoe, S. Rubinow, and J. Geller (1972). Nonverbal behavior and nonverbal communication. *Psychological Review*, **79**, 185–214.

Wiener, M., and A. Mehrabian (1968). *Language within language: Immediacy, a channel in verbal communication*. New York: Appleton-Century-Crofts.

Wiens, A. N., J. D. Matarazzo, and G. Saslow (1965). The Interaction Recorder: An electronic punched paper tape unit for recording speech behavior during interviews. *Journal of Clinical Psychology*, **21**, 142–145.

Williams, E. (1974). An analysis of gaze in schizophrenics. *British Journal of Social and Clinical Psychology*, **13**, 1–8.

Woodmansee, J. J. (1965). An evaluation of the pupil response as a measure of attitude toward Negroes. Unpublished doctoral dissertation, University of Colorado.

Woodmansee, J. J. (1970). The pupil response as a measure of social attitudes. In G. Summers (Ed.), *Attitude measurement*. New York: Rand McNally.

CHAPTER 6

Proxemics: The Study of Space

INTRODUCTION

In this chapter we discuss the manner in which individuals use physical space in their interactions with others and how physical space influences behavior. Most researchers have labelled this area of nonverbal research as the study of proxemics, a term introduced by Edward T. Hall, the noted anthropologist who first systematically studied human use of space. In her recent review, Shirley Weitz (1974) has noted that "Proxemics . . . is clearly linked to anthropology. The meaning and use of space in different cultures is a primary focus of study, and naturalistic methods of observation are generally used" (p. 199). Personal space, in contrast, is a social psychological term (introduced by Robert Sommer) which, as Weitz noted,

chiefly deals with the meaning of space to the individual in terms of the effects of crowding, territoriality, architectural design, and so on, and is only peripherally concerned with intercultural variations. Controlled laboratory and field studies are used, in contrast to proxemics, which mainly relies on observational studies. The difference between proxemic and personal space research is analogous to that between the structural and experimental approaches. (Weitz, 1974, p. 199)

Both proxemic and personal space research are considered in this chapter.

Though we are interested primarily in the empirical research, Hall's observations and classification schemes are too important not to be considered in some detail. His 1966 book, *The Hidden Dimension,* is "a model of clarity and precision in social science writing" (Weitz, 1974, p. 200) and fascinating reading for the expert and novice alike. Hall (1966) defined proxemics as the "interrelated observations and theories of man's use of space as a specialized elaboration of culture" (Hall, 1966, p. 1); "The study of how man unconsciously structures microspace—the distance between men in the conduct of daily transactions, the organization of space in his houses and buildings and ultimately the layout of his towns" (Hall, 1963b, p. 1003). Hall (1966) described three kinds of spatial organization: fixed feature, semi-fixed feature, or informal space. *Fixed* feature space refers to arrangement of environmental space such as houses, rooms, even cities and towns. *Semi-fixed features* are such movable objects as a table, chairs, and the like. *Informal space* pertains to interpersonal distance, which is of primary interest here.

Hall (1968) reviewed proxemics on an interpersonal level as "a constellation of sensory inputs . . . coded in a particular way" (p. 94). He formulated a comprehensive "proxemic notational system" that covers the following eight different "dimensions": (a) postural-sex identifiers (sex and postural status of the interactants), (b) sociofugal-sociopetal axis (face-to-face vs. back-to-back positioning of shoulders), (c) kinesthetic factors (the different distances between persons that provide a capability for touching one another), (d) touch code, (e) visual code (based on retinal areas used, e.g., foveal for direct gaze), (f) voice loudness, (g) thermal code (the heat transmitted by a human body), (h) olfaction code (the presence and degree of undifferentiated breath and body odors). The reader will note that many of these dimensions encompass some aspects of the nonverbal behaviors considered in previous sections on the voice, kinesics, and visual behavior. However, underlying all of these dimensions is the factor of physical distance which, other things held constant, will determine how much we hear, see, feel, smell, etc. Indeed, at the risk of pointing out the obvious, distance can be considered a necessary (but not sufficient) condition for nonverbal communication itself.

Less obvious is the fact that distance determines the kind of communication that takes place. One of Hall's most important contributions was his description of four distance zones that were based on his observation of normal middle-class Americans. These include the intimate, personal, social, and public distances. *Intimate* distances begin with a close phase ("the distance of love-making and wrestling, comforting and protecting" (Hall, 1966, p. 110), where olfactory and thermal sensations are maximal, perception of very fine visual detail (e.g., skin texture) is at its greatest, while large objects (e.g., the head) are blurred, and most important, where physical contact is most probable. Speech, interestingly, plays a relatively minor role, given the abundance of other sensory stimulation from other modalities. A distance from 6 to 18 inches constitutes the far phase of the intimate distance, where 'heads, thighs, and pelvis are not easily brought into contact but hands can reach and grasp extremities" (p. 111). Even at these distances, visual perception of the face is somewhat distorted, and the voice is kept at a whisper or at a very low level. Olfaction, touch, and thermal perception are still quite salient. Hall noted that "much of the physical discomfort that Americans experience when foreigners are inappropriately inside the intimate sphere is expressed as a distortion of the visual system" (p. 111).

Personal distances can range from 1.5 to 2.5 feet (close phase) to 2.5 to 4 feet (far phase). At these distances, visual distortion no longer occurs and thermal perception is effectively dimished, olfaction to a lesser extent. Interactants can reach and touch each other with their extremities but, at the far phase, only if both extend their limbs. Where a person stands signals the nature of the relationship (the closer, generally, the more involved and physically intimate). At the far phase, subject matter of a personal nature is appropriate in conversation and the voice level is moderate.

Social distances range from 4 to 7 feet (near phase) and from 7 to 12 feet (far phase). Most impersonal informal business occurs at the closer of these distances, where the taller of two interactants can look down at the other (such as a businessman at his secretary). Formal business interactions occur at the longer distances where vision and hearing are the two primary modalities of sensory input. Visual contact is most important to interaction at these distances as gaze aversion is tantamount to terminating communication. Hall observed that the far social distances permit initiation or termination of social interaction without rudeness, and they are employed in situations (e.g., a large office) where persons need to be insulated or screened from other potential interactants.

Finally, there are what Hall describes as *public* distances, ranging from 12 to 20 feet, or 25 feet or more. Mandatory recognition of others is no longer socially required as at the social distances. Here defensive or socially evasive actions can be taken (e.g., changing direction of one's walk) and fine details of the face and other body parts begin to become indistinguishable. Far public distances are, according to Hall (1966), "automatically set around important public people" (p. 177) (e.g., the President). Also at these distances, "the subtle shades of meaning conveyed by the normal voice are lost as are the details of facial expression and movement. Not only the voice but everything else must be exaggerated or amplified. Much of the nonverbal communication shifts to gestures and body stance" (p. 120).

The above distances apply only to Americans and possibly a relatively pure cultural group (Northern European) within this country. Based on his cross-cultural research, Hall (1968) asserted that "what crowds one people does not necessarily crowd another " (p. 84). Unlike the evidence that Paul Ekman amassed on universals of facial expression, it appears that there are no universals in distance setting. Man's use and conceptualization of space in relation to structures and other people varies across cultures which have developed rules and uses of space which, once learned, are largely unconscious:

Proxemic patterns, once learned, are maintained largely out of conscious awareness and thus have to be investigated without resort to probing the conscious minds of one's subjects. Direct questioning will yield few if any of the significant variables, as it will with kinship and house type, for example. In proxemics one is dealing with phenomena akin to tone of voice, or even stress and pitch in the English language. Being built into the language, these are hard for the speaker to consciously manipulate. (Hall, 1963b, p. 1003)

That proxemic variables are of paramount importance in cross cultural interaction can be seen from a number of Hall's brilliant and lucid observations. Consider the following description by Hall of his experience training Americans overseas:

Americans overseas were confronted with a variety of difficulties because of cultural differences in the handling of space. People stood "too close" during conversations, and when the Americans backed away to a comfortable conversational distance, this was taken to mean that Americans were cold, aloof, withdrawn, and disinterested in the people of the country. (Hall, 1963a, p. 423).

Persons of other cultures often find it difficult to interact with Americans. For example, Hall (1963b) noted:

Arabs complained of experiencing alienation particularly when interacting with that segment of the U.S. population which can be classed as noncontact (predominantly of North European origin, where touching strangers and casual acquaintances is circumscribed with numerous proscriptions). When approached too closely, Americans removed themselves to a position which turned out to be outside the olfactory zone (to be inside was much too intimate for the Americans). Arabs also experienced alienation traceable to a suspiciously low level of the voice, the directing of the breath away from the face, and a much reduced visual contact. Two common forms of alienation reported by American subjects were *self-consciousness at the cost of involvement* and *other consciousness*. Americans were not only aware of uncomfortable feelings, but the intensity and the intimacy of the encounter with Arabs was likely to be anxiety provoking. The Arab look, touch, voice level, the warm moisture of his breath, the penetrating stare of his eyes, all proved to be disturbing. The reason for these feelings lay in part in the fact that the relationship *was not defined as intimate,* and the behavior was such that in the American culture is only permissible on a non-public basis with a person of the opposite sex.

In a different cultural setting, a Chinese experienced alienation during an interview when he was faced directly and seated on the opposite side of a desk, for this was defined as *being on trial.* (pp. 1005–1006)

Though we do not consider Hall's anthropological observations in much greater detail, it is fair to say that much of the empirical data generated overlaps with Hall's formulations. For example, Altman and his colleagues studied territoriality, which they defined as an individual's preference for areas and objects (Altman and Haythorn, 1967, p. 171), a concept that clearly corresponds to Hall's semi-fixed and fixed space notion but not to his concept of informal space. Little (1965), however, proposed the term "personal distance" as "the area immediately surrounding the individual in which the majority of his interactions with others take place" (p. 237). And even before Little, Sommer (1959) proposed his term "personal space," which was characterized by an absence of fixed geographic reference points (i.e., it moves with the individual, and expands and contracts in different circumstances). Kuethe (1962a, 1962b) introduced the term "social schema," a construct by which people perceive themselves and others as belonging or being organized together much like objects in a Gestalt sense. Finally, Jourard (1966) systematically studied tactile communication, which is one of the proxemic dimensions specified by Hall.

An important technical distinction that Watson (1972) has made and which concerns all the research that we consider is the *emic-etic* distinction, originally made by linguists. An emic level of analysis involves studying the relationships of behaviors within a specific system (such as a particular culture), i.e., the internal structure of the behavioral system. In contrast, "the *etic* approach involves viewing a system of behavior from outside the system, using criteria which are external to the system. . . . The *etic* approach provides an initial base from which the observer can begin his analysis of the system" (p. 454). In particular, Watson (1972) pointed out that "so far proxemic research has been cast almost entirely in an etic framework" (p. 454), based upon some variations of the etic notation system developed by Hall. We do not belabor this distinction further in this review though the reader should be aware of it in considering research in this area as a whole.

In the following sections we consider the empirical research which has been conducted on proxemics. The studies conducted can generally be organized into the following areas: (a) individual and group differences in personal space where personality, demographic, and cultural variables are the primary focus; (b) studies focusing on interpersonal variables such as interpersonal attraction, interpersonal distance, and arousal and responses to invasions of personal space; (c) the effects of environment and variations in physical setting that affect population density; (d) studies on touch. Finally, we consider some of the most recent theories developed which attempt to explain the significance of space to humans in relation to their needs for "territory," "privacy," distance from others, and the like.

Before turning to these various areas, some general consideration should be given briefly to the methods of study employed in proxemic research so that the reader can better appreciate the strengths and weaknesses of the various studies we are considering. Watson (1972), himself an anthropologist, noted that there are essentially two basic ways of obtaining information concerning human behavior: naturalistic observation and laboratory experimentation. He noted that the second is "less often as creative, less often as intellectually stimulating, and almost always less exciting than the first method, but always of equal importance . . . [and] at least in the case of proxemics . . . more necessary" (p. 446). As we noted earlier, Hall's own research was based upon naturalistic observation. One of the most important tools in such research is a camera, preferrably one which is power driven, permitting rapid shooting. Skill is needed, however, in unobtrusive recording and (important for cross-cultural research) the photographer must be knowledgeable about and sensitive to the culture being studied (e.g., a member of the culture). This latter consideration is crucial if one is to be sure that the behavior being observed is the result of some proxemic factor and not some other confounding influence specific to a particular culture.

Laboratory investigations, of course, permit control over extraneous influences, but even here it is important to consider "what kinds of factors must be neutralized, rendered constant in order to isolate proxemic behavior from their differential influence" (Watson, 1972, p. 447). To answer this question, Watson turned to the work of Altman and Lett (1969) who proposed that interpersonal behavior was influenced by *environmental* as well as *interactant characteristics.* Not only do physical (appearance), physiological (e.g., state of arousal, fatigue), or personality factors influence proxemic behavior, but so also do environmental variables such as the available space in the laboratory, lighting, noise, and room temperature. Each can be conceptualized as antecedent factors that play an important role in the social interaction: "When people engage in face to face interaction they derive from certain factors antecedent to the interaction the definition of the situation . . . in which interactants find themselves" (Watson, 1972, p. 447). How subjects define the situation is a particularly important matter and very difficult to control, especially in cross-cultural research where even the same laboratory situation may have different meanings for different persons.

As we see, a number of different experimental methods have been employed, few of which have been psychometrically sophisticated. In their review, Duke and Nowicki (1972) stated, "The empirical literature on interpersonal distance is, for the most part, naturalistic-correlations. . . . Perhaps the assumption is made that since interpersonal distance is such an 'obvious' phenomenon, any measure will do" (p. 121). One experimental "real-life" measure was to obtain self-reports from subjects at what point they begin to feel uncomfortable as others physically approached them (e.g., Frankel and Barrett, 1971), or as they physically approached another. Horowitz, Duff, and Stratton (1964) had experimenters approach subjects from various angles (e.g., back, front, side) to obtain "body buffer zone" measurements. Cozby (1973) more recently reported correlations ranging from .69 to .90 between four approach measures (i.e., where the subject approaches and is approached by two experimenters). Meisels and Canter (1970), however, reported a correlation of only .65 between physical distance and perceived closeness.

A less obtrusive method is determining the distance or location (opposite vs. side-by-side) at which a person seats himself in relation to an interactant. A whole area of research pioneered by Robert Sommer (1959, 1969) has been devoted to the study of seating distances, seating arrangements, and invasions of personal space (e.g., sitting too close). Subjects can be exposed to "free seating situations," where they can choose a distance available, or they can be made to "intrude" when seating is possible only in areas already occupied. Where distance is manipulated as an independent variable (i.e., others approaching or "invading" a subject's personal space) various dependent measures of comfort-discomfort are possible, such as physiological recording (McBride, King, and James, 1965) or other expressive nonverbal behaviors (e.g., gaze-aversion, posture-shifts, agonistic facial expressions) or instrumental acts (i.e., leaving the situation).

Another approach has been to employ "simulated" measures of personal space. Kuethe (1962a) proposed that humans develop "social schemas" whereby personal relationships are organized along Gestalt principles. To measure social schemas Kuethe employed a felt board on which cut out figures and nonhuman objects are placed, the area between them presumably representing "psychological distances." Kuethe employed this technique in two ways: (a) by having subjects *place* the figures directly on the felt board, or (b) by having subjects *replace* the figures in an arrangement previously made by the experimenter. This latter method was called the figure replacement technique, the changes in distances (nearer or farther) from the original setting representing each individual's particular "social schema." Kuethe's technique was extensively employed by Tolor (1968) who also developed a paper-and-pencil measure called the Psychological Distance Scale (PDS) whereby the subject indicates his distance from certain figure "concepts" (e.g., father, mother, sister, stranger). Recently, Pedersen (1973a) developed the Pedersen Personal Space Measure by which the subject places a movable human profile as close as is comfortable to a profile drawn on a page. The drawn profile shows a man facing left, front, right, and viewed from the top.

Whereas the real-life measures are subject to conscious control by subjects, the simulated measures suffer from a question concerning their validity. Some support for the validity of simulated measures comes from Shontz and McNish (1972) who, in their research on body image, recently demonstrated that "recognition of a stimulus as a human body activates cognitive processes . . . and produces perceptual responses that differ systematically from those that occur to stimuli which are not so recognized" (p. 24). This was true for distance estimations of others' bodies, mirror images of the body, and drawings of the body. However, Gottheil, Corey, and Paredes (1968) obtained only a correlation of .40 between "real life" (seating distance) and simulated personal space measures. Other investigators (Dosey and Meisels, 1969; Pedersen, 1973a) have also reported poor agreement among personal space measures, including questionnaires, sillhouette, seating, and approach distances.

A paper-and-pencil instrument recently developed and subjected to considerable validation is the CIDS or Comfortable Interpersonal Distance Scale (Duke and Nowicki, 1972). This scale consists of a plane with eight radians emanating from a common point. Subjects are to imagine themselves at the center of a room and are to indicate on each particular radian (representing a direction of approach) where they would allow an imaginary other to approach them. Duke and Nowicki demonstrated that the measure was not significantly correlated with confounding factors such as a social desirability response set, and they reported relatively high correlations (.65 to .84) between the CIDS and actual approach measures. More recently Gordon and Duke (1975) constructed a paper-and-pencil scale to measure group space, defined as "the invisible boundary surrounding an interacting group" (p. 1). This consisted of two parallel lines representing a hallway on an $8\frac{1}{2} \times 11$-inch sheet of paper and two circles representing persons conversing near the center of the paper at a distance from each other that would correspond to a real distance of about $2\frac{1}{2}$ feet. Subjects are asked to draw a line indicating the path they would follow if they were walking down a hallway to class. Six different sheets of paper were employed with the circles corresponding to two male students, two female students, two female teachers, two male teachers, and two wastebaskets. With a validation sample of high school student seniors, greater distances were shown in the hypothetical paths for "high status" authority figures (e.g., policemen, teachers) than low-authority stimuli (e.g., students and wastebaskets). A similar task using four circles to depict a larger group yielded essentially the same results. In addition, there was an interaction between locus of control and preferred distance, with external locus-of-control subjects showing greater distances. Test-retest reliability of the stimuli ranged from .70 for female students to .84 for policemen, with only male students as stimuli ($r = .40$) yielding unacceptably low reliability. Further research with the instrument is needed but it would be interesting to see its intercorrelation with personal-space invasion measures, dominance behaviors, and the CIDS measure.

All these approaches have been extensively used in the literature we will review. The point to be made here is that no single measure of personal space is totally adequate. As Meisels and Dosey (1971) reported, how a person is instructed to approach another can influence interpersonal distance seating. Since most measurement techniques have been subject to conscious awareness (and hence control) of the subject, experimentally produced artifacts must be suspect. Evans and Howard (1972), for example, found a poor correspondence between various behavioral, subjective, and physiological changes as a function of decreasing distance. Zanni (1976) in particular noted that interchangeability among personal space measures (e.g., actual interpersonal distance vs. figure placement vs. paper-and-pencil tests) rested on the assumptions that (a) subjects' awareness of the dependent variable does not contaminate the measure and (b) that subjects' spatial preferences based on figure placement or paper-and-pencil measures accurately mirror real life spatial preferences. To investigate these assumptions, Zanni manipulated perceived similarity of an experimental accomplice by giving subjects information that the subject was either in the same or different experimental condition. Zanni reasoned that since perceived similarity is associated with shorter interaction distances, different personal space measures should reflect this if they are valid. Five personal space measures were used: (a) subjects actually chose a seat next to a similar or dissimilar experimental accomplice; (b) subjects chose a seat next to a chair on which the accomplice's belongings were placed; (c) subjects were to use a feltboard; (d) subjects indicated their seating placement on a paper-and-pencil diagram without awareness of seating preference as a dependent measure; (e) seating choices on a diagram were made with awareness of seating preferences. For the first four measures subject personal space was greater when the experimental confederate was perceived as dissimilar. In contrast, subject awareness of the dependent measure obviated this well known effect, suggesting that awareness will contaminate subject performance in an experiment. Zanni did conclude, however, that the figure placement technique and paper-and-pencil measure did provide an adequate index of subjects' real use of personal space. Despite Zanni's findings and the new apparently objective measures (e.g., the CIDS), the following cautionary remarks by Evans and Howard in their review (1973) still probably describe the state of the art in proxemics:

Given the complex nature of human environment variables, exploration in this area of personal space should employ a combination of techniques that seek to minimize bias and maximize data generalizability. Piecemeal examination of individual variables based upon a single dependent measure will continue to provide us with much data and little insight into the nature of personal space. (Evans and Howard, 1973, p. 338)

INDIVIDUAL DIFFERENCES

Here we consider differences in the use of personal space and distance as a function of sex, race, cultural factors, personality, and age. Several reviews covering these areas have been provided by Lett, Clark and Altman (1969), Evans and Howard (1973), and Patterson (1974). Lett, Clark, and Altman (1969), in particular, sampled the proxemic literature and generated a useful set of propositions to which they attached varying degrees of certainty based upon the research findings. Where appropriate, we note their propositions and the studies they reported in support of them, including more recent studies available to us for review.

Sex Differences

Lett, Clark, and Altman (1969) generated four hypotheses or propositions based on sex differences. Their best supported hypothesis and one that has been generally supported in subsequent research was that females maintain closer interpersonal distances than males. This has been demonstrated in a variety of ways: by seating position (e.g., females preferred sitting corner to corner, as in Hare and Bales, 1963, and Sommer, 1959; or side-by-side as in Norum, Russo, and Sommer, 1967, and Sommer, 1959); by figure placements (Long, Ziller, and Henderson, 1968; although Lerea and Ward, 1966, obtained nonsignificant results). Willis (1966) demonstrated that females tended to approach closer to certain conversational partners. Hartnett, Bailey, and Gibson (1970) found that females allowed an experimenter to approach closer to them than males, and Leibman (1970) obtained findings that generally suggested females had smaller personal space zones, based upon seating patterns of subjects.

As might be expected, these relationships become more complicated when other variables are considered. In particular, the sex of the other interactant is most important. For example, Leibman (1970) found that females tended to sit closer to other females than other males. Other researchers found that white females tended to approach closer to one another (e.g., Aiello and Jones, 1971; Dosey and Meisels, 1969; Pellegrini and Empey, 1970), even in social situations larger than dyads (Mehrabian and Diamond, 1971; Patterson and Schaeffer, 1974). Leibman (1970) suggested that prevailing social norms foster closer female-female interaction than male-male interpersonal distances.

Opposite sex interaction produces yet more complicated findings. Based upon his figure placement task, Kuethe (1962a, 1962b; Kuethe and Weingartner, 1964) found that the "social schemata" of male-female pairings reflected less personal space than same sex pairings. Kleck (1967) obtained similar results using a photograph placement technique, as did Long, Henderson, and Ziller (1967) using geometric symbols representing people. In all of these studies, opposite sex pairs were depicted closer together than same-sex pairs. Hartnett, Bailey, and Gibson (1970) observed a tendency for males high on heterosexuality to move closer to female decoys than males. In contrast, however, Campbell, Kruskal, and Wallace (1966) observed that students tended to seat themselves in same sex arrangements and Lewit and Joy (1967) reported that female observers viewed a male-male dyad as closer together than a male-female pair. Dosey and Meisels (1969) found that females actually approached another female closer than another male, whereas males approached females and other males at about the same distance. Finally, McBride, King, and James (1965) noted that subjects' galvanic skin responses were greater when approached by an opposite-sex experimenter.

An important distinction emphasized by Patterson (1974) is whether the subject is approaching another or is approached by another person. Several researchers found that females allowed closer approach to themselves than males (Hartnett, Bailey, and Gibson, 1970; Mehrabian and Friar, 1969; Willis, 1966). In particular, Hartnett, Bailey, and Gibson found that while females tolerated a closer approach by others, they maintained a greater distance from others when actually making an approach themselves. Patterson (1974) commented: "Females appear to be more reserved than males not only in actively approaching someone of the opposite sex, but also in passively limiting the closer approach of such a person" (p. 3).

Petri, Huggins, Mills, and Barry (1974) administered the Comfortable Interpersonal Distance Scale (Duke and Nowicki, 1972) to males and females. Subjects were asked to show schematically the extent to which they would allow an imaginary, same-aged "stranger" to approach them from each of eight different directions. Their findings were as follows: (a) subjects of both sexes kept male strangers farther away, regardless of the approach; (b) females kept strangers of both sexes more distant from rear approaches than from frontal approaches (although this was true only for females over 20); (c) males did not maintain a greater personal space behind them; however, they allowed females to approach closer from behind. For males, the sex of the stranger was important:

If a female stranger approached a male subject, the personal space approximated a circle, but if the approaching stranger was male the personal space became elliptical. While males allowed strangers of either sex to approach to essentially the same distance in front, a significantly greater distance was required for male strangers approaching from the rear. (Petri, Huggins, Mills, and Barry, 1974, p. 5)

Gordon and Johnson (1975) measured the distance that college students passed by a male and female experimental assistant who either faced towards or away from them. Subjects walked farther away from the male when he faced them than the female assistant or when he was not facing them. The female assistant's position had no significant effect on the distance allotted her. Male subjects walked farther away from the assistants than females and farther away when the assistant faced them than when not.

It is not surprising, given the multiplicity of methods employed (i.e., seating arrangements, actual approach tasks, figure placement methods), that the findings would be somewhat inconsistent. Indeed, it seems rather naive to assume that these relationships can be studied without considering also such crucial variables as the nature of the relationship and interpersonal transaction. Allgeier and Byrne (1973), for example, found that interpersonal attraction resulted in decreases in interpersonal distance between opposite-sex pairs. Little (1968) noted that the social context and degree of acquaintance were major factors in determining dyadic schema for his subjects. Willis (1966) found that females only approached closer to "best friends," whereas they stayed further than males from "friends." Cook (1970) observed that intimacy was a major factor in a person's choice of seating arrangements in real life settings. Klukken (1972) found that while females tended to use shorter interaction distances (especially for discussion of intimate topics with friends), they and male subjects employed greater distances when interacting with a stranger concerning an intimate topic. Rohner and Aiello (1976) studied proxemic behavior of same-sex and opposite-sex dyads with a group of high school students. Unlike much prior research, special care was taken to control interpersonal affect level, degree of acquaintance of interactants, topic of conversation, and experimental situation. Subject dyads were asked to stand in a specific 9 × 11-foot area in front of the desk of a woman observer and discuss their least and most preferred television shows. The degree of acquaintance and interpersonal affect level did not influence the two proxemic measures, body orientation, and interpersonal distance. As predicted, female-female dyads interacted with a more direct orientation and shorter interpersonal distances than males. Mixed-sex dyads showed an intermediate level of intimacy of body orientation but not on interpersonal distance, where they stood at approximately the male-male dyadic distances. The unexpected distance setting for mixed-sex dyads may possibly have been due to adolescent discomfort with heterosexual interaction stiuations.

It is also not surprising that different findings might emerge when people are merely asked to make representational arrangements of social situations as compared to when they actually engage in proxemic behavior with others. This latter point is illustrated in a study by Fromme and Beam (1974) who investigated the behavior of high- and low-dominant male and female subjects who were interacting with a confederate engaging in high and low eye contact. Under conditions of low confederate eye contact, dominant females evidenced the smallest personal space whereas nondominant females and males and dominant males differed only very slightly. However, when confederate eye contact was high (presumably a "dominance challenge"), high-dominant males dramatically decreased their interpersonal distance by approaching rapidly whereas all other subjects tended to increase their distance. Interestingly, dominant females responded with a marked increase in eye contact, apparently the female response to a dominance challenge. This study illustrates the importance of situational factors (behavior of the interactant) and individual difference variables (e.g., dominance) that must be also considered as contributing to proxemic behavior.

The uses and meanings of social approach-avoidance behaviors may also differ in important ways for the sexes. Some evidence for this point may be seen in some studies investigating the effects of crowding. Both Freedman, Levy, Buchanan, and Price (1972) and Ross, Layton, Erickson, and Schopler (1973) reported that females were more positive to other females in crowded conditions, whereas males reacted negatively to males in the same circumstances. However, in Freedman, Levy, Buchanan, and Price (1972) when mixed-sex groups in crowded and uncrowded situations were compared, no differences emerged. Freedman, Levy, Buchanan, and Price (1972) hypothesized that females were expected to be more affiliative and would find crowding circumstances facilitating for interpersonal attraction whereas males, who were expected to be dominant and competitive, would react negatively to a physically crowded situation. In contrast, a more recent finding by Marshall and Heslin (1975) showed that males preferred a crowded situation when working on a long and involving task, whereas females preferred a less crowded condition. Apparently the task orientation allowed men to develop a common goal and sense of comraderie, whereas females found the task orientation and crowding situation frustrating to their affiliative needs, especially when there was close personal contact. Mixed-group subjects also apparently preferred the more crowded situation. Other findings showing such sex differences in crowding situations are noted later.

Finally, Fisher and Byrne (1975) examined sex differences in reaction to personal space intrusions in a library situation. Several previous experiments had shown that males preferred approaching others from the side and females preferred a direct frontal approach to others (Horowitz, Duff, and Stratton, 1964; Jones, 1971), but that males were most sensitive to frontal invasions and females to invasions from the side (Patterson, Mullins, and Romano, 1971). Fisher and Byrne (1975) elaborated on the latter finding by having confederates of both sexes invade the personal space of students sitting in a library. As predicted, males noticed more often, reacted more negatively to, and erected more "barriers" to others who sat opposite them than beside them, whereas females showed a similar response to invasions from the side. Interestingly, the sex of the invader had no apparent effect.

More recently, Buchanan, Juhnke, and Goldman (1976) investigated sex differences concerning the propensity for violation of the personal space of others. In their first experiment a male or female confederate was positioned at different times one foot away from one of two floor selection panels in a large downtown elevator. In this situation 78% of males chose to avoid using the floor selection panel next to the male confederate and 85% of the males similarly avoided the female confederate. Eighty-five percent of the female subjects avoided male personal space violations and 74% avoided female personal space violations. In a second study a male and female confederate were positioned in the elevator at the same time, thereby forcing subjects to make a personal space violation using one of the floor selection panels. In this situation 72% of male subjects chose to use the panel occupied by female subjects and 62% of females chose to violate the female confederates' personal space. In both studies female choices were not significantly different from chance preferences, suggesting that norms for personal space violations are less strong for females. In contrast, males showed a greater avoidance of violation of female personal space when a choice was possible (as in the first experiment), but when forced to do so, chose to use the control panel by the female rather than the male confederate. These findings illustrate the importance of the situational context and complex social norms in determining individual proxemic behavior. Males may avoid violating male personal space more than females, but perhaps only when no choice exists.

In summary, the findings most generally suggest that: (a) females require less personal space than men, especially with other females, in tolerating approach and in approaching others; (b) opposite-sex interactions are not necessarily closer than male-male interactions except in research utilizing projective personal space measures.

Age

Relatively little research has been conducted on developmental aspects of personal space. Willis (1966) reported that peers approached one another more closely than older individuals. Fry and Willis (1971), using 5, 8, and 10 year old boys and girls as subjects, found that the older children who effected invasions in the personal space of adults waiting in line for a movie, were regarded negatively whereas 5 year olds who crowded the adults were received positively. Meisels and Guardo (1969) studied the development of social schemas and found that children require less personal space as they grow older. In addition, they found that the children initially utilized less personal space for same-sex pairs, but as they grew older (i.e., by the sixth or seventh grade), they began to place themselves closer to figures of opposite-sex peers. Duke and Nowicki (1972) tested this latter relationship using their Comfortable Interpersonal Distance Scale and found that there was a decrease in the distancing from the opposite-sex persons as subjects approached adolescence. Pedersen (1973b) employed his own projective personal space measure (Pedersen Personal Space Measure-Children's Form) with children of both sexes from grades 1–6. Consistent with the just noted findings on sex differences, he found that males indicated a need for larger personal space for all ages. This was most true at the third grade level; at the sixth grade, both sexes showed approximately the same personal space. These relationships held when the imaginary other person was a man, woman, and same-sexed child. In addition, children's personal space toward other opposite-sexed children tended to be smaller regardless of grade level.

In contrast to projective personal space measures, other research based on "real life" proxemic measures suggests that personal space may actually increase with age. Dennis and Powell (1972) found that children's interaction distance with other peers and teachers was greater for the older children. In addition, Baxter (1970) observed a direct relationship between age and distance when comparing children, adolescents, and adults conversing in natural settings. Finally, Aiello and Aiello (1974) studied the standing interpersonal distance set by same-sex pairs of children who were supposedly waiting to begin an experimental task. The age range was 6 to 11. Interpersonal distance increased with age and by early adolescence (age 12) males assumed greater distances than females and stood at greater angles as well. That adult personal space distances appeared at early adolescence was considered reflective of socially learned norms governing proxemic behavior.

Cultural and Ethnic Differences

This is an area of research that Hall (1966) first systematically elaborated with his observational data. For example, Hall reported that Germans, in particular, required more space and were more rigid in their spatial behavior than Americans, Latin Americans, French, and particularly Arab peoples, members of the latter three cultures having a higher tolerance for close interaction than Americans. Watson and Graves (1966) tested some of Hall's propositions in a study with Arab and American students. They found that Arabs talked louder, interacted at closer distances, touched more, and looked more at their interactant than Americans. Sommer (1968) reported intimacy ratings based on seating arrangements to be essentially the same for English, American, and Swedish subjects, whereas the Dutch required slightly more and Pakistanis slightly less interpersonal distance. Contrary to predictions, Forston and Larson (1968) found no differences in proxemic behavior in a problem solving situation between dyads consisting of either Latin American students or American students. However, the subjects were seated, and this may have limited the range of their proxemic behavior.

Little (1968) used a simulated personal space measure (doll figures) with five national groups (American, Swedish, Scottish, Greek, and Southern Italian). In addition, the relationship between the doll figures (e.g., friends, acquaintances, strangers; intimacy level; superior vs. subordinate) and topic of conversation (pleasant, neutral, unpleasant) was studied. As predicted, subjects from Northern European countries produced social schemas reflective of greater interpersonal distances than subjects from the Southern Mediterranean countries. Contrary to expectations, females were not seen as interacting closer together unless the interaction was of either an intimate or unpleasant nature. When seen in a superior-subordinate relationship, the female-female distances obtained were greater than the male-male doll placement distances. Little concluded that, in addition to cultural distances, the relationship and affective nature of the transaction were the determining variables. Shuter (1976) trained observers to reliably estimate the interaction distance and axis of orientation of adult male, female, and mixed-sex Latino dyads conversing in their native Costa Rica, Panama, and Colombia. Shuter found that Costa Rican dyads interacted at closer distances and more direct orientations than Panamanian and Colombian dyads. Female dyads consistently interacted at shorter distances and more direct orientation than male dyads in the same culture. The image of Latinos interacting at close distances is evidently most true for Central Americans, diminishing as one goes further South.

In addition to cross-cultural studies, a number of researchers have investigated racial differences. Baxter (1970) made unobtrusive ratings of Chicano, black, and white interactants in their natural settings and found interpersonal distances were least for the Chicanos and greatest for the blacks. Baxter also found that as age increased from child to adolescent to adult, so did interpersonal distance, and male-female groups interacted most proximally, female-female pairs less so, and male-male pairs were most distant. (The sex findings must be treated with caution, however, given that his procedure permitted no control over relationship variables.) In addition, he noted that while Anglos interacted at about the same distances indoors and in outside settings, Chicanos interacted more closely outdoors, whereas, the reverse was true of blacks. In his study of speaking distance, Willis (1966) found that mixed racial dyads (e.g., black-white) interacted at greater distances than same race pairs. Frankel and Barrett (1971) reported that white subjects allowed a closer approach by a white experimenter than a black experimenter, especially if the subjects were low in self-esteem or high in authoritarianism.

Tolor (1968), using a figure placement task, found that racially homogeneous figures were placed closer together than racially heterogeneous groups. More recently, Duke and Nowicki (1972) have reported similar results with their Comfortable Interpersonal Distance Scale. However, Leibman (1970) found that white subjects in taking a seat were not affected by the race of a seated confederate, although black females showed a tendency to favor sitting by black males rather than white males in a personal space intrusion situation. Jones (1971) employed a naturalistic observational method in New York City using Hall's notational system. However, no significant differences emerged for proxemic variables (including interaction distance) for dyads belonging to black, Puerto Rican, Italian, and Chinese subcultures. Most recently, Thayer and Alban (1972) reported the interesting experimental strategy of varying the perceived similarity of an interactant with members of different subcultures. Specifically, they found that when the experimenter was wearing an American flag decal on his clothing, New Yorkers from the Little Italy section interacted with him at closer distances than when he was wearing a Peace symbol; the reverse occurred (but not significantly) when the experimenter interacted with Greenwich Villagers. The authors argued that perceived similarity between the interactants was an important factor in "releasing" cultural variations in proxemic behavior.

Several researchers have investigated subcultural differences in proxemic behavior among children. Aiello and Jones (1971) studied first- and second-grade children in a school setting and found greater distances among middle-class white children than lower-class black and Puerto Rican children. White boys maintained significantly greater distances from each other than girls, whereas these relationships were not significant for blacks and Puerto Ricans. The axis of orientation also differed among groups of blacks maintaining a less direct orientation than whites and Puerto Ricans. In addition, females stood at slightly more direct orientations than males but the differences, while significant, were small. In a subsequent investigation, Jones and Aiello (1973) made unobtrusive observations for first-, third-, and fifth-grade black and white children. While first grade black children stood closer and less directly towards each other, only their more indirect orientation distinguished fifth-grade blacks from whites. Consistent with other findings noted earlier, females were more direct in their orientation than males. Dennis and Powell (1972) observed interracial dyadic interaction among children aged 7–8, 9–10, and 11–14. As predicted, they found a marked increase in the interaction distance for black-white dyads as a function of age. However, they obtained no control data for same-race dyads, rendering any conclusions from the data rather speculative.

Finally, in an important study, Scherer (1974) photographed black and white children interacting racially in homogeneous dyads in a school yard setting, subjecting the photographs to a special analysis to obtain accurate measures of interpersonal distance as a function of race. Considering social class as a variable, Scherer found that children from lower social classes interacted more closely but that no subcultural differences were apparent. In addition to introducing an important new research tool, this study forces a reconsideration of the previous findings and conclusions regarding subcultural differences.

Personality Differences

In one of the earliest studies on personal distance, Smith (1954) ingeniously employed a slide projector which subjects could control in viewing faces at various distances (based on picture image size). Male subjects also filled out the Bell Adjustment Inventory and Knutson Personal Security Inventory. Those subjects who appeared better adjusted on these measures tended to employ larger image settings. One obvious variable to be related to interpersonal distance setting is introversion-extraversion. Liepold (1963), Patterson and Holmes (1966), Patterson and Sechrest (1970), and Cook (1970) all reported that extraverts (as classified on the Maudsley Personality Inventory) had smaller personal space (based on seating distance). In contrast, Meisels and Canter (1970) found no relationship between seating distance and subjects' introversion-extraversion scores or their scores on three MMPI scales (K, Sc, and Pt scales) of deviancy. Porter, Argyle, and Salter (1970) also found no relationship. Eberts (1972) did report that individuals who lived alone and had lower self-acceptance scores preferred larger interaction distances. Klukken (1972) found no relation between personality scores from the Cattell 16 PF Questionnaire and personal distance seating.

A study by Williams (1971) illustrates that the method employed in measuring personal space is important. In separate experiments, Williams had introverted and extraverted subjects (a) seat themselves next to a discussant; (b) indicate on a questionnaire their distance preferences, density preferences, and feeling states when their personal space was intruded upon; and (c) choose their comfortable and uncomfortable conversational distances based upon the experimenter actually approaching them. While extraverts and introverts did not differ in their seating behavior or distance preferences, extraverts did consistently indicate (on the questionnaire and in the experimenter approach situation) that they could tolerate closer inter-action distances than introverts. Higgins, Peterson, and Dolby (1969) employed Kuethe's social schema technique with subjects who were described as good or poor in social adjustment and found that subjects with good social adjustment placed the son nearer to the mother. In contrast, the family schema of poorly adjusted males showed greater distances and more interventions between mother and son.

Related to the above findings, Patterson (1974) has suggested a positive relationship between social anxiety and interaction distances. Luft (1966) reported that in dyad pairs, the individuals having the greater anxiety score recalled a prior interaction distance as being significantly closer than their less anxious partners. Clore (1969) and Mehrabian and Diamond (1971) found that subjects high on affiliation approach others more closely in interaction situations. Given such findings, Patterson (1974) concluded:

> While the results on social anxiety, extraversion, and affiliation may seem somewhat unrelated, there is evidence indicating substantial correlations between test measures of these three dimensions. In fact, a majority of items from each of those dimensions loads on a common social approach–avoidance factor (Patterson & Strauss, 1972). Thus these nominally different scales may all be tapping a common underlying dimension which is at least marginally predictive of interaction distances (p. 5)

Several researchers have attempted to relate projective test measures to personal space. Frede, Gautney, and Baxter (1968) obtained body-image Barrier scores from the Holtzman Inkblot performance of subjects. A "projective" interpersonal distance measure was obtained from subjects on the Make a Picture Story Test (MAPS Test). Subjects with high Barrier scores (i.e., theoretically, well delineated body-image boundaries) tended to place MAPS characters closer together and depict more interactions and approach behaviors in their stories than did low-Barrier subjects. The authors concluded that high-Barrier subjects are "people who not only deal with others on more proximal bases in social settings, but also see them as communicating more with each other and utilizing forms of interaction generally defined as approach or prosocial in orientation" (p. 578). In contrast, Dosey and Meisels (1969) obtained measures of subjects' Barrier scores and anxiety from the Rorschach and their interaction distance preferences (based upon actual approach behavior, seating behavior, or silhouette drawings of persons). No significant relationships were observed between the personality and personal space measures and, indeed, the personal space measures themselves were not consistently interrelated. Most recently, however, Greene (1976) hypothesized that individuals with indefinite body boundaries, when faced with an unstructured social situation involving potential personal threat, would engage in physical distancing from others. Subjects selected as having high or low Barrier scores on the Rorschach attended a small group process session. As predicted, more low Barrier subjects chose distant seating positions from the leader. Subject self-report data suggested that the near the leader seating locations were perceived as aversive by the subjects with lower Barrier scores.

In another study, Meisels and Dosey (1971) obtained TAT and Word Association Test measures of defensiveness against hostility expression in subjects. One group of subjects was then exposed to an anger arousing interaction with an experimenter. Compared to subjects not so aroused, the angered subjects showed a greater approach towards the experimenter when instructed to approach him but not when asked only to set a comfortable conversational distance. More significantly, angered subjects with defenses against hostility expression approached less closely to the experimenter than other angered subjects. It was concluded that increased interpersonal distance may serve as a defense against impulse expression when one is angered but at the same time inhibited in expressing it.

In the study by Meisels and Dosey (1971) subject personality characteristics interacted with the characteristics of the experimental confederate. Frankel and Barrett (1971) found that whites high in authoritarianism and low in self-esteem sat greater interpersonal distances from black confederates than from a white confederate. In contrast, high-authoritarian–high self-esteem white subjects maintained the shortest distances. Low-authoritarian subjects did not differ in their distancing from confederates. Likewise, Hartnett, Bailey, and Gibson (1970) observed that males high in heterosexuality approached closer to female interactants. Finally, the reader will recall the interaction between sex and dominance of subject and confederate eye contact in the study by Fromme and Beam (1974). In particular, low-dominant males showed a decrease in proxemic behavior under conditions of high confederate eye contact (the opposite behavior of high-dominant males), and they rated the interaction as more unpleasant than high-dominant males and high- and low-dominant females.

Several recent studies related Rotter's Locus of Control scale (LOC) to interpersonal distance seating. Tolor, Brannigan, and Murphy (1970), using a newly developed "Psychological Distance Scale" (PDS), found that Internally oriented college student females showed greater psychological closeness to "sister" and "father" concepts. However, no such relationships were observed for males. Some support was obtained for a hypothesized association between a Future Expectancy measure and subjects' PDS scores. Subsequently however, Duke and Nowicki (1972), as part of their validation procedure for their CIDS measure, found that LOC (as a measure of socially learned expectancies) did not predict interpersonal distances for "friends." However, LOC did relate to subjects' distance setting with unfamiliar others, "for which no specific expectancies were assumed available" (1972, p. 129). Specifically, "internals" produced shorter interpersonal distances when hypothetically interacting with strangers, including various authority figures (e.g., LOC correlated .62 with the distance set for interaction with a policeman). In another study to be described in more detail later, Schopler and Walton (1975) reported that internally oriented subjects found the same group situation less crowded than externally oriented subjects. In a study on environmental crowding that we will review later in greater detail, Cozby (1973) obtained measures of personal space (based on subject approach and experimenter approach) which were intercorrelated with a number of other personality and background variables. Modest but significant relationships (positive or negative) were obtained between females' personal space measures and measures of self-esteem (negative), social avoidance tendencies (positive), dominance (negative), and "house density when growing up" (positive).

Although numerous personality characteristics seem related to interpersonal distance setting, a possibility is that these relationships might not hold across situations. Long, Calhoun, and Selby (1976) investigated the relationship between personality measures and consistency in selection of interpersonal distance. Subjects were given a seating preference questionnaire in which they were to indicate their seating choice for themselves and a same-sex or opposite-sex acquaintance. Different high-anxiety situations (e.g., waiting for a job interview, for results of medical tests) and low-anxiety situations (e.g., choosing a study area in the library) were described. Multiple regression analysis was employed to relate the personality measures (The Personality Research Form, Maudsley Personality Inventory). Neuroticism was the strongest predictor of consistency being negatively related to interpersonal distance setting across situations, although higher multiple correlations between personality measures and specific seating situations were obtained. The results suggest that at least some personality factors may be predictive of both specific interpersonal and cross-situational interpersonal distance setting.

Finally, two highly interesting studies have used personal space as a dependent measure of dramatic life experiences of individuals. Hetherington (1972) compared proxemic behavior of adolescent girls who had experienced early separations from their fathers due to divorce or death. Specifically, he found that daughters of divorcees showed significant proximity seeking with male interviewers, whereas daughters of widowed mothers tended to distance themselves from males. In another study, Spinetta, Rigler, and Karon (1974) compared the placement of dolls (representing nurse, doctor, mother, and father) in a replica model of their hospital setting by terminally ill leukemia children and chronically ill hospitalized children. For both groups, doll placement distances increased with the number of admissions. However, even more dramatic, the leukemic childrens' distances increased significantly more so than their chronically ill counterparts, "lending strong support to the hypothesis that the sense of isolation grows stronger as the child nears death" (1974, p. 751).

Psychiatric Populations

One of the propositions that Lett, Clark, and Altman (1969) considered well established was that personal space was greater for psychologically disturbed individuals than for normals. Hutt and Vaizey (1966), for example, noted that their autistic children spent more time at the boundary of the play room than did normal children. Weinstein (1965), using Kuethe's felt placement technique demonstrated that emotionally disturbed boys placed the child figures farther apart than did the normals. Weinstein proposed that the earliest social schema to develop is that between mother and child, and that this may be disturbed in maladjusted children. Fisher (1967) subsequently replicated this finding with emotionally disturbed children. She also obtained a significant positive relationship ($r = .57$) between hostility present in the mothers as measured by the Buss-Durkee Hostility scale and the distance the children placed the figures.

Most of the studies on disturbed populations have focused on schizophrenics who are typically thought to show the greatest social withdrawal. Contrary to this impression, Sommer (1959) reported that his schizophrenic subjects either chose distant, diagonally placed seats or immediately adjacent seats next to a designated person, whereas normals showed a preference for corner to corner seating. Further, Tolor (1970a), using Kuethe's technique, has reported that his group of schizophrenics did not show greater personal space needs than normals. Indeed, their replacement errors were consistently in the direction of closer distances. On the other hand, Horowitz, Duff, and Stratton (1964) instructed schizophrenics and normals to approach an inanimate object (a hat rack) or a male and a female by walking forwards, backwards, sideways, and at an angle to the stimulus. Subsequently, the subjects also made self-ratings of personal space based upon drawing a line around silhouette figures (seen from above, frontally, and in profile). The findings showed that schizophrenics preferred consistently greater distances than normals when approaching persons but not objects. Horowitz, Duff, and Stratton proposed that "an area of personal space appears to surround every individual, which seems to be reproducible and may be regarded as an immediate *body-buffer zone*" (p. 655). Horowitz (1968) subsequently replicated this procedure, this time examining the stage of illness of schizophrenic, depressed, or neurotic inpatients. As before, schizophrenic patients tended to show the greatest interpersonal distances but the differences were primarily significant during the acute states of illness (i.e., just after admission). When measured at the final stages of their hospitalization they showed significant reduction in their interpersonal distances, as did patients with depression as the primary symptom. Interestingly, the neurotic patients showed an increase in their personal space, reflective of the interpersonal difficulties many evidenced with staff during the course of their treatment.

Some question has been raised about the use of projective personal space tasks with schizophrenics. Thornton and Gottheil (1971) used Kuethe's technique and reported that "schizophrenic males . . . did not display the schema that 'people belong together'" (p. 192). Further, they overestimated at least one of the parental figure distances (woman-boy or man-boy), which they did not do for any nonparental figure sets. In contrast, Blumenthal and Meltzoff (1967) employed the Make A Picture Story test with schizophrenics and normals, examining figure placements under immediate and delayed figure replacement conditions for hostile and neutral interaction scores. The nature of the relationships between the figures did not affect the placements and all subjects were inaccurate in the delayed reproduction condition. Of primary interest was the fact that schizophrenics were less accurate than normals, particularly so when a time delay was imposed. The authors argued that the greater errors by schizophrenics were due to their cognitive disorganization. They also contended, in view of the overall negative findings, that "it is questionable whether social schemas are as pervasive a phenomenon as previous research has suggested" (1967, p. 127). It is interesting to note, however, that in the study by Thornton and Gottheil (1971), where a simpler task was used, "the schizophrenic *S*s . . . were neither more variable nor less accurate in their replacements than were the normal *S*s" (p. 193). The complexity of the task is thus an important consideration in working with disturbed populations.

Approaching the question of personal space from a different vantage point, Boucher (1972) evaluated interview interactions with schizophrenics and alcoholics who were seated at either Hall's intimate, personal, or social distances from the interviewer. As predicted, the schizophrenics reported greater interpersonal attraction towards the interviewer when seated at the farther distances (personal and social) as compared to the intimate distance. However, when allowed to subsequently "pull up a chair" next to the interviewer, schizophrenic subjects previously exposed to the intimate seating distances chose nonsignificantly greater distances than those schizophrenics who interacted at the other distances. In contrast, alcoholics exposed to the intimate interview distance did place their chair significantly farther away, although they did not show the expected differences in interpersonal attraction. While the results thus were not entirely consistent, Boucher nevertheless deserves credit for his innovative method in studying proxemic behavior.

Finally, Aronow, Reznikoff, and Tryon (1975) studied several interpersonal distance measures of process and reactive schizophrenics and normal controls. The measures included a "live" measure of seating distance, Kuethe's technique, the Make A Picture Story test, and the Tolor Psychological Distance Scale, a paper-and-pencil measure of personal space. Contrary to expectations, no differences on any of the measures were obtained for the groups. However, the authors noted that all the patients were hospitalized less than 6 months, thus excluding the more extreme process subjects. (It may also be that the patients were past the acute stage of their illness, an important factor identified by Horowitz, 1968). This latter point received some support from a study by Tolor and Donnon (1969), who found that the social schema of patients hospitalized for longer periods of time showed a greater desire for social interaction than patients hospitalized for a short time.

Many of the studies on schizophrenics point to the characteristic social withdrawal that occurs with that illness. Booraem and Flowers (1972) provided seven psychotic inpatients with an assertive training program at the beginning and end of treatment. A personal space measure (based upon approach of an experimental associate) and a measure of self-report anxiety were also obtained. The treatment efficacy was evident from an earlier release of the assertive training patients (compared to other control patients receiving milieu therapy); further, the assertively trained patients showed significant decreases in pre-post anxiety and in their personal space measures, whereas controls did not.

In a study with diagnostically heterogeneous outpatients, Tolor (1970b) employed his Psychological Distance Scale in which a person marks his position between all possible pairs of the following "concepts": sister, brother, stranger, neighbor, best friend, mother, and father. Several significant but difficult to interpret findings emerged. Patients as a group showed greater distance to the Mother concept whereas hospitalized male patients showed closer distances to Sister and Brother and a greater distance to Best Friend concept.

Finally, several studies have investigated personal space in special subject populations. In a classic study, Kuethe and Weingartner (1964) obtained social schema from homosexual and nonhomosexual penitentiary inmates. While the nonhomosexual inmates employed schema (man-woman pairings) similar to heterosexual noninmates, the homosexuals failed to show man-woman pairings when free placement was allowed. In addition, the homosexuals tended to place two men figures too close during the replacement task, whereas a similar error occurred for nonhomosexuals for the man-woman pairings. Kinzel (1970) measured "body buffer zones" of violent inmates by approaching them from eight different directions until asked to stop. Kinzel reported that the body buffer zones of the violent prisoners were almost four times larger than those of nonviolent prisoners. Further, their rear zones were significantly larger than their frontal zones, the opposite being true for nonviolent subjects. Although the distances measured decreased over time (12 separate weekly measurements), the violent group maintained larger zones "despite the fact that the intruder [the experimenter] had clearly come to be perceived more as friend than foe" (1970, p. 103). An interesting anecdotal observation concerned an increase in one patient's rear zone, despite a decreasing frontal zone, which coincided with a homosexual panic following a sexual proposition from another inmate.

INTERPERSONAL RELATIONSHIPS

As noted in the discussion of Hall's observations, physical distance literally determines the kinds of interaction possible, ranging from love making to impersonal information exchange when individuals are out of reach except for sight and hearing. It is thus not surprising that perhaps the majority of studies on proxemic behavior have focused on aspects of interpersonal interaction. As we shall see, interpersonal distance has been used both as a dependent and independent variable and as a function of seating arrangements or interacting with population density factors.

Familiarity and Liking

One of the most strongly held propositions of Lett, Clark, and Altman (1969) was that the more familiar and/or liked another is, the closer one interacts with him. Kuethe (1962a), in his first study of social schemas, reported that strangers were placed at greater distances than friends. Little (1965) also examined this relationship in the abstract, or "projectively," by having subjects place figures on a board under different instructional sets. When identified as friends, the stimuli were grouped together closer than when they were seen as acquaintances, and least closely if they were identified as strangers. These relationships held in another experiment when subjects actually had confederates assume various distances from one another based on the same instructional sets. In another study, Little, Ulehla, and

Henderson (1968) replicated this relationship between degree of acquaintance and figure placement distance. When instructed to adopt an approval seeking role as opposed to an approval avoiding role, subjects in Rosenfeld's experiment positioned themselves significantly closer to an experimental confederate (Rosenfeld, 1965). In three studies, Mehrabian (1968a, 1968b; Mehrabian and Friar, 1969) found that distance decreased as subjects imagined themselves being more positive toward a hypothetical addressee. Willis (1966) tested this relationship in "real-life" situations by instructing 40 subject "experimenters" to interact with strangers, acquaintances, friends, close friends, and parents. Each interaction ended with the experimenter measuring the distance at which the conversation took place. Friends approached the experimenters closer than their parents or strangers. Kiesler and Goldberg (1968) presented subjects an audiotape of a speaker following which they were asked to schematically diagram where they would sit with the person in the same room. The closer the seating position, the more liking shown for the speaker. In another study, when provided with information that another person was "warm and friendly" (rather than cold and unfriendly), subjects chose more proximate seating (Kleck, 1969).

Goldring (1967) presented students with cartoonlike drawings at near or far interaction distances. Adjective check list ratings of the drawings showed that the pairs depicted at closer distances were described more favorably (e.g., warm, active, excited, responsive). Duke and Nowicki (1972) reported that their subjects depicted significantly smaller distances between themselves and same sex and opposite sex friends on their Comfortable Interpersonal Distance Scale. Aiello and Cooper (1972) studied both physical distance and body axis orientation in relation to mutual liking. Subjects were junior high school students paired into conversational dyads on the basis of positive and negative sociometric choices. Significantly closer interaction distances (but not more direct orientations) were unobtrusively observed in the dyads whose members liked each other. Aiello and Cooper, in particular, proposed distance setting rather than orientation as the most sensitive measure of interpersonal relationships.

Several researchers have investigated social acceptance in relation to various measures of social schema of "psychological distance." Weinstein (1965), for example, reported that disturbed and presumably less accepted boys placed human figures farther apart, as did children less accepted by their parents (Weinstein, 1967). That some caution is necessary in the use and interpretation of social schemas, however, is evident in a study by Tolor (1969), who found that unpopular children (based on peer sociometric choice) produced closer interaction distances on a figure replacement task. Weinstein (1967) failed to obtain a relationship between her social schema measure of personal space and children's acceptance by their classmates. Blumenthal and Meltzoff (1967) also found no distance effect as a function of neutral and hostile relationships represented on the Make a Picture Story Test.

Finally, several recent studies have investigated interpersonal distance and heterosexual attraction. Byrne, Ervin, and Lamberth (1970), for example, found that standing distance between couples who had just dated varied inversely with their affective ratings for each other. Allgeier and Byrne (1973) aroused subjects interpersonal attraction by manipulating perceived similar or dissimilar attitude compatibility between themselves and an opposite-sex confederate. Just as was shown in a study of same-sex pairs (Byrne, Baskett, and Hodges, 1971), subjects who rated the confederate as more attractive chose closer seating distances. In addition, subjects' interpersonal distance setting was also related to composite self-report indexes of anxiety, hostility, and depression. Subsequently, Griffitt, May, and Veitch (1974) employed erotic material to sexually arouse male and female subjects. While sexual arousal did not produce closer seating proximity in the subjects, an interesting finding emerged: sexually aroused subjects who responded negatively to sexual stimulation tended to avoid heterosexual persons in terms of their seating proximity.

Intimacy, Arousal, and Interpersonal Distance

Consistent with Argyle and Dean's equilibrium theory (see Chapter 5) there is considerable evidence that as interpersonal distance decreases, so does interpersonal arousal. McBride, King, and James (1965), for example, found subjects' GSRs increased as they were approached by an experimenter. A frontal approach produced the greatest arousal, followed by approach from the side and the rear. Kleck (1970) observed an increase in subjects' self-manipulations as interaction distance decreased. Aiello, Epstein, and Karlin (1975) subsequently found increases in subjects' electrodermal activity as a function of crowding, an effect that did not habituate over time. Other investigators, however, failed to obtain such a relationship with heart rate (Efran and Cheyne, 1974) or palmar sweating measures (Dabbs, 1971).

Recently Middlemist, Knowles, and Matter (1975) pointed out that in these studies compensatory behavioral responses are often possible which can reduce subjects' physiological arousal during crowding or invasions of personal space. In an ingenious study they investigated a personal space invasion in a situation where compensatory responses would be impossible. Specifically, they varied personal space invasions of subjects urinating in a lavatory by placing confederates adjacent to or one urinal removed from the subject, or leaving the subject alone during micturation. As predicted, the dependent measures (time to micturation and micturation duration) were affected as a function of presence and distance, showing a clear arousal effect.

Thus, as intimacy increases, compensatory behaviors may occur to reduce the arousal to an appropriate level. This concept of intimacy is directly analogous to what Mehrabian (1969) has described as "immediacy." As mentioned in Chapter 5, Argyle and Dean (1965) demonstrated that as distance decreased so did mutual gazing in compensatory fashion. We will not attempt to review again here all of the studies reported in the section on visual behavior. However, we should note that one common criticism concerning the equilibrium theory is that as physical distance between interactants increases, eye contact may seem to increase due to observer error or to a desire for information rather than a compensatory response to decreased intimacy. Indeed, not all studies of this relationship have been positive or persuasive (e.g., for negative findings see Kleinke, Staneski, and Berger, 1975; Kleinke, Staneski, and Pipp, 1975). However, Argyle and Ingham (1972) replicated their earlier relationship between distance and looking employing a more sophisticated method of analysis (see Chapter 5 on visual behavior) that tended to support the intimacy hypothesis.

Finally, Edwards (1973) conducted an experiment with implications for equilibrium theory in which orientation and distance were studied as a function of the need for, and tolerance of, eye contact in doll figure interactants. Subjects were given descriptions of social situations in which the interactants were similar or dissimilar in their need for and tolerance of eye contact. As predicted, orientation asymmetry was greater in those situations where the interactants were dissimilar in their social needs, and eye contact tolerance and distances were greater. Where an individual was depicted as having high eye contact needs, the figure was generally shown with a more direct orientation. Significant individual differences were noted in subjects' placements of the doll figures, suggesting to the author that this technique might be used as a clinical projective device.

In addition to compensatory changes in eye contact as a function of variations in distance, changes in interactants' body orientations may occur. In their cross cultural study, Watson and Graves (1966) reported that as physical distance decreased, body orientation between American and Arab dyads became less direct, as did also mutual gaze for American but not Arab interactants. While Aiello and Jones (1971) reported that black and Puerto Rican children tended to stand significantly closer to one another, they also noted that they engaged in less direct body orientations. Clore (1969) found that the approach of one subject to another subject's chair (marked by a coat and book) became less direct as seated distance decreased. Pellegrini and Empey (1970) also noted that as distance decreased between two interactants, so did directness of approach. Patterson (1973b) reported that approach, orientation, and distance for individuals are stable over time (e.g., over 25-minute and 1-week intervals). Indeed, Patterson and Sechrest (1970) observed that even trained experimental accomplices tended to approach at less direct orientations when approaching closer to another, despite experimental instructions to the contrary.

In contrast to "encoding" studies on intimacy, several researchers have obtained judgments of perceived intimacy based on photographs or diagrams of individual seating arrangements. Sommer (1968) found that for five nationalities side by side seating was considered most intimate, followed by a corner to corner seating arrangement. Scherer and Schiff (1973) obtained ratings of photographic slides depicting two males seated at various distances (3, 4, 5, and 6 feet) and orientation angles (0, 30, 45, 60, and 90°). Perceived intimacy varied inversely with physical proximity of the interactants and directly with eye contact. In contrast to Sommer's findings, side-by-side seating was judged less intimate than corner to corner seating. By separating out perceived looking behavior from the orientations of interactants, the authors found no effect for body orientation as a proxemic behavior, leading to the conclusion that "body orientation is important only as it affects eye contact" (Scherer and Schiff, 1973, p. 840). In summary then, while there is considerable support for the intimacy equilibrium theory for physical distance and orientation as well as looking behavior, the conditions under which it applies and the exact relationship between the nonverbal behaviors have yet to be precisely delineated. Patterson (1973a) has provided an excellent review of these issues in a recent paper.

Finally, distance may affect "intimacy" on a verbal level. For example, Jourard and Friedman (1970) varied "distance" by having subjects talk into a tape recorder without the interviewer present and with the interviewer present, but either with or without eye contact. While males did not vary in their disclosure at varying distances, females tended to disclose less as "distance" decreased. Lassen (1973) had psychiatric residents conduct initial interviews with psychiatric patients at seating distances of 3, 6, and 9 feet. All therapists indicated a preference for the 6 foot interaction distance. The patients showed an increase in their Speech Disturbance Ratio (see Chapter 2) from 3 to 6 to 9 feet. In addition, they tended to feel they were unclear at the 9-foot distance, whereas at 6 feet they reported being most open and raters judged that they talked most about their fears and anxieties. Most recently, Stone and Morden (1976) investigated the relationship between verbal productivity for personal and nonpersonal topics (e.g., academic, social, material) and interaction distance. For female interviewee-interviewer pairs there was greater discussion of personal topics at an intermediate (5-foot) distance, compared to a close (2-foot) and far (9-foot) distance. The results of these last two studies suggest, in particular, that cultural norms for appropriate interaction distances do have implications for verbal communication.

Interpersonal Similarity

In addition to familiarity and liking, interpersonal similarity has been studied. Indeed, as mentioned above (Allgeier and Byrne, 1973), it has been employed as a manipulation to induce liking. Little, Ulehla, and Henderson (1968) found that figures identified as politically compatible (e.g., both voting for Goldwater or both for Johnson) were placed closer together in the figure replacement task. That the kind of similarity is important was evident in a study by Tolor and Salafia (1971), who varied high and low intelligence, prestigiousness, similarity, adjustment, and support. Figures with positive attributes ascribed to both were placed closer than those given unfavorable characteristics. In a study comparing nine ethnic groups, Brislin (1974) reported that the perceived attitude similarity of the different groups was the best predictor of proximate seating arrangements in an open group.

Kleck and his colleagues have studied the effect of physical dissimilarities (i.e., physical abnormalities) on interpersonal interaction. On a figure placement task subjects placed an amputee farther apart from self-representation than a friend, blind person, and a black; but epileptic and mental patient stimuli were placed even more distant (Kleck, Buck, Goller, London, Pfeiffer, and Vukcevic, 1968). In a second experiment, subjects who actually interacted with a confederate described as an epileptic chose significantly greater seating distances. Kleck (1970) also observed subjects' conversational behavior towards a confederate seated 4 or 10 feet away whose comments reflected attitudes similar to those of the subject. Significantly more nonverbal agreement cues (i.e., head nods) were shown by subjects in the close seating distance, suggesting a stronger influence of the confederate at closer distances. This interpretation was also corroborated by an increase in subjects' self-manipulations that also occurred at the closer distances, most likely a reflection of subjects' greater arousal. Finally, Fisher (1974) varied interpersonal seating distance (2, 4, 5.5, and 13 feet) between subjects and a confederate who was attitudinally similar or dissimilar to the subjects. Those subjects interacting with a similar confederate judged the environment to be aesthetically of higher quality and less crowded. In addition, they felt more positive towards the confederate.

Influence of Proxemic Behavior on Interpersonal Perception

Few investigators have experimentally employed distance as an independent variable. What few findings there are suggest no simple or consistent relationship between interpersonal distance and the judgements made about another. To investigate the effect of distance on interpersonal perception, Porter, Argyle, and Salter (1970) had experimental confederates seat themselves at distances of 2, 4, and 8 feet from English high school children. Contrary to predictions, closer seating proximity did not result in the confederate being perceived as more friendly or better adjusted. In contrast, the role subjects assumed towards the confederate as an "interviewer" for a job or as a "new acquaintance" did affect how the confederates were perceived. There was some suggestion that the closer the confederates' seating distance came to the subject's preferred interpersonal distance (also measured in the study), the more "excited" versus "bored," "at ease" versus "self-conscious," and "performer" versus "audience" confederates were judged to be. Patterson and Sechrest (1970) also varied seating distance of a confederate (from 2, 4, 6, and 8 feet) who was ostensibly being interviewed by subjects whose task it was to form an impression of the confederate. Subjects in this experiment saw the confederate as less friendly, less aggressive, less extraverted, and less dominant as a function of increased interpersonal distance (i.e., 4 vs. 6 vs. 8 feet). Mehrabian (1968a) has reported that subjects rated a communicator as being more positive towards an addressee when standing closer to him.

Albert and Dabbs (1970) varied both seating distance (1–2, 4–5, and 14–15 feet) and behavior of a confederate speaker (hostile versus friendly) while employing attitude change as a dependent measure of the effect of speaker persuasion at various interaction distances. Subject attitude change decreased linearly with distance, becoming negative for the hostile speaker at the close distance. However, perception of the speaker per se was generally unaffected by the distance at which he sat, although attention to the message itself was greatest at the middle (i.e., most appropriate) distance. At the close and far distances subjects' attention apparently shifted to the physical characteristics of the speaker. Thus there is some evidence that the closer and/or most appropriate social distances can lead to more positive impressions but the strength of the effect may be weak relative to other variables (e.g., subject role, confederate behavior).

Interpersonal Distance and Negative Social Experience

A consistent finding is that negative social interactions lead to greater interpersonal distance. Martin and Van Dyke (1968) had female subjects interact with a hostile or friendly experimenter. As predicted, the subjects exposed to the negative interaction placed cut out figures significantly farther apart than subjects exposed to the friendly experimenter, presumably "protecting" their negative affect. Dosey and Meisels (1969) also found that a stress manipulation (i.e., questioning subjects' interpersonal attractiveness) resulted in both significantly farther approach distances, figure placements, but not seating distances for subjects so stressed. However, as we noted earlier, Meisels and Dosey (1971) also demonstrated that arousal of hostility may result in decreased interpersonal distance when that serves as a counter-aggressive act (invasion of personal space) in individuals capable of directly expressing aggression. In the study cited above by Albert and Dabbs (1970) a social schema produced by subjects exposed to a hostile speaker at close distances reflected greater figure distances than subjects in the other conditions.

Most recently, Sanders (1976) investigated the effect duplicity had on interpersonal distance setting. Subjects were placed in a room where they "overheard" a conversation by an alleged friend and an interviewer in which they were described positively, negatively, or in a neutral fashion. Upon subsequently filling out the Comfortable Interpersonal Distance Scale the greatest distance set by subjects was with the alleged friend who was overheard making negative comments. Graves and Robinson (1976) studied the effect of consistent and inconsistent verbal and nonverbal messages on subjects' proxemic behaviors. College students were recruited to role play a client while interacting with a counselor who exhibited either positive or negative nonverbal behavior (i.e., constant eye contact, forward trunk-lean, legs forward and parallel versus infrequent eye contact, backwards body-lean, legs crossed to side) which was consistent or inconsistent with the (positive–negative) verbal behavior. Subsequent to this interaction the subject joined the counselor in a room and the interpersonal distance was measured. Inconsistent messages resulted in greater subject interpersonal distance setting, especially when the nonverbal behavior was negative. Finally, Barrios and Giesen (1976) showed that subjects' positive or negative expectations of a group interation affected their choice of seating distance from one another but not the group moderator. Specifically, subjects expecting hostile interactions seated themselves significantly more distant from one another.

Interpersonal Task Orientation

How individuals go about performing a task is influenced by their positions relative to one another. In several studies Sommer (1965, 1969) and Norum (1966) demonstrated that side-by-side seating arrangements facilitated cooperative task interactions, whereas opposite seating arrangements were associated with competing interactions. Conversing subjects sat corner to corner. Batchelor and Goethals (1972) gave subjects a problem with instructions to come to an individual or collective decision. When making a collective decision, subjects were observed to come closer together and have more visual contact.

A number of researchers have recently investigated distance as an independent variable in cooperative versus competitive dyadic interactions with the Prisoner's Dilemma Game. This game:

Tempts each player to competitive responses in seeking individual gain or comparative success in relation to the other participant. If both players adopt a competitive or exploitive strategy, both lose. Mixed cooperative-competitive play by the two participants result in variable outcomes. Profit by both players, however, is assured if each responds cooperatively. (Sensenig, Reed, and Miller, 1972, p. 105)

Sensenig, Reed, and Miller (1972) had subjects play the Prisoner's Dilemma Game at either 3- or 20-foot distances. For the greater distances, fewer mutually cooperative choices, smaller earnings, and more disparate outcomes were observed, mutual cooperation virtually extinguishing late in the experiment. The authors concluded: "Not only does distance influence initial interaction, but that this influence may become increasingly determinate with continued interaction" (1972, p. 106).

One variable not controlled for in many studies on personal distance is eye contact, which plays a well documented role in interpersonal attraction. Gardin, Kaplan, Firestone, and Cowan (1973) either allowed or prevented visual contact while varying subject seating arrangement from a side by side to opposite seating positions. As predicted, a side by side seating arrangement facilitated subjects' cooperativeness and positive interpersonal attitudes on the Prisoner's Dilemma Game more so than the opposite seating positions, but only when visual contact was prevented. When subjects could see each other the opposite seating arrangement produced more cooperative behavior and positive interpersonal attitudes, in addition to producing a stronger sociometric choice response. It was concluded: "When available, the effects of eye contact tended to dominate those of seating proximity per se" (p. 17).

In addition to seating arrangement facilitating different kinds of task performance, the nature of social interaction may be reflected in subsequent seating choices. Tedesco and Fromme (1974) utilized confederates to provide subjects with cooperative, competitive, or neutral Prisoner's Dilemma Game experiences. A subsequent seating measure of personal space showed that subjects exposed to the cooperative confederate seated themselves significantly closer than did other subjects who were exposed to the neutral or negatively cooperative confederates. Boles and Patterson (1974) also varied distance (7 vs. 2.5 feet) and orientation (face to face versus side by side) in a study employing the Prisoner's Dilemma Game. Although none of these manipulations affected subject cooperativeness, a post experimental measure of seating showed that subjects seated themselves closer to the experimental confederate (their partner in the Prisoner's Dilemma Game) when they had sat either facing the confederate or closer to the confederate during the game. As in Gardin, Kaplan, Firestone and Cowan (1973), a face-to-face seating orientation but not distance was associated with more positive post game sociometric ratings. Finally, Ryen and Kahn (1975) examined intergroup orientation in relation to group attitudes and proxemic behavior. Subjects placed into three-member groups acted alone, cooperatively, or competitively, and with or without feedback. Subjects who acted independently later selected random seating patterns without showing attitudinal preferences for any of the groups including their own. Cooperative group subjects showed a slight attitudinal bias for their group while sitting equidistant from the other groups. Competitive group subjects sat near their own group members and far from others if they received no feedback, and especially so if they received losing feedback. In contrast, winning competitive group subjects sat nearer to the losing group, and they also produced high nongroup attitude ratings towards the other group. Ryen and Kahn (1975) observed:

The fact that such differences in evaluation and proxemic behavior were found with only minimal interaction both within the between groups, and in a situation where there was no tangible reward for the behaviors of the groups, suggests that both own group bias and group proxemic behavior are quite robust phenomena. (p. 16)

Seating Arrangements and Interpersonal Interaction

Thus far in our discussion of interpersonal relationships we have noted in various studies the frequent use of seating arrangements and seating distances in proxemic studies. Perhaps no researcher has contributed more systematically to the study of seating arrangements than Robert Sommer. Sommer (1967a) emphasized the importance of isolating the effect that seating position has on a person's relationship to others or his role in a group. In his review Sommer (1967a) noted that "all studies agreed that choice of seats is nonrandom with respect to status and personality" (p. 244). Earlier Sommer (1961) evaluated Hall's notion about interaction distances in situations where the interactants are seated. Sommer (1961) found that the upper limit for comfortable conversation between two individuals was 5½ feet. However, he noted that this distance was for individuals instructed to interact in an experimental setting. At home, comfortable conversational distances of 8–10 feet were also observed.

In his book, *Personal Space: The Behavioral Basis of Design,* Sommer (1969) reported a study in which seating positions of persons interacting in a cafeteria were compared with those not interacting. For square tables interactants favored corner-to-corner seating while noninteractants sat opposite one another. However, both opposite and corner seating were used by interactants with rectangular table arrangements, while noninteractants were typically separated by chairs or a diagonal seating arrangement across the table. Mehrabian and Diamond (1971) systematically studied the effect of different furniture arrangements in facilitating affiliative behavior in strangers in three studies. Their principal finding of interest here is that side-by-side seating (e.g., as on a couch) was less facilitating of interaction than more direct orientations, especially for highly affiliative pairs.

One of the better documented effects that seating position can have on interaction is in influencing leadership and status roles. Felipe (1966) obtained semantic differential ratings for various seating positions. The head seating position was seen as being unequal with other seating positions (e.g., at the sides of the table). Strodtbeck and Hook (1961) simulated a jury trial with subjects and found that the subjects seated at the ends of the table tended to be elected as foreman of the jury. Lott and Sommer (1967) administered questionnaires to subjects concerning where they would sit in relation to a person of higher, lower, or equal status. For rectangular tables, the head position was associated with higher status. With square tables, subjects indicated a preference for seats further away from higher or lower status persons than equals. Subsequently, these same findings were observed for subjects in a live experimental situation where subjects interacted with confederates of a higher, lower, or equal status. Ward (1968) employed five-man discussion groups. Subjects facing the largest number of discussants engaged in the most talking and were most likely to be judged as leaders by the other members.

In an interesting study DeLong (1970) studied the effect of "territorial" seating arrangements over time on dominance relationships in a graduate seminar. DeLong found that two subgroups emerged at the time the professor diminished his active participation. One subgroup was aligned with the most verbally dominant student, another with the professor. Interestingly, members of both subgroups aligned themselves on their respective leader's right-hand side. When the existence of the two subgroups was taken into account, significant relationships emerged between the students' "leadership ranks" based on peer ratings and their "territorial rank," as determined by the seats they consistently chose in class. Further, when the primary leadership role in seminar shifted from the professor to the verbally dominant student, subjects to the right of the new (student) leader perceived themselves in their ratings as more superior, and the students to the right of the professor regarded themselves as inferior. DeLong noted:

Here we find a complex superimposed, dual-imagery consistent with the popular folk association of right hand with goodness and dominance, and the left hand with evil and submissiveness. Alliances and loyalties are communicated through the assumption of right-hand orientations between leaders and followers. (1970, p. 184)

Considerable research in proxemics and particularly seating arrangements also has focused on the counseling or psychotherapy situation. Noting the findings of earlier studies that communication across a desk corner
is psychologically more intimate (Haase and DiMattia, 1969; Lott and
Sommer, 1967; Sommer, 1959), Haase and DiMattia (1970) presented
clients, counselors, and administrators pictures of different seating arrangements. Based on semantic differential ratings, seating positions across a
desk corner were seen by all subjects as most preferable for counseling
relationships. Considering the separate groups, administrators showed the
greatest preference for an across-the-table interviewing arrangement. Interestingly, while counselors favored a seating situation where no desk was
intervening, clients most preferred the desk corner seating position where
there was some "protected sociopetal space." Noting that counselors often
utilize the seating arrangement most preferable to themselves, the authors
commented, "This might offer grounds for speculation about the client's
reaction to being maneuvered into an interaction where the furniture arrangement is suited to the counselor and not to the feelings and perhaps the
eventual benefit of the client" (1970, pp. 323–324).

In another study Haase (1970) gave subjects instructional sets to respond
to seating arrangements as if they were seeking personal counseling or academic assistance. As predicted, the closer distances were considered most
appropriate for a counseling relationship. Kelly (1972) presented male psychiatric patients pictures of a therapist with a client depicting various "therapist proxemic cues" (i.e., varied distance, eye contact, body-lean, arm/leg
openness, orientation). Closer interaction distances, more eye contact, forward trunk lean, and a more direct orientation all connoted a more positive
therapist attitude. Haase and Tepper (1972) similarly varied distance, eye
contact, trunk-lean, verbal empathy, and body orientation. All of the first
four variables contributed significantly to higher judged empathy, although
seating distance produced the weakest effect.

Dinges and Oetting (1972) had subjects given a counseling set, or no
instructional set, rate photographs depicting various interaction distances.
Measures of "concept-specific anxiety" showed that the counseling situation photograph produced higher ratings of potential anxiety, the most anxiety being associated with the very near (30 inches) and far (88 inches)
distances. A distance of about 50 inches was judged as least anxiety arousing for a counseling situation. Broekmann and Moller (1973) obtained subject ratings of seating arrangements for counseling, formal, home, and
same- and opposite-sex social situations. In contrast to the previous findings noted above, subjects preferred an across-the-table position for counseling, formal, and opposite-sex interaction situations, whereas a corner

seating position was most preferred for same-sex interactions. In addition, seating distances were varied for the different positions. The middle distance was most preferred but subjects who were described as submissive and dependent and socially controlled preferred the more distant position, whereas subjects with the opposite traits preferred the middle and closer distances. As in the study by Boucher (1972) with alcoholics and schizophrenics, distance preferences may vary with personality and should thus be considered in research of this kind.

Finally, Knight and Bair (1976) actually had 9 male counselors each interview 3 male subjects in face to face unobstructed seating distances of 18, 30, and 48 inches. A Semantic Differential covering four topics (counselor, interview setting, closeness, and seating) was subsequently filled out by subjects. An unspecified behavior rating scale filled out by observers viewing the 15-minute interview through a one-way mirror constituted a second dependent measure of interviewee comfort. Both the observer ratings and interviewee semantic differential ratings showed that the 30-inch distance was most comfortable, followed by the 48 and then 18-inch distance.

Most studies of seating arrangement have involved choice of chair positions around a table with little recognition of the potential significance of the table. Recently, Weiss and Keys (1975) varied seating distance (near or far) with the presence or absence of a table, which was hypothesized to provide a form of psychological distance. Postexperimental questionnaires were utilized to provide the dependent measures of perceived distance by male subject dyads engaged in a discussion. While seating distance had no significant effect, subjects separated by a table rated themselves as feeling more distant from their partner and as perceiving their partner as better adjusted.

"Territorial Invasion" of Personal Space

In addition to studying the significance of seating arrangements in social interaction, Sommer also investigated normative violations of individuals' personal space. In their now classic study, Felipe and Sommer (1966) employed confederates to intrude on the personal space of others in natural settings. The basic method involved the confederate seating himself at an inappropriately close distance (e.g., 6 inches) from the unsuspecting subject, also sometimes staring or acting in a way to assert his dominance; the dependent measure being the time before the individual vacated his seat. One study was conducted at a state hospital. In addition to obtaining support for the hypothesis that invaded patients would vacate their space, Felipe and Sommer observed:

Many more subtle indications of the patient's discomfort were evident. . . . Typically the victim would immediately face away from E, pull in his shoulders, and place his elbows at his sides. Mumbling, irrelevant laughter, and delusional talk also seemed to be used by the victim to keep E at a distance. (1966, p. 209)

In a second experiment the subjects were students seated in a university library. A female experimenter seated herself at a variety of distances from already seated students: (a) in a chair 3 inches away; (b) in the same chair 15 inches away; (c) the empty seat 2.5 feet away; (d) two empty seats 5 feet away; (e) directly across from the student, 4 feet away. More students left in condition (a) but conditions (b)–(d) also produced more rapid evacuation of spaces than students not invaded. Observation of student subjects' behaviors prior to leaving showed that they attempted to look away or shift their position, interpose a barrier, move farther away, with marked individual differences in subjects' reactions.

Sommer (1967b) also investigated various strategies that a person might employ in avoiding others or in aggressively "defending" his space against intrusion by others. On a questionnaire showing seating positions students given the instructional set to "avoid intrusion" chose the middle chair. Subsequently Sommer and Becker (1969) again employed a questionnaire depicting a room seating situation with two instructional sets (passive versus active defenses) and two room density descriptions (crowded versus uncrowded). As predicted, students chose the center seating areas when engaged in active defense and the end chairs closest to the wall during the passive avoidance condition. Subjects under the passive avoidance instructions also tended to favor seating with their backs to the door, whereas relatively more subjects actively defending tended to face the door. More subjects under avoidance instructions favored seating in the rear of the room. Subjects also tended to choose small tables and tables against the wall. Under high density instructions, more subjects given the passive avoidance set sat towards the rear nearest a wall.

In other studies of spatial intrusion, Patterson, Mullens, and Romano (1971) varied the immediacy of intruders in a university library setting by having a confederate seat herself adjacent, across, or two or three seats adjacent from an unsuspecting student. As predicted, various compensatory behaviors (e.g., leaning away, blocking by turning away or using a hand or elbow) were observed to increase as a function of increasing confederate immediacy. Contrary to predictions, cross glances also increased with immediacy either due to a need for increased information or vigilance towards disliked others. Unlike Felipe and Sommer's experiment, few subjects actually left the situation. Johnson (1972) investigated various privacy signals in public settings by observing seated individuals. The most commonly observed nonverbal behaviors included the following privacy signals: sitting straight up and forward, with books in front of them, reading or writing. Table markers tended to reduce privacy by apparently facilitating approach by others.

Fry and Willis (1971) conducted invasions of personal space using children of ages 5, 8, and 10 years to approach adults in a movie theater line. Five year old children were received positively, eight-year-olds with indifference, and ten year olds were reacted to negatively. McDowell (1972) hypothesized that if a person is engaged in an interaction with the invader of his personal space he would feel compelled to remain in the interaction but would react with hostility. Confederates interacted with subjects at normal (98-centimeter) or "violated" (48-centimeter) distances. Contrary to the hypothesis, subjects whose personal space was violated moved away significantly more from the confederate (male or female), but they did not assume a less direct orientation, decrease their looking, or evaluate the intruding confederate more negatively.

Given the evidence that personal space invasions are unpleasant and tend to evoke flight responses, it might be hypothesized that under normal circumstances individuals would avoid such normative violations. Barefoot, Hoople, and McClay (1972) seated experimenters 1, 5, and 10 feet from a drinking fountain. Significantly fewer male passersby stopped to drink at the fountain when the distance was 1 foot than when it was 5 and 10 feet, although those who did drink did not consistently appear to reduce their drinking time. Efran and Cheyne (1973) placed confederates in a hallway at personal and social distances and found that significantly fewer persons crossed in between the confederates at personal distances than expected by chance, whereas this was not the case at social distances. Subsequently, Efran and Cheyne (1974) reported that subjects forced to violate the shared space of two confederates displayed more agonistic facial behaviors and reported more negative moods than subjects who did not so intrude.

In a series of six studies too numerous to describe individually, Sommer and Becker (1969) left "territorial markers" (e.g., personal objects such as books, coats, journals, which signal legitimate occupancy of the space) in study hall seats with the finding that most served to protect the seat from being taken by other students. Indeed, naive students even participated in defending the space of confederate subjects who had left markers. Sommer and Becker concluded these findings represented a start in understanding how markers reserve and legitimize space against invasion by potential intruders.

More recently, Becker (1973) compared the value of markers against actual occupancy in a library situation. As predicted, occupancy by people served to affect the choice and duration of seating of other naive students more than the presence of markers alone. Markers, however, did delay occupancy of seats nearby. A subsequent questionnaire study employing photographs of various tables with markers present revealed that no subject would sit at a marked location or risk a confrontation with an intruder or owner of a marker. Becker concluded that markers are highly effective in reducing conflict and hostility about the use of space by acting as warning devices for "jurisdictional control" (i.e., temporary use of space).

Recently, Shaffer and Sadowski (1975) justly argued that spatial markers do not necessarily represent "territorial behavior" unless one can presume that the individuals who marked spatial locations would defend them against invasion. Subjects in the study by Becker and Mayo (1971), for example, did not defend their marked cafeteria space when it was violated. Shaffer and Sadowski chose an overcrowded barroom setting for an experimental field study, reasoning that this was a situation where empty but marked tables would be both susceptible to invasion (i.e., being occupied by someone else) and also likely to be defended by the individual who left the marker. A male and a female experimenter thus occupied various tables selected as being high or low in potential for interacting with others in the bar. Each sat at the table for 15 minutes and then left, leaving a personal belonging behind to mark their seat as being occupied. As predicted, the authors found that markers by either sex protected the seating condition longer than when no marker was left, although masculine belongings were more effective than female items. However, females were equally likely to "invade" such marked spaces as males. When the table location was high in its potential for facilitating social interaction, markers were less effective than when the table location was more peripheral in its location and thus less ideal for social interaction. Most recently, Arenson (1976) pointed out that the potential discomfort resulting from invasion of a marked space may have a bearing on the degree of defense. Arensen used four psychology undergraduate students who visited a race track and occupied marked seats vacated by spectators in between horse races. Of 32 invasions perpetrated there were 20 defenses by neighbors of the person who marked the space. However, 14 of the 20 defenders were relatives or friends who presumably felt a commitment to the absent person.

ENVIRONMENTAL FACTORS

In the studies reviewed so far, the experimental manipulations have focused on direct manipulation of interpersonal or seating distance in relation to personality or social factors. A third way interpersonal distance can vary is by modifications in the environmental setting. If ten people are moved to a smaller room their interpersonal distance will, of necessity, shrink. Much of this research can be considered as "ecological psychology," or the study of crowding, population density, and the like. Since our focus is primarily on the individual, we will not attempt a comprehensive review but rather will consider some of the recent research which exemplifies some of the current thinking in this area as it affects proxemic research in general.

In a study of territorial behavior in psychiatric patients, Esser, Chamberlain, Chapple, and Kline (1965) reported that patients behaved more asocially on a crowded ward. Dabbs (1971) varied the room size for subjects, hypothesizing that as interpersonal proximity increased, so would subjects' arousal and the emotional climate of the situation. Pairs of subjects were left in rooms either 3.5 × 5 feet or 12 × 23 feet, which provided seating positions 2 and 6 feet apart, respectively. Subjects were given materials to discuss and instructional sets to either induce argumentative or friendly conversation. As expected, subjects placed in the small room felt more pressure and tended to disagree more with their partners, but they also tended to shy away more from open disagreement. Interestingly, subjects who engaged in "friendly conversation" in the small room appeared less attentive to the conversational content, perhaps because of the distraction resulting from the unnatural interpersonal distance. In contrast, argumentative discussion may have served to draw subjects' attention away from the interpersonal intimacy. Indeed, subjects who argued in the small room showed a significant decrease in palmar sweat measures reflective of an "attentional withdrawal" from the situation.

Griffitt and Veitch (1971) examined two variables: room density (3.5 subjects vs. 12–16 in one room) and temperature (93.5 vs. 73.4°F). Subjects completed a number of questionnaires including an attitude measure towards a hypothetical similar or dissimilar stranger. As predicted, subjects reported less positive personal and social affective reactions and less liking towards a stranger under conditions of high density and high temperature. Rawls, Trego, McGaffey, and Rawls (1972) obtained measures of subjects' personal space preferences based on their actual approach distances. Subsequently, they were given psychomotor and arithmetic problems while sitting at a table with 2, 4, and 8 other subjects. General support was obtained for the hypothesis that performance of high personal space subjects would deteriorate under the more crowded conditions. Freedman, Klevansky, and Ehrlich (1971), in contrast, found no significant effect of room density on a task performed by their subjects. However, Freedman, Klevansky, and Ehrlich also noted that the task chosen was one which subjects could complete without being affected by the crowding. Pedersen and Shears (1974) had pairs of subjects engage in a competitive interpersonal game, remain in a confined cubicle crowded together, or spend an equivalent amount of time separately. Before and after the experiment, measures of subjects' personal space were obtained on the Pedersen Personal Space Measure and from actual approach distances. Comparable reductions in personal space were obtained on both measures for subjects who interacted in the competitive game and crowded room situations as compared with subjects who were kept separated. However, even control subjects showed a reduction in personal space measured by experimenter approach distance. The results suggested that degree of acquaintance, either produced by interaction or crowding, in the absence of negative interaction, may result in people becoming "more approachable."

In an important study Cozby (1973), noting the negative results of Freedman, Klevansky, and Ehrlich (1971), argued that "the 'crowding is bad' theory of crowding is too simple. . . . High density may be seen as good or bad, depending upon the individual's current goals and whether the presence of others facilitates or inhibits those goals" (p. 46). Cozby (1973) obtained personal space measures on subjects in addition to a number of personality and background variables. Employing a model of a room with varying numbers of person-figures in it, he obtained subjects' ratings of liking for the room situation when it (a) represented a party, or (b) represented a study room setting. As he predicted, liking for the crowded room was greatest for the party situation; the uncrowded room was liked best for the study situation. In addition, subjects with small personal space needs preferred the high density room to large personal space subjects, particularly when it represented a party situation. These results show that crowding per se may not be necessarily undesirable, depending on the goals and personal qualities of individuals in the situation.

Consistent with this reasoning, Schopler and Walton (1975) hypothesized that crowding was "a joint function of high physical density and potential behavioral interferences" (p. 3). Employing six-person, same-sexed groups, Schopler and Walton varied subjects' expectations of high or low group structure (by creating a "chain of command" among members or by instructing subjects to solve the problem differently each time) or their expectations about the pleasantness or unpleasantness of the experience. Subjects were also classified as to Internal or External orientation on the Locus of Control Scale. As predicted, subjects in the low structure situation reported experiencing more crowding when differences in subject external-internal orientation were controlled for. In particular, subjects high in internal control felt less crowded than subjects high in external control. Expectations of pleasantness had no apparent effect.

Seta, Paulus, and Schkade (1975) have also noted that whether the situation is competitive or cooperative can determine the effect of crowding. In their study groups of four, subjects performed individual tasks at 2-foot (close) or 5-foot (far) interaction distances with the expectation that they would either be evaluated as a group (cooperative condition) or individually (competitive situation). As predicted, cooperative subjects' performance was enhanced by the near seating condition, whereas the far seating condition resulted in improved performance for subjects in the competitive situation. Subsequently, Petty (1976) exposed a same-sex group of four subjects to a "high density" (7 square feet per person) or a "low density" (19 square feet per person) experimental situation in which they engaged in a competitive or cooperative task. Although subjects reported feeling more crowded and uncomfortable in the high density situation, they did not behave less cooperatively or evaluate each other more negatively. As such, the perception of being crowded did not necessarily lead to undesirable interpersonal consequences. Paulus, Annis, Seta, Schkade, and Matthews (1976) employed a 2 × 2 × 2 factorial design where group size, room size, and interpersonal distance were independently varied. That is, subjects engaged in a maze tracing task where the mazes were either 6 (close distance) or 18 inches away (far distance) in a large or small room, as part of a mixed-sex group of four or eight persons. Performance in the maze task was affected by group size but not distance or room size. However, in a second study, manipulation of distance alone (other factors held constant) did result in decreased task performance, and in a third study males performed more poorly in a small room whereas females performed better in a large room. Density thus was a factor in task performance although it affected the sexes differentially.

In an important study Worchel and Teddlie (1976) noted that in most studies interaction distance was confounded with density, and that the previous findings concerning high density may be due to the effects of closer interaction distances rather than number of persons per se. For example, in a study by Epstein and Karlin (1975) subjects in the center of a crowded room (who had the least personal space) reported more discomfort than subjects on the room periphery. Worchel and Teddlie placed groups of 7 subjects in large and small rooms where seating distance (close and far) was independently varied. In addition, for half the groups pictures were placed in the experimental room to test the additional hypothesis that the presence of distractors would divert subjects' attention from the others and lessen their experience of crowding. Subjects in each group performed two tasks: (a) forming as many words as possible from a master word; (b) hearing and passing judgment on a case of juvenile delinquency. The results showed that subjects reported experiencing more crowding in the near than far interaction distance. However, greater crowding was experienced in the high density compared to the low density condition only when the interaction distances were far. Interaction distance rather than density affected subjects in a number of ways. Subjects in the close interaction situation overestimated the experimental time (a reflection of their discomfort with the situation); their performance on the word forming task was worse; and, they were more punitive in their judgement of the delinquent. When the pictures were present in the room in the near interaction condition, this reduced the above mentioned effects of crowding, as predicted. These findings very nicely illustrate the complexity of factors operating in situations where crowding occurs.

In addition to task differences, sex differences also play a role in the effect of environmental crowding. Ross, Layton, Erickson, and Schopler (1973) compared the effects of crowding on males and females given some choice dilemma questions to discuss. Males evaluated themselves and others more positively and gazed more at others in the uncrowded situation, whereas females gazed more and rated themselves and others more positively in the crowded room situation. These findings are similar to those obtained by Freedman, Levy, Buchanan, and Price (1972), who varied room size and sex. In two studies men were more competitive, or gave more severe "court sentences," when situated in small rather than large rooms while women showed the opposite behavior. Mixed sex groups showed no apparent effects. Marshall and Heslin (1975) varied group density for same sex and mixed sex groups while measuring member attraction towards the group. They also separately examined both variations in group size and room density (i.e., varying room size, holding subject number constant), either of which can be manipulated to produce crowding. (Earlier studies had not made this distinction.) While their findings in entirety are too complex to report here we can note that: (a) for same-sex subjects, small groups led to greater member attraction than large groups, especially among males; (b) for mixed-sex groups, member attraction was greater for the large groups for female subjects; and (c) group size per se had more effect than room density. Epstein and Karlin (1975) also noted that crowded males in general were less cohesive and more competitive than crowded females.

Baum and Greenberg (1975) induced subject expectations that they would face a 10-person or 4-person group in a relatively small room. In actuality, all subjects were exposed to two confederates who entered the room after them. As predicted, however, subjects expecting to interact with 10 persons perceived the room as being more crowded. In addition, they showed room corner seating preferences, looked less at the first confederate to enter, reported more personal discomfort, liked the confederate less, and liked the room less than subjects anticipating only 4 others. Whether or not the confederate actually sat close to subjects or farther away had little effect on the subjects' ratings. Baum and Greenberg (1975) concluded the following:

Subjects appear to be preparing for crowding by seeking positions in the room that will remove them from the majority of the group that is to assemble, and that will afford maximum defense and control over the high frequencies of social encounter that they are expecting. Similarly, reduced facial regard may be interpreted as a signal indicating that the subject does not want to interact. (1975, p. 667)

A number of studies have investigated the effect of other variables on the perception of crowding. Gochman and Keating (1967a) compared the perception of crowding among students who performed poorly, or well, during a quiz in a high, or low, density classroom, and found that the students performing more poorly rated the classroom as more crowded. Gochman and Keating (1976b) then assessed student perception of classroom crowding on different occasions when they were either filling out personality questionnaires (i.e., inwardly directed attention), or when they were listening to a lecture (outer directed attention). The results supported the prediction that when a person's focus of attention is inward, judgments of the environmental circumstances would be negative. Miller and Nardini (1976) investigated individual differences in the perception of crowding. Male and female subjects were asked to place as many pipe cleaner figures in a model room until they perceived the room as being crowded. Subjects of both sexes high on affiliative seeking tendencies showed a higher tolerance for crowding.

In addition to studies on crowding, where too many people are brought together, it is also possible that persons can become "too close" as a result of social isolation. Proxemics can be viewed in terms of the dimension of time as well as distance. Altman and his colleagues have studied social isolation in some detail. Thus, Haythorn, Altman, and Myers (1966) exposed dyads made up of Navy recruits to 10 days isolation. Subjects were matched, or varied, according to personality characteristics (need achievement, need affiliation, dominance, and dogmatism) to produce high-homogeneous or heterogeneous combinations or low-homogeneous or heterogeneous combinations. Both the experimental isolation and nonisolated control group worked at their regular task. Based upon questionnaires, personal stress, and emotional symptomatology, the following findings emerged: (a) isolation itself produced more subjective stress but not more emotional symptomatology; (b) isolated dyads heterogeneous for dogmatism reported more emotional symptoms; (c) isolated and nonisolated dyads heterogeneous for need achievement experienced more stress and emotional symptomatology; (d) subjects heterogeneous for dominance reported less stress and emotional symptomatology than high- or low-dominant pairs, the high-dominant pairs showing less recovery from stress than other pairs; (e) contrary to predictions, homogeneous high-dominant and low-dominant isolated pairs did not differ in the stress they experienced.

In another study employing similarly constituted dyads, Altman and Haythorn (1967) examined the territorial behavior of subjects. For isolated dyads "territorial behavior" increased over time (e.g., subjects claiming beds and chairs as their "own"), as did relative social isolation. In addition, dyads incompatible on dominance (e.g., both dominant), or affiliation, "traits directly associated with interpersonal matters," showed especially high territorality, whereas incompatibility in subjects' achievement needs and dogmatism scores did not effect such changes. Incompatibility on "ego-centric" characteristics (e.g., high-low dominance) resulted in active member interactions, whereas incompatibilities in "sociocentric" characteristics, such as affiliation and achievement, resulted in social withdrawal.

Continuing this line of research, Altman (1971) reported a study in which isolated dyads were exposed to varying degrees of privacy, outside stimulation, and expectations for continued isolation. All groups were actually to be kept isolated for 8 days, but half were told it would be for 20 days and half that it would be for 4 days. However, half the subjects chose to terminate the isolation experience prior to the planned 8 days when the experiment was to actually end. Subject pairs with extended isolation expectancies (20 days) or violated expectancies (e.g., subjects with a 4-day expectancy who went into the fifth day in isolation), or subjects in less private and less stimulated situations, terminated their isolation earlier than the others. Interestingly, early terminators characteristically showed lower territorial behavior and social interaction early in isolation and greater territorial and social behavior later, whereas the opposite was true for dyads that completed the 8-day period. From these results the author proposed the hypothesis that "aborter groups had 'misread' the demands of the situation and had not gone about the business of adapting to their environments and to one another in terms of group formation processes (Altman, 1971, p. 297).

In contrast to the above research, Beussee, Ahearn, and Hammes (1970) obtained diaries of the experiences of men, children, and women in experimental tests of fall out shelters. Confinement periods ranged from 1 day to 2 weeks. While subjects experienced no deleterious psychological and social consequences, complaints centered about space, sleeping, excessive temperatures, and water. Interestingly, negative comments began to decrease and positive comments increase as the end of confinement neared. It would thus seem that cognitive variables, particularly one's expectations in an isolated situation are an important factor in determining adjustment to the isolation.

Several researchers have studied dominance behavior in relation to "natural" territorial situations. Esser, Chamberlain, Chapple, and Kline (1965) studied the behavior of psychiatric patients by keeping records of patients' location in relation to floor grids and by their interactional behavior. Rankings of patients' dominance behavior were obtained based upon number of contacts, duration of interactions, and initiative taken in patient-patient and patient-staff contacts. Territorial locations were defined as spaces where patients spent more than 75% of their time. Patients who were most dominant roamed freely in the ward situation, whereas less assertive patients appeared to establish their own particular territorial areas and withdraw socially. In addition, it appeared to the authors "that a person's instability in the dominance hierarchy and his possession of territory are both related to aggressive behavior . . . a person whose position in the hierarchy is established and who does not occupy a specific spot will not show aggressive behavior" (1965, p. 43).

More recently, Sundstrom and Altman (1974) studied territorial and dominance behavior among institutionalized juveniles. Subjects' use of areas in the institution was observed, especially the desirable areas, and peer rankings of dominance were obtained. Under social conditions in which the group composition remained stable, the most dominant individuals maintained priority use of desirable areas but when the group composition changed, use of space broke down and more individuals shared the desirable spaces. Sundstrom and Altman (1974) concluded:

Under stable conditions, there was a positive dominance-territorial behavior relationship, and dominant members frequently used desirable spaces. When the social structure underwent change, the stable space-use system broke down, and conflict emerged, perhaps reflecting interference with resource-distribution and interaction-control functions served by a space-use system. (pp. 123–124)

Finally, in an interesting but complex study, Edney (1975) examined behavioral differences among unacquainted domitory student pairs. The experiments were conducted in one of the student's rooms making him the "resident" and the other a "visitor." One subject (either the "visitor" or "resident") was assigned to a "control" role (i.e., to act as the experimenter's assistant in carrying out a series of tasks). These tasks included making the other subject do various things (e.g., sending him outside the room, moving furniture) and establishing control over the room situation (by designating his personal area with a string). The dependent measures included an interpersonal distancing task, a "density tolerance questionnaire," and other self-report questionnaires. In addition, FIRO-B measures of active and passive control were obtained, the latter considered representative of "territorial aggressiveness" (i.e., resisting control). The results showed that controlling subjects found the room as "more pleasant" and "stimulating" than those who were controlled. "Residents" generally viewed the room as more pleasant and private, and they attributed their own behavior to the room, whereas "visitors" employed personality as an explanation for the behaviors in the situation. Subjects who were high on active control indicated smaller space needs and a higher tolerance for crowding. When in the role of assistant they also chose shorter interpersonal distances. Regardless of personality or situational role factors, however, "visitors" tended to see "residents" as being more "at home." As a result of these findings, Edney (1975) argued that the concept of control "is broader than the unitary concept of dominance, and that one form (passive control) can be articulated meaningfully to territory while another form (active control) related to other spatial behaviors" (p. 13).

Valins and Baum (1973) studied students living in dormitories and the effect of different architectural designs on them. For example, they found that corridor design, as opposed to suite design (the latter design forcing far fewer interpersonal contacts), was associated with subjects' reports that they felt too crowded, that there were too many residents, and too many disliked residents. These same subjects (who lived in corridor design dormitories) also tended to perceive model replicas of rooms to be more crowded for unstructured social situations. Further, in an experimental situation, corridor design residents felt more uncomfortable, sat farther away from, and looked less at confederates during a waiting period. In a subsequent study, corridor resident subjects reported more personal discomfort and sat farther away from confederates in a cooperative situation but not in a competitive situation where social interaction was less likely. Finally, in performing anagram tasks, corridor residents performed better in competitive and "coaction" (acting independently) situations whereas suite residents did better in the cooperative situation and while working alone. These unusually consistent results strongly suggest that environmental living situations can profoundly affect one's perception of social situations and their mood and behavior when interacting with others.

Glassman, Burkhart, Grant, and Vallery (1976) had the opportunity to study the effects of natural crowding on female college freshman dormitory students, some of whom were required to live in groups of three in two-person dwellings. Compared to women living two per room, those living three per room obtained lower grade point averages, were less satisfied, made more complaints about other dormitory residents and their room, and made more room change requests. In particular, those who had expected more living space than they encountered expressed the least satisfaction with their situation. It should be noted that these findings were obtained in a natural setting with subjects facing interminable crowding, in contrast to laboratory studies of crowding.

Desor (1972) examined subjects' reactions to various fixed spaces (i.e., room dimensions). Based upon models of rooms and a figure placement task subjects showed greater tolerance for "crowding" and physical closeness when there were more partitions, doors, and the area (which was held constant) was rectangular in shape. Interestingly, it made no difference whether the partitions were complete or only partial (e.g., half the wall height, opaque); visual stimulation did not appear as important as the potential for physical or personal contact resulting from the room arrangements. The type of social activity was also important: more persons could be added to the room situation when it was used for a cocktail party than when room occupants were engaged in reading.

In a field study Eoyang (1974) surveyed residents of a trailer park. Two variables investigated were the number of occupants per living unit and relative privacy (i.e., living alone in a bedroom). With living space constant, the number of occupants per unit was the most significant determinant of living satisfaction, more so than privacy, time in situation, or personal attributes of the individuals. This finding is consistent with an important paper by Galle, Gove, and McPherson (1972), who divided population density into four factors: persons per room, rooms per housing unit, housing units per structure, and structures per acre. Through complicated statistical analyses, they determined the number of persons per room is the most important factor in population density for mortality, fertility, public assistance, and juvenile delinquency. Social structure had relatively little effect on the above pathologies except through its influence on this component of density. However, for admissions to mental hospitals, number of rooms per housing unit was the best single predictor (perhaps reflecting a self-selection process where disturbed individuals tend to live alone).

Finally, Paulus, Cox, McCain, and Chandler (1975) visited a prison setting to study the effect of crowding. Social density (number of individuals per housing unit) and spatial density (square feet of space per individual) measures were obtained for the male prisoners in the study. Subjects were asked to add miniature human figures to a model room until they considered it crowded; in addition, various measures of affective state were obtained. The results showed that inmates living in the more crowded environments tended to prefer less crowded environments. The length of confinement was also negatively related to tolerance of crowding. Social density (more so than spatial density) was more related to negative affect, and negative affect was related to an intolerance of crowding. Subsequently, Cox, Paulus, McCain, and Schkade (1976) took palmar sweat prints of prisoners and found that social density was related ($r = .33$) to this physiological measure of arousal. In addition, prisoners in more crowded living conditions evidenced more physical complaints and illnesses. The authors also visited workers on offshore oil drilling platforms and found that workers on crowded platforms (11 square feet per worker) were reluctant to be interviewed and expressed more negative reactions about their living condition compared to workers on less crowded platforms.

One final concept we will introduce briefly in relation to environmental variables and personal space is the concept of "manning." This refers to the number of people needed to carry out an activity. A condition of under-manning exists when there are not enough persons to fill various roles required for completion of activities; this corresponds to a situation of low population density. Overmanning, in contrast, occurs when there are too many persons for a job. Wicker (1973) investigated the effects of overman-ning by placing groups of three persons in a two man task or groups of two or three persons working on tasks suitable for that number. Overmanned groups tended to perform more poorly on the task and to perceive less need for an additional member. While the effects and findings were not particu-larly strong, this study points out that the number of persons in relation to task requirements is also an important variable in studying environment and personal space.

RESEARCH ON TOUCHING BEHAVIOR

Though most proxemic research has been devoted to interpersonal conver-sational distance, one must not forget that body contact and touching are proxemic phenomena. This is an area, in psychological research, that has been relatively unstudied until recently. In sampling some of the research conducted on touching, we will again neglect the more structural ap-proaches in favor of experimental studies. However, the reader should not forget Hall's comment that many investigators "have failed to grasp the deep significance of touch, particularly active touch. They have not under-stood how important it is to keep the person related to the world in which he lives" (1966, p. 57). Along with Hall, several other anthropologists have focused upon the study of touching behavior. Lawrence Frank wrote one of the earliest papers on tactile communication (Frank, 1966), and a later paper by Kauffman (1971) outlined essentially a structuralist approach to "tacesics, the study of touch." While such works tend to fall short on empir-ical findings, they do synthesize and integrate ideas that are useful for empirical investigation. Kauffman has proposed a "processual model" by which touching behavior can be predicted based upon a person's past expe-rience, present situational factors, and motivational characteristics. Her goal, however, is to identify "tacemes," "tacemorphs," and "tacemorphic constructions," an approach similar to the linguistic-kinesic analogy devel-oped by Birdwhistell. Our interest here will be upon more rigorously con-trolled, experimental, perhaps more "atomistic" findings.

Jourard (1966) was one of the first psychologists to consider studying touch systematically. Commenting on the lack of research in this area, Jour-ard noted:

As investigators, we have encroached upon many realms deemed sacrosanct. We have enquired into people's sex lives, probed their religious sentiments, peeped into their unconscious fantasies, we have even eavesdropped on the psychotherapeutic interview. But for all this, we know little about the conditions under which a person will permit another to touch him, the meanings people attach to touching and being touched, the loci of acceptable touch, and little of the consequences of body-contact. It is as if the touch–taboo most of us learned in childhood has produced a scotoma of our professional vision, making us describe man in our text-books as if he did not get closer to his fellows than a foot or so. (p. 221)

In his original study Jourard administered a "body-accessibility question-naire" to unmarried college students of both sexes. This questionnaire consists of the human figure divided into various areas on which the students were to indicate the extent to which they allow parents and close friends to touch their body and the extent to which they have touched them. Subjects also indicated whether or not the particular body areas were visually observed. Frequency, circumstances, or meaning of contact was not taken into account. As might be expected, the hands, arms, shoulders, back, and head areas were most frequently touched among all subjects. There were significant relationships between being seen and seeing others' bodies, touching and being touched. The most touching occurred between subjects and their closest opposite sex friends. Interestingly, males were touched more by their mothers than they touched their mothers, whereas females exchanged more physical contact on different areas of the body than did males. There were also significant relationships among the touching measures for individuals, suggesting that body accessibility is a generalized phenomenon for an individual and is perhaps related to personality factors. Specifically, individuals who rated themselves as unattractive reported being touched on less of their body surface, and Protestant and Catholic girls reported more body contact with their boyfriends than did Jewish girls.

Most recently, Rosenfeld, Kartus, and Ray (1976) replicated Jourard's 1966 study to see whether touching has changed over the last decade. They found that very little change in body accessibility has occurred for touching by mothers, fathers, and same-sex friends or unmarried males and females between the ages 18–22. However, they did find that females touched male friends more often in the chest, stomach, and hip region and males increased in their touching of female friends in the area from the chest to the knees. One might speculate that these differences are a reflection of changes stemming from the sexual revolution.

In their study of Arab and American student interactions, Watson and Graves (1966) noted that the only touching occurred among Arab students, and those instances of touching were more unintentional than intentional. Jourard (1966) also reported naturalistically observing touching in coffee houses in different countries. For pairs of individuals during 1-hour sittings, 180 touches were observed for Puerto Ricans, 110 for French, none for English, and 2 for Americans. In a study reported by Shuter (1976), observations were made of the frequency of contact (touching and holding) of Costa Rican, Panamanian, and Colombian dyads. As with distance and axis of orientation the Costa Ricans were the most tactile people followed by Panamanians and Colombians. As in the American culture, female dyads engaged in more physical contact, but unlike our culture, all male dyads showed more contact than mixed-sex dyads.

Jourard also noted that the French in their mental hospitals deliberately encourage touching including massage, whereas body contact in American culture is generally limited to such acts as pulse taking. Aguilera (1967) also described a study of touching within a psychiatric setting. In an experimental group, nurses employed simple, appropriate touch gestures and verbal communication with their patients; control patients only received verbal communication. As expected, use of touch gestures resulted in increased verbal interaction, rapport, and approach behaviors on the part of patients after approximately 8 days of interaction. At about the same time, decreases in interaction were noted among control patients. The delay in patient response was attributed to learning on the part of nurses of how to use touch effectively; however, many variables were uncontrolled and no statistical tests were employed.

Jourard and Rubin (1968), using questionnaires, related touching with a special form of verbal productivity, self-disclosure. Male and female college students filled out the body contact questionnaire (Jourard, 1966) and a self-disclosure questionnaire listing 40 personal topics and whether or not they had been discussed with the particular target person (e.g., mother, father, opposite sex friend, etc.). Jourard and Rubin found that, for most practical purposes, the two measures of intimacy were essentially independent. There was a low but significant ($r = .31$) tendency for males to touch and disclose more to a same-sex friend and a similar relationship ($r = .38$) between females and opposite-sex friends. Interestingly, analysis of the body accessibility questionnaires suggested that for males, the degree to which they were touched by their mothers was predictive of how much they would allow their father or same sex friends to touch them, but not with touching by their girlfriends.

Subsequently Jourard and Friedman (1970) varied intimacy or psychological distance by having an interviewer vary his behavior in the following fashion (in order of decreasing distance): (a) verbally respond impersonally; (b) touch the subject when entering the room; (c) disclose to the subject; (d) touch and disclose to the subject. The number of seconds spent talking was the dependent measure of self-disclosure. Contrary to Argyle and

Dean's intimacy-distance equilibrium theory, subjects talked more as "distance" decreased. Subjects in interviewer conditions (c) and (d) also reported more positive affect and more impression change. Jourard and Friedman, however, pointed out that in contrast to Argyle and Dean's experiments, their subjects were dealing with interviewers who were behaving quite positively toward them. This situation may result in movement toward the interviewer, consistent with interpersonal attraction which must be held constant for equilibrium theory to be fairly tested. Indeed, a correlation of .73 was noted between subjects' positive feelings towards the interviewer and their self-disclosure. Finally, Cooper and Bowles (1973) had an experimental group engage in encounter group physical contact exercises. As predicted, experimental subjects, following their encounter group session, showed a greater willingness to self-disclose to group members based on scores from the Jourard Self-Disclosure Questionnaire.

Though touches can communicate, they also produce other effects, one of which is physical arousal. Geis and Viksne (1972) explored this aspect by obtaining fingertip "sweat prints" from subjects. After engaging in some physical exercise, subjects received and gave a back rub to an opposite-sex confederate under the rationale that they needed to relax prior to engaging in social conversation. Compared to subjects who did not engage in physical contact, experimental subjects showed a significant reduction in arousal. This finding was considered consistent with Harlow's "contact comfort" theory. However, one might speculate that the opposite could have occurred had there simply been touching and no expectation given to subjects that they were to relax. Subsequently, Nicosia and Aiello (1976) measured skin conductance in same-sex groups of subjects who were crowded and touching one another, or who were separated by barriers of artificial plexiglass partitions or a string. Crowded men increased in skin conductance, especially men touching one another, compared to noncrowded men. In contrast, noncrowded women's skin conductance increased. Subjects who touched showed the lowest tolerance for frustration. Self-report indexes of somatic arousal, awareness of interpersonal proximity, and annoyance all were greater for crowded, especially touching subjects. The results demonstrated a sex difference in response to touching in crowded situations, men becoming more uncomfortable and women becoming more comfortable, with barriers reducing the discomfort for males but having no apparent effect for females.

Boderman, Freed, and Kinnucan (1972) examined the implicit assumption among encounter group enthusiasts that touching facilitates interpersonal attraction. Employing bogus ESP (Extra Sensory Perception) experiments with subjects, some of whom were touched by a confederate, they found that touching subsequently resulted in more favorable ratings of the confederate. Breed and Ricci (1973) repeated this experiment but added warm-cold confederate behavior in addition to touching. Contrary to the results just mentioned, touching did not produce any effect, although the warm-cold manipulation did. For some reason, subjects in the experiment by Breed and Ricci found the confederate less accessible.

In an interesting study, Silverman, Pressman, and Bartel (1973) examined self-esteem in relation to tactile communication. After a confederate non-verbally conveyed several emotions (i.e., love, pity, hurt, and hate) to the subject by touching them, subjects were in turn required to communicate "love to a friend" through touch. Both the location of touch (intimacy) and duration of touching were observed. High self-esteem subjects engaged in more intimate touching than low self-esteem subjects, but there was no difference observed in duration of touching. In addition, high self-esteem subjects reported that they felt they communicated the emotion more easily, and males felt the task was easier.

Touching in relation to status of an individual (e.g., sex, race, age, socioeconomic level) was studied by Henley (1973). Henley hypothesized that higher-status persons would touch more and reciprocate more touch by lower-status individuals. Based upon naturalistic observation of touching frequency of individuals in indoor and outdoor settings, high-status individuals (e.g., older vs. younger; male vs. female, white vs. black) did engage in more touching of their lower status partners. Limited support was also obtained for the hypothesis that higher-status individuals will reciprocate touch more. One recent study examined the role of touching in relation to self-exploration in a counseling relationship. Pattison (1973) trained counselors to employ hand-touching at times when more information was being sought. As predicted, touching in this fashion resulted in a greater depth of self-exploration by clients, even though touching did not alter client perception of their relationship with the counselor. Watson (1975) studied touching behavior in a geriatric nursing setting. Instrumental and expressive touching by the staff to the patients were distinguished. The former pertained to acts that fulfill the performance of another act (e.g., changing a bandaid); expressive touching constitutes part of communication of feelings. Watson reported that instrumental acts were related to the nature of the jobs performed by staff. However, the amount of touching was positively related to the status or rank of the nursing person, senior nurses exhibiting far more touching of patients than nurse's aides. This was especially true when touching accompanied some form of criticism or censure of the patients. The number of observations was relatively small, however, and the disproportionate number of males serving as aides and females serving as nurses pose important limitations for the interpretation of their findings.

Heslin (1974) recently proposed a classification of touching behavior based upon which he and his colleagues have conducted several studies. Five categories of touching are specified based upon the nature of the interpersonal relationship. At the *Functional/Professional* level, use of touch is on an impersonal "manipulator-to-object" level, as during a physician's examination where the motivation is to do something to the other person who is regarded largely as an object. Touches such as handshakes represent the *Social/Polite* level (where physical contact occurs on a very restricted, socially prescribed level). In contrast to Henley (1973), Heslin sees this kind of touching as neutralizing status disparities rather than signifying them by signaling recognition of the other as a "person." Touches that convey *Friendship/Warmth* are often the most difficult for persons to interpret because the relationship is close enough for love or sexual attraction to develop. Heslin thus hypothesizes that when two friends are alone, this kind of touching will decrease as a result of the association of privacy with sex and love. He also hypothesized that "it is in the areas of *Friendship/Warmth* that the greatest cross-cultural variability occurs" (1974, p. 2) given the varying cultural norms about sexual behavior. *Love/Intimacy* touches (e.g., hand on cheek) also require an appropriate interpersonal context if they are not to disturb others by conveying sexual intentions. The "touch" level of *Sexual Arousal* is obviously the most intense, and the kinds of touches which convey this meaning are probably somewhat idiosyncratic among partners. Heslin (1974) proposed two competing models relating these five classifications to one another. The first was that "as you move from Functional/ Professional to Sexual Arousal there is a corresponding increase in the extent to which you individualize and humanize the other person" (p. 3). Alternatively, one could argue that "the most appreciation of the other as an individual occurs in the Friendship/Warmth relationship" (pp. 3–4) whereas recipients of Love/Intimacy or Sexual Arousal are regarded as love and sex "objects," respectively.

White (1975) studied the nonverbal behavior of engaged and dating college couples in relation to measures of romantic love and intimacy. Based on analysis of 3-minute videotaped interactions, there were significant correlations between duration of male initiated body contact and measures of intimacy and romantic love. This was true for females only, however, Nguyen, Heslin, and Nguyen (1975) recently investigated male-female differences in their perception of the meaning of various touches (a pat, squeeze, brush, and stroke) to different body areas if they were to touch a close friend of the opposite sex. Ratings were made in terms of the following meaning categories: playfulness, warmth/love, friendship/fellowship, sexual desire and pleasantness. Both sexes agreed that the pat was the most friendly and playful and that the stroke was most loving, sexual, and pleasant. Touches to the legs were viewed as most playful and to the hands as most loving, sexual, and pleasant. Subjects relied more on the mode than the location of touch in rating playfulness, warmth/love, and pleasantness whereas the body area was more important in determining sexual desire or friendship/fellowship. The results showed that both sexes agreed that touches to the genital area, regardless of kind, conveyed sexual meaning. However, males associated touches by females indicating sexual desire with positive ratings on pleasantness and warmth/love whereas females gave essentially opposite and negative ratings for these touches by males in terms of pleasantness, love/warmth, friendliness, and playfulness. Interestingly, the authors reported that on further investigation that "females dislike of sexual touching was replaced with a strong positive response after marriage" (p. 103).

Following up on this sex difference in interpreting touches, Fisher, Rytting, and Heslin (1976) trained a library clerk to accidently brush the hand of a student in the process of returning his library card (a touch essentially Professional/Functional in nature). Following this touch (or no touch) manipulation, students were approached by the experimenter and asked to complete a rating scale, ostensibly to evaluate their feelings about library facilities and personnel. In general, touching by the library clerk resulted in more positive evaluations by students of the touches and the library settings. This was particularly true for females, whereas males appeared somewhat more ambivalent. In particular, this effect was true even if the student was not aware of being touched. The authors observed: "If this is the case, then the potency of the act of touching another person becomes very striking: a touch of less than one second has the power to make people feel better, and this effect can generalize to evaluation of associated stimuli" (1975, p. 10).

Silverthorne, Micklewright, O'Donnell, and Gibson (1975) investigated the effect of touching on interpersonal judgement when two persons meet. Male and female subjects were introduced to a male or female confederate who either nodded and gave a firm handshake, or gave a firm handshake accompanied by a left handed squeeze on the subject's upper right arm. The male confederate was generally perceived more positively the more that touching was involved in the greeting. For females, the nod or handshake plus arm clasp produced consistently the best ratings on interpersonal attraction. Most interestingly, touching for male confederates was positively related to female subjects' ratings of them as an acceptable marriage partner, whereas the opposite relationship obtained for female confederates introduced to male subjects. Finally, Heslin and Boss (1976) have extended their naturalistic investigation of touching to airport departure and arrival situations. Randomly selected "target" pairs of travelers and nontravelers were carefully observed for touching behavior and then interviewed concerning the nature of the relationship. A detailed observational coding procedure was followed. The authors found that men were less comfortable about touching and used less intimate forms of touching than women. As predicted, males and older people were more intense (i.e., intimate) in touching and initiated contact more often than females and young persons. Unexpectedly, kissing on the mouth was the most common behavior even in comparison to handshaking. Finally, the amount of and intensity of touching among target pairs was related to the amount of physical contact generally occurring in the crowd. These behaviors were seen as strongly normatively prescribed for a situation involving public intimacy behavior.

RECENT THEORETICAL DEVELOPMENTS

With the tremendous expansion in empirical research on proxemic phenomena, it should not be surprising that many researchers have tried to organize the multiplicity of findings into some theoretical or conceptual framework. We will note some of these efforts briefly in this concluding section which the interested reader may want to consider in greater detail. Pedersen and Shears (1973), for example, reviewed the recent literature on personal space from the standpoint of a general system theory. Distance setting behavior is viewed as a steady state mechanism for both "person systems" and "group systems." These systems operate to: (a) process input or incoming information; (b) evaluate the input against internal criteria within the system; and (c) transmit output which are responses to environmental events affecting the internal state. Modifications in the steady state are a result of negative feedback occurring within the individual (person system) or group situation (group system). Within the person system, verbal and nonverbal expressive behaviors and physiological reactions may signal the perception of an environmental change (input) by an individual who then evaluates this against his "normative or idiosyncratic social schema." The instrumental behavior that follows is defined as "output," i.e., the person's response to the environment. A reduction in eye contact or shift in body orientation, for example, might occur in response to an invasion of personal space which upsets the person system. This whole process is conceptualized in terms of a "feedback loop" analogous to communications systems. Kaplan (1974) has recently also proposed a structural model for studying interpersonal distancing employing an "intimacy-immediacy" dimension ("defined as an integration across proxemic, kinesic, paralinguistic, and linguistic interpersonal modalities," p. 1).

On a more modest level, Duke and Nowicki (1972) applied social learning theory and Rotter's locus of control theory to their concept of personal space. Interpersonal distancing is seen as a function of an individual's social reinforcement history and his current expectancies for reinforcement. When a person interacts with someone about whom he has some expectancy then he "should be responded to with preferred interpersonal distances which are not related to (mediated by) the locus of control orientation" (p. 128). However, when dealing with strangers for whom no expectancies are available, the person's locus of control orientation (i.e., whether they see reinforcements as being under self-control or the control of others) should be related to their interpersonal distance setting. Specifically, Duke and Nowicki predicted that for strangers there should be a positive relationship between externality and the interpersonal distance chosen, inasmuch as externals do not expect to be able to control what happens to themselves socially.

Sundstrom and Altman (1974) conceptualized interaction distance in terms of various interpersonal variables: the relationship and degree of liking of the interactants; their expectation of interaction; the intimacy of their conversation; and such situational constraints as room density. Various relationships are proposed between interpersonal comfort and interaction distance for strangers (who have no expectancy of interaction), friends or acquaintances, and strangers expecting to interact. Variables which may modify these distances are the sex of interactants, stand-seating positions, and intimacy of conversation topic. Room density appears to modify interaction distances such that in dense settings closer interaction distances may still be experienced as comfortable. Other factors such as the kind of interaction, the formality of the situation, and setting all need to be taken into account in studies of personal space.

Most recently, Sundstrom (1975) has conceptualized crowding as an interpersonal phenomenon that can be characterized by a sequential process. That is, a high room density may lead to interpersonal disturbance and stress, which in turn produces individual coping responses to alleviate the stress. Interpersonal disturbances occurring as a result of crowding include intrusion by others who are too close, and interference in obtaining goals. Sundstrom operationalized these concepts in a $2 \times 2 \times 2$ experimental design in which room size was varied (i.e., small versus large); intrusion by confederates occurred consisting of forward-leaning and high (80%) eye contact and physical contact (e.g., confederate knee rests against subject's leg); and goal-blocking (confederates preventing the subject from finishing statements by interruptions, looking away, etc.). Three subjects interacted with each of 3 confederates either in a small or large room. Topics varying in intimacy were chosen for discussion. Subjects filled out self-report scales following each interaction. Videotapes of the interactions were taken and later viewed by trained observers. Small room size, intrusion, and goal blocking all led to self-report ratings of discomfort and stress. Interestingly, these ratings declined over the three interaction periods with the exception of stress due to goal-blocking, which increased. Various verbal and nonverbal measures of affiliative behavior were coded, the results showing that small room size lowered topic intimacy and subject head-nodding; intrusion lowered facial regard by subjects, and goal-blocking decreased facial regard, gesturing, and head-nodding. Contrary to expectation, combined small room size, intrusion and goal-blocking did not lead to intensified stress though it did result in further reductions in facial regard. While each of the variables associated with crowding (i.e., density, intrusion, goal-blocking) independently produced interpersonal stress, apparently the reductions in subject-affiliative behavior noted above served to compensate for, or facilitate adaptation to the conditions, except where the confederate was being interruptive and inattentive (i.e., "rude") in the goal-blocking situation. Since such behavior will evoke interpersonal offense and is not necessarily a consequence of crowding (as would be the intrusion of conversation by another party in the subject-confederate conversation) the particular manipulation of goal blocking may not have been. most appropriate.

Several other researchers have dealt with environmental and proxemic phenomena from a social psychological standpoint. Altman (1974) wrote an important paper on privacy which he defined as "the selective control of access to the self" (p. 22). Privacy is described as an "interpersonal boundary control process" where the person is made more or less accessible to others at various times, given the circumstances of the social situation. An individual's privacy may be considered in terms of the privacy desired versus the actual degree of privacy achieved. Crowding or intrusion occurs when desired privacy is discrepant from achieved privacy; where the reverse is true, a state of isolation is considered to exist. In particular, various nonverbal behaviors are employed to regulate privacy including distancing, variation in the angle of orientation, and use of objects or areas for territorial defense.

Stokols (1974) reviewed various theories of crowding, including "stimulus overload" models, behavioral constraint models, and ecological models, and has argued that the experiential aspect of crowding has been neglected by current theories. Stokols proposed:

(1) the experience of crowding involves the perception of insufficient control over the environment; (2) perceived crowding evokes the desire to augment physical or psychological space as a means of gaining control over the environment and avoiding actual or anticipated interferences; and (3) feelings of crowding will be most intense, persistent, and difficult to resolve where the failure to augment space maximizes security threats. (1974, p. 14)

Stokols described various kinds of control interferences which he calls neutral (unintentional and impersonal), or personal "thwarting" which produce experiences of personal and neutral crowding. Situational determinants are important in this analysis and Stokols proposed a distinction between primary and secondary environments, the former being those locations where an individual "spends much of his time, relates to others on a personal basis, and engages in a wide range of personality-important activities" (p. 19). In an empirical investigation of his theory, Stokols and Resnick (1975) predicted that "personal thwarting" (where subjects have inadequate control over the spatial and social aspects of their environment), compared to "neutral thwarting" experiences (i.e., where the lack of control only is environmental), will result in greater feelings of being crowded, more critical evaluations of others in the situation, stronger feelings of being evaluated critically, and greater interpersonal distance setting when the opportunity permits. In their study, groups of 4 male and 4 female subjects were placed in a bare room ostensibly to be acquainted prior to performing an experimental task. Half the groups were told to become acquainted as this would facilitate their performance (neutral thwarting), the other half were told that they should assess each others' strengths and weaknesses prior to the task (personal thwarting). Following this interaction period the subjects were taken to a room to seat themselves (by positioning chairs at a table) and work on another task. The results generally bore out the predictions with the exception of chairseating arrangements where distances did not differ. In addition, subjects in the "personal thwarting" condition stood (rather than sat on the floor) for a longer period of time, engaged in more self-manipulations, and could remember fewer names of their group members than subjects who expected that their interaction would facilitate later group task performance. Although there was some support for his theory, it seems reasonable that the manipulations of having subjects critically "size up" one another could produce the experimental effects without any necessity for postulation of a concept of "personal thwarting."

Attacking popularized notions of territoriality and aggressive behavior, Edney (1974) has conceptualized human territoriality in more psychological terms. Territoriality is proposed as an organizing construct which operates on a community level and in small group and interpersonal relations. On the latter levels one can identify "behavior-setting congruences" and role ascriptions "which govern peoples' behavior in various places. The primary functions of territorial behavior are to reduce randomness and create order. Rather than employing dominance as a territorial concept (which inevitably leads to aggression, as Ardrey, 1966, argued), Edney proposes the concept of control which is "a better antonym and antidote for randomness and disorder, and since it has a broader meaning which embraces concepts like the temporal ordering of behavior" (1974, p. 13).

Finally, Evans and Eichelman (1975) wrote a paper whose title perhaps best sums up the present state of the art: "Preliminary models of conceptual linkages among some proxemic variables." Concerning the various models proposed thus far, they noted:

These conceptualizations are not explicit nor are they directive in the sense that they have stimulated integrative programs of research. In particular, most proxemic research exists as a disconnected array of independent studies that are often performed with questionable research methodologies. The task of examining how the various data fit together is left to others. (p. 1)

Evans and Eichelman reviewed the major theoretical models underlying proxemic research. One is the "stress model" which views crowding and invasions of personal space as psychologically and physiologically discomforting. Evans and Eichelman pointed out, however, that this model in its present form is probably crude. Short-term stresses differ in their effect on individuals more than long term stresses; often deleterious physiological changes do not occur until after mastery of the stressful situation. Task and incentive are important aspects of situations interacting with stress. Arousal has been postulated as a more specific construct, but here too empirical evidence is contradictory. Further, cognitive variables such as perceived control or expectancies and situational appraisals (e.g., Lazarus, 1966) interact with arousal in complex ways which make this variable difficult to study in isolation.

Perhaps the most prevalent theoretical construct employed with proxemic research has been the "information overload model" which follows from Hall's notion that crowding and decreased interpersonal distances forces us to process more information than we normally do, this "overload" producing confusion and discomfort. However, many variables modify this relationship. For example, Loo (1973) has noted that spatial restrictions in structured situations are less disturbing than when the situation is unstructured. Territorial familiarity may modify the impact of crowding or invasions of space. Evans and Eichelman (1975) also noted that "though personal space invasions may indeed change the quantity and quality of the information present in an array, it is the interpretation of the information that will determine whether an individual feels stressed or aroused" (pp. 15–16). They suggested, in addition, that the information overload phenomena be considered more in terms of "variables such as stimulus saliency and priority information processing biases" (p. 18). Finally, Sommer (1969, 1972) and others conceptualized much of the proxemic research in terms of the conflict between individual and group or social needs. Crowding heightens the likelihood that social intrusions may interfere with individual needs. Altman's concept of privacy mentioned earlier plays an important role here.

In their own paper, Evans and Eichelman (1975) proposed their own functional model governing human use of space. They saw man as differing from animals in that he was an information processor who provided for his needs through energy utilization and production by mapping out territories. Social and physical expectations are important aspects of spatial behavior in that they are derivatives of our "maps" which make our world predictable. Individual differences in response to crowding might be viewed as a function of differences in cognitive mapping ability. In concluding they noted:

Clearly this model is unsatisfactory as it stands. It is too general and marshals only preliminary suggestions of evidence . . . but hopefully this kind of analysis avoids the pitfalls of premature overspecialization and reliance on pet paradigms of inquiry. (1975, pp. 33–34)

REFERENCES

Aguilera, D. C. (1967). Relationship between physical contact and verbal interaction between nurses and patients. *Journal of Psychiatric Nursing*, **5**, 5–21.

Aiello, J. R., and T. C. Aiello (1974). The development of personal space: Proxemic behavior of children 6 through 16. *Human Ecology*, **2**, 177–189.

Aiello, J. R., and R. E. Cooper (1972). Use of personal space as a function of social affect. Summary in *Proceedings of the 80th Annual Convention of the American Psychological Association*. Washington, D.C.: American Psychological Association, pp. 207–208.

Aiello, J. R., Y. M. Epstein, and R. A. Karlin (1975). Effects of crowding on electrodermal activity. *Sociological Symposium*, **14**, 42–57.

Aiello, J. R., and S. E. Jones (1971). Field study of the proxemic behavior of young school children in three subcultural groups. *Journal of Personality and Social Psychology*, **19**, 351–356.

Albert, S., and J. M. Dabbs, (1970). Physical distance and persuasion. *Journal of Personality and Social Psychology*, **15**, 265–270.

Allgeier, A. R., and D. Byrne (1973). Attraction toward the opposite sex as a determinant of physical proximity. *Journal of Social Psychology*, **90**, 213–219.

Altman, I. (1971). Ecological aspects of interpersonal functioning. In A. H. Esser (Ed.), *Behavior and environment: The use of space by animals and men*. New York: Plenum Press. Pp. 291–306.

Altman, I. (1974). *Privacy: A conceptual analysis*. Paper presented at the meeting of the American Psychological Association, New Orleans. Altman, I., and W. W. Haythorn (1967). The ecology of isolated groups. *Behavioral Science*, 1967, **12**, 169–182.

Altman, I., and E. E. Lett (1969). The ecology of interpersonal relationships: A classification and conceptual model. In J. E. McGarth, *Social and psychological factors in stress*. New York: Holt, Rinehart, and Winston. Pp. 159–176.

Ardrey, R. (1966). *The territorial imperative*. New York: Atheneum.

Arenson, S. J. (1976). *Reactions of invasions of marked seats at a race track*. Paper presented at the meeting of the Eastern Psychological Association, New York.

Argyle, M., and J. Dean (1965). Eye-contact, distance, and affiliation. *Sociometry*, **28**, 289–304.

Argyle, M., and R. Ingham (1972). Gaze, mutual gaze, and proximity. *Semiotica*, **6**, 32–49.

Aronow, E., M. Reznikoff, and W. W. Tryon (1975). The interpersonal distance of process and reactive schizophrenics. *Journal of Consulting and Clinical Psychology,* **43,** 94.

Barefoot, J. C., H. Hoople, and D. McClay (1972). Avoidance of an act which would violate personal space. *Psychonomic Science,* **28,** 205–206.

Barrios, B., and M. Giesen (1976). *Getting what you expect: Effects of expectation on intragroup attraction and interpersonal distance.* Paper presented at the meeting of the Southeastern Psychological Association, New Orleans.

Batchelor, J. P., and G. R. Goethals (1972). Spatial arrangements in freely formed groups. *Sociometry,* 1972, **35,** 270–279.

Baum, A., and C. I. Greenberg (1975). Waiting for a crowd: The behavioral and perceptual effects of anticipated crowding. *Journal of Personality and Social Psychology,* **32,** 671–679.

Baxter, J. C. (1970). Interpersonal spacing in natural settings. *Sociometry,* **33,** 444–456.

Becker, F. D. (1973). Study of spatial markers. *Journal of Personality and Social Psychology,* **26,** 439–445.

Becker, F. D., and C. Mayo (1971). Delineating personal distance and territory. *Environment and Behavior,* **3,** 375–382.

Beussee, M. P., T. R. Ahearn, and J. A. Hammes (1970). Introspective reports of large groups experimentally confined in an austere environment. *Journal of Clinical Psychology,* **26,** 240–244.

Blumenthal, R., and J. Meltzoff (1967). Social schemas and perceptual accuracy in schizophrenia. *British Journal of Social and Clinical Psychology,* **6,** 119–128.

Boderman, A., D. W. Freed, and M. T. Kinnucan (1972). "Touch me, like me": Testing an encounter group assumption. *Journal of Applied Behavioral Science,* **8,** 527–533.

Boles, W. E., and A. H. Patterson (1974). *The effects of personal space variables upon approach and attitudes toward the other in a prisoner's dilemma game.* Paper presented at the meeting of the American Psychological Association, New Orleans.

Booraem, C. D., and J. V. Flowers (1972). Reduction of anxiety and personal space as a function of assertion training with severely disturbed neuropsychiatric inpatients. *Psychological Reports,* **30,** 923–929.

Boucher, M. L. (1972). Effect of seating distance on interpersonal attraction in an interview situation. *Journal of Consulting and Clinical Psychology,* **38,** 15–19.

Breed, G. R., and J. S. Ricci (1973). "Touch me, like me." Artifact? Summary in *Proceedings of the 81st Annual Convention of the American Psychological Association.* Washington, D.C.: American Psychological Association, pp. 153–154.

Brislin, R. W. (1974). Seating as a measure of behavior: You are where you sit. *Topics in Culture Learning,* **2,** 103–118.

Broekmann, N. C., and A. T. Moller (1973). Preferred seating position and distance in various situations. *Journal of Counseling Psychology,* **20,** 504–508.

Buchanan, D. R., R. Juhnke, and M. Goldman (1976). Violation of personal space as a function of sex. *Journal of Social Psychology,* **97,** 187–192.

Byrne, D., G. D. Baskett, and L. Hodges (1971). Behavioral indicators of interpersonal attraction. *Journal of Applied Social Psychology,* **1,** 137–149.

Byrne, D., C. R. Ervin, and J. Lamberth (1970). Continuity between the experimental study of attraction and real-life computer dating. *Journal of Personality and Social Psychology,* **16,** 157–165.

Campbell, D. T., W. H. Kruskal, and W. P. Wallace (1966). Seating aggregation as an index of attitude. *Sociometry,* **29,** 1–5.

Clore, G. (1974). *Attraction and interpersonal behavior.* Paper presented at the meeting of the Southwestern Psychological Association, Austin.

Cook, M. (1970). Experiments on orientation and proxemics. *Human Relations,* 1970, **23,** 61–76.

Cooper, C. L., and D. Bowles (1973). Physical encounter and self-disclosure. *Psychological Reports,* **33,** 451–454.

Cox, V. C., P. B. Paulus, G. McCain, and J. K. Schkade (1976). Field research on the effects of crowding in prisons and on offshore drilling platforms. Unpublished manuscript.

Cozby, P. C. (1973). Effects of density, activity, and personality on environmental preferences. *Journal of Research in Personality,* **7,** 45–60.

Dabbs, J. M., Jr. (1971). Physical closeness and negative feelings. *Psychonomic Science,* **23,** 141–143.

DeLong, A. J. (1970). Dominance-territorial relations in a small group. *Environment and Behavior,* **2,** 170–191.

Dennis, V. C., and E. R. Powell (1972). Nonverbal communication in across-race dyads. Summary in *Proceedings of the 80th Annual Convention of the American Psychological Association.* Washington, D.C.: American Psychological Association, pp. 557–558.

Desor, J. A. (1972). Toward a psychological theory of crowding. *Journal of Personality and Social Psychology,* **21,** 79–83.

Dinges, N. G., and E. R. Oetting (1972). Interaction distance anxiety in the counseling dyad. *Journal of Counseling Psychology,* **19,** 146–149.

Dosey, M. A., and M. Meisels (1969). Personal space and self-protection. *Journal of Personality and Social Psychology,* **11,** 93–97.

Duke, M. P., and S. Nowicki, Jr. (1972). A new measure and social-learning model for interpersonal distance. *Journal of Experimental Research in Personality,* **6,** 119–132.

Eberts, E. H. (1972). Social and personality correlates of personal space. In W. J. Mitchell (Ed.), *Environmental design: Research and practice. Proceedings of the EDRA III/AR VIII Conference.* Los Angeles: University of California Press.

Edney, J. J. (1974). *Human territories: Comment on functional properties.* Paper presented at the meeting of the American Psychological Association, New Orleans.

Edney, J. J. (1975). Territoriality and control: A field experiment. *Journal of Personality and Social Psychology,* **31,** 1108–1115.

Edwards, D. J. A. (1973). The determinants of the symmetry or asymmetry of social orientation schemata. *Journal of Experimental Social Psychology,* **9,** 542–550.

Efran, M. G., and J. A. Cheyne (1973). Shared space: The cooperative control of spatial areas by two interacting individuals. *Canadian Journal of Behavioural Science,* **5,** 201–210.

Efran, M. G., and J. A. Cheyne (1974). Affective concomitants of the invasion of shared space: Behavioral, physiological, and verbal indicators. *Journal of Personality and Social Psychology,* **29,** 219–226.

Eoyang, C. (1974). Effects of group size and privacy in residential crowding. *Journal of Personality and Social Psychology,* **30,** 389–392.

Epstein, Y. M., and R. A. Karlin (1975). Effects of acute experimental crowding. *Journal of Applied Social Psychology,* **5,** 34–53.

Esser, A. H., A. S. Chamberlain, E. D. Chappel, and N. S. Kline (1965). Territoriality of patients on a research ward. In J. Wortis (Ed.), *Recent advances in biological psychiatry,* Vol. 7. New York: Plenum Press. Pp. 37–44.

Evans, G. W., and W. Eichelman (1975). Preliminary models of conceptual linkages among some proxemic variables. Unpublished manuscript.

Evans, G. W., and R. B. Howard (1972). A methodological investigation of personal space. In W. J. Mitchell (Ed.), *Environmental design: Research and practice. Proceedings of the EDRA III/AR VIII Conference.* Los Angeles: University of California Press.

Evans, G. W., and R. B. Howard (1973). Personal space. *Psychological Bulletin,* **80,** 334–344.

Felipe, N. J. (1966). Interpersonal distance and small group interaction. *Cornell Journal of Social Relations,* **1,** 59–64.

Felipe, N. J., and R. Sommer (1966). Invasions of personal space. *Social Problems,* **14,** 206–214.

Fisher, J. D. (1974). Situation-specific variables as determinants of perceived environmental aesthetic quality and perceived crowdedness. *Journal of Research in Personality,* **8,** 177–188.

Fisher, J. D., and D. Byrne (1975). Too close for comfort: Sex differences in response to invasions of personal space. *Journal of Personality and Social Psychology,* **32,** 15–21.

Fisher, J. D., M. Rytting, and R. Heslin (1976). Hands touching hands, *Sociometry,* **39,** 416–421.

Fisher, R. L. (1967). Social schema of normal and disturbed school children. *Journal of Educational Psychology,* **58,** 88–92.

Forston, R. F., and C. U. Larson (1968). The dynamics of space: An experimental study in proxemic behavior among Latin Americans and North Americans. *Journal of Communication,* **18,** 109–116.

Frank, L. K. (1966). Tactile communication. In A. G. Smith (Ed.), *Communication and culture: Readings in the code of human interaction.* New York: Holt, Rinehart, and Winston. Pp. 199–209.

Frankel, A. S., and J. Barrett (1971). Variations in personal space as a function of authoritarianism, self-esteem, and racial characteristics of a stimulus situation. *Journal of Consulting and Clinical Psychology,* **37,** 95–98.

Frede, M. C., D. B. Gautney, and J. C. Baxter (1968). Relationships between body image boundary and interaction patterns on the MAPS test. *Journal of Consulting and Clinical Psychology,* **32,** 575–578.

Freedman, J. L., S. Klevansky, and P. R. Ehrlich (1971). The effect of crowding on human task performance. *Journal of Applied Social Psychology,* **1,** 7–25.

Freedman, J. L., A. S. Levy, R. W. Buchanan, and J. Price (1972). Crowding and human aggressiveness. *Journal of Experimental Social Psychology,* **8,** 528–548.

Fromme, D. K., and D. C. Beam (1974). Dominance and sex differences in nonverbal responses to differential eye contact. *Journal of Research in Personality,* **8,** 76–87.

Fry, A. M., and F. N. Willis (1971). Invasion of personal space as a function of the age of the invader. *Psychological Record,* **21,** 385–389.

Galle, O. R., W. R. Gove, and J. M. McPherson (1972). Population density and pathology: What are the relations for man? *Science,* **176,** 23–30.

Gardin, H., K. J. Kaplan, I. J. Firestone, and G. A. Cowan (1973). Proxemic effects on cooperation, attitude, and approach-avoidance in a prisoner's dilemma game. *Journal of Personality and Social Psychology,* **27,** 13–18.

Geis, F., and V. Viksne (1972). Touching: Physical contact and level of arousal. Summary in *Proceedings of the 80th Annual Convention of the American Psychological Association.* Washington, D.C.: American Psychological Association, pp. 179–180.

Glassman, J. B., B. R. Burkhart, R. D. Grant, and G. G. Vallery (1976). *Crowding, expectation, and extended task performance: An experiment in the natural environment.* Paper presented at the meeting of the Southeastern Psychological Association, New Orleans.

Gochman, I. R., and J. P. Keating (1976a). *Inner and outer directed attention and the perception of crowding.* Paper presented at the meeting of the Western Psychological Association, Los Angeles.

Gochman, I. R., and J. P. Keating (1976b). *Perceived crowding as a function of unsuccessful goal attainment.* Paper presented at the meeting of the Western Psychological Association, Los Angeles.

Goldring, P. (1967). Role of distance and posture in the evaluation of interactions. Summary in *Proceedings of the 75th Annual Convention of the American Psychological Association.* Washington, D.C.: American Psychological Association, pp.343–344.

Gordon, G. G., and M. P. Duke (1975). *A new measure of social learning theoretical analysis of group space.* Paper presented at the meeting of the Southeastern Psychological Association, Atlanta.

Gordon, M. A., and T. L. Johnson (1975). *Body territoriality: Effects of sex and position of assistant and sex of subject.* Paper presented at the meeting of the Southwestern Psychological Association, Houston.

Gottheil, E., J. Corey, and A. Paredes (1968). Psychological and physical dimensions of personal space. *Journal of Psychology,* **69,** 7–9.

Graves, J. R., and J. D. Robinson (1976). Proxemic behavior as a function of inconsistent verbal and nonverbal messages. *Journal of Counseling Psychology,* **23,** 333–338.

Greene, L. R. (1976). Body image boundaries and small group seating arrangements. *Journal of Consulting and Clinical Psychology,* **44,** 244–249.

Griffitt, W., J. May, and R. Veitch (1974). Sexual stimulation and interpersonal behavior: Heterosexual evaluative responses, visual behavior and physical proximity. *Journal of Personality and Social Psychology,* **30,** 367–377.

Griffitt, W., and R. Veitch (1971). Hot and crowded: Influences of population density and temperature on interpersonal affective behavior. *Journal of Personality and Social Psychology,* **17,** 92–98.

Haase, R. F. (1970). The relationship of sex and instructional set to the regulation of interpersonal interaction distance in a counseling analogue. *Journal of Counseling Psychology,* **17,** 233–236.

Haase, R. F., and D. J. DiMattia (1969). *Counselor preference for proxemic arrangement in dyads.* Counseling Center Research Report No. 2. Amherst: University of Massachusetts.

Haase, R. F., and D. J. DiMattia (1970). Proxemic behavior: Counselor, administrator, and client preference for seating arrangement in dyadic interaction. *Journal of Counseling Psychology,* **17,** 319–325.

Haase, R. F., and D. T. Tepper, Jr. (1972). Nonverbal components of empathic communication. *Journal of Counseling Psychology,* **19,** 417–424.

Hall, E. T. (1963a). Proxemics—The study of man's spatial relations and boundaries. In I. Galdston (Ed.), *Man's image in medicine and anthropology.* Monograph Series No. 4. New York: International University Press. pp. 422–435.

Hall, E. T. (1963b). A system for the notation of proxemic behavior. *American Anthropologist,* **65,** 1003–1026.

Hall, E. T. (1966). *The hidden dimension.* Garden City, N. Y.: Doubleday.

Hall, E. T. (1968). Proxemics. *Current Anthropology,* **9,** 83–108.

Hare, A. P., and R. F. Bales (1963). Seating position and small group interaction. *Sociometry,* **26,** 480–486.

Hartnett, J. J., K. G. Bailey, and F. W. Gibson, Jr. (1970). Personal space as influenced by sex and type of movement. *Journal of Psychology,* **76,** 139–144.

Haythorn, W. W., I. Altman, and T. I. Myers (1966). Emotional symptomatology and subjective stress in isolated pairs of men. *Journal of Experimental Research in Personality,* **1,** 290–305.

Henley, N. M. (1973). Status and Sex: Some touching observations. *Bulletin of the Psychonomic Society,* **2** (2), 91–93.

Heslin, R. (1974). *Steps toward a taxonomy of touching.* Paper presented at the meeting of the Midwestern Psychological Association, Chicago.

Heslin, R., and D. Boss (1976). Tactile behavior in arrival and departure at an airport. Unpublished manuscript. (Available from Richard Heslin, Department of Psychological Science, Purdue University, West Lafayette, Indiana.)

Hetherington, E. M. (1972). Effects of father absence on personality development in adolescent daughters. *Developmental Psychology,* **7,** 313–326.

Higgins, J., J. C. Peterson, and L. L. Dolby (1969). Social adjustment and familial schema. *Journal of Abnormal Psychology,* **74,** 296–299.

Horowitz, M. J. (1968). Spatial behavior and psychopathology. *Journal of Nervous and Mental Disease,* **146,** 24–35.

Horowitz, M. J., D. F. Duff, and L. O. Stratton (1964). Body buffer zones. *Archives of General Psychiatry,* **11,** 651–656.

Hutt, C., and M. J. Vaizey (1966). Differential effects of group density on social behavior. *Nature,* **209,** 1371–1372.

Johnson, P. K. (1970). *Privacy signals in public areas: An exploratory investigation.* Doctoral dissertation, University of Washington. [*Dissertation Abstracts International,* **32,** (1972), 4843B–4844B. University Microfilms No. 72-7372, 75.]

Jones, S. E. (1971). A comparative proxemics analysis of dyadic interaction in selected subcultures of New York City. *Journal of Social Psychology,* **84,** 35–44.

Jones, S. E., and J. R. Aiello (1973). Proxemic behavior of black and white first-, third-, and fifth-grade children. *Journal of Personality and Social Psychology,* **25,** 21–27.

Jourard, S. M. (1966). An exploratory study of body-accessibility. *British Journal of Social and Clinical Psychology,* **5,** 221–231.

Jourard, S. M., and R. Friedman (1970). Experimenter-subject distance and self-disclosure. *Journal of Personality and Social Psychology,* **15,** 278–282.

Jourard, S. M., and J. E. Rubin (1968). Self-disclosure and touching: A study of two modes of interpersonal encounter and their interrelation. *Journal of Humanistic Psychology,* **8,** 39–48.

Kaplan, K. J. (1974). *Structure and process in interpersonal "distancing."* Paper presented at the meeting of the American Psychological Association, New Orleans.

Kauffman, L. E. (1971). Tacesics, the study of touch: A model for proxemic analysis. *Semiotica,* **4,** 149–161.

Kelly, F. D. (1972). Communicational significance of therapist proxemic cues. *Journal of Consulting and Clinical Psychology,* **39,** 345.

Kiesler, C., and G. Goldberg (1968). Multi-dimensional approach to the experimental study of interpersonal attraction: Effect of a blunder on the attractiveness of a competent other. *Psychological Reports,* **22,** 693–705.

Kinzel, A. F. (1970). Body buffer zone in violent prisoners. *American Journal of Psychiatry,* **127,** 99–104.

Kleck, R. E. (1967). The effects of interpersonal affect on errors made when reconstructing a stimulus display. *Psychonomic Science,* **9,** 449–450.

Kleck, R. E. (1969). Physical stigma and task oriented interactions. *Human Relations,* **22,** 53–60.

Kleck, R. E. (1970). Interaction distance and nonverbal agreeing responses. *British Journal of Social and Clinical Psychology,* **9,** 180–182.

Kleck, R. E., P. L. Buck, W. L. Goller, R. S. London, J. R. Pfeiffer, and D. P. Vukcevic (1968). Effect of stigmatizing conditions on the use of personal space. *Psychological Reports,* **23,** 111–118.

Kleinke, C. L., R. A. Staneski, and D. E. Berger (1975). Evaluation of an interviewer as a function of interviewer gaze, reinforcement of subject gaze, and interviewer attractiveness. *Journal of Personality and Social Psychology,* **31,** 115–122.

Kleinke, C. L., R. A. Staneski, and S. L. Pipp (1975). Effects of gaze, distance, and attractiveness on males' first impression of females. *Representative Research in Social Psychology,* **6,** 7–12.

Klukken, P. G. (1971). *Personality and interpersonal distance.* Doctoral dissertation, University of Florida. [*Dissertation Abstracts International,* **32** (1972), 6033B. University Microfilms No. 72-12, 484.]

Knight, P. H., and C. K. Bair (1976). Degree of client comfort as a function of dyadic interaction distance. *Journal of Counseling Psychology,* **23,** 13–16.

Kuethe, J. L. (1962a). Social schemas. *Journal of Abnormal and Social Psychology,* **64,** 31–38.

Kuethe, J. L. (1962b). Social schemas and the reconstruction of social object displays from memory. *Journal of Abnormal Psychology,* **65,** 71–74.

Kuethe, J. L., and H. Weingartner (1964). Male-female schemata of homosexual and nonhomosexual penitentiary inmates. *Journal of Personality,* **32,** 23–31.

Lassen, C. R. (1973). Effect of proximity and anxiety and communication in the initial psychiatric interview. *Journal of Abnormal Psychology,* **81,** 226–232.

Lazarus, R. S. (1966). *Psychological stress and the coping process.* New York: McGraw-Hill.

Leibman, M. (1970). The effects of sex and race norms on personal space. *Environment and Behavior,* **2,** 208–246.

Lerea, J., and B. Ward (1966). The social schema of normal and speech-defective children. *Journal of Social Psychology,* **69,** 87–94.

Lett, E. E., W. Clark, and I. Altman (1969). *A propositional inventory of research on interpersonal distance.* Research Report No. 1, Bethesda. Naval Medical Research Institute.

Lewit, D. W., and V. Joy (1967). Kinetic versus social schemas in figure grouping. *Journal of Personality and Social Psychology,* **7,** 63–72.

Liepold, W. E. (1963). Psychological distance in a dyadic interview. Unpublished doctoral dissertation, University of North Dakota.

Little, K. B. (1965). Personal space. *Journal of Experimental Social Psychology,* **1,** 237–247.

Little, K. B. (1968). Cultural variations in social schemata. *Journal of Personality and Social Psychology,* **10,** 1–7.

Little, K. B., Z. J. Ulehla, and C. Henderson (1968). Value congruence and interaction distances. *Journal of Social Psychology,* **75,** 249–253.

Long, B. H., E. H. Henderson, and R. C. Ziller (1967). Self-social correlates of originality in children. *Journal of Genetic Psychology,* **111,** 47–57.

Long, B. H., R. C. Ziller, and E. H. Henderson (1968). Developmental changes in the self-concept during adolescence. *The Social Review,* **76** (2), 210–230.

Long, G. T., L. G. Calhoun, and J. W. Selby (1976). *Personality characteristics related to cross-situational consistency in interpersonal distance.* Paper presented at the meeting of the Southeastern Psychological Association, New Orleans.

Loo, C. T. M. (1973). Important issues in researching the effects of crowding on humans. *Representative Research in Social Psychology,* **4,** 219–226.

Lott, D. F., and R. Sommer (1967). Seating arrangements and status. *Journal of Personality and Social Psychology,* **7,** 90–95.

Luft, J. (1966). On nonverbal interaction. *Journal of Psychology,* **63,** 261–268.

Marshall, J. E., and R. Heslin (1975). Boys and girls together: Sexual composition and the effect of density and group size on cohesiveness. *Journal of Personality and Social Psychology,* **31,** 952–961.

Martin, D. G., and W. K. Van Dyke (1968). The expression of social experience in a figure placement task. *Psychonomic Science,* **12,** 355–356.

McBride, G., M. G. King, and J. W. James (1965). Social proximity effects of galvanic skin responses in adult humans. *Journal of Psychology,* **61,** 153–157.

McDowell, K. V. (1972). Violations of personal space. *Canadian Journal of Behavioral Science,* **4,** 210–217.

Mehrabian, A. (1968a). Inference of attitudes from the posture, orientation, and distance of a communicator. *Journal of Consulting and Clinical Psychology,* **32,** 296–308.

Mehrabian, A. (1968b). Relationship of attitude to seated posture, orientation, and distance. *Journal of Personality and Social Psychology,* **10,** 26–30.

Mehrabian, A. (1969). Some referents and measures of nonverbal behavior. *Behavior Research Methods and Instrumentation,* **1,** 203–207.

Mehrabian, A., and S. G. Diamond (1971). Seating arrangement and conversation. *Sociometry,* **34,** 281–289.

Mehrabian, A., and J. T. Friar (1969). Encoding of attitude by a seated communicator via posture and position cues. *Journal of Consulting and Clinical Psychology,* **33,** 330–336.

Meisels, M., and F. M. Canter (1970). Personal space and personality characteristics: A nonconfirmation. *Psychological Reports,* **27,** 287–290.

Meisels, M., and M. A. Dosey (1971). Personal space, anger-arousal, and psychological defense. *Journal of Personality,* **39,** 333–344.

Meisels, M., and C. J. Guardo (1969). Development of personal space schemas. *Child Development,* **40,** 1167–1178.

Middlemist, R. D., E. S. Knowles, and C. F. Matter (1976). Personal space invasions in the lavatory: Suggestive evidence for arousal. *Journal of Personality and Social Psychology,* **33,** 541–546.

Miller, S., and K. M. Nardini (1976). *Individual differences in the perception of crowding.* Paper presented at the meeting of the Eastern Psychological Association, New York.

Nguyen, T., R. Heslin, and M. L. Nguyen (1975). The meanings of touch: Sex differences. *Journal of Communication,* **25,** 92–103.

Nicosia, G. J., and J. R. Aiello (1976). *Effects of bodily contact on reactions to crowding.* Paper presented at the meeting of the American Psychological Association, Washington, D.C.

Norum, G. A. (1966). Perceived interpersonal relationships and spatial arrangements. Unpublished master's thesis, University of California, Davis.

Norum, G. A., N. J. Russo, and R. Sommer (1967). Seating patterns and group task. *Psychology in the Schools,* **4** (3), 276–280.

Patterson, M. L. (1973a). Compensation in nonverbal immediacy behaviors: A review. *Sociometry,* **36,** 237–252.

Patterson, M. L. (1973b). Stability of nonverbal immediacy behaviors. *Journal of Experimental Social Psychology,* **9,** 97–109.

Patterson, M. L. (1974). *Factors affecting interpersonal spatial proximity.* Paper presented at the meeting of the American Psychological Association, New Orleans.

Patterson, M. L., and D. S. Holmes (1966). Social interaction correlates of the MMPI extraversion-introversion scale. *American Psychologist,* **21,** 724–725.

Patterson, M. L., S. Mullens, and J. Romano (1971). Compensatory reactions to spatial intrusion. *Sociometry,* **34,** 114–121.

Patterson, M. L., and R. E. Schaeffer (1974). Effects of size and sex composition on interaction distance, participation, and satisfaction in small groups. Unpublished manuscript, University of Missouri at St. Louis.

Patterson, M. L., and L. B. Sechrest (1970). Interpersonal distance and impression formation. *Journal of Personality,* **38,** 161–166.

Patterson, M. L., and M. E. Strauss (1972). An examination of the discriminant validity of the social–avoidance and distress scale. *Journal of Consulting and Clinical Psychology,* **39,** 169.

Pattison, J. E. (1973). Effects of touch on self-exploration and the therapeutic relationship. *Journal of Consulting and Clinical Psychology,* **40,** 170–175.

Paulus, P. B., A. B. Annis, J. J. Seta, J. K. Schkade, and R. W. Matthews (1976). Density does affect task performance. *Journal of Personality and Social Psychology,* **34,** 248–253.

Paulus, P. B., V. Cox, G. McCain, and J. Chandler (1975). Some effects of crowding in a prison environment. *Journal of Applied Social Psychology,* **5,** 86–91.

Pedersen, D. M. (1973a). Development of a personal space measure. *Psychological Reports,* **32,** 527–535.

Pedersen, D. M. (1973b). Developmental trends in personal space. *Journal of Psychology,* **83,** 3–9.

Pedersen, D. M., and L. M. Shears (1973). A review of personal space research in the framework of general system theory. *Psychological Bulletin,* **80,** 367–388.

Pedersen, D. M., and L. M. Shears (1974). Effects of an interpersonal game and of confinement on personal space. *Journal of Personality and Social Psychology,* **30,** 838–845.

Pellegrini, R. J., and J. Empey (1970). Interpersonal spatial orientation in dyads. *Journal of Psychology,* **76,** 67–70.

Petri, H. L., R. G. Huggins, C. J. Mills, and L. S. Barry (1974). *Variables influencing the shape of personal space.* Paper presented at the meeting of the American Psychological Association, New Orleans.

Petty, R. M. (1976). *The effects of crowding on cooperation and interpersonal evaluations.* Paper presented at the meeting of the Western Psychological Association, Los Angeles.

Porter, E., M. Argyle, and V. Salter (1970). What is signalled by proximity? *Perceptual and Motor Skills,* **30,** 39–42.

Rawls, J. R., R. E. Trego, C. N. McGaffey, and D. J. Rawls (1972). Personal space as a predictor of performance under close working conditions. *Journal of Social Psychology,* **86,** 261–267.

Rohner, S. J., and J. R. Aiello (1976). *The relationship between the sex of interactants and other nonverbal behaviors.* Paper presented at the meeting of the Eastern Psychological Association, New York.

Rosenfeld, H. M. (1965). Effect of an approval-seeking induction on interpersonal proximity. *Psychological Reports,* **17,** 120–122.

Rosenfeld, L. B., S. Kartus, and C. Ray (1976). Body accessibility revisited. *Journal of Communication,* **26,** 27–30.

Ross, M., B. Layton, B. Erickson, and J. Schopler (1973). Affect facial regard and reactions to crowding. *Journal of Personality and Social Psychology,* **28,** 69–76.

Ryen, A. H., and A. Kahn (1975). The effects of intergroup orientation on group attitudes and proxemic behavior. *Journal of Personality and Social Psychology,* **31,** 302–310.

Sanders, J. L. (1976). Duplicity by a friend and its effect on personal space. *Perceptual and Motor Skills,* **42,** 246.

Schaffer, D. R., and C. Sadowski (1975). *This table is mine: Respect for marked barroom tables as a function of gender of spatial marker and desirability of locale.* Paper presented at the meeting of the Southeastern Psychological Association, Atlanta.

Scherer, S. E. (1974). Proxemic behavior of primary school children as a function of their socioeconomic class and sub-culture. *Journal of Personality and Social Psychology,* **29,** 800–805.

Scherer, S. E., and M. R. Schiff (1973). Perceived intimacy, physical distance, and eye contact. *Perceptual and Motor Skills,* **36,** 835–841.

Schopler, J., and M. Walton (1975). The effects of expected structure, expected enjoyment, and participants' internality-externality upon feelings of being crowded. Unpublished manuscript. (Available from Department of Psychology, University of North Carolina, Chapel Hill, North Carolina.)

Sensening, J., T. E. Reed, and J. S. Miller (1972). Cooperation in the prisoner's dilemma as a function of interpersonal distance. *Psychonomic Science,* **26,** 105–106.

Seta, J. J., P. B. Paulus, and J. K. Schkade (1975). *The effects of group size and proximity under cooperative and competitive conditions.* Paper presented at the meeting of the Southwestern Psychological Association, Houston.

Shontz, F. C. and R. D. McNish (1972). The human body as stimulus object: Estimates of distances between body landmarks. *Journal of Experimental Psychology, 95,* 20–24.

Shuter, P. (1976). Proxemics and tactility in Latin America. *Journal of Communication, 26,* 46–52.

Silverman, A. F., M. E. Pressman, and H. W. Bartel (1973). Self-esteem and tactile communication. *Journal of Humanistic Psychology, 13,* 73–77.

Silverthorne, C., J. Micklewright, M. O'Donnell, and R. Gibson (1975). *Attribution of personal characteristics as a function of touch on initial contact.* Paper presented at the meeting of the Western Psychological Association, Sacramento.

Smith, G. H. (1954). Personality scores and the personal distance effect. *Journal of Social Psychology, 39,* 57–62.

Sommer, R. (1959). Studies in personal space. *Sociometry, 22,* 247–260.

Sommer, R. (1961). Leadership and group geography. *Sociometry, 24,* 99–110.

Sommer, R. (1965). Further studies of small group ecology. *Sociometry, 28,* 337–348.

Sommer, R. (1967a). Small group ecology. *Psychological Bulletin, 67,* 145–152.

Sommer, R. (1967b). Sociofugal space. *American Journal of Sociology, 72,* 654–660.

Sommer, R. (1968). Intimacy ratings in five countries. *International Journal of Psychology, 3,* 109–114.

Sommer, R. (1969). *Personal space: The behavioral basis of design.* Englewood Cliffs, N.J.: Prentice-Hall.

Sommer, R. (1972). *Design awareness.* San Francisco: Rinehart.

Sommer, R., and F. D. Becker (1969). Territorial defense and the good neighbor. *Journal of Personality and Social Psychology, 11,* 85–92.

Spinetta, J. J., D. Rigler, and M. Karon (1974). Personal space as a measure of a dying child's sense of isolation. *Journal of Consulting and Clinical Psychology, 42,* 751–756.

Stokols, D. (1974). *The experience of crowding in primary and secondary environments.* Paper presented at the meeting of the American Psychological Association, New Orleans.

Stokols, D., and S. M. Resnick (1975). *An experimental assessment of neutral and personal crowding experiences.* Paper presented at the meeting of the Southeastern Psychological Association, Atlanta.

Stone, G. L., and C. J. Morden (1976). Effect of distance on verbal productivity. *Journal of Counseling Psychology, 23,* 486–488.

Strodtbeck, F. L., and L. H. Hook (1961). The social dimensions of a twelve-man jury table. *Sociometry, 24,* 397–415.

Sundstrom, E. (1975). An experimental study of crowding: Effect of room size, intrusion, and goal blocking on nonverbal behavior, self-disclosure, and self-reported stress. *Journal of Personality and Social Psychology, 32,* 645–654.

Sundstrom, E., and I. Altman (1974). Field study of territorial behavior and dominance. *Journal of Personality and Social Psychology, 30,* 115–124.

Tedesco, J. F., and D. K. Fromme (1974). Cooperation, competition, and personal space. *Sociometry, 37,* 116–121.

Thayer, S., and L. Alban (1972). A field experiment on the effect of political and cultural factors on the use of personal space. *Journal of Social Psychology, 88,* 267–272.

Thornton, C. C., and E. Gottheil (1971). Social schemata in schizophrenic males. *Journal of Abnormal Psychology, 77,* 192–195.

Tolor, A. (1968). Psychological distance in disturbed and normal children. *Psychological Reports, 23,* 695–701.

Tolor, A. (1969). Children's popularity and psychological distance. Summary in *Proceedings of the 77th Annual Convention of the American Psychological Association,* Washington, D.C.: American Psychological Association, pp. 545–546.

Tolor, A. (1970a). The fallacy of schizophrenic deficit in the interpersonal sphere. *Journal of Consulting and Clinical Psychology,* **35,** 278–282.

Tolor, A. (1970b). Psychological distance in disturbed and normal adults. *Journal of Clinical Psychology,* **26,** 160–162.

Tolor, A., G. G. Brannigan, and V. M. Murphy (1970). Psychological distance, future time perspective, and internal-external expectancy. *Journal of Projective Techniques and Personality Assessment,* **34,** 283–294.

Tolor, A., and M. Donnon (1969). Psychological distance as a function of length of hospitalization. *Psychological Reports,* **25,** 851–855.

Tolor, A., and W. R. Salafia (1971). The social schemata technique as a projective device. *Psychological Reports,* **28,** 423–429.

Valins, S., and A. Baum (1973). Residential group size, social interaction, and crowding. *Environment and Behavior,* **5,** 421–439.

Ward, C. D. (1968). Seating arrangement and leadership emergence in small discussion groups. *Journal of Social Psychology,* **74,** 83–90.

Watson, O. M. (1972). Conflicts and directions in proxemic research. *Journal of Communication,* **22,** 443–459.

Watson, O. M., and T. D. Graves (1966). Quantitative research in proxemic behavior. *American Anthropologist,* 1966, **68,** 971–985.

Watson, W. H. (1975). The meanings of touch: Geriatric nursing. *Journal of Communication,* **25,** 104–112.

Weinstein, L. (1965). Social schemata of emotionally disturbed boys. *Journal of Abnormal Psychology,* **70,** 457–461.

Weinstein, L. (1967). Social experience and social schemata. *Journal of Personality and Social Psychology,* **6,** 429–434.

Weiss, M., and C. Keys (1975). *The influence of proxemic variables on dyadic interaction between peers.* Paper presented at the meeting of the American Psychological Association, Chicago.

Weitz, S. (Ed.) (1974). *Nonverbal communication: Readings with commentary.* New York: Oxford University Press.

White, G. T. (1975). *The mating game: Nonverbal interpersonal communication between dating and engaged college couples.* Paper presented at the meeting of the Western Psychological Association, Sacramento.

Wicker, A. W. (1973). Undermanning theory and research: Implications for the study of psychological and behavioral effects of excess populations. *Representative Research in Social Psychology,* **4,** 185–206.

Williams, J. L. (1971). Personal space and its relation to extraversion–introversion. *Canadian Journal of Behavioral Science,* **3,** 156–160.

Willis, F. N., Jr. (1966). Initial speaking distance as a function of the speakers' relationship. *Psychonomic Science,* **5,** 221–222.

Worchel, S., and C. Teddlie (1976). The experience of crowding: A two factor theory. *Journal of Personality and Social Psychology,* **34,** 30–40.

Zanni, G. R. (1976). *An investigation of five personal space measures.* Paper presented at the meeting of the Eastern Psychological Association, New York.

Epilogue

In concluding our review of nonverbal communication research we would like to make some personal observations as well as to consider briefly some aspects of research that we have not specifically covered in this book. In a recent review of Weitz's book *Nonverbal Communication* (Weitz, 1974), Koivumaki (1975) noted that "the only real weakness of the book is a unidimensional organization scheme . . . to divide a field along channel lines is an obvious but not necessarily the best way to organize the material" (p. 214). The danger of such a unidimensional approach is that it leads the reader into viewing each channel (e.g., face, voice, eye) separately, when in fact interpersonal communication is a "multichannel" phenomenon. Since Weitz herself did include a section on multichannel communication, this criticism is perhaps even more applicable to this book. Certainly attitudes, internal psychological states, and social interaction sequences involve face, hand, body, and eye movements and paralinguistic variables occurring simultaneously and not independently of one another. On the other hand, in reviewing the literature for this book we found that the majority of studies clearly fell into the categories chosen for the chapters. Further, it is our feeling, especially in psychological research, that researchers do frequently focus on single nonverbal channels, especially given the time and difficulty in measuring many nonverbal behaviors. It thus seemed both important and appropriate to consider the nonverbal behaviors (e.g., face, eye, voice) in separate sections, while still noting obvious interrelationships between the various topic areas (e.g., between looking and interpersonal distance). Finally, it was not our intention to focus on psychological variables (e.g., attitude, mood, personality) and their various nonverbal correlates. Rather, our interest is on the nonverbal behaviors specifically so that the researcher interested in studying one or more of them may be able to see the major methodological issues and many examples of how these variables were used in studies to date. This goal could be most appropriately met through a single-channel approach.

It is also true, however, that as the functions and meanings of nonverbal behaviors become better understood, future research will focus more extensively on the interrelationships between nonverbal and verbal behaviors. A prominent example of such new research comes in the area of deception, where researchers look for nonverbal cues indicative of emotional or factual dissimulation. Here one is by definition looking for discrepancies in the information provided by verbal and nonverbal channels or by different nonverbal channels (e.g., the face vs. the body). Likewise, research on interpersonal attitudes involves consideration of the verbal and different nonverbal channels, and indeed the careful reader of this book will note many experiments (e.g., Mehrabian, 1972) in which multiple nonverbal behaviors were studied in just such a fashion. More research of this kind can be expected in the future, especially experiments in which the relative contribution of particular nonverbal behaviors is assessed.

In addition to the issue of multichannel communication there are some other areas of nonverbal research not covered in this review that are emerging as important. Specifically, the "encoding" and "decoding" of nonverbal behaviors has begun to attract attention, including our own, in recent years. We know from everyday experience that people differ dramatically in the degree to which they are nonverbally expressive, in either one or more channels (e.g., face, voice, body movements,). Some of these group (e.g., sex) differences were noted in the section on facial expression and voice, but much more systematic research is needed. In particular, there is little theory and even less empirical verification to explain why individual differences in "encoding" exist. The same problems apply to differences in "decoding" ability: we know people differ in their sensitivity to nonverbal cues, but the reason why is unclear. Rosenthal and his associates at Harvard developed the only multichannel test of nonverbal sensitivity, but as yet most of their findings are in unpublished form. Only a few researchers (e.g., Cupchik, 1973; Lanzetta and Kleck, 1970; Levy, 1964; Mehrabian and Ferris, 1967; Zuckerman, Lipets, Koivumaki, and Rosenthal, 1975) have addressed the important issue whether and how encoding and decoding are related. We have begun to study these issues in our own laboratory. However, this area is so new and sufficiently lacking in both theory and an established body of research findings that we feel special discussion devoted to this topic is best deferred until more research has been completed. It is also our feeling that encoding-decoding issues will become a major area of interest to students of nonverbal communication and that the reader should be sensitive to current papers and forthcoming publications.

Finally, we would like to make some personal comments regarding nonverbal behavior research. These are based both on our own observations of this field gained in conducting this literature review and on our own research experiences. First, with but few exceptions, conducting good research on nonverbal behavior is very expensive, tedious, and exacting work. In evaluating facial expression by the FAST procedure, Ekman noted that 1 minute required 3 hours' coding time. In our own laboratory we found that to obtain accurate frequency and duration measures of hand (illustrator, adaptor) and gaze behavior an average of 20 hours of coder time for a 30-minute interview was needed. The result is that research findings take a longer time to compile and undoubtedly many investigators find the "payoff" not great enough to warrant a continuing program of research. There are notable exceptions (Paul Ekman and Wallace Friesen, Starkey Duncan, and Phoebe Ellsworth, to name a few), and it should be clear from this review how valuable their research programs have been to the field. However, where techniques are especially difficult, as in facial expression research, the bulk of such research may actually be provided by only one investigator (e.g., Ekman). That one laboratory provided almost all the findings in a specific area over the past decade speaks poorly for the development of the field as a whole, if highly for that particular research team. Unfortunately, a large number of the studies reviewed are "one-shot affairs" where the findings raise as many questions and issues as they answer. The net product can be as much clutter as clarity when one looks at the research as a whole. While we hope that this book stimulates new researchers to enter the field, we also hope that their interest will be sustained over time.

With a Presidential election now behind us, we are again reminded of the public interest in "experts" who read "body language" to provide information concerning the character and intentions of important public figures. Unfortunately, past and present popular works devoted to this subject have been based upon limited research findings; indeed, some works (best left unnamed) appear to be essentially acts of creative writing. From the findings described in this book, it should be clear how important the social psychological context (i.e., interpersonal and situational factors) is in relation to nonverbal behavior. However, this should not discourage the researcher from merely looking just for group differences and main effects. More research needs to be conducted on individual differences in relation to interpersonal and situational variables if we are to extract all the information that can be derived from the tedious coding of nonverbal behavior. Our own experience highlights this point. In a study just completed on interview behavior in normal and conversational stress situations there were a large number (approximately 100) of personality correlations with measures of the frequency and duration of nonverbal behaviors (hand, gaze, and temporal speech behaviors) within and across interview situations. Although 2 to 3 extra hours of individual subject time were added to the project, this addition seemed clearly worthwhile in terms of the extra yield of information. Much replication and refinement lie ahead before any solid conclusions can be drawn, but it may be that limited generalizations about personality in given social contexts can be reliably obtained from nonverbal behavior. Such a prospect should be exciting for anyone who wishes to enhance the reliability and power of his observations in standardized interpersonal interactional contexts (e.g., interviews).

In attempting such a review as this we were aware that it could be incomplete and dissatisfying in many respects to potential readers. By doing this work we have tremendously increased our own knowledge of nonverbal communication research. Obviously, we cannot expect the reader to benefit as much as we have from the final product, which represents a distillation of much effort. We do hope, however, that the reader who is "willing to work" and read carefully the seemingly endless descriptions of studies will gain a better appreciation of not only the difficulties but also the excitement that one can expect to encounter in conducting research in this long neglected but important area of human behavior.

REFERENCES

Cupchik, G. C. (1972). Expression and impression: The decoding of nonverbal affect. Doctoral dissertation, University of Wisconsin. [*Dissertation Abstracts International*, 1973, **33**, 5536B. (University Microfilms No. 73-7184)]

Koivumaki, J. H. Recent but comprehensive. (Review of *Nonverbal communication: Readings with commentary* by S. Weitz). *Journal of Communication*, 1975, **25**, 213–215.

Lanzetta, J. T., and R. E. Kleck (1970). Encoding and decoding of nonverbal affect in humans. *Journal of Personality and Social Psychology*, **16**, 12–19.

Levy, P. (1964). The ability to express and perceive vocal communication of feeling. In J. R. Davitz (Ed.), *The communication of emotional meaning*. New York: McGraw Hill.

Mehrabian, A. (1972). *Nonverbal communication*. Chicago: Aldine-Atherton.

Mehrabian, A., and S. R. Ferris (1967). Inference of attitudes from nonverbal communication in two channels. *Journal of Consulting Psychology*, **31**, 248–252.

Weitz, S. (Ed.) (1974). *Nonverbal communication: Readings with commentary*. New York: Oxford University Press.

Zuckerman, M., M. S. Lipets, J. H. Koivumaki, and R. Rosenthal (1975). Encoding and decoding nonverbal cues of emotion. *Journal of Personality and Social Psychology*, **32**, 1068–1076.

Author Index

323

Subject Index